Cognitive Psychotherapy
of Psychotic and
Personality Disorders

Cognitive Psychotherapy of Psychotic and Personality Disorders
Handbook of Theory and Practice

Edited by

Carlo Perris

*Norrlands University Hospital, Umeå, Sweden
& the Swedish Institute of Cognitive Psychotherapy,
Stockholm, Sweden*

and

Patrick D. McGorry

*Centre for Young People's Mental Health, North-
Western Healthcare Network, Australia*

JOHN WILEY & SONS

Chichester · New York · Weinheim · Brisbane · Singapore · Toronto

Other Wiley Editorial Offices

John Wiley & Sons, Inc., 605 Third Avenue,
New York, NY 10158-0012, USA

WILEY-VCH Verlag GmbH, Pappelallee 3,
D-69469 Weinheim, Germany

Jacaranda Wiley Ltd, 33 Park Road, Milton,
Queensland 4064, Australia

John Wiley & Sons (Asia) Pte Ltd, 2 Clementi Loop #02-01,
Jin Xing Distripark, Singapore 129809

John Wiley & Sons (Canada) Ltd, 22 Worcester Road,
Rexdale, Ontario M9W 1L1, Canada

Library of Congress Cataloging-in-Publication Data

Cognitive psychotherapy of psychotic disorders: handbook of theory and practice / [edited by]
   Carlo Perris and Patrick D. McGorry.
       p.   cm.
   Includes bibliographical references and index.
   ISBN 0-471-98221-0 (cased)
   1. Psychoses—Treatment. 2. Cognitive therapy. I. Perris, Carlo. II. McGorry, Patrick D.
   [DNLM: 1. Psychotic Disorders—therapy. 2. Cognitive Therapy—methods. WM 200
C6765 1998]
   RC512.C556   1998
   616.89'142—dc21
   DNLM/DLC
   for Library of Congress   98-3825
                                                                         CIP

British Library Cataloguing in Publication Data

A catalogue record for this book is available from the British Library

ISBN 0-471-98221-0

Typeset in 10/12pt Times by Best-set Typesetter Ltd., Hong Kong
Printed and bound in Great Britain by Bookcraft (Bath) Ltd, Midsomer Norton, Somerset
This book is printed on acid-free paper responsibly manufactured from sustainable forestry, in which
at least two trees are planted for each one used for paper production.

Contents

About the Editors

Carlo Perris MD, MDhc (Timisoara) is Emeritus Professor of Psychiatry and former Chairman at the Department of Psychiatry, Umeå University, and WHO Collaborating Center for Research and Training in Mental Health. He is also the Co-director of The Swedish Institute for Cognitive Psychotherapy in Stockholm. He is Honorary President of the World Federation of Biological Psychiatry, and the President of the Swedish Association of Cognitive Psychotherapy. He was seminal in the distinction between unipolar and bipolar affective disorders in the 1960s. He has been a visiting research fellow/visiting professor in Switzerland, the USA, the UK, Japan, Italy and Romania. He has authored several books on cognitive psychotherapy in English, Italian and French. His main interest is the metacognitive treatment of severely disturbed patients (schizophrenics and personality disordered), for whom he has developed and implemented a chain of small treatment units throughout Sweden and elsewhere. He has published widely on various psychiatric subjects and also on transcultural research, e.g. parenting. This last research work has been summarized in an edited book (together with W. Arrindell & Martin Eisemann), *Parenting and Psychopathology*, published by Wiley.

Patrick D. McGorry MB, BS, PhD, MRCP(UK), FRANZCP is Professor at the Department of Psychiatry, University of Melbourne. First-episode psychosis in young people is his major area of interest. Professor McGorry was instrumental in leading the development of the Early Psychosis Prevention and Intervention Centre (EPPIC) and has been closely involved in the Centre's development as its Director. He is also the Director of the Centre for Young People's Mental Health, a programme of the Royal Melbourne Hospital, of which EPPIC is an integral part. In 1995 Professor McGorry received the Ian Simpson Award for his contribution to research related to first-episode psychosis, and was winner of the 1996 Gold Achievement Award from the Australian and New Zealand Mental Health Services Conference for the most outstanding individual contribution to theory, education and practice.

List of Contributors

Lucio Bizzini PhD *Hôpitaux Universitaires de Genéve, Dèpartment de Psychiatrie, Clinique de Psychiatrie gériatrique, UTCA, Geneva, Switzerland*

Dr Bizzini is a clinical psychologist, Head of the Cognitive Therapy Unit for the Elderly (Geriatric Psychiatric Clinic) at the University Hospital of Geneva (HUG, Department of Psychiatry), and granted for the Swiss National Research Programme on Aging. He is also the President of the Swiss Association for Cognitive Psychotherapy, and Lecturer at the University of Fribourg, Switzerland

José Valls Blanco MD *Fundación "Castilla del Pino", Reyes Catolicos Córdoba, Spain*

Professor Valls Blanco is Professor of Psychiatry at the Medical Faculty of the University of Córdoba. He is the Secretary of the "Fundacion Castilla del Pino", also in Córdoba, and the Editor of the *Proceedings* of the Foundation

Hans D. Brenner MD, PhD *Direktion Mitte/West der Universtären Psychiatrischen Dienste Bern, Bolligenstrasse 111, 3072 Ostermundigen, Switzerland*

Professor Brenner is Professor of Psychiatry and Chairman at the Department of Psychiatry of Bern University, Switzerland. He has co-edited several books on the psychosocial treatment of schizophrenia, and is the author of several articles on the cognitive therapy of schizophrenia

Massimo Casacchia MD *Service Hospitalo-Universitaire de Psychiatrie, Centre Hospitalier du Vinatier, 95 Bd Pinel, F-69677 Bron cedex, France*

Professor Casacchia is Professor of Psychiatry and Chairman at the Department of Psychiatry of the L'Aquila, Italy. He is also the Vice President of the Italian Society of Psychiatric Rehabilitation

Oliver Chambon MD *Service Hospitalo-Universitaire de Psychiatrie, Centre Hospitalier du Vinatier, 95 Bd Pinel, F-69677 Bron cedex, France*

Dr Chambon is a psychiatrist at the Department of Psychiatry of Lyon University at Bron, France. He has co-authored (with M. Marie-Cardine)

Psychothérapie des psychoses chroniques (Masson, 1994), *Le réadaptation sociale des psychotiques chroniques* (Presse Universitaire de France, 1992) and (with C. Perris & M. Marie-Cardine) *Techniques de psychothérapie cognitive des psychoses chroniques* (Masson, 1997). He has also co-authored (with M. Marie-Cardine & R. Meyer) *Psychothérapies. L'approche intégrative et éclectique* (Le Courdier, 1994: LEA, 1994)

Larry Davidson PhD   *Department of Psychiatry, Yale University School of Medicine, 34 Park Street, New Haven, CT 06519, USA*
   Professor Davidson is Assistant Professor of Psychiatry at the Yale University School of Medicine and Director of the Psychosis Program at the Connecticut Mental Health Center in New Haven, CT, USA

Jane Edwards PhD   *Centre for Young People's Mental Health, North-Western Healthcare Network, 35 Poplar Road, Parkville, Victoria 3052, Australia*
   Dr Edwards is Assistant Director (Clinical), Early Psychosis Prevention and Intervention Centre (EPPIC), and Associate of the Departments of Psychology and Psychiatry, University of Melbourne

David Fowler PhD   *Clinical Psychology, University of East Anglia, Norwich NR4 7TJ, UK*
   Dr Fowler is Lecturer in Clinical Psychology, Health Policy and Practice Unit, University of East Anglia, Head of Psychological Therapies for Psychosis Service, Norfolk Mental Health Trust, and co-author (with P. Garety and E. Kuipers) of *Cognitive Behaviour Therapy for Psychosis* (Wiley, 1995)

Philippa Garety PhD   *Department of Clinical Psychology at UMDS, 3rd Floor, Riddell House, St Thomas' Hospital, London SE1 7EH, UK*
   Professor Garety is Professor of Clinical Psychology at UMDS, St Thomas' Hospital, London, UK

Gillian Haddock   *Department of Nursing, University of Manchester, Oxford Road, Manchester M13 9PL, UK*
   Dr Haddock is Senior Lecturer in Clinical Psychology, Department of Nursing, University of Manchester, and Honorary Consultant Clinical Psychologist for Tameside and Glossop Community and Priority Services Trust, UK. She has carried out work evaluating the effectiveness of cognitive-behavioural treatments in chronic, recent-onset and acute schizophrenia

Lisa Henry MSc   *Early Psychosis Prevention and Intervention Centre (EPPIC), Centre for Young People's Mental Health, Western Healthcare Network, 35 Poplar Road, Parkville, Victoria 3052, Australia*
   Lisa Henry is a doctoral student with an interest in the recovery process in early psychosis and its influence on the long-term course.

Bettina Hodell PhD   *Direktion Mitte/West der Universtären Psychiatrischen Dienste Bern, Bolligenstrasse 111, 3072 Ostermundigen, Switzerland*
   Dr Hodell is a Research Psychologist at the Department of Psychiatry, Bern University, Switzerland. She has published several articles on the cognitive therapy of schizophrenic conditions

Bruno Intreccialagli MD   *Viale Dell'Astronomia 21, 00144 Rome, Italy*

Dr Intreccialagli is a Psychiatrist and Psychotherapist. He is an officer in the Directive Committee of the Italian Society of Cognitive Therapy (SITCC) in Rome. He has contributed articles and chapters in the field of attachment theory and psychopathology

Henry J. Jackson PhD FAPS   *Department of Psychology, University of Melbourne, Parkville, Victoria 3052, Australia*

Professor Jackson is Associate Professor of Psychology and Convenor of the Postgraduate Clinical Psychology Training Program in the Department of Psychology at the University of Melbourne. He is also Co-Director of the Early Psychosis Research Centre, Parkville, Victoria, Australia

David G. Kingdon MD   *Mental Health Group, Southampton University, Royal South Hants, Brinton's Terrace, Southampton SO14 OYG*

David Kingdon is Professor of Mental Health Care Delivery at University of Southampton UK. He has co-authored (with D. Turkington) *Cognitive-Behavioral Therapy of Schizophrenia* (LEA, 1994), and is the author of several articles on the cognitive therapy of schizophrenic conditions

Elizabeth Kuipers PhD   *Department of Psychology, Institute of Psychiatry, De Crespigny Park, Denmark Hill, London SE5 8AF, UK*

Elizabeth Kuipers is Professor of Clinical Psychology at the Institute of Psychiatry, London

Michael Kyrios PhD   *Departments of Psychology & Psychiatry, University of Melbourne, Royal Melbourne Hospital, Parkville, Victoria 3050, Australia*

Dr Kyrios is senior lecturer in the Department of Psychology and has a major clinical and research interest in obsessive-compulsive disorder.

Virginia Lafond MSW, CSW   *Schizophrenia Service, Royal Ottawa Hospital, 1145 Carling Avenue, Ottawa, Ontario, Canada K1Z 7K4*

Virginia Lafond works in the Schizophrenia Service at the Royal Ottawa Hospital, Canada. She is the author of *Grieving Mental Illness: A Guide for Patients and Their Caregivers* (University of Toronto Press, 1994)

Stacey Lambert PsyD   *Department of Psychiatry, Yale University School of Medicine, 34 Park Street, New Haven, CT 06519, USA*

Stacey Lambert is an Associate Research Scientist in the Department of Psychiatry at the Yale University School of Medicine and practises as a Clinical Psychologist at the Connecticut Mental Health Center in New Haven, CT, USA

Giovanni Liotti MD   *Viale Dell'Astronomia 21, 00144 Rome, Italy*

Giovanni Liotti is the Director of Training of the Italian Association for Cognitive Therapy (SITCC). He is also the President of an Association of Psychotherapists in Rome, whose aim is to systematically explore how the activation of a maladaptive attachment system throughout an individual′s developmental history may contribute to the shaping of psychopathological syndromes. He is also co-author (with V.F. Guidano) of *Cognitive Processes and the Emotional Disorders* (1983) and has contributed over 100 chapters and articles to various edited books and scientific journals published in Italy, the UK, the USA and Germany

Roberto Lorenzini MD   *Corso di Portanuova 12, Milan, Italy*
   Roberto Lorenzini is a psychiatrist and a teacher at the SITCC. He is in charge of the 5th Department of Mental Health in Viterbo, and works in Rome as a psychotherapist. He has co-authored (most often with S. Sassaroli) several books in Italian on various theoretic aspects of cognitive therapy

Dana Maude MA, EPPIC   *Centre for Young People's Mental Health, 35 Poplar Road, Parkville, Victoria, Australia 3052*
   Dana Maude is a doctoral student focusing on factors influencing the recovery process and early treatment resistance in psychotic disorders.

Thomas H. McGlashan MD   *Department of Psychiatry, Yale University School of Medicine, 34 Park Street, New Haven, CT 06519, USA*
   Professor McGlashan is Professor of Psychiatry, Yale University School of Medicine, and Executive Director, Yale Psychiatric Institute

Patrick D. McGorry MB, PhD   *Centre for Young People's Mental Health, Western Healthcare Network, 35 Poplar Road, Parkville, Victoria 3052, Australia*
   Professor McGorry is Professor and Director of the Centre for Young People's Mental Health

Hjördis Perris Dr Med Sci   *The Swedish Institute of Cognitive Psychotherapy, Dalagatan 9A, Box 6401, 113 82 Stockholm, Sweden*
   Professor Perris is Associate Professor of Medical Psychology, Umeå University, Co-Director of The Swedish Institute of Cognitive Psychotherapy, Stockholm, co-author of a book on personality disorders (in Swedish) and co-editor of *Cognitive Psychotherapy: Theory and Practice*

Carlo Perris MD   *The Swedish Institute of Cognitive Psychotherapy, Dalagatan 9A, Box 6401, 113 82 Stockholm, Sweden*
   Professor Perris is Co-director of the Swedish Institute of Cognitive Psychotherapy, Stockholm, and Professor of Psychiatry at Umeå University Department of Psychiatry, Norrlands University Hospital, 901 85 Umeå, Sweden

Elizabeth Peyton   *Graduate Faculty, New School for Social Research, 65 Fifth Avenue, New York, NY 10003, USA*
   Elizabeth Peyton is a doctoral student in the Psychology Department at the New School for Social Research in New York, USA

James Pretzer PhD   *Cleveland Center for Cognitive Therapy, 24100 Chagrin Blvd., #470, Beachwood, OH 44122-5535, USA*
   Professor Pretzer is the Director of the Cleveland Center for Cognitive Therapy and is an Assistant Clinical Professor of Psychology in the Department of Psychiatry at the Case Western Reserve University School of Medicine. He also is a Consulting Editor at Behavior OnLine where he hosts an open discussion of Cognitive Therapy. He has co-authored *Clinical Applications of Cognitive*

Therapy (Plenum, 1990) and *Cognitive Therapy of Personality Disorders* (Guilford, 1990)

Jörg Richter   *Department of Psychiatry, University of Rostock, Gehlsheimer Strasse 20, D-181 47 Rostock, Germany*
   Professor Richter is Associate Professor, Department of Psychiatry, University of Rostock, Germany

Rita Ronconi MD   *Department of Psychiatry of the L'Aquila University, L'Aquila, Italy*
   Professor Ronconi is an Assistant Professor of Psychiatry and a Research Associate at the Department of Psychiatry of the L'Aquila University, L'Aquila, Italy

Jeremy D. Safran   *Graduate Faculty, New School for Social Research 65 Fifth Avenue, New York, NY 10003, USA*
   Professor Safran is Professor of Psychology at the New School for Social Research in Manhattan. He is a former Director of the Clinical Psychology Program and is co-author of *Interpersonal Process in Cognitive Therapy* (with Zindel Segal) and *Emotion in Psychotherapy* (with Leslie Greenberg)

Lisa Phillips MSc   *Centre for Young People's Mental Health, 35 Poplar Road, Parkville, Victoria, Australia 3052*
   Lisa Phillips in the coordinator of the PACE clinic, a preventive clinical service for young people at incipient risk of psychosis.

Sandra Sassaroli MD   *SITCC, Corso di Portanuova 12, Milan, Italy*
   Dr Sassaroli is a psychiatrist and a teacher at the SITCC. Formerly in Rome, she works now in Milan where she is the Director of a Training Institute for Cognitive Therapy. She has co-authored (mostly with R. Lorenzini) several books in Italian on various theoretical aspects of cognitive therapy

Annette Schaub PhD   *Department of Psychiatry, Ludwig Maximilian University of Munich, Nussbaumstrasse 7, 80336 Munich, Germany*
   Dr Schaub is at present a research assistant at the Department of Psychiatry, University of Munich. Main interests: coping with psychiatric illness, quality of life, cognitive functioning, cognitive therapy, evaluation of treatment programmes in psychiatry

Paul Schlette PhD   *Department of Psychiatry, Nyköping Hospital, Nyköping, Sweden*
   Dr Schlette is a clinical psychologist at the Department of Psychiatry, Nyköping Hospital, Nyköping Sweden

Lars Skagerlind   *Department of Psychiatry, Norrlands University Hospital, 901 85 Umeå, Sweden*
   Lars Skagerlind is a psychiatric nurse and a registered cognitive psychotherapist. He is in charge of the Ersboda Cognitive Psychotherapy Center for severely disturbed patients at the Norrlands University Hospital in Umeå, and a research student at the Department of Psychiatry of the Umeå University, Umeå, Sweden

Douglas Turkington MD   *Collingwood Clinic, St Nicholas' Hospital, Gosforth, Newcastle upon Tyne NE3 3XT, UK*

Dr Turkington is a Consultant Psychiatrist at the Collingwood Clinic, St Nicholas' Hospital, Newcastle upon Tyne. He has co-authored (with D.G. Kingdon) *Cognitive-behavioral Therapy of Schizophrenia* (LEA, 1994)

T. Michael Vallis PhD   *Queen Elizabeth II Health Sciences Centre, Psychology Department, 1278 Tower Road, Halifax, Nova Scotia B3H 249, Canada*

Dr Vallis works in the Departments of Psychology and Psychiatry, Dalhousie University, Halifax. He has co-authored (with J.L. Howes & P.C. Miller) *The Challenge of Cognitive Therapy* (Plenum, 1991)

Lawrence Yusupoff   *25 St John Street, Manchester M3 4DT, UK*

Lawrence Yusupoff is an independent Consultant Clinical Psychologist, based in Manchester. His principal research interest has been the evaluation of cognitive-behavioural therapies for persistent hallucinations and delusions. He is currently involved in the training and supervision of mental health professionals who are developing their therapeutic skills with psychotic patients. He also has a private therapy and medico-legal practice

Foreword

I am delighted to have the opportunity to introduce this present volume to the various types of professionals dealing with severe psychiatric disorders: psychiatrists, psychologists, psychiatric nurses, social workers, etc.

In a way, the chapters in this volume reflect various aspects of my own work with the psychotherapy of patients. My very first psychiatric article, published in 1961, dealt with a kind of cognitive intervention with a chronically schizophrenic young man who had the delusion that he was being followed by FBI men. My practical approach to this patient was to have him attempt to describe in great detail exactly what were the characteristics of his "followers". As he started to operationalize his definition of these individuals, it became necessary for him to observe them more and more closely. In so doing, they became "real people" rather than homogeneous stereotypes.

In the course of time, as he attempted apply the profile of these supposed typical FBI men to people whom he saw, it became increasingly difficult to fit them into this mold. In the course of time, he came to the conclusion that perhaps he was wrong in his identifications—actually, misidentifications—and that he was jumping to conclusions about people without actually observing them very closely.

Another aspect of the psychopathology that helped to drive this delusion was his belief that he was guilty for various misdemeanors of his father. As a result of this "borrowed guilt" he concretized the punishment into the form of government agents who would be punishing him. With this understanding and, of course, a strong, supportive therapeutic relationship, the patient was able to refocus his attention on more realistic aspects of living and the delusions gradually dissipated.

It was not until many years later that I had an opportunity to return to the early observations that I had made regarding the empirical testing of one's beliefs. I teamed up with a medical student (Richard Hall) and one of my psychiatric residents (John Rush), and selected six patients from the psychiatric service who had delusions. We found, in keeping with our earlier experiences, that the process of focusing on the supposed characteristics of "persecuted" patients and attempting to apply a derived set of criteria for diagnosing them, helped to fortify the patients' reality testing and, at the same time, to diminish the impact of the delusions. It was thus a two-fold process, simultaneously priming the individual's ability to subject his/her conclusions to rational and empirical scrutiny; and additionally actually applying this to the phenomenology of the patient's thinking.

Many years elapsed before this work was taken up again and applied in a more systematic way by investigators such as Perris, Kingdon, Turkington, Bentol, Chadwick, Lowe and others. As a result of the stimulation of these other authors, I then prepared a paper with Brad Alford, drawing on his experience as well as my own in dealing with delusions.

Another facet of my work has been dealing with more severely depressed patients; perhaps the most difficult in this group are those who receive the diagnosis of "bipolar affective disorder". Of particular interest and challenge have been the patients with rapid-cycling bipolar disorder. Although the conventional wisdom asserts that the bipolar cycles are driven emotionally, the very important cognitive infrastructure tends to be neglected. Actually, in our work with rapid cyclers, we found that a surge of either manic excitement or depressive feelings was initiated subjectively by a particular type of interpretation. Thus, when a patient heard some good news, she would fantastically exaggerate it and when the news was not so good, she would see this as something really awful. One patient, for example, had a kind of manic excitement over the fact that she was going to have a family reunion with her adult children and grandchildren. The very thought was highly romanticized, and she envisioned them standing or sitting around the piano, like the Trapp family. This manic excitement continued until the family got together. Then, when the children started to squabble with one another, she had the thought, "They hate each other. I've really failed them as a parent", and started to feel acute depressive feelings. Although the cognitive interventions in this and other cases occurred in the context of the patients receiving medications such as lithium, we found that it was possible to effect a far more penetrating change in the patients' psychopathology through the cognitive interventions.

We also found that bipolar patients would adhere much more effectively to their medication if their various beliefs about the effects and side effects of the medication were addressed in a cognitive fashion. Thus, the focus on the belief during the manic phase that medication would rob a patient of his/her originality and good feelings and was a deterrent, and during the depressed phase, the belief that nothing would help and that the side effects were intolerable also served as a deterrent.

My other major experience with the sicker patients occurred in the context of the rapid inpatient treatment of depressed patients. We found that a highly structured activity schedule provided the framework for introducing a practically all-day exposure to cognitive-behavioral techniques. Thus, the patients were instructed in filling out the daily schedule of activities every morning, recognizing and evaluating their negative thoughts and responding to them. Two group therapy sessions a day allowed the patients an opportunity to develop their cognitive skills and to address important issues such as hopelessness, suicidal wishes, family problems, occupational and interpersonal problems. The patients also did "homework" during the day and would have their own patient-led group meetings in which they would discuss their reading and their homework assignments. Using this technique allowed us to reduce the number of patient days from approximately 21 down to 7 days.

Various authors of the different chapters in the book have been successful in addressing and applying many of the principles that evolved in the history of cognitive therapy, and have added much more in verifying the treatment of conditions such as dissociative disorders and personality disorders.

Aaron T. Beck

Preface

In recent years the concept of "serious mental illness" has become popular in developed countries, partly as a device for containing mental health budgets and targeting finite and often shrinking resources. It has also been used constructively in some countries as a mechanism to prevent the dissipation of funding released from the dissolution of the old state psychiatric hospital system, acting as an organising principle for the allocation of resources in a community-based system. People suffering from disorders, such as schizophrenia and borderline personality disorder, which fall within this rubric, not only have a profile of severe morbidity and mortality, but have traditionally been the most neglected when it came to the quality of their psychiatric care. The essence of the serious mental illness profile is that a disorder of this type typically has its onset during adolescence or early adult life (Mrazek and Haggerty, 1994) and is associated with a pervasive disturbance of mental functioning which puts at risk the normal life trajectory and quality of life for the person. The early course is one of several years of relapsing illness with background disability, suffering and distress, punctuated by illness episodes or crises, a significant risk of suicide (at least 10%), and ultimately, in most cases, an amelioration of the disorder over time as the person matures or the vulnerability lessens. The latter is qualified by the degree of irreversible damage done while the disorder is at its peak, and by the risk of not surviving the fury of the early years of illness. Clearly many disorders, not only schizophrenia, can be characterised by such a profile. It is somewhat ironic that these disorders are now being given priority by funders of mental health services, while formerly more attractive disorders and patients, impugned inappropriately by some as the "worried well", are being excluded from care. Such an unnecessary corollary of an increased emphasis on serious disorders creates a new type of discrimination. Nevertheless, for people who do live with the more severe and pervasive disorders, there is a lot of catching up to be done.

The facilities and environments in which treatment has been offered have been extremely neglected and underfunded in the past, and this is beginning to be addressed in some countries by more sophisticated deinsitutionalisation programmes, though in others serious new errors have been made. For some, notably people with borderline personality disorder, it has typically been very difficult to gain adequate access to treatment facilities at all. While of dubious value in personality disorder, pharmacological treatments for psychotic disorders have been effective but have had severe side-effects, and have been crudely employed by many clinicians. Fortunately there have been major advances in this field recently, and a new generation of antipsychotics and antidepressants with better efficacy and lower side effects is now available. Psychotherapeutic treatments for these disorders were, if anything, even more inappropriate and ineffective, narrowly deployed, and too arcane or too inflexible to meet the needs of these severely ill patients. Despite the efforts of pioneers such as Fromm-Reichmann, Arieti, Kohut and others, to adapt traditional psychoanalytic approaches to the more severely disturbed groups of patients, these attempts, developed as they were in isolation from other treatment approaches, ultimately failed. Behaviour therapies had a similar history of very limited success. Psychological treaments in general suffered from a highly reductionistic approach which interfered with integrated biopsychosocial treatment. Clinical trials failed to show advantages for specialised dynamic psychotherapy, and this led along with other factors to a destructive scenario in which psychological treatments became discredited and even contraindicated in some quarters. Certainly, no "blueprint" survived to guide the average practitioner who wanted include a person-centred psychological approach in the management of psychotic or personality disorders. Clinicians found themselves unsure about how to talk with patients with serious disorders and personal psychotherapy was felt to be no longer a valid part of the treatment. Fortunately, there is now renewed hope too for this aspect of the management of these patients.

The cognitive revolution, which has emerged from and drawn on the two great tributaries of behaviourism and psychoanalysis, has finally over the past decade reached the shores of serious mental illness. During the 1980s, neither of us could find evidence of cognitive psychotherapy research or treatment in psychotic disorders. Fortunately, there is now a burgeoning level of activity including several randomised clinical trials from Europe and North America showing its effectiveness, even in treatment refractory cases. A similar situation exists in other severe disorders, such as severe personality disorder, where cognitive interventions have been developed. The attractiveness of cognitive interventions is that they are empowering and humanistic in their respect for the person. Furthermore, they can be based on clinically testable theories in individuals and groups of patients, are highly compatible with biological models of vulnerability and disorder, are pragmatic in terms of length and depth of intervention, and they can be offered as part of a multimodal treatment approach. Within the cognitive approach, as evidenced by this volume, there can be a range of approaches to the patient. All of these have in common, with each other and with many other forms of psychological treatment, an optimistic and humane approach to the patient and their disorder. The foundation for all improvement and progress is a healthy and stable relationship with the patient, which is actively nurtured. An understanding of each individual as a unique person with idiosyncratic sets of schemas and constructions of the world is the next building block, and this is combined with a knowledge of similar patterns in others with these disorders. The acknowledgment of an internal world, some aspects of which are out of awareness is another common feature, which gives the cognitive approach its depth. The influence of constructivism, acknowledged by many as a variant of cognitive psychology, is apparent in a number of the contributions in this volume. Indeed, in developing cognitive interventions for the seriously mentally ill, it is an undoubted advantage to incorporate other theoretical ideas to broaden and deepen the approach, another good example of this being attachment theory. This pluralist capacity allows the psychological approach to coexist with and catalyse biological and social elements within the treatment programme. When used as part of the treatment for complex disorders with multifactorial aetiology, such integrative pluralism is essential. At the coal-face with the patient, however, the therapy must remain flexible and pragmatic without being superficial. This is a difficult balancing act. In the real world, many patients are young, immature, not introspective or particularly insightful or especially intelligent. Their disorders have often further impaired their capacity to reflect and to contain disturbing emotions, as well as, in many cases, their cognitive capacity. If we are serious about developing a blueprint for personal psychotherapy with people with serious mental illness, we need to develop a therapeutic approach which can engage and help a broad spectrum of people, not just a select minority. A staged approach with a series of levels to be mastered, as pioneered by Hogarty and colleagues, is one solution to this practical problem.

There are a number of continuing challenges from a theoretical point of view. Firstly, the integration of the metatheories underpinning cognitive therapies with the cognitive neuropsychology of the psychotic disorders in particular, and more broadly with other neuroscientific aspects, notably neuroimaging paradigms, is an important task. Including cognitive remediation therapies within the cognitive "church" helps to foster such an integration, which has been explored most extensively by Brenner and colleagues in Berne. Secondly, as is widely acknowledged, a more satisfactory understanding of the relationship between cognition and affect is required by the cognitive behaviour therapy field in general. This is an issue central to the more serious and pervasive disorders, where greater disturbance of the relationship between cognition and affect occurs, and careful study of the early phases of these disorders could provide more clues to such understanding. Indeed, partly because of the special psychological opportunities available at this phase of illness, we have included a special focus on the early phases of psychotic disorder as a feature of this book.

The collection of authors in this volume are part of a growing group of clinicians and researchers who are tackling one of the most challenging and rewarding tasks in psychiatry, one which was originally thought impossible by both Kraepelin and Freud, namely to establish personal contact with and help through psychological methods people with the most serious mental illnesses. The contributions in this volume as well as other emerging literature demonstrate that this is not only feasible, but that the way of doing it can be reproduced and described. Perhaps the next and equally critical step will be to show that these are practical enough skills for routine use by reasonably well trained mental health professionals.

The editors would like to thank all the contributors for their excellent co-operation, all the patients and their families whose experiences and wisdom gave rise to the new knowledge contained within this volume. We would like to sincerely thank our colleagues, some of whom have contributed directly to this volume, but also the many others whose contribution has been indirect but of considerable importance nonetheless. We are most grateful to Michael Coombs and Lesley Valerio from John Wiley & Sons whose patience and forbearance as well as their professionalism were key variables in producing the book. We would also like to acknowledge the support and tolerance of our families which also critical elements enabling the task to be completed.

REFERENCE

Mrazek, P.J. & Haggerty, R.J. (eds) (1994). *Reducing Risks for Mental Disorders: Frontiers for Preventive Intervention Research*. Washington, DC: National Academy Press.

Carlo Perris
Patrick D. McGorry
April, 1998

Chapter 1

Psychotherapeutic and Cognitive-behavioral Treatments for Schizophrenia: Developing a Disorder-specific Form of Psychotherapy for Persons with Psychosis

Larry Davidson*, Stacey Lambert and Thomas H. McGlashan
Department of Psychiatry, Yale University School of Medicine, New Haven, CT, USA

A number of factors have contributed to a diminution of interest in the potential utility and effectiveness of psychotherapy for people with psychotic disorders. Certainly among the most influential of these factors was the advent of psychotropic medications in the 1950s and the ascendancy of the neurobiological paradigm of serious mental illness over the last 20 years. In addition, psychotherapy outcome studies appearing in the early 1980s (e.g. Gunderson et al., 1984) suggested that intensive, investigative forms of psychodynamic psychotherapy not only lacked efficacy for people with these disorders, but might actually cause harm to them as well. Most recently, utilization review guidelines of managed care organizations have restricted access to these forms of long-term psychotherapy for most individuals, and have moved increasingly toward time-

---

* Author for correspondence.

Cognitive Psychotherapy of Psychotic and Personality Disorders: Handbook of Theory and Practice.
Edited by C. Perris and P.D. McGorry.
© 1998 John Wiley & Sons Ltd.

limited, problem-focused and empirically-based approaches to psychotherapy. In their current form, most of these brief psychotherapies are limited in their relevance to, and in their effectiveness in addressing, the kinds of problems experienced by people with prolonged psychotic disorders. As a result, there has been a noticeable decrease in literature on psychotherapy for people with psychosis over the last 20 years, with many trainees and other newcomers to the field assuming that there is little point to such efforts and that they might, in fact, cause more harm than good.

Despite this decrease in scholarly interest in psychotherapy for psychosis, most mental health providers who work with people with prolonged psychotic disorders are not themselves psychiatrists, and consequently do not prescribe medications. While they continue to want to care for and assist these individuals, they may feel that there is little for them to do in this regard other than to provide case management services that attend to the individual's basic and everyday needs (Milton, Patwa & Hafner, 1978). On the other hand, many mental health providers still develop relationships with, and talk to, their psychotic patients. At least in these cases, it would appear that some of the principles first derived from the psychotherapeutic tradition continue to live on in conventional treatments for psychosis; having gone "underground" as it were, but remaining implicit in the practices of "supportive psychotherapy" (McGlashan, 1994) and "clinical case management" (Harris & Bachrach, 1988) that constitute the core of current non-somatic treatments for this population. The lack of research exploring the nature and utility of these approaches to the care of people with psychosis may represent more of a lack of interest in these modalities on the part of the academic community than reflect an actual decrease in their use in day-to-day clinical practice. To the extent that clinicians working routinely with such patients continue to attempt to develop useful relationships with them and talk with them in a supportive way about their problems and concerns, more research, examination and discussion of these approaches seems warranted and perhaps overdue.

Fortunately, several reviews of psychotherapeutic and other psychosocial treatments for people with psychosis have appeared in just the last few years (Bellack & Mueser, 1993; McNally, 1994; Kane & McGlashan, 1995; Penn & Mueser, 1996; Scott & Dixon, 1995), indicating that there may now be renewed interest in just such efforts. One line of investigation that appears to be particularly promising involves the application of cognitive-behavioral principles in the development of a new form of psychotherapy that specifically addresses some of the core symptoms associated with psychosis. Although there may only be a handful of empirical studies produced to date that have evaluated this approach, there is a growing body of literature exploring the potential usefulness of a number of cognitive-behavioral interventions in treating some of the symptoms and dysfunctions associated with psychosis that have been refractory to medications.

The following chapter reviews the core elements and current status of this new form of psychotherapy for schizophrenia as it is being developed in English-speaking countries. We begin with a brief review of the history of psychotherapy for schizophrenia as a backdrop for discussing these more recent attempts to introduce cognitive-behavioral aspects into the treatment of this population. Next, we provide an introduction to the core elements of the cognitive-behavioral approach to psychosis as it is beginning to be practiced in the UK and the USA. We follow the example of delusions through each of the iterations of psychotherapeutic approaches in order to highlight their differences, and then review each of the major approaches developed to date applying cognitive-behavioral principles to the treatment of psychosis. We close by suggesting that at this point in the development of this new treatment, a dialogue between the psychotherapy and cognitive-behavioral traditions would be productive in exploring the ways in which psychotherapy may benefit from the disorder-specific focus of the cognitive-behavioral approach, but also the ways in which lessons learned from psychotherapy about so-called "non-specific" factors may better inform cognitive-behavioral interventions with this population as well.

A BRIEF HISTORY OF THE PSYCHOTHERAPY OF SCHIZOPHRENIA

Attempts to develop a "talking cure" for schizophrenia probably began at the turn of the century with Adolph Meyer's (1950) "psychobiology". Meyer held the perspective that the course of many psychiatric disorders, including psychosis, could be understood in the context of the person's life story as functional reactions to the person's encounter with the environment. Harry Stack Sullivan (e.g. 1931, 1953, 1962) elaborated this perspective into the treatment modality of interpersonal psychotherapy on his innovative inpatient unit for acutely psychotic men at Sheppard-Pratt Hospital in the 1920s. Sullivan regarded schizophrenia as a disturbance in the person's capacity to relate to others that was not biological in origin, but rather reflected the history of the patient's interactions with significant others. Freida Fromm-Reichmann (e.g. 1960) integrated more classical psychoanalytic thinking and terminology with Sullivan's interpersonal perspective during her tenure at Chestnut Lodge in the 1930s, 1940s, and 1950s. In her work there with more chronically psychotic patients, she developed what eventually became the prototype of psychodynamic psychotherapy.

In its earliest forms, psychodynamic psychotherapy was closest to psychoanalysis in theory and practice. The psychodynamic model of the mind regards psychopathology as generated by active and sustained psychological conflict between drive-created wishful impulses, on the one hand, and antithetical wishes, reality or conscience on the other. This conflict generates defenses against the wishful impulse, and these defenses can often be seen in the form of symptoms. Furthermore, any or all of this drama may occur outside of awareness, i.e. unconsciously.

According to the conflict/defense model, schizophrenic symptoms result from conflict and defense, just as in neurotic psychopathology. The differences between schizophrenia and the neuroses are quantitative, not qualitative, in nature, with schizophrenia being more severe. In the latter syndrome, conflict is more intense and requires frequent use of very primitive—i.e. developmentally earlier—defenses such as denial and projection, which often involve a break with reality. The mind of a patient with schizophrenia regresses to developmentally earlier stages or levels of organization, the exact level being determined (or fixated) by past psychological trauma(s) of an experiential nature. The differences between schizophrenia and neurosis lie in the depth of regression and the fixation point, which for schizophrenia is located in the pre-oedipal phase of development.

Given the conflict/defense model, the therapeutic strategies of psychodynamic psychotherapy for psychotic patients follow many of those outlined for classic psychoanalysis of neurotic patients. Among these are: (a) the position of the therapist as a neutral explorer of the interactional process who is after the truth about the patient's experience, rather than after change *per se* (e.g. "social recovery"); (b) the centrality of the one-to-one transference relationship; (c) the admonition to interpret negative transference but not positive transference; and (d) the importance of identifying and removing defenses.

The conflict/defense model also suggests that there is a hierarchy of validity to the process material (i.e. the patient's thoughts, feelings and behaviors in the session). Further, higher validity corresponds to greater depth. Truer meaning lies behind defenses, behind conflict, closer to the drives of sex and aggression. The ultimate aim of this process is to remove the person's developmental fixations through insight, abreaction and working-through, thus allowing the resumption of normal emotional growth.

Based upon their experience with treating psychotic patients, Sullivan & Fromm-Reichmann modified classical technique by sitting patients up, and seeing them less frequently than daily, but being more interactive with them in sessions. Nevertheless, the treatment remained intensive, exploratory and long-term, with the principal work of therapy being understanding. Symptom formation was regarded as dynamic, i.e. psychological, and triggered by stress that was specifically meaningful vis-à-vis the patient's past, personal development. Treatment, therefore, meant confronting, clarifying and interpreting that meaning to the patient.

The transition from psychodynamic psychotherapy to supportive psychotherapy began in the late 1950s, with the introduction of chlorpromazine to the treatment of psychosis. Neuroleptics not only added to the treatment modalities available for schizophrenia but also introduced a paradigm shift in the conception of schizophrenia. The effectiveness of the new drugs suggested a somatic factor in the disorder, a notion that found further support in the genetic studies soon to follow. Medications and genetics ultimately translated into the more contemporary vulnerability–stress model of the mind, in which disorder is seen as an interaction between a biological vulnerability to psychosis and experiential stress which triggers psychotic symptom formation or mental state breakdown. The nature and source of the biological vulnerability is unknown, but unlike the psychodynamic model, a somatic vulnerability is acknowledged. The nature of stress in this model also is different, being more generic and quantitative than the more personally meaningful stress of the psychodynamic model.

Empirical research in the 1960s and 1970s aided the transition to biological treatments and biological causes by demonstrating clearly the efficacy of drug treatments and the lack of efficacy of psychotherapeutic treatments. The clear utility of drugs re-medicalized the relationship between the treatment pair; therapist–client turned again to doctor–patient. The provider changed from an analyst who does "with" the patient to the doctor who "supports" treatment in the traditional way, with the treatment defined as medication and the therapeutic relationship serving that exchange.

The treatment model of what has since come to be called "supportive psychotherapy" diverges considerably from its psychodynamic roots. The process of treatment is more medical in nature, with the doctor/therapist doing to and for the patient with medication and support. Since the stress that triggers symptoms is seen as more external and general, efforts are made to help the patient reduce stress by developing better coping strategies, by avoiding stress more effectively, or by removing the stress *for* the patient through manuevers that are basically custodial. The aims of this treatment are: (a) palliative, i.e. to reduce the intensity and disruptive nature of symptoms; and (b) rehabilitative, i.e. to help the patient adjust to and/or cope with ongoing dysfunction.

As a result of their differences in perspective and aims, psychodynamic and supportive psychotherapy diverge from each other technically in many of their goals and process strategies. A summary of these differences is presented in Table 1.1 (Goals) and Table 1.2 (Strategies).

Despite the divergence in their etiologic models and aims, however, psychodynamic and supportive psychotherapies also share many technical and treatment process elements. Some of these are: (a) setting a contract or working relationship and the concrete details of place, frequency, limits, expectations, etc.; (b) establishing a trusting relationship; (c) elucidating the patient's experiences in the here and now, both symptomatic and non-symptomatic, and tolerating what the patient brings to the work without losing structure and direction; and (d) remaining available, committed to continuity, and at peace with the necessity for patience, practice and adherence to task. These common elements, combined

Table 1.1 Goals

SUPPORTIVE	INVESTIGATIVE
Social recovery	Personality change
Re-establish homeostasis	Resume emotional growth
Removal of symptoms	Removal and understanding of symptoms
Strengthen defenses	More mature defenses
Sealing-over	Integrating

Table 1.2 Strategies

SUPPORTIVE	INVESTIGATIVE
Defines reality	Explores patient's reality
Reassurance	Abstinence
Gives advice	Remains neutral
Maintains family contact	Investigates concerns about family
Does to and for the patient	Does with the patient
Ignores psychotic symptoms	Explores psychotic symptoms
Structure against regression	Regressions tolerated
Liberal with anti-psychotic drugs	Sparse with antipsychotic drugs
Sides with defenses	Explores defenses
Fosters positive transference	Does not manipulate transference
Avoids negative transference	Interprets negative transference

with an attention to the formative life experiences and growth and development needs of the patient, have since been integrated with an active focus on the patient's basic, everyday needs into a concept of "clinical case management" which has moved the therapeutic frame outside of the clinician's office into the community settings where the patient lives, works and socializes (Harris & Bachrach, 1988).

THE COGNITIVE-BEHAVIORAL APPROACH TO SCHIZOPHRENIA

Continuing this historical perspective, the cognitive-behavioral approach to psychosis can be traced to an article by Beck (1952) appearing in the 1950s entitled "Successful outpatient psychotherapy of a chronic schizophrenic with a delusion based on borrowed guilt". While a few articles were produced in the intervening 40 years (e.g. Hartman & Cashman, 1983; Hole, Rush & Beck, 1979), this line of investigation began in earnest only in the early part of this decade with a related body of work emerging independently around the world (e.g. Chadwick & Lowe, 1990; Fowler, Garety & Kuipers, 1995; Hodel & Brenner, 1994; Hogarty et al., 1995; Kingdon & Turkington, 1994; Perris & Skagerlind, 1994; Tarrier et al., 1993a,b). This work consists of efforts first to identify, and then to reduce, core target symptoms and behaviors associated with psychosis, such as delusions and hallucinations, through highly structured interventions. Most approaches also are time-limited in nature, typically spanning 4–16 sessions, and all strive for an ideal of being manualized, empirically-tested and replicable.

The model of the mind employed by cognitive-behavioral approaches developed independently both of psychoanalytic thought and of theories of the etiology of psychosis. A key assumption of this model is that people develop and maintain cognitive sets or schemata that allow them to make sense of their experiences (Beck et al., 1979; Lambert & Davidson, 1997; Meichenbaum, 1977).

Social-cognitive, information-processing and inferential processes do not follow strictly the rules of formal logic, but employ these schemata as heuristics to screen, limit and organize perceptual stimuli (Kingdon, Turkington & John, 1994). Such schemata are necessary due to the brain's limited ability to process information, and typically are adaptive and useful in enabling the person to navigate through his or her immediate social environment.

In this view, psychopathology is thought to result from distortions in the formation or use of schemata; distortions which may be generated through a variety of mechanisms (Roberts, 1992). For example, as first suggested by Maher (1974), abnormal perceptual experiences (such as auditory hallucinations) may result—through an otherwise normal inferential process—in the production of maladaptive beliefs (such as God or the CIA talking to me). Alternatively, normal perceptual experiences may be distorted through the rigid use of schemata that are inappropriate to the context and content of the experiences. In this case, it is the inferential process itself which is skewed, leading the person to adopt narrow or biased beliefs that maintain only a minimal connection with objective facts or new experiences (Meichenbaum, 1977). In either case, however, the processes that underlie the generation of such beliefs are viewed as basically similar to those underlying normal cognitive processes, differing only by matter of degree (Strauss, 1969, 1991). As in depression, in which people consistently maintain negative views of themselves, the world and the future irrespective of disconfirming evidence, delusional beliefs, for example, are viewed as reflecting overly narrow or inflexible cognitive sets that are resistant to disconfirmation (Alford & Correia, 1994; Hartman & Cashman, 1983) and which, as a result, lead to the misinterpretation of new events in accordance with their belief system (Lowe & Chadwick, 1990; Roberts, 1992).

Such a model of the mind is consistent with the assumptions of supportive psychotherapy in relation to psychosis, being based in a broadly defined vulnerability–stress paradigm. This model promises to move the paradigm a step further, however, by generating new techniques and interventions to address specific aspects of psychosis that are lacking in the armamentarium of supportive psychotherapy. In addition, this model of the mind allows for a more interactive interplay between biology and environment as mediated through perceptual and social-cognitive processes. Should "hard-wired" neurocognitive deficits be discovered at the core of psychosis, these deficits could assume a prominent role in explaining the production of distorted cognitive schemata. In such a case, structural or neuroanatomical dysfunction would be generating cognitive dysfunction. On the other hand, it also is possible within this view for abnormal or distorted perceptual experiences (whether due again to neurobiological causes or to environmental sources) to produce maladaptive schemata. In either case, locating some of the core symptoms of psychosis at the level of cognitive schemata suggests a number of specific foci for cognitive-behavioral interventions.

The specific foci targeted for intervention have been identified through a review of the descriptive, phenomenological, behavioral, cognitive and neurocognitive literatures, and comprise a range of social-cognitive and behavioral deficits associated with psychosis. These include: vulnerability to acute disorganization; perceptual distortions; attentional and memory impairments; impairments in inferential reasoning and social judgment; emotional disturbances and impairments in affect regulation; social disability; and distortions in sense of self and others. It is perhaps most useful to illustrate the kinds of interventions developed to address these problem areas, and to highlight their departure from the technical and process elements of both investigative and supportive psychotherapy, through the example of the conceptualization and treatment of delusions.

In keeping with its focus on internal conflict and the role of defenses, investigative psychotherapy is primarily interested in the content of delusional beliefs, rather than in their form *per se*. The assumption in this view is that delusions are structural manifestations of primitive defenses, and that the route to resolution of the need for such defenses lay in clarification, confrontation, interpretation and working-through of the unconscious conflicts (latent content) that lay behind or underneath the delusional material (manifest content). The generation of new delusions will only be disrupted by a resumption of normal development that would move the patient beyond the pre-oedipal phase in which such primitive defenses operate.

In contrast to this approach, supportive psychotherapy is interested primarily in the form and timing of delusional beliefs rather than in their content. Although little attention has been paid to the nature of specific symptoms such as delusions within this approach, the broad assumption is that symptoms are produced (in a non-specific way) by a necessary neurobiological vulnerability to psychosis associated with sufficient environmental stress. In this regard, symptoms represent little more than the situational emergence of pre-wired pathology, and are best managed through biological treatments and the reduction of precipitating stressors. The primary interventions utilized by practitioners of supportive psychotherapy are therefore psychoeducation of patients and their families about symptoms, the need for medications, and strategies for stress management. To the extent that patients choose to discuss their delusions in treatment, therapists may first point out or remind the patient of the delusional nature of these beliefs, and then strive to help the patient *contain* the beliefs within the frame of the relationship to lessen their detrimental impact on the patient's day-to-day life (e.g. "If you talk this way to your boss, you may get fired").

In contrast both to investigative and to supportive psychotherapy, the cognitive-behavioral approach maintains an interest in both the form *and* content of delusional beliefs. The content of delusions are assumed to represent the person's attempts to make sense of some prior experiences. These experiences may themselves be abnormal in nature—as is the case with delusions generated as explanations for hallucinatory experiences—or they may be relatively normal experiences which are processed in distorted ways. In both cases, the thought processes involved in delusional beliefs are conceptualized as being similar to "normal" thought processes, differing from non-delusional beliefs only quantitatively on a spectrum of degree of resistance to modification by disconfirming events and evidence (Hole, Rush & Beck, 1979; Strauss, 1969). While the content thus represents the experiences the person has a need to make sense of, the form represents possible distortions, biases, or limitations in the ways the person has been able to make sense of these experiences.

In the cognitive-behavioral approach, both of these elements of form and content then become targets for intervention. The goal of intervention is to help the patient replace his/her maladaptive beliefs with more accurate beliefs, or at least with beliefs that make more adaptive sense of the experiences in question; and, in the process, to learn to question and evaluate his/her beliefs according to the available evidence. Building upon the base first established by cognitive therapy, this process consists primarily of Socratic questioning and behavioral tests (Beck et al., 1979). The therapist begins this process by establishing a trusting, working alliance with the patient, characterized by an air of "collaborative empiricism" (Beck et al., 1979; Chadwick & Lowe, 1994; Fowler & Morley, 1989; Kingdon & Turkington, 1994). This means that the clinician positions him/herself as an ally rather than as an opponent of the patient, avoiding direct confrontations or challenges to the patient's beliefs that can threaten or disrupt rapport. Instead of education and containment (as in supportive psychotherapy), and instead of interpretation of the content of the delusion (as in investigative psychotherapy), the cognitive-behavioral clinician invites the patient to explore with him/her the evidence for the delusional beliefs and the possibility of alternative explanations that account for that evidence. Should the patient resist this exploratory approach and insist on the therapist's validation of the delusional beliefs, the therapist is to strive for an ideal in which the two can "agree to differ" until some later time at which the impasse can be resolved (Kingdom & Turkington, 1994). This approach involves several phases.

In the initial phase of treatment, the therapist conducts a comprehensive assessment of the patient's delusions, including an evaluation of the degree of conviction with which the patient holds each belief. Once this is completed, the therapist targets the least firmly held beliefs for intervention first, in order to increase the probability of success and increase the patient's trust and confidence in the process (Chadwick & Lowe, 1990; Watts, Powell & Austin, 1973). Two main strategies are then employed to undermine the patient's conviction in these beliefs and to introduce alternative explanations (Beck et al., 1979; Chadwick & Birchwood, 1994; Chadwick & Lowe, 1994; Kingdon & Turkington, 1994).

The first strategy is that of "verbal challenge", in which the therapist begins to sow a seed of doubt in the patient's mind by questioning his/her evidence for the delusional beliefs, and pointing out and discussing discrepancies in the patient's account. Once the possibility of doubt has been introduced, the therapist also begins to offer alternative explanations to account for the evidence presented, and to encourage the patient to reconsider the delusional beliefs in light of hypothetical contradictions. The second strategy then builds upon the first, engaging patients in "behavioral experiments" or "planned reality testing" to evaluate the evidence for the delusional beliefs as compared to alternative accounts. The patient is encouraged to consider the delusional belief as only one possible hypothesis that should be tested, and to carry out such tests. The specific behavioral experiments to be conducted are negotiated with the patient to assure their relevance and meaningfulness to him/her, and that they have the potential to invalidate the delusion should they fail. Finally, the actual behavioral experiments may be carried out, with discussions with the patient following in terms of their implications for the maintenance or dissolution of the delusions. The goal of this process is to guide the patient to let go gradually of the delusions and to accept in their place more adaptive explanations for his/her experience.

EMERGING FORMS OF COGNITIVE-BEHAVIORAL PSYCHOTHERAPY FOR PSYCHOSIS

Several related forms of cognitive-behavioral psychotherapy for persons with psychosis have been developed in the English-speaking world over the last few years. Most of these efforts have taken place in the UK, with the one exception being the work of Hogarty and his colleagues in Pittsburgh. In this section, we review briefly each of the major approaches that have been developed, and consider the limited empirical support that has been generated for each form of treatment to date.

Cognitive Therapy

Perhaps the most broadly-developed and rigorously studied form of treatment emerging from the UK is the "cognitive therapy" of Chadwick, Birchwood, Lowe, Drury, and their colleagues (Chadwick & Birchwood, 1994; Chadwick, Birchwood & Trower, 1996; Chadwick & Lowe, 1990, 1994; Chadwick et al., 1994; Drury et al., 1996a, 1996b; Lowe & Chadwick, 1990). This group of investigators have applied a common model of cognitive change to several different populations and settings, having developed an individual approach for the treatment of delusions and hallucinations in chronic, medication-refractory patients as well as an individual and group approach for the treatment of patients in acute episodes.

The individual treatment approach to refractory delusions consists of the combination of *verbal challenge* and *planned reality testing* described above. In the context of a relationship characterized by the spirit of "collaborative empiricism", verbal challenge consists of focused discussions on the nature and feasibility of delusional beliefs, with the gradual introduction of the possibility of there being alternative explanations for the experiences the delusions are thought to be making sense of. Planned reality testing consists of "behavioral experiments" in which patients are walked through empirical tests that should provide evidence for the accuracy or falseness of delusional beliefs. Most of the studies of this approach have used small numbers of patients in multiple-baseline designs to determine the effectiveness of this combined strategy and to determine specifically which of these two components is the active ingredient of therapeutic change.

In their approach to hallucinations, these investigators have adapted these same two principles of intervention to address beliefs patients hold about their persistent auditory hallucinations. Through initial exploratory work, they identified the relevant dimensions of voices that they think impact on subjective responses to hallucinations, including the identity, power and meaning of the voices and patients' attitudes toward compliance with the voices, and then use verbal challenge and planned reality testing to offer patients alternative explanations for why they hallucinate and for how they might deal differently with their voices. This process begins with identification of beliefs about voices and the evidence used to generate and support these beliefs, discussion of the costs in terms of distress and disruption to their lives attributable to those beliefs, and the connection between these costs and beliefs about the specific dimensions outlined above. Interventions similar to those used with delusions then build upon this base in order to open up more options for coping with the hallucinatory experiences.

Most recently, this approach has been expanded to include a group treatment module and has been adapted to the needs of inpatients in acute episodes. The acute, inpatient treatment package includes individual sessions involving identifying, challenging and testing of key beliefs as described above; participation in small group meetings in which patients are encouraged to consider the adaptive and maladaptive nature of each others' beliefs, to suggest alternative explanations for each others' experiences, to learn new coping strategies, and to challenge their negative attitudes toward psychosis and accept and integrate their disability into their lives; a family component that introduces the cognitive paradigm to treatment and elicits the family's participation in stress and symptom management; and a structured, ward activity program focused on skill development and improving interpersonal relationships.

Empirical support for the individual treatment of refractory symptoms (Chadwick & Lowe, 1990, 1994; Chadwick et al., 1994; Lowe & Chadwick, 1990) has thus far been garnered from small-sample (a total of 12 patients), multiple-baseline studies that suggest that delusions are amenable to a combination of verbal challenge and planned reality testing, that these interventions are most effective in this order, and that verbal challenge may actually be sufficient in and of itself to bring about significant change in delusions. Planned reality testing may be best used as a complement to verbal challenge when that has not proved sufficient in and of itself (i.e. for refractory patients). Additional evidence from four patients who had persistent hallucinations (Chadwick & Birchwood, 1994) suggests that verbal challenge and reality testing can not only produce clinically significant reductions in the strength of these problematic beliefs, but also can reduce the frequency and duration of the hallucinations themselves, suggesting a more substantive connection between the hallucinatory activity itself and the cognitive, behavioral and affective dimensions originally thought to be reactions to it.

Most impressive, however, have been the results of a controlled trial of the inpatient treatment approach to patients in acute episodes (Drury et al., 1996a, 1996b). This trial involved the randomization of 20 patients to each of two conditions, the experimental condition of cognitive therapy consisting of the treatment package described above, and the control condition consisting of "informal support" and participation in a therapeutic activities program. Significant effects were found for cognitive therapy in the reduction of positive symptoms and in decreases in delusional conviction by week 7 of treatment in comparison to the control group. Perhaps more importantly, cognitive therapy also showed significant effects at 9-month follow-up, with 95% of the cognitive therapy patients vs. 44% of the control patients reporting no or only minor positive symptoms. Such differences were not found in negative or disorganized symptoms during the course of treatment or at follow-up. Finally, in addition to symptom remission, cognitive therapy led to a more rapid resolution of the psychotic episode, cutting time to discharge in half, and tripling the number of patients who had recovered from the episode at 6-month follow-up.

Coping Strategy Enhancement

This approach has been developed by Tarrier and his colleagues (Tarrier, 1992a, 1992b; Tarrier et al., 1990, 1993a, 1993b), and involves identifying coping strategies already implicitly used by patients and building on these systematically to train the patient in a battery of coping techniques to compensate for and/or minimize residual psychotic symptoms. Using a biopsychosocial model of hallucinations and delusions, coping strategy enhancement (CSE) aims to decrease symptoms by training patients to cope with both the environmental cues that precipitate symptom exacerbation and their cognitive, behavioral, and physiological reactions to these cues and the resulting symptoms. CSE is conducted in a three-stage process involving an assessment of the environmental factors that maintain psychotic symptoms and their emotional consequences, and an attempt to modify these factors to reduce symptoms and the accompanying negative affects: (a) identifying and monitoring symptoms of voices and delusions and their situational contexts (on the same basis as one would in cognitive-behavioral treatments with anxious or depressed patients); (b) developing coping strategies in response to these symptoms; and (c) practicing new strategies *in vivo* and with homework between sessions.

Empirical support for this treatment has been garnered from a controlled clinical trial comparing CSE and a cognitive-behavioral problem-solving approach not specific to psychotic symptomatology. Twenty-three patients were assigned to either problem-solving or CSE and participated in twice-weekly sessions over a 5-week period. CSE decreased delusions by 50% in 60% of patients, as compared to 25% of problem-solving patients, and most patients retained this decrease at 6-month follow-up.

Cognitive-behavioral Therapy for Schizophrenia using a Normalizing Rationale

Two similar approaches to a manualized cognitive-behavioral psychotherapy for schizophrenia have been developed by Kingdon & Turkington (1991, 1994) and Fowler, Garety & Kuipers (1995). Kingdon & Turkington base their "normalizing" approach on the importance of the cognitive-behavioral premise that the symptoms of schizophrenia vary only quantitatively from "normal" processes and occur at the end of a continuum or spectrum that spans from "normal" to "pathological". For example, delusional beliefs occupy an endpoint on a continuum of degrees of conviction in a belief. Similarly, hallucinations are located at the extreme end of a continuum that ranges from dreams and normal imagination to illusions to hallucinations, with even "normal" individuals experiencing hallucinations during periods of sensory or sleep deprivation. The aim of this treatment is to move maladaptive beliefs, behaviors and symptoms to a less extreme position on the continuum through the use of reasoning, and to reduce the fear, confusion, and uncertainty associated with these symptoms in patients' experiences by relating them to the normal experiences of which they are exaggerations. As they describe, the goal is "that of explaining and destigmatizing confusing and frightening experiences, while not losing sight of the fact that something is seriously wrong" (Kingdon & Turkington, 1994).

This treatment approach incorporates several key steps. A thorough assessment including psychiatric, psychological and social factors is conducted and detailed information about the period directly prior to the adoption of delusion is obtained. Target symptoms are identified and normalizing explanations of the illness are provided. This includes psychoeducation about the vulnerability–stress model of schizophrenia and typical sensory, perceptual and communication deficits associated with formal thought disorder, filling in gaps in "real-world" knowledge, and a discussion about "delusional mood". The concept of "delusional mood" is a hallmark of this particular cognitive approach. It is related to the increased suggestibility people experience in times of stress. Specifically, "delusional mood" refers to the phenomenon in which patients experience increased anxiety, confusion and even an acute exacerbation of psychotic symptoms prior to the genesis of a delusion. This increase in stress and disturbing feelings renders them suggestible and the delusion then serves to alleviate the confusion and unpleasant feelings, regardless of its veracity. The techniques of verbal challenge, behavioral experiments and teaching coping strategies, described earlier in this chapter, also are incorporated into this phase.

The approach developed by Fowler, Garety & Kuipers (1995) utilizes a similar basic conceptual foundation, suggesting that psychotic symptoms exist at the opposite end of a continuum that begins with normal processes, and that delusions serve to explain seemingly inexplicable experiences, such as hallucinations, mysterious somatic concerns and confusing social stimuli. This approach involves six stages which include: (a) engagement and assessment; (b) teaching coping strategies for self-management of psychotic symptoms; (c) the collaborative development of a new model of the disorder based on this conceptual model and the vulnerability–stress model of psychosis, but also tailored to the individual; (d) cognitive strategies to address delusional beliefs; (e) cognitive strategies to address dysfunctional assumptions; and (f) social disability and relapse management strategies.

Empirical support for the Kingdon & Turkington (1994) approach has been derived from a naturalistic study of the treatment of 64 patients over a 5-year period in one catchment area in the UK. Evidence is found in the low admission rate, symptomatic improvement, and functional status of the patients, and in the lack of adverse events such as suicides or homicides. A number of other changes were introduced into the system during this 5-year period, however, including the introduction of sophisticated community-based services. It is therefore impossible to tell which if any of these positive outcomes are attributable to this treatment *per se*, and the authors are currently pursuing controlled trials to demonstrate its effectiveness.

Empirical support for the approach of Fowler, Garety & Kuipers comes from single-case experiments (Fowler & Morley, 1989) and from a small controlled trial (Garety, 1994). Early single case experiments involved five cases and utilized approximately 10 sessions of cognitive behavioral therapy (CBT) aimed at both belief change and teaching coping strategies. These studies found moderate improvements and suggested that belief change is not necessary but yields more substantial improvements. A later study (Fowler, 1992) involved 19 cases and distinguished between subjects with predominately negative symptoms and those with predominately positive symptoms. Patients with negative symptoms were unable to participate in CBT, and none showed improvements. Patients with positive symptoms received an average of 22 sessions of CBT and tended to make significant improvements. The only clinical trial to date (Garety et al., 1994) involved 12 patients who received CBT compared to seven patients in a control group, and found that the patients who received CBT showed significant reductions in both delusional conviction and overall severity of symptoms.

Personal Therapy

This form of treatment, developed by Hogarty and his colleagues (1995, in press a, b) in the USA, involves disorder-specific practice principles, gradual staging of interventions (over 3 stages), and the "centrality of affect dysregulation" in schizophrenia. Conceptualized as a modification of psychotherapy based on an understanding of the basic social-cognitive and affective dysfunctions associated with the disorder, "personal therapy" aims to cultivate adaptive strategies that facilitate self-control of affect and the managing of underlying neuropsychological vulnerability. The treatment starts with an understanding of the patient's subjective stages, including intense and troublesome affects and the influence of these affects on behavior, and uses traditional behavioral techniques of modeling, rehearsal, practice, feedback and homework assignments to teach patients new coping skills. The phases of the treatment are cumulative in nature, and involve the following interventions and goals:

Phase I: *Interventions*
            Therapeutic joining (involving communication, trust, empathy, and hope).
            Establishment of a treatment contract and minimum effective medication dosing.
            Supportive therapy (active listening, acceptance, problem-solving and advocacy, health promotion, and reinforcement of positive behaviors and perceptions).
            Psychoeducation, including stress avoidance and prosocial "internal coping" strategies (i.e. drawing initial relationship between stressors as triggers and exacerbation of symptoms).
            Gradual resumption of self-care responsibilities.
            Goal
            Clinical stabilization.

Phase II: *Interventions*
            Psychoeducation regarding relapse prevention and self-protective coping.
            Teaching of adaptive strategies for managing stress and affect, and enhancing social perception abilities and ameliorating social behavior deficits (e.g. social skills, relaxation techniques, conflict resolution).
            Goals
            Adjustment to disability and resumption of interests in work.
            Basic understanding of vulnerability and ways to cope and be proactive in avoiding relapses, as well as of how to handle affects.

Phase III: *Interventions*
            Application of basic and intermediate coping skills in naturalistic settings.
            Focus on information processing and social cognitive deficits, including advanced principles of criticism management and conflict resolution.
            Goals
            Advanced "internal coping" skills applied in social contexts, including an awareness of the effect of behavior and expression on others.
            Community integration and resumption of normative activities.

Empirical support for this form of treatment (Hogarty et al., in press a, b) has been derived from two concurrent clinical trials over 3 years involving 97 patients living with family and 54 patients living alone. In the combined sample, 8% of patients failed to move beyond the basic phase, 38% entered but did not advance beyond the intermediate phase, and 54% completed the intermediate phase and entered and/or completed the advanced phase. As in all of the studies reviewed, all patients received appropriate medications. Personal therapy (PT) proved to be more effective than two randomly assigned comparison treatments (of supportive and family therapies) in forestalling or preventing "late relapse" in the first year for patients living with their families, but not for those living alone (possibly due to the stress of basic needs and residential and clinical instability). The more dramatic effects of PT appear to occur in the second and third years, with significant improvements in both personal and social adjustment domains as compared to both supportive and family therapies. Specific improvements were in the enhancement of work performance and relationships with external family for patients living alone, and in intrapersonal competence and interpersonal effectiveness, as well as a reduction in negative symptoms and withdrawal, for patients living with family. Particularly striking in these studies was the continued improvement in year 3, showing no sign of a plateau in gains as found in the comparison conditions. Residual symptoms and deficits that may limit improvement are found in the area of social cognition, particularly in the inability to take the "second person" perspective and to read informal social norms and cues in novel contexts. Current work of this group is focusing on these residual problem areas.

DISCUSSION

This brief review of a body of work that has been developing over the past several years suggests that the cognitive-behavioral approach to psychosis has promise in decreasing some of the positive symptoms of schizophrenia and also in improving the functional capacity of patients. This approach represents a step forward in the evolution of psychotherapy for schizophrenia, in that it specifically addresses some of the core symptoms and deficits associated with the disorder which prior approaches to psychotherapy, both investigative and supportive, did not. It employs a clear and empirically testable conceptual framework to generate new techniques for the assessment and management of these phenomena, and in this way achieves a more disorder-relevant approach. Such an approach can make a valuable addition to the package of treatments currently available to clinicians working with psychotic patients, providing them with concrete guidelines for responding to patient needs and behaviors beyond the mere provision of support. In addition, by being goal-orientated and problem-focused, this treatment promises to combat the therapeutic nihilism that many practitioners experience when facing psychotic patients, offering hope to patients and clinicians alike that more can be done in recovering from psychosis than simply waiting for the medication to take effect.

Despite the significant progress represented by the disorder-specificity of cognitive-behavioral treatment, it also is possible, however, that something important may be getting lost in the translation from investigative to supportive to cognitive-behavioral psychotherapy. What may be getting lost is precisely the emphasis placed on, and attention paid to, what have since come to be called the "*non*-specific" elements of psychotherapy; those elements that pertain to cultivating a trusting, accepting, empathic and supportive connection to patients who have become isolated and alienated from the world. In addition to offering a context for interpretation, insight and understanding, this relationship has been used as a vehicle for resocialization and as a bridge back to the broader human community. While cognitive-behavioral approaches typically assume the establishment of rapport and a working alliance as the basis for more advanced techniques, little attention is paid in this literature to how such a relationship can be established with patients suffering from psychosis. Clinicians experienced with this population, in contrast, know just how complicated and difficult the initial engagement process can be, how long such a process may take (i.e. to be measured in years, not weeks), and how advanced some of the skills must be just for this initial phase. In addition, these clinicians know the variety of daily life issues and needs that can interfere with and undermine treatment, from non-compliance, to substance abuse, to unemployment, poverty and homelessness (Lambert & Davidson, 1997).

Cognitive-behavioral approaches may be limited in their effectiveness with this population if they do not develop a more sustained interest in these "non-specific" factors as well, if they do not attend to basic needs and the context of care, if they do not broaden their frame beyond a 4–16 session timeline, and if they do not pause to benefit from some of the other lessons learned by investigative and supportive psychotherapists and clinical case managers in how to engage, relate to and assist people with psychosis (e.g. Lambert & Davidson, 1997). These limitations suggest the value of a dialogue between the various approaches, so that the strengths and contributions of each can be preserved in a comprehensive treatment approach that moves beyond a focus on only one or two elements in isolation—whether these be conflicts, symptoms, or cognitive schemata—to addressing the entirety of the person with the disorder in the context of his/her daily life.

REFERENCES

Alford, B.A. & Correia, C.J. (1994). Cognitive therapy of schizophrenia: theory and empirical status. *Behavior Therapy*, **25**, 17–33.

Beck, A.T. (1952). Successful outpatient psychotherapy of a chronic schizophrenic with a delusion based on borrowed guilt. *Psychiatry*, **15**, 305–312.

Beck, A.T., Rush, A.J., Shaw, B.F. & Emery, G. (1979). *Cognitive Therapy of Depression*. New York: Guilford.

Bellack, A.S. & Mueser, K.T. (1993). Psychosocial treatment for schizophrenia. *Schizophrenia Bulletin*, **19**, 317–336.

Chadwick, P. & Birchwood, M. (1994). The omnipotence of voices: a cognitive approach to auditory hallucinations. *British Journal of Psychiatry*, **164**, 190–201.

Chadwick, P.D.J., Birchwood M. & Trower, P. (1996). *Cognitive Therapy for Hallucinations, Delusions, and Paranoia*. Chichester: Wiley.

Chadwick, P.D.J. & Lowe, C.F. (1990). Measurement and modification of delusional beliefs. *Journal of Consulting and Clinical Psychology*, **58**, 225–232.

Chadwick, P.D.J. & Lowe, C.F. (1994). A cognitive approach to measuring and modifying delusions. *Behavior Research and Therapy*, **32**, 355–367.

Chadwick, P.D.J., Lowe, C.F., Horne, P.J. & Higson, P.J. (1994). Modifying delusions: the role of empirical testing. *Behavior Therapy*, **25**, 35–49.

Drury, V., Birchwood, M., Cochrane, R. & MacMillan, F. (1996a). Cognitive therapy and recovery from acute psychosis: a controlled trial. I. Impact on psychotic symptoms. *British Journal of Psychiatry*, **169**, 593–601.

Drury, V., Birchwood, M., Cochrane, R. & MacMillan, F. (1996b). Cognitive therapy and recovery from acute psychosis: a controlled trial. II. Impact on recovery time. *British Journal of Psychiatry*, **169**, 602–607.

Fowler, D. (1992). Cognitive behavior therapy in management of patients with schizophrenia: preliminary studies. In A. Werbatt & J. Gullberg (eds), *Psychotherapy of Schizophrenia: Facilitating and Obstructive Factors*. Oslo: Scandinavian University Press.

Fowler, D. & Morley, S. (1989). The cognitive-behavioral treatment of hallucinations and delusions: a preliminary study. *Behavioral Psychotherapy*, **17**, 267–282.

Fowler, D., Garety, P. & Kuipers, E. (1995). *Cognitive Behaviour Therapy for Psychosis: Theory and Practice*. Chichester: Wiley.

Fromm-Reichmann, F. (1960). *Principles of Intensive Psychotherapy*. Chicago: University of Chicago Press.

Garety, R.A. (1992). Making sense of delusions. *Psychiatry*, **55**, 282–291.

Garety, P.A., Kuipers, E.L., Fowler, O., Chamberlain, F. & Dunn, G. (1994). Cognitive behavior therapy for drug-resistant psychosis. *British Journal of Medical Psychology*, **67**, 259–271.

Gunderson, J.G., Frank, A.F., Katz, H.M., Vannicelli, M.L., Frosch, J.P. & Knapp, P.H. (1984). Effects of psychotherapy in schizophrenia: II. Comparative outcome of two forms of treatment. *Schizophrenia Bulletin*, **10**, 564–598.

Harris, M. & Bachrach, L.L. (eds) (1988). Clinical case management. *New Directions for Mental Health Services*, **40**.

Hartman, L.M. & Cashman, F.E. (1983). Cognitive-behavioral and psychopharmacological treatment of delusional symptoms: a preliminary report. *Behavioral Psychotherapy*, **11**, 50–61.

Hodel, B. & Brenner, H.D. (1994). Cognitive therapy with schizophrenic patients: conceptual basis, present state, future directions. *Acta Psychiatrica Scandinavica*, **90**, 108–115.

Hogarty, G.E., Kornblith, S.J., Greenwald, D., DiBarry, A.L., Cooley, S., Flesher, S., Reiss, D., Carter, M. & Ulrich, R. (1995). Personal therapy: a disorder-relevant psychotherapy for schizophrenia. *Schizophrenia Bulletin*, **21**, 379–392.

Hogarty, G.E., Kornblith, S.J., Greenwald, D., DiBarry, A.L., Cooley, S., Ulrich, R., Carter, M. & Flesher, S. (in press a). Effects of personal therapy on schizophrenia relapse. I. Description and results of three-year trials among patients living with or independent of family. *American Journal of Psychiatry*.

Hogarty, G.E., Greenwald, D., Ulrich, R.F., Kornblith, S.J., DiBarry, A.L., Cooley, S., Carter, M. & Flesher, S. (in press b). Effects of personal therapy on the adjustment of schizophrenic patients. II. Results of three-year trials among patients living with or independent of family. *American Journal of Psychiatry*.

Hole, R.W., Rush, A.J. & Beck, A.T. (1979). A cognitive investigation of schizophrenic delusions. *Psychiatry*, **42**, 312–319.

Kane, J. & McGlashan, T.H. (1995). Treatment of schizophrenia. *The Lancet*, **346**, 820–825.

Kingdon, D.G. & Turkington, D. (1991). The use of cognitive-behavior therapy with a normalizing rationale in schizophrenia: preliminary report. *Journal of Nervous and Mental Disease*, **179**, 207–211.

Kingdon, D.G. & Turkington, D. (1994). *Cognitive-behavioral Therapy of Schizophrenia*. New York: Guilford.

Kingdon, D.G., Turkington, D. & John, C. (1994). Cognitive-behavior therapy of schizophrenia: the amenability of delusions and hallucinations to reasoning. *British Journal of Psychiatry*, **164**, 581–587.

Lambert, S. & Davidson, L. (1997). Cognitive-behavioral treatment of delusions in the context of community-based care: a case study. Manuscript under review.

Lowe, C.F. & Chadwick, P.D.J. (1990). Verbal control of delusions. *Behavior Therapy*, **21**, 461–479.

McGlashan, T.H. (1994). What has become of the psychotherapy of schizophrenia? *Acta Psychiatrica Scandinavica*, **90**, 147–152.

McNally, R.J. (1994). Innovations in cognitive-behavioral approaches to schizophrenia. *Behavior Therapy*, **25**, 1–4.

Maher, B.A. (1974). Delusional thinking and perceptual disorder. *Journal of Individual Psychology*, **30**, 98–113.

Meichenbaum, D. (1977). *Cognitive-behavior modification: an integrative approach*. New York: Plenum.

Meyer, A. (1950). *The Collected Papers of Adolf Meyer*. Baltimore, MD: Johns Hopkins University Press.

Milton, F., Patwa, V.K. & Hafner, R.J. (1978). Confrontation vs. belief modification in persistently deluded patients. *British Journal of Medical Psychology*, **51**, 127–130.

Penn, D.L. & Mueser, K.T. (1996). Research update on the psychosocial treatment of schizophrenia. *American Journal of Psychiatry*, **153**, 607–617.

Perris, C. & Skagerlind, L. (1994). Cognitive therapy with schizophrenic patients. *Acta Psychiatrica Scandinavica*, **89**, 65–70.

Roberts, G. (1992). The origins of delusion. *British Journal of Psychiatry*, **161**, 298–308.

Scott, J.E. & Dixon, L.B. (1995). Psychological interventions for schizophrenia. *Schizophrenia Bulletin*, **21**, 621–630.

Strauss, J.S. (1969). Hallucinations and delusions as points on continua function. *Archives of General Psychiatry*, **21**, 581–586.

Strauss, J.S. (1991). The person with delusions. *British Journal of Psychiatry*, **159**, 57–61.

Sullivan, H.S. (1931). The modified psychoanalytic treatment of schizophrenia. *American Journal of Psychiatry*, **2**, 519–540.

Sullivan, H.S. (1953). *The Interpersonal Theory of Psychiatry*. New York: W.W. Norton.

Sullivan, H.S. (1962). *Schizophrenia as a Human Process*. New York: W.W. Norton.

Tarrier, N. (1992a). Psychological treatment of schizophrenic symptoms. In D. Kavanagh (ed.), *Schizophrenia: an Overview and Practical Handbook*. London: Chapman & Hall.

Tarrier, N. (1992b). Management and modification of residual psychotic symptoms. In M. Birchwood & N. Tarrier (eds), *Innovations in the Psychological Management of Schizophrenia*. Chichester: Wiley.

Tarrier, N., Sharpe, L., Beckett, R., Harwood, S., Baker, A. & Yusupoff, L. (1993b). A trial of two cognitive-behavioral methods of treating drug resistant residual psychotic symptoms in schizophrenic patients. II. Treatment-specific changes in coping and problem-solving skills. *Social Psychiatry & Psychiatric Epidemiology*, **28**, 5–10.

Tarrier, N., Beckett, R., Harwood, S., Baker, A., Yusupoff, L. & Ugarteburu, I. (1993a). A trial of two cognitive-behavioral methods of treating drug-resistant residual psychotic symptoms in schizophrenic patients. I. Outcome. *British Journal of Psychiatry*, **162**, 524–532.

Tarrier, N., Harwood, S., Yusopoff, L. et al. (1990).   Coping strategy enhancement (CSE): a method of treating residual schizophrenic symptoms. *Behavioral Psychotherapy*, **18**, 283–293.
Watts, F.N., Powell, G.E. & Austin, S.V. (1973).   The modification of abnormal beliefs. *British Journal of Medical Psychology*, **46**, 359–363.

Chapter 2

Defining the Concept of Individual Vulnerability as a Base for Psychotherapeutic Interventions

Carlo Perris
Swedish Institute of Cognitive Psychotherapy,
Stockholm, Sweden

INTRODUCTION

This chapter deals with an abridged description of a theoretical frame of reference for the study of mental disorders and for the planning of their treatment, which our research group has been developing for some decades. Since more detailed accounts of this framework have been given in previous publications, where some results of research work by our group have also been reported (Perris, 1981a, 1989, 1991a,b; Perris & Perris, 1985, 1997), only its main aspects will be highlighted at this juncture.

There has been considerable progress during the past decades towards a systematic standardization of psychiatric diagnoses. However, although standardization imposes uniformity and comparability, as Zubin, Magaziner & Steinhauer (1983) have pointed out, it can also lead to a rigidity which may rule out innovative findings and further developments. The "disease" conception of mental disorders, in fact, subtly conveyed by operationalized categorical diagnoses, regardless of its validity, undoubtedly influences the expectancies that the community and the various categories of mental health workers (be they psychologists, doctors or therapists) hold toward an individual who has been given such a diagnosis.

Cognitive Psychotherapy of Psychotic and Personality Disorders: Handbook of Theory and Practice.
Edited by C. Perris and P.D. McGorry.
© 1998 John Wiley & Sons Ltd.

Another important problem arising from emphasis on practical operationalized diagnostic systems, is that reliable description of a syndrome does not imply valid understanding of its underlying cause (Zubin & Spring, 1977). Also, only modest understanding of the patients or their therapeutic requirements is provided by the diagnosis (Carpenter & Strauss, 1979). Zubin and his co-workers, Carpenter and Strauss, and many others (e.g. Bentall, 1990; Jackson, 1990) question the usefulness of a category diagnosis "schizophrenia". One aspect that those authors underscore, and on which we agree, is that regardless of the emphasis on stringent diagnostic criteria, we continue to identify a wide range of psychopathologies and multiple illness syndromes under the rubric "schizophrenia". As pointed out elsewhere (Perris 1988, 1989, 1993), it is very likely that the term "schizophrenia", as currently used, covers many aetiologic and pathogenic subgroups of disorders that we are unable to disentangle. Kety (1973) suggested, in this context, that the likelihood that one is dealing with a number of different disorders with a common symptomatology must be recognized. A similar opinion has been maintained more recently by several other authors (Carpenter & Strauss, 1979; Crow, 1980; Jackson, 1990). One logical consequence of the criticism of a conception of "schizophrenia" as a discrete disease entity, should be a consistent substitution of the term "schizophrenic disorder" or syndrome for that of "schizophrenia" in order to avoid the image of a very specific and unitary disease. Such a substitution would put the schizophrenic disorders in line with the other "disorders" taken into account by current classification systems, and would permit avoidance of the acrobatic diagnostic exercises which become necessary to keep separate schizophreniform or schizoaffective syndromes from "schizophrenia". In addition, it would become easier if the ideas of a unitary disease were relinquished, to pay greater attention to the possibility that what we term "schizophrenia" exists on a continuum with what we might call normal behaviour (Strauss, 1969; Heilbrun, 1973; Ciompi, 1982/1988; Perris, 1988, 1993; Claridge, 1990).

A corresponding critique of categorical diagnoses applied to personality disorders has been reported elsewhere (Perris & Perris, 1997). In brief, if a categorical diagnosis gives very limited information about the real therapeutic requirements of the patients with a diagnosis of "schizophrenia" or "major depression", such information, if anything, is even less compelling concerning patients who receive a categorical diagnosis of a specific type of personality disorder (Perris & Perris, 1997). Millon & Davis (1996) have recently emphasized that:

> Personality disorders are not disorders at all in the medical sense. Rather, personality disorders are reified constructs employed to represent varied styles or patterns in which the personality system functions *maladaptively* [emphasis in the original] in relation to its environment (p. 86).

The approach followed by Perris & Perris is in line with this opinion. Hence, we have pointed out that a more suitable conceptualization of personality disorders,

with implications for treatment, would be in terms of enduring behaviour disturbances in interpersonal relationships. In particular, we suggest that a meaningful
conceptualization of disturbances in interpersonal relationships can be made in
terms of dysfunctional internal workings models of self and others, and hence in
terms of the vulnerability that the individual has developed throughout his life-
span (see below). This kind of conceptualization, as pointed out by Perris &
Perris (1997), has important implications for treatment.

There can be little doubt, in fact, that the approach which is taken to the
treatment of patients suffering from a mental disorder depends not only on the
immediate therapeutic goals to be achieved (e.g. emergency interventions), but
also upon the attitude of the care-giver to the nature of mental disturbances, their
origins and their expected outcome.

Let us consider the schizophrenic disorders as an example. If it is thought,
as it occasionally was in the early 1970s, that "schizophrenia" is not a mental
disorder at all but merely a "style of life", then no efforts will be made to find
suitable treatments. On the other hand, if disorders labelled as "schizophrenic"
are more or less implicitily assumed to have a genetically determined, irrevocably
progressive deteriorating course with a malignant outcome, then such a belief
will inevitably affect the setting of goals for treatment. Marshall (1990) points
out that:

> The notion that schizophrenia is a discrete entity and the belief that it is a disorder
> of largely genetic origins are mutually reinforcing and, in turn, both assist in the
> transformation of an abstract, hypothetical concept into a "thing" (p. 91).

One recent example of the dyscomfort induced by implicit attitudes concealed
behind a diagnostic system (the American Diagnostic and Statistical Manual,
DSM in its various revisions—American Psychiatric Association 1980, 1987,
1994), which otherwise claims to be "atheoretical", is that some American authors who aimed to investigate developmental processes in schizophrenic disorders (Nuechterlein et al., 1992), decided not to rely on DSM-III or DSM-III-R
criteria as the diagnostic basis for inclusion in their project. Their explanation for
doing thus was that the use of a diagnostic system demanding a continuous period
of illness of 6 months or more would exclude study of the earliest months of
active symptomatology, and tend to narrow the range of psychotic cases to those
with poorer prognosis, without shedding any light on possible determinants of the
poor prognosis.

Obviously, if the duration criterion is considered as essential, many claims
concerning early interventions in schizophrenic psychotic manifestations, in the
hope of preventing further negative developments, would be regarded as disput-
able. Also, it must be emphasized that several authors concur in maintaining that
a poor outcome is not a given result for all patients who are labelled as schizophrenics, and may, in fact, be an artifact (Bentall, 1990; Bleuler, 1972; Ciompi,
1980, 1982/1988; Harding, Zubin & Strauss, 1987; Perris, 1981b, 1989; Zubin &
Spring, 1977).

Alongside with the development of diagnostic criteria for use in psychiatric research (Feighner et al., 1972), and the proposals of multi-axial classifications of mental disorders (Rutter et al., 1969; Ottosson & Perris, 1973; Perris et al., 1979), which in due time became one source of inspiration for the development of the DSM, an intellectual atmosphere has been developing that allows for the importance of multiple physical and psychological factors in the aetiology and pathogenesis of the psychological disorders.

Regarding the aetiology of mental disorders, in fact, psychiatry has traditionally seemed to polarize itself into psychological and biological camps. Each has argued the essential validity of its approaches, and within the two major camps minor warring tribes have emerged. Even though attempts at integration occur, the most widespread common practice is that all too often single factors of biological, intrapsychic or social nature are given decisive importance, the only difference being that the emphasis is placed on one type of causal explanation or another, depending on the arbitrary preferences of the particular author. On the other hand, the main problem is that anyone who reads carefully the various theories of "schizophrenia" presented in the literature, cannot but admit that here is something convincing in all of them, and that "schizophrenia" can indeed be conceived as a biological disorder, or as a result of maladaptive intrapsychic processes, or as a failure in a struggle against pathogenic social forces. However, the trouble is that each author, as in the tale of the blind Indians and the elephant, has perceived only one aspect of the truth, and has therefore described "schizophrenia" (and to some extent also other mental disorders) on the basis of only one of its many-sided aspects, all too often without considering that explanatory models about health and illness are nothing but a subset of rationalizations that individuals and groups make about the world in general.

The standpoint of this chapter is that assumptions exclusively based on in depth psychologies, biochemical hypotheses or social explanations are but reductionistic. Hence, the concept that genes, environment and life experience all interact to determine behaviour must be incorporated into any theory with which mental disorders are to be understood. A focus on these interactions is crucial in models emphasizing individual vulnerability.

THE CONCEPT OF INDIVIDUAL VULNERABILITY

Among the concepts with which we sympathize are those that regard the occurrence of psychopathological manifestations within a theoretical framwork which is focused on *individual vulnerability*. For several years, in fact, our group has adopted a critical attitude to all reductionistic attempts to explain the occurrence of most mental disorders—especially the major psychotic ones—in terms of simple, linear, causative relationships (Perris & d'Elia, 1964; Perris 1966, 1987, 1988, 1991a,b, 1993; Perris & Perris, 1985, 1997; Perris, H, 1982; Eisemann, 1985). Our opinion, instead, has been that a more holistic approach to the understand-

ing of mental disturbances and to the planning of treatment should be consistently used.

The approach that we propound is based on a comprehensive framework that
takes into account not only the continuous interactions that in a given cultural
context affect the susceptibility of an individual to develop a psychopathological
disorder, but also the continuous dialectical interplay between the ("vulnerable")
individual and his/her environment. Hence, our framework allows for taking
into account an exploration of the developing individuals' active role in creating
and interpreting their experience (Magnusson, 1983; Magnusson & Öhman, 1987;
Sameroff, 1975; Lerner, 1982; Scarr, 1992). As emphasized by Plomin (1995),
environmental theory has moved away from passive models of development in
favour of models that recognize the active role of children in selecting, modifying
and creating their environments.

This proposal, of course, is neither new (Jaspers, 1913; Freud, 1920; Slater &
Slater, 1944; Meehl, 1962) nor unique. Rather, it accords well with opinions that
are becoming increasingly accepted in psychiatric circles, especially concerning
the development of schizophrenic syndromes and their further course (Bleuler,
1981; Ciompi, 1982/1988; May, Gritti & Calderisi, 1985; Mirsky & Duncan, 1986;
Nuechterlein & Dawson, 1984; Nuechterlein et al., 1992; Zubin, 1987; Zubin &
Spring, 1977; Zubin et al., 1983; Gottesman & Shields, 1971, 1982; Brody, 1981),
but also regarding the occurrence and development of other mental disorders,
inclusive those of personality (Marsella, 1988; Perris, 1987, 1991b; Perris &
Perris, 1997; Hammen et al., 1985; Power & Dalgleish, 1997; Teasdale & Dent,
1987). In the following, the main characteristics of the basic frame of reference
postulated by our group will be highlighted. In the next section, instead, a closer
definition of the concept of individual vulnerability will be sketched.

A schematic illustration of the framework that we propose is presented in
Figure 2.1, in which the main elements of the model are pointed out. The figure
underscores that within a given cultural context every individual not only is
determined by the biological and psychosocial factors which contribute to
his development as a person, but he himself continuously interacts with such
factors, modifying their impact. This conception bears some resemblance with
that of "reciprocal determinism" proposed by Bandura (1978) and also with the
concept of "dynamic interaction" as used by Magnusson & Endler (1977). The
theoretical ground of the model, however, is mostly laid on knowledge that
is accumulating in the domain of developmental psychopathology (Sroufe &
Rutter, 1984; Cicchetti & Cohen, 1995). It relates also to concepts that have been
originally propounded by Meyer (1958) and by Bowlby (1969, 1973, 1980, 1988)
and which, concerning the latter, have been inspired, among others, by
Waddington (1957).

Developmental psychopathology, as Rutter (1988) points out, serves as a
means of bringing together a set of strategies that have been little used until now
and that carry the potential of throwing new light on old topics (e.g. the use of
genetic research strategies to identify where to look for environmental influence;
Plomin, 1994, 1995). It also provides a framework for integrating knowledge

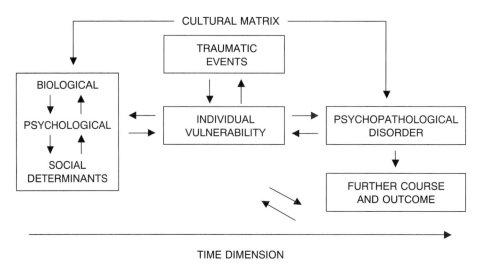

TIME DIMENSION

Figure 2.1 A basic illustration of an interactionistic conception of individual vulnerability

within and across disciplines, contexts and domains of inquiry (Cicchetti & Cohen, 1995). Among the core conceptual tenets of developmental psychopathology, Cicchetti & Cohen enumerate the following:

> (a) there are multiple contributors to disordered outcomes in any individual; (b) the contributors vary among individuals who have the disorder; (c) among individuals with a specific disorder, there is heterogeneity in the features of their disturbance; and (d) there are numerous pathways to any particular manifestation of disordered behaviour (p. 8).

Bowlby, (1973, 1988) drew his model of developmental pathways from Waddington (1957). The basic metaphor is that of one among a group of growing stems deviating from its normal development. Bowlby (1973) postulates human development as occurring unceasingly along one or another of an array of possible and discrete pathways. All pathways are thought to start together, so that initially the individual has access to a large range of pathways, along any one of which he might travel. Thus, as pointed out by Sroufe (1989), individuals may all begin on the same major pathway and, because of subsequent "choices", ultimately show quite different patterns of adaptation. Moreover, individuals who begin on a path deviating from the mainstream may nonetheless return to adaptation within the normal range, through subsequent corrective changes. Pathology, then, is viewed as the result of a series of deviations, always taking the individuals further from normal patterns of adaptation. Such a concept of pathology is clearly consonant with opinions about psychopathology as occurring along a continuum with normal behaviour, as mentioned above.

The model presented in Figure 2.1 is not reductionistic. A continuously ongoing transaction is assumed to occur between the individual, on the one hand, and the factors belonging to the different domains on the other hand, which influence his (normal or deviant) development. Thus, what ultimately becomes pathogenic is assumed to be the result of such interactions, and not the effect of any single factor, even though the phenotypical manifestations can be very similar. In particular, neither genetic factors, nor particular social influences, nor intrapsychic processes occurring very early in life *per se* are regarded as necessary and sufficient determinants of psychopathological manifestations occurring later in life. In line with basic concepts in behavioural genetics, genetic influences are understood in terms of *probabilistic propensities* rather than in terms of *deterministic genes* (Plomin, 1995; Rende & Plomin, 1995).

One distinguishing element of the vulnerability model that we propound consists of the importance given to the cultural context, both as a pathoplastic determinant of the development of vulnerability (e.g. the concept of *empty self*, described by Cushman, 1990, or that of narcissistic culture, described by Lasch, 1979) and for the impact that cultural, characteristics have, not only on the type of treatment that will be chosen, but also, as Stern (1995) points out, on the development and successive maintenance of a therapeutic relationship if the treatment of choice is psychotherapy.

A further important distinction between the vulnerability model discussed here and those propounded so far by other authors is that the latter consider vulnerability almost exclusively in relation to some given mental disorder (e.g. "schizophrenia" or "depression") and prevalently in biological terms. Zubin & Spring (1977, p. 8), for example, on the one hand, maintain that their vulnerability model:

> ...proposes that each of us is endowed with a degree of vulnerability that under suitable circumstances will express itself in an episode of schizophrenic illness.

On the other, they specify that vulnerability to schizophrenia has to be regarded as a *relatively permanent, enduring trait*. Our model of vulnerability is not limited to any specific disorder, but extends to all kinds of psychopathological manifestations (Perris, 1991a, 1993). We believe, in fact, that if a concept of vulnerability were limited to only a specific type of mental disorder, at the same time as vulnerability for that very disorder were regarded as enduring, then there would be the trap of having to explain that specific vulnerability without becoming reductionistic. In other words, there would be a risk of regressing on the ancient concept of *diathesis*, already known to Greek and Roman doctors, that has been of limited use in the progress of our knowledge. Hence, the first part of Zubin & Spring's postulate, to our view, should be reformulated as follows:

> Each of us is endowed with a degree of vulnerability that under suitable circumstances can express itself in a psychopathological disorder. Such a disorder may assume the characteristics of a schizophrenic syndrome.

Also, the indication of a time dimension in Figure 2.1 clearly emphasizes that we do not regard individual vulnerability as a static, unaltering condition. It is assumed, in fact, that because of the continuous dialectical interactions taken into account in the model, vulnerability changes continuously throughout a person's life-span (Perris, 1989, 1993). This possibility of changing, which has been stressed both by developmental psychologists (e.g. Magnusson, 1983; Sameroff, 1975) and in the field of psychopathology (e.g. Erlenmeyer-Kimling, 1979; Brody, 1981) is an important prerequisite in stipulating the goals of therapeutic interventions.

Any model of vulnerability that takes into account interactive process focuses not only on the possible potentiation of various factors but also allows for taking into account the possibility of neutralizing effects to occur, which enhance an individual's resilience in the face of negative experiences (Anthony & Cohler, 1987; Rutter, 1985).

The vulnerability model proposed by Ciompi (1982/1988) is the model which lies closest to our own. Ciompi's model, in fact, not only downplays the role of a "specific" genetic vulnerability to schizophrenia, but also takes into account the internalization of important *affective–logical systems of reference (schemata or affect-logic)*, which are assumed to become equilibrated and structured over the course of development on the basis of experience, in a circular process of assimilation and accommodation to the outside world. Those hierarchically organized *systems of reference* are akin to our conception of *internal working models*, to be described below. They are assumed, in fact, to comprise instructions for feeling, thinking and acting, and to affect one's behaviour once activated by certain contexts or precipitating factors. Ciompi does not mention, however, whether his model can be understood as generalizable to other mental disorders besides the schizophrenic ones for which it was developed.

One further aspect of the model in Figure 2.1 to be commented upon is that it emphasizes a conceptualization of life events in terms of an interaction with the individual experiencing them. In fact, not only it has been repeatedly shown, e.g. in research on depression, that vulnerability enhances the individual's reactivity to stressfuls events (Brown & Harris, 1978; Perris, H, 1982; Paykel, 1982), but it has also been maintained that each individual is idiosyncratically vulnerable to particular events which might leave another person unaffected (Erlenmeyer-Kimling, 1979; Perris H, 1982; Strauss & Carpenter, 1981). Obviously, this is quite in line with what any cognitive psychotherapist knows well—that it is an individual's own perception of the stressfulness of an event that utltimately defines the severity of the load.

It is also well known that many stressful situations do not occur by chance, but result from the interplay between a certain individual and his environment at a certain point in time. Erlenmeyer-Kimling (1979) has pointedly emphasized that "life events are obviously handled or mishandled in different ways by different people". The concept of *vulnerability* as understood by Zubin & Spring, Ciompi, and ourselves implicitly comprises a general assumption about the crucial importance of the subjective interpretation of life events, that is, the meaning that the individual gives to them. In addition, the stress that we put on the interaction among the various factors comprised in our framework allows for genetic factors influencing experiential input (Ginsburg, 1967). In the context of life events and schizophrenic disorders, finally, special mention should be made of the contribution of Day (1985, quoted by Ciompi, 1987), who emphasized the impact of a long-lasting "toxic" environmental influence (e.g. an overdemanding or invading milieu), as opposed to critical single life-events. We believe that a similar negative influence might apply to other disorders as well, especially those of personality.

Independently of how vulnerability is conceptualized, there is a fair agreement among several of the models presented so far about the crucial importance of individual vulnerability on the further course, and possibly the outcome, of psychopathological manifestations after an initial breakdown (Zubin & Spring, 1977; Ciompi, 1982/1988; Nuechterlein et al., 1992; Perris, 1991; Perris & Perris, 1998). Zubin (1987) points out that the model we adopt for the "aetiology of schizophrenia" is bound to determine our approach to its management, because acceptable forms of treatment for the psychoses have always reflected the dominating conception of the nature and the cause of the disorders. In particular, as emphasized by Perris & Perris (1985), a multifactorial conception of vulnerability, as in the model in Figure 2.1, implies that even treatment should be conceived multifactorially and integrated.

TOWARD A CLOSER CONCEPTUALIZATION OF "VULNERABILITY"

Even though the concepts of vulnerability described so far imply a progress towards an understanding of the occurrence of mental disorders beyond reductionistic conceptions, they have little to say concerning possible interventions aimed at modifying an individual's vulnerability.

To the extent that vulnerability is conceived as a relatively invariant trait, most treatment procedures are aimed at improving the ability of the vulnerable individual to cope with stressful events, or consists of interventions aimed at mitigating the impact of external factors, without pretending to modify vulnerability in itself. Interventions with the families, directed at influencing the level of "expressed emotions", or various approaches focused on the enhancement of coping strategies are to be understood as examples of efforts aimed at mitigating the impact of external factors, without altering vulnerability.

In our effort to reach a closer definition of vulnerability from a constructivistic and interactionistic developmental perspective, we (Perris, 1988, 1991a; Perris & Perris, 1997) have elaborated a more comprehensive schema, shown in Figure 2.2 which represents a proposal of criteria for an integrated theory of psychopathological disorders, and from which various hypotheses can be derived to be tested in empirical studies.

Briefly, it is assumed that individual vulnerability is not exclusively biological, but results from the continuous interactions which occur during development

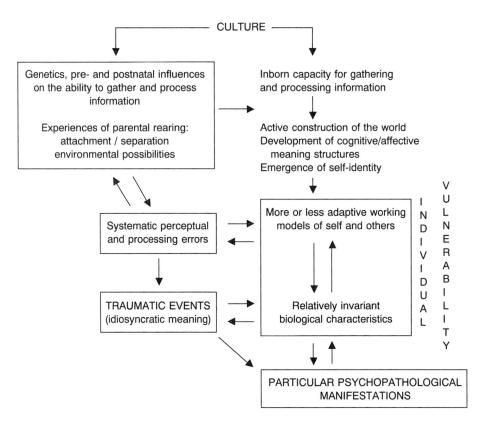

Figure 2.2 An expanded illustration of the model shown in figure 2.1. Individual vulnerability is defined by the continuous interactions between the individual's biological characteristics and the internal working models that he has developed

between biological and psychosocial factors (also in the context of early relationships), and result in the internalization of more or less adaptive internal working models of self and others (Bowlby, 1969; Main, 1981; Crittenden, 1990, 1994).

It is a currently accepted view in developmental psychology that the individual enters the world equipped with a rudimentary set of genetically determined structures and inborn neural patterns, together with their associated information-processing programs which, in turn, subsequently develop along a genetically controlled course. These programs make it possible for the individual to deal in an adaptive manner with all the stimulation by information to which he is exposed. It must be stressed, however, that the further development of cognitive/affective structures does not represent qualitative changes derived solely from maturationally-based (and genetically determined) preformations totally independent of experiential contributions. It has already been stressed above that genetic and environmental influences may be linked in different ways, both as genetic effects on environment, and through the effects of environmental interventions on genetic conditions (Rende & Plomin, 1995). The structures of the brain which support the cognitive/affective functions mentioned above require sensory experiences for maturation. Hence, neuronal activity becomes an important factor in the re-organizazion of these structures. To the extent that neuronal activity is modulated by sensory signals, it is obvious that different environmental factors can affect the development of the neuronal matrix. Singer (1986) has drawn attention to the fact that experience-dependent self-reorganization of the brain must be treated as an active dialogue between the brain and its surroundings. Meyersburg & Post (1979) pointed out that a parallelism between neural and behavioural sequences certainly exists in early childhood. Of particular relevance in this connection are the early interactions between the child and its caregivers, among which those underlying the process of attachment described by Bowlby (1969, 1973, 1980) occupies a most prominent place.

Obviously, I cannot explicate at this juncture the evidence supporting the validity of attachment theory and its paramount relevance for both developmental psychopathology and psychoherapy. Recent overviews have been made available, to which the interested reader is referred (Sperling & Berman, 1994; West & Sheldon-Keller, 1994; Perris, 1996; Atkinson & Zucker, 1997). At this junction, however, a few words have to be spend on the concept of *internal working models of self and others*, since they represent the core of our concept of individual vulnerability.

Starting at birth, the infant begins to construct a self from interaction with innately given sequences of maturation and evironmental events. In describing the development of self, developmental psychologists refer to a dual process of development that includes both what goes on within the infant, and what goes on between the child and the caregiver. Stern (1985), for example, maintains that even the very young infant has some abilities to abstract, average and represent information preverbally. Stern labels the very early interactive experiences which are averaged and represented preverbally "RIGs", that is, Representations of Interactions that have been Generalized. RIGs can thus constitute, Stern maintains, a *basic unit of the core self* and can, according to him, be conceputalized as the basic building blocks from which working models, as described by Bowlby, are constructed.

Bowlby (1969, 1973) maintained that for a secure attachment to develop, the attachment figure has to be both accessible and willing to respond in an appropriate way. Attachment theory postulates that confidence in the availability of attachment figures, or lack of it, is built up slowly during the years of immaturity, and that whatever expectations are developed during those years tend to persist relatively unchanged throughout the rest of life. Bowlby emphasizes that the varied expectations of the accessibility and responsiveness of attachment figures that different individuals develop are tolerably accurate reflections of the experiences those individuals have actually had.

Bowlby proposed that each individual constructs complementary mental representations of the world and of him/herself in it—*internal working models of self and others*—with the aid of which he/she perceives events, forecasts the future, and constructs his/her plans. In the working model of the world that anyone builds, a key feature is his/her notion of who these attachment figures are, where they may be found, and how they may be expected to respond. Similarly, in the working model of the self that anyone builds, a key feature is his/her notion of how acceptable or unacceptable the person him/herself is in the eyes of his/her attachment figures. Thus, as emphasized by Crittenden (1994), an internal working model is a mental structure consisting of an individual's representation of (a) him/herself (in the context of a specific attachment relationship); (b) the attachment figure (in the context of the relatonship with the self); and (c) the affect associated with the relationship. Affect is especially important because, according to Bowlby, affect ties certain kinds of situations with certain kinds of responses. Affect, in other words, functions, according to Crittenden, as a primitive, rapid and efficient appraisal system. Cognitions functions to mediate the relations among perception, affect and behaviour.

It is assumed that all working models are changed by the very information received. They must constantly be updated, adapted and re-adapted by mechanisms of assimilation and accommodation. Those more central for one's self-concept and for the conception of one's relations with others (core structures), however, are assumed to be far more resistant to change (Bowlby, 1973; Liotti, 1987)

To support the relative stability of working models and their effect on later personality, Bowlby (1973) maintains that it is not only environmental pressures that tend to maintain development on a particular pathway. He acknowledges, also, that structural features of personality, once developed, have their own means of self-regulation that tend also to maintain the current direction of development. In particular, Bowlby emphasizes that current working models determine:

> . . . what is perceived and what is ignored, how a new situation is constructed, and what plan of action is likely to be constructed to deal with it (1973, p. 417).

The occurrence of systematic perceptual and processing errors, indicated in Figure 2.2, contributes through biased self-verification processes to the relative stability of the core structures. The potential for at least some modification of developmental patterns through corrective experiences (e.g. successful psychotherapy), however, should always be kept in mind. It is this potential for change that is exploited in the metacognitive approach to psychotherapy described in the chapter by Liotti and Intreccialagli and in that by Perris and Skagerlind in this volume. Metacognitive approaches, thus, aim at a restructuring of core structures. If interventions have been successful, then the vulnerability of the treated individual is substantially lowered.

In conclusion, it should be emphasized, finally, that our focus on dysfunctional internal working models of self and others as the core feature of individual vulnerability does not contrast with concepts of psychopathology that focus on information-processing disorders. In line with Ciompi (1987), in fact, we assume that the concept of dysfunctional working models of self and others (or disturbed affective/cognitive reference systems, in Ciompi's terminology) establishes a logical connection between vulnerability and information-processing while integrating many possible partial causes, whether biological or psychosocial, inborn or acquired.

REFERENCES

American Psychiatric Association (1980–1994). Diagnostic and Statistical Manual of Mental Disorders (3rd–4th edns). Washington, DC: American Psychiatric Association.
Anthony, E.J. & Cohler, B.J. (eds) (1987). *The Invulnerable* Child. New York: Guilford.
Atkinson, L. & Zucker, K.J. (eds) (1997). *Attachment and Psychopathology*. New York: Guilford.
Bandura, A. (1978). The self system in reciprocal determinism. *American Psychologist*, **33**, 344–358.
Bentall, R.P. (1990). The syndromes and symptoms of psychosis. In R.P. Bentall (ed.), *Reconstructing Schizophrenia*. London: Routledge, pp. 23–60.
Bleuler, M. (1972). *Die schizophrenen Geistesstörungen im Lichte langjähriger Kranken- und Familiengeschichten*. Stuttgart: Thieme.
Bleuler, M. (1981). Einzelkrankheiten in der Schizophreniegruppe? In G. Hober (ed.), *Schizophrenie: Stand und Entwicklungstendenzen der Forschung*. Stuttgart: Schattauer.
Bowlby, J. (1969). *Attachment and Loss. Vol. 1, Attachment*. London: Hogarth.
Bowlby, J. (1973). *Attachment and Loss. Vol. 2, Separation*. London: Hogarth.
Bowlby, J. (1980). *Attachment and Loss. Vol. 3, Loss*. London: Hogarth.
Bowlby, J. (1988). Developmental psychiatry comes of age. *American Journal of Psychiatry*, **145**, 1–10.
Brody, E.B. (1981). Can mother–infant interaction produce vulnerability to schizophrenia? *Journal of Nervous and Mental Disease*, **169**, 72–81.
Brown, G.W. & Harris, T. (1978). *Social Origins of Depression. a Study of Psychiatric Disorder in Women*. London: Tavistock.
Carpenter, W.T. & Strauss, J.S. (1979). Diagnostic issues in schizophrenia. In L. Bellak (ed.), *Disorders of the Schizophrenic Syndrome*, pp. 291–319. New York: Basic Books.
Cicchetti, D. & Cohen, D.J. (eds) (1995). *Developmental Psychopatholog*. (2 Vols). Chichester: Wiley.
Ciompi, L. (1980). Ist die chronische Schizophrenie ein Artefakt?—Argumente und Gegenargumente. *Fortschritte der Neurologie und Psychiatrie*, **48**, 237–248.
Ciompi, L. (1982/1988). *Affektlogik*. Stuttgart: Klett Verlag. Also in English: *The Psyche and Schizophrenia. The Bond between Affect and Logic* (1988). Cambridge, MA: Harvard University Press.
Ciompi, L. (1987). Toward a coherent multidimensional understanding and therapy of schizophrenia: converging new concepts. In J.S. Strauss, W. Böker & H.D. Brenner (eds), *Psychosocial Treatment of Schizophrenia*. Bern: Huber, pp. 48–62.
Claridge, G. (1990). Can a disease model of schizophrenia survive? In R.P. Bentall (ed.), *Reconstructing Schizophrenia*. London: Routledge, pp. 157–183.
Crittenden, P.M. (1990). Internal representational models of attachment relationships. *Infant Mental Health Journal*, **11**, 259–277.
Crittenden, P.M. (1994). Peering into the black box: an exploratory treatise on the development of self in young children. *Rochester Symposium on Developmental Psychology*, **5**, 79–148.
Crow, T.J. (1980). Molecular pathology of schizophrenia: more than one disease process? *British Medical Journal*, **280**, 66–68.

Cushmman, P. (1990).   Why the self is empty. *American Psychologist*, **45**, 599–611.

Day, R. (1985).   Social stress and schizophrenia: from the concept of recent life events to the notion of toxic environments (quoted by Ciompi, 1987).

Eisemann, M. (1985).   Psychosocial aspects of depressive disorders. *Umeå University Medical Dissertations, New Series*, No. **139**.

Erlenmeyer-Kimling, L. (1979).   Advantages of a behavior-genetic approach to investigating stress in the depressive disorders. In R.E. Depue (ed.), *The Psychobiology of Depressive Disorders*, New York: Academic Press, pp. 391–408.

Feighner, J., Robins, E., Guze, S., Woodruff, R., Winokur, G. & Munoz, R. (1972).   Diagnostic criteria for use in psychiatric research. *Archives of General Psychiatry*, **26**, 57–63.

Freud, S. (1920).   *Drei Abhandlungen der Sexualtheorie (Ges. Werke)*. London: Imago.

Ginsburg, B.E. (1967).   Genetic parameters in behavioral research. In J. Hirsch (ed.), *Behavior-genetic Analysis*, New York: McGraw-Hill, pp. 135–153.

Gottesman, I.I. & Shields, J. (1971).   Schizophrenia. Geneticism and environmentalism. *Human Heredity*, **21**, 517–522.

Gottesman, I.I. & Shields, J. (1982).   *Schizophrenia. The Epigenetic Puzzle.* Cambridge: Cambridge University Press.

Hammen, C., Marks, T., Mayol, A. & de Mayo, R. (1985).   Depressive self-schemas, life stress, and vulnerability to depression. *Journal of Abnormal Psychology*, **94**, 308–319.

Harding, C.M., Zubin, J. & Strauss, J.S. (1987).   Chronicity in schizophrenia: fact, partial fact, or artifact? *Hospital and Community Psychiatry*, **38**, 477–486.

Heilbrun, A.B. (1973).   *Aversive Maternal Control.* New York: Wiley.

Jackson, H.-F. (1990).   Are there biological markers of schizophrenia? In R.P. Bentall (ed.), *Reconstructing Schizophrenia*. London: Routledge, pp. 118–156.

Jaspers, K. (1913).   *Allgemeine Psychopathologie.* Heidelberg: Springer.

Kety, S.S. (1973).   Problems in biological research in psychiatry. In J. Mendels (ed.), *Biological Psychiatry*, New York: Wiley, pp. 15–34.

Lasch, C. (1979).   *The Culture of Narcissism. American Life in an Age of Diminishing Expectations.* New York: Norton.

Lerner, R.M. (1982).   Children and adolescents as producers of their own development. *Developmental Review*, **2**, 342–370.

Liotti, G. (1987).   The resistance to change of cognitive structures. A counterproposal to psychoanalytic metapsychology. *Journal of Cognitive Psychotherapy*, **1**, 87–104.

Magnusson, D. (1983).   Implications of an interactional paradigm for research on human development. *Reports of the Department of Psychology, University of Stockholm*, **59** (suppl), Sept 1983.

Magnusson, D. & Endler, N.S. (eds) (1977).   *Personality at the Crossroads: Current Issues in International Psychology.* Hillsdale, NJ: Erlbaum.

Magnusson, D. & Öhman, A. (eds) (1987).   *Psychopathology. An Interactional Perspective.* New York: Academic Press.

Main, M. (1981).   Metacognitive knowledge, metacognitive monitoring, and singular (coherent) vs. multiple model of attachment: findings and directions for future research. In C.M. Parkes, J. Stevenson-Hinde & P. Marris (eds), *Attachment across the Life Cycle*, London: Routledge, pp. 127–159.

Marsella, A. (1988).   Cross-cultural research on severe mental disorders: issues and findings. *Acta Psychiatrica Scandinavica*, **78** (suppl 344), 7–22.

Marshall, R. (1990).   The genetics of schizophrenia. Axiom or hypothesis? In R.P. Bentall (ed.), *Reconstructing Schizophrenia*, London: Routledge, pp. 89–117.

May, M., Gritti, P. & Calderisi, S. (1985).   La "diathesis-stress theory" della schizofrenia. Basi teoriche ed implicazioni terapeutiche. *Neurologia, Psichiatria, Scienze Umane*, **5**, 140–156.

Meehl, P.E. (1962).   Schizotaxia, schizotypy, schizophrenia. *American Psychologist*, **17**, 827–838.

Meyer, A. (1958). *Psychobiology: a Science of Man.* Springfield, IL: Charles C. Thomas.

Meyersburg, H.A. & Post, R.M. (1979). An holistic developmental view of neural and psychological processes: a neurobiologic–psychoanalytic integration. *British Journal of Psychiatry,* **135**, 139–155.

Millon, T. & Davis, R.D. (1996). *Disorders of personality. DSM-IV and Beyond.* New York: Wiley.

Mirsky, A.F. & Duncan, C.C. (1986). Etiology and expression of schizophrenia. *Annual Review of Psychology,* **37**, 291–319.

Nuechterlein, K.H. & Dawson, M.E. (1984). A heuristic, vulnerability/stress model of schizophrenic episodes. *Schizophrenia Bulletin,* **10**, 300–312.

Nuechterlein, K.H., Dawson, M.E., Gitlin, M. et al. (1992). Developmental processes in schizophrenic disorders: longitudinal studies of vulnerability and stress. *Schizophrenia Bulletin,* **18**, 387–424.

Ottosson, J.-O. & Perris, C. (1973). Multidimensional classification of mental disorders. *Psychological Medicine,* **3**, 238–243.

Paykel, E.S. (1982). Life events and early environment. In E.S. Paykel (ed.), *Handbook of Affective Disorders.* Edinburgh: Churchill Livingstone, pp. 146–161.

Perris, C. (1966). A study of bipolar (manic depressive) and unipolar recurrent depressive psychoses. *Acta Psychiatrica Scandinavica,* **42**, **194** (whole suppl).

Perris, C. (1981a). Recent developments and current issues in the study of depression. *Ideggyogyaszati Szemle,* **34**, 481–490.

Perris, C. (1981b). Course of schizophrenia and some organic psychoses. In H.M. van Praag, M.H. Lader, O.J. Rafaelsen & E.J. Sachar (eds), *Handbook of Biological Psychiatry, Part IV.* Basel: Dekker: pp. 81–158.

Perris, C. (1987). Towards an integrating theory of depression focusing on the concept of vulnerability. *Integrative Psychiatry,* **5**, 27–39.

Perris, C. (1991a). Ein Vulnerabilitätsmodell der Psychopathologie. Ein integrative Theorie. In G.-E. Kühne (ed.), *Aktuelle Aspekte der Psychiatrie.* Jena: Universitätsverlag, pp. 22–30.

Perris, C. (1991b). An interactionistic integrating view of depressive disorders and their treatment. *Acta Psychiatrica Scandinavica,* **84**, 413–423.

Perris, C. (1988). *Kognitiv psykoterapi vid schizofrena störningar.* Stockholm: Pilgrim Press.

Perris, C. (1989). *Cognitive Therapy with Schizophrenic Patients.* New York: Guilford.

Perris, C. (1993). *Psicoterapia del paziente difficile.* Lanciano, Italy: Métis.

Perris, C. (1996). *Ett band för livet. Bowlbys anknytningsteori och psykoterapi.* Stockholm: Natur och Kultur.

Perris, C. & d'Elia, G. (1964). Pathoplastic significance of the premorbid situation in depressive psychoses. *Acta Psychiatrica Scandinavica,* **40** (suppl 180), 87–100.

Perris C. & Perris, H. (1985). A biological, psychological, and social approach to the study of depression and its implications for treatment. *Neurologia, Psichiatria, Scienze Umane,* **5** (suppl), 67–93.

Perris, C. & Perris, H. (1998). *Personlighetsstörningar. Uppkomst och behandling ur ett utvecklingspsykopatologiskt perspektiv.* Stockholm: Natur och Kultur.

Perris, C., Eriksson, U., Jacobsson, L., Lindström, H., von Knorring, L. & Perris, H. (1979). The use of a multi-aspects classification model (MACM) in psychiatry. In J. Obiols, C. Ballús, E. González-Monclús & J. Pujol (eds), *Biological Psychiatry Today.* Amsterdam: Elsevier/North Holland, pp. 1377–1381.

Perris, H. (1982). *A Multifactorial Study of Life Events in Depressed Patients.* Medical Dissertations, New Series, No. 78, Umeå University.

Plomin, R. (1994). The Emanuel Miller Memorial Lecture 1993. Genetic research and identification of environmental influences. *Journal of Child Psychology and Psychiatry,* **35**, 817–834.

Plomin, R. (1995). Genetics and children's experiences in the family. *Journal of Child Psychology and Psychiatry*, **36**, 33–68.

Power, M. & Dalgleish, T. (1997). *Cognition and Emotion. From Order to Disorder*. London: Psychology Press.

Rende, R. & Plomin, R. (1995). Nature, nurture, and the development of psychopathology. In D. Cicchetti & D.J. Cohen (eds), *Developmental Psychopathology*, Vol. 1. Chichester: Wiley, pp. 291–314.

Rutter, M. (1985). Resilience in the face of adversity. *British Journal of Psychiatry*, **147**, 598–611.

Rutter, M. (1988). Epidemiological approaches to developmental psychopathology. *Archives of General Psychiatry*, **45**, 486–495.

Rutter, M., Lebovici, S., Eisenberg, L. et al. (1969). A triaxial classification of mental disorders in childhood. *Journal of Child Psychology and Psychiatry*, **10**, 41–61.

Sameroff, A.J. (1975). Transactional models in early social relations. *Human Development*, **18**, 65–79.

Scarr, S. (1992). Developmental theories for the 1990s: development and individual differences. *Child Development*, **63**, 1–19.

Singer, W. (1986). The brain as a self-organizing system. *European Archives of Psychiatry and Neurological Sciences*, **236**, 4–9.

Slater, E. & Slater, P. (1944). A heuristic theory of neurosis. *Journal of Neurology, Neurosurgery and Psychiatry*, **7**, 49–55.

Sperling, M.B. & Berman, W.H. (eds) (1994). *Attachment in Adults. Clinical and Developmental Perspectives*. New York: Guilford.

Sroufe, L.A. (1989). Pathways to adaptation and maladaptation: psychopathology and developmental deviation. In D. Cicchetti (ed.), *The Emergence of a Discipline. Rochester Symposium on Developmental Psychopathology*, Vol. 1. Hillsdale, NJ: Erlbaum, pp. 13–40.

Sroufe, L.A. & Rutter, M. (1984). The domain of developmental psychopathology. *Child Development*, **55**, 317–325.

Stern, D.N. (1985). *The Interpersonal World of the Infant*. New York: Basic Books.

Stern, D.N. (1995). *The Motherhood Constellation*. New York: Basic Books.

Strauss, J.S. (1969). Hallucinations and delusions as points on continua function. *Archives of General Psychiatry*, **21**, 581–586.

Strauss, J.S. & Carpenter, W.T. (1981). *Schizophrenia*. New York: Plenum.

Teasdale, J.D. & Dent, J. (1987). Cognitive vulnerability to depression: an investigation of two hypotheses. *British Journal of Clinical Psychology*, **26**, 113–126.

Waddington, C.H. (1957). *The Strategy of the Genes*. London: Allen & Unwin.

West, M.L. & Sheldon-Keller, A.F. (1994). *Patterns of Relating. An Adult Attachment Perspective*. New York: Guilford.

Zubin, J. (1987). Possible implications of the vulnerability hypothesis for the psychosocial management of schizophrenia. In J.S. Strauss, W. Böker & H.D. Brenner (eds), *Psychosocial Treatment of schizophrenia*. Bern: Huber, pp. 30–41.

Zubin, J. & Spring, B. (1977). Vulnerability—a new view of schizophrenia. *Journal of Abnormal Psychology*, **86**, 103–126.

Zubin, J., Magaziner, J. & Steinhauer, S.R. (1983). The metamorphosis of schizophrenia: from chronicity to vulnerability. *Psychological Medicine*, **13**, 551–571.

Chapter 3

When the Going Gets Tough: Cognitive Therapy for the Severely Disturbed

T. Michael Vallis
Queen Elizabeth II Health Sciences Centre, Dalhousie University, Halifax, Nova Scotia, CANADA

The development of cognitive therapy over the past two decades has been nothing short of remarkable. Careful consideration of cognitive therapy by clinicians of many disciplines (psychologists, psychiatrists, social workers, nurses, etc.), theoreticians and academics, as well as the public, has resulted in overwhelmingly positive responses from all sectors. Cognitive therapy has become one of the most prominent, if not the most prominent, form of time-limited psychotherapy. Virtually all clinical service units offer cognitive therapy as a therapeutic approach for a wide range of problems. Similarly, cognitive therapy is standard in the curriculum of most training programs in psychology (e.g. Howes et al., 1996). Testimony to the growth of cognitive therapy is the number of distinct variants that have been identified. In 1988, Mahoney enumerated 17 distinct forms of cognitive therapy. While modality-specific differentiation has fallen out of vogue (in favour of cross-modality rapprochement and integration) this statistic, if outdated, reflects widespread interest in cognitive therapy. Keeping pace with the development of intervention techniques has been the number of distinct problem areas to which cognitive therapy has been applied. The problems for which cognitive therapy offers solutions include depression (Elkin et al., 1989; Hollon & Najavits, 1989; Shea, Elkin & Hirshfield, 1989; Vallis, 1992), anxiety (Barlow, 1988; Chambless & Gillis, 1996), eating disorders (Garner & Bemis, 1985; Garner, Fairburn & Davis, 1987), pain (Eimer, 1989; Miller, 1991; Turk, 1996), irritable bowel syndrome (Payne & Blanchard, 1995) and marital difficulties

Cognitive Psychotherapy of Psychotic and Personality Disorders: Handbook of Theory and Practice.
Edited by C. Perris and P.D. McGorry.
© 1998 John Wiley & Sons Ltd.

(Epstein & Baucom, 1989; Margolin, 1987). Recent interest has also been paid to using cognitive therapy to treat problems such as post-traumatic stress disorder, bereavement, post partum depression, psychosis and family dysfunction (see Alford & Correia, 1994; Dobson & Craig, 1996; Vallis, Howes & Miller, 1991). Unfortunately, empirical data validating the efficacy of cognitive therapy has not kept pace with the widespread implementation of cognitive therapy principles (see Howes & Vallis, 1996).

Given the strong positive data regarding efficacy it can be concluded that cognitive therapy has "come of age". Cognitive therapy does appear to be very useful for the problem areas that define most of the range of affective experience and, therefore, distress (i.e. sadness, fear, anxiety, anger, and pain). As well, cognitive therapy is time-efficient and, given the central nature of the collaborative relationship and phenomenology, user-friendly (Vallis, 1991). Yet we must remain aware of the need to demonstrate, not assume, efficacy, especially in novel areas of implementation. Similarly, any clinician with experience is aware of the frequency with which individual patients present with difficult issues that defy the efficacy of even the most well-validated methods. It is the "difficult" cases that are the focus of this chapter. Specifically, the purpose of this chapter is to present a meta-model of cognitive therapy that can guide the therapist when treating cases outside the traditional limits of cognitive therapy. Applying cognitive therapy to the treatment of schizophrenia and personality disorders is discussed as a means of illustrating the use of this model. This meta-model is best appreciated in the context of the developmental history of cognitive therapy. Therefore, I will begin with a discussion of where we have been, where we now are, and where we are going with cognitive therapy.

WHERE HAVE WE BEEN?

Nowhere is the scientist-practitioner model of clinical practice better illustrated than with cognitive therapy. Consider the following. First, the theoretical underpinnings of cognitive models of psychopathology and change have been clearly operationalized and tested (see Goldberg & Shaw, 1989; Rush & Giles, 1982). There can be no question that cognition, at the levels of content, process, and structure (Hollon & Kriss, 1984) play a significant but non-exclusive (Riskind & Steer, 1984; Silverman, Silverman & Eardley, 1984) role in mediating affect, behaviour and even motivation[1] (e.g. Prochaska, DiClemente & Norcross, 1992). As well, within cognitive therapy, change appears to occur through the process of cognitive restructuring, although not exclusively so (Simons, Garfield & Murphy, 1984). Second, cognitive therapy intervention strategies have been specified and

---

[1] Prochaska's transtheoretical model of the stages of change, which relies heavily on cognitive factors, provides a framework to assess and intervene on motivation for behaviour change. The key constructs in assessment and intervention are cognitive in nature, including self-efficacy, decisional balance (pros and cons of changing or not changing) and self-perceptions.

evaluated. Cognitive therapy-specific techniques blend pure cognitive with behavioural techniques and include activity scheduling, mastery and pleasure techniques, graded task assignments, role play, cognitive rehearsal, experimentation, rational restructuring and re-attribution, among others (Beck et al., 1979; J. Beck, 1995). Cognitive therapy was perhaps the first of the psychotherapies to provide a therapy "manual" (Beck et al., 1979). Such manuals have become recognized as a necessary criteria for therapeutic legitimacy. For instance, in order to meet criteria for inclusion in the American Psychological Association's list of "empirically supported treatments" a detailed therapy manual must be available (Chambless, 1993). Third, the cognitive therapy model has been evaluated in controlled randomized outcome studies and shown to be effective (Shea, Elkia & Hirschfield, 1989; Hollon & Najavits, 1989). Fourth, training models, both intramural and extramural, have been developed to facilitate the development of therapist competency (e.g. at the Centres for Cognitive Therapy in Philadelphia and California, USA). Fifth, methodologies for assessing therapist adherence and competence have been developed, and used as predictors of outcome (DeRubeis et al., 1982; Dobson, Shaw & Vallis, 1985; Vallis, Shaw Dobson, 1986). For instance, within the National Institute of Mental Health's Treatment of Depression Collaborative Research Program (1980–1985) the cognitive therapy trainers used a competency scale (the Cognitive Therapy Scale; Dobson, Shaw & Vallis, 1985; Vallis, Shaw & Dobson, 1986) to determine the readiness of the trainees to participate in the main outcome phase of the trial as competent cognitive therapists. As well, during the main outcome phase competency was evaluated and criteria established to institute remedial supervision if competency fell below a predetermined level (the "redline" concept; Shaw, 1984). Sixth, process markers have been identified to help guide the implementation of intervention techniques. Safran (Greenberg & Safran, 1987; Safran & Muran, 1996) has led much of this work, advancing concepts such as "hot cognition", affective immediacy and "alliance rupture" to guide the implementation of cognitive therapy. Finally, suitability criteria have been identified to help select those most likely to respond to intervention (Safran et al., 1990a,b, 1993). It seems clear that cognitive therapy is not equally suitable for all individuals. Criteria that appear associated with favourableness of protocol-based cognitive therapy include accessibility of cognition and affect, personal responsibility for change, alliance potential and security operations, among others (see Safran et al., 1993). This list of scientific credentials is impressive indeed and, in all likelihood, unequalled in the area of psychotherapy.

The tremendous amount of work that has gone into the development and validation of cognitive therapy as a form of therapy has occupied the attention of scientists and clinicians for more than a decade. This groundwork can be considered the *first stage* (or *first generation*) of cognitive therapy. It has been extremely valuable and has provided psychotherapists with a solid foundation on which to build. I would suggest, however, that this stage of development has reached a close, and we currently exist within the *second stage* (or *second generation*) of cognitive therapy.

WHERE ARE WE NOW?

There was a time when cognitive therapy was limited to small specialty groups (either therapist or patient specialty groups), first in academic institutions, then in specialty clinics. No longer is this the case. By virtue of its success, cognitive therapy has "gone public". Now the vast majority of psychotherapists are familiar with cognitive therapy. This is both a blessing and a curse, as familiarity does not ensure competency. At best, society benefits greatly from the availability of a highly effective form of intervention in the skilled hands of the broad therapeutic community. At worst, those familiar with the language and outcome potential of cognitive therapy who implement interventions with little to no training compromise the benefit to society of cognitive therapy. I recall my personal ambivalence that developed in the mid-1980s after several years of offering half-day and full-day workshops on cognitive therapy for depression (in collaboration with Dr Brian Shaw). Over time we would encounter individuals who labelled themselves as trained cognitive therapists after one or two of these sessions (competency by acclamation), which included no direct supervision or even experiential learning opportunities! I was committed to promote the dissemination of cognitive therapy but became concerned about the danger of too little competence paired with enthusiasm and overconfidence. My ambivalence became acute when I reflected on my experience as a cognitive therapy trainer within the NIMH Treatment of Depression Collaborative Research Program. Within this program, we would not credential a therapist as competent until he/she successfully completed a 3-day workshop and between 100 and 150 hours of weekly individual, and monthly group, supervision over a period of at least 18 months, during which between four and six different patients were treated.

Regardless of the advantages or disadvantages of cognitive therapy going public, several significant changes have resulted that greatly impact on the practice of cognitive therapy. First, the settings in which cognitive therapy is implemented have broadened to the mainstream of clinical practice; clinic-based outpatient, day hospital, and inpatient settings, mental health units and private practice. Second, the clinical problem issues to which cognitive therapy is applied have changed. Patients are not selected to fit the therapy, as is a necessary condition in the empirical evaluation of cognitive therapy (e.g. unipolar, non-suicidal depressed outpatients with no substance abuse). Instead the therapy is adapted to the clinical situations in which therapists work. Thus, it is probably more appropriate to talk about cognitive psychotherapy than specific subtypes of cognitive therapy (e.g. cognitive therapy for depression, cognitive therapy for bulimia, etc.). Third, those of us who call ourselves cognitive therapists have had sufficient experience in the implementation of "standard" cognitive therapy (e.g. the protocol-based 20 session format summarized by Beck et al., 1979) that we have begun to see its limitations. This has resulted in revisions to theory and technique. This represents, in my opinion, the most significant outcome of the second generation of cognitive therapy. The primary constructs that have guided these revisions include; affect, development, interpersonal process and the therapeutic relationship, constructivism, and psychotherapy integration.

Collective experience, based on decades of psychotherapy research, is overwhelming in indicating that "single-cause, single-effect" models of therapy are inappropriate. To say that depression is selectively "caused" by faulty cognitions and that therapeutic change is uniquely mediated by "cognitive restructuring" is untrue and has been unhelpful to the field. This reductionistic approach has led to the "horse-race" mentality of psychotherapy evaluation (see Elkin et al., 1985). That is, attempts to find which therapy is superior to others and what the effective ingredients in a therapy are (the ill-fated component analysis) have not produced solid results for the most part. Despite an enormous amount of careful work guided by these goals, the results have been disappointing (at best) and possibly misleading (at worst). Take, for example, the general conclusion in the comparative psychotherapy outcome literature that "all have won, and all must have prizes" (Luborsky, Singer & Luborsky, 1975). This is a misleading conclusion, one that could have dire consequences in the current economic climate of restraint and cut-back. It is more accurate to conclude that there probably is differential efficacy of differing psychotherapies. The problem has been the methodology. Recent process-based research, which takes person by situation by intervention interactions into account, is likely to confirm differential efficacy (Safran & Muran, 1996; Rice & Greenberg, 1984). Dispensing with the "winner takes all" model of psychotherapy outcome research breaks down the barriers between therapies. The work on integration has been very influential here (Norcross & Goldfried, 1992). Integration necessarily leads to a theoretical eclecticism which crosses traditional technique boundaries. It would be short-sighted of cognitive therapists to ignore this influential work and try to "hold the fort" in favour of protocol-bound cognitive therapy. In fact, I would suggest, and hope to demonstrate, that cognitive therapy can be in the lead with regard to broad integrationist models of intervention.

The central role of affect in psychotherapy cannot be denied. Yet early cognitive therapy approaches placed affect in a secondary position, as a problem to be overcome rather than an important knowing process in itself (see Greenberg & Safran, 1987; Mahoney, 1985, 1988). Recognizing the importance of emotional experiencing *per se* in the change process has led to changes in therapeutic style. Take for, example the process markers of hot cognition and in-session affective shifts (Greenberg & Safran, 1987). Knowing that cognition and affect are inseparable (Greenberg & Safran, 1987; Leventhal, 1984; Lang, 1979) elevates the importance of attending to emotion directly. Identifying the experience of affect in sessions, either by homing in on cognitions that are discussed with experienced emotion (hot cognition) or being guided by the affective shifts demonstrated in session (as opposed to the agenda established at the beginning of the session) become as legitimate as a meaning inquiry or review of a thought record. Further, recognition of the central role of affect makes exploration *per se* as important an intervention as rational restructuring, role play, behavioural rehearsal, etc. In fact, exploration of affectively-charged material often leads to decentering, which is a spontaneous reappraisal, based not on rationality but on elaboration (see Guidano & Liotti, 1983; Greenberg & Safran, 1987).

Initially, cognitive therapy took an ahistorical stance (Beck et al., 1979). Development was seen as secondary to current experiencing. Clinical experience, however, has led cognitive therapists to reconsider the role of development in cognitive dysfunction, especially with regard to schematic processing. Guidano & Liotti (1983) provide an excellent model of a developmental approach to cognitive therapy. Their approach relies heavily on developmental theory (Bowlby, 1985) and structural models of knowledge. They differentiate tacit from explicit knowing, and highlight the central role of self-knowledge in emotional dysfunction and well-being. Attachment is seen as playing a major role in the development of self-knowledge. Further, Guidano & Liotti (1983), as well as others (Safran et al., 1986; Meichenbaum & Gilmore, 1984) differentiate core from peripheral cognitive events. *Core* cognitive events are defined as being central to the experience of the self, often with onset early in the developmental process (see Young's notion of early maladaptive schemata, 1990). In contrast, *peripheral* cognitive events are non-central to the experience of the self (see Safran et al., 1986). As such, changes in core cognitive processes are thought to lead to greater and more lasting clinical change. Interventions designed to alter core cognitive structure are embedded within a developmental reconstruction and include; in-depth examination/reconstruction of the developmental stages leading to the formation of deep structure self-knowledge (Guidano & Liotti, 1983); emotional exploration to produce decentering and cognitive differentiation (Safran & Segal, 1990); and the use of the therapeutic relationship to promote cognitive change (Rothstein & Robinson, 1991).

Interpersonal process and the nature of the therapeutic relationship have also become central issues to cognitive therapists. Safran's (1990a; 1990b) concepts of the interpersonal schemata and interpersonal cycles open new avenues for the practising cognitive therapist. An interpersonal schemata is "... a generic cognitive representation of interpersonal events ..." (Safran, 1990a, p. 89) that is "... abstracted on the basis of interactions with attachment figures and that permits the individual to predict interactions in a way that increases the probability of maintaining relatedness with these figures ..." (p. 93, Safran, 1990a). With these interpersonal schemata as a base, Safran emphasizes the interpersonal nature of an individual's functioning and distress, and has developed therapeutic interventions directed toward facilitating change, at a core level, in interpersonal schemata. Many of these interventions are based on detailed exploration of the patient–therapist interaction and its relationship to the patient's distress and self-schemata.

The foray of cognitive therapists/theorists into areas outside the traditional cognition-focused boundaries of first generation cognitive therapy has been very productive. Retrospectively, two conceptual models of cognitive therapy can be differentiated, each with its own set of assumptions about the nature of cognition in psychopathology, and each with its own set of intervention guides. These models have been labelled by Mahoney (1988) as the *rationalist* and *constructivist* models of cognitive therapy. This work represents the *second stage*, or *second generation*, cognitive therapy. It is essential to note that differentiating rationalist from constructivist approaches is not to imply that one is better than the other. The situation is more akin to evolution, not revolution. This notwithstanding, the distinction between *rationalist* and *constructivist–developmental* approaches to cognitive therapy warrants elaboration.

In distinguishing these approaches Mahoney (1985, 1988) highlights differences in the conceptualization of the nature of reality (ontology) as well as assumptions regarding the nature of knowledge and the process of change (epistemology). Rationalists view reality as largely external and stable, something that can be confirmed and validated (e.g. collecting *data* and appealing to the *evidence* to correct cognitive *distortions*). In contrast, constructivists view reality as totally subjective and idiosyncratic, with an emphasis on the active creation of reality in a feed-forward fashion (Mahoney, 1988). Thus, relative differences in the view of reality can be found between therapy models influenced by rationalist perspectives (Beck's and Ellis's, 1977, models) and those influenced by constructivist perspectives (Guidano & Liotti's, and Mahoney's models). Rationalists and constructivists also differ on their views of the nature of knowledge and the process of change. According to a rationalist perspective, knowledge is validated by logic and reason, with priority given to thought over emotion. The notion of controlling emotions by controlling thoughts follows from this. In contrast, constructivism maintains that knowledge is an integrated cognitive–behavioural–affective experience (Mahoney, 1988). Rationalists and constructivists also differ in their notions of human change, in which change proceeds according to cause-and-effect relationships, characterized by associationism (rationalism) or via structural differentiation, where mental representations are transformed and refined in an evolutionary fashion (constructivism; Mahoney, 1988).

In summary, cognitive therapy has been marked by a series of developmental stages. There are currently a number of different frameworks within which to develop cognitive conceptualizations, and from which to plan interventions. As a result, an explicit meta-model of cognitive therapy can identified, with rationalist-based and constructivist-based theories as overarching theoretical guideposts (Vallis, 1991). This meta-model can provide therapists with systematic choices about which cognitive conceptualization to follow in a specific case (Howes & Parrott, 1991; Howes & Vallis, 1996).

WHERE ARE WE GOING?

Contemporary cognitive therapists are in a position to reap the benefits of the tremendously productive efforts made during the first and second stages of cognitive therapy. However, in order to realize this potential a meta-perspective on cognitive therapy is needed. Otherwise, there is a potential that cognitive models will become either rigidly isolationist or will lose their identity to methodological eclecticism. A meta-perspective can allow cognitive therapists to

maintain conceptual/theoretical fidelity and yet blend rationalist and constructivist models to maximize flexibility and address cognition, affect, development and relationship issues. This is particularly important when working with
difficult cases. After explicating a meta-model of cognitive therapy I will attempt
to illustrate its value by discussing cognitive therapy for schizophrenia and personality disorders. These two clinical conditions are useful to juxtapose, because
it would appear that schizophrenia and psychotic disorders are best approached
guided by a flexible rationalist-based model, and personality disorders by a
flexible constructivist-based model.

Cognitive Therapy: A Meta-Model

Perhaps the most tangible benefit of past work on cognitive therapy is the
availability of multiple conceptual frameworks to guide assessment and treatment and yet maintain treatment fidelity (Howes & Vallis, 1996; Howes &
Parrott, 1991). Five specific conceptual sets have been identified: conceptualizations based on cognitive content alone; cognitive content vs. cognitive
process vs. cognitive structure (the tripartite conceptualization); core vs. peripheral cognitive processes; constructivist and developmental processes; and finally,
cognitive–interpersonal processes (see Figure 3.1).

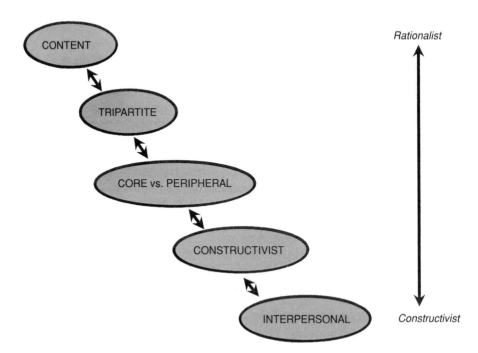

Figure 3.1 Levels of conceptualization within cognitive therapy

Content-based conceptualizations focus on the accessible content of the patient's experience; that is, their self-statements, stream of consciousness, or automatic thoughts (e.g. Meichenbaum, 1977). There is considerable empirical support for the efficacy of interventions targeted at cognitive content related to depression, anxiety, pain, anger and behavioural impulsivity (see Hollon & Najavits, 1989). Therapy interventions using this conceptual model tend to be reductionistic and learning-based, with predominance on self-monitoring and self-statement modification. These interventions can be extremely effective when working with problem issues that are specific in nature, where cognitions are easily accessible, responses are observable (e.g. pain tolerance, impulse control), and the working alliance (goal, task and bond components; Bordin, 1979) is intact. Conceptualizing at a content level has the advantages of accessing cognitive material that directly influences affect and behaviour, and of allowing the construction of an idiosyncratic model of a patient's phenomenology that is immediately verifiable to the patient. This is a particular advantage when working with non-traditional populations, where *a priori* cognitive models often do not exist. A primary disadvantage is that content-based conceptualizations do not address non-accessible cognitive processes or structures.

With *tripartite conceptualizations*, cognitive content, process and structure form the basis of assessment and intervention (Hollon & Kriss, 1984; Turk & Salovey, 1985). This model is best illustrated by Beck and his colleagues in treating depression (Beck et al., 1979). This tripartite conceptualization advances our understanding of patients' problems by addressing non-conscious cognitive issues (faulty information-processing styles, dysfunctional assumptions regarding personal worth) but is limited by not addressing the differential importance of some cognitive issues over others, and in not addressing developmental and interpersonal factors (Howes & Parrott, 1991). It is this conceptual model for which there are the greatest number of cognitive therapy-specific interventions. Again, this is best illustrated by the Beck et al. (1979) protocol for treating depression. J. Beck (1995) provides a detailed and clear manual of how to implement standard cognitive interventions, both behavioural (graded task assignment; role play, etc.) and cognitive (cognitive restructuring; empirical testing, etc.).

Conceptualization at the level of core cognition developed from attention to cognitive structure, especially the self-schemata. Distinguishing surface-level (peripheral) from deeper-level (core) cognitions has been tremendously helpful in guiding therapists to select targets of intervention (Guidano & Liotti, 1983; Safran et al., 1986). Core cognitions differ from peripheral cognitions in that they can be used to predict a patient's emotional/behavioural responses across situations. Attempts to change core or central beliefs are assumed to create greater anxiety, but longer-lasting change (Guidano & Liotti, 1983; Safran et al., 1986). Core conceptualizations appear to facilitate assessment and treatment by identifying those cognitive structures which may serve an organizing function for the individual and therefore identify cognitive constructs (content, process, structure) that are stable and generalizable. The interventions associated with this conceptual model are less recognizable as standard cognitive interventions than with the content or tripartite models, and involve exploration (meaning inquiries, elaboration of relevance to self) and decentring. As such, these interventions tend to be more affect-focused than technique-focused. This approach may be useful in guiding treatment with more difficult patient populations, given its idiosyncratic focus. Disadvantages of this approach include the following: accessing core cognitive structures is time-consuming and may not be suitable in some therapy situations; core beliefs are hypothetical constructs (i.e. tentative); and the reliability of a core-peripheral distinction may be questionable, given the current lack of empirical validation of this approach (Howes & Parrott, 1991).

As mentioned above, Guidano & Liotti (1983) have been instrumental in advancing a *developmental–constructivist conceptualization* in cognitive therapy. In this approach, deep structures are viewed as having a developmental basis. That is, early developmental events contribute to core cognitive structures. Thus, it is important to focus on the patient's cognitive, as well as emotional, development in assessment and treatment. The interventions associated with this model cross therapeutic boundaries, although they remain highly cognitive. That is, meaning and appraisal characteristics remain central to these interventions. Change in deep structure requires an in-depth examination of the developmental stages leading to the formation of deep structure self-knowledge. Thus, the therapists influenced by these notions spend extensive amounts of time on historical and process-focused issues, relative to therapists focused on problem solving and symptom resolution.

Advocates of the *interpersonal-based conceptualization*, such as Safran (1990a,b; Safran & Segal, 1990) highlight the value of Sullivan's (1953) interpersonal theory to cognitive therapy. Safran emphasizes the importance of the "cognitive–interpersonal cycle", and states that cognitive, interpersonal and interactional factors (i.e. "me–you patterns") are linked, and that information processing in the real world involves "hot cognitions" (i.e. emotionally laden cognitions; see Greenberg & Safran, 1987; Safran, 1984). Jacobson (1989) also advocates the use of the therapeutic relationship as a means to evaluate, test and help the patient to change core beliefs. An interpersonal-based conceptualization tends to result in greater attention being paid to the patient's cognitions, behaviours and affect during the therapy session, as well as the therapist's feelings and responses that the patient evokes (Jacobson, 1989; Rothstein & Robinson, 1991). The therapeutic relationship can be helpful in identifying core cognitions, but can also become a means to develop healthier interpersonal relationships. The therapist may focus more specifically on the "here and now", may employ more gestalt techniques to help deal with "hot cognitions", and may utilize behavioural strategies such as modelling and role playing within the context of the relationship, as well as more standard cognitive techniques (see Rothstein & Robinson 1991; Safran & Segal, 1990).

These conceptual models form a hierarchy of complexity that can guide a cognitive therapist in working with the severely disturbed. As one proceeds from the content-focused models to the developmental and interpersonal models, much changes. These changes include both conceptual and procedural issues. Conceptually, there is broadening from dealing with accessible cognition ("What is going through your mind right now?") to non-accessible cognition ("You seem to operate as if you require everyone's approval to be worthwhile"), to affect, development and relationships ("Can you see how your experience of yourself as a helpless child contributed to your belief in yourself as powerless and relates to your feelings of dependancy on me and the therapy?"). Procedurally, we see movement from cognitive therapy-specific techniques (self-statement training, cognitive restructuring, etc.) to more general interventions, often ones integrated from others therapy models (e.g. affective exploration, gestalt two-chair technique).

The availability of multiple frameworks allows the therapist to approach conceptualization in a flexible manner, by selecting the framework that best matches the patient's individual difficulties. These conceptual models, and the interventions that follow, form a meta-model of cognitive therapy. This meta-model will allow a therapist to implement cognitive therapy in a highly flexible manner, and to maintain treatment fidelity even when faced with difficult issues (resistance).

These conceptual models need to be viewed from the context in which they were developed. They are not mutually exclusive but are evolutionary transformations based on the positive attributes associated with developmentally prior models. Therapists should be encouraged to use these models as a template to guide the process of assessment, conceptualization and treatment planning/intervention. This is particularly true when working with difficult, treatment-resistant cases, or in novel areas where a model of intervention is in its infancy (e.g. schizophrenia or personality disorders). The template maximizes the therapist's options because it allows the therapist to make informed choices regarding the handling of cognition, affect, development and relationships (in and out of session). As a rough heuristic, the principle of parsimony is a useful one. Unless one has evidence to the contrary, one might begin working from rationalist-based models. These models are learning-based and the interventions that follow lend themselves well to empirical evaluation and time-limited administration. To the extent that interventions based on these models are not productive, or where comprehensive conceptualization requires going beyond cognition, the therapist might expand his/her model to address more fully affect, development and relationships. It is often at the point that rationalist-based interventions are of limited efficacy that therapists abandon the cognitive model and switch to another theoretical model, such as time-limited dynamic therapy, or refer patients for pharmacotherapy. While there are clear strengths of other systems of therapy cognitive therapists need to appreciate that cognitive models exist that can allow therapy fidelity and blend rationalist and constructivist interventions.

Table 3.1 presents a schematic of this meta-model of cognitive therapy. The range of therapeutic targets, including cognition, affect, development and interpersonal functioning are identified and for each, rationalist and constructivist models are contrasted in terms of conceptual content and approach to

Table 3.1 A meta-model of cognitive therapy

Construct	Model	Intervention
Cognition	Distorted thoughts vs. ongoing representations of self	Self-control to correct distortions vs. exploration to produce decentering and differentiation
Affect	A problem to be solved vs. an essential knowing process	Self-control vs. exploration
Development	Unimportant relative to the present vs. essential to current experience of self	Addressed in hit-or-miss fashion vs. detailed developmental reconstruction
Interpersonal functioning	Therapeutic relationship technical vs. therapeutic relationship a safe place for cognitive change	Focus on out of session content, problems reflect resistance vs. focus on in session content, problems necessary part of change

intervention. Therapists would be expected to focus more on cognitive content and process than cognitive structure when following a rationalist-based perspective. This would follow from a view of knowledge as being validated by logic and reason, with priority given to thought over emotion (change the way you think and this will change the way you feel). In contrast, therapists who adopt a constructivist-based perspective would be expected to focus more on cognitive structure than cognitive content or process. Thus. cognitive therapy applied according to a rationalist perspective tends to be content-focused, structured and orientated toward education and skills acquisition.

In contrast to therapy based on the rationalist perspective, therapy based on the constructivist model is more focused on cognitive structure and its development, within the context of the therapeutic relationship. As noted earlier, Guidano & Liotti (1983) illustrate this approach clearly. Their approach is less didactic, structured and educational than that of Beck et al. (1979), Meichenbaum (1977) or Rehm (1981). While symptom relief is sought, it is not, initially at least, the primary focus. Instead, therapy is orientated toward the identification of core organizing schemata. Therapists spend a great deal of their time trying to understand the patients phenomenology *vis-à-vis* these core schemata (deep structure vs. surface structure; Arnkoff, 1980). Therapists' interventions are likely to be less distinctive than those deriving from a rationalist perspective. Therapists work to help patients come to appreciate (not learn) how they see themselves and how this view influences their distress. This is done in an experiential fashion (see Guidano & Liotti, 1983; Mahoney, 1988; Safran & Segal, 1990). Considerable emphasis is placed on decentring (being able to observe one's own thought processes and appreciate their impact), as opposed to development of specific coping strategies (e.g. record-keeping, disputing negative automatic thoughts, using "flash cards"; see Young & Beck, 1982). Further, in following a constructivist perspective, cognitive therapists would explore the patient's developmental context in greater detail. Such a focus is designed to aid in identifying core dysfunctional beliefs and the decentring process. Thus, more weight is given to the process of therapy than to intervention techniques.

Therapists guided by constructivist notions often use their own relationship with the patient in therapy to a greater extent than therapists guided by rationalist notions (Jacobson, 1989; Safran & Segal, 1990). As a consequence of the therapist's conceptualization, constructivist-based cognitive therapy tends to be more flexible and more integrated with non-cognitive therapies than rationalist-based cognitive therapy. However, it runs the risk of being a less distinctive form of therapy.

This meta-model can be used by attending to the process of therapy; that is, it requires a focus on in-session markers. As all psychotherapy is grounded in the therapeutic relationship, this is the first issue to consider. Can the patient relate to the therapist in a stable manner, in which boundaries (between cognitive domains and cognition-affect) are maintained and the nature of the therapeutic exchange is based on education and rational thought? If so, rationalist-based interventions are likely to be effective; if not, more constructivist models of intervention are appropriate. Careful examination of past relationship patterns, especially past therapy relationships, is necessary here. Second, to intervene productively on cognition with cognitive therapy-specific interventions, the patient must be able to access cognition and differentiate between cognitions associated with different affects and cognitions of varying intensity. Third, the patients' capacity to experience and moderate affect is extremely important. Those able to differentiate among emotions (content and intensity) and those able to work with affect (experience emotion in a manner that is sufficiently non-threatening that they can sustain a focus on it and learn something from it) are likely to do well with rationalist-based interventions.

While scientific responsibility requires us to continue to demonstrate that novel applications of cognitive therapy are efficacious through controlled experimentation, the model presented above provides us with a strong framework to guide therapeutic intervention in novel areas and when working with difficult cases. Perhaps the most challenging areas for the adaptation of cognitive therapy are with psychotic disorders and personality disorders. At first blush, one might dismiss treating these problems with cognitive therapy. This might be justified by opinions such as; "since the psychoses, by definition, involve loss of touch with reality, cognitive therapy has nothing to offer". Similarly, "since personality disorders are by definition chronic and developmental in nature, dynamic approaches are preferable to cognitive approaches". Certainly treating these problems with cognitive therapy presents challenges, but the meta-model of cognitive therapy allows therapists to meet this challenge. Central to this is the cognitive therapist's willingness to be *flexible*. To the extent that a therapist sticks with one model of cognitive therapy (e.g. the Meichenbaumian self-instructional model) or insists on following a specific protocol (e.g. the standard Beck 20-session protocol for treating depression), cognitive therapy is likely to be of limited use in treating psychosis and personality disorder. The flexible cognitive therapist, however, will find him/herself with much to offer in working with psychoses and personality disorders. Let's discuss each of these problems separately.

Treating Schizophrenia

The application of cognitive therapy to schizophrenia represents an important advance in cognitive therapy. Traditionally, schizophrenia has been the purview of psychiatric treatment, with antipsychotic medication as primary intervention and psychosocial rehabilitation as secondary (Bellack & Mueser, 1993; Penn & Mueser, 1996). As such, psychological interventions have focused on social skills training and family therapy. Both of these models of intervention have been shown to be effective and are important components in the comprehensive treatment of schizophrenia. Yet none of these well-developed interventions (antipsychotic drugs, social skills training, family therapy), or their combination, are sufficiently powerful to obviate the need for additional interventions. Drug-resistant positive symptoms are common in schizophrenia (see Tarrier et al., 1993), as are chronic psychosocial sequelae. Cognitive therapy offers great potential by focusing specifically on the cognitive aspects of functioning. It should be noted, however, that cognitive interventions should be seen as adjunctive to "treatment as usual", and not as alternative interventions. For the purposes of this chapter, treating schizophrenia is a good illustration of how to implement flexible rationalist-based (content and tripartite models of conceptualization) cognitive therapy.

Cognitive therapy interventions for treating schizophrenia are relatively recent and can be categorized as either process-based (cognitive deficits) or content-based (cognitive biases). The process-based approaches focus on cognitive abilities from a neuropsychological perspective; that is, attention, concentration and memory. These models of intervention are referred to as "cognitive rehabilitation". The interventions typically involve repetitive training in the micro-skills conceptualized to be deficient in the cognitive abilities of schizophrenics (see Bellack, 1992, for a critical discussion of the validity of specified cognitive deficits). Cognitive rehabilitation efforts have been likened to cognitive rehabilitation with traumatic brain injury (see Spring & Ravdin, 1992). The potential of cognitive rehabilitation has been highlighted by a number of authors (Spring & Ravdin, 1992; Brenner et al., 1992; Liberman & Green, 1992).[2]

---

[2] Brenner et al. (1992) describe Integrated Psychological Treatment (IPT), which involves five hierarchical stages: cognitive differentiation; social perception; verbal communication; social skills; and interpersonal problem solving. Cognitive differentiation involves learning stimulus discrimination, concept formation and systematic search strategies. Social perception training involves graded training in social discrimination. Verbal communication deals with both receptive and expressive aspects of communication, using parroting, paraphrasing, and interactive communication techniques. The final two elements of the program, social skills and interpersonal problem solving, involve standard behaviour therapy methods (modelling, role playing and directive feedback) with a special emphasis on the cognitive components of these tasks. Brenner et al. report positive, if preliminary, data supporting the efficacy of IPT in enhancing attention, concept formation and abstract thinking (although see Bellack, 1992; Hogarty & Flesher, 1992).

Content-based interventions are more familiar to the cognitive therapist. Alford & Correia (1994) review cognitive therapy for schizophrenia and suggest that the key features for successful intervention include; a special focus on maintaining a working therapeutic relationship, self-concept as it relates to the experience of psychotic symptoms, and directive interventions that emphasize perspective-taking (decentring) over challenging validity of beliefs. While there are relatively few studies on the application of cognitive therapy to schizophrenia (especially positive psychotic symptoms) several encouraging studies should be noted.

Chadwick et al. (1994) compared empirical testing of beliefs (reality testing) to verbal challenging of psychotic symptoms in a small ($n = 1$) design (multiple baseline across subjects) and reported evidence that verbal challenging was more effective than empirical testing (contrary to general opinion within cognitive therapy). Interestingly, empirical testing was more effective when it followed verbal challenging than when it preceded it (Chadwick et al., 1994). Bentall, Haddock & Slade (1994) advocate a cognitive model of auditory hallucinations in which internal mental events are mistattributed as external to the self in the context of specific beliefs and expectations, all of which are targets for cognitive therapy. They present preliminary data to support the efficacy of focusing therapy (self-monitoring, detailed analysis of form and content of hallucinations, re-attribution) with a small number of schizophrenics. Tarrier et al. (1993) compared coping skills training to problem-solving therapy in their efficacy with residual positive symptoms. Both interventions were found to produce change, unlike the wait-time within subject control period, with some data to suggest that coping skills training was superior to problem-solving. Interventions did not produce change on negative symptoms, and expectations of treatment benefit did not play a role in the outcome of this study (Tarrier et al., 1993). Garety et al. (1994) report data on a preliminary non-random controlled trial comparing cognitive therapy to treatment as usual in a small group of schizophrenics. The cognitive therapy protocol was complex and individualized, including the following components: reduction of distress secondary to the experience of psychotic symptoms (Strauss et al., 1989); increasing understanding of the disease and developing self-control motivation; and reducing hopelessness. Specific interventions included standard cognitive restructuring to cope with positive symptoms (à la Beck et al., 1979), relabelling and education (normalizing therapy; Kingdon & Turkington, 1994), goal setting, and modification of delusional beliefs and dysfunctional assumptions.

The collective results of these studies, while not conclusive, are encouraging and suggest that cognitive therapy can play a significant role in the treatment of schizophrenia and related psychotic disorders. The meta-model of cognitive therapy identified earlier is ideal to guide cognitive therapists in this area. The available studies indicate that implementing cognitive therapy with schizophrenia requires special attention to the therapeutic relationship, flexibility, cognitive restructuring based on exploration, differentiation, functionality (not on external validity checks) and developmental reconstruction (Garety et al., 1994).

While early data, particularly that of Meichenbaum & Cameron (1973) promoted a content-based conceptualization of cognitive therapy (i.e. self-
instructional training) with schizophrenia, replication of these data have not been
encouraging (Bellack, 1992). Instead, a tripartite model of conceptualization
predominates, with a particular focus on content and structure. The need for
flexibility is great, given that the nature of the symptoms (e.g. paranoid ideation)
easily impair the therapeutic relationship (alliance ruptures are likely; see Safran
& Muran, 1996) and some of the confrontative interventions can easily elicit
symptoms (e.g. alternative generation and socratic questioning can increase
paranoia). Managing the therapeutic relationship requires special attention,
guided less by therapist-as-educator and more by the notion of collaborative
examination. Timing interventions based on the quality of the alliance is critical.
The therapist needs to be able to shift from restructuring activities to normalizing
activities to exploration in a highly flexible manner. If one views cognitive
therapy as a meta-system, rather than as a protocol, this flexibility is maximized.
The only way to maintain this degree of flexibility is to stay process-focused ("in
the moment"), not content-focused. Working from a single-model protocol is
likely to be insufficiently flexible for treating schizophrenia. Rationalist-only
models may be too rigid, as the nature of the therapeutic relationship is based on
the "student and teacher" model. This role differential may be fine at times,
but at other times is likely to evoke suspicion and threaten trust. Similarly, a
constructivist-only model may overemphasize exploration. With neurotic-type
problems, careful exploration (guided by affective immediacy and coreness)
often leads to cognitive differentiation, decentring and spontaneous reappraisal.
Psychotic cognition is unlikely to be associated with spontaneous reappraisal and
careful re-analysis (i.e. cognitive restructuring) is probably required to produce
change. As well, normalizing therapy will require guided rehearsal, best conducted from a rationalist perspective.

Garety et al. (1994) illustrate how the role of development needs to be incorporated into therapy with schizophrenia. In their description of interventions
targeted at dysfunctional assumptions they emphasize that,

> ... to address such assumptions the therapist starts by attempting to clarify the
> nature of the assumptions held. Most often this is done by a longitudinal assessment,
> a process involving questioning about the origins of assumptions and how they
> affected the person's life since the time they started to the present. Once dys-
> functional assumptions have been clarified, cognitive therapy procedures are
> used to restructure such assumptions and develop more adaptive and positive
> self-appraisal ... (p. 263).

The importance of developmental reconstruction is obvious in this therapy,
which is among the more comprehensive of the cognitive therapy approaches to
treating schizophrenia.

Considerable research, both conceptual and empirical, needs to be conducted
to evaluated the value of cognitive therapy for treating schizophrenia and psy-

chotic disorders in general. Yet it appears clear that whatever protocol(s) is(are) operationalized it(they) will need to be highly flexible, with a strong focus on the relationship and maintaining a working therapeutic alliance, and a blending of re-attribution (normalizing), restructuring and exploration interventions. The meta-model of cognitive therapy presented here will be useful, both in guiding larger scale research studies in the process of protocol determination, and also in guiding the individual therapist working within novel areas or with particularly difficult cases.

Treating Personality Disorders

There can be little dispute that individuals with personality disorders tend to be difficult therapy cases. The nature of the disorders themselves, in terms of chronicity, pervasiveness and self-perpetuation, make change, especially lasting change, difficult to achieve. Yet cognitive therapy is important to consider when treating those with personality disorder, for several reasons. First, those with personality disorder display many of the symptom disorders for which cognitive therapy has been shown to be a highly effective intervention (depression, anxiety; see Mavissakalian & Hamann, 1988; Millon, 1981; Shea et al., 1987). In fact, the more severe the personality disturbance, the more likely the individual will display distressing clinical symptoms (Millon, 1981). Second, given that cognitive therapy has received such strong empirical validation in the treatment of many symptom disorders, it is worth implementing it with personality disorders on the basis of impact alone. It must be emphasized, however, that there are virtually no empirical data validating cognitive therapy as a treatment for personality disorders. Efficacy must be *demonstrated*, not assumed.

Some of the specific features of cognitive therapy that offer potential for the treatment of personality disorder include: its phenomenological focus, which may be helpful in developing a strong working therapeutic alliance, clearly something that is a challenge in treating personality disorders; the active development of self-control, a major deficit in most individuals with personality disorders; therapeutic flexibility that allows blending of problem-solving strategies with a focus on underlying dysfunctional processes; and recent theoretical developments that lend themselves particularly well to personality disorder.

Working with personality disorders illustrates the value of the meta-model presented earlier. In contrast to schizophrenia and psychotic disorders, where the content and tripartite conceptual models are generally well-suited, it is the constructivist–interpersonal conceptual models that are most appropriate for personality disorders. Flexibility, based on immediate therapy process, is central to this work. Flexibility is required in both conceptualization and intervention. Those cognitive therapy approaches to personality disorders that specify highly differentiated cognitive models of each of the different personality disorders (models which serve as a blueprint for intervention) overlook what is known about the nature of personality disorders as diagnostic categories (Beck et al.,

1990; Young, 1990). Evidence is overwhelming that personality disorder diagnoses represent dimensional prototypes (fuzzy sets), not discrete categories (Cantor & Genero, 1986; Cantor et al., 1980; Frances & Widiger, 1986; Millon, 1986; Widiger et al., 1987). Prototypes describe a theoretical ideal or standard against which real people can be compared and consist of the most common features of members of a category (Millon, 1986). Within a prototypical model, categories are not homogeneous, they do not have distinct boundaries, and defining characteristics vary in their validity (Frances & Widiger, 1986). As such, one can expect greater variability in presentation between individuals with the same personality disorder diagnosis, and greater overlap between diagnoses (i.e. a larger proportion of mixed personality disorder diagnoses). The increased variability that follows from a prototypical model of personality disorder implies that a highly idiographic approach is needed when working with this population. At best, a cognitive profile for any personality disorder category is prototypical; exceptions to the rule and fuzzy cases are likely to be the norm. Until validating data are available, it appears more appropriate to focus on process-based adaptations to the standard cognitive protocol than to base interventions on categorical conceptualizations of unproven validity.

The successful implementation of standard cognitive interventions requires the following patient characteristics: an ability to view problems in a way that is (or becomes) compatible with the cognitive therapy rationale; a willingness to learn coping strategies and to accept the therapist as an educator; an ability to implement cognitive therapy techniques (e.g. monitor and record dysfunctional thoughts, collect evidence, role play, challenge negative thoughts); and an ability to follow a structured approach. Several recent studies have confirmed that these characteristics are indeed, central to the efficacy of cognitive therapy (Fennell & Teasdale, 1987; Persons, Burns & Perloff, 1988). Interestingly, Persons, Burns & Perloff also report that the presence of personality disorder was a significant predictor of premature termination in their study of depressed outpatients in a private practise setting. In related work, Safran et al. (1990a, 1993) reported that suitability for short-term cognitive therapy (assessed by the Suitability for Short-Term Cognitive Therapy (SSCT) interview scale) was predictive of outcome for a mixed anxious–depressed group.[3] Many, if not most, individuals with personality disorder would score low on the items of this scale, suggesting poor suitability for cognitive therapy. Recent data collected by Vallis, Howes & Standage (in press) confirm this. In this study, degree of personality dysfunction was assessed using the Personality Disorders Examination (PDE; Loranger, 1988) and suitability for cognitive therapy was assessed using the SSCT on a group of mixed psychiatric patients. Results confirmed a negative relationship between degree of personality dysfunction and suitability for stand-

---

[3] This scale assesses: accessibility of automatic thoughts; awareness and differentiation of emotions; acceptance of personal responsibility for change; compatibility with the cognitive therapy rationale; alliance potential (both in, as well as out of, session alliance); chronicity of problems; security operations; focality; and patient optimism/pessimism.

ard cognitive therapy for a number of the DSM-III-R personality disorder categories.

There appears to be a conflict between what is known about the general characteristics of individuals with personality disorder and what is known about protocol-based cognitive therapy and how it works. Individuals with personality disorder have, by definition, longstanding problems that impair adaptive functioning at a number of levels, including self issues, interpersonal functioning and role adaptation. The presence of these characteristics is likely to interfere with many of the structure and technique-orientated features of cognitive therapy. This suggests that cognitive therapy should be adapted to address the particular problems presented by those with personality disorder. Clearly, one important criterion on which to judge the value of current cognitive models for cognitive therapy with personality disorder is the extent to which these issues are addressed. There are several models proposed to treat personality disorder with cognitive therapy. These models can be divided into content-based vs. process-based approaches. Content-based approaches have been presented by Beck et al. (1990), Young (1990), and Turner (for Borderline Personality Disorder, 1989) and have been reviewed by Howes & Vallis (1996). While very descriptive, and therefore clinically rich, these models are threatened by the questionable differential validity of the personality disorder categories themselves. In a sense, they are top-heavy with content. Process-based approaches have been proposed by Vallis and his colleagues (Howes & Vallis, 1996; Rothstein & Vallis, 1991; Vallis, 1991) for personality disorders as a whole, and by Linehan (1993) for treating borderline personality disorder. The model of Vallis and colleagues best illustrates the meta-model of cognitive therapy.

Since individuals with personality disorder have difficulty following through on many of the specific tasks of cognitive therapy, cognitive therapy is best implemented within the context of a conceptual model that integrates technique with process variables (such as the development of dysfunctional self-beliefs, interpersonal schemata, and the meaning of the therapeutic relationship). This requires conceptual, procedural and process adaptations of many common practices within cognitive therapy.

Conceptually, cognitive therapy needs to be seen as an integrated, systemic form of psychotherapy, in which the central focus of therapy is on dysfunctional beliefs concerning the self and one's world (i.e. core beliefs; Safran et al., 1986), and in which the therapist's conceptualization includes cognitive processes, both conscious (automatic thoughts) and non-conscious (dysfunctional schemata; Turk & Salovey, 1985). The constructivist–developmental and interpersonal models of cognitive therapy, described earlier, serve as guides for intervention. The constructs addressed by these models most closely fit with issues presented by personality disorder patients.

Integrating the constructivist-developmental model into cognitive therapy when treating personality disorder patients has a number of advantages. First, there is increased *flexibility* that allows the therapist to track the patient more closely. Second, there is greater attention placed on *developmental* issues. Third, more focus is placed on the *process* of therapy, including the meaning of the therapeutic relationship itself. This allows a range of problem issues such as trust, intimacy and resistance to be addressed.

Procedurally, modification of the structure of cognitive therapy is required because of the difficulty personality disorder patients often have with issues such as compatibility with the cognitive therapy rationale, the ability to implement homework exercises, and so on. The following structural adaptations are recommended. First, cognitive therapy should not be guided by a strict limit on the number of sessions. Second, the structure of an individual session should be guided by relevant process issues, as opposed to a standard protocol.

Attention to the process of cognitive therapy is important because the development and maintenance of a working therapeutic alliance with personality disorder patients is often tenuous. The therapist needs to be highly sensitive to the state of the alliance, and much work goes into establishing and maintaining a functional alliance (see Jacobson, 1989). For this reason the therapist should be prepared to deviate from ongoing or planned interventions, in order to maintain the alliance. In fact, the relationship between the patient and therapist becomes a powerful therapeutic tool (Jacobson, 1989; Safran & Segal, 1990; Rothstein & Robinson, 1991; Young, 1990). As part of the relationship, exploration of resistance as a form of self-protection is often a therapeutic focus.

Rothstein and Vallis (1991) outline general strategies for implementing process-focused cognitive therapy with personality disorder, which is composed of two major phases. Phase one involves the development of a comprehensive cognitive *conceptualization* of the problem and phase two involves active *intervention* strategies based on this conceptualization. In developing the case conceptualization it is essential to consider a number of issues and their meaning. These issues include: understanding the symptoms presented by the patient in the context of his/her current situation and developmental history (e.g. current dysfunction might reflect persistent patterns that were functional at a past point in one's development); consideration of the therapeutic process and how it can be used in developing a comprehensive conceptualization (e.g. detailed exploration of the patient's reactions to the process of assessment/treatment, and how this relates to important intra- and interpersonal processes); exploration of the cognitive–developmental process (e.g. tracing the development and maintenance of beliefs about the self); and finally, conceptualizing core schemata.

In implementing this process-based approach to cognitive therapy, guided by the constructivist model, standard cognitive and behavioural strategies are important, but are not the sole defining characteristics. Instead, the bulk of the initial therapeutic effort is committed to helping the individual identify, appreciate and re-evaluate core dysfunctional processes. Strategies to accomplish this consist of an *exploration* of the patient's thoughts, beliefs and assumptions, the patient's core and peripheral cognitions, affect–cognition relationships, and the capacity of the patient to de-centre (see Rothstein & Vallis, 1991; Safran & Segal, 1990). *Interventions per se* include standard cognitive-behavioural change strategies, as well as the use of the therapeutic relationship to facilitate reappraisal of self- and interpersonal schemata, and focus on the patient's developmental context to facilitate reappraisal of self-schemata.

SUMMARY

In this chapter, I have attempted to present a meta-model of cognitive therapy that accomplishes several goals. First, this model integrates the tremendous amount of scientific knowledge that has accumulated regarding the validity of the cognitive therapy approach to assessment and treatment of psychopathology. Second, by linking the available cognitive conceptual models along a rationalist–constructivist dimension, the flexibility of cognitive therapy is maximized. One important outcome of this linkage is that the cognitive therapist can be flexible but maintain treatment fidelity. Third, the uses of this meta-model are illustrated by focusing on two relatively novel, and difficult, areas for intervention—schizophrenia and personality disorders. These two clinical conditions are interesting to juxtapose as they appear to require the therapist to make full use of the meta-model; focusing on content-tripartite models when working with schizophrenia, and constructivist models when working with personality disorders. The meta-model is not intended to imply that there is not blending of models and movement from one model to the next. In fact, this fluidity is the primary strength of the model.

It is clear that we must turn our attention to empirical studies of cognitive therapy as applied to non-traditional populations. If the results of the first generation studies of cognitive therapy are any indication, the future for cognitive therapy is bright indeed!

REFERENCES

Arnkoff, D. (1980). Psychotherapy from the perspective of cognitive theory. In M. Mahoney (ed.), *Psychotherapy Process*. New York: Plenum, pp. 339–361.

Alford, B.A. & Coreia, C.J. (1994). Cognitive therapy of schizophrenia: theory and empirical status. *Behavior Therapy*, **25**, 17–34.

Barlow, D.H. (1988). *Anxiety and Its Disorders: the Nature and Treatment of Anxiety and Panic*. New York: Guilford.

Beck, J.S. (1995). *Cognitive Therapy: the Basics and Beyond*. New York: Guilford.

Beck, A.T., Freeman, A. & Associates (1990). *Cognitive Therapy of Personality Disorders*. New York: Guilford.

Beck, A.T., Rush, A.J., Shaw, B. & Emery, G. (1979). *Cognitive Therapy of Depression*. New York: Guilford.

Bellack, A.S. (1992). Cognitive rehabilitation for schizophrenia. Is it possible? Is it necessary? *Schizophrenia Bulletin*, **18**, 43–50.

Bellack, A.S. & Meuser, K.T. (1993). Psychosocial treatment for schizophrenia. *Schizophrenia Bulletin*, **19**, 317–336.

Bentall, R.P., Haddock, G. & Slade, P.D. (1994). Cognitive behaviour therapy for persistent auditory hallucinations: from theory to therapy. *Behavior Therapy*, **25**, 51–66.

Bowlby, J. (1985). The role of childhood experience in cognitive disturbance. In M. Mahoney & A. Freeman (eds), *Cognition and Psychotherapy*. New York: Plenum, pp. 181–200.

Bordin, E. (1979). The generalizability of the psychoanalytic concept of the working alliance. *Psychotherapy*, **16**, 252–260.

Brenner, H.D., Hodel, B., Roder, V. & Corrigan, P. (1992). Treatment of cognitive dysfunctions and behavioral deficits in schizophrenia. *Schizophrenia Bulletin*, **18**, 21–25.

Cantor, N. & Genero, N. (1986). Psychiatric diagnosis and natural categorization: a close analogy. In T. Millon & G.L. Klerman (eds), *Contemporary Directions in Psychopathology: Towards the DSM-IV*. New York: Guilford, pp. 233–256.

Cantor, N., Smith, E., French, R.D. & Mezzick, J. (1980). Psychiatric diagnosis as a prototype categorization. *Journal of Abnormal Psychology*, **89**, 81–89.

Chadwick, P.D.J., Lowe, C.F., Horne, P.J. & Higson, P.J. (1994). Modifying delusions: the role of empirical testing. *Behavior Therapy*, **25**, 35–50.

Chambless, D.L. (1993). Task force on promotion and dissemination of psychological procedures. Washington, DC: Report of the Division 12 of the American Psychological Association.

Chambless, D.L. & Gillis, M.M. (1996). Cognitive therapy of anxiety disorders. In K.S. Dobson & K.D. Craig (eds), *Advances in Cognitive-Behavioral Therapy*. Thousand Oaks, CA: Sage, pp. 116–144.

DeRubeis, R., Hollon, S., Evans, M. & Bemis, K. (1982). Can psychotherapies for depression be discriminated? A systematic investigation of cognitive therapy and interpersonal therapy. *Journal of Consulting and Clinical Psychology*, **50**, 744–756.

Dobson, K.S. & Craig, K. (1996). *Advances in Cognitive Behavior Therapy*. Thousand Oaks, CA: Sage.

Dobson, K., Shaw, B. & Vallis, T.M. (1985). The reliability of competency ratings on cognitive-behavior therapists. *British Journal of Clinical Psychology*, **24**, 295–300.

Elkin, I., Parloff, M., Hadley, S. & Autry, J. (1985). NIMH treatment of depression collaborative research program: background and research plan. *Archives of General Psychiatry*, **42**, 305–316.

Elkin, E., Shea, M.T., Watkins, J. et al. (1989). NIMH treatment of depression collaborative research program: general effectiveness of treatments. *Archives of General Psychiatry*, **46**, 971–983.

Ellis, A. (1977). The basic clinical theory of rational–emotive therapy. In A. Ellis & R. Grieger (eds), *Handbook of Rational–Emotive Therapy*. New York: Springer, pp. 3–34.

Eimer, B.N. (1989). Psychotherapy for chronic pain. In A. Freeman, K.M. Simon, L.E. Beutler & H. Arkowitz (eds), *Comprehensive Handbook of Cognitive Therapy*. New York: Plenum, pp. 449–466.

Epstein, N. & Baucom, D.H. (1989). Cognitive-behavioral marital therapy. In A. Freeman, K.M. Simon, L.E. Beutler & H. Arkowitz (eds), *Comprehensive Handbook of Cognitive Therapy*. New York: Plenum, pp. 491–513.

Fennell, M. & Teasdale, J. (1987). Cognitive therapy for depression: individual differences and the process of change. *Cognitive Therapy and Research*, **11**, 253–272.

Frances, A. & Widiger, T. (1986). Methodological issues in personality disorder diagnosis. In T. Millon & G. Klerman (eds), *Contemporary Directions in Psychopathology: Towards the DSM-IV*. New York: Guilford, pp. 381–400.

Garety, P.A., Kuipers, E.L., Fowler, D., Chamberlain, F. & Dunn, G. (1994). Cognitive behavioural therapy for drug-resistant psychosis. *British Journal of Medical Psychology*, **67**, 259–271.

Garner, D.M. & Bemis, K.M. (1985). Cognitive therapy for anorexia nervosa. In D.M. Garner & P.E. Garfinkel (eds), *Handbook of Psychotherapy for Anorexia and Bulimia*. New York: Guilford, pp. 107–146.

Garner, D.M., Fairburn, C.G. & Davis, R. (1987). Cognitive-behavioral treatment of bulimia nervosa: a critical appraisal. *Behavior Modification*, **11**, 398–431.

Goldberg, J.O. & Shaw, B.F. (1989). The measurement of cognition in psychopathology: clinical and research applications. In A. Freeman, K.M. Simon, L.E. Beutler & H. Arkowitz (eds), *Comprehensive Handbook of Cognitive Therapy*. New York: Plenum, pp. 37–60.

Greenberg, L. & Safran, J. (1987). *Emotions in Psychotherapy*. New York: Guilford.

Guidano, V.F. & Liotti, G. (1983). *Cognitive Processes and Emotional Disorders: a Structural Approach to Psychotherapy*. New York: Guilford.

Hogarty, G.E. & Flesher, S. (1992). Cognitive remediation in schizophrenia: proceed . . . with caution! *Schizophrenia Bulletin*, **18**, 51–57.

Hollon, S. & Kriss, M. (1984). Cognitive factors in clinical research and practice. *Clinical Psychology Review*, **4**, 35–76.

Hollon, S.D. & Najavits, L. (1989). Review of empirical studies on cognitive therapy. In A. Frances & R. Hales (eds), *Review of Psychiatry*, Vol. 7. New York: American Psychiatric Press, pp. 643–666.

Howes, J.L. & Parrott, C. (1991). Conceptualization and flexibility in cognitive therapy. In T.M. Vallis, J.L. Howes & P.C. Miller (eds), *The Challenge of Cognitive Therapy: Applications to Non-traditional Populations*. New York: Plenum, pp. 25–41.

Howes, J.L. & Vallis, T.M. (1996). Cognitive therapy with non-traditional populations. Application to personality disorders and post-traumatic stress disorder. In K.S. Dobson & K. Craig (eds), *Advances in Cognitive Behavior Therapy*. Thousand Oaks, CA: Sage, pp. 237–272.

Howes, J.H., Vallis, T.M., Wilson, A., Ross, M. & Louisy, H. (1996). Predoctoral internship training in Canada. I: Internship settings and supervisory issues. *Canadian Psychology*, **37**, 173–179.

Jacobson, N.S. (1989). The therapist–client relationship in cognitive behavior therapy: implications for treating depression. *Journal of Cognitive Psychotherapy*, **3**, 85–96.

Kingdon, D. & Turkington, D. (1994). *Cognitive Behavioural Therapy of Schizophrenia*. New York: Guilford.

Lang, P.J. (1979). A bio-informational theory of emotional imagery. *Psychophysiology*, **16**, 495–512.

Leventhal, H. (1984). A perceptual–motor theory of emotion. In L. Berkowitz (ed.), *Advances in Experimental Social Psychology*. New York: Academic Press.

Liberman, R.P. & Green, M.F. (1992). Whither cognitive-bahavioural therapy for schizophrenia? *Schizophrenia Bulletin*, **18**, 27–35.

Linehan, M.M. (1993). *Cognitive-Behavioral Treatment of Borderline Personality Disorder*. New York: Guilford.

Loranger, A.W. (1988). *Personality Disorder Examination (PDE) Manual*. Yonkers, NY: DV Communications.

Luborsky, L., Singer, B. & Luborsky, L. (1975). Comparative studies of psychotherapies: is it true that "all have won and all must have prizes?". *Archives of General Psychiatry*, **32**, 995–1008.

Mahoney, M. (1985). Psychotherapy and human change processes. In M. Mahoney & A. Freeman (eds), *Cognition and Psychotherapy*. New York: Plenum, pp. 3–48.

Mahoney, M. (1988). The cognitive sciences and psychotherapy: patterns in a developing relationship. In K. Dobson (ed.), *Handbook of Cognitive-behavior Therapies*. New York: Guilford, pp. 357–386.

Margolin, G. (1987). Marital therapy: a cognitive–behavioral–affective approach. In N.S. Jacobson (ed.), *Psychotherapists in Clinical Practice: Cognitive and Behavioral Perspectives*. New York: Guilford, pp. 232–285.

Mavissakalian, M. & Hamann, M.S. (1988). Correlates of DSM-III personality disorder in panic disorder and agoraphobia. *Comprehensive Psychiatry*, **29**, 535–544.

Meichenbaum, D.M. (1977). *Cognitive Behaviour Modification*. New York: Plenum.
Meichenbaum, D.M. & Cameron, R. (1973). Training schizophrenics to talk to themselves: a means of developing attentional control. *Behaviour Therapy*, **4**, 515–534.
Meichenbaum, D. & Gilmore, B. (1984). The nature of unconscious processes: a cognitive-behavioral perspective. In K.S. Bowers & D. Meichenbaum (eds), *The Unconscious Reconsidered*. New York: Wiley.
Miller, P.C. (1991). The application of cognitive therapy to chronic pain. In T.M. Vallis, J.L. Howes & P. Miller (eds), *The Challenge of Cognitive Therapy: Application to Non-traditional Populations*. New York: Plenum, pp. 159–181.
Millon, T. (1981). *Disorders of Personality: DSM-III, Axis II*. New York: Wiley.
Millon, T. (1986). Personality prototypes and their diagnostic criteria. In T. Millon & G. Klerman (eds), *Contemporary Directions and Psychopathology: Towards the DSM-IV*. New York: Guilford, pp. 671–712.
Norcross, J.C. & Goldfried, M.R. (1992). *Handbook of Psychotherapy Integration*. New York: Basic Books.
Payne, A. & Blanchard, E.B. (1995). A controlled comparison of cognitive therapy and self-help support groups in the treatment of irritable bowel syndrome. *Journal of Consulting and Clinical Psychology*, **63**, 779–786.
Penn, D.L. & Mueser, K.T. (1996). Research update on the psychosocial treatment of schizophrenia. *American Journal of Psychiatry*, **153**, 607–617.
Persons, J., Burns, D. & Perloff, J.M. (1988). Predictors of dropout and outcome in cognitive therapy for depression in a private practice setting. *Cognitive Therapy and Research*, **12**, 557–576.
Prochaska, J.O., DiClemente, C.C. & Norcross, J.C. (1992). In search of how people change: applications to addictive behaviors. *American Psychologist*, **47**, 1102–1114.
Rehm, L. (1981). A self-control therapy program for the treatment of depression. In T. Clarkin & H. Glazer (eds), *Depression: Behavioral and Directive Intervention Strategies*. New York: Garland, pp. 68–110.
Rice, L. & Greenberg, L. (1984). *Patterns of Change*. New York: Guilford.
Riskind, J. & Steer, R. (1984). Do maladaptive attitudes cause depression: misconceptions of cognitive theory. *Archives of General Psychiatry*, **41**, 1111.
Rothstein, M.M. & Robinson, P.J. (1991). The theraputic relationship and resistance to change in cognitive therapy. In T.M. Vallis, J.L. Howes & P.C. Miller (eds), *The Challenge of Cognitive Therapy: Application to Non-traditional Populations*. New York: Plenum, pp. 43–55.
Rothstein, M. & Vallis, T.M. (1991). The application of cognitive therapy to personality disorders. In T.M. Vallis, J.L. Howes & P. Miller (eds), *The Challenge of Cognitive Therapy: Application to Non-traditional Populations*. New York: Plenum.
Rush, A.J. & Giles, D.E. (1982). Cognitive therapy: theory and research. In A.J. Rush (ed.), *Short-term Psychotherapies for Depression*. New York: Guilford, pp. 143–181.
Safran, J.D. (1984). Assessing the cognitive–interpersonal cycle. *Cognitive Therapy and Research*, **8**, 333–348.
Safran, J.D. (1990a). Toward a refinement of cognitive therapy in light of interpersonal theory. I. Theory. *Clinical Psychology Review*, **10**, 87–106.
Safran, J.D. (1990b). Toward a refinement of cognitive therapy in light of interpersonal theory. II. Practice. *Clinical Psychology Review*, **10**, 107–122.
Safran, J.D. & Muran, J.C. (1996). The resolution of ruptures in the therapeutic alliance. *Journal of Consulting and Clinical Psychology*, **64**, 447–458.
Safran, J.D. & Segal, Z.V. (1990). *Cognitive Therapy: an Interpersonal Process Perspective*. New York: Basic Books.

Safran, J.D., Segal, Z., Shaw, B.F. & Vallis, T.M. (1990a). Patient selection for short-term cognitive therapy. In J.D. Safran & Z. Segal (eds), *Cognitive Therapy: an Interpersonal Process Perspective.* New York: Basic Books.

Safran, J.D., Segal, Z., Vallis, T.M. & Shaw, B.F. (1990b). Suitability for short-term cognitive interpersonal therapy: interview and rating scales. In J.D. Safran & Z. Segal (eds), *Interpersonal Process in Cognitive Therapy.* New York: Basic Books.

Safran, J.D., Segal, Z., Vallis, T.M. & Shaw, B.F. (1993). Assessing patient suitability for short-term cognitive therapy. *Cognitive Therapy and Research*, **17**, 23–38.

Safran, J.D., Vallis, T.M., Segal, Z.V. & Shaw, B.F. (1986). Assessment of core cognitive processes in cognitive therapy. *Cognitive Therapy and Research*, **10**, 509–526.

Shaw, B.F. (1984). Specification of the training and evaluation of cognitive therapists for outcome studies. In J. Williams & R. Spitzer (eds), *Psychotherapy Research: Where Are We and Where Should We Go?* New York: Guilford.

Shea, M.T., Elkin, I. & Hirschfield, R.M.A. (1989). Psychotherapeutic treatment of depression. In A.J. Frances & R.E. Hales (eds), *Review of Psychiatry*, Vol. 7. New York: American Psychiatric Press, pp. 235–255.

Shea, M.T., Glass, D.R., Pilkonis, P.A., Watkins, J. & Docherty, J.P. (1987). Frequency and implications of personality disorders in a sample of depressed outpatients. *Journal of Personality Disorders*, **1**, 27–42.

Silverman, J., Silverman, J. & Eardley, D. (1984). Do maladaptive attitudes cause depression? *Archives of General Psychiatry*, **41**, 28–30.

Simons, A., Garfield, S. & Murphy, G. (1984). The process of change in cognitive therapy and pharmacotherapy for depression: changes in mood and cognition. *Archives of General Psychiatry*, **41**, 45–51.

Strauss, J.S., Rakfeldt, J., Harding C.M. & Lieberman, P. (1989). Psychological and social aspects of negative symptoms. *British Journal of Psychiatry*, **155**(suppl. 7), 128–132.

Spring, B.J. & Ravdin, L. (1992). Cognitive remediation in schizophrenia: should we attempt it? *Schizophrenia Bulletin*, **18**, 15–20.

Sullivan, H.S. (1953). *The Interpersonal Theory of Psychiatry.* New York: Norton.

Tarrier, N., Beckett, R., Harwood, S., Baker, A., Yusupoff, L. & Ugarteburu, I. (1993). A trial of two cognitive-behavioral methods of treating drug-resistant residual psychotic symptoms in schizophrenic patients. I. Outcome. *British Journal of Psychiatry*, **162**, 524–532.

Turk, D.C. (1996). Cognitive factors in chronic pain and disability. In K.S. Dobson & K. Craig (eds), *Advances in Cognitive Behavior Therapy.* Thousand Oaks, CA: Sage, pp. 83–115.

Turk, D. & Salovey, P. (1985). Cognitive structures, cognitive processes and cognitive behavior modification. I. Client issues. *Cognitive Therapy and Research*, **9**, 1–18.

Turner, S.M. (1989). Case study evaluations of a bio-cognitive-behavioral approach for the treatment of borderline personality disorder. *Behavior Therapy*, **20**, 477–489.

Vallis, T.M. (1991). Theoretical and conceptual basis of cognitive therapy. In T.M. Vallis, J.L. Howes & P. Miller (eds), *The Challenge of Cognitive Therapy: Application to Non-traditional Populations.* New York: Plenum.

Vallis, T.M. (1992). The current status of cognitive therapy in the treatment of depressive disorders. *Medicine North America*, **July**, 4221–4223.

Vallis, T.M., Howes, J.L. & Miller, P. (eds) (1991). *The Challenge of Cognitive Therapy: Application to Non-traditional Populations.* New York: Plenum.

Vallis, T.M., Howes, J.L. & Standage, K. (in press). Is cognitive therapy mitable for treating individuals with personality disorders? *Cognitive Therapy and Research.*

Vallis, T.M., Shaw, B.F. & Dobson, K.S. (1986). The cognitive therapy scale: psychometric properties. *Journal of Consulting and Clinical Psychology*, **54**, 381–385.

Widiger, T., Trull, T., Hurt, S., Clarkin, J. & Frances, A. (1987).   A multi-dimensional scaling of the DSM-III personality disorders. *Archives of General Psychiatry*, **44**, 557–563.

Young, J.E. (1990).   *Cognitive Therapy for Personality Disorders: Schema-focused Approach*. Sarasota, FL: Professional Resource Exchange Inc.

Young, J.E. & Beck, A.T. (1982).   Cognitive therapy: clinical applications. In A.J. Rush (ed.), *Short-Term Psychotherapies for Depression*. New York: Guilford, pp. 182–214.

Chapter 4

The Assessment of Dysfunctional Working Models of Self and Others in Severely Disturbed Patients: a Preliminary Cross-national Study

Carlo Perris*, D. Fowler, L. Skagerlind, O. Chambon,
L. Henry, J. Richter, J. Valls Blanco, A. Schaub,
M. Casacchia, R. Ronconi and P. Schlette
Swedish Institute of Cognitive Psychotherapy, Stockholm, Sweden

Several of the contributions to this book have emphasized that one aspect of the conceptual adaptations of cognitive psychotherapy (CPT), which have been required to treat severely disturbed patients with a personality disorder, refers to a focus on basic views of self and others and on core beliefs (Freeman & Leaf, 1989; Beck et al., 1990; Rothstein & Vallis, 1991; Wessler, 1988). In short, it could be said that one major focus of the treatment of such patients is on dysfunctional self-schemata and on their restructuration.

The term "dysfunctional" self-schema derives from those theorists who have used concepts such as *self-schema* (Markus, 1977; Fong & Markus, 1982), *internal working models of self and others* (Bowlby, 1969; Main, 1991; Guidano & Liotti, 1983; Perris, 1993; Perris & Perris, 1998), *interpersonal schemata* (Safran & Segal, 1990) and *early maladaptive schemas* (Young, 1990), to describe cognitive struc-

* Author for correspondence.

Cognitive Psychotherapy of Psychotic and Personality Disorders: Handbook of Theory and Practice.
Edited by C. Perris and P.D. McGorry.
© 1998 John Wiley & Sons Ltd.

tures which are laid down in memory, accessed by threat cues and speculated to represent the results of earlier social/emotional learning and adaptation to emotional threats.

Also concerning CPT with patients with a schizophrenic disorder, the ultimate aim of a metacognitive approach, as pointed out by Perris & Skagerlind (this volume), is to achieve the restructuring, or at least a substantial modification, of dysfunctional internal working models of self and others.

However, despite such an emphasis on core schemata in the CPT of patients with a diagnosis of personality disorder, and of those with a schizophrenic disorder, research on the systematic assessment of dysfunctional schemata in this kind of patient is still almost completely lacking.

Commenting on this state of affairs, Hammen (1993) has recently pointed out that although there are a number of speculations about the contents and characteristics of schemata held by people with different disorders, and personality disorders in particular, there has been little attempt to verify or measure such constructs. Schmidt et al. (1995) agree on this opinion. These authors underscore that despite the central role that schemata are assumed to play in the cognitive conceptualization and treatment of personality disorders, few guidelines exist regarding schema identification and assessment. In particular, Hammen emphasized that although the *working model* concept suggested by Bowlby is a very important one, e.g. for a definition of vulnerability for depression (however, see the chapter by Perris C., this volume), development of measures of representations of others and the self in relationship is still awaited. A similar consideration applies to the concept of *interpersonal schemata* proposed by Safran & Segal (1990).

Self-report questionnaires, despite their limitations (Segal, 1988; Hammen, 1993), still represent the most popular ways of operationalizing self-schema concepts. The most commonly used instrument to assess dysfunctional assumptions associated with dysphoric emotions is the *Dysfunctional Attitude Scale* (DAS; Weissman, 1979; Weissman & Beck, 1978). The DAS is hypothesized to identify assumptions underlying idiosyncratic thinking typical of depression (Beck, 1984), even though its specificity has been questioned (see below).

Originally, two parallel 40-item forms (DAS-A and DAS-B) were developed, which were assumed to be equivalent. However, repeated investigations (e.g. Parker, Bradshaw & Blignault, 1984; Oliver & Baumgart, 1985) have failed to support the hypothesis of equivalence, since the two forms seem to measure different constructs. Of late, DAS-B has apparently been dropped altogether and only DAS-A has been used in research work, especially in studies aimed at investigating cognitive vulnerability for depression or the effect of CPT in depressive disorders.

DAS-A has reasonable reliability and construct validity. The results obtained in different samples of depressed patients with this scale have been quite consistent, with mean scores around 140–150 across several studies (Dobson & Shaw, 1986; Parker, Bradshaw & Blignault, 1984; Hollon, Kendall & Lumry, 1986;

Peselow et al., 1990; Fava et al., 1994). Significantly lower scores (mean values 100–115) have been found in healthy controls (Weissman, 1979; Parker et al., 1984; Dobson & Shaw, 1986; Peselow et al., 1990; Hollon, Kendall & Lumry 1986). On the other hand, a significant decrease in mean scores, with mean values within the normal range, has been repeatedly shown in depressed patients who respond to pharmacological treatment (for a review, see Blackburn, 1988). Such a decrease in DAS score in relation to changes in the severity of depression, independently of any treatment with cognitive psychotherapy, suggests that high scores in the DAS are state-dependent rather than a trait variable that could be assumed to be a marker of vulnerability for depression (Hollon, Kendall & Lumry, 1986; Blackburn, 1988; Dohr, Rush & Bernstein, 1989; Peselow et al., 1990; Fava et al., 1994; Miranda & Persons, 1988). On the other hand, Reda et al. (1985) were able to show that, although many of the 37 DAS items which had been included in a longitudinal study of depressive beliefs in patients treated with a tricyclic antidepressant showed significant change by the end of each client's depressive episode, five beliefs appeared to be quite resistant to change, persisting even 1 year after discharge. The beliefs which did not change suggest an attitude toward oneself corresponding to what in terms of Bowlby's internal working models would be called *compulsive self-reliance*. The finding by Reda and his co-workers is an important one, since it points to the necessity of distinguishing between more central assumptions (core assumptions), which could be assumed to be resistant to changes in levels of psychopathology, and more peripheral attitudes which could be regarded as state-dependent. However, to our knowledge, no replication of that study has been reported in the literature.

Also, a poor specificity of the DAS has been found in comparisons between depressive and schizophrenic populations (Hollon, Kendall & Lumry, 1986; see also below), suggesting that rather than tapping a cognitive structure unique to depressives, scores on the DAS may simply reflect a general distress or self-worth factor associated with psychiatric disorder (Segal & Shaw, 1986; Segal, 1988).

To our knowledge, studies in which the DAS has been used in patients with a personality disorder have not been reported in the literature. Hollon, Kendall & Lumry (1986) have reported high DAS scores (mean 154.3) in a small group of non-depressed schizophrenic patients. This result is consistent with one of another study reported by Silverman, Silverman & Eardley (1984), who found a mean of 148.1 in a group of non-depressed schizophrenic controls. As yet unpublished results obtained in small series of schizophrenic patients by Fowler and his co-workers (mean 145.6, SD 23.3, $n = 14$), and by Skagerlind & Perris (mean 138.2, SD 37.5, $n = 28$) also point to mean scores which are above non-patient normative means, and closely approximate those obtained in depressed patients. Very likely, a total score on the DAS, as suggested by Segal (1988), is a blunt measure for assessing dysfunctional cognitions specific to any mental disorder. On the other hand, neither in the study by Silverman, Silverman & Eardley (1964) nor in that by Hollon, Kendall & Lumry (1986) has a detailed item analysis been carried out. Hence, it is impossible to decide whether clusters of particular items would differentiate schizophrenics from depressed patients.

Young and his co-workers (Young, 1990; Schmidt et al., 1995) have described a *Schema Questionnaire* (SQ) for assessing "early maladaptive schemas" assumed to be relevant to personality disorders. The SQ is a 205-item self-report inventory designed to measure 16 early maladaptive schemas hypothesized by Young (1990) "to develop during childhood *vis-à-vis* relationships with significant caretakers". Those 16 schemata are grouped within six higher-order areas of functioning: (a) "instability/disconnection"; (b) "impaired autonomy"; (c) "undesirability"; (d) "restricted self-expression"; (e) "restricted gratification"; and (f) "impaired limits". In a factor-analytic study carried out in healthy subjects, 13 of the original 16 scales hypothesized by Young were retrieved. Those scales showed adequate test–retest reliability (ranging from 0.50 to 0.82), and satisfactory alpha internal consistency coefficients. Applications of the SQ in psychiatric populations, however, have so far been limited in scope. Schmidt et al. (1995) have used the Personality Diagnostic Questionnaire—Revised (PDQ-R; Hyler & Rieder, 1987) as a criterion measure to assess the validity of the SQ. The authors have divided 163 patients into a high and a low PDQ-R score according to a median split. Subjects in the high PDQ-R group showed, also, significantly higher values on all SQ scales than subjects in the low PDQ-R group. These results were interpreted by the authors to support the view that high scores on the SQ scales can be obtained in personality-disordered patients. They do not allow, however, for definite conclusions to be drawn, either concerning the specificity of the SQ for personality disorders, or concerning the independence of SQ scores from levels of psychopathology.

Beck et al. (1990) have reported a list of "Contents of schemas in personality disorders" as an appendix in their book. This list is an extension of a similar one previously reported by Freeman & Leaf (1989). It includes "typical beliefs" supposedly associated with each specific personality disorder taken into account in the Diagnostic and Statistical Manual (DSM) of the American Psychiatric Association, with the exception of that of the borderline type. As a reason for excluding borderline personality disorder, the auhors maintain that this disorder is less specific in content than the other ones.

Although the list presented by Beck et al. (1990) is suggestive, it is unclear whether it refers to "core" or "conditional" schemata, or to what extent it includes basic views of self and others. Since all these concepts are used by the authors in discussing the conceptualization of cases in the CPT of personality disorders (Beck et al., 1990, Table 16.1, p. 352), it would help to specify in what respect "basic views of self and others" are assumed to differ from "core schemata". Also, it would be helpful if a distinction were made in the list between core schemata and more secondary assumptions. Westen (1991) regards the conceptualizations suggested by Freeman & Leaf (1989) and Beck et al. (1990) as very preliminary and, largely, as representing a mere translation of DSM-III-R criteria into schema language. On the other hand, and independently of any critical opinion concerning the status of the beliefs included in the list of

"Contents of schemas in personality disorders", it remains that any research work aimed at verifying the occurrence and the assumed specificity of those beliefs in the various personality disorders has not yet been reported.

The vulnerability–stress model of psychopathology proposed by C. Perris (this volume) suggests that individual vulnerability should be understood as the result of a continuous interaction between the individual's biological characteristics and dysfunctional internal working models of self and others. The model not only underscores that each individual is determined by multiple biological and psychosocial factors which contribute to his development as a person (that is, with his specific "vulnerability"), but also that each individual interacts with those factors modifying their impact.

This conceptual framework would predict idiosyncratic differences in the content of the assumptions about self and the world among different people in general and particularly between schizophrenic groups, and groups of people with non-psychotic disorder, or personality disorder (Perris & Perris, 1998).

In the following, we will report on the preliminary results of a cross-national application of a new instrument: the *Dysfunctional Working Models Scale* (DWM-S), developed by Perris et al. (1996, 1998). The DWM-S was intended to assess the content of dysfunctional internal working models of self and others (core schemata) in severely disturbed patients with a schizophrenic or a personality disorder.

DESCRIPTION OF THE DWM-S

The DWM-S is a self-report questionnaire comprising 35 items. The choice of the items to be included in the scale was made by the two senior authors (C.P. & D.F.). Thirty of the items, selected from a larger original pool, reflect dysfunctional representations of self and others in relationships which had been identified by the authors in the course of conducting CPT with patients with a schizophrenic or personality disorder. Five additional items, mostly reflecting a perfectionistic attitude, slightly modified from the DAS, were added to make a total of 35 items. The format of DWM-S is similar to that of the DAS. Each item is scored on a seven-point scale ranging from "I totally agree" to "I totally disagree". The items are worded so that for some of them, total agreement suggests dysfunctionality, whereas for others the reverse is true. The lowest obtainable score is 35 and the highest 245.

Preliminary investigations carried out in convenience samples of patients and healthy controls in Sweden ($n = 150$; Perris et al., 1998) suggest that the DWM-S has a highly satisfactory internal consistency (alpha = 0.97) and also highly satisfactory test–retest coefficients, both in healthy subjects and in patients (rho coefficients = 0.90 and 0.86 respectively). Results on the DWM-S are not influenced by sex and do not show any significant correlation with age. Between groups, comparisons have shown significant differences between the healthy subjects and all the patients' groups and between the non-psychotic Axis I patients and both the personality disorder patients and the schizophrenic patients. On the other hand, no significant difference was found between schizophrenics and patients with a personality disorder.

Several explanations of this last-mentioned finding can be taken into account. One is that the personality disorder group in the study only comprised patients with a cluster A or B personality disorder. Hence, it is not known whether the inclusion of patients with a personality disorder belonging to cluster C would have yelded different results. Another possible explanation derived from clinical practice is that there are pronounced similarities in aversive experiences and disturbed patterns of attachment in childhood and adolescence, both in patients with a schizophrenic disorder and in those with a severe personality disorder. These experiences may lead to the development of similar dysfunctional working models of self and others, mostly expressing fear of closeness and poor self-esteem.

The results mentioned so far were obtained in samples of Swedish patients. Hence, no conclusion could be drawn on the generalizability of the findings to patients from other cultural contexts. Also, no investigation had been made in the Swedish sample of any possible correlation between DWM-S results and levels of psychopathology.

To find an answer to those questions a larger multinational study has been planned, coordinated by the WHO Collaborating Centre for Research and Training in Mental health in Umeå. This study, which is still in progress, has so far included six centres, one from each of the following countries: France (Lyon), Spain (Córdoba), Italy (L'Aquila), Australia (Melbourne) and two centres from Germany (Munich and Rostock).

In each centre, at least 30 patients of both sexes with a (DSM-IV, or ICD-10) diagnosis of schizophrenia had to be collected. Also, it has been left open for each centre to collect patients with other diagnoses, when this has been feasible. However, this first phase of the study has been focused on schizophrenic patients. To assess a possible relationship between DWM-S scores and levels of psychopathology, two procedures have been followed. One has been of searching for possible correlations with ratings of psychopathology. For this purpose the patients were rated with the *Brief Psychiatric Rating Scale* (BPRS, Overall & Gordham, 1962) at the time when they completed the DWM-S. The other approach has been of calculating possible correlations between DWM-S scores and duration of illness (in years) from the first onset of manifest psychopathology. It could be suspected, in fact, that a longer duration of illness could have negatively influenced the view of self and others reflected in the DWM-S.

In this phase of the study a total of 289 patients (150 male and 139 female) have been collected at the six centres, 185 of them with a diagnosis of schizophrenia (96 male and 89 female). The remaining 104 were a miscellaneous group of patients (mostly from German and Italy) with too few representatives in the different diagnostic categories to allow for the creation of any meaningful diagnostic subgroup.

The results obtained in the total series and in the whole group of schizophrenic patients are shown in Table 4.1, while the distribution of the results in the series from the various centres is shown in Table 4.2. Neither in the whole series nor in the group of schizophrenic patients was there any significant difference in DWM-S scores between male and female patients. Neither was there any significant correlation with age, either in the whole series ($n = 289$, rho coeff $= 0.10$) or in the schizophrenic group ($n = 185$, rho coefficient $= 0.10$). In all centres highly satisfactory internal consistency coefficents were found (see Table 4.3).

Table 4.1 Means and standard deviations for the various measures in the whole series and in the group of schizophrenic patients

	Total			Male			Female		
	n	Mean	SD	n	Mean	SD	n	Mean	SD
Whole series									
AGE	289	36.4	11.7	150	35.4	11.3	139	37.6	12.2
BPRS	211	34.7	15.8	101	35.1	16.3	110	34.3	15.3
DWM-S	289	138.8	40.7	150	137.1	39.2	139	140.6	42.4
AGE ONSET	163	26.8	10.0	74	26.5	10.3	89	27.0	9.7
Schizophrenics									
AGE	185	33.5	10.2	96	32.4	9.9	89	34.8	10.6
BPRS	140	33.7	17.9	68	35.1	18.7	72	32.4	17.3
DWM-S	185	130.6	38.6	96	126.0	34.5	89	135.3	42.7
AGE ONSET	105	24.8	6.7	43	23.7	5.3	62	25.9	8.1

Table 4.2 Means and standard deviations for the varius measures in the whole series and in the schizophrenic subgroup at the various centres

	AGE			BPRS			DWM-S			AGE ONSET		
		Mean	SD		Mean	SD		Mean	SD		Mean	SD
Whole series												
France:	25	34.8	10.6	25	47.8	8.1	25	134.5	31.4	16	27.8	9.0
Australia:	29	23.0	3.5	29	7.5	5.7	29	100.3	29.0	29	21.3	3.2
Spain:	35	34.7	9.3	—	—	—	35	118.4	33.5	—	—	—
Germany 1:	30	38.0	10.3	30	36.3	11.1	30	110.4	31.4	30	26.7	8.4
Italy:	82	39.2	11.4	82	42.5	11.7	82	136.0	31.1		—	—
Germany 2:	88	38.9	12.4	45	29.6	8.3	88	173.1	33.8	88	28.5	11.5
Schizophrenics												
France:	25	34.8	10.6	25	47.8	8.1	25	134.5	31.4	16	27.8	9.0
Australia:	27	23.2	3.5	27	7.6	5.8	27	101.7	29.5	27	21.5	3.3
Spain:	35	34.7	9.3	—	—	—	35	118.4	33.5	—	—	—
Germany 1:	30	38.0	10.3	30	36.3	11.1	30	110.4	31.4	30	26.7	8.4
Italy:	36	36.3	10.2	36	45.8	14.4	36	138.8	32.1	—	—	—
Germany 2:	32	32.8	9.9	22	26.1	7.0	32	174.2	28.3	32	24.9	6.2

Table 4.3 Cronbach's alpha coefficients in the various countries

Centre	n	Alpha coefficient
France	25	0.86
Australia	29	0.91
Spain	35	0.86
Germany 1	30	0.90
Italy	82	0.87
Germany 2	88	0.94
All centres	286	0.93

As shown in Figure 4.1, no significant difference in mean DWM-S score was found between the schizophrenic patients from the various centres and those previously collected in Sweden (Mann–Whitney $U = 4475.1$; $z = -1.73$; $p = 0.08$). On the other hand, significant differences occur between patients from the various centres. In particular, Australian patients show the lowest scores (however, not significantly different from the scores in the Spanish and in the German 1 patients) and the German 2 patients the highest (significantly different from all other groups). The high values in the German 2 sample, however, cannot be explained by higher values in BPRS scores in this sample (see Table 4.2).

No significant correlations have been found, either in the whole series or in the schizophrenic group, between DWM-S scores and BPRS scores. Also, no significant correlation emerged in the schizophrenic group between DWM-S scores and duration of illness in years (Table 4.4).

Neither in the Australian series with the lowest mean age and the lowest mean BPRS score nor in the German 2 series with the highest mean BPRS score was there any significant correlation between DWM-S and BPRS scores (Spearman rho = 0.27 in the Australian and 0.18 in the German 2 series).

The preliminary results of the ongoing multinational study presented in this chapter support the view that the findings previously obtained in Sweden are generalizable within the studied cultural contexts. Also, it seems that core assumptions which can be assessed by the DWM-S are relevant for schizophrenic patients at the various centres.

As in the previous Swedish study, no significant influence of age and sex on the DWM-S scores has been demonstrated. Also, neither the level of current psychopathology, as assessed by the BPRS, nor the duration of illness seem to have any impact on DWM-S scores. These results contradict the assumption that results obtained by the DWM-S could be state-dependent, at least in schizophrenic patients. A few cases reported in the previous article, who had markedly improved after having been treated for about 2 years with schema-focused cognitive psychotherapy, showed a decrease in DWM-S scores. This type of decrease, if verified in a large series, would support the view already underscored by Bowlby (1969), that revisions of the internal working models of self and others can indeed

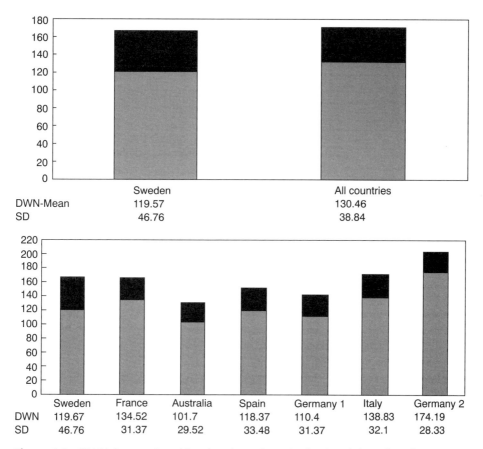

Figure 4.1 DWN-S score in schizophrenic patients in the Swedish and in the present material

Table 4.4 Spearman rho coefficients between DWM-S acores and BPRS acores, and between DWM-S scores and duration of illness

DWM-S with BPRS	Total series schizophrenic	rho 0.08	ns
	group	rho 0.14	ns
DWM-S with duration of illness (years)	Schizophrenic group	rho 0.13	ns

NS = not significant.

occur, for example, as a consequence of psychotherapy. To validate this assumption, however, it will be necessary to show, as in the study by Reda et al. (1985), that core schemata do not change as a mere consequence of a decrease in level of psychopathology.

REFERENCES

Beck, A.T. (1984). Cognition and therapy. *Archives of General Psychiatry*, **41**, 1112–1114.

Beck, A.T., Freeman, A. & Associates (1990). *Cognitive Therapy of Emotional Disorders*. New York: Guilford.

Blackburn, I.M. (1988). Cognitive measures of depression. In C. Perris, I.M. Blackburn & H. Perris (eds), *Cognitive Psychotherapy. Theory and Practice* (pp. 98–119). Heidelberg: Springer-Verlag.

Bowlby, J. (1969). *Attachment and Loss, Vol. 1: Attachment*. London: Hogarth.

Dobson, K.S. & Shaw, B.F. (1986). Cognitive assessment with major depressive disorders. *Cognitive Therapy and Research*, **10**, 13–29.

Dohr, K.B. Rush, A.J. & Bernstein, I.H. (1989). Cognitive biases and depression. *Journal of Abnormal Psychology*, **98**, 263–267.

Fava, M., Bless, E., Otto, M.W., Fava, J.A. & Rosenbaum, J.F. (1994). Dysfunctional attitudes in major depression. *Journal of Nervous and Mental Disease*, **182**, 45–49.

Fong, G.T. & Markus, H. (1982). Self-schemas and judgments about others. *Social Cognition*, **1**, 191–204.

Freeman, A. & Leaf, R.C. (1989). Cognitive therapy applied to personality disorders. In A. Freeman, K.M. Simon, L.E. Butler & H. Arkowitz (eds), *Comprehensive Handbook of Cognitive Therapy*. New York: Plenum, pp. 403–434.

Guidano, V.F. & Liotti, G. (1983). *Cognitive Processes and Emotional Disorders*. New York: Guilford.

Hammen, C. (1993). Cognition and psychodynamics: a modest proposal. *Clinical Psychology and Psychotherapy*, **1**, 15–20.

Hollon, S.D., Kendall, P.C. & Lumry, A. (1986). Specificity of depressotypic cognitions in clinical depression. *Journal of Abnormal Psychology*, **95**, 52–59.

Hyler, S.E. & Rieder, R.O. (1987). *PDQ-R: Personality Diagnostic Questionnaire—Revised*. New York: New York State Psychiatric Institute.

Main, M. (1991). Metacognitive knowledge, metacognitive monitoring, and singular (coherent) vs. multiple (incoherent) model of attachment: findings and directions for future research. In C.M. Parkes, J. Stevenson-Hinde & P. Marris (eds), *Attachment Across the Life Cycle*. London: Routledge, pp. 125–159.

Markus, H. (1977). Self-schemata and processing information about the self. *Journal of Personality and Social Psychology*, **35**, 63–78.

Miranda, J. & Persons, J.B. (1988). Dysfunctional attitudes are mood-state dependent. *Journal of Abnormal Psychology*, **97**, 76–79.

Oliver, J.M. & Baumgart, E.P. (1985). The Dysfunctional Attitude Scale: psychometric properties and relation to depression in an unselected adult population. *Cognitive Therapy and Research*, **9**, 161–167.

Overall, J.E. & Gordham, D.R. (1962). The brief psychiatric rating scale. *Psychological Reports*, **10**, 799–812.

Parker, G., Bradshaw, G. & Blignault, I. (1984). Dysfunctional attitudes: measurements, significant constructs and links with depression. *Acta Psychiatrica Scandinavica*, **70**, 90–96.

Perris, C. (1993). *Psicoterapia del paziente difficile*. Lanciano, Italy: Métis.

Perris, C. & Perris, H. (1998). *Personlighetsstörningar. Uppkomst och behandling ur ett utvecklingspsykopatologiskt perspektiv*. Stockholm: Natur & Kultur.

Perris, C., Fowler, D., Skagerlind, L., Olsson, M. & Thorsson, C. (1996). Development and preliminary applications of a new scale for assessing dysfunctional working models of self and others. Paper presented at the European Association of Behavioural and Cognitive Therapy, Budapest, Hungary.

Perris, C., Fowler, D., Skagerlind, L., Olsson, M. & Thorsson, C. (1998). Development and prelimninary application of a new scale for assessing working models of self and others (DWM-S) in severely disturbed patients. *Acta Psychiatrica Scandinavica*, **98**, 219–223.

Peselow, E.D., Robins, C., Block, B., Barouche, F. & Fieve, R.R. (1990). Dysfunctional attitudes in depressed patients before and after clinical treatment and in normal control subjects. *American Journal of Psychiatry*, **147**, 439–444.

Reda, M.A., Carpiniello, B., Secchiaroli, L. & Blanco, S. (1985). Thinking, depression, and antidepressants: modified and unmodified depressive beliefs during treatment with amitriptyline. *Cognitive Therapy and Research*, **9**, 135–143.

Rothstein, M.M. & Vallis, T.M. (1991). The application of cognitive therapy to patients with personality disorders. In T.M. Vallis, J.L. Howes & P.C. Miller (eds), *The Challenge of Cognitive Therapy*. New York: Plenum, pp. 59–84.

Safran, J.D. & Segal, Z.V. (1990). *Interpersonal Processes in Cognitive Therapy*. New York: Basic Books.

Schmidt, N.B., Joiner, T.E., Young, J.E. & Telch, M.J. (1995). The Schema Questionnaire: investigation of psychometric properties and the hierarchical structure of a measure of maladaptive schemas. *Cognitive Therapy and Research*, **19**, 295–321.

Segal, Z.V. (1988). Appraisal of the self-schema construct in cognitive models of depression. *Psychological Bulletin*, **103**, 147–162.

Segal, Z.V. & Shaw, B.F. (1986). Cognition in depression: a reappraisal of Coyne and Gotlib's critique. *Cognitive Therapy and Research*, **10**, 779–793.

Silverman, J.S., Silverman, J.A. & Eardley, D.A. (1984). Do maladaptive attitudes cause depression? *Archives of General Psychiatry*, **41**, 28–30.

Weissman, A.N. (1979). The dysfunctional attitude style: a validation study (Doctoral dissertation, University of Pennsylvania, 1978). *Dissertations Abstracts International*, **40**, 1389–1390B.

Weissman, A.N. & Beck, A.T. (1978). Development and validation of the Dysfunctional Attitudes Scale: a preliminary investigation. Paper presented at the meeting of the American Educational Research Association, Toronto, Canada.

Wessler, R.L. (1988). Cognitive appraisal therapy: a new multidimensional treatment for certain disorders of personality. Paper presented at the 1st International Congress on the Disorders of Personality, Copenhagen, Denmark.

Westen, D. (1991). Cognitive-behavioral interventions in the psychoanalytic psychotherapy of borderline personality disorders. *Clinical Psychology Review*, **11**, 211–230.

Young, J.E. (1990). *Cognitive Therapy for Personality Disorders: a Schema-focused Approach*. Sarasota, FL: Professional Resource Exchange, Inc.

Chapter 5

State-of-the-art Approaches in the Treatment of Information-Processing Disorders in Schizophrenia

Bettina Hodel and Hans D. Brenner
Department of Psychiatry, Bern University, Bern, Switzerland

THEORETICAL AND EMPIRICAL BACKGROUND

The term "cognitive impairment" in schizophrenia is used to refer to dysfunctions in information processing (Spaulding, 1992) and to thought disorders, e.g. hallucinations and delusional beliefs (Kingdon & Turkington, 1994; Yusupoff & Haddock, this volume). This chapter will discuss the former aspect, i.e. the so-called cognitive dysfunctions, and the methods to treat them.

Results of recent experimental studies show that in schizophrenia cognitive dysfunctions are primarily a consequence of attentional deficits (Spaulding et al., 1997, Bellack, 1996). Disorders like deficient activation of stored experiences or deficient conceptual behavior planning, however, also play a principal role (Hemsley, 1994; Magaro, 1980). The severity of these disturbances in information processing varies across patients (Freedman & Chapman, 1973; Spring, Leman & Fergeson, 1990), and may fluctuate within patients over time as well (Corrigan et al., 1994). These disturbances have been detected before the onset of an acute psychotic episode (Nuechterlein et al., 1992) and may even predate adulthood (see studies of Schreiber et al., 1992, on adolescents and studies of Mednick, 1996, on children). Summarized, these disorders are considered to represent a "core psychological deficit" (Hemsley, 1987, 1993; Nuechterlein et al., 1992).

Cognitive Psychotherapy of Psychotic and Personality Disorders: Handbook of Theory and Practice.
Edited by C. Perris and P.D. McGorry.
© 1998 John Wiley & Sons Ltd.

A widespread discussion about the etiology of disordered information processing has arisen over the past few years. Current speculation on this issue follows various lines: some authors postulate a "limited capacity" as the basic underlying deficit involved, which is in turn probably related to deficits of neuronal differentiation of the neocortex (van den Bosch, Rombouts & van Asma, 1993; Green, 1993). Based on findings of experimental studies, Hemsley (1994) proposes that both behavioral abnormalities and psychiatric symptoms typical of patients with schizophrenia are linked with a deterioration in the relationship between stored experience and ongoing input. In normal cognition, contextual information—both spatial and temporal—controls the activation of appropriately stored materials and results in "expectancies or response bias". In schizophrenia, dysfunctional brain-processes, mainly spatial and temporal irregularities, lead to a weakening in the influence of memories on current perception. The result is a deficiency in rapid and automatic assessment of the significance of aspects of current sensory input. Also based on research data, Spaulding et al. (1994) tried to create a unified conceptual model to optimize therapeutic interventions and rehabilitation efforts. They proposed three factors as the main impairments in schizophrenia: Factor 1 is vulnerability-linked and can be detected before the onset of schizophrenia or in vulnerable subjects who may never have experienced an acute episode. The factor's origin is presumed to be based on disordered periventricular limbic structures (see Bogarts, 1989). This leads to impairments hypothesized to be relatively insensitive to fluctuations in mental status, as well as to changes in the course of illness. Factor 1 represents molecular cognitive impairments like pre-attentional processes which can be measured in backward masking and span of apprehension tasks. Pervasive effects of this Factor 1 on molar levels, however, are supposed as well: concept formation, problem solving and executive functioning could be affected. Factor 2 is symptom-related and can first be detected during episodes of psychotic exacerbation. It then decreases to a pre-episode level when the psychosis remits. Factor 2 represents molar cognitive impairments in concept formation and modulation, in short-term or working memory and in problem-solving abilities. This factor is hypothesized to be a fairly direct consequence of the neurophysiological processes associated with psychotic relapses. Therefore, it seems to be an important clinical indicator in the context of rehabilitation. Factor 3 is qualitatively similar to Factor 2, but is residual rather than episode-linked, and appears later in the course of the disorder. In contrast to pre-existing or worsening vulnerabilities observed under progressive limbic degeneration, Factor 3 is not cumulative or progressive but represents an impaired neurophysiological process which simply takes longer to normalize than the processes associated with Factor 2.

Several years ago, Brenner (1989) devised a mainly heuristic model which will be briefly described here for two reasons; First, because it attempts to explain the cognitive disorders manifested in schizophrenia from a comprehensive approach; and second, because it addresses the interrelations between neuronal, cognitive and emotional processes of behavior control. The model's basis is the arousal and activation system of the human brain. The neurochemical substrate of the arousal system represents reciprocal norepinephrinergic and serotonergic neuronal pathways. Their neuronal activity is closely related to perceptual information processing and to external control. The activation system, on the other hand, is regulated by dopaminergic nigrostriatal and mesolimbic–mesocortical neuronal circuits as well as their interconnections. By its activity attention is directed to internal control. It therefore corresponds to processes of conceptual information processing. In both systems, there is a regulative negative feedback mechanism. The norepinephrinergic-activating neuronal pathways of the arousal system habituate with repeated sensory input and ensure that novel or unexpected events can change information-processing, thus providing external control. Neuronal activity then primarily corresponds to novel information and less to information that is activated by the working memory. The dopaminergic activation system, on the other hand, provides for a rapidly increasing redundancy of information. Neural activity then mainly refers to information that is already represented, thus providing for internal control. In the first phases of coping with a complex situation, a great amount of novel information usually has to be processed, without having already passed through structures which are relevant for cognitive organization. Here, the perceptual control properties of the arousal system, with its bias towards habituation, constitute an advantage. They permit the global representation of a broad array of stimuli. In a latter phase of processing the bias of the activation system towards redundancy is more advantageous. It permits a limitation of the information processed and thus is the basis for a differentiation of the situation into specific elements.

However, behavior patterns are not only dependent on the neuronal and cognitive processes described, but on emotional processes as well. Emotional processes are distinguishable in participatory and episodic ones (cf. Pribram & McGuiness, 1975). Participatory processes are characterized by involvement and engagement with external stimuli. The correlations between perceptual information processing and the arousal system are also features of the participatory processes. They tolerate incongruity for a short period of time between the perception of situations and learned values, so that new or relevant external stimuli can be recognized and processed as such. If new or surprising environmental stimuli are judged as relevant—if, in other words, intensified perception can be expected to reduce incongruency, thereby controlling the situation—optimistic feelings arise. There is a connection between believing that success is possible and interest, hope and social support. All these feelings serve as an incentive to behave in a way that changes situations. Episodic processes, however, tend to reach a relatively lasting kind of stability by returning to previous forms of control. The correlations between the activation system and conceptual information processing are features of episodic processes. They tend to be relatively stable over time and to stem from earlier levels of organization. External stimuli are processed and selected only when they are relevant to inner processes and do not interfere with them. If they are disruptive, they will be considered to be irrelevant and will be filtered out. Internal configurations can thus be conserved. If there is an expectation that the perception of a situation cannot be used to ultimately reduce incongruency, negative feelings such as dismay and pessimism may arise. They are coupled with awareness of poor competence, fear and social alienation. In schizophrenia the constant overstimulation of the activation system and its inherent bias towards a predominance of internal control leads to rigid perception and behavioral planning. Therefore, schizophrenic patients are easily "frozen" into a state of negative outcome expectancies. This can be further increased by a negative self-image and by a pronounced external locus of control, both of which are common in schizophrenia. Efforts to change this situation by active behavior are therefore rare and short-lived. Participatory and episodic processes, as well as perceptual and conceptual information processing, become increasingly dissociated. Consequently, the schizophrenic patient withdraws from reality more and more, and relates to his/her environment in an increasingly fragmentary and irregular manner.

THERAPEUTIC INTERVENTIONS

Interventions for Improving Cognitive Information Processing

The importance of developing interventions specifically directed at reducing dysfunctional information processing for the rehabilitation of patients with schizophrenia was explicitly postulated only a few years ago (Carpenter & Schooler, 1988; Möller, 1988; Häfner, 1988). There are several reasons why it took a relatively long time for experimental findings to be translated into therapeutic action. One of them might be the difficulty of operationalizing dysfunctional information processing, as such processing can vary inter- and intra-individually in schizophrenia (Corrigan et al., 1994). Another reason could be that earlier approaches in the treatment of information-processing disorders showed only isolated and short-term effects, due to methodological limitations of the respective studies (Spaulding et al., 1986; Brenner, Hodel & Merlo, 1995; Hodel & Brenner, 1996a). Over the last 10 years, however, a lot of investigations have been carried out to improve information processing in schizophrenia. Currently there exist four main kinds of intervention: direct, indirect and combined interventions, as well as interventions for improving emotional processing (cf. Hodel & Brenner, 1994).

Direct Interventions

Direct interventions aim at reducing isolated information processing disorders or cognitive deficits. Usually they include rehearsing cognitive tasks to improve attentional and mnemonic functions (the stimulation approach; see Green, 1993). Early attempts at attentional training can, for instance, be traced back to Rosenbaum, Mackavey & Grisell (1957), who used punishment, and to Meiselman (1973), who used contingent reinforcement to improve performance in reaction time. Wagner (1968) trained schizophrenic patients to scan a visual field by instructing them how to match task and test stimuli. Wishner & Wahl (1974), as well as Benedict & Harris (1989), optimized selective attentional skills in letter recognition training under auditory distraction conditions. Hammond & Summer (1972) and Larsen & Fromholt (1976) improved short-term memory functions by means of serial rehearsal of syllables and words.

Some of the newer methods of cognitive skills training attempt to replicate or to specify the results obtained in earlier methods. For instance, Classen & Laux (1989) replicated Meiselmans' (1973) study on contingent reinforcement of correct reactions. Along the lines of Hammond & Summer (1972), Mussgay, Olbrich & Ihle, (1991) trained patients how to recognize and reproduce visual stimuli and how to distinguish between relevant and irrelevant elements within them. Also, Jaeger & Douglas (1992) offered systematic training in attentional and short-term recall tasks. Delahunty, Morice & Frost (1993) trained patients how to maintain and shift focused attention and how to logically structure time-dependent information. Other recent studies focus on conceptual functions by providing training procedures in the Wisconsin Card Sorting Task (WCST; Heaton & Pendelton, 1981). Goldberg et al. (1987)—the first researchers to conduct repeated WCST training with schizophrenic patients—observed only a trend of improvement after the training, which was short-term and reversible. In contrast to this, Bellack et al. (1990) reported a significantly improved test performance by giving contingent reinforcement for correct answers. Summerfelt et al. (1991) and Green et al. (1992) reported significant gains by supplying a combination of contingent reinforcement and instructions for problem-solving. In single-case studies, Hellmann et al. (1992) found that this combination even produces durable gains.

Other, newer, developments of direct interventions include computerized training programs. Lamberti, Wieneke & Brauke (1988) reported positive changes in selective visual attention after the use of an attentional training. Gestrich & Hermanutz (1991) succeeded in reducing schizophrenic patients' reaction time in learning tasks involving computerized visual and auditory stimuli. Gansert & Olbrich (1992) and Olbrich (1996) reported positive experiences with computerized training for improving attentional, mnemonic and conceptual skills (verbal and non-verbal ones). After completion of education in computerized text processing, Schöttke (1993) found no improvements in attentional functions. A relationship was shown, however, between the number of mistakes and the severity of dysfunctional attentional processing.

Indirect Interventions

Indirect approaches in the treatment of cognitive dysfunctions in schizophrenia focus primarily on improving poor social skills and behavioral control. However, cognitive dysfunctions are taken into consideration as well. Cognitive and behavior-related dysfunctions are remediated by making circumscribed changes in behavior planning (the behavior modification approach; see Green, 1993). One of the first indirect methods used to normalize attentional/perceptual and conceptual processes in schizophrenic patients was devised by Meichenbaum & Cameron (1973). They trained patients in the techniques of self-instructions to improve attentional focusing and maintenance during concentration exercises. These procedures also involved techniques of self-encouraging in the case of failure. Later, Diaz & Colon (1985) trained schizophrenic patients in Kanfer's (1977) method of self-monitoring, a procedure of self-instructions in which the present situation is compared with the desirable one. Self-instructions are here a means of focusing attentional skills in specific social situations.

New developments in cognitive-behavioral modification pay attention to empirical data which show that, in schizophrenia, cognitive dysfunctions also play a central role in the acquisition of social skills (Teuber & Liberman, in preparation). Liberman (1988) developed training modules which provide patients with the social and the problem-solving skills needed to lead an independent and satisfying life in the community. Modules include areas like symptom self-management or recreation for leisure. Based on the training concept of Wallace (1982), all modules are highly structured and include the three principles of problem solving (problem definition, goal definition and generating a solution). Bellack et al. (1990) elaborated similar procedures for social skills training with schizophrenic patients. His training includes not only a cognitive preparation of the subsequently played situation but also interventions for improving para-, non-verbal and motor skills, as well as procedures for correcting social cognition and perception (Bellack, 1986, 1989, 1996; Bellack & Morrison, 1982). Current training procedures additionally focus on cognitive dysfunctions by using the principle of overlearning as in step-repetition in which videotapes and other media are applied. Concerning the effects of such social skills training methods, gains in skill attainment and skill utilization were found at a 1- and even at a 2-year follow-up (Eckman et al., 1992; Vaccaro et al., 1992; Wallace et al., 1992). Other training concepts address deficits in perceiving and interpreting affective stimuli (Bellack, 1996). In particular, skills are trained which are needed to discriminate one level of an emotion from another, such as benevolent from negative criticism. However, no stepwise procedures have been devised that incorporate these concepts, neither have any relevant evaluative studies been carried out to date (Bellack, 1996).

Combined Interventions

Combined procedures to treat cognitive deficits in schizophrenia can be characterized as a combination of the stimulation, the behavior modification and the substitution–transfer approaches. The latter means that specific training tasks generate compensatory processes on the treated level which are transferable on other levels of functioning (see Green, 1993).

Adams et al. (1981) were one of the first research groups to present results of combined interventions. They offered a patient with severe delusional beliefs training in both attentional tasks devised by Wagner (1968) and in self-instruction in order to focus attention on reality. Additionally, they taught him to understand beliefs in a situation-related manner. The training was effective not only in reducing psychopathological symptoms but also in improving global cognitive functioning and overt behavior. Recent single-case studies have demonstrated that social skills training procedures are more effective if they are preceded by attentional training (Massel et al., 1991; Wong & Woolsey, 1989).

The Integrated Psychological Treatment (IPT) for schizophrenic patients may also be regarded as a combined approach (Brenner et al., 1987, 1990, 1994; Roder et al., 1988, 1992, 1995). It is based on a model of two vicious circles interacting between cognitive and behavioral dysfunctions. A vicious circle is a positive feedback loop in which elements in the loop exacerbate one another so that deficits worsen continually. A first vicious circle describes how deficits in elementary and more complex cognitive processes mutually debase each other. The second vicious circle shows how cognitive deficits prevent sufficient acquisition of interpersonal coping skills. Postulations of this model are: first, that elementary impairments of cognitive functions have a pervasive effect on more complex levels of cognitive functioning; second, it claims that impaired elementary and complex functions have a negative influence on the acquisition and utilization of social skills (Brenner et al., 1992). IPT translates the inverse corollary of this model into treatment interventions: it addresses not only cognitive deficits, but also their impact on social competence, and provides step-by-step skills training for groups of five to seven patients along five subprograms. Training always proceeds from cognitive to more complex social skills demands. Even though the content of this therapy program focuses on a combination of cognitive and behavioral deficits, the emotional aspects involved are given secondary attention as well. For instance, emotionally-loaded concepts, such as aggravation and sadness, are analyzed, visual aids depicting emotionally-loaded social situations are interpreted, and social skills and problem-solving skills are rehearsed to teach patients to cope with emotionally-loaded social interactions in an well-adjusted manner. The results of various studies have shown that IPT does have a positive impact on cognitive and social functioning and reduces psychopathological symptoms in schizophrenia (for overviews, see Brenner, Hodel & Merlo, 1991; Roder et al., 1992; Blumenthal et al., 1993). All the same, these evaluative studies have also revealed that emotional distress can reduce gains in cognitive skills and social behavior and can hinder further progress (Brenner, 1989; Hodel, Brenner & Merlo, 1990).

This short review of empirical studies on cognitive training procedures shows that, especially in the current procedures, a wide range of cognitive skills can be learned and maintained in schizophrenia. Such results reflect a more differentiated understanding of the role of basic cognitive dysfunctions in schizophrenia. However, in these empirical studies the correlations between cognitive disorders and symptomatology are seldom discussed. This is astonishing, since Brenner et al. (1990), Nuechterlein et al. (1992) and Liberman et al. (1993) presented a considerable body of empirical and clinical evidence which suggests that emotional distress can lead to an increase in cognitive and behavioral dysfunctions as well as in psychopathology.

Interventions for Improving Emotional Information Processing

In schizophrenia, cognitive dysfunctions lead to a failure in producing and controlling behavioral sequences. As a consequence, distress may arise. This, in turn, can negatively influence emotional information processing. The exact nature of disorders in the area of emotional information processing is even harder to establish than that of cognitive dysfunctions. First attempts were made by Gjerde (1983). He showed that emotional distress can aggravate the information-processing deficits typical of schizophrenic patients. Braff (1991) found that under emotional strain a schizophrenic person reacts with worsened attentional functioning. Gaebel & Woelwer (1992), Hellewell, Connell & Deakin (1994) and Bellack (1996) believe that—independent of situational distress—a deficient emotional perception is based on attentional dysfunctions. Nuechterlein et al. (1992) reviewed a considerable body of the literature and concluded that intensive or long-lasting emotional stress can completely overwhelm the patients' limited capacity to process information, and thus trigger ensuing psychotic episodes.

There are only a few empirically tested approaches to modifying emotional distress in schizophrenia. One of the first approaches for treating deficient emotional processing, i.e. deficient attentional processing under emotional stress, included self-instructions. Meichenbaum & Cameron (1973) taught patients in self-instructing to cope with anxiety-ridden situations in an effective manner. Over a decade later, Falloon (1987) trained a patient to reduce his states of arousal by the use of the thought-stopping technique. Kraemer, Dinkhoff-Awiszus & Möller (1988) and Kraemer, Zinner & Möller (1991) also developed a stepwise method for improving problem-solving behavior in stressful situations. We recently developed Emotional Management Training (EMT) for schizophrenic patients. In this training patients learn to cope with emotions in a well-adjusted way and, concomitantly, in their very own individual manner (Hodel & Brenner, 1996a, 1996b). The EMT consists of two subprograms that are divided into several steps. It has undergone evaluation in a multicenter study with 67 chronic schizophrenic patients (Hodel et al., 1997). Its treatment effects were compared with an anti-stress training (Andres, Brenner & Bellwald, 1992) and with a tutoring program to improve basic information processes (Roder et al., 1995). EMT was found to have a significantly more substantial impact on cognitive functioning, e.g. short-term memory, and on psychopathology (Hodel et al., 1997).

DISCUSSION

Therapeutic interventions for reducing information processing disorders are one of the main topics of present rehabilitation procedures in schizophrenia. Current contributions to the discussion can be summarized as follows:

1. Positive training results are seldom generalized to higher or more complex processes such as the overall level of cognitive functioning, or to social competence or independent living skills (Mussgay, Olbrich & Ihle, 1990; Hellman et al., 1992; Bellack, 1992; Bellack & Mueser, 1993; Corrigan & Green, 1993; Green, 1993). The following findings, however, could broaden the view of a poor generalizability: Spaulding (1992) postulated that isolated or time-limited gains in cognitive mastery are comparable in relevance to cognitive improvements that are durable and have been acquired directly. This is due to the fact that time-limited gains help to stabilize the effects of subsequent psychosocial interventions. According to Kern, Green & Satz (1992), Corrigan, Wallace & Green, (1992) and Corrigan et al. (1994), verbal memory is related to improvements in social skills. Hypothetically, such an interrelationship should include the pervasive effects of mutual improvements. For example, Eckman et al. (1992) and Wallace et al. (1992) showed that the effects of social skills training were generalizable to various cognitive functions.

2. Interventions for reducing cognitive dysfunctions are used in a relatively undifferentiated manner, even though there is compelling evidence that cognitive dysfunctions differ inter-individually, both in qualitative and in quantitative terms (Green, 1993; Spaulding et al., 1994). Therapeutic corollaries of the following findings could be used to improve the differentiation of interventions. As mentioned at the beginning of this paper Spaulding et al. (1997) differentiated cognitive dysfunctions into three factors. Factor 1 is caused by neuropsychological abnormalities and is vulnerability-linked. It is even detectable in first-degree relatives and in "high-risk" children (see Green, 1993). In contrast, Factors 2 and 3 are symptom-related and can be characterized as episode-linked or residual. Differentiations such as these can help a lot to tailor and clearly operationalize cognitive interventions in schizophrenia.

3. The effectiveness of interventions for reducing cognitive deficits is dependent on motivational factors. Several studies have revealed that the severity of deficits in reaction time or in recall can be influenced by motivation (Koh et al., 1981; Summerfelt et al., 1991; Hodel, 1993). The procedure of the dynamic assessment, however, has opened new vistas in differentiating such moderating factors as the patients' motivation from their learning capacity, or from improvements in functioning (Guthke & Wiedl, 1996). This assessment includes three steps. In a first step, tests are administered without any help. In the subsequent step, the same tests are presented together with task-relevant instructions. In a final step, test repetitions show learning effects. Variations in performance during subsequent testing procedures represent the range of variance caused by motivational factors.

The evaluation of cognitive treatment interventions and efforts to improve their effectiveness should also take into account non-cognitive aspects of the illness and environmental factors. Examples of factors having an important impact on the course of illness are the quantity and quality of the re-emergence of symptoms, patient compliance, and the way in which patients and their relatives cope with the illness (Gjerris & Kissling, 1994). Their possibilities of coming to terms emotionally with the illness seem to play an important role in outcome (Hogarty et al., 1995; Wiedl, 1997). Taking into account such factors may enhance future developments in the cognitive rehabilitation of schizophrenic patients. Based on the discussion presented above, the following hypothetical propositions can be formulated (see also Hodel & Brenner, 1994):

1. Interventions for reducing cognitive disorders might be improved by paying greater attention to emotional processing.
2. Improvements might be made by determining the indication for the use of group therapy or individual therapy in cognitive remediation: therapeutic interventions in group settings seem more suitable for treating vulnerability-linked cognitive disorders which are found inter-individually. Individual therapy, however, should preferably be applied in cases of symptom-related, episode-linked or residual cognitive disorders (Spaulding et al., 1997).
3. Approaches that provide a combination of direct and/or indirect treatment for information-processing disorders should receive greater attention, since combined interventions have been proved to be more effective (Brenner, Hodel & Giebeler, 1995).
4. More attention should be paid to aspects other than cognitive ones, such as re-emergence of symptoms, compliance to therapy, etc. These not only contribute to the effectiveness of a specific treatment but also to the course of illness in general.
5. Results of psychobiological research, especially those pertaining to the field of brain research, which have broadened our understanding of the relationships between structural or functional abnormalities and cognitive disorders, might enhance the specificity and effectiveness of future training procedures.

Considerably more ideas than those mentioned above could be elaborated on future developments of cognitive treatment for schizophrenic patients. Even so, on the basis of the directions outlined above, multimodal approaches that provide psychiatric rehabilitation for different areas of dysfunctioning, and which also include non-cognitive aspects of the illness as well as environmental factors, seem to be most promising.

REFERENCES

Adams, H.E., Brantley, P.J., Malatesta, V. et al. (1981). Modifications of cognitive processes: a case study of schizophrenia, *Journal of Consulting and Clinical Psychology*, **49**, 460–464.
Andres, K., Brenner, H.D. & Bellwald, L. (1992). Körperzentrierte Arbeit mit schizophrenen Patienten, *Swiss Med*, **1–2**(92), 40–42.
Bellack, A.S. (1986). Das Training sozialer Fertigkeiten zur Behandlung chronisch Schizophrener. In W. Böker & H.D. Brenner (eds), *Bewältigung der Schizophrenie*. Bern: Huber.

Bellack, A.S. (1989). A comprehensive model for the treatment of schizophrenia. In A.S. Bellack (ed.) *A Clinical Guide for the Treatment of Schizophrenia*. New York: Plenum, pp. 1–21.

Bellack, A.S. (1992). Cognitive rehabilitation for schizophrenia: is it possible? *Schizophrenia Bulletin*, **18**, 43–50.

Bellack, A.S. (1996). Defizitäres Sozialverhalten und Training sozialer Fertigkeiten: Neue Entwicklungen und Trends. In W. Böker & H.D. Brenner (eds), *Integrative Therapie der Schizophrenie*. Bern: Huber, pp. 191–202.

Bellack, A.S. & Morrison, R.L. (1982). Interpersonal dysfunction. In A.S. Bellack, M. Hersen & A.E. Kazin (eds), *International Handbook of Behavior Modification and Therapy*. New York: Plenum, pp. 717–747.

Bellack, A.S. & Mueser, K.T. (1993). Psychosocial treatment for schizophrenia. *Schizophrenia Bulletin*, **19**, 317–336.

Bellack, A.S., Morrison, R.L., Wixted, J.T. et al. (1990). An analysis of social competence in schizophrenia. *British Journal of Psychiatry*, **156**, 809–818.

Benedict, R.H. & Harris, A. (1989). Remediation of attention deficits in chronic schizophrenic patients: a preliminary study. *British Journal of Clinical Psychology*, **28**, 187–188.

Blumenthal, S., Bell, V., Schöttler, R. et al. (1993). Ausprägung und Entwicklung von Basissymptomen bei schizophrenen Patienten nach einem kognitiven Therapieprogramm. *Schizophrenie*, **8**(1), 20–28.

Bogarts, B. (1989). Limbic and paralimbic pathology in schizophrenia: interaction with age- and stress-related factors. In S.C. Schulz & C.A. Tamminga (eds), *Schizophrenia: Scientific Progress*. New York: Oxford University Press, pp. 216–226.

Braff, D.L. (1991). Information processing and attentional abnormalities in schizophrenic disorders. In P.A. Magaro (ed.), *Cognitive Bases of Mental Disorders*. Newbury Park, CA: Sage, pp. 262–307.

Brenner, H.D. (1989). Die Therapie basaler psychischer Dysfunktionen aus systemischer Sicht. In W. Böker & H.D. Brenner (eds), *Schizophrenie als systemische Störung*. Bern: Huber, pp. 170–188.

Brenner, H.D., Hodel, B. & Merlo, M.C.G. (1991). Non-pharmalogical treatment concepts of negative symptomatology. In A. Marneros (ed.), *Proceedings of the European–American Workshop "Negative versus Positive Schizophrenia"*. Berlin: Springer.

Brenner, H.D., Hodel, B. & Giebeler, U. (1995). Kognitive Therapien bei schizophren Erkrankten: Theoretische Grundlagen, empirische Befunde und zukünftige Entwicklungen. In W. Bender, W. Hubmann & F. Mohr (eds), *Neuere Entwicklungen in der Behandlung schizophrener Psychosen*. Munich-Haar: VTS, pp. 11–35.

Brenner, H.D., Hodel, B., Kube, G. et al. (1987). Kognitive Therapie bei Schizophrenen: Problemanalyse und empirische Ergebnisse. *Nervenarzt*, **58**, 72–83.

Brenner, H.D., Hodel, B., Roder, V. et al. (1992). Treatment of cognitive dysfunctions and behavioral deficits. *Schizophrenia Bulletin*, **18**, 21–26.

Brenner, H.D., Kraemer, S., Hermanutz, M. et al. (1990). Intervention programs: cognitive treatment in schizophrenia. In E.R. Straube & H. Hahlweg (eds), *Schizophrenia: Concepts, Vulnerability and Intervention*. New York: Springer, pp. 161–191.

Brenner, H.D., Roder, V., Hodel, B. et al. (1994). *Integrated Psychological Therapy for Schizophrenic Patients (IPT)*. Seattle: Hofgrefe & Huber.

Carpenter, W.T. & Schooler, N.R. (1988). Treatment, services, and environmental factors. *Schizophrenia Bulletin*, **14**(3), 427–437.

Classen, W. & Laux, C. (1989). Comparison of sensimotor and cognitive performance of acute schizophrenic impatients treated with remoxipride or haloperidol. *Neuropsychobiology*, **21**(3), 131–140.

Corrigan, P.W. & Green, M.F. (1993). The situational feature recognition test: a measure of schema comprehension for schizophrenia. *International Journal of Methods in Psychiatric Research*, **3**, 29–35.

Corrigan, P.W., Wallace, C.J. & Green, M.F. (1992). Deficits in social schemata in schizophrenia. *Schizophrenia Research*, **8**, 129–135.

Corrigan, P.W., Wallace, C.J., Schade, M.L. et al. (1994). Learning medication self-management skills in schizophrenia: relationships with cognitive deficits and psychiatric symptoms. *Behavior Therapy*, **25**(1), 5–15.

Delahunty, A., Morice, R. & Frost, B. (1993). Specific cognitive flexibility rehabilitation in schizophrenia. *Psychological Medicine*, **23**, 221–227.

Diaz, A. & Colon, F. (1985). Autocontrol: una revision bibliografica [Self-control: a bibligraphic review]. *Annual Modification Conducta*, **11**, 441–458.

Eckman, T.A., Wirshing, W.C., Marder, S.R. et al. (1992). Technology for training schizophrenics in illness self-management: a controlled trial. *American Journal of Psychiatry*, **149**, 1549–1555.

Falloon, I.R.H. (1987). Cognitive and behavioral interventions in the self control of schizophrenia. In J.S. Strauss, W. Böker & H.D. Brenner (eds), *Psychosocial Treatment of Schizophrenia*. Toronto: Huber, pp. 180–190.

Freedman, B. & Chapman, L.J. (1973). Early subjective experience in schizophrenic episodes. *Journal of Abnormal Psychology*, **82**, 46–54.

Gaebel, W. & Woelwer, W. (1992). Facial expression and emotional face recognition in schizophrenia and depression. *European Archives of Psychiatry and Clinical Neuroscience*, **242**, 46–52.

Gansert, U. & Olbrich, R. (1992). Die Einführung eines computergestützten kognitiven Trainings für schizophrene Kranke in Gruppenform: ein Erfahrungsbericht. *Schizophrenie*, **7**, 26–31.

Gestrich, J. & Hermanutz, M. (1991). Computer-gestütztes Aufmerksamkeitstraining mit Schizophrenen. In R. Schüttler (ed.), *Theorie und Praxis kognitiver Therapieverfahren bei schizophrenen Patienten*, Munich: Zuckerwerdt, pp. 95–101.

Gjerde, P.F. (1983). Attention capacity dysfunction and arousal in schizophrenia. *Psychological Bulletin*, **93**, 57–72.

Gjerris, A. & Kissling, W. (eds) (1994). The role of compliance in the treatment of schizophrenia. *Acta Psychiatrica Scandinavica*, **89**(suppl 382).

Goldberg, T.E., Weinberger, D.R., Berman, K.F. et al. (1987). Further evidence for dementia of the profrontal type in schizophrenia? A controlled study of teaching the Wisconsin Card Sorting Test. *Archives of General Psychiatry*, **44**, 1008–1014.

Green, M.F. (1993). Cognitive remediation in schizophrenia: is it time yet? *American Journal of Psychiatry*, **150**, 178–187.

Green, M.F., Satz, P., Ganzell, S. et al. (1992). Wisconsin Card Sorting Test performance in schizophrenia remediation of a stubborn deficit. *American Journal of Psychiatry*, **149**, 62–67.

Guthke, J. & Wiedl, K.H. (1996). *Dynamisches Testen*. Göttingen: Hofgrefe.

Häfner, H. (1988). Rehabilitation Schizophrener. *Zeitschrift für Klinische Psychologie*, **17**(3), 187–209.

Hammond, K.R. & Summer, D.A. (1972). Cognitive control. *Psychological Revue*, **79**, 58–67.

Heaton, R.K. & Pendleton, M.G. (1981). Use of neuropsychological test to predict adult patients' everyday functioning. *Journal of Consulting and Clinical Psychology*, **49**, 807–821.

Hellman, S., Green, M.F., Kern, R.S. et al. (1992). The effects of instruction versus reinforcement on the Wisconsin Card Sorting Test. *Journal of Clinical and Experimental Neuropsychology*, **14**, 63.

Hellewell, J.S.E., Connell, J. & Deakin, J.F.W. (1994). Affect judgement and facial recognition memory in schizophrenia. *Psychopathology*, **27**, 255–261.

Hemsley, D.R. (1987). Psychological models of schizophrenia. In E. Miller & P. Cooper (eds), *Textbook of Abnormal Psychology*. London: Churchill Livingstone.

Hemsley, D.R. (1993).   A simple (or simplistic?) cognitive model for schizophrenia. *Behaviour Research Therapy*, **7**(31), 633–645.

Hemsley, D.R. (1994).   A cognitive model for schizophrenia and its possible neural basis. *Acta Psychiatrica Scandinavica*, **90**(suppl 384), 80–86.

Hodel, B. (1993).   Weiterentwicklung des IPT: Das Training "Umgang mit Emotionen" im Vergleich mit dem Training "Kognitive Differenzierung" (abstr). *Schizophrenie Sonderheft*, **1**, 18.

Hodel, B. & Brenner, H.D. (1994).   Cognitive therapy with schizophrenic patients: conceptual basis, present state, future directions, *Acta Psychiatrica Scandinavica*, **90**(suppl 384), 108–115.

Hodel, B. & Brenner, H.D. (1996a).   Ein Trainingsprogramm zur Bewältigung von maladaptiven Emotionen bei schizophren Erkrankten: Erste Ergebnisse und Erfahrungen. *Nervenarzt*, **67**, 564–571.

Hodel, B. & Brenner, H.D. (1996b).   Weiterentwicklung des "Integrierten Psychologischen Therapieprogramms für schizophrene Patienten" IPT: Erste Ergebnisse zum Training "Bewältigung von maladaptiven Emotionen". In W. Böker & H.D. Brenner (eds), *Integrative Therapie der Schizophrenie*, Bern: Huber, pp. 170–188.

Hodel, B. & Brenner, H.D. (1997).   Kognitive Therapieverfahren bei schizophren Erkrankten. In W. Böker & H.D. Brenner (eds), *Behandlung schizophrener Psychosen*. Stuttgart: Enke.

Hodel, B., Brenner, H.D. & Merlo, M.C.G. (1990).   Cognitive and social training for chronic schizophrenic patients: a comparison between two types of therapeutic interventions. In C.N. Stefanis (ed.), *Psychiatry, a World Perspective*, Vol. 3. Amsterdam: Elsevier, pp. 768–773.

Hodel, B., Sandner, M. & Brenner, H.D. (1997a).   Ein Training zur Bewältigung maladaptiver Emotionen bei schizophren Erkrankten. In P. Hofmann, M. Laux, C. Probst et al. (eds), *Klinische Psychotherapie*. Vienna: Springer, pp. 261–269.

Hodel, B., Zanello, A., Welling, A. et al. (1997b).   Ein Therapieprogramm zur Bewältigung von maladaptiven Emotionen bei schizophren Erkrankten: Ergebnisse einer Multicenter-Studie. In C. Mundt, M. Linden & W. Barnett (eds), *Psychotherapie in der Psychiatrie*. Vienna: Springer.

Hogarty, G.E., Kornblith, S.J., Greenwald, D. et al. (1995).   Personal therapy: a disorder-relevant psychotherapy for schizophrenia: description and preliminary findings. *Schizophrenia Bulletin*, **21**(3), 379–393.

Jaeger, J. & Douglas, E. (1992).   Neuropsychiatric rehabilitation for persistent mental illness. *Psychiatric Quarterly*, **63**(1), 71–94.

Kanfer, F.H. (1977).   Selbstmanagement-Methoden. In F.H. Kanfer & A.P. Goldstein (eds), *Möglichkeiten der Verhaltensänderung*. Munich: Urban & Schwarzenberg.

Kern, R.S., Green, M.F. & Satz, P. (1992).   Neurophysiological predictors of skills training for chronic schizophrenic patients. *Journal of Psychiatric Research*, **4**, 223–230.

Kingdon, D.G. & Turkington, D. (1994).   *Cognitive-behavioral Therapy of Schizophrenia*. New York: Guilford.

Koh, S.D., Grinker, R.R., Marusarz, T.W. et al. (1981).   Affective memory and schizophrenic anhedonia. *Schizophrenia Bulletin*, **7**, 292–303.

Kraemer, S., Dinkhoff-Awiszus, G. & Möller, H.J. (1988).   Modifikationen des Integrierten Psychologischen Therapieprogramms (IPT). In V. Roder, H.D. Brenner, N. Kienzle et al. (eds), *Integriertes Psychologisches Therapieprogramm für schizophrene Patienten (IPT)*, Munich: Psychologie Verlags Union, pp. 141–146.

Kraemer, S., Zinner, H.T. & Möller, H.J. (1991).   Kognitive Therapie und Sozialtraining: Vergleich zweier verhaltenstherapeutischer Behandlungskonzepte für chronisch schizophrene Patienten. In R. Schüttler (ed.), *Theorie und Praxis kognitiver Therapieverfahren bei schizophrenen Patienten*. Munich: Zuckerwerdt, pp. 102–117.

Lamberti, G., Wieneke, K.H. & Brauke, N. (1988). Der Computer als Hilfe beim Aufmerksamkeitstraining—eine klinisch-experimentelle Studie. *Rehabilitation*, **27**, 190–198.

Larsen, S.F. & Fromholt, P. (1976). Mnemonic organisation and free recall in schizophrenia, *Journal of Abnormal Psychology*, **85**, 61–65.

Liberman, R.P. (1988). *Psychiatric Rehabilitation of Chronic Mental Patients*. Washington DC: American Psychiatric Press.

Liberman, R.P., Jacobs, H., Boone, S.E. et al. (1997). Skills training for the community adaption of schizophrenia. In J.S. Strauss, W. Böker & H.D. Brenner (eds), *Psychosocial Treatment of Schizophrenia*. Toronto: Huber, 94–109.

Liberman, R.P., Lillie, F., Falloon, I.R.H. et al. (1984). Social skills training for relapsing schizophrenics: an experimental analysis. *Behavior Modification*, **8**, 155–179.

Liberman, R.P., Massel, H.K., Mosk, M.D. et al. (1985). Social skills training for chronic mental patients. *Hospital and Community Psychiatry*, **36**, 396–403.

Liberman, R.P., Wallace, C., Blackwell, G. et al. (1993). Innovations in skills training for the seriously mentally ill: the UCLA social and independent living skills modules. *Innovations & Research*, **2**, 43–60.

Magaro, P.A. (1980). *Cognition in Schizophrenia and Paranoia: the Integration of Cognitive Processes*. Hillsdale, NJ: Erlbaum.

Massel, H.K., Corrigan, P.W., Liberman, R.P. et al. (1991). Conversational skills training in thought-disordered schizophrenics through attention focusing. *Psychiatry Research*, **38**, 51–61.

Mednick, S. (1996). The implication of high risk studies for early intervention in schizophrenia. *Verging on Reality, the First International Conference on Strategies for Prevention in Early Psychosis, 28–29 June*, Melbourne: Abstracts Book, p. 12.

Meichenbaum, D. & Cameron, R.C. (1973). Training schizophrenics to talk to themselves: a means of developing attentional controls. *Behavior Therapy*, **4**, 515–534.

Meiselman, K. (1973). Broadening dual modality cue utilization in chronic non-paranoid schizophrenics. *Journal of Consulting and Clinical Psychology*, **41**, 447–453.

Möller, H.J. (1988). Neuere Ergebnisse zur Prognostik und neuroleptischen Behandlung schizophrener Psychosen. In S. Haas & B. Ende-Scharf (eds), 3rd Psychiatrie-Symposium des Psychiatrischen Krankenhauses Eichberg, Germany.

Mussgay, L., Olbrich, R., Ihle, W. et al. (1991). Das Training kognitiver Fertigkeiten bei schizophrenen Patienten und seine Effekte auf elementare Informationsverarbeitungsmasse. *Zeitschrift für Klinische Psychologie*, **20**, 103–114.

Nuechterlein, K.H., Snyder, K.S. & Mintz, J. (1992). Paths to relapse: possible transactional processes connecting patient illness onset, expressed emotion, and psychotic relapse. *British Journal of Psychiatry*, **161**(suppl 18), 88–96.

Olbrich, R. (1996). Psychophysiologische Vulnerabilitätsmechanismen bei schizophrenen Psychosen: Stand der Forschung und eigene Untersuchungen. In H.J. Möller & A. Deister (eds), *Vulnerabilität für affektive und schizophrene Erkrankungen*. Vienna: Springer, pp. 103–112.

Olbrich, R. & Mussgay, L. (1990). Reduction of schizophrenic deficits by cognitive training: an evaluative study. *European Archives of Psychiatry and Neurological Sciences*, **239**, 366–369.

Pribram, K.H. & McGuinness, D. (1975). Arousal, activation, and effort in the control of attention. *Psychological Review*, **82**, 116–149.

Roder, V., Brenner, H.D., Kienzle, N. et al. (1988). *Integriertes Psychologisches Therapieprogramm für schizophrene Patienten (IPT)*. Munich: Psychologie Verlags Union.

Roder, V., Brenner, H.D., Kienzle, N. et al. (1992). *Integriertes Psychologisches Therapieprogramm für schizophrene Patienten (IPT); 2. überarbeitete und ergänzte Auflage*. Munich: Psychologie Verlags Union.

Roder,V., Brenner, H.D., Kienzle, N. et al. (1995). *IPT Integriertes psychologisches Therapieprogramm für schizophrene Patienten*. Weinheim: Beltz, Psychologie Verlags Union.

Rosenbaum, G., MacKavey, W.R. & Grisell J.L. (1957). Effects of biological and social motivation on schizophrenic reaction time. *Journal of Abnormal and Social Psychology*, **54**, 364–368.

Schöttke, H. (1993). Schizophrene Patienten lernen elektronische Textverarbeitung: Bedeutung von Informationsverarbeitung. Symptomatik und Zustandsangst. *Verhaltenstherapie*, **3**, 35–43.

Schreiber, H., Stolz-Born, G., Heinrich, H. et al. (1992). Attention, cognition, and motor perseveration in adolescents at genetic risk for schizophrenia and control subjects. *Psychiatry Research*, **44**, 125–140.

Spaulding, W.D. (1992). Design prerequisites for research on cognitive therapy for schizophrenia. *Schizophrenia Bulletin*, **18**(1), 39–42.

Spaulding W.D., Sullivan, M., Weiler, M. et al. (1994). Changing cognitive functioning in rehabilitation of schizophrenia. *Acta Psychiatrica Scandinavica*, **90**(suppl 384), 116–124.

Spaulding, W.D., Reed, D., Elting, D. et al. (1997). Cognitive changes in the course of rehabilitation. In H.D. Brenner, W. Böker & R. Genner (eds), *Towards a Comprehensive Therapy for Schizophrenia*. Seattle: Hofgrefe and Huber, pp. 106–117.

Spaulding, W.D., Storms, L., Goodrich, V. et al. (1986). Application of experimental psychopathology in psychiatric rehabilitation. *Schizophrenia Bulletin*, **12**, 560–577.

Spring, B.J., Leman, M. & Fergeson, P. (1990). Vulnerabilities to schizophrenia: informations-processing markers. In E.R. Straube & K. Hahlweg (eds), *Schizophrenia. Concepts, Vulnerability, and Intervention*. Berlin: Springer, pp. 97–114.

Summerfelt, A.T., Alphs, L.D., Funderburk, F.R. et al. (1991). Impaired Wisconsin Card Sort performance in schizophrenia may reflect motivational deficits. *Archives of General Psychiatry*, **48**, 282–283.

Teuber, J. & Liberman, R.P. (in preparation). Community skills in schizophrenia. *Rehab Rounds*.

Vaccaro, J.V., Liberman, R.P., Blackwell, G. et al. (1992). Combining social skills training and assertive case management. In R.P. Liberman (ed.), *New Directions for Mental Health Services: Effective Psychiatric Rehabilitation*. San Fransisco: Jossey-Bass.

van den Bosch, R.J., Rombouts, R.P. & van Asma, J.O. (1993). Subjective cognitive dysfunction in schizophrenic and depressed patients. *Comprehensive Psychiatry*, **34**(2), 130–136.

Wagner, B.R. (1968). *Lehrbuch der psychosomatischen Medizin*. Munich: Urban und Schwarzenberg.

Wallace, C.J. (1982). The social skills training project of the mental health clinical research center for the study of schizophrenia. In J.P. Curran & P.M. Monti (eds), *Social Skills Training: a Practical Handbook for Assessment and Treatment*. New York: Guilford, pp. 57–89.

Wallace, C.J., Liberman, R.P., MacKain, S.J. et al. (1992). Effectiveness and replicability of modules for teaching social and instrumental skills to the severely mentally ill. *American Journal of Psychiatry*, **149**, 654–658.

Wiedl, K.H. (1997). Coping-orientated therapy with schizophrenic patients: general guidelines, starting points and issues of evaluation. In H.D. Brenner, W. Böker & R. Genner (eds), *Towards a Comprehensive Therapy for Schizophrenia*. Seattle: Hofgrefe & Huber, pp. 209–227.

Wishner, L. & Wahl, O. (1974). Dichotic listening in schizophrenia. *Journal of Consulting and Clinical Psychology*, **42**, 538–546.

Wong, S.E. & Woolsey, J.E. (1989). Re-establishing conversational skills in overtly psychotic, chronic schizophrenic patients: discrete trials training on the psychiatric ward. *Behavior Modification*, **13**, 415–430.

Chapter 6

Cognitive-behavioural Coping-orientated Therapy for Schizophrenia: a New Treatment Model for Clinical Service and Research

Annette Schaub
Department of Psychiatry, University of Munich, Germany

Cognitive therapy has recently gained prominence in the treatment of schizophrenia with process and content interventions being two general approaches to address cognitive dysfunctions (Spaulding et al., 1986). Whereas process interventions aim at remediating basic information-processing skills that serve as vulnerability markers for further episodes, content approaches focus on changing the nature of, or one's response to, dysfunctional thoughts and, unlike the latter, put more emphasis on stress management. Coping-orientated cognitive therapy aims at modifying dysfunctional beliefs about the illness, self and environment (e.g. Perris and Skagerlind, this volume), beliefs held about symptoms (e.g. Fowler, Garety & Kuipers, this volume) as well as teaching more adaptive coping strategies (for an overview, see Schaub & Böker, 1997).

RESEARCH ON COPING IN SCHIZOPHRENIA

Recent research on coping with schizophrenia indicates that patients employ a wide range of active problem-orientated coping strategies at different stages of the illness (for an overview, see Böker & Schaub, 1997). Studies show that a high

Cognitive Psychotherapy of Psychotic and Personality Disorders: Handbook of Theory and Practice.
Edited by C. Perris and P.D. McGorry.

proportion of schizophrenic patients are aware of early warning signs of relapse as well as situations that provoke relapse (Herz & Melville, 1980). Some specific ways of managing the illness appear to be more beneficial than others in improving outcome, including: (a) awareness of early warning signs combined with cooperation with mental health professionals (Heinrichs, Cohen & Carpenter, 1985); (b) specific coping strategies, e.g. changing one's expectancies with respect to goals of life, maintaining a positive morale, compliance with treatment (Schaub, 1994); (c) a broad repertoire of coping strategies (Thurm & Häfner, 1987; Schaub, 1994; Mueser, Valentiner & Agresta, 1997). Significant correlations have been found between basic symptoms (i.e. discrete self-perceived phenomena) and problem-orientated coping reactions (Süllwold, 1977; Böker et al., 1984; Brenner et al., 1987). Only Wiedl (1992) found a relationship between high levels of negative symptoms and emotion-orientated, less cognitive ways of coping (Wiedl, 1992). Relatives's coping may play an important role too, as relatives with more knowledge about schizophrenia use more coping strategies and report higher levels of coping efficacy (Mueser, Valentiner & Agresta, 1997). The effectiveness of coping strategies is usually evaluated in terms of the course of the illness, subjective distress and coping efficacy, although aspects of social integration and quality of life should be considered too.

ILLNESS MANAGEMENT PROGRAMMES IN SCHIZOPHRENIA

During the last 15 years, group format psychoeducational and coping-orientated treatment programmes combined with pharmacotherapy have gained prominence in the treatment of schizophrenia (Wienberg, 1995; Schaub & Böker, 1997). The limited effect of neuroleptics on negative symptoms and psychosocial functioning, problems related to medication compliance, and the reduction of length of inpatient stay have intensified the search for more effective psychosocial treatment programmes. Current concepts of schizophrenia, such as the vulnerability–stress–coping model (Zubin & Spring, 1977) and its modifications (Nuechterlein & Dawson, 1984; Liberman et al., 1986) that highlight the interactions between biological vulnerability, stressors and protective factors, as well as recent research on coping, have played important roles in the development of these programmes.

The term "psychoeducational" was used by Anderson, Hogarty & Reiss (1980) to refer to education about schizophrenia in the context of family therapy. Whereas there used to be a reluctance to inform patients about their illness, education about schizophrenia is now widely accepted as a treatment standard. But in addition to family interventions (e.g. Falloon et al., 1985; Hogarty et al., 1991), information about schizophrenia is now offered to patients themselves in individual or group settings. Providing information about schizophrenia and its treatment based on the vulnerability–stress model demystifies the illness and develops a more constructive understanding of the illness. Programmes that focus on education and the enhancement of coping strategies to deal with stress and illness-related impairments are called "coping-orientated" programmes. Although the influence of life events, stressors (e.g. family communication styles), and coping on the course of schizophrenia has been repeatedly documented (Bebbington et al., 1993; Norman & Malla, 1993; Schaub, 1994), only a few psychosocial interventions have emphasized specifically improving the patient's competence to cope with these stressors.

Table 6.1 shows some current mainly group format illness management programmes for which guidelines are available (Schaub, Andres & Schindler, 1996). Individual programmes focusing on coping with persistent positive symptoms (e.g. Tarrier et al., 1993) were excluded. In spite of differences concerning the groups of reference (i.e. whether they address patients, families or both), treatment goals, setting (single vs. group setting), time-frame, and structure (highly structured vs. flexible), these programmes are all based on the vulnerability–stress model and employ behavioural learning principles. They all include psychoeducational elements and the patient is seen as an active partner in the treatment process. Manuals for family interventions include those by Anderson, Reiss & Hogarty (1986), Falloon, Boyd & McGill (1984), Mueser & Glynn (1995) and Hahlweg, Dürr & Müller (1995).

The Medication Management Module (Liberman, 1986) and the Symptom Management Module (Liberman, 1988) had a strong impact on the development of German treatment programmes (e.g. Kieserg & Hornung, 1996; Wienberg, Schünemann-Wurmthaler & Sibum 1995; Bäuml, Pitschel-Walz & Kissling, 1996). The majority of the programmes help patients identify and manage warning signs of relapse, develop an emergency plan and manage medication issues. The Symptom Management Module (Liberman, 1988) is the only group format to focus on chronic symptoms (see chapter by Fowler, Garety and Kuipers, this volume). All German programmes focus on developing a constructive concept of the illness (Süllwold & Herrlich, 1992) by providing information about the vulnerability–stress–coping model and its treatment. The personal therapy of Hogarty et al. (1995) attempts to provide a growing awareness of personal vulnerability, including the "internal cues" of affect dysregulation, by means of teaching graduated, internal coping strategies. The programme by Schaub et al. (1997) also puts more emphasis on teaching coping strategies, similiar to the programmes of Süllwold & Herrlich (1992) and Wiedl (1994).

In contrast to psychoeducational family interventions that have been found to be effective in several studies (Penn & Mueser, 1996), there are only a few controlled studies of illness management programmes provided for the patients alone or in combination with their families (see Table 6.2). The Medication and Management Modules showed that specific illness-related skills can be learned and internal locus of control increased (Eckman et al., 1992; Schaub et al., 1998a). The first results of the Hogarty et al. (1995) study have been encouraging with a finding that relapses were decreased and there was an increase in personal and social adjustment over the 3 years of treatment. In Germany, two centres in

Table 6.1 Summary of illness management programmes in schizophrenia

Focus	Liberman (1986)[a]	Liberman (1988)[b]	Hogarty et al. (1995)[c]	Kieserg & Hornung (1996)[d]	Wienberg et al. (1995)[e]	Bäuml et al. (1996)[f]	Schaub et al. (1997); Schaub (1997)[g]
	Patients	Patients	Patients and relatives	Patients and relatives	Patients	Patients and relatives	Patients and relatives
Information about the vulnerability–stress model	No	No	Yes	Yes	Yes	Yes	Yes
Early warning signs and emergency plan	No	Yes	Yes	Yes	Yes	Yes	Yes
Coping with persistent symptoms	No	Yes	(No)	No	No	(No)	(No)
Social skills training	Yes	Yes	Yes	No	No	No	Yes
Problem solving	Yes	Yes	Yes	No	No	No	Yes
Medication management	No	No	Yes	Yes	Yes	Yes	Yes
Stress management	No	No	Yes	(No)	(No)	(No)	Yes

Setting
  Inpatient (i)
  Outpatient (o)
  Day hospital (d)
	i/o/d	i/o/d	i/o	o/d	i/o	i/o	i/o

Number of sessions	20–25	20–25	94	14	15	16	24/16

[a] Medication Management Module (MMM; German version; Brenner, 1989).
[b] Symptom Management Module (SMM; German version; Brenner, 1990).
[c] Personal Therapy (PT) (individual setting).
[d] Psychoeducational training for schizophrenic patients (PTS).
[e] Psychoeducational group therapy for people suffering from schizophrenic and schizo-affective psychosis (PEGASUS).
[f] Psychoeducational groups for patients and their relatives (PIP) with eight sessions for patients and their relatives separately.
[g] Coping-orientated treatment programme for schizophrenic and schizo-affective patients including their relatives (BOT).
Parentheses refer to a less explicit use of the treatment element.

Table 6.2 Controlled studies on illness management programmes described in Table 6.1

Study	Treatment conditions	n	Frequency and duration of treatment	Results
Eckman et al. (1992)	Skills training in symptom (SMM) + medication management (MMM) Supportive group therapy (SGT)	20 21	Twice-weekly sessions for 6 months (ca. 50 sessions)	Attainment and retention in skills: post-treatment: MMM + SMM > SGT ($p < 0.0001$) 6 months: MMM + SMM > SGT ($p < 0.0001$ / $p < 0.02$) 1 year: MMM + SMM > SGT ($p < 0.0001$ / $p < 0.005$)
Buchkremer & Fiedler (1987) Lewandowski, Buchkremer & Stark (1994)	"Cognitive therapy", i.e. psychoeducation on relapse prevention (CT) Social skills training (SST) Extended standard treatment (EST) including psychoeducation and medication management All included groups for relatives	21 21 24	10 Weekly sessions	Rehospitalization: 1 year: CT (6%**) < SST (37%) < EST (42%**) (**$p = 0.009$) 2 year: CT (17%†) < SST (42%) = EST (42%†) (†$p = 0.08$) 5 year: CT (27%) < SST (61%) ($p < 0.05$) Relapse: 1 year: CT (22%*) < SST (53%) < EST (54%*) (*$p = 0.04$) 2 year: CT (33%) < SST (53%) < EST (54%) (n.s.)
Hornung et al. (1995) Buchkremer et al. (1997)	Psychoeducational medication management training (PMT) PMT + cognitive psychotherapy (CP) PMT + Key-person counselling (KC) PMT + CP + KC Leisure time group (LTG)	32 34 35 33 57	PMT: 10 sessions CP: 10 sessions KP: 10 sessions LTC: 25 sessions	Rehospitalization: 1 year: PMT + KC + CP (15%) < LTG (23%) < PMT + KC (27%) < PMT (31%) < PMT + CP (32%) (n.s.) 2 year: PMT + KC + CP (24%*) < PMT + KC (39%) < PMT + CP (44%) = PMT (44%) < LTG (50%*) (*$p < 0.05$)
Kissling et al. (1995) Bäuml et al. (1996)	Psychoeducational groups for patients and relatives (PE) Standard treatment (ST)	80 83	Eight sessions for patients and relatives covering 3 months	Rehospitalization: 1 year: PE (21%) < ST (38%) ($p = 0.03$) 2 year: PE (41%) < ST (58%) ($p = 0.03$)
Hogarty et al. (1995)	Personal therapy (PT) Standard treatment (ST)	54	Three sessions a month for 1 year Two sessions a month for 2 years	Relapse: 3 year: PT < ST Over the 3 years: gains in personal and social adjustment PT > ST

Münster (Buchkremer & Fiedler, 1987; Lewandowski, Buchkremer & Stark, 1994; Hornung et al., 1995; Buchkremer et al., 1997) and Munich (Kissling, Bäuml & Pitschel-Walz, 1995; Bäuml, 1997) evaluated their programmes, including patients and relatives. Both programmes focus on a better understanding of the illness and improving compliance by managing medication issues. In controlled studies there was a lower relapse rate at 2-year and even 5-year follow-up.

A COPING-ORIENTATED TREATMENT PROGRAMME IN SCHIZOPHRENIA

Rationale and Implementation of the Treatment Programme

In contrast to purely psychoeducational treatment, the programme decribed in Table 6.3 emphasizes stress management and developing rewarding activities (Schaub & Möller, 1990; Schaub et al., 1997; Schaub, 1997). It has been developed for stabilized patients suffering from schizophrenia and schizo-affective disorder. The programme includes psychoeducational elements (e.g. hand-outs for important topics) and cognitive-behavioural learning principles (e.g. role playing, cognitive restructuring, problem-solving). The manual was conceptualized as a guideline that encourages flexibility in having a dialogue with participants, but providing structure for conveying essential information. The therapeutic principles are explained to the patients as well as the contents and time-frame of the sessions. The long version of the programme lasts an average of 24 sessions over 2.5 months, and the short version lasts 16 sessions, with 4 sessions scheduled on an outpatient basis.

Table 6.3 Description of the coping-orientated treatment programme

1. Education about schizophrenia and treatment options based on the vulnerability–stress–coping model
   - Providing information about schizophrenia (symptoms, course of the illness)
   - Providing information about treatment options (pharmacotherapy; benefits and side-effects; psychosocial interventions, e.g. behavioural therapy)
   - Identifying, monitoring and coping with early warning signs of relapse
2. Coping with stressors
   - Identifying stressful situations related to psychopathology and psychosocial functioning
   - Recognizing signs of stress, i.e. psychophysiological, cognitive and emotional aspects
   - Stress management: relaxation techniques, problem solving, social skills training, cognitive restructuring and coping strategy enhancement
3. Improving quality of life
   - Identifying pleasant situations
   - Learning to engage in pleasant situations

Teaching a concept of the illness that enables the patient to understand the nature of his illness and how he can influence its course and severity plays an important role in this treatment programme. With regard to the vulnerability–stress–coping model, participants are taught about the interactions between vulnerability, stressors, coping, deterioration in well-being and relapse, as well as information about treatment and coping. According to the transactional concept of coping by Lazarus (1991), stress occurs when specific internal or external demands are appraised as taxing or exceeding the person's resources, and damage to self-esteem is possible. Coping refers to the person's cognitive and behavioural efforts to manage (reduce, minimize, master, tolerate) the stress. Multiple stressors may lead to a worsening in symptoms and relapses. Therefore, participants need to learn how to recognize their personal signs of stress, to identify stressful situations, to avoid very stressful situations, and to cope more effectively when they experience stress. Stress management refers to both meeting challenges and preventing overstimulation. The patients learn to become sensitive about their own individual level of stimulation and to live a life maintaining a good balance between meeting demands and times of leisure and recreation. The definition of stress includes not only overstimulation but also understimulation. This points to the importance of helping clients structure their time with meaningful but not overly demanding activities. In every session there is a focus on stressors as well as topics that promote well-being. Whereas former treatment approaches tried to avoid emotionally charged situations or illness-related or private topics in group therapy with clients suffering from schizophrenia, this programme addresses these topics in order to help clients better deal with these situations when they encounter them in their day-to-day lives.

The programme can be implemented in individual therapy, although there are several advantages of the group format, such as opportunities for observational learning from other patients and sharing their experiences with the illness. The programme should be provided in combination with comprehensive treatment that includes case management and short-term psychoeducational family therapy or groups for relatives. Families are provided with information about schizophrenia, its treatment, and guidelines for stress management. This information can help relieve negative feelings many relatives experience related to coping with an ill family member, such as anxiety, guilt and depression. Communication training can help to improve social skills for expressing positive or negative feelings. In cooperation with the patient, an emergency plan is developed in the event of a crisis. The groups for relatives should include a mimimum of eight sessions (on a bi-weekly or monthly basis), and at least four single family sessions should be conducted.

Description of the Coping-orientated Treatment Programme

The coping-orientated treatment programme consists of three subprogrammes (see Table 6.3). The *first subprogramme* focuses on *education about schizophre-*

nia and its treatment based on the vulnerability–stress–coping model. The participants share their ideas, information, and experiences with schizophrenia. The therapist informs them about the vulnerability–stress–coping model. Psychotic symptoms are explained as the result of breakdown in coping when a vulnerable person is confronted with excessive demands. The participants are taught that their vulnerability is reflected by processes such as disturbances in brain metabolism and problems in information processing. Stress can worsen this vulnerability and stabilizing factors such as personal coping competencies, self-efficacy, social networks and treatment can minimize the negative effects of stress on vulnerability. During the discussion of the model the participants are invited to provide examples from their own experience. They are asked which stressors provoked the current or previous exacerbations and what was helpful for them to cope with the crisis. With reference to their experiences, topics like diagnosis, positive and negative symptoms, the course of the illness, and treatment are discussed. The participants are informed about neuroleptics, their effects and side-effects, as well as about behavioural psychotherapy (e.g. family therapy and social skills training). The benefits of these treatments are outlined, based on the vulnerability–stress model (e.g. how the use of neuroleptics influences biological liability to stress).

In order to assess *early warning signs of relapse*, the participants are asked which changes in thinking, feeling, body sensations and behaviours they experienced before their most recent relapse. Participants identify their own early warning signs by using a checklist designed by Herz & Melville (1980). This questionnaire is complemented by individual changes not listed and statements about changes in taking medication. If the participant agrees, significant others are asked about their observations. The participants monitor the severity and frequency of these signals throughout treatment, and are encouraged to continue doing this after the end of treatment. In collaboration with significant others, as well as health care providers, contracts are made based on these warning signs, in which steps are identified to be taken if the warning signs occur and an emergency plan is developed.

The *second subprogramme* deals with *coping with stressors*. First the participants are asked to *identify stressful situations in different areas of living* and to classify them with regard to illness and psychosocial functioning. For patients with severe negative symptoms or very chronic psychosis, who may find it difficult to identify stressors, the therapist facilitates a discussion of personal situations the patient and others have experienced. Stressors may arise with regard to the *illness*, such as negative symptoms (e.g. loss of energy, poor concentration), positive symptoms (e.g. hearing voices), and treatment (e.g. medication side-effects), as well as *psychosocial functioning* (e.g. associated with relationships with other people, work, living situation). Constructing a hierarchy of stressful situations illustrates the amount of burden experienced by each patient in the various areas of life.

Many patients in groups worry about relapse. They also are afraid to be confronted with stereotypes and prejudices in conversations about the illness. With regard to psychosocial functioning, they report problems developing close relationships, loss of friends and colleagues, lack of tolerance of others, and loneliness. From their viewpoint, disputes (especially with the parents) are often based on discrepancies between their resources and the expectations of significant others. With regard to work, patients complain about being under too much pressure because of very high demands (especially time-limits). They complain about criticism by supervisors, competition between colleagues, problems in keeping a job, unemployment, and an uncertain future.

Next, the participants are asked to *recognize signs of stress* and to analyse stressful situations according to a scheme that includes the activating event, the eliciting beliefs, psychophysiological, cognitive and emotional changes, as well as coping reactions and their consequences. According to Lazarus (1991), emotions are influenced by different processes, including the eliciting environmental and internal conditions that produce a special person–environment relationship, the mediating process of appraisal of that relationship, the coping process, as well as the response itself. *Physical changes* may refer to "psycho-vegetative" complaints in general (e.g. sweating, shivery, trembling), to a specific organ (e.g. heart palpitations) or sore muscles (e.g. neck pain). *Changes in thinking* can be differentiated in content of cognition (e.g. appraisals or inner monologues that possibly refer to self-defeating beliefs and irrational ways of thinking) and processes (e.g. poor concentration, distractability, thought blocking). *Mood changes* may relate to helplessness, irritability, anxiety and depression. Examples of *changes in behaviour* are withdrawal or communication problems due to poor listening skills, inability to express oneself, or poor non-verbal behaviours (e.g. poor eye contact). The participants are also asked to fill out a "stress questionnaire" about stressful situations, thoughts and reactions in these situations, and activities that might reduce stress and coping strategies they want to learn and unlearn.

> To illustrate this approach a stressful situation is described by *Mr B*, a 30 year-old patient with a schizoaffective psychosis. *Place, time, action*: he felt stressed at work. *Appraisals, inner monologue*: he thought that he could not keep up with his boss's expectations. *Feelings:* he worried about it. *Body sensations*: his back felt stiff. *Cognitive processes*: his thinking was slow and repetitive. *Coping behaviour*: he withdrew more and more, catastrophized about what would happen, and started heavy smoking. *Consequences of the situation*: in the long run he felt dissatisfied and did not know what to do.

Stress management employs a wide range of different techniques. Relaxation techniques, such as a short form of *muscle relaxation training* (Jacobson, 1938) or *breathing techniques* (Tausch, 1996), combined with positive imagery, are offered at the beginning of each session in this subprogramme. Emphasis is placed on improving *problem solving*, *social skills training* (i.e. self-assertive behaviour and communication skills) and *identifying and changing maladaptive cognitions* (i.e. cognitive restructuring). Problem solving includes teaching different steps, such as a precise definition of the problem, brainstorming solutions, discussing pros and cons, deciding on the most effective solution, and planning its implementation. The stressful situations described by the participants are discussed in the group and different ideas about how to deal with the situation are elicited and evaluated. When possible, participants role-play the response they think is best.

With regard to social skills training, a list of personal competencies and deficits in social skills as well as a list about strategies to be learned and unlearned for social situations are developed. For social skills training it is important to explain the goals of these exercises, to provide information about the main elements of assertiveness, and to set up individualized situations that can be used in roleplays to practice the skill (Bellack et al., 1997). Stressful situations can be also triggered by dysfunctional cognitions that hinder assertive behaviour and achieving personal goals. In cognitive restructuring the participants are taught how to confront their irrational thinking patterns, such as, "I should not make any mistakes" or "I must be loved by everyone", and together alternatives are worked on.

> With regard to the stressful situation previously described by *Mr B*, the group members came up with the following solutions in problem solving: (a) stop taking medication; (b) decrease the dosage of medication; (c) do not let others put you under too much stress; (d) ask your boss for less work; (e) talk with your boss about your present situation; (f) look for a less demanding job; (g) another colleague should be hired; (h) accept lower salary. Mr B decided on the third and fourth proposals. However, he expressed anxiety about talking with his boss. Therefore, the situation was role-played. Mr B thanked the group for their support after this meeting. At the next session he reported that he had talked with his boss and a resolution had been arrived at. The talk went much better than he had expected. He appeared very relieved.

In addition, participants are helped to *learn specific coping skills*. Coping strategies can be classified as beneficial or maladaptive, as well as preventive or related to short- or long-term stressors. Maladaptive strategies refer to ineffective behaviours, such as taking alcohol and drugs, rumination, aggressive behaviours, as well as excessive behaviours (e.g. with regard to caffeine and nicotine, eating, sleep, and avoidance of specific situations). The participants are asked which strategies they have found helpful in stressful situations, and what they plan to do in the future if they get stressed again. Together with other participants, potentially effective coping strategies are identified and a plan is made to put them into action (cf. Mueser & Gingerich, 1994). The participants are asked what recreational behaviours they neglect most when under stress and what they can do to resume them. In subsequent sessions, the participants are asked for feedback on whether the strategies they identified have been useful. They are asked to continue to identify and monitor stressful situations, so that they will become more aware of stressors and ways of dealing with them. Possible cognitive coping strategies include setting reasonable expectations, positive self-instructions and planning recreational activities. Possible behavioural coping strategies are exercising regularly, practising relaxation techniques and structuring daytime activities. Possible social coping strategies include comumnicating directly about stress and asking other people about support.

At the end of this sub-programme the focus shifts to *the management of crisis and the prevention of relapse*. The concept of warning signs is again focused on and together with the patient a more detailed analysis of the most recent relapse with regard to his biography is conducted. The development of symptoms, the conditions under which they occurred, and the coping strategies are assessed. The participants are asked how the crisis developed, what happened before the crisis, how they tried to deal with the crisis, and which strategies they thought were helpful or not. In order to learn from past experiences, participants are asked what they could have done that might have been helpful and what they plan to do in the future. However, crisis management alone is not sufficient. Relapse prevention and health behaviour are also critical for improving the course of the illness.

The goal of the third and final subprogramme, *improving quality of life*, is to foster positive personal assets and to develop a life style which promotes health and well-being. Patients are also helped to develop a concept of the self that is not exclusively defined in terms of their illness, but is based on a conception of their individuality and on the remaining possibilities of their life. Similiar to analysing stressors, patients are encouraged to identify pleasant situations, so that they become aware of these situations in which they feel well. They are encouraged to engage in activities they find enjoyable (e.g. developing interests, organizing and planning leisure time).

Two Case Reports

To illustrate the programme, two case-reports are presented:

> *Mr K* was a 35 year-old teacher, suffering from his third episode of a paranoid schizophrenia. He had been ill for 12 years and had been hospitalized for about 6 months. Stressors that appeared to precipitate his most recent relapse were problems at work and difficulty in developing close relationships. On the one hand, he had difficulty managing the stress related to working as a teacher; on the other hand, he did not want to give up his profession, which he had put so much effort into achieving.
>
> At the beginning of the group, Mr K spoke very frankly about his experiences and symptoms such as suspicion, compulsions and poor concentration, as well as problems in developing close relationships. He then reported feeling stressed because of this disclosure. After being told that he was allowed to share experiences as well as keep them to himself he reported feeling very relieved. He attended the groups very regularly and became an active and very interested participant. He found the vulnerability–stress model helpful in understanding his illness. He reported his warning signs, including sleeping problems, irritability, uncontrollable fits of rage, social withdrawal and poor concentration. He chose to work with his sister to develop an emergency plan based on these signs. With regard to stress management, he focused on being under too much pressure. He was able to analyse his dysfunctional thinking pattern, "I have to be perfect", and change it to, "I am allowed to make mistakes". At the end of the group he changed his expectations with regard to his goals of life and decided to work at a less demanding job. He often

volunteered for role-plays and found them helpful in gaining self-confidence and getting to know others' perspectives. He focused on coping with rumination, and found thought-stopping and relaxation, as well as positive self-instructions, to be helpful. At the beginning of the group he spent most of his leisure time reading the Bible and praying, but towards the end of the group he spent time gardening as well as talking to other people.

At first his parents complained about his laziness, inability to follow through, and difficulty maintaining an adequate level of personal hygiene, problems which they believed to be under his voluntary control. They found the vulnerability–stress model helpful in understanding the illness and realizing that those behaviours were common symptoms of schizophrenia. Family work began with helping the parents process their mourning that their son did not fulfil their expectations of becoming a successful teacher. The talks then focused on guidelines for effective problem solving and managing stress. At the end of the sessions they reported that they believed that their son had gained insight and that he behaved in an acceptable manner. They were pleased about his new hobby of gardening.

In Mr K's feedback to the group he reported that he had learned much about his illness and gained more self-confidence in coping with it and everyday problems. He valued most that the group gave him opportunity to deal with his conflicts and was a source of comfort and appreciation from others. At the 2 year follow-up he had not had a relapse and had achieved a higher level of psychosocial functioning.

MRS S was a 42 year-old married woman with a daughter aged 17 years and a son aged 13 years who had suffered her fifth episode of a schizo-affective disorder. She had been ill for 24 years and had been hospitalized for 22 months. The possible reasons for her recent relapse were the recent death of her mother, with whom she had had an intense relationship, marital problems and poor medication compliance. With regard to the vulnerability–stress model, she mainly addressed psychosocial stressors, but neglected the biological aspects of vulnerability and biological factors. After the first sub-programme it appeared that she had benefited from education about medication as she reported that now she understood its purpose. She was able to recognize her early warning signs and, together with her family, an emergency plan was developed. The first stressful situations Mrs S reported in group referred to the missing of a dog's lead. What seemed quite a trivial situation at first gave a hint to one of the main problem areas: Mrs S felt responsible for everything at home and had difficulties expressing her negative feelings to others who she felt demanded too much of her. Exploration of her maladaptive thinking resulted in identifying a self-defeating belief that, "I am the only one in charge for everything". She reported marital problems as well as lack of understanding by her adolescent daughter and her sister, who thought that she was not ill but made up all these problems to get attention. Role-plays on how to be more assertive and how to talk with others about her illness seemed helpful to her, as well as sharing experiences on this topic with other people. Mrs S focused on these topics one at a time and developed coping strategies to be put in action. Her competencies included her social skills, high performance at her job, and an outgoing attitude.

Mrs S's husband and her children attended family sessions. At the beginning they mainly expressed their anger and fear about Mrs S's inappropriate behaviours that occurred during a psychotic episode. The children were less understanding than Mrs S's husband, who supported her in regaining her authority in the family. Although there were still some problems in their marital relationship and the relationship with her daughter and her son, Mrs S accepted her husband's support in monitoring her warning signs and the two seemed to become closer.

Mrs S valued the group sessions for giving her more competence in dealing with difficult situations, as well as providing a better understanding of her illness. At a follow-up 2 years later, Mrs S had not had a relapse or rehospitalization. Her daughter had moved to her own apartment. Mrs S reported that the relationship with her husband as well as with her daughter and son had improved markedly.

First Results

Several studies have supported the clinical feasibility of this treatment programme (Schaub and Möller, 1990; Schaub et al., 1997; 1997). A randomized controlled study with 20 patients at the University of Berne, supported by the Swiss National Funds compared the coping-oriented treatment programme ($n = 11$) with a supportive control group ($N = 9$) in a two-year follow-up study (Schaub et al., 1997). Fifteen patients were diagnosed as schizophrenic, mainly paranoid, and five patients as schizo-affective. The patients were 32.20 years (SD = 16.85) old on average; mean duration of illness: 8.03 (SD = 5.95); mean number of hospitalizations. 5.85 (SD = 3.75); mean duration of hospitalization: 97.27 (SD = 68.50) weeks; years of education: 9.93 (SD = 1.40). In contrast to the structured and manualized proceeding of the experimental group, the supportive group engaged in unstructured discussions with topics chosen by the participants. Training took place twice a week for 1.5 hours with 24 sessions and lasting 2.5 months on average. There were up to four additional sessions offered to each family. Before and after treatment, psychopathology was assessed with the Brief Psychiatric Rating Scale (Overall & Gorham. 1962) and the Scale for the Assessment of Negative Symptoms (Andreasen, 1981). The Stress Coping Questionnaire (Janke, Erdman & Kallus, 1985) was adminstered to identify the coping strategies typically used and the Frankfurt Self-concept Scale (Deusinger, 1986) to assess relevant aspects of the self-concept. Knowledge about the illess was assessed by the Knowledge Test about Psychosis (Schaub et al., 1997) and quality of life by the Social Interview Schedule (Hecht, Faltermaier & Wittchen, 1987). There were no differences in the decrease of psychopathological symptoms (BPRS, SANS) in either group at post-treatment. Both groups gained knowledge about psychosis and its treatment, however, this increase was more pronounced in the coping-orientated group. Already from pre- to post-treatment the score increased from 79% to 87% right answers and was stable on this high level at 6, 12 and 18 month follow-up. With regard to standard of living (Hecht et al., 1987) both groups improved on living conditions and leisure time activities. The patients in the experimental group reported closer social contacts in their social network and an increase in well-being whereas in the control group the social support decreased. With regard to self-confidence the patients in the coping-orientated treatment gained significantly more assertiveness in social contacts than those in the control group (Deusinger, 1986). Coping strategies showed no signifcant differences between the two groups. Comparing the days of hospitalization one year before and one year after the group treatment, patients in the coping-oriented therapy showed a significant lower duration of hospitalization than those in the control group. These results were affirmed in an extended study with 33 patients including 17 patients in the coping-oriented treatment and 16 patients in the control group.

Since 1995 the shorter coping-orientated treatment programme has been evaluated at the Department of Psychiatry, University of Munich (Schaub et al., 1998c). Up to now 119 patients with schizophrenia or schizo-affective psychosis attended this group and 78% of these filled out comprehensive feedback questionnaires. 91% rated the programme as helpful to very helpful with regard to its contents as well as the mutual stimulation and support by other participants. More than two-thirds of the patients reported feeling well educated about psychosis and that their coping strategies had improved. They also found the programme helpful in instilling a greater sense of control over their illness and its course. The patients favoured topics such as relapse prevention, aetiology and course of the illness, treatment options as well as the recognition of individual stress thresholds and coping strategy enhancement. There was a significant reduction of psychopathological symptoms (BPRS, SANS) and a significant increase in knowledge about the illness and its treatment in a subsample of 45 patients. Up to now 42 patients have been recruited for a one-year follow-up assessment showing a relapse rate of 21%. This result is identical to the psychoeducational intervention by Bäuml et al. (1996) comparing it to standard treatment with a relapse rate of 38%. At follow-up the majority of the patients in this study had insight into their illness, were compliant with treatment and knew much about stress management and coping with early warning signs. They were satisfied with their living and working situation as well as leisure time activities; they complained, however, about their low income. The majority of the patients followed the treatment guidelines recommended by the clinic with atypical antipsychotics being the medication most prescribed. At Munich up to now 37 patients have been recruited in a randomized controlled study that is to assess the course of the illness, social integration and qualify of life in a longitudinal study of three years.

DISCUSSION

According to Goldstein (1992), psychoeducational programmes tap deep-seated issues of personal identity and one's role in a family unit that cannot be ignored. Alternative therapeutic strategies have to be added in order to permit the psychoeducational approach to be effective at fostering coping strategies and social skills. Interventions that provide information about the psychiatric disorder and its treatment to patients and relatives, as well as guidelines for stress management, have become more widely practised. Recent controlled research on these interventions provides a basis for cautious optimism about the impact of these interventions on the course of the illness. The coping-orientated group format treatment program for patients with a post-acute schizophrenic or schizo-affective episode provides information about the illness and its treatment, as well teaching strategies for how to deal with stressors more effectively and how to prevent relapse. In a controlled study, patients treated with the coping-orientated treatment programme showed more treatment gains with regard to knowledge about psychosis, quality of life, and social competence, compared to the control group. Long-term outcomes need to be assessed to determine whether the programme helps to prevent relapses and rehospitalizations. At this point it is unknown whether possible treatment effects are due to improved compliance, the family atmosphere, ability to cope with stress, or altered dysfunctional beliefs of the illness.

Although standardized programmes involve teaching a predetermined set of information and skills, there is always a need to adapt the programme to address specific patient needs. Patients are better motivated when they can relate the contents of therapy to their own personal lives. When rehabilitation can be provided on an inpatient basis, patients should be recruited as soon as they are able to attend the sessions. To facilitate the generalization of skills to patients' natural environments, booster sessions should be provided on an outpatient basis. The integration of relatives into treatment is a very important component. The negative feelings many relatives experience in coping with an ill family member are alleviated and relatives are supported to function as informed caregivers who reinforce patients' improvements.

Further research is needed to determine the extent to which trained coping skills generalize from the training setting to "real life" environments. There is an urgent need to develop appropriate procedures to measure the transfer of psychosocial and coping skills from the training setting to naturalistic settings in the community. These procedures need to incorporate multiple perspectives (i.e. the patient, the family and clinicians). There is also a need to focus on a wider range of potential outcomes, including the impact on vocational functioning, quality of life, family well-being and satisfaction with services. Research needs to aim at identifying which patients benefit from which treatment programmes in order to make differential treatment recommendations and to tailor interventions to meet specific patient needs (see Schaub et al., 1998b). As biological advances over the next decade continue to contribute to a better understanding of the aetiology and pharmacologic treatment, it is likely that the role of psychological interventions in enhancing social functioning, coping with schizophrenia and re-integrating patients into the community will become even greater than it is today.

ACKNOWLEDGEMENTS

The further development of this treatment programme was supported by the Swiss National Funds (NF 32-39762.93). This paper is dedicated to Michael Goldstein, one of the pioneers in psychosocial interventions in psychiatry, who passed away in March 1997.

REFERENCES

Anderson, C.M., Hogarty, G.E. & Reiss, D.J. (1980).   Family treatment of adult schizo-phrenic patients: a psychoeducational approach. *Schizophrenia Bulletin*, **6**, 490–515.

Anderson, C.M., Reiss, D.J. & Hogarty, G.E. (1986).   *Schizophrenia and the Family*. New York: Guildorf.

Andreason, N.C. (1981).   *Scale for the Assessment of Negative Symptoms (SANS)*. Iowa City: University of Iowa.

Bäuml, J. (1997).   *Psychoeduaktive Gruppenarbeit bei schizophrenen Patienten* (Psychoeducational group treatment for schizophrenic patients). *Psycho*, **23**, 38–45.

Bäuml, J., Pitschel-Walz, G. & Kissling, W. (1996).   Psychoedukative Gruppen bei schizophrenen Psychosen für Patienten und Angehörige. In A. Stark (ed.), *Verhaltenstherapeutische und psychoedukative Ansätze im Umgang mit schizophren Erkrankten* (Behavioural and psychoeducational approaches in the treatment of patients with schizophrenia). Tübingen: Deutsche Gesellschaft für Verhaltenstherapie, pp. 217–255.

Bebbington, P., Wilkins, S., Jones, P., Förster, A., Murray, R., Toone, B., & Lewis, S. (1993).   Life events and psychosis, Initial results from the Camberwell Collaborative Psychosis Study. *British Journal of Psychiatry*, **162**, 72–79.

Bellack, A.S., Mueser, K.T., Gingerich, S. & Agresta, J. (1997).   Social Skills Training for Schizophrenia. New York: Guilford.

Böker, W., Brenner, H.D., Gerstner, G., Keller, F., Müller, J. & Spichtig, L. (1984).   Self-healing strategies among schizophrenics: attempts at compensation for basic disorders. *Acta Psychiatrica Scandinavica*, **69**, 373–378.

Böker, W. & Schaub, A. (1997).   Bewältigungsversuche Schizophrener. In W. Böker & H.D. Brenner (eds), *Behandlung schizophrener Psychosen* (Treatment in Schizophrenia). Stuttgart: Enke, pp. 165–185.

Brenner, H.D., Böker, W., Müller, J., Spichtig, L. & Würgler, S. (1987).   On autoprotective efforts of schizophrenics, neurotics and controls. *Acta Psychiatrica Scandinavica*, **75**, 405–414.

Buchkremer, G. & Fiedler, P. (1987).   Kognitive vs. handlungsorientierte Therapie (Cognitive vs. action-orientated treatment). *Nervenarzt*, **58**, 481–488.

Buchkremer, G., Klingberg, S., Holle, R., Schulze Mönking, H. & Hornung, W.P. (1997).   Psychoeducational psychotherapy für schizophrenic patients and their key relatives or care-givers: results of a 2-year follow-up. *Acta Psychiatrica Scandinavica*, **96**, 483–491.

Deusinger, I. (1986).   *Die Frankfurter Selbstkonzeptskalen (FSKN)* (The Frankfurt Scales for Assessing Self-concepts). Göttingen: Hogrefe.

Eckman, T.A., Wirshing, W.C., Marder, S.R., Liberman, R.P., Johnston-Cronk, K., Zimmerman, K. & Mintz, J. (1992).   Technology for training schizophrenics in illness self-management: a controlled trial, *American Journal of Psychiatry*, **149**, 1549–1555.

Falloon, I.R.H., Boyd, J.L., McGill, C.W., Williamson, M., Razani, J., Moss, H.B., Gilderman, A.M. & Simpson, G.M. (1985).   Family management in the prevention of morbidity of schizophrenia. Clinical outcome of a two-year longitudinal study. *Archives of General Psychiatry*, **42**, 887–896.

Falloon, I.R.H., Boyd, J.L. & McGill, C.W. (1984).   *Family Care of Schizophrenia*. New York: Guilford.

Goldstein, M. (1992).   Psychosocial strategies for maximizing the effects of psychotropic medications for schizophrenia and mood disorder. *Psychopharmacology Bulletin*, **28**, 237–240.

Hahlweg, K., Dürr, H. and Müller, U. (1995).   *Familienbetreuung schizophrener Patienten* (Family management with schizophrenic patients). Weinheim: Beltz, Psychologie-Verlags-Union.

Hecht, H., Faltermaier, A. & Wittchen, H.-U. (1987). *Social Interview Schedule (SIS)*, Regensburg: Materialien zur Klinischen Psychologie und Psychotherapie, Roderer Verlag.

Heinrichs, D.W., Cohen, B.P. & Carpenter, W.T. (1985). Early insight and the management of schizophrenic decompensation. *Journal of Nervous and Mental Diseases*, **173**, 133–138.

Herz, M.I. & Melville, C. (1980). Relapse in schizophrenia. *American Journal of Psychiatry*, **137**, 801–805.

Hogarty, G.E., Anderson, C.M., Reiss, D.J., Kornblith, S.J., Greenwald, D.P., Ulrich, R. & Carter, M. (1991). Family psychoeducation, social skills training and maintenance therapy in the aftercare treatment of schizophrenia: II. Two-year effects of a controlled study on relapse and adjustment. *Archives of General Psychiatry*, **48**, 340–347.

Hogarty, G.E., Kornblith, S.J., Greenwald, D., DiBarry, A.L., Cooley, S., Flesher, S., Reiss, D., Carter, M. & Ulrich, R. (1995). Personal therapy: a disorder-relevant psychotherapy for schizophrenia. *Schizophrenia Bulletin*, **21**, 379–393.

Hornung, W.P., Holle, R., Schulze-Mönking, H., Klingberg, S. & Buchkremer, G. (1995). Psychoedukativ-psychotherapeutische Behandlung von schizophrenen Patienten und ihren Bezugspersonen—Ergebnisse einer 1-Jahres-Katamnese (Psychoeducational-psychotherapeutic treatment of schizophrenic patients and their relatives. Results of a 1-year follow-up). *Nervenarzt*, **66**, 828–834.

Jacobson, E. (1938). *Progressive Relaxation*. Chicago: University of Chicago Press.

Janke, W., Erdman, G. & Kallus, W. (1985). *Der Streßverarbeitungsbogen* (The Stress Coping Questionnaire). Göttingen: Hogrefe.

Kieserg, A. & Hornung, W.P. (1996). *Psychoedukatives Training für schizophrene Patienten (PTS)* (Psychoeducational training for schizophrenic patients), Materialie Nr. 27, überarbeitete und erweiterte Auflage. Tübingen: Deutsche Gesellschaft für Verhaltenstherapie.

Kissling, W., Bäuml, J. & Pitschel-Walz, G. (1995). Psychoedukation und Compliance bei der Schizophreniebehandlung (Psychoeducation and compliance in the treatment of schizophrenia). *Münchner Medizinische Wochenzeitschrift*, **137**, 801–805.

Lazarus, R.S. (1991). *Emotion and Adaptation*. New York: Oxford University Press.

Lewandowski, L., Buchkremer, G. & Stark, M. (1994). Das Gruppenklima und die Therapeut-Patient-Baziehung bei zwei Gruppentherapiestrategien für schizophrene Patienten—ein Beitrag zur Klärung differentieller Therapieeffeckre. *Psychotherapie Psychosomatik Medizinische Psychologie*, **44**, 115–121.

Liberman, R.P. (1986). *Social and Independent Living Skills. The Medication Management Module*. Trainer's manual and patient handbook. Los Angeles, CA: Clinical Research Center for Schizophrenia and Psychiatric Rehabilitation.

Liberman, R.P. (1988). *Social and Independent Living Skills. The Symptom Management Module*. Trainer's manual and patient handbook. Los Angeles, CA: Clinical Research Center for Schizophrenia and Psychiatric Rehabilitation.

Liberman, R.P., Mueser, K.T., Wallace, C.J., Jacobes, H.E., Eckman, T. & Massel, H.K. (1986). Training skills in the psychiatrically disabled: learning coping and competence. *Schizophrenia Bulletin*, **12**, 631–647.

Mueser, K.T. & Gingerich, S. (1994). *Coping with Schizophrenia. A Guide for Families*. Oakland, CA: New Harbinger Publications.

Mueser, K.T. & Glynn, S.M. (1995). *Behavioral Family Therapy for Psychiatric Disorders*. Needham Heights, MA: Allyn and Bacon.

Mueser, K.T., Valentiner, D.P. & Agresta, J. (1997). Coping with negative symptoms of schizophrenia: patient and family perspectives. *Schizophrenia Bulletin*, **23**, 329–339.

Norman, R.M. & Malla, A.K. (1993). Stressful life events and schizophrenia. I. A review of research. *British Journal of Psychiatry*, **162**, 161–166.

Nuechterlein, K.H. & Dawson, M.E. (1984).   A heuristic vulnerability–stress model of schizophrenic episodes. *Schizophrenia Bulletin*, **10**, 300–312.

Overall, J.E. & Gorham, D.R. (1962).   The Brief Psychiatric Rating Scale. *Psychological Reports*, **18**, 799–812.

Penn D.L. & Mueser, K.T. (1996).   Research update on the psychosocial treatment of schizophrenia. *American Journal of Psychiatry*, **153**, 607–617.

Schaub, A. (1994).   Relapse and coping behaviour in schizophrenia. *Schizophrenia Research*, **11**(2), 188.

Schaub, A. (1997).   Bewältigungsorientierte Gruppentherapie bei schizophren und schizoaffektiv Erkrankten und ihren Angehörigen (Description of a coping-orientated treatment programme for schizophrenic and schizo-affective patients and their relatives). In U. Trenckmann & M. Lasar (eds), *Psychotherapeutische Strategien der Schizophreniebehandlung* (Psychotherapeutic strategies in the treatment of schizophrenia). Lengerich, Berlin: Pabst Science Publishers, pp. 95–120.

Schaub, A. & Böker, W. (1997).   Bewältigungsorientierte Therapieansätze (Coping-orientated treatment programs). In W. Böker & H.D. Brenner (eds), *Behandlung schizophrener Psychosen* (Treatment in schizophrenia). Stuttgart: Enke, pp. 186–208.

Schaub, A. & Möller, H.J. (1990).   Training kognitiver und sozialer Defizite bei schizophrenen Patienten. *Zentralblatt für Neurologie und Psychiatrie*, **255**, 277.

Schaub, A., Andres, K. & Schindler, F. (1996).   Psychoedukative und bewältigungsorientierte Gruppentherapien in der Schizophreniebehandlung (Psychoeducational and coping-orientated group therapy in the treatment of schizophrenia). *Psycho*, **22**, 713–721.

Schaub, A., Andres, K., Brenner, H.D. & Donzel, G. (1997).   Developing a novel coping-orientated treatment programme for schizophrenic patients. In H.D. Brenner, W. Böker & R. Genner (eds), *Integrative Therapy of Schizophrenia*. Bern: Huber, pp. 228–251.

Schaub, A., Andres, K., Brenner, H.D., Donzel, G. & Schindler, F. (1997).   Bewältigungsorientierte Therapie bei psychisch Erkrankten—ein gruppentherapeutisches Konzept zum Umgang mit einer schizophrenen Psychose. In C. Mundt, M. Linden & W. Barnett (eds), *Psychotherapie in der Psychiatrie*. Vienna: Springer, pp. 93–96.

Schaub, A., Behrendt, B. & Brenner, H.D. (1998a).   A multi-hospital evaluation of the Medication and Symptom Management Modules in Germany and Switzerland. *Internal Review of Psychiatry*, **1**, 42–46.

Schaub, A., Behrendt, B., Brenner, H.D., Mueser, K.T. & Liberman, R.P. (1998b).   Training schizophrenic patients to manage their symptoms: predictors of treatment response to the German version of the symptom management module. *Schizophrenia Research*, **31**, 121–130.

Schaub, A., Wolf, B., Forschmayr, S., Gartenmaier, A. & Möller, H.J. (1998c).   Description and evaluation of a coping-oriented treatment programme in schizophrenia and schizoaffective psychosis. VI. World Congress. World Association for Psychosocial Rehabilitation (WAPR), Hamburg, p. 59.

Spaulding, W., Storms, L., Goodrich, V. & Sullivan, M. (1986).   Applications of experimental psychopathology in psychiatric rehabilitiation. *Schizophrenia Bulletin*, **12**, 560–577.

Süllwold, L. (1977).   *Symptome schizophrener Erkrankungen. Uncharakteristische Basisstörungen* (Symptoms of schizophrenia. Uncharacteristic basic disorders). Monographs on the Entire Field of Psychiatry, Vol. 13. Berlin: Springer.

Süllwold, L. & Herrlich, J. (1992).   Providing schizophrenic patients with a concept of illness. An essential element of therapy. *British Journal of Psychiatry*, **161**(suppl 18), 129–132.

Tausch, R. (1996).   *Hilfen bei Streß und Belastung* (Helpful strategies for stress and burden). Reinbek bei Hamburg: Rowohlt.

Tarrier, N., Beckett, R., Harwood, S., Baker, A., Yusupoff, L. & Ugarteburu, I. (1993). A trial of two cognitive-behavioral methods of treating drug-resistant residual psychotic symptoms in schizophrenic patients. I. Outcome. *British Journal of Psychiatry*, **162**, 524–532.

Thurm, L. & Häfner, H. (1987). Perceived vulnerability, relapse risk and coping in schizophrenia. *European Archives of Psychiatry and Neurological Sciences*, **237**, 46–53.

Wiedl, K.H. (1992). Assessment of coping with schizophrenia. Stressors, appraisals and coping behaviour. *British Journal of Psychiatry*, **161**(suppl 18), 114–122.

Wiedl, K.H. (1994). Bewältigungsorientierte Therapie bei Schizophrenen (Coping-orientated therapy in schizophrenia). *Zeitschrift für Klinische Psychologie, Psychopathologie und Psychotherapie*, **42**, 89–117.

Wienberg, G. (1995). *Schizophrenie zum Thema machen. Psychoedukative Gruppenarbeit mit schizophren und schizoaffektiv erkrankten Menschen: Grundlagen und Praxis* (Focusing on schizophrenia. Psychoeducational group therapy for patients with schizophrenia and schizo-affective psychosis: basics and practice). Bonn: Psychiatrie Verlag.

Wienberg, D., Schünemann-Wurmthaler, S. & Sibum, B. (1995). *Schizophrenie zum Thema machen, Manual und Materialien* (Focusing on schizophrenia: manual and working sheets). Bonn: Psychiatrie-Verlag.

Zubin, J. & Spring, B. (1977). Vulnerability—a new view of schizophrenia. *Journal of Abnormal Psychology*, **86**, 103–126.

Chapter 7

Options and Clinical Decision Making in the Assessment and Psychological Treatment of Persistent Hallucinations and Delusions

Lawrence Yusupoff
Private Practice, Manchester, UK
and
Gillian Haddock
Department of Nursing, University of Manchester, UK

The standard mental health service response to patients presenting with psychotic symptoms is to prescribe neuroleptic medication. Since their introduction in the 1950s, neuroleptics have revolutionized the treatment of psychosis, although there are still substantial numbers of medicated patients whose psychotic symptoms persist (Curson, Patel & Liddle, 1988). In addition, the side effects associated with this type of medication preclude or limit their use for some patients. As a result of these observations, alternative or complementary psychosocial treatments for psychotic patients have been developed. The recent advances which have been made in the psychological treatment of psychosis suggest that these should be offered as routine services to the majority of patients. Psychological approaches evaluated so far include family interventions (Barrowclough & Tarrier, 1992), early intervention and prodromal signs monitoring (Birchwood, 1996) as well as psychological treatments aimed at reducing the occurrence and distress associated with persistent positive symptoms (Sellwood et al., 1994). The latter is the focus of this chapter, which highlights specific clinical issues, and provides an overview of the assessment and treatment

Cognitive Psychotherapy of Psychotic and Personality Disorders: Handbook of Theory and Practice.
Edited by C. Perris and P.D. McGorry.
© 1998 John Wiley & Sons Ltd.

options recently available to clinicians whose caseloads include hallucinating and deluded patients.

ASSESSMENT

Initial Decision-making and Planning

Assessment of individuals with persistent hallucinations or delusions needs to be both structured and comprehensive to determine whether individual cognitive-behaviour therapy is a clinical priority and, if offered to the patient, will result in meaningful quality of life changes. The traditional cognitive-behavioural scenario of patient and therapist collaborating to diminish specified symptoms may well apply to those with psychotic symptoms; however, an expanded clinical frame-work is called for. The needs of this population are often complex (Fowler, Garety & Kuipers, 1995) and "intrinsic impairments" associated with schizophre-nia (such as delusions, cognitive deficits and negative symptoms) may be further complicated by their secondary, social and psychological consequences, such as family disharmony, dependency and diminished self-esteem (Birchwood, Hallett & Preston, 1988). Ideally, an initial assessment should highlight the clinical issues which might affect decisions regarding whether psychological therapy is offered at all and, if so, the adjustments which will be required which reflect unique aspects of any case. A series of questions are presented below to give some idea as to the breadth and type of information which may be required to arrive at decisions about the nature, timing and limits of a possible intervention.

1. Are there any priority social, financial or medical needs which, if resolved, would either directly impact psychotic symptoms or free the patient to engage in therapy more fully?
2. Are there any non-psychotic clinical states or symptoms which are best dealt with prior to embarking on treatment of psychotic symptoms?
3. To what extent have family members or carers adjusted their life styles and roles to accommodate the patient's enduring needs and what are the implications for them of the patient being less symptomatic?
4. What are the potential limits, in terms of outcome, of a symptom-focused therapy for the individual, given his/her pre-morbid level of social and psychological adjustment?
5. What are the implications for the patient of an unsuccessful clinical outcome?
6. What is the patient's relapse history and does any aspect of therapy expose the patient to the kinds of stressors previously associated with acute episodes?
7. Do the other support agencies and professionals understand what the therapy involves and do they all agree that therapy should be offered?

8.   Are other agencies and professionals offering interventions which will con-
     tradict or undermine psychological therapy?
9.   In the event of relapse during the period of active therapy, have plans
     been made together with the multidisciplinary team as to the therapeutic
     strategy?
10. Once therapy is complete what resources might the patient require to
     maintain clinical gains?
11. Is there a history of psychological trauma, and how might the patient be
     supported to be able to tolerate the resultant stress of having memories
     re-activated, if the psychotic symptoms are related to that trauma?
12. What additional therapeutic modalities, e.g. social skills training, family
     therapy, etc., might be of value to support the symptom-focused therapy
     and should these be offered concurrently or sequentially and by whom?
13. What are the likely short- and long-term consequences of the patient not
     receiving individual therapy for symptoms and how do these risks balance
     against the risks associated with a course of therapy?

Some of the issues raised by these questions currently pre-date formal research in these areas; the point, however, remains the same, and what is intended
is to draw attention to the diverse conditions and contexts which need to be
included in clinicians' models of therapeutic change for this client group. Intelligent coordination of therapeutic efforts is therefore required and choosing
an appropriate case management model of service delivery is essential (e.g.
Lancashire et al., 1997). Having drawn attention to the preliminary considerations affecting early clinical decisions and planning, specific assessment options
follow.

Eliciting Symptoms

Patients' reports of psychotic experiences and beliefs are often incomplete unless
specific prompt questions designed to elicit these symptoms are asked. Use of
reliable psychiatric interview schedules, like the Present State Examination
(Wing, Cooper & Sartorius, 1974) is recommended to elicit a complete profile of
psychotic and non-psychotic symptoms.

The number of symptoms may vary considerably and negotiation is often
required to select an appropriate target symptom initially from a range of distressing phenomena. This may be based on the patient's priorities, the discrete-
ness of occurrence of a symptom and whether there is the possibility of selecting
one key phenomenon which might result in a "domino effect", i.e. other symptoms automatically dissipating by intervening with just one. Another possibility is
to select symptoms hierarchically to minimize distress or reduce the threat associated with the possibility of symptom change, where motivational factors are
complex (see section below on assessment of motivation).

Rating Scales and Dimensions of Psychotic Symptoms

The development of assessment tools for hallucinations and delusions has, until recently, been largely for diagnostic purposes, hence these symptoms have usually been classified in terms of their presence or absence. The therapist's focus, however, is on the symptom itself and the assessment of its behavioural and cognitive correlates with a view to intervening at this level. Monitoring changes and outcome measurement thus requires scales which tell us about the nature of the individual dimensions of symptoms and how they co-vary as a result of treatment (Garety, 1992). For example, a patient who experiences a reduction in hallucination loudness as a result of treatment may not show a concurrent change in frequency or duration, therefore the improvement will not be picked up on standard measures of severity. Two scales are available which have been developed to measure the severity of a number of different dimensions of auditory hallucinations and delusions (the Auditory Hallucination Rating Scale, AHRS; and the Delusions Rating Scale, DRS; Haddock et al., 1997). Thirteen dimensions of auditory hallucinations (frequency, duration, amount of distress, intensity of distress, location, conviction of beliefs regarding origin, disruption, controllability, loudness, amount of negative content, degree of negative content, number, form) and six dimensions of delusions (amount of preoccupation, duration of preoccupation, amount of distress, intensity of distress, conviction, disruption) are elicited and rated by an interviewer on a five-point scale which has specified anchor points. These instruments can be used at the beginning, during and following treatment to track changes over time and to assess specific changes in individual dimensions.

Assessment of Motivation

Persistent hallucinations and delusions are frequently distressing and patients' motivation to complete a course of therapy might well be related to the need to obtain psychological relief. Therapeutic engagement may not be straightforward, however; patients may have competing motivations which may undermine good outcomes. Attitudes to symptoms may be mixed in terms of their perceived disadvantages as well as benefits which the clinician may not be party to initially. There is some evidence that psychiatric inpatients who report that their voices are associated with advantages, even if distress is also experienced, are more likely to continue hallucinating post-treatment (Miller, O'Connor & DiPasquale, 1993).

Attitudes may not be static and assessment procedures which enable patients to discuss openly the merits and demerits of their psychotic experiences, may be crucial in establishing therapeutic alliances. The practice of "motivational interviewing" described for the treatment of alcohol-dependent individuals (Miller, 1983; Miller & Rollnick, 1991) may have some relevance to patients with persistent psychotic symptoms. Simple assessment methods, however, may be sufficient in many cases (e.g. asking patients to complete a checklist of pros and cons) as long as patients are clear that the therapist expects to hear both sides of their story.

A related issue is to do with patients' expectations about the consequences of symptom loss or change. An initial motivational analysis might suggest that the patient clearly favours symptom change, but there may well be as yet undisclosed fears. Again, merely asking the patient to systematically outline the imagined effects of reduced symptomatology, including any deleterious ones, is advisable. A common fear is that once the symptom is absent or less problematic, the State's financial support of the individual will cease; once this belief is elicited it is usually relatively simple to dispel. Similarly, some patients believe that their guarantee of continued psychiatric support from hospital and community teams is contingent on the presence of distressing symptoms.

A case example may illustrate the value of considering motivational factors during assessment:

> A 27 year-old man with a 5-year history of persistent auditory hallucinations and a number of delusional beliefs requested assistance with his distress about one delusional system in particular. He was convinced that a miniature video camera had been surgically implanted in his left eye by supreme beings, during a brief period of unconsciousness a number of years previously. He believed that the camera was connected to an electrode at the back of his head, which controlled some of his bodily functions and also transmitted the pictures from the camera to millions of homes around Europe via a satellite system. He was unclear as to why the supreme beings had arranged this. When asked to specify the imagined benefits of having the electronic apparatus either surgically or psychologically removed (he preferred the latter option when the choice was put to him), he believed that his other symptoms, including his voices, would vanish, as would his problems with concentration, anxiety and low mood. He did not spontaneously offer any possible negative effects. The patient was encouraged to consider some. It was put to him that if his account were true then he was a well-known international figure and that he might well feel pretty ordinary without any role to play in life; he agreed that this was a risk. A more serious risk of symptom loss was then disclosed; he recalled that the electronic equipment had been inserted when he had in fact died, as opposed to just being unconscious, which might mean that symptom change might lead to his death. The therapist accepted his concern and agreed that the risk of the patient dying would interfere with the therapeutic process. The patient then became aware of the humorous angle to this discussion and having been assisted with identifying a number of cognitive maintaining factors he arrived at his second therapy session, having lost the delusional system in question.

Motivational considerations extend beyond the initial assessment and therapists might be alerted to these issues either during stuck points in therapy or after a dramatic therapeutic change. At every stage, it is recommended that the clinician hypothesizes about the implications of symptom change and checks these out with the patient; the therapist may need to be proactive in this regard as the patient may not necessarily have access to these cognitions. One implication worth examining, particularly for patients who have been chronically preoccupied with their psychotic experiences, is the realization that their beliefs are without foundation and thus there may well be a sense of "lost years" (Chadwick, 1992; Yusupoff & Tarrier, 1996). Under such circumstances the patient may have a strong investment in maintaining symptoms, unless this issue is sensitively addressed and the psychotic experiences are re-legitimized, for example by pointing out that the patient had little choice about the factors which resulted in the onset of the psychosis in the first place.

Another implication of symptom change for patients is the removal of the perceived block to social and occupational success—"If only I didn't experience X, then I would be able to . . . . . .". Cognitive-behavioural procedures are potentially powerful and the patient may realize early on that symptom change is indeed obtainable; this may be threatening if the individual perceives that he no longer has a reason to "fail". Perhaps there may be a more fundamental fear of success associated with the person's self-concept (Epstein, 1987) or purely because of the perceived demands of having to learn new skills and adjusting to a new role. Identification of these beliefs gives the therapist some options; assisting the patient to reconsider therapeutic goals, in a more "realistic" light, is often reassuring rather than demoralizing. An alternative is to advise the patient to obtain goals in a paced, step-wise fashion and to talk of plateaux of functioning rather than an all-or-nothing view of therapeutic outcome. Judicious use of paradox may also have some merit; in one case the patient was reassured to hear that he ought to remain "just a little suspicious" by the end of therapy when he expressed a powerful fear of losing his chronic persecutory delusion.

Cognitive-behavioural Interviewing

General aspects of cognitive-behavioural assessment are described elsewhere (e.g. Kirk, 1989), however, a number of (semi-)structured interviews such as the Maudsley Assessment of Delusions Schedule (MADS; Buchanan et al., 1993) and the Antecedent and Coping Interview (ACI; Tarrier, 1992) are specifically designed for psychotic symptoms. The MADS is a structured interview, designed to elicit information from the patient about his/her delusions in terms of a large number of different variables, e.g. the behaviours associated with the belief, the evidence the patient holds which contributes to their conviction, etc. The ACI is a structured interview which is designed to elicit symptom determinants (e.g. environmental and cognitive antecedents), emotional reactions and the consequences associated with any psychotic symptom, as well as coping strategy use. For example, a delusional belief may be maintained by particular behavioural sequences. A paranoid patient may selectively attend to evidence consistent with his belief that his local community is against him and his actions (following activation of his belief) may be consistent with his delusional inferences, such that he rapidly escapes to safety. A detailed analysis of this is essential to provide the basis for intervention, which might involve helping the patient to re-consider his interpretation of events and to experiment with alternative non-persecutory responses.

A good experiential account of the symptom is often a prerequisite to effective clinical work with this population and the general recommendation is that the more detailed the picture the more finely-tuned the intervention. Obtaining detailed phenomenological accounts may also enhance rapport. Anecdotally, some patients report that despite numerous previous psychiatric interviews, much of their subjective experience of symptoms had remained unexpressed until the time of their first cognitive-behavioural interview, and clinical changes are not uncommon during the initial assessment, prior to formal psychological intervention. If there is a sufficiently good rapport, and the patient is forthcoming about his experiences, then a more in depth enquiry may be possible, perhaps to go well beyond the detail normally disclosed at interview. The purpose of this is to engage the patient in an unrehearsed dialogue about aspects of the experience which may never have been thought about fully or consciously processed. Such a procedure may elucidate the "rules" which govern what is and what is not possible in the patient's alternative reality and which behaviours the patient is free to engage in (Brehm, 1976), in order to construct suitable reality-testing tasks. Also, obtaining such a detailed account is more likely to generate inconsistencies which can be discussed when jointly reviewing the evidence which support particular beliefs.

With regard to delusions, examples might include asking about persecutors' motivations for undermining the patient, what their goal is, their source of funding (if they belong to an organization), and mechanisms by which unusual things are achieved (e.g. "How does the electrode in the back of your head control your actions? . . . How is it connected to the neurones? . . . How did they manage that?"). In summary, "facts" as stated by the patient are not taken at face value by the interviewer, who, by his questioning, models a logical, normalizing thinking style, which potentially disrupts the fixed, habitual thinking processes which maintain symptoms (Kanfer & Schefft, 1988). In one case, the patient had always assumed that the named individual who had possessed him over the years, who made him commit indecent assaults, was motivated only to inflict suffering and undermine the patient. Careful questioning resulted in the patient continuing to believe that he was possessed, but that the possessor was also a victim, controlled by more powerful forces. Although subtle, this kind of shift potentially alters the personal meaning of the psychotic experience, such that distress is diminished and a new plateau of social functioning might then become available to the patient.

This style of interviewing needs to be conducted with sensitivity, as patients' responses vary considerably; some may respond with expressions of surprise or relief and it may well be relevant to introduce humour, to facilitate the therapeutic process. Others, however, who have mixed motivations with regard to changing symptoms, may use the process to strengthen their convictions by either expanding the rules to accommodate the inconsistent information (Brett-Jones, Garety & Helmsley, 1987), by minimizing the relevance of the inconsistencies or by incorporating the therapist in the delusional system, thereby invalidating his contribution, by classing his intentions as malevolent. As soon as this becomes apparent, the interviewer has the option of shifting style, by discussing things more generally, by spending some time on clarifying competing motivations or to continue with other aspects of the interview, e.g. eliciting symptom determinants.

In vivo Assessments

Assessment of psychotic symptoms is potentially enhanced by the activation of the target experiences during a session, once it is established that the patient will be able to tolerate the resultant emotional reaction. This can be achieved by asking the individual to bring on the voices (Fowler & Morley, 1989) or by the use of guided imagery to recall the last major episode of symptom occurrence that week. "Hot" cognitions are more readily accessible under such circumstances as are subtle physiological, behavioural and affective changes. Aspects of the emotional reaction will be publicly observable, such as postural changes, breathing rate and facial pallor, which can be fed back to the patient and accompanying cognitions checked out. Another form of *in vivo* assessment is to accompany the patient to situations outside the clinic or home where symptoms are typically experienced. An example is the patient who was unable to recall accurately his reaction to his delusional beliefs and voices during sessions, but when walking along a busy road with his therapist was able to provide an on-going detailed report of triggers, interpretation of events and emotional response.

Continued Assessment and Monitoring during Treatment

Instruments such as the AHRS and the DRS can be used throughout treatment to monitor the effects of therapy over time. In addition, more detailed rating scales and monitoring tools can be used to test hypotheses generated by a formulation. For example, early assessment may reveal that an individual's voices are associated with certain types of interactions or events. It may be useful for the patient to concurrently monitor these situations by recording the antecedent and consequent events surrounding symptom occurrence, in terms of behavioural, physiological and cognitive factors. This may help the therapist and patient to identify the types of thoughts and emotions which are contributing to symptom occurrence or worsening and provide an ideal place for intervention. A patient who expresses persecutory beliefs may utilize this type of monitoring tool to keep an objective record of the evidence collected during times when the belief is held most strongly, to be reviewed during therapy sessions.

Monitoring tools may also play an important part of intervention in itself, with patients experiencing auditory hallucinations; it has been noted that concurrent monitoring may reduce symptom severity (Reybee & Kinch, 1973). Focusing on voices may reduce the distress associated with them (i.e. serve a desensitization purpose) and allow patients to explore the content, their respondent thoughts and feelings as well as extract the underlying beliefs which may be contributing to distress (Chadwick & Birchwood, 1996). Strategies which can aid this type of focusing approach have been described in detail by Haddock and colleagues (Bentall, Haddock & Slade, 1994; Haddock, Bentall & Slade, 1996) and are summarized in the treatment section below.

Informal and Observational Assessment

Effective clinical decisions are unlikely to be based solely on the formal assessment procedures described so far. Sensitive adjustment of the content, structure and timing of sessions may be required for this clinical population. Some psychotic patients' tolerance of stress may be well below that of traditional cognitive-behaviour therapy cases, and premature withdrawal from therapy may be the result. Psychotic symptom content may also directly influence the quality of the patient–therapist relationship. It is not uncommon for patients' voices to comment on the therapist, sometimes disparagingly, and persecutory belief systems potentially may extend to include the therapist. It is for these reasons that changes in state during sessions (speech becoming more incoherent, sleepiness, agitation, guardedness, etc.) should be monitored closely and reasons for the change established and acted upon. A decision may be reached with the patient that session length should be kept short or that discussion of sensitive topics is delayed, or that training is offered to manage uncomfortable states during sessions. Missed appointments also might alert the therapist to hypothesize about the possible relationship of these to session content and/or style.

FORMULATIONS AND SYMPTOM MEANING

A psychological formulation represents a conceptual re-organization of the information obtained during assessment to account for symptom onset and maintenance. The degree of complexity of the formulation varies in each case, as does the timing of its communication. A formulation typically includes an individualized cognitive-behavioural model of maintenance, i.e. an account of the way symptom-related beliefs and physiological, behavioural and affective changes are all reciprocally related such that the experience persists.

Symptom explanations might be offered which are consistent with the patient's historical narrative, which might incorporate early experiences, previous relationship conflicts, psychological traumas, bereavement and significant life events around the time of the first onset of psychosis. Romme & Escher (1996), for example, describe a number of case studies where patients were assisted to relate their hallucinatory content to conflicts in their lives and, by resolving these, reductions in the severity of the voices were noted. Selecting personally significant rationalizations potentially expands the subjective meaning of psychotic phenomena for the patient. There may well be therapeutic advantages for acknowledging the content-relevance of symptoms in this way by linking them with key aspects of the patient's life history. The more powerful the link for the patient, the greater the likelihood of therapeutic collaboration; delusional conviction may be such that shifting away from his view of reality will be too threatening unless legitimized in some personally meaningful way.

In one case, a woman, in her 30s, with a diagnosis of schizo-affective disorder, described a distressing belief that she was somehow responsible for catastrophic world events, including wars and serious climatic changes; this central belief appeared to be related to a series of secondary beliefs, including some persecutory concerns. The core theme of the patient's "hyper-responsibility" was used as a template to examine her personal history. There were indeed a series of relevant past events. The patient's mother had died when she was only 5 years old and she was sexually molested by a stranger some months later; high conviction ratings were obtained for the belief that she might have been responsible for both events. Furthermore, there had been a further attempt at molestation in her teens; she recalled disclosing this event to her husband some years later and within just 1 day of telling him, the institution where she was at risk was featured in national news programmes, because of a serious event. She attributed the "trouble" to herself and the disclosure. The symbolic links between the current symptom and the significant previous life events were included in the formulation. Initially, therapeutic work involved a re-appraisal of her sense of responsibility for the earlier events, using traditional cognitive therapy techniques, which resulted in rapid reductions in psychotic symptomatology.

A formulation might also include what the symptom represents to the individual in terms of expected future functioning and quality of life compared to prior life goals. For example, the symptom may be associated with fleeting imagery of the individual finally being overcome by the symptom some time in the future and, by implication, life having become intolerable. Including this additional type of symptom meaning might suggest some useful cognitive-behavioural interventions, including imagery re-training.

TREATMENT OPTIONS WITH HALLUCINATIONS AND DELUSIONS

Sophisticated cognitive-behavioural treatment protocols for the psychoses are now available (Perris, 1989; Kingdon & Turkington, 1994; Fowler, Garety & Kuipers, 1995; Chadwick, Birchwood & Trower, 1996), so what follows represents a brief account of some therapeutic options and draws attention to two approaches in particular, "focusing" and "coping strategy enhancement".

Once a formulation is made explicit (with the proviso that further adjustments might be required), this then serves as a structure for therapist and patient to negotiate the direction of the intervention, guided by the specific problems highlighted in the formulation. Treatment might address the symptom itself, its behavioural, physiological or cognitive correlates, or might target non-psychotic clinical states, which may be contributing to a worsening of the psychotic symptoms.

Focusing vs. Distraction for Voices

With respect to auditory hallucinations, there are two main themes regarding the orientation of the intervention: (a) techniques designed to assist the individual to distract himself more from the voices; or (b) techniques which help the individual to focus more on the voices. Distraction techniques have been shown to be effective for some individuals, although their benefit is usually restricted to the time of use and generalization to other situations is minimal (Margo, Hemsley & Slade, 1981; Nelson, Thrasher & Barnes, 1991). These approaches have been hypothesized to be successful at reducing hallucinatory activity because of their ability to block subvocalization, a phenomenon which has been linked to the occurrence of auditory hallucinations. The most commonly used distraction techniques involve listening to music or speech through a personal stereo, subvocal counting, reading out loud, humming, or even gargling. Obviously, there are social constraints attached to using these, as they prevent the individual from engaging in simultaneous social interaction. Generalization is also a problem, although this can be improved by helping the individual to integrate the techniques optimally into their everyday lives and to help them to select techniques which they find easiest to implement. For example, a form of activity scheduling (Haddock, Bentall & Slade, 1996) has been shown to optimize the use of distraction techniques (and may be especially useful if the individual also has problems with motivation or depression). It involves careful monitoring of everyday or planned activities to discover those distraction approaches which have most impact on the severity of voices. Using data from this monitoring exercise, an activity schedule can be devised which incorporates activities shown to have most impact on the severity of the individual's voices, and limits those activities which contribute to an increase in severity of voices. The individual can rate the effectiveness of each technique or activity when it is implemented so that the schedule can become fine-tuned to optimize those techniques which have been most effective.

Cognitive approaches such as focusing (Bentall, Haddock & Slade, 1994), attempt to explore the content of an individual's voices and relate this to his/her beliefs about the voices and themselves. The approach combines concurrent monitoring with a desensitization programme, and involves the patient gradually exposing him/herself to increasingly emotive aspects of the voices. Initially, the patient is asked to monitor concurrently only the physical characteristics of his/her voices. When the patient feels comfortable with this, he/she can then move on to monitoring the content and his/her resultant thoughts, and to focus on the beliefs which are activated as a result of the voices. Verbal and written shadowing (immediately repeating the content out loud, or writing down the content) can aid focusing on voice content and thoughts and help the patient to discuss his/her beliefs. This type of focusing may in itself reduce voice severity by helping the individual to identify correctly the nature of the symptom and discuss its content, whilst keeping arousal to a minimum. The content often relates to meaningful personal issues, and may be linked to an individual's current worries or past memories. Careful questioning may reveal common themes in the patient's voice content, cognitions and beliefs about him/herself and the world. Chadwick & Birchwood (1996) have shown that the distress associated with voices is related to the beliefs the individual has about them, rather than the actual content of the voices. The beliefs can be explored, modified and lead to a reinterpretation of the voices; this in turn may reduce anxiety and the frequency and intrusiveness of the voice. Negative automatic thoughts which accompany voices, as well as the voices themselves, can be monitored, and individuals helped to evaluate these and practise alternative responses.

Delusions

Cognitive-behavioural interventions may well be applied successfully to delusional beliefs; such belief modification and reality testing procedures have been described by Watts, Powell & Austin (1973) and recently refined by Chadwick & Lowe (1990). The approach involved careful identification of the individual characteristics of the beliefs and questioning to elicit the evidence underlying the belief. This might then lead to the therapist and patient collaborating to devise a series of behavioural experiments to test out the evidential basis of the belief. This type of approach has been used successfully to reduce belief conviction and associated distress.

As with any symptom-based intervention, whether it is to modify a delusional belief or modify the beliefs surrounding a voice, careful assessment of the function that the belief is serving for the individual is essential before embarking on methods which may result in a reduction in the occurrence of the symptom. This might be obviously relevant where the belief is grandiose in nature, but other symptoms may well have some self-esteem preserving function (Chadwick, Birchwood & Trower, 1996). Alternative interventions might then be planned or the patient adequately prepared in order that symptomatic changes can be tolerated and benefited from.

Coping Strategy Enhancement (CSE)

A pragmatic therapeutic approach for both persistent hallucinations and delusions is that of coping strategy training. This is based on the finding that patients often develop coping behaviours naturalistically to manage their symptoms or the resultant distress (Falloon & Talbot, 1981; Breier & Strauss, 1983; Cohen & Berk, 1985; Tarrier, 1987; Carr, 1988). Patients might then benefit from a systematic training to enhance partially effective strategies, to promote more consistent usage or to add new techniques to existing repertoires. In Tarrier's (1987) sample of symptomatic subjects, coping strategies elicited were classified into four modalities, which included cognitive (e.g. distraction or self-instruction), behavioural (e.g. increasing social or independent activities), physiological (e.g. relaxation) or sensory (e.g. playing recorded music).

A previous randomized controlled trial (Tarrier et al., 1993a) gives some empirical support for this approach and there was some indication that successful reductions in symptomatology were related to patients having developed more effective coping repertoires (Tarrier et al., 1993b). A second, larger-scale investigation has now been completed and patients are currently being followed up 1 and 2 years post-treatment. Initial results clearly favour the CSE approach over and above routine psychiatric care and supportive counselling conditions.

In practice, the CSE approach requires careful cognitive-behavioural analyses of symptoms, and interventions vary considerably; in some cases belief modification procedures might be the preferred option and a coping model may not be relevant if the initial intervention results in such symptomatic improvement that the individual no longer feels that coping is necessary. The current CSE approach is described more fully elsewhere (Yusupoff & Tarrier, 1996), although formulation-driven therapeutic options tend to fall into the following categories:

1. *Training the patient to manipulate symptom determinants.* In one case, a patient's persecutory concerns were activated when listening to exciting radio programmes, which then resulted in an increase in physiological arousal, which cognitively was associated with his history of violent offenses and his fear of losing control again. The patient was then encouraged to experiment with modulating his physiological state by changing the radio volume or by listening to exciting sports matches half-way through.

2. *Training to change the components of the emotional reaction to voices or delusional belief activation.* This option is relevant where the patients' habitual response to psychotic phenomena are hypothesized maintaining factors. The patient is then guided to experiment with exaggerating or reducing his/her typical cognitive, physiological or behavioural responses, monitoring the effects and then practising *in vivo* for homework.

3. *Eliminating maladaptive coping strategies.* This is especially relevant where the patient's existing strategy is effective in the short term, but may contribute to longer-term symptom maintenance. A maladaptive strategy is defined as one which is used by the individual as a protection from imminent danger or unacceptable personal risk. Thus, the symptom is resisted at all costs and therefore the patient is never in a position to assess the true risk. A patient who always shouts back at his voices, as if their accusations and directives have true potential to threaten his psychological integrity or cause real physical harm, may experience temporary relief by counter-attacking in this way, especially if his response is associated with the symptom stopping. The therapeutic intervention might parallel the cognitive-behavioural treatment of obsessive-compulsive patients (Salkovskis, 1989) and involve training-up of

non-responding to facilitate reality-testing. Such training might best be conducted using symptom simulation role plays, as described in four below.

4. *Provision of realistic training conditions.*   This refers to strategies aimed to maximize skills acquisition by either generating the symptom *in vivo* (Fowler & Morley, 1989), e.g. instructing patients "to bring on voices", or by simulating aspects of the psychotic experience. Symptom-simulation role play may be a powerful therapeutic technique (Tarrier et al., 1990). This involves the therapist role-playing voices, making sure all relevant symptom parameters (e.g. voice content, tone, loudness, etc.) are accurately represented. Role play reversal is important with this technique, so that therapists can display their patient's standard emotional response and model the alternative more effective possibilities. Another version is for the patient to record onto tape his/ her own imitations of his/her voices, which are then played back to elicit hot cognitions, train up rational responding or to use the recording for graded exposure trials.

    Delusional beliefs also may be amenable to such methods, once the patient has acquired the requisite skills to evaluate his/her beliefs. The patient's deliberations may be tried out as the therapist plays devil's advocate by presenting evidence in favour of the delusional interpretation of events, and then reversing roles. Actual delusional scenarios might also be re-enacted. An example here is the man whose persecutory concerns were triggered when seeing orange-coloured street lights, the purple after-image representing for him his first psychotic episode induced by LSD, 20 years previously. His automatic thoughts typically related to the idea that he was relapsing, and would end up being moved from the community to an institution, being separated from his wife and losing the respect of his family. His coping repertoire included some weak rational responses. Symptom simulation involved darkening the room (to re-create his fear of twilight/street lights) and the therapist recited out aloud the patient's typical thoughts, whilst the patient had the opportunity to practise and overlearn more effective rational responses. Such dramatic methods are far more memorable to patients than the usual therapy conversations, and generalization of skills to the non-clinic environment more likely.

5. *Multiple strategy sequences.*   Single coping strategies may be ineffective and the patient may benefit from training to combine individual strategies in a given sequence. Self-instructional training might be used to organize effective coping behaviours. Symptom simulations would be used, perhaps carefully grading symptom intensity, to establish that the individual has indeed acquired the skill, and can apply his strategy sequences under trying conditions. Written instructions or flashcards might also be of value, either during training or when practising "in the field".

6. *Using symptom recurrence to cue adaptive changes in interpersonal behaviour and lifestyle.*   This option typically becomes available only towards the end of therapy, and is usually relevant for patients who have achieved a fairly sophisticated psychological model of their psychotic symptoms. An example

here would be the woman who was taught to use the start of any period of symptom exacerbation as a cue to asking herself a series of self-help questions; these were based on the insights concerning early maladaptive schemas (Young, 1994), previously gained during therapy. The questions included: (a) is there an emotional need I am not acknowledging (or am I putting everyone else first)?; (b) what relevant adjustment can I make to my life-style at the moment?; (c) is there something which I would like to say to someone, but have not taken the risk so far?; (d) what specific requests can I make of someone or others to change this situation?; (e) am I still using my specific symptom coping strategies which I learnt during therapy?

CONCLUDING REMARKS

It would be difficult to dispute now, in the late 1990s, that a breakthrough in the psychological treatment of psychotic symptoms had not been made (e.g. see Haddock & Slade, 1996). The principles and practices of cognitively-orientated psychotherapies do seem to be applicable to psychosis. The foregoing sections above illustrate how our traditional methods may be adapted to voices and delusional beliefs. Psychosis is a new territory for the cognitive-behaviour therapist and the landscape is unlikely to be uniform. If we were to remain dominated by the conceptual framework generated by psychiatric diagnostic systems then we might continue to be misled that one patient with voices and delusions was aetiologically equivalent to the next. The availability of clear psychological treatment protocols for psychotic symptoms is a welcome development, and the opportunity now exists for an increasingly refined appreciation of the human diversity represented in the population of patients we call "psychotic".

REFERENCES

Barrowclough, C. & Tarrier, N. (1992). *Families of Schizophrenic Patients: Cognitive-behavioural Interventions*. London: Chapman & Hall.

Bentall, R.P., Haddock, G. & Slade, P.D. (1994). Psychological treatment for auditory hallucinations: from theory to therapy. *Behavior Therapy*, **25**, 51–66.

Birchwood, M., Hallett, S. & Preston, M. (1988). *Schizophrenia: An Integrated Approach to Research and Treatment.* London: Longman.

Birchwood, M. (1996). Early intervention in psychotic relapse: cognitive approaches to detection and management. In G. Haddock & P.D. Slade (eds), *Cognitive Behavioural Interventions for Psychotic Disorders.* London: Routledge.

Brehm, S.S. (1976). *The Application of Social Psychology to Clinical Practice.* New York: Wiley.

Brett-Jones, J., Garety, P.A. & Hemsley, D.R. (1987). Measuring delusional experiences: a method and its application. *British Journal of Clinical Psychology*, **26**, 257–265.

Breier, A. & Strauss, J.S. (1983). Self-control in psychotic disorders. *Archives of General Psychiatry*, **40**, 1141–1145.

Buchanan, A., Reed, A., Wessely, S., Garety, P., Taylor, P., Grubin, D. & Dunn, G. (1993). Acting on delusions. 2: The phenomenological correlates of acting on delusions. *British Journal of Psychiatry*, **163**, 77–81.

Carr, V. (1988). Patients' techniques for coping with schizophrenia: an exploratory study. *British Journal of Medical Psychology*, **61**, 339–352.

Chadwick, P. (1992). *Borderline: a psychological Study of Paranoia and Delusional Thinking*. London: Routledge.

Chadwick, P. & Birchwood, M. (1996). Cognitive behaviour therapy with voices. In G. Haddock & P.D. Slade (eds), *Cognitive Behavioural Interventions for Psychotic Disorders*. London: Routledge.

Chadwick, P., Birchwood, M. & Trower, P. (1996). *Cognitive Therapy for Delusions, Voices and Paranoia*. London: Wiley.

Chadwick, P. & Lowe, C.F. (1990). The measurement and modification of delusional beliefs. *Journal of Consulting and Clinical Psychology*, **58**, 225–232.

Cohen, C.I. & Berk, B.S. (1985). Personal coping styles of schizophrenic outpatients. *Hospital and Community Medicine*, **36**, 407–410.

Curson, D.A., Patel, M. & Liddle, P.F. (1988). Psychiatric morbidity of a long-stay hospital population with chronic schizophrenia and implications for future community care. *British Medical Journal*, **297**, 819–822.

Epstein, S. (1987). Implications of cognitive self-theory for psychopathology and psychotherapy. In N. Cheshire & H. Thomae (eds), *Self, Symptoms and Psychotherapy*. New York: Wiley.

Falloon, I.R.H. & Talbot, R.E. (1981). Persistent auditory hallucinations: coping mechanisms and implications for management. *Psychological Medicine*, **11**, 329–339.

Fowler, D. & Morley, S. (1989). The cognitive-behavioural treatment of hallucinations and delusions: a preliminary study. *Behavioural Psychotherapy*, **17**, 267–282.

Fowler, D., Garety, P. & Kuipers, E. (1995). *Cognitive Behaviour Therapy for Psychosis: Theory and practice*. Chichester: Wiley.

Garety, P. (1992). The assessment of psychotic symptoms. In M. Birchwood & N. Tarrier (eds), *Innovation in the Management of Schizophrenia*. Chichester: Wiley.

Haddock, G., Bentall, R.P. & Slade, P.D. (1996). Focusing vs. distraction in the psychological treatment of auditory hallucinations. In G. Haddock & P.D. Slade (eds), *Cognitive-behavioural Interventions with Psychotic Disorders*. London: Routledge.

Haddock G. & Slade, D. (eds) (1996). *Cognitive-behavioural Interventions with Psychotic Disorders*. London: Routledge.

Haddock, G., McCarron, J., Tarrier, N. & Faragher, E.B. (1997, Submitted). The auditory hallucinations and delusions rating scales.

Kanfer, F.H. & Schefft, B.K. (1988). *Guiding the Process of Therapeutic Change*. Research Press.

Kingdon, D.G. & Turkington, D. (1994). *Cognitive-behavioural Therapy of Schizophrenia*. Hove: Erlbaum.

Kirk, J. (1989). Cognitive-behavioural assessment. In K. Hawton, P.M. Salkovskis, J. Kirk & D.M. Clark (eds), *Cognitive Behaviour Therapy for Psychiatric Problems*. Oxford: Oxford Medical Publications, pp. 315–338.

Lancashire, S., Haddock, G., Tarrier, N., Baguley, I., Butterworth, A.C. & Brooker, C. (1997). Effects of training in psychosocial interventions for community psychiatric nurses in England. *Psychiatric Services*, **48**, 39–46.

Margo, A., Hemsley, D.R. & Slade, P.D. (1981). The effects of varying auditory input on schizophrenic hallucinations. *British Journal of Psychiatry*, **139**, 122–127.

Miller, L.J., O'Connor, E. & DiPasquale, T. (1993). Patients' attitudes toward hallucinations. *American Journal of Psychiatry*, **150**, 584–588.

Miller, W.R. (1983). Motivational interviewing with problem drinkers. *Behavioural Psychotherapy*, **11**, 147–162.

Miller, W.R. & Rollnick, S. (eds) (1991). *Motivational Interviewing: Preparing People to Change Addictive Behaviour*. New York: Guilford.

Nelson, H.E., Thrasher, S. & Barnes, T.R.E. (1991). Practical ways of alleviating auditory hallucinations. *British Medical Journal*, **302**, 327.

Perris, C. (1989). *Cognitive Therapy with Schizophrenic Patients*. London: Cassell.

Reybee, J. & Kinch, B. (1973). Treatment of auditory hallucinations using focusing. Unpublished study.

Romme, M. & Escher, S. (1996). Empowering people who hear voices. In G. Haddock & P.D. Slade (eds), *Cognitive-behavioural Interventions with Psychotic Disorders*. London: Routledge.

Salkovskis, P.M. (1989). Obsessions and compulsions. In J. Scott, J.M.G. Williams & A.T. Beck (eds), *Cognitive Therapy in Clinical Practice: an Illustrative Casebook*. London: Routledge.

Sellwood, W., Haddock, G., Tarrier, N. & Yusupoff, L. (1994). Advances in the psychological management of psychotic symptoms. *International Review of Psychiatry*, **6**, 210–215.

Tarrier, N. (1987). An investigation of residual psychotic symptoms in discharged schizophrenic patients. *British Journal of Clinical Psychology*, **26**, 141–143.

Tarrier, N. (1992). Management and modification of residual psychotic symptoms. In M. Birchwood & N. Tarrier (eds), *Innovations in the Psychological Management of Schizophrenia*. Chichester: Wiley.

Tarrier, N., Beckett, R., Harwood, S., Baker, A., Yusupoff, L. & Ugarteburu, I. (1993a). A trail of two cognitive-behavioural methods of treating drug-resistant residual psychotic symptoms in schizophrenic patients. I. Outcome. *British Journal of Psychiatry*, **162**, 524–532.

Tarrier, N., Sharpe, L., Beckett, R., Harwood, S., Baker, A. & Yusupoff, L. (1993b). A trial of two cognitive-behavioural methods of treating drug-resistant residual psychotic symptoms in schizophrenic patients. II. Treatment-specific changes in coping and problem-solving skills. *Social Psychiatry & Psychiatric Epidemiology*, **28**, 5–10.

Tarrier, N., Harwood, S., Yusupoff, L., Beckett, R. & Baker, A. (1990). Coping strategy enhancement (CSE): a method of treating residual schizophrenic symptoms. *Behavioural Psychotherapy*, **18**, 283–293.

Watts, F.N., Powell, E.G. & Austin, S.V. (1973). The modification of abnormal beliefs. *British Journal of Medical Psychology*, **46**, 359–363.

Wing, J.E., Cooper, J. & Sartorius, N. (1974). *The Description and Classification of Psychiatric Symptoms: an Instruction Manual for the PSE and Catego System*. London: Cambridge University Press.

Young, J.E. (1994). *Cognitive Therapy for Personality Disorders: A Schema-focused Approach*. Satasota, FL: Professional Resource Press.

Yusupoff, L. & Tarrier, N. (1996). Coping strategy enhancement for persistent hallucinations and delusions. In G. Haddock & P. Slade (eds), *Cognitive Behavioural Interventions with Psychotic Disorders*. London: Routledge.

Chapter 8

Understanding the Inexplicable: an Individually Formulated Cognitive Approach to Delusional Beliefs

David Fowler*
Health Policy and Practice Unit, University of East Anglia, Norwich, UK
Phillippa Garety
Department of Clinical Psychology, UDMS, St Thomas' Hospital, London, UK
and
Elizabeth Kuipers
Department of Psychology, Institute of Psychiatry, London, UK

INTRODUCTION

The idea of treating delusional beliefs with psychological therapy is still a relatively radical perspective to those who have been trained within Western psychiatry. Many still believe that delusional beliefs cannot be understood from a psychological perspective and that they derive directly from some type of organic disorder. This perspective suggests that attempting to make sense of delusional beliefs in collaboration with the patient, and attempting to alter beliefs by discus-

* Author for correspondence.

Cognitive Psychotherapy of Psychotic and Personality Disorders: Handbook of Theory and Practice.
Edited by C. Perris and P.D. McGorry.
© 1998 John Wiley & Sons Ltd.

sion, would be futile. However, there is a strong case for adopting a more flexible view about the degree to which delusional beliefs can be understood, and the degree which they may be amenable to psychological intervention. In this chapter we start by arguing the case for psychological intervention. We briefly discuss the psychiatric perspective on delusions and review recent observations about delusions which suggest a need for a new approach to thinking in this area. Next we highlight the key clinical problems associated with delusions and outline the basis of a psychological formulation of delusions. We describe what we believe are the four key factors responsible for change in delusional thinking by cognitive therapy. These include the establishment of a working therapeutic relationship with the deluded client, collaborative discussion of a shared formulation of the client's beliefs, cognitive restructuring of specific delusional interpretations, and work on negative evaluations of self and others. Finally we describe three cases to illustrate the process of cognitive therapy for delusions.

THE PSYCHIATRIC PERSPECTIVE ON DELUSIONS

Psychiatric classification schemes define delusions as fixed, immutable and inexplicable beliefs, which are held with strong conviction and resistant to argument (APA, 1994); and psychiatric theory suggests that such beliefs derive directly from biological disturbance (Kraepelin, 1919/1971; Berrios, 1991). It is therefore worthwhile reviewing the reasons for the development of classification schemes and the scientific status of the psychiatric hypothesis concerning delusions.

The classification of delusions as a set of inexplicable (or non-understandable) anomalies of speech derive from the observations of a school of German psychopathologists, of whom Jaspers (1963) and Schneider (1959) have been the most influential. Careful and detailed observations of people with psychotic disorders highlighted the presence of a set of experiences which, it was suggested, could not be understood in terms of either the patient's life history or current circumstances. These symptoms included delusions of thought insertion (patients believing that thoughts were coming into their mind from an outside source); delusions of control (patients believing that their actions were being controlled by an outside force) and delusions of reference (in which the actions and gestures of strangers are believed to have special relevance for the individual). Frith (1992) notes that, although being classified as delusions, such symptoms have the characteristics of anomalous experiences. The theoretical suggestion was that as such experiences could not be understood, they were more likely to be primary symptoms which derive from organic rather than psychological causes. This is not an unreasonable hypothesis, given the nature of the phenomena: however, it is a hypothesis and one which is still as yet unproven, although recent cognitive neuropsychological theories provide an innovative new perspective on these ideas and are consistent with experimental findings (see Frith, 1992; Hemsley, 1993).

The term "delusion" does not only refer to delusional experiences—indeed it more commonly refers to the more systematized delusional beliefs of paranoia, guilt and grandiosity. It is of interest that Kraepelin 1919/1971, Jaspers (1963) and Bleuler (1950) all explicitly suggested that such systematized beliefs were secondary symptoms which often appeared to derive from the attempt of the individual to make sense of his/her life and experiences. Early psychiatric theorists then suggested there were two types of delusion: secondary delusions which were explicable and which seemed to arise from similar processes to normal beliefs; and primary delusions which did not. This theoretical position about the nature of delusions has led to attempts to search for classifications and definitions which seek to draw a neat boundary between primary and secondary symptoms. Unfortunately, the phenomenon of delusions has resisted such simple categorization. Psychological and social theorists have suggested that difficulties in categorization of delusions according to their content may be due to the fact that it is impossible to be wholly objective about a criterion of understandability (Maher, 1988). They argue that judgements about whether beliefs are understandable or not depend on one's social perspective. What some may view as bizarre and inexplicable, others may view as metaphors, or judge as meaningful. Laing (1960) provided a seminal illustration of this in describing an alternative perspective on the meaning of the delusions of one of Kraepelin's cases. Criticisms of the classification of delusions does not invalidate enquiry into disease models. It does suggest that opinions about the inexplicable, fixed and unchangeable nature of delusions should not be accepted *a priori*.

In summary, from a scientific perspective the degree to which different types of delusional phenomena are open to modification is an open question requiring investigation. Acceptance of the opinion that all delusions are fixed, immutable, inexplicable and resistant to psychological therapy has probably hindered understanding of these important symptoms. Furthermore, even if one accepts the possibility that some delusional experiences may arise from biological causes (and there appears some support for this hypothesis) there is a broad consensus, which includes Kraepelin amongst many other theorists, that many systematized paranoid and other delusions can be understood in terms of psychological processes. It is the possibility of understanding delusions that opens the way toward psychological therapy.

EMPIRICAL EVIDENCE ABOUT DELUSIONS

What do careful observations and experiments reveal about the nature of delusions? Careful longitudinal studies suggest that delusional beliefs wax and wane naturally over time and lie on a continuum with eccentric and overvalued ideas (Strauss, 1969, Chapman & Chapman, 1988). Furthermore different dimensions of delusional experience, i.e. conviction (the degree of belief), fixity (the degree to which alternative perspectives may be considered) and preoccupation (the degree to which someone thinks about a belief) may vary independently over time (Garety, 1985; Brett Jones, Garety & Hemsley, 1987). Close examination of content of delusional ideas suggests that there are broad similarities between the content of beliefs, widely held in the population (beliefs in hypnosis, telepathic contact, in the spiritual influences of malevolent forces) and the delusional beliefs of psychiatric patients (for review see Kingdon and Turkington, 1994). Other studies have reported that large subgroups of the non-psychiatric population report anomalies of experience with high frequency (such schizotypal experiences include *deja vu*, visual and auditory hallucinations and odd perceptions) (Chapman & Chapman, 1988; Romme & Escher, 1989). Related studies have shown that individuals who report such experiences show biases in cognitive processing similar to those of people who have had frank psychotic experiences (Claridge, 1985). There is a strong case for arguing that there may be a continuity between normal beliefs and delusions, and that strongly held delusional ideas may be points on a continuum with overvalued ideas and normal beliefs.

Most pertinent to the idea that delusions can be modified is direct evidence from intervention studies. There are now several well conducted trials which demonstrate that delusions may be subject to modification. These include single case experiments (Fowler & Morley, 1989; Chadwick & Lowe, 1990; Lowe & Chadwick, 1990; Fowler, 1992) and controlled trials (Garety et al., 1994; Kuipers et al., 1997, 1998). These studies demonstrate that psychological therapy can have an impact on patients' self-report ratings of conviction in delusional beliefs and on symptom rating scales. Although these studies provide a clear justification for attempting to intervene with deluded patients, our understanding of the impact of psychological therapy on delusions is still in its infancy. We need to undertake further research to examine carefully what can be achieved by intervention and to explore the limits of understanding and therapy.

THE CLINICAL EXPERIENCE OF WORKING WITH THE DELUDED PATIENT

While the evidence above points to an exciting time for those therapists interested in delusions, it is important to be clear what has been achieved. From a clinical perspective it is all too easy to read a study reporting significant changes and draw an implication that all delusions are easy to modify by psychological therapy. This is not so. Not all patients change. There are dropouts and treatment failures to consider. Furthermore, successful interventions are more often characterized by amelioration rather than cure. Changes are often achieved only after several sessions of psychological intervention over a period of months. We cannot yet reliably predict success, although there are indications that those individuals who respond are most likely to be those who have a cognitive flexibility about their delusions in the initial stages (Sharp et al., 1996; Garety et al., 1997). We also have a long way to go in seeking answers to exactly who changes and why. Successful therapy with people with delusions requires commitment and persistence and the ability to face challenges within sessions, such as dealing with paranoid thoughts about the therapist, which are rarely encountered when working with other types of clients.

The initial experience of working with deluded patients, especially to those who have had little experience of people with psychosis, can sometimes lead therapists to recall vividly the psychiatric perspective that delusions are bizarre, inexplicable, fixed and unmodifiable. Typically the experience is of meeting people who hold strange ideas that are patently and obviously incorrect. Despite this, such people may hold on to their ideas tenaciously and may be unwilling to consider alternatives. Initial analysis of the content of the beliefs can often be highly confusing and it is rare that in the first session one is able to grasp how such beliefs could have any sensible connection with any real events in the person's life. People with delusions can also sometimes present as threatening to others, and can be difficult to engage in a therapeutic relationship. Perhaps most importantly, premature attempts to provide some reality test almost always lead to rejection. It is rare indeed that a deluded patient, on being directly told he/she has a mental illness or that his/her beliefs are probably incorrect, will start to alter his/her perspective and develop insight.

Some case examples may illustrate typical experiences in the first session:

> *Andrew* presented in a fearful state, saying, "Everyone is against me, I see evil around in people everywhere, they look at me. People are influencing me. I can feel it in my body, they are changing the sensations in my stomach". Andrew looked suspiciously at the therapist; it was a major task to keep him calm. The challenge in the initial stages of working with Andrew was simply to contain his severe anxiety and prevent spread of fear to the therapist.

> *Jane* presented as a friendly person. However, within a few minutes of meeting her, she started to talk about how her name was Anne, how she was the daughter of the Queen, and how Prince Philip had made her pregnant and that her children had been hidden away. She also said that she was rich and was prevented from taking up her money. She described seeing people around her conspiring against her. During the session she handed the therapist a sheet of paper which was a letter she was writing to the Queen. No one sentence made sense—instead it was a list of jumbled ideas and sentences. Jane seemed to think that it was a reasonable piece of prose. The challenge initially was to make sense of all these bizarre statements and to try to get a grip on what any threads of meaning in what Jane was saying. It was hard at times not to wonder whether it was of any use at all to sit and listen to what appeared to be a stream of nonsense.

> *Paul* presented very angrily. He said "There is a plot against me. People are plotting and making things up at work. I have been to the police and doctor. I don't need therapy, I just need this to stop. Why are they doing this to me? What are you going to do about it? The therapist felt attacked and put on the spot.

During initial contacts with deluded patients it is rare that delusions make sense. It is very easy for the therapist to give up and fall back on the idea that delusions are inexplicable and not amenable to psychological intervention. Our experience in the clinic suggests, however, that often what initially seems very unclear eventually, after detailed collaborative inquiry, starts to make sense if one looks at events from the patient's perspective. Therapists working in this area need to be able flexibly to apply quite sophisticated therapeutic skills associated with containing anxiety and building therapeutic relationships. They also need a theoretical framework to help them make sense of some of the odd beliefs and behaviour they are faced with. In the next section we outline the basic features of a psychological formulation of delusions.

OUTLINE OF A PSYCHOLOGICAL FORMULATION OF DELUSIONS

In a recent review we described how various different types of psychological processes may contribute to the formation and maintenance of delusions and other psychotic symptoms (Fowler, Garety & Kuipers, 1995). The literature offers several competing theories to explain delusions. Theorists such as Hemsley (1993) and Frith (1992) have suggested that some of the primary anomalies of experience associated with delusions may result from cognitive-neuropsychological deficits and probably some type of brain dysfunction. Others have suggested that delusions may arise as explanations of anomalous experiences (Maher, 1988) or may be viewed as unsignalled metaphors (Bannister, 1983). Cameron (1959) suggested that delusions may arise as a result of social learning and Southard (1912) that they may be viewed as misinterpretation of bodily experiences. Still other theorists suggest that paranoid and grandiose delusions may arise as a reaction to emotional threats and may serve a function of defending against threats to self-esteem (Freud, 1915; Bentall, Kinderman & Kaney, 1994). We have argued that there is no single pathway to delusions instead different delusional beliefs may arise from different processes (Garety & Hemsley, 1994). In some cases careful assessment may suggest that one type of process may satisfactorily explain the presence of delusion, but in most cases delusions appear to be the product or final common pathway of several interacting processes and biological, psychological and social processes may be involved.

In clinical practice, a useful starting point is that the beliefs of people with delusions may be seen to arise from the way people have attempted to make sense of their lives and experiences. Like us, people with delusions are subject to many biases in their judgement and reasoning which can lead to maintaining strong beliefs with little rational support. Unlike many of us, some people with delusions may have episodes of having unusual anomalies of experience. Such experiences often feel of strong personal significance for the individual and typically demand explanation and suggest to the person that the world has changed, not themselves. Even these gross initial assumptions provide a basis for understanding. The clinical implication is for therapists armed with psychological understanding about the way both normal and abnormal biases can influence thinking and belief formation to look for sense where often to the lay person there only appears nonsense. Our clinical experience suggests that, in almost all cases, some sense can emerge over time if one is prepared to carefully examine the individual's history and experiences. In therapy, taking a developmental or historical approach to delusions is a useful starting point. This involves starting from the point when the patient first formed the belief and then carefully and systematically examining the basis of evidence which supports it.

FROM THEORY TO THERAPY

Psychological understanding can then open the way for therapeutic intervention for delusions. A psychological perspective suggests that delusional beliefs can be located in the context of an individual's life experience. Cognitive theory aids the understanding of anomalies of experience and misinterpretations as products of cognitive processes. The use of such perspectives in therapy opens the way to making sense of delusions in collaboration with patients and assisting patients to adopt new perspectives of their problems which are less distressing and more likely to lead to adaptive ways of managing the person's life difficulties. It implies an approach to cognitive therapy which is based on understanding and making sense of delusions, and which is collaborative rather than argumentative. We are still unclear about exactly what is necessary or sufficient to achieve belief change but we think it likely that the success of cognitive-behavioural therapy is rooted in its ability to provide understanding, and its focus on the following four factors.

Building and Maintaining a Therapeutic Empathic Relationship

The clinical effectiveness of any therapy depends largely on the capacity of the patient to engage in a therapeutic alliance and the skill of the therapist in fostering this. This is true of any therapy but is particularly important in therapy with people with psychosis. Some people with psychosis, although not all, can be difficult to engage in working alliances. We believe the key to addressing these problems is establishing a relationship in which the client feels understood and involved. Achieving this can be problematic, in particular with paranoid clients, where frequently there is a mismatch between the therapist' and the patient's view of their predicaments. The solution involves a flexible approach to therapy which is sensitive to changes in the client's mental state and interpretations, and starts by working from the client's perspective. The starting point is a neutral stance on the part of the therapist in which the therapist carefully listens and attempts to tease out the particular life circumstances and current events that provided the context for the formation and maintenance of the belief. However, there may be a need for the therapist to monitor for signs of paranoid interpretations occurring about the therapists in the sessions and to attempt to manage such problems in a way that provides the opportunity for reality testing, but is least threatening for the person.

Collaboratively Making Sense of Delusions in the Context of the Person's Life History and Individual Vulnerabilities

We noted above that cognitive therapy is often characterized as attempting to modify beliefs. This may imply to some that therapy consists in arguing with patients to attempt to remove beliefs. In fact the direction of therapy may be opposite. We suggest that effective cognitive therapy consists of constructing a new model of events with the patient. An important aspect of our approach to cognitive-behavioural therapy is that it focuses on developing the patients' understanding of their beliefs, and places the development of their beliefs in the context of their individual life histories and vulnerabilities. Work in this area builds on the work above. Careful listening often leads to a detailed analysis of the events leading up to the formation of beliefs, including precipitating events and current and past psychotic experiences. Experience in conducting structured cognitive-behavioural assessments can assist therapists significantly in this process. There are two aspects to conducting a cognitive-behavioural assessment of delusions. First, it is important to take a good history to identify possible vulnerability factors, triggering events and psychotic experiences in previous episodes. Detailed examination of the circumstances surrounding the initial emergence of delusional ideas is particularly important. Such assessment often clarifies the evidence supporting the belief and the context in which it emerged. Second, it is important to analyse in detail current experiences and delusional ideas and their precipitants and consequences. Such assessment involves a collaborative process focused on making sense of the development of the delusional beliefs from the patient's perspective. There are many different developmental histories leading to delusions but typically, people remembering the onset of delusional ideas report a period of crisis accompanied by dysphoria which then worsens and may be accompanied by a variety of psychotic experiences. The experience of puzzlement and emotional upheaval is very common. The therapist tries to identify a thread of meaning which links the individual's life history, the specific context in which the delusion was formed, the emotional upheaval and the themes of the delusions. These ideas are shared and discussed with the patient.

Compensating for Cognitive Biases and Distortions in Interpreting Events

Probably the most familiar set of cognitive therapy techniques are those associated with reinterpreting appraisals of specific events; these are the cognitive restructuring methods used in cognitive therapy of depression (Beck et al., 1979). Delusions are often maintained by misinterpreting specific events on a day-to-day basis. There are various reasons why this may be so. Simply having a belief system can lead to a tendency to seek confirmatory evidence for the belief, i.e. interpreting events in terms of the belief rather than looking for alternative interpretations. In some cases misinterpretations may be facilitated by a tendency to have reasoning biases, such as a "jumping to conclusions" reasoning style (Garety & Hemsley, 1994). Delusional interpretations of events may also be facilitated by emotional processing biases, as suggested by Bentall, Kinderman & Kaney (1994). Compensating for such misinterpretations is therefore an important aspect of cognitive therapy. Typically this involves identifying specific delusional interpretations of events, then seeking alternative explanations. The techniques used are often direct applications of rational restructuring techniques widely described for other types of psychiatric problem (see Hawton et al., 1989).

Addressing Negative Self-evaluations

Negative self-evaluations (e.g. believing that the self is evil or worthless) are closely intertwined with delusional beliefs and may underpin aspects of the emotional reaction to delusions. Negative self-evaluations may also be closely linked to the content of hallucinations. It is often possible to make meaningful links between the content of delusions and hallucinations and the characteristics of threatening and traumatic events in the patient's life. Addressing negative self-evaluations where present is highly important. Typically, the first stage is to identify the content of the negative self-evaluation. Following this, the therapist aims to assist the patient to review and re-evaluate such evaluations according to a realistic appraisal of the patient's life circumstances. In individuals who have had severe life difficulties, the re-appraisal may be in the form of assisting the patient to view his/her life challenges as one of struggling with adversity or even "self as hero in the face of tragedy", rather than an appraisal as a "worthless victim" or "bad person in need of punishment". Josephs (1988) has described a somewhat similar approach from a psychoanalytic perspective in a paper entitled "Witness to Tragedy".

In the following we describe three cases to provide a more detailed illustration of therapeutic processes in cognitive-behavioural therapy for delusions.

Case 1—Andrew: Seeking to Be Good in the Face of Evil

Background.   Andrew was referred because he felt he was being influenced by evil forces. He had had these beliefs for 12 years since a breakdown while at university. Since then he had been gradually rehabilitated after attending a day centre for several years. Currently, he described experiencing feelings of paranoia nearly all the time at work and at home, and interpreted many day-to-day events as evidence for a conspiracy against him. He worked but was under threat of redundancy because of a poor absence record. He lived with his partner, another service user.

Therapy processes in the early sessions.   Andrew was very frightened in the initial sessions. In describing his beliefs he sweated, shook and looked about him fearfully. After observing this the therapist made a empathic comment about Andrew's looking fearful. He gently encouraged Andrew to describe his fears about being in the session. Eventually, Andrew disclosed that he was worried about talking to the therapist because discussing his problems with someone else might make it worse for Andrew, and may even be dangerous for the therapist. This issue became a focus for further discussion. The therapist first empathized with Andrew's dilemma and explicitly recognized his fears. He then took a neutral stance, not putting pressure on Andrew to discuss what he did not wish to, but encouraging him to examine the advantages and disadvantages of talking about his fears in therapy. Andrew described that he believed that evil people were capable of harming both Andrew and the therapist and that they were telling him to stop talking. The therapist noted the difficulty of the dilemma that the conspirators were placing Andrew in. The therapist also noted that it was difficult to make sense of the problem without knowing exactly what the problem was. He also said he was willing to take a risk about listening to Andrew's problems so that he could find out. The therapist suggested that they could proceed slowly and carefully, and monitor any threats together and stop if the threats got worse. The decision about whether to disclose and in what detail was left with Andrew. This discussion appeared to give some comfort to Andrew and he began to talk. The therapist used a open listening approach, clarifying and reflecting Andrew's perspective and attempting to gain a coherent story of events relating to the belief from its initial emergence. During this period Andrew was frequently asked if he felt threatened about what he was talking about. The advantages and disadvantages of disclosing were reviewed regularly. Andrew continued to worry about the possible threat associated with disclosing. These fears appeared to be outweighed by his feelings of relief about talking to someone who was willing to listen in detail to his view of events. Because of Andrew's fears the therapist arranged for Andrew to make telephone contact with his office if he felt threatened between sessions. Only once did Andrew make use of this, and a brief phone call helped to contain his worries on that occasion.

Factors involved in the development of the delusion. Andrew identified various factors involved in development of his beliefs concerning an evil threat. In describing his childhood he said he had always felt an outsider in the family and at school, although he had had a close relationship with his elder brother who was protective of him. The feelings of being different and an outsider continued when he went to University. At university he began to have doubts about his sexual orientation. Triggering events leading to his first experience of psychosis included sexual and relationship problems with a Nigerian girlfriend and his brother dying. He also started to take amphetamines. During this period he remembered what he described as "feeling panicky about myself" and strong feelings of anxiety. He then experienced a full-blown psychotic episode and was compulsorily admitted to hospital. In this episode he experienced delusions of reference, critical and abusive voices, and feelings of thought interference and of being controlled by external forces. The initial experience of this was terror and perplexity but he described gradually becoming more and more convinced that these experiences were being caused by a conspiracy of evil against him. He believed that this was due to the influence of his girlfriend, who he decided was a witch doctor, and his mother, who was involved in the plot via telepathy. The task for Andrew also became clear at this time; he had to struggle to stay good to survive. He described this as a personal battle with evil. Andrew had continued to believe this since that time. He also regularly experienced other mild psychotic symptoms and had had two severe psychotic episodes.

Fostering an alternative perspective. During Andrew's description of the emergence of the belief the therapist had focused on empathizing with Andrew's difficult struggle to make sense of his experiences and to cope with the stresses he felt. After four sessions the therapist gently started to offer an alternative explanation for Andrew's predicament. Drawing from what Andrew had described, the therapist suggested that there seemed to be two aspects to Andrew's vulnerability to developing psychotic problems. First, these was his emotional vulnerability: what Andrew described as his feelings of being unsure about himself and sensitive. This sensitivity appeared to be compounded by his doubts about his sexuality. Second, the therapist highlighted what was probably a biological vulnerability which had been either triggered by, or exacerbated by, drug abuse and particularly amphetamine abuse. After outlining these factors in general terms the therapist asked whether Andrew might find it useful to elaborate further how factors such as these might make sense of Andrew's experiences. Andrew agreed to further discussion but still described himself as doubtful about whether this could really account for his troubles.

In later sessions attention was focused on attempting to explain the nature of some of the psychotic experiences Andrew had found so personally significant during his initial psychotic episode. Andrew continually returned to argument that the only possible explanation of such experiences was in terms of evil forces and telepathic contact. The therapist empathized with Andrew's perspective, and in particular suggested that it was both logical and rational for Andrew to have made sense of his experience in this way. He said explicitly that almost anyone confronted with similar experiences would probably view things in a similar manner. However, alongside this, the therapist continued to suggest that there might be another way of looking at these events and asked if Andrew would be interested in discussing this.

They decided to have some sessions focused on attempting to explain psychotic experiences. Initially the therapist asked if Andrew thought anyone else had such experiences. The therapist then briefly outlined accounts of other cases who had reported experiences similar to Andrew. On stimulating Andrew's interest, text-book accounts of such experiences and case accounts, including autobiographical accounts, were given to Andrew to read in sessions. Discussion focused on the implications of other people having such experiences, and did Andrew think that these other people were being persecuted by evil? Andrew was interested in these discussions but still returned to his beliefs when pressed. The next focus for discussion concerned how changes in the way mind works could lead to such experiences. First, the therapist provided a general outline of a cognitive model of how the mind forms conscious experiences, highlighting that events are shaped by interpretation. Following Frith (1992), a model of how some of the symptoms such as delusions of control and thought interference could occur was also outlined. Much of the discussion about these issues took the form of thought experiment, asking Andrew to think what his experiences might be if some of the basic cognitive processes underlying perception became altered. One of the key aspects of these discussions was repeatedly emphasizing that although the experiences may have arisen from a breakdown in certain fundamental cognitive processes, there was nothing to tell Andrew that this had happened. His experience would have been that the world had changed, not himself, and that the ideas he created at the time had made the best sense possible of the information available to him. Andrew was intrigued and interested in these ideas. It was emphasized that he had made sense of things in order to cope, to make sense of his life and to keep himself together, but what had been initially helpful was now negative and that it might now be the time to leave that behind and look for a new way of looking at his life. It was put to Andrew that perhaps it would be useful to explore which explanation was most useful for him, the evil conspiracy or making misinterpretations.

Raising the possibility of another general explanation for Andrew's experiences led to a period in which the main focus was reviewing specific delusional experiences and events, both those in the past and those occurring in the present. Andrew interpreted many day-to-day events in terms of his belief. Cognitive-behavioural analysis of his paranoid thoughts revealed that typical triggers included minor ambiguities or social misunderstanding, gossip at work, and particularly conversations with his mother. Close analysis of such situations revealed that most such situations would normally be accompanied by slight aversive feelings, i.e. critical comments by his mother, adverse comments by work colleagues, ambiguous situations. Andrew was asked to monitor such thinking on a daily basis and to bring back events and specific thoughts for discussion in therapy. These were re-evaluated in much the similar way as to negative automatic thoughts in cognitive therapy of depression. The way in which Andrew's beliefs were being maintained by a self-fulfilling prophecy of expectation and evidence was highlighted.

Andrew gradually became more aware of the factors responsible for the development of what he came to call his "myth" of an evil conspiracy. He became able to explicitly outline the advantages and disadvantages of continuing with the myth. Among the advantages were the excitement and esteem associated with being involved in a personal struggle with evil, as opposed to living a more mundane life. In the early stages the therapist suggested that he need not give it all up at once and could always return to the belief, but that it might be useful to occasionally peek from the shield and entertain and alternative perspective. Gradually Andrew became more able to identify alternatives to his delusional thinking himself, and his preoccupation and conviction in beliefs about the evil conspiracy weakened considerably. In the later stages, therapy addressed Andrew's emotional vulnerability. It appeared that delusional thinking often occurred in situations when Andrew was feeling threatened or vulnerable. An example of this was Andrew's tendency to feel threatened in situations and therefore deluded in work and family situations when he felt the centre of attention. Analysis of this issue revealed that Andrew felt threatened because, although a lively and gregarious man, he thought it was wrong and was therefore scared to act confidently and make jokes. Discussion of this issue focused on the validity of his belief that it is always wrong and inappropriate to be a warm, open and even loud person. Therapy involved 22 sessions over 9 months. At the end of therapy Andrew was no longer deluded, although still occasionally having mild schizotypal experiences, including murmuring voices on a regular basis. He remained free from delusions at 18-month and 5-year follow-up.

Case 2—Jane: the Confused Royal Relative

Background.   Jane was a lady who lived alone in a rented council flat. She attended day care regularly and had social contacts with friends and relatives. She looked after herself well and was co-operative with health professionals. She was friendly and keen to talk with a therapist. She described herself as feeling quite down and had moderate to severe depression. Despite her obvious willingness to engage in a therapeutic alliance and ease of ability to disclose her delusional ideas the first session with Jane, as described above, was very confusing. In discussing her problems Jane's talk showed signs of thought disorder. She described mixed delusional ideas which had no coherence. It seemed to the therapist that confusion was a central part of Jane's problem. She appeared not to be able to make sense of the sequence of events in her life, or of many of the events themselves. She appeared driven to make sense of her problems to the degree that she had tried to write down an account (which was hopelessly garbled). Possibly, she was trying to compensate for the confusion about her past but, in the process of attempting to make sense of her life, was becoming more and more confused. Some regular themes recurred: that Jane believed she had a relationship with the Royal Family; that she thought someone was sexually interfering with her at night; that she thought her neighbours and others were watching her; that she often mistook children she saw in the street for her own children; and that she misidentified strangers as lovers.

At the end of the first session the therapist suggested to Jane that possibly confusion about what had happened to her was a central problem. Given this possibility, the most useful place to start would be to try to make sense of her past and attempt to get a clear picture of what events had occurred, and how her beliefs about these had developed over time. Jane agreed that this would be useful, and also agreed to the therapist talking to other professionals who had known Jane and having a detailed look at her notes. Using various sources of information, the therapist then proceeded in a structural way to try to piece together Jane's history and the development of her delusions over time. In sessions this involved carefully listening in a highly structured way, taking careful notes, and continually returning to events and their time patterns and pointing out gaps and inconsistencies in time and place. What coherence emerged was fed back to Jane and integrated with information from other professionals and the notes.

Over time, by working collaboratively, a more coherent shared picture of Jane's life and beliefs emerged. Jane had had a very difficult life. She had grown up in a troubled family. Her mother had had psychotic episodes. Her father had left the family when Jane was an infant. Her stepfather had been violent and abusive to her mother and had repeatedly threatened to leave. Jane had felt frightened of her stepfather most of her childhood and described being beaten and sexually molested by him from the age of 11. She had been unhappy at school and regularly teased. The problems continued into early adulthood. She married at age 17 and went to live in London. At 18 she had a child, and a second a year later. She then separated from her husband as he was violent and alcoholic and returned her home town. She became severely depressed and was admitted to hospital voluntarily after taking an overdose. Soon after that, her husband returned and began threatening her and the children. The children were subsequently taken into care after reports of sexual abuse of the children. The process of care proceedings was instigated by Jane herself. She then left her husband. Soon after this, she had her first psychotic episode, which was preceded by a period of severe depression and another suicide attempt. In the psychotic episode she experienced voices and persecutory ideas that people wanted to kill her. She also started to have grandiose feelings that she was the Princess of Wales. These partially resolved, then recurred in a subsequent admission 6 months later. Since that time she had continually presented with delusional ideas and mixed psychotic symptoms, occasionally being readmitted because of pestering strangers but most of the time managing independently at home.

Jane continually held a number of delusional beliefs. She had ideas that she was the daughter of the Queen and also that her father was named Chris Moore. She referred to these people as her "real family" and said that the Queen had had a blood test proving that she was Jane's mother. She talked about her memories of being brought up by the Queen, and said that there was a large amount of money being held in trust for her. Jane said that she took part in royal engagements as part of her "second life", a life that ran alongside her day-to-day life and took place at night when she was asleep. She believed that when she went to sleep she became blind and "anything could happen". She also said that she had been and was still being sexually abused. She believed that she had been abused by the Queen and was currently being abused by her brother and father. This abuse took place at night and she could tell who the abuser was. She had put a chain on her door to stop people getting in at night, but said that sometimes they came down from the loft to abuse her. She said she had 13 children and that the children were proof of the abuse, as there was no other way they could have been conceived.

Offering an alternative perspective. The first strategy involved gently empathizing with what the examination of Jane's life troubles appeared to have indicated. The therapist therefore gently redescribed what he appeared to have discovered. The therapist highlighted Jane's struggle to develop and escape from her family, then her struggle to be a mother in tremendously adverse circumstances and her coping with the loss of her children and her struggles with psychotic breakdown. The therapist highlighted her struggle against what appeared to be tremendous adversity. At this Jane became tearful and wept. She described severe feelings of loss and longing for her children as the most difficult to cope with. Jane described feelings of considerable relief from such discussions and afterwards became more able to discuss events a little more coherently. Typically, the therapist emphasized the positive aspects of Jane's struggle to be a caring and good person despite her difficulties. This was not difficult, as she was clearly a caring and kind individual and the social worker involved in the care proceedings had highlighted the fact that it was at Jane's initiative to protect the children that she had let them go.

The life review sessions described above provided a basis from which to review the delusional ideas. Regarding the ideas about her relationship with the Royal Family, Jane described periods of time spent actively fantasizing as she sat watching television and was aware that she sometimes got lost in these fantasies. The therapist suggested the possibility that one of her problems was distinguishing between reality and fantasy. Jane accepted this as a possibility but was ambivalent about giving the beliefs up. She had thought about applying to see her birth certificate to prove that she was entitled to trust money, and some time was spent discussing what the implications of seeing different names on this might be. The therapist noted that he thought it most probable that it would say her name rather a person connected to the Royal Family. While these issues were occasionally discussed in therapy at Jane's instigation, the beliefs in connection with the Royal Family were not a central target for intervention. These aspects of Jane's delusions appeared to be a harmless extension of fantasy and appeared to be a pleasurable escape. It was left with Jane whether she wanted to proceed with getting her birth certificate. She talked about it occasionally but never proceeded with it. The therapist did not push.

What was clearly distressing for Jane was the thought that she was being abused at night. She described members of her family coming in at night and abusing her. These were experiences involving both tactile hallucinations and voices. In reviewing her history it was clear that she had been the subject of violent sexual assault in both childhood and as an adult. Given these indications and the fact that they occurred as she was just going off to sleep, the therapist asked Jane if it was possible that she might be confusing dreams and memories with reality. The aim in offering this perspective was to help Jane to distance herself from the distressing experiences which she believed to be current. There was no attempt to recall specific events in the past. Indeed, given Jane's obvious problems in recall of autobiographical events, attempting to establish firmly the presence or absence of specific events would have been impossible. Instead, the aim was to help her to relabel her experiences as images which most likely reflected and elaborated on events which had happened in the past and which were no longer current. When Jane discussed her abuse, the therapist empathized with these events as another of the dreadful challenges she had faced in her life and suggested that it was unsurprising that she was still tormented by images of this. The focus was on helping her manage the images and to put such events behind her and build a future.

The general formulation that Jane's problems reflected problems in overcoming severe and repeated trauma and a confusions between memories, fantasies and reality also helped make sense of day-to-day experiences. For example, periods when she was overwhelmed with grief and the loss of her children would often be accompanied by her seeing children of her own family in the town, and feelings of guilt would be associated with ideas of reference which had the content that everyone knew Jane was bad. Discussion focused on reinterpreting such ideas when they occurred and relabelling her experiences in terms of the model. It was suggested that the confusion between memory, fantasy and reality constituted as aspect of Jane's illness, which probably partially came from biological causes. The idea the Jane had an illness was readily accepted by her. Acceptance of a partial sick role appeared to help decrease some of her painful feelings of blame for her life difficulties.

What appeared to be the most useful aspects of therapy in this case was the sessions spent helping Jane to come to terms with her life difficulties. Jane showed considerable courage in confronting her past. A feature of this case was Jane's quiet dignity in facing her problems and her ability to face her emotional reactions and the depth of her grief when this was brought out. This is not always the case—some patients cannot face such emotion. It is necessary in such cases to understand and accept this. The outcome assessments at the end of therapy showed that Jane continued to have psychotic experiences but was less distressed by them. She was less preoccupied by, and less convinced of, her delusional beliefs. This was maintained at follow-up.

Case 3—Paul: the Angry Victim of a Set-up

Background.   Paul described that, years previously, he had been set up by the people he worked with. He said they sabotaged his work to make him ill and leave his job. They went to various lengths to sabotage things, including arson and damage, and eventually suggested he was involved with murder. Currently he was continually brooding over these ideas to such a degree that he could think of nothing else. He believed his wife was involved in the conspiracy and was plotting against him; he also described seeing people who he thought were part of the conspiracy following him around. He felt he was being continually watched by people who parked cars outside his house. He believed the police and health professionals were also involved in the conspiracy. As described above, in the initial sessions Paul was very angry. He said he did not want help from a therapist. Instead he believed the only solution was for the Police to arrest the conspirators. The therapist empathized with Paul's feelings of frustration and suggested that perhaps the best place to start was to try to get the full story. Paul remained angry and doubtful about the value of this but agreed to see the therapist again to discuss the background to the set up.

His family practitioner had reported that Paul came from an extremely troubled family of seven brothers. The family were known to social services and he had spent childhood in various foster homes. Paul declined to elaborate on has childhood but would say only that meeting his wife at 17 was the best and only good thing that had ever happened to him, and helped him leave his childhood behind. Careful examination of the events preceding the development of Paul's paranoid ideas suggested that these had begun during a period in which he had had some severe difficulties at work in a factory and had been the subject of cruel practical jokes and bullying. He had continued to work hard during a time in the factory when an industrial dispute had led many of his colleagues to work to rule. He had also refused to join in with petty pilfering, which was rife amongst his colleagues. This had alienated him from his peers. In addition, at this time his relationship with his wife had clearly been very difficult; it later became clear that she had been having an affair. These problems had at first triggered severe anxiety, but he then described having a range of psychotic experiences. In particular he reported looking at certain people at work and seeing their eyes going red and spinning round and glowing. He became more and more suspicious that strange events were happening and began hearing things on the TV and radio as relating to him. Amongst these were a series of murders and sexual assaults in the region. He began to make sense of all these events as part of a general conspiracy against him.

Offering an alternative framework.   The therapist gently suggested that it sounded as though Paul had had a very difficult time at work and that this, combined with problems in his relationship with his wife, must have been almost unbearable.

Paul agreed and this provided an initial basis for developing a shared view about the nature of his problems. Unfortunately, however, Paul was extremely resistant to developing this model any further and, despite accepting the possibility that he had been confused and emotionally upset, showed no sign of accepting the idea that his valid feelings of being threatened may have led him to misperceive a much wider conspiracy.

Paul continued to come for therapy and the main focus was the therapist gently offering alternative interpretations of specific events in the past and present. With Paul this was an effortful and demanding process. His difficulty in accepting a general alternative view made reinterpretation of specific events much more difficult. Sometimes systematic analysis of events would occasionally lead to minor shifts in his interpretation but usually he would return to his beliefs in the following sessions. Paul would also occasionally start to believe that the therapist was involved in the set-up, and secretly liaising with the police. The therapist addressed this issue by making a clear statement along the lines that his role with Paul was as a psychologist attempting to help him with his problems and that he had had no communications with any conspirators or with the police. Paul appeared satisfied with these statements and later said that he had tended to believe them largely because the therapist's non-verbal behaviour appeared to indicate that he was not lying. Independent assessment of Paul's beliefs after 7 months of this type of work indicated little change in his ratings of preoccupation, conviction or distress at his beliefs. However, at follow-up 9 months later he appeared to have given up the beliefs and have developed considerable insight into his problems. A key event seemed to have been that his wife, who had been threatening to leave, had indeed left. This had initially led to a severe depressive reaction, but in recovering from this he had found himself no longer believing in the set-up. Possibly during the therapy he had not been able to face the emotional consequences of the threat of his wife leaving and this had had an effect on the rigidity to which he held his beliefs. The subsequent event of her departure had exposed him to the fear and may have loosened his need for the delusional beliefs. Paul later described that what had been discussed in therapy had helped him considerably in making sense of his life after his wife had left.

CONCLUSION

We are still at an early stage in evaluating cognitive approaches to therapy for delusions. The evidence suggests that some delusions are open to change, while others are not. The reasons for this are still unclear. However, perhaps the most important aspect of the cognitive approach is the implication for understanding patents offered by the cognitive perspective or formulation. Therapy may not work for all, but the perspective suggests that all those working with deluded patients should make an attempt to understand what initially appears inexplicable. In working with patients who have long histories it is often the case that the events which have happened to them, and which triggered and maintained their difficulties, have been lost in the mists of their psychiatric notes. An approach which involves working collaboratively with patients to make sense of their lives and distress is often greatly appreciated. Such an approach can provide the building blocks for a humane approach to working with people with severe psychotic illness.

REFERENCES

American Psychiatric Association (1994). *Diagnostic and Statistical Manual of Psychiatric Disorders*: 4th edn. Washington, DC: American Psychiatric Association.

Bannister, D. (1983). The Psychotic Disguise. In W. Dryden (ed.), *Therapists' Dilemmas*. London: Harper and Row.

Beck, A.T., Rush, A.J., Shaw, B.F. & Emery, G. (1979). *Cognitive Therapy of Depression*. Chichester: Wiley.

Bentall, R.P., Kinderman, P. & Kaney, S. (1994). The self, attributional processes and abnormal beliefs: towards a model of persecutory delusions. *Behaviour Research and Therapy*, **32**, 331–341.

Berrios, G. (1991). Delusions as wrong beliefs: a conceptual history. *British Journal of Psychiatry*, **159**(suppl 14), 6–13.

Bleuler, E. (1950). *Dementia Praecox or the Group of Schizophrenias* (originally published 1911; English Translation; Zinkin, E.). New York: International Universities Press.

Brett-Jones, J., Garety, P. & Hemsley, D. (1987). Measuring delusional experiences: a method and its application. *British Journal of Clinical Psychology*, **26**, 257–265.

Cameron, E. (1959). The paranoid pseudocommunity revisited. *American Journal of Sociology*, **65**, 52–58.

Chadwick, P.D.J. & Lowe, C.F. (1990). Measurement and modification of delusional beliefs. *Journal of Consulting and Clinical Psychology*, **58**, 225–232.

Chapman, L.J. & Chapman, J.P. (1988). The genesis of delusions. In T.F. Oltmanns & B.A. Maher (eds), *Delusional Beliefs*. New York: Wiley, pp. 167–183.

Claridge, G. (1985). *Origins of Mental Illness*. Oxford: Blackwell.

Fowler, D.G. (1992). Cognitive behaviour therapy for psychosis: preliminary studies. In *The Psychotherapy of Schizophrenia: facilitating and obstructive factors*. Oslo: Scandinavian University Press.

Fowler, D.G., Garety, P. & Kuipers, E. (1995). *Cognitive Behaviour Therapy for Psychosis: Theory and Practice*. Chichester: Wiley.

Fowler, D. & Morley S. (1989). The cognitive-behavioural treatment of hallucinations and delusions: a preliminary study. *Behavioural Psychotherapy*, **17**, 267–282.

Freud, S. (1915/1956). A case of paranoia running counter to the psychoanalytic theory of disease. *Collected papers, Vol. II. London: Hogarth*.

Frith, C.D. (1992). *The Cognitive Neuropsychology of Schizophrenia*. Hove: Erlbaum.

Garety, P. (1985). Delusions: problems in definition and measurement. *British Journal of Medical Psychology*, **58**, 25–34.

Garety, P., Fowler, D., Kuipers, E., Freeman, D., Dunn, G., Bebbington, P., Hadley, C. & Jones, S. (1997). London–East Anglia randomised controlled trial of cognitive-behavioural therapy for psychosis II: Predictors of outcome. *British Journal of Psychiatry*, **171**, 420–426.

Garety, P.A., Kuipers, L., Fowler, D., Chamberlain, F. & Dunn, G. (1994). Cognitive-behavioural therapy for drug-resistant psychosis. *British Journal of Medical Psychology*, **67**, 259–271.

Garety, P.A. & Hemsley, D.R. (1994). Delusions: investigations into the psychology of delusional reasoning. Oxford: Oxford University Press.

Hawton, K., Salkovskis, P.M., Kirk, J. & Clark, D.M. (1989). *Cognitive Behaviour Therapy for Psychiatric Problems*. Oxford: Oxford University Press.

Hemsley, D. (1993). Perceptual and cognitive abnormalities as the basis for schizophrenic symptoms. In A.S. David & J. Cutting (eds), *The Neuropsychology of Schizophrenia*. London: Erlbaum.

Jaspers, K. (1963). *General Psychopathology* (trans. J. Hoenig & M.W. Hamilton). Manchester: Manchester University Press.

Josephs, L. (1988).   Witness to tragedy: a self psychological approach to the treatment of schizophrenia. *Bulletin of the Menninger Clinic*, **52**(2 March).

Kingdon, D.G. & Turkington, D. (1994).   *Cognitive Behaviour Therapy of Schizophrenia*. Hove: Erlbaum.

Kraepelin, E. (1919).   *Dementia Praecox and Paraphrenia* (1971). (trans. R.M. Barclay). New York: Robert E. Kreiger Publishing Co., Inc.

Kuipers, E., Garety, P., Fowler, D., Dunn, G., Bebbington, P., Freeman, D. & Hadley, C. (1997).   London–East Anglia randomized controlled trial of cognitive-behavioural therapy for psychosis. 1: Effects of the treatment phase. *British Journal of Psychiatry*, **171**, 319–327.

Kuipers, E., Fowler, D., Garety, P., Dunn, G., Bebbington, P., Freeman, D. & Hadley, C. (1998). London—East Anglia randomized controlled trial of cognitive-behavioural therapy for psychosis. III: Follow up and economic evaluation at 18 months. British Journal of Psychiatry, **173**, 61–68.

Laing, R.D. (1960).   *The Divided Self*. London: Tavistock.

Lowe, C.F. & Chadwick, P.D.J. (1990).   Verbal control of delusions. *Behavior Therapy*, **21**, 461–479.

Romme, M.A.J. & Escher, A.D.M. (1989).   Hearing voices. *Schizophrenia Bulletin*, **15**(2), 209–216.

Schneider, K. (1959).   *Clinical Psychopathology*. New York: Grune & Stratton.

Maher, B.A. (1988).   Anomalous experience and delusional thinking: the logic of explanations. In T.F. Oltmanns & B.A. Maher (eds), *Delusional Beliefs*. New York: Wiley.

Sharp, H.M., Fear, C.F., Williams, J.M.G. et al. (1996).   Delusional phenomenology— dimensions of change. *Behaviour Research and Therapy*, **34**, 123–142.

Southard, E.E. (1912).   On the somatic sources of somatic delusions. *Journal of Abnormal Psychology*, **7**, 326–339.

Strauss, J.S. (1969).   Hallucinations and delusions as points on continua function. *Archives of General Psychiatry*, **21**, 581–586.

Chapter 9

Pathogeny and Therapy

Sandra Sassaroli and Roberto Lorenzini
SITCC, Milan, Italy

WHAT IS A DELUSION?

In everyday usage, the words "madness" and "delusion" are nearly synonymous: it would almost seem that delusion is the most obvious and easily recognizable form of mental pathology, providing a very clear-cut line between what is normal and what is not.

Yet, if we look closer we will see that the dividing line between normality and delusion is not as clear-cut as it might first appear. Not only is there a rather wide strip of no man's land wedged in between the two territories, but there are also many points of mutual infiltration, chinks, breaches and secret passageways connecting the two. Indeed, the task of finding an exact definition for delusion and of distinguishing just how delusion differs from normal thought has always been a key issue in the history of psychopathological inquiry (Kraepelin, 1919; Weitbrecht, 1963).

Many different criteria by which a delusion may be distinguished have been proposed. Taken individually, all these criteria are insufficient and tend to be far too wide in applicability. Considered together, superimposed one upon the other, they furnish too narrow and rigid a definition for delusion.

Jaspers' Criteria

One author who has dedicated much research to the analysis of the experience of delusion is Jaspers. His ideas have influenced the whole of twentieth century psychiatry. He identified three basic characteristics of delusion (Jaspers, 1965):

Cognitive Psychotherapy of Psychotic and Personality Disorders: Handbook of Theory and Practice.
Edited by C. Perris and P.D. McGorry.
© 1998 John Wiley & Sons Ltd.

1. First, *absolute subjective certainty*: the content of the subject's delusion is experienced by him as being absolutely obvious, as if it were a certainty perceived by him beyond all shadow of a doubt. There is no need for proof, as it is absolutely obvious that things are actually as they appear to him.

   This criterion undoubtedly contains some truth, but is too widely applicable. In our daily lives and in our existential striving, we are often guided by absolute certainties that modify our experiences. Convictions such as, "You can't ever trust a man"; "The best make it to the top"; "You can trust your friends"; "Everyone needs to be loved"; "There is a god" all constitute patterns of meaning that organize and give significance to our experiences as we live them and, in turn, are confirmed by those experiences. Therefore, although absolute certainty is one characteristic of delusion, it does not serve to identify delusion alone and thus cannot furnish us with a reliable dividing line.

2. Jaspers' second criterion defines delusion as a *judgement that remains uninfluenced and incorrigible* in the face of all logical experience and confutation.

   Although some of the ideas we listed above belong to "normal" individuals, these convictions share this second characteristic and, like delusion, use nearly every attempted confutation as a further corroboration. Despite this, we find this second criterion to be more significant.

   At this point we would like to say that we believe that the "incorrigibility of delusion" is indeed a peculiarly characteristic feature, offering fertile ground for further reflection. We agree with Popper that knowledge does not grow through a process of induction, but through conjecture and later confutation: a person's theories come to be modified through the process of taking stock of his errors in predicting. Consequently, delusion may be described as a block or a slowing down in the growth of knowledge in a particular area due to a system's failure to take stock of invalidation.

3. Last, Jaspers identifies *absurdity or impossibility of content* as the third characteristic of delusion. Of all the three criteria, this one seems to us the weakest. Children have ideas that are clearly absurd and impossible, but this does not mean that they suffer from delusions. Neither can we consider as delusional those primitive people who adhere to beliefs which seem as bizarre to our eyes as our own beliefs must appear to them.

   Absurdity and impossibility are the criteria most often used by ordinary people to define people suffering from delusion. Delusional people say things that are false, sane people say things that are true. Obviously, this is not always the case. The delusion of a man convinced that his wife is cheating on him does not cease to be a delusion if his wife really begins to betray him. He remains a victim of both delusion and betrayal. Thus an idea may be true in that it may correspond to a situation that really exists in the outer world and yet at the same time constitute a delusion. By contrast, a conviction may be false (e.g. one may be convinced that the sun is shining outdoors, whereas in reality it is night), but this does not necessarily constitute a delusion. It would become a delusion, however, if the window were opened and the subject continued to insist that it was day-time, except that the sun had been momentarily darkened by an eclipse that no one had foreseen or predicted— or worse, that someone had concealed the sun on purpose (Lorenzini & Sassaroli, 1992a,b).

The Incomprehensibility of Delusion

According to Jaspers, primary delusion is characterized by the fact of being incomprehensible. That is to say, it appears as a phenomenon that has no comprehensible psychological link with the subject's history. This does not mean that the subject makes incomprehensible affirmations, for indeed, these could be not only possible but even true. What is incomprehensible is the psychological trajectory that has led the person to formulate these affirmations and the reason that, at a certain point, has compelled him to plunge headlong into delusion.

It must be underlined that Jaspers emphasizes the fact that there is absolutely no connection between the experience of delusion and the subject's psychological history. He is not suggesting that it is difficult for an outside observer to retrace and identify the connecting link, over the course of time, from the earliest stages of delusion and the process of construing it. It is not that the link is difficult or impossible to track down—there simply is no link.

Where a link may be found, we are not dealing with delusion. If it is possible to understand why a person is suffering from a delusion, then his/her state cannot be described as a true delusion. In such cases we are dealing with secondary delusion. Secondary delusion may occur in cases of emotional disturbance, as in the development of personality disorders, or as a response to extremely stressful traumas or to particular external situations.

Thus, Kretschmer's (1949, 1962) enormous and laudable effort to find a psychological continuity in the experience of a few patients suffering from paranoid psychosis, by reconstructing the interior meshwork of meaning upon which their lives were woven, has had a curious, twofold outcome. On the one hand, Kretschmer has linked his name forever with a new diagnostic category: the *delusion of sensitive relationship*; on the other hand, the result of this was that this particular form has been discarded from the category of primary delusion, where Jaspers's dogma of incomprehensibility reigns unchallenged.

It is our belief that the theory of the incomprehensibility of delusion is not only false but harmful, given the paralysing effect it has on therapeutic efforts. These efforts are always focused on the reconstruction of meaning wherever it may seem lost in hopes of opening the narrow and constrained existence of the person suffering from delusion to new meanings, thereby increasing his degree of freedom. Incomprehensibility reinforces the dividing wall between normality and madness, widens the gap, and ends up by corroborating itself (Rossi Monti, 1984).

Paranoia and DSM

In the various editions of DSM, paranoia has assumed the name "delusional disorder", the main characteristics of which are delusions which are not bizarre, last longer than 1 month, and are associated with psychosocial behaviour which is not impaired in any significant way, except for the direct consequences of the delusion itself.

Delusional disorder, which generally first manifests itself in mid- or late adulthood, with a prevalence of 0.03% of the population, is distinguished from schizophrenia and from schizophreniform disorders on the basis of the absence of other symptoms characteristic of schizophrenia in its active phase (auditory or visual hallucinations, bizarre delusions, disorganized speech, grossly disorganized and catatonic behaviour, negative symptoms, impairment of social and work behaviour). The distinction between delusional disorder and Paranoid Personality Disorder lies in the absence of genuine, clearly evident and persistent delusional beliefs in the case of the latter.

Here we refer the reader to the Diagnostic Criteria of the DSM-IV for delusional disorder and for paranoid personality disorder.

These criteria provide the basis for the most widely used diagnostic test, the Structured Clinical Interview for the DSM-III-R (SCID; American Psychiatric Press, 1990). The diagnostic criteria of the DSM-IV for delusional disorder and paranoid personality disorder are as set out in Table 9.1.

PATHOGENY OF DELUSION

Modes of Knowledge Growth

The explicative principle that we will use to describe the behaviour of living beings is that of the maximizing of predictive capacity. That is to say that every cognitive system tends towards, prefers and operates in order to bring about those situations (and those descriptions of self) that are the richest in constructive implications (Kelly, 1955). It may seem that we are undertaking an extremely difficult task in assuming this theoretical perspective in order to explain the behaviour of a person suffering from delusion whose prediction capacities appear to an outside observer to be greatly reduced, but this is not always the case (Winter, 1992; Lorenzini & Sassaroli, 1992a,b).

We agree with Popper that there is only one mode of knowledge growth: the modification of previous knowledge through a process of trial and elimination of errors, a process that is set in motion by an unsolved problem (falsification or

Table 9.1 Diagnostic criteria for E22.0, delusional disorder

A. Non-bizarre delusions (i.e. involving situations that occur in real life, such as being followed, poisoned, infected, loved at a distance, or deceived by spouse or lover, or having a disease) of at least 1 month's duration.

B. Criterion A for schizophrenia has never been met. Note: Tactile and olfactory hallucinations may be present in delusional disorder if they are related to the delusional theme.

C. Apart from the impact of the delusion(s) or its ramifications, functioning is not markedly impaired and behaviour is not obviously odd or bizarre.

D. If mood episodes have occurred concurrently with delusions, their total duration has been brief relative to the duration of the delusional periods.

E. The disturbance is not due to the direct physiological effects of a substance (e.g. a drug of abuse, a medication) or a general medical condition. *Specify type* (the following types are assigned based on the predominant delusional theme):

- Erotomanic type: delusions that another person, usually of higher status, is in love with the individual
- Grandiose type: delusions of inflated worth, power, knowledge, identity or special relationship to a deity or famous person
- Jealous type: delusions that the individual's sexual partner is unfaithful
- Persecutory type: delusions that the person (or someone to whom the person is close) is being malevolently treated in some way
- Somatic type: delusions that the person has some physical defect or general medical condition
- Mixed type: delusions characteristic of more than one of the above types, but no one theme predominates
- Unspecified type

Table 9.2 Diagnostic criteria for F60.0, paranoid personality disorder

A. In a variety of contexts, as indicated by four (or more) or the following:

1. Suspects, without sufficient basis, that others are exploiting, harming or deceiving him/her.
2. Is preoccupied with unjustified doubts about the loyalty or trustworthiness of friends or associates.
3. Is reluctant to confide in others because of unwarranted fear that the information will be used maliciously against him/her.
4. Reads hidden demeaning or threatening meanings into benign remarks or events.
5. Persistently bears grudges, i.e. is unforgiving of insults, injuries or slights.
6. Perceives attacks on his/her character or reputation that are not apparent to others and is quick to react angrily or to counter-attack.
7. Has recurrent suspicions, without justification, regarding fidelity of spouse or sexual partner.

B. Does not occur exclusively during the course of schizophrenia, a mood disorder with psychotic features, or another psychotic disorder, and is not due to the direct physiological effects of a general medical condition.

Note: If criteria are met prior to the onset of schizophrenia, add "premorbid", e.g. "paranoid personality disorder (premorbid)".

invalidation). This is valid in both phylogenesis and ontogenesis (Popper, 1934, 1969, 1972).

In phylogenesis we have, through the succession of generations, a modification of the gene pool over a very long period of time in which the process of trial and new hypotheses is represented by mutation of the species. The elimination of errors occurs by means of natural selection: unsuitable solutions to problems come to be discarded through death or sterility.

In ontogenesis, the process is much more rapid and less cruel. Innate expectations are inscribed in the genetic make-up of an individual, but from the moment of birth onwards these expectations are enriched and modified through error and failure: in order to overcome these failures, new, individual solutions are tried out. The new solutions that do not bring desired results will be abandoned without the individual having to perish with them. In the human being the possibility of changing our ideas has eliminated the need to perish with our mistakes. Those solutions which bring desired results are adopted and thus acquired expectations are produced which will be continually modified whenever they fail to predict reality.

The growth of knowledge occurs through conjecture and confutation. Cognitive systems may differ in the way they deal with the confutation of their hypotheses and in how they choose to deal with invalidations.

In our view (Lorenzini & Sassaroli, 1995) there are four basic ways of dealing with invalidation. They are: (a) active exploration; (b) avoidance; (c) hostility; and (d) immunization. Furthermore, we maintain that these modes are learned in the earliest attachment relationships and that each of the four attachment patterns tends to generate a specific mode of dealing with invalidation. We have found a correspondence between active exploration and secure attachment; between avoidance and insecure ambivalent attachment; between hostility and disorganized attachment; and between immunization and insecure avoidant attachment. Let us briefly examine the peculiarities of these four styles of knowledge:

1. *Active seeking or exploration.* The system seeks continually to widen its boundaries and thus constantly puts its hypotheses to the test of falsification. This is a complex system that can allow itself to meet invalidation head on without risking a collapse of its capacity to predict. The attitude is typically explorative. When confronted with failure, the behaviour that led to failure is abandoned and, at the same time, explorative behaviour is reinforced as a more general class, in that its aim to acquire information has been reached (Bateson, 1984).

   A system that tends towards the explorative attitude knows that it learns from its mistakes even though they may be painful. Thus, whenever it encounters failure, it takes stock of this and tries to learn from the experience. It does not stop exploring.

2. *Avoidance.* The system tries not to encounter invalidations by narrowing its field of exploration. In testing its hypotheses, it limits itself to narrow and

familiar areas, avoiding uncertain situations which are perceived as threatening to the system's stability. The movement here is the opposite of exploration. Being excessively cautions, one attempts to avoid encountering
innovation or unfamiliarity.

Gradually a vicious circle is created: the subject renounces his exploration
while the unknown areas continue to grow. Therefore, his need to withdraw
to more restricted areas increases.

When faced with an unfamiliar stimulus, the choice to explore or avoid it
depends upon the system's evaluation of whether it is able to deal with and
make use of the new stimulus, or whether it runs the risk of succumbing to it.
If the new stimulus is not seen as threatening to the system's stability, the
subject will choose to explore. In contrast, if the system sees itself as incapable of dealing with the new stimulus, which is perceived as destabilizing—
if it is unable to adapt—it will prefer to avoid the stimulus.

3. *Hostility*. This is a way of getting around invalidation. Kelly (1955) describes it as "reproposing a construction of reality that has already been
shown to be erroneous". The subject, when faced with admitting a mistake,
will raise his voice and repeat his point of view with even greater firmness. He
does not avoid confrontation with newness, neither does he attempt to minimize its effects, rather he imposes with force his own explanation of things.
Other people, who are in a social environment, such as the one human beings
are immersed in, represent the source of the invalidation of our ideas; but
in this case, others are no longer seen as interlocutors but as enemies, and
thereby lose their power of invalidation. Others, then, are ignored or ma-
nipulated as if they were inanimate things that must necessarily yield to the
needs of the only existing subject.

The need to impose one's own truth, refusing to listen to the views of
another or forcing him to confirm to one's own truth, is the essence of the
hostile attitude.

4. *Immunization*. This is the strategy through which the system minimizes
invalidation to the point of nullifying the consequences this invalidation has
on its structure. The data provided by reality loses all its meaning, is discredited, underestimated, ignored or reconstructed in such a way as to lose
all power of falsification over the subject's theories. Whereas in both exploration and avoidance, other people and the environment are highly
significative, in the case of immunization an autarchic attitude prevails that
empties the individual's relationship with reality and his relationship with
others of all meaning.

This way of handling invalidation is, as in the case of the avoidant style,
based on the prediction that the system will be unable to adapt to the
invalidation that it has received, and thus must somehow immunize the
effects that the invalidation has had. The two typical modes of immunization
are: (a) the development of *ad hoc* hypotheses; and (b) the emptying of
hypotheses of their empirical content so that they become vague and inconsistent and so that no concrete events able to confute them exist any longer.

When manifest on a modest level, these two modes become stubbornness in the first case, and vagueness and inconsistency in the second. If manifest markedly they become delusion: the defence, at all costs, of one's own way of seeing things, imperviousness to criticism and to all outside events.

Immunization and Insecure Avoidant Attachment

The immunization style of knowledge finds the groundwork for its development within an insecure avoidant attachment relationship. We will briefly discuss a few characteristics of this type of relationship (Ainsworth et al., 1978; Bowlby, 1969, 1973, 1980; Bretherton, 1985): Here we are dealing with the case of children who have often experienced difficulty in having access to the attachment figure and who have gradually learned to do without it, focusing on the world of inanimate things rather than of people. The hub around which their experience of attachment is organized is rejection, and at the same time, the denial of rejection.

Once they have become adults, people with avoidant attachment try to rely on themselves alone, do not recognize any weakness in themselves, and never ask others for help.

In setting a distance between himself and the attachment figure and in not trusting it, the child is not pursuing an aim which is opposite to the general aim of attachment behaviour (which is maintaining closeness to an adult; Crittenden, 1994). Rather, he does this keeping in mind the particular situation in which he must operate and in which he must deal with an attachment figure who does not desire this closeness. Distancing oneself is therefore an adaptive strategy that allows the child to maintain, in any case, a relationship with the attachment figure by learning to rely on himself and by remaining distant. Maximum possible nearness is guaranteed by distance.

It is within this type of relationship that the cognitive style we have defined as "immunization" develops, because consensus with the other person loses its importance in the absence of a relationship. It is as if the other person does not exist and thus the child becomes accustomed to considering his world of meaning autarchically, as if no-one else existed.

In the vast majority of cases, the source of invalidation is other human beings. And if others are not taken into consideration, one immunizes oneself even from the risk of being subjected to invalidation. The immunizing of oneself against invalidation corresponds, on a cognitive level, to "doing it by yourself", which we have described on the behavioural level.

The pathogeny of such a style of knowledge lies in the fact that the attachment figure "does not interact" with the child, does not listen to him, and has no exchange with the child.

This non-interaction or communicative silence can occur in two apparently opposite ways. In the first, the attachment figure is absent, distant, disinterested or objectively unable to interact. In the second case he is, on the contrary, even too present physically speaking, but he does not listen to the child, is too over-bearing, incapable of a true communicative dialogue or of considering the needs of others, usually making his own needs prevail over those of the child.

In both cases, the loss of consensus, which is the evolutionary foundation of the cognitive mechanism of immunization, occurs because of a lack of dialogue with the significant other. In this communicative silence, a cognitive autarchy, a form of egocentrism slowly comes to be established, eventually leading to the experience of delusion.

This communicative block may develop either due to the absence of the attachment figure or to its overbearingness. Both have in common scarce atten-tion for the interlocutor and in both cases communication fails to occur. The subjective worlds of meaning remain isolated from each other and cognitive autarchy is established.

Attachment, Knowledge and Pathology

Thus a weak system, lacking in complexity, poor in alternatives, which must maintain its existing structure by protecting itself from invalidation, may do so in three ways: (a) avoiding any encounter whatsoever with invalidation, renouncing all exploration (avoidance); (b) ignoring invalidation by discrediting its source and insisting even more forcefully on one's own construction of the facts (hostil-ity); and (c) nullifying the impact of the invalidation on its structure through *ad hoc* hypotheses or through the reduction of empirical content (immunization).

Every individual tends to prefer one of these three modes and this preference comes to be established through the influence of the attachment relationship.

In our view, the style of knowledge is a very fixed trait that is formed at an extremely early age in the mother–child relationship. It then becomes the hub of the entire structure of an individual's personality. As a basic determining factor of personality, it also influences the development of many psychopathological traits.

Up until now, all attempts to show the relationship between attachment pat-terns and the various types of psychiatric syndromes have failed, or at least have been rather awkward. This may be because the two levels are too distant from each other, too inhomogeneous for such an operation to be successful.

The style of knowledge may provide the necessary mediation lacking between these two levels. Delusion may be the expression of a cognitive system that has undergone a massive radical invalidation that is poor in alternatives, and that has developed the tendency to immunize invalidations within the context of a par-ticularly extreme avoidant attachment relationship.

Natural History of Paranoid Delusion

Paranoid delusion is a complex system of lucid thought, consistent, with a strong, logical structure, not confused and capable of extremely detailed predictions that regularly are self-confirming (Cameron, 1959; American Psychiatric Association, 1995). Basing himself on a central idea which no criticism may touch, the subject correctly draws all further deductions and is thus able to give consistent explanations that are always the same for every vital event. The untouchable nucleus of his delusion is defended through the profuse proliferation of *ad hoc* hypotheses that immunize it in the face of every confutation.

The paranoid subject is unfamiliar with the mechanism of adaptation and is forced to assimilate as good or bad all data perceived. He seems to attain absolute certainty by excluding all incongruous data, rc-interpreting it and simplifying it and, above all, banishing all doubt. He is totally incapable of distancing himself from his delusion, or of believing that different points of view and different explanations of things may exist. He is completely in tune with his delusion; it provides the very support for the subject's identity. His cognitive system is absolutely monolithic and every event has a bearing on the central nucleus of the self. Nothing is peripheral, nothing is irrelevant, nothing is due to chance, everything is intentional and refers to his delusion (Lorenzini, Sassaroli & Rocchi, 1989).

Even prior to full manifestation, we are dealing here with a system that is moving progressively towards rigidity, increasingly unable to change predictions that become more and more detailed and have greater and greater bearing on the central aspects of the self. A structure of this kind is monolithic, rigid and apparently immutable. Yet it is also extremely fragile in that it has no viable alternatives in the event that it should receive a major, serious invalidation that cannot be ignored and that deprives it of an essential part of its way of seeing itself. A typical manifestation occurs when, for example, having reached a certain age, the subject must deal with the fact that he is not what he believed himself to be.

It is impossible for the paranoid subject to construe himself differently. It must be underlined that it is not that he does not want to do so, or that he prefers not to do so, but simply that, given the structure of his system, he is absolutely unable to do so. Only by withdrawing into his suppositions can he manage to maintain a certain level of predictablity. For him the only alternative is an absolute void. Delusion is the only road open to him (Adams Webber, 1979).

Early Manifestation

Concerning paranoia, Arieti (1974, p. 909) has stated:

> One important point that must be considered is the relevance of the original episode. It is not only an event which incites the subject but a dynamic factor of great importance in whose absence the patient would be able to arrest or even to compensate for his inclination towards psychosis.

An event so devastating upon the as yet healthy equilibrium can only be an intolerable invalidation of one of the central constructs regarding the subject's identity.[1]

The descent into delusion proceeds gradually. The subject first experiences a feeling of astonishment and amazement. He feels that something very important is changing without being able to explain it to himself. This is the so-called "pre-delusion mood". The first ideas are still unconnected, asystematic, not yet linked together or structured. Confusion and uneasiness prevail. The subject enters a state of alarm.

In order to escape from this gravely confused situation, the structure of the paranoid system suddenly grows rigid and stresses internal consistency, to the disadvantage of the likeliness of its predictions. Thus the subject moves towards a dogmatic attitude that becomes more and more a caricature and towards an absolute submission of all data to his theories. The delusional system becomes more and more consistent and structured. It is able to find an explanation for everything and to metabolize every attempted confutation through the proliferation of its auxiliary *ad hoc* hypotheses.

Continuing Manifestation

After a period of uncertainty following the early invalidation, the formulation of the delusional idea appears to the subject as a saving anchor, through which his system recovers its lost ability to predict. The new idea becomes the hub of all later experience, a light allowing him to move in the dark and to give significance to what seemed to have lost all meaning.

The system sacrifices the likeliness of its predictions to absolute inner consistency, becoming impervious to all outside criticism, given that the only alternative reconstruction possible is either too poor or too empty. Thus he can only maintain the earlier construct, which is far richer, and not take into account the invalidation. The invalidation may be completely ignored, or explained through an *ad hoc* hypothesis, or transformed into a corroboration of his theories, or be considered as an anomaly still requiring explanation.

According to the hypothesis of falsificationism, the overcoming of a theory may occur only in the presence of a better theory that may substitute it (Popper & Lorenz, 1989).

What the paranoid person lacks and what the psychotherapist attempts to construct or reconstruct is precisely this better theory, which allows the patient to abandon the only theory upon which he has built his fortification, despite the better alternatives that may be available to him. Unfortunately this attempt is not easy, because the patient will interpret it in the light of the only theory he has as something threatening and persecutory. The guiding rule remains that the thera-

---

[1] It is not of the content of the invalidation that makes it intolerable, but the subject's absolute lack of any alternatives to this particular idea of self that has been invalidated.

pist must never invalidate a delusional patient's system without first having constructed an alternative, as the patient's delusion has been erected as a defence for his predictive capabilities when faced with the danger of absolute chaos.

THERAPY

Modifying the Cognitive Style

It is obvious that the aim of all therapies is to be able to deal with and resolve all specific problems with which the patient must struggle by modifying the patterns of meaning that generate and keep the problem alive. Thus, all efforts are aimed at specific contents.

It is equally obvious that, in order for a therapy to be considered successful, it must not limit itself to solving individual problems (for fear of lapsing immediately into other analogous ones) but must modify the patient's way of dealing with things that has been shown to be the source generating these problems.

Recovering the dynamism of knowledge, and thus reactivating the process of conjecture and confutation, can occur in this case through the escape from cognitive egocentrism which immunizes the system from all possible invalidation stemming from others, and which at the same time, by relegating the system to absolute autarchy, sterilizes it.

The escape from cognitive egocentrism, depending on the gravity of the case, occurs in two phases. The first consists in the distinction between the self and others in order to begin structuring a world with a plurality of subjects, overcoming the idea that there exists only one absolute subject, with no interlocutors. This distinction is uncertain in subjects with mental disorders of both a paranoid and a schizophrenic character (Lorenzini & Sassaroli, 1992a,b). The second phase consists in the construction of shared universes of meaning between the self and others within which a shared language is possible that allows the subject to listen to others.

The therapeutic relationship is an ideal situation, allowing the patient a way out from cognitive egocentrism through the recognizing of others and the sharing of meaning with them. The task of the therapist in this case is "being present". A constant, discreet presence is needed that does not intrude upon the subject but which cannot be ignored. A delicate balance must be found between "understanding and speaking the same language", and "substituting the other, speaking in his place". The main concern must be that of always maintaining a borderline between the two subjectivities, a dividing line that allows both to exist and co-exist. The dividing line that creates two close and communicating subjectivities is always very precarious. On the one hand, it may be in danger of vanishing, of bringing about a fusion of the two and a loss of identity, and on the other hand, it may grow rigid, becoming a wall behind which the other may vanish, impeding all communication and giving sanction once again to the new autarchy.

Strategies in Delusion

The general aim of intervening in delusion is to foster the subject's predictive capacity, that is to say, his ability to formulate hypotheses, to take invalidations into account, to re-construe events differently, and thus reactivate the growth and complexity of his cognitive system. In doing thus, it must be taken into account that his mental disturbance represents an extreme, desperate attempt to maintain some vestige of his predictive capacity and not plunge straight into chaos.

By definition, delusion is the resistance to all criticism. Any attempt to convince the patient by a demonstration of the facts or by trying to reason logically with him is thus destined to fail. This is what all the others around the patient have attempted to do—his friends and relatives—before he sought help from a therapist or, more usually, before he was taken to a therapist.

The therapist is not immune from entering the patient's world. Thus, the patient is in danger of enlarging the army of persecutors around him. The more the therapist attacks the patient's delusion, the more he will be considered a threat to the order that the patient has managed to create in his inner world.

Here we must underline that delusion remains, for the patient, the best if not the only explanation he is able to give of the things around him. The old cannot be abandoned before being sure there is something new to replace it with. Change means changing from one situation to another, and not from one situation to nothing at all.

Attempting to demonstrate as false the patient's delusional theories before modifying the conditions which have created them is tantamount to pushing him towards the breakdown of his predictive capacities, which he has managed to salvage through the solution of his psychosis. Such an ingenuous attempt normally leads to further rigidity and withdrawal into his ideas and to an interruption of the therapeutic relationship, which amounts to a healthy defence.

The approach is decidedly much easier when the paranoid world is not of a persecutory nature. When it is not, in fact, it is easier for the therapist to become a significant and reliable point of reference without becoming just one more persecutor among many.

The certainty of delusion is such that it is very rare for a paranoid patient to turn to a therapist of his own free will for help in dealing with his ideas, which are for him the only solid and sure feature of his reality. He will turn spontaneously to a therapist for different reasons, which are, however, connected with his pathology: for example, a continuous state of tension, the fact that others maltreat him, or to request certification of the abuse he has received from others.

In the initial contract, the therapist must respond cautiously to the patient's requests as they represent the only element motivating him to undergo therapy. However, the therapist must absolutely avoid collusion with the patient's ideas (even when this seems to kindle feelings of goodwill and trust in the patient). The negative impact of such collusion will be felt by the therapist sooner or later when he must modify his position of complicity with the patient. Acceptable requests involve firstly comprehension and later changes in the patient's emotional states or behaviour, and not changes in his outer reality. The therapist, therefore, must suspend his judgement concerning the patient's delusion, and try to neither attack or reinforce it, but simply leave it aside. The patient's ideas must be kept out of the discussion as much as possible. They will be spontaneously and gradually abandoned when the patient comes to have better theories available to him to explain his situation and predict his future.

One theory may be considered better than another, following Popper's falsificationism, if:

1. It explains what the previous theory explained (in our case delusion).
2. It explains what the previous theory was unable to explain.
3. It is falsifiable but not falsified, and thus has received important corroboration (validation).

One feels immediately discouraged. In fact, one realizes how difficult it is for a new theory to manage to explain everything that the delusion explained and also what it failed to explain, as the delusion is by definition absolutely all-encompassing. Nothing escapes its explanation, nothing invalidates it, everything corroborates it. Its weak point and its evil power lie indeed in its ability to "explain everything", and thus on this level it is invincible in the face of all other theories.

This consideration suggests some possible strategies. The new theory must grow without ever having to measure itself in its early phase against the patient's delusion, as this encounter would be fatal. Thus, the therapist must not try to show that the new explanation gradually being elaborated is truer than the patient's ideas. Rather he must simply show that it is another possibility.

Popper's third characteristic of falsifiable potential is what distinguishes a delusional mind from a normal one. This characteristic is indeed in favour of the new theory and to the disadvantage of the delusion, but only if the judge is an impartial external observer familiar with Popper's epistemology. Instead, the choice between the two theories must be made by the delusional system itself, which cannot allow itself the luxury of being wrong. Thus, before the subject can appreciate the advantages gained through having theories that may be falsified, he must be placed in a condition in which he may make mistakes. This means that he must be able to choose between two predictions, one of which may be richer than the other, yet for which an alternative does exist.

Therapeutic progress does not start at the point where the patient first considers his ideas as true, and then, further on, judges them as false, although this does occur and is the most certain signal that the therapy has been successful. Rather, therapeutic progress is the effect of a shift that occurs in the patient from experiencing his ideas as "necessary" at first and then as "superfluous" later on. Delusions, in fact, become less necessary and obligatory when the undeveloped parts of the system begin to develop. Only then will the patient be able to appreciate a new way of being in the right, and unlike before, he will be able to contemplate the possibility of being in the wrong.

At least at the beginning, the new theories must be compatible with the patient's only point of view, which is of course, his delusional perspective. Or at least, they must not measure themselves against it in order not to fail. In order to achieve this, it is necessary to follow a certain strategy.

First, "alternative explanations" must be constructed for the patient by asking him, "If things were not as you claim they are, how else could they be?"However, in order to assure that these attempts are not experienced by the patient as a threatening attack on his delusional world, it would be preferable to refer these alternative explanations to other people. For example, "You tell me that you were fired from your job because there was a plot against you. Now, let's examine the case of another person and try to figure out several reasons why he might have been fired". It is also necessary that the new explanations be considered as hypothetical and not referred to the patient himself, as if the therapist were playing an imaginary game with him or writing a screenplay for a film. In this way, the patient will discover that different points of view may exist, even if he is still unable to refer them to his own situation.

This type of operation of creating alternatives is necessary if the patient wishes to focus discussion on his delusion; otherwise, the more this part of his delusion structure is left out of the discussion in the early phases of treatment, the better. It must be considered only as a sign of deep distress which can be accepted in therapy.

At the same time, the dark zones of the system must be explored in order to create new implications of meaning among those penalized areas that have remained undeveloped. In order to foster this development of the "shadow", the therapist must recognize the patient's idea of self, to which he clings most tenaciously and which he is by no means willing to abandon. Thus, those opposing polarities that the patient most fears must be stressed.

Each negative polarity must be brought out into the open and elaborated in order to enrich it. The therapist could ask, "What would life be like for someone who is unsuccessful at his work? How would a person who is unsuccessful at his work spend his time? How could a person who is unsuccessful at his work have self-esteem?". The therapist in this case plays a very active role as "expert companion in exploration", who encourages the discovery of new territories, points out unexpected perspectives and underlines unforeseen possibilities, and indicates solutions adopted by other people whom the patient knows.

During the phase of discovery, all critical judgement is suspended, as otherwise negative judgement will impede the exploration of the "unfamiliar", thereby creating a vicious circle. In fact, it is the unfamiliarity of an event that makes the subject judge it as unpleasant. In other words, the therapist must help the patient "fill a void", put meaning and predictions where previously absolute darkness existed in order to render it less frightening.

Further on, one may retrace the patient's history in order to understand how he came to develop such a rigid and unilateral mode of constructing himself and his reality and to see how it has been reinforced through repeated use. Recognizing the context in which a certain idea has been constructed allows one to realize how that idea may be congruous, reasonable and effective in that one particular situation and how, by changing context, it may become inadequate and harmful.

Lastly, new hypothesized points of view may be explored by applying them to the patient himself in order to discover how they would allow him to adapt better and bring him a growing sense of well-being, because they would allow him to change. "Being able to change one's mind" and "realizing one has made a mistake" are proposed as elements of strength, rather than of weakness. In fact those who take into account invalidation stemming from reality are better able to exploit their opportunities, modifying what may be modified without stubbornly attempting to modify what cannot be modified.

At this point, delusion may be taken into consideration once again in order to criticize it thoroughly. In analysing its first appearance, its continuing existence, its structure and its gradual loss of importance, the therapist will retrace the therapeutic journey, underlining constantly the basic error, i.e. that in order to affirm one is in the right, it is necessary to be able to indicate those conditions in which one would admit being wrong.

This mode of approach to patients suffering from delusion may be put into practice within the contexts of both private and public mental health care. Paranoid patients are more frequently found in public mental health care facilities, where they have been brought by their relatives or committed by public authorities, rather than of their own free will.

In this case, the therapist must abstain from any judgement concerning the patient's delusional ideas and work towards reformulating the malaise experienced by the patient—which will surely be present, even if only as a conflict with his environment—into a request for help. Every slight suffering expressed by the patient may give the therapist something to seize on in order to initiate the therapeutic contract, without this necessarily having to do with the content of his delusion.

The therapist's attitude must be sincere, never deceitful, and careful not to display an excessive involvement, which would only make the patient suspicious and encourage delusional ideas concerning the therapist as well.

Especially in some of the initial phases, the presence of several professional figures in the role of co-therapists may be useful in order to avoid a situation of excessive intimacy, which these patients often find it difficult to tolerate.

Clinical Case Study

William had been brought in for therapy after an episode of violent aggression against his boss, during which it had been necessary to commit forcefully him to an institution in an emergency situation.

William was 26 years old, and an only child in a well-to-do family. His mother, a cultivated woman, came from a family of musicians, writers and historians, and she had successfully devoted herself to politics. She expected her son to become a great artist or man of letters. His father came from a humble rural background and had become a successful entrepreneur in the field of agriculture. He had made a lot of money and was generally known for being a highly efficient, practical and successful man. He expected his son to become an up-and-coming manager in one of the family business enterprises.

Two sets of expectations converged on William from both his mother's and his father's side (for both he was the only descendant), and these expectations were very much in conflict with each other. Furthermore, they were also way beyond the range of William's real capacities. He had managed to finish secondary school with just barely passing grades, despite his parents attempts to "recommend him". At university, he had changed his major several times without getting anywhere, and had done only about four or five exams. Then the family decided that going to university was too far below the standards of a genius like William. It wasn't worth his while and he would only waste time there. So he had attended courses in computer science, marketing, graphics and journalism, all very expensive, and despite the fact that a diploma was guaranteed by the payment of the high enrollment fees, he nearly failed his final exam.

This had done nothing to change his family's mind about the fact that William was an extraordinary young man, a true genius. In the eyes of his mother, he was gifted with rare artistic talent. In the eyes of his father, he possessed a brilliant, practical intelligence. William too shared their convictions concerning himself.

Then he had found a job for 6 months as an errand boy for a labour union office. This experience had been construed by his parents as "a way for the young genius to come to know the concrete difficulties of life in order to develop his character and come to know the world of humble people who must earn their bread with the sweat of their brow. An experience to cite in his biography".

The crisis exploded when William's boss told him that if he continued to work so little and so poorly, he would be fired. In William's mind it was impossible to think of himself as "inadequate" for any job, thus there had to be another explanation for his boss's behaviour. For a while, he was dismayed, but then everything became clear to him. The director of the office feared William for his great intelligence. He wanted to get rid of William in order to keep him from rapidly and inevitably ascending to the top and becoming a success. This was the only plausible explanation for the event which did not question his extraordinary qualities.

The first phase of therapy consisted in getting him to express reasons why ordinary people (not himself of course) sometimes are fired from their jobs. This first phase was very difficult because the only explanation he proposed at the beginning was that of the boss's envy of his dependants who were superior to him.

In the meantime there were two other crises of violence following two social failures (failing his exams, and not being hired for another job), which had been predicted by the therapist and which were explained by William with the usual interpretative scheme: "I am perfect and if they do not want me, it is because they are afraid of me, and that is why they have organized a plot against me".

His therapy passed through two successive phases. In the first, patient and therapist began to construe what life would be like for a young man his age who was not a genius but just a normal person. At the beginning gaped an absolute void, but gradually, the terror of nothingness was substituted by the curiosity for possible activities, interests and goals that William had never imagined existed. Slowly the idea began to dawn that it was possible to live, and to live a good life. without necessarily having to be a genius, superior to everyone.

In the second phase, the story of his development was revisited with a new awareness of his situation, and with a critical attitude towards the ideal models he had learned from his parents, which had deprived him of being a normal and happy person, and had forced him to be a genius and madman.

His criticism of his delusion occurred spontaneously and marked its end. William moved out of his parents' house, went to live on his own, and found a girlfriend. He earns a living working in a fast food restaurant, and has gone back to university to continue his studies.

CONCLUSION

Paranoia is a disorder rarely studied by clinical psychologists because, more often than not, it lurks for decades in the shadows, without ever expressing itself as a request for help on the part of the patient, and sometimes without ever manifesting itself in the subject's environment. Sometimes it diminishes and even resolves itself spontaneously in the course of time. Very frequently, it accompanies the subject to his death, gradually becoming the central theme of his long-suffering existence. More rarely it explodes dramatically and unexpectedly.

It must be admitted that most therapists are quite happy to avoid having to do with paranoid patients, given the impotence they experience when faced with the inner world of a paranoid patient, apparently so inaccessible, inexplicable, and thus, threatening.

But that which we avoid continues to become even more unknown and frightening. This chapter will have achieved its aim if it has helped therapists to glimpse the reasons for the patient's delusion and to perceive it as the patient's last, desperate attempt to keep his world of meanings from falling apart, a world which already appears to him as having no alternatives. If that were so, a new curiosity might replace the therapist's bewilderment and threatened feelings and kindle in him a keen desire to take on such a demanding therapeutic challenge. In which case, we would certainly see more paranoid cases among our clients.

REFERENCES

Adams Webber, J. (1979). *Personal Construct Theory*. Chichester: Wiley.
Ainsworth, M.D.S. et al. (1978). *Patterns of Attachment: a Psychological Study of the Strange Situation*. Hillsdale, NJ: Erlbaum.
American Psychiatric Association (1995). *Diagnostic and Statistical Manual of Mental Disorders* (DSM-IV). Washington, DC: American Psychiatric Association.
American Psychiatric Press (1990). *Structured Clinical Interviews for the DSM-III-R* (SCID). Washington, DC: American Psychiatric Press.
Arieti, S. (1974). *Interpretation of Schizophrenia*. New York: Basic Books.
Bateson, G. (1984). Steps Toward an Ecology of Mind. New York: Ballantine.
Bowlby, J. (1969). *Attachment and Loss, Vol. I—Attachment*. London: Hogarth.
Bowlby, J. (1973). *Attachment and Loss, Vol. II—Separation Anxiety and Anger*. London: Hogarth.
Bowlby, J. (1980). *Attachment and Loss, Vol. III—Sadness and Depression*. London: Hogarth.
Bretherton, I. (1985). Attachment theory, retrospect and prospect. In I. Bretherton & E. Waters (eds), *Growing points of Attachment Theory and Research*. Monographs of the Society for Research in Child Development. Chicago, IL: University of Chicago Press.
Cameron, N. (1959–1966). Paranoia states and paranoia. In S. Arieti (ed.), *American Handbook of Psychiatry*. New York: Basic Books.

Crittenden, P. (1994).   Peering into the black box: an exploratory treatise on the develop-
    ment of self in young children. In D. Cicchetti & S. Toth (eds), *Rochester Symposium
    on Developmental Psychopathology, Vol. 5: The Self and its Disorders*. Rochester, NY:
    University of Rochester Press, pp. 79–148.
Jaspers, K. (1965).   Psicologia generale. Rome: Il Pensiero Scientifico.
Kelly, G.A. (1955).   The Psychology of Personal Construct. New York: Norton.
Kraepelin, E. (1919)   *Dementia Praecox and Paraphrenia*. Edinburgh: E. and E.
    Livingstone.
Kretschmer, E. (1949).   *Psychotherapeutische Studien*. Stuttgart, Thieme.
Kretschmer, E. (1962).   Medizinische Psychologie, 12th edn. Stuttgart, Thieme.
Lorenzini, R., Sassaroli, S. & Rocchi, M.T. (1989).   Schizophrenia and paranoia as a
    solution to predictive failure. *International Journal of Personal Construct Psychology*,
    2(2), 417–32.
Lorenzini, R. & Sassaroli, S. (1992a).   *Cattivi Pensieri: I disturbi del pensiero
    schizofrenico, paranoico, ossessivo*. Rome: NIS.
Lorenzini, R. & Sassaroli, S. (1992b).   *La verita privata: Il delirio e i deliranti*. Rome: NIS.
Lorenzini, R. & Sassaroli, S. (1995).   *Attaccamento, conoscenza e disturbi di personalità*.
    Raffaello Cortina Editore.
Popper, K. (1934)   *Logik der Forschung*. Vienna: Springer-Verlag.
Popper, K. (1969).   *Conjectures and Refutations*. London: Routledge and Kegan Paul.
Popper, K. (1972).   *Objective Knowledge: An Evolutionary Approach*. Oxford:
    Clarendon.
Popper, K. & Lorenz, K. (1989).   Die Zukunft ist offen. In R. Piper (ed.), *Das Altenberger
    Gespräch mit den Texten der Wiener Popper Symposium*. Munich: R. Piper GmbH.
Rossi Monti, M. (1984).   *La Conoscenza Totale*. Milan: Il Saggiatore.
Weitbrecht, H.J. (1963, 1968).   *Psychiatrie im Grundriss*. Heidelberg: Springer-Verlag.
Winter, D. (1992).   *Personal Construct Psychology in Clinical Practice*. London:
    Routledge.

Chapter 10

Early Intervention in Psychotic Disorders: a Critical Step in the Prevention of Psychological Morbidity

Jane Edwards and Patrick D. McGorry
Centre for Young People's Mental Health, Parkville, Australia

What we've got to be very astute about is getting in *early* with the best treatments because if someone is at the formative stages of their lives, of their careers, of interpersonal relationships . . . If they miss one year due to an episode of schizophrenia they are falling behind; if they miss two or three or four years then it is almost impossible to make up that time (James, 1996).

Too many first-episode patients experience subsequent episodes and a serious decline in functioning. The continued search for interventions to secure better outcomes and prevent the accrual of disabilities is warranted (Fenton, 1997, p. 43).

Early intervention around the onset of psychotic disorders is a highly attractive theoretical notion which is receiving increasing international interest (McGlashan, 1996a; McGorry & Edwards, 1997). It involves, first, deciding when a psychotic disorder has commenced and offering effective treatments at the earliest possible point and, second, ensuring that the interventions provided constitute best practice for this phase of illness. The relative effectiveness of these two strategies in terms of outcome has not been determined. Indeed, it should be acknowledged that the efficacy and effectiveness, including cost-effectiveness, of specific phase-related treatments is in need of extensive and rigorous research (Kane, 1997; McGorry, in press).

Cognitive Psychotherapy of Psychotic and Personality Disorders: Handbook of Theory and Practice.
Edited by C. Perris and P.D. McGorry.
© 1998 John Wiley & Sons Ltd.

This chapter elaborates on the logic of early intervention in psychotic disorders and our attempts to both develop and deliver best practice treatments for early psychosis, based on more than 14 years of experience. To this end, the Early Psychosis Prevention and Intervention Centre (EPPIC) is described, advanced as a clinical "laboratory" for the study of first-episode psychosis, which is now in its sixth year of development. This chapter focuses on the operational aspects of this evolving "real world" program, with particular emphasis on the psychological aspects of care in relation to individuals who have experienced a frank psychotic disorder. Issues concerning treatment for the prepsychotic phase of schizophrenia are detailed elsewhere (McGorry & Singh, 1995; Yung & McGorry, 1996) and the prodrome clinic is only briefly described in this text. For descriptions of our approach to the biological aspects of treatment of the first-episode patient, the reader is referred to McGorry and Jackson (in press).

While empirical "evidence" for the interventions proposed in this chapter is thin, there is sufficient knowledge available from clinical practice to inform treatment guidelines for working with individual and families with early psychosis. Indeed, a number of groups in Australia and New Zealand are moving towards drafting such guidelines as a means of commencing a dialogue (Pennell et al., 1997). We would argue that a consensus opinion about treatment in first-episode psychosis would, in its final form, look significantly different from practice guidelines developed for more established psychotic illnesses, such as those developed by the American Psychiatric Association for the treatment of patients with schizophrenia (American Psychiatric Association, 1997). Evidence-based approaches to medicine do not rely solely on randomized controlled trials with their inherent limitations (Jackson & Judd, 1997) but also take into account current practice and expert opinion (Andrews, 1997). Our endeavours are described in the spirit of contributing towards the accrual of evidence essential to the development of best practice standards, encouraging other clinicians and researchers to assist in this undertaking.

THE LOGIC OF EARLY INTERVENTION

Preventative Opportunity

The opportunity for secondary prevention in psychotic disorders is readily apparent (McGorry, 1992; McGorry & Singh, 1995). First, prolonged delays are common prior to first effective treatment for psychosis (Beiser et al., 1993; Loebel et al., 1992; McGorry et al., 1996), averaging a year or more in developed countries. Much of the occupational and social decline in psychosis occurs before treatment is initiated (Jones et al., 1993). It has been suggested that the duration of untreated psychosis (DUP) is an important predictor of outcome in first-episode schizophrenia; delays in treatment are associated with slower and less complete recovery (Crow et al., 1986; Helgason, 1990; Larsen, McGlashan & Moe, 1996; Loebel et al., 1992; Rabiner, Wegner & Kane, 1991; Wyatt, 1991; Wyatt, Piña

& Henter, in press) and with substantially higher health costs for at least 3 years after first treatment (Moscarelli, Capri & Neri, 1991). Testing the hypothesis that reduction in DUP results in improvement in outcome is a complex endeavour (McGlashan, 1996b), clearly requiring adoption of a clinical epidemiological perspective. Second, disability and handicap are most likely to develop during the early years after illness onset (Carpenter & Strauss, 1991; McGlashan & Johannessen, 1996)—a "critical period" of maximum vulnerability (Birchwood & MacMillan, 1993; Birchwood, McGorry & Jackson, 1997). For the portion of the critical period which follows entry into treatment, there is the issue of the quality, range, and intensity of treatment provided (McGorry et al., 1996).

Best practice treatment for later stages of the disorder may not constitute best practice for early psychosis (McGorry, 1992). Age- and phase-specific variants of existing clinical approaches, or completely novel approaches, may be required. This is a particularly important consideration with regard to early treatment resistance or "prolonged recovery" (Edwards et al., in press). Frequency of relapse appears to peak during the early years following illness onset (Eaton et al., 1992) and, given the suggestion that time to remission increases with increasing number of episodes of illness (Lieberman et al., 1996), should be a focus of treatment (McGorry, in press). On a more general level, we also need to be aware of the iatrogenic effects of "care", including depression and post-trauma reactions to admission to hospitalization (McGorry et al., 1991). In summary, a realistic secondary preventive approach would involve reducing the duration of untreated psychosis and optimizing the management during the early years following detection.

Conceptual Framework

In view of the inadequacies of the neo-Kraepelinian "disease" concept of schizophrenia in the setting of early psychosis (McGorry, Copolov & Singh, 1990; McGorry, 1991, 1995), we have suggested the more general term "psychosis" to be more useful in first-episode and early psychosis samples (McGorry, 1995). Psychosis is a global syndrome, defined narrowly by the presence of clear-cut delusions or hallucinations, or more broadly by including marked thought disorder and severe catatonic features. It may occur in association with major depression, mania, or primary negative or deficit symptoms, and it is the different combinations of these syndromes with psychosis which gives rise to categories of psychotic disorder. Course should be separated from syndromes, and here the concept of staging (Fava & Kellner, 1993) is useful. The model which is detailed in McGorry et al. (1996), is a matrix of phase of illness, patterns of syndromes present during and between episodes of relapse, and the associated levels of disability and handicap. The transitions from one phase to another (e.g. from prodrome to first psychotic episode, from first episode to critical period, and from critical period to prolonged psychosis) are key processes, with only a proportion of individuals making the transition across each phase. In clinical practice we have further divided the critical period into four phases: acute, early, late, and prolonged recovery (Edwards, Cocks & Bott, in press), which serves to remind the clinician that recovery is to be expected (Lieberman et al., 1993; McGorry, 1992). The conceptual model is reflected in the content of psychoeducation provided throughout the clinical program (EPPIC, 1997a; Ioannides & Hexter, 1994a; McGorry, 1995).

Developmental Framework

The period of maximum risk for the onset of a psychotic disorder, particularly in males, is late adolescence or early adulthood (Häfner et al., 1995; Kosky & Hardy, 1992). This is a critical developmental phase, involving the consolidation of identity, the process of separation from parents, key educational and vocational steps, and the construction of a peer group (Winnicott, 1965). Adolescence has been characterized as a period of great risk to healthy development (Takanishi, 1993), being a period of rapid change which can be highly stressful (Rice, Herman & Petersen, 1993). When a major psychiatric disorder such as a psychosis strikes during this life stage there is the potential for personal disaster—maturation may be put on hold, social and family relationships can be strained or severed, and vocational prospects are frequently derailed. Secondary problems, such as unemployment, substance abuse, depression, self-harm and law breaking, frequently develop or intensify. It is has been suggested that developmental factors may need to be considered in phenomenological differences between adolescent and adult mania (McElroy et al., 1997). Adult psychiatric services tend to overlook and/or underestimate the significance of this key perspective in treatment provision.

EARLY PSYCHOSIS PREVENTION AND INTERVENTION CENTRE

The Early Psychosis Prevention and Intervention Centre (Edwards et al., 1994; McGorry, 1993; McGorry et al., 1996) is a multicomponent service that was developed in order to address the needs of older adolescents, and young adults and adolescents in the early stages of a psychotic disorder.

Historical Origins

It is important to note that the historical origins of EPPIC lie in an inpatient ward located on the grounds of a major psychiatric hospital servicing the inner-city area of Melbourne (Copolov et al., 1989; Edwards et al., 1994; McGorry et al.,

1996). Our experience with the first-episode admission group led to a better understanding of the particular clinical needs of these patients and the special preventive approach required for their care. However, the psychosocial elements of the inpatient unit were largely restricted to a group-based recovery program (see Edwards et al., 1994, for details). The usual limitations of a group based program became apparent—the range of presentations in terms of intellectual functioning, impairments and disabilities, and premorbid personalities rendered group work difficult. The short-term inpatient focus had implications for continuity of care, with patients being referred to routine adult area mental health services upon discharge, resulting in loss of the quarantined early psychosis environment. In addition, the stand-alone inpatient unit had limited ability to tackle the duration of untreated psychosis, its referral base dependent on the acute units of the parent hospital and the limited community development strategies of the associated generic outpatient clinics.

It became increasingly obvious that "assessing the impact of early detection and prevention programs requires a co-ordinated catchment-based health service" (Fenton, 1997, p. 43). Following the dedication of additional funds by the Victoria State Government, EPPIC commenced operation in October 1992. The Centre aims to reduce the level of both primary and secondary morbidity in individuals with early psychosis through the twin strategy of identification of patients at the earliest stage from onset of psychosis and provision of intensive phase-specific treatment up to 18 months. Selection criteria for the new service were: age 15–30; experiencing a first episode of psychosis; resident in the service catchment area; and prior treatment (if any) restricted to a maximum of 6 months.

The service has been increasingly moving towards a community-based approach. In June 1995 the inpatient unit was annexed from the psychiatric hospital and relocated to a less stigmatizing environment at the Parkville site; at the same time a reduction in bed numbers occurred and the considerable savings achieved were used to provide additional specialized treatment options required.

Context

EPPIC's catchment area is approximately 820 000, covering the Western Metropolitan Region of Melbourne, an area serviced by two public psychiatric hospitals and five community mental health clinics. Census data indicated that in 1991 the number of people within EPPIC's catchment area and age range was 208 104 (Australian Bureau of Statistics, 1991), a population base expected to yield about 200 new cases of psychosis per annum—estimates of local expected incidence figures were based on WHO data (Jablensky et al., 1992). Important features of the region include: a large proportion of people who have been born overseas or have parents born overseas (35% of the catchment population was born outside Australia; Australian Bureau of Statistics, 1991); a high proportion from the lowest socio-economic status groups; significant unemployment; and poor public transport infrastructure in parts of the locality. This region has very few private psychiatrists.

The clients are young, with the average age for both men and women being 22 years; 81% live with family members/relatives. Approximately 70% have schizophrenia spectrum disorders (i.e. schizophrenia, schizophreniform delusional disorder and schizo-affective disorder), 25% have affective psychoses, and 5% other, often transient, psychotic disorders. More than one-third of first-episode patients are managed without requiring inpatient admission (Power et al., in press). More than 90% achieve remission from the first psychotic episode (Edwards et al., in press). Substance abuse is a major clinical issue (Rolfe, 1997) with approximately 70% of all first-episode patients having used cannabis within 12 months prior to initial presentation for treatment and about 50% having used in the month prior to assessment.

Program Description

The program has evolved considerably since 1993. The initial blueprint comprised six clinical components (McGorry, 1993)—the early psychosis assessment team (EPAT), a single outpatient case management team, the original inpatient unit, a day program, family work, and cognitively orientated psychotherapy for early psychosis. The development of four smaller programs followed—accommodation, assertive outreach, a treatment-resistance team, and a prodrome clinic (Edwards et al., 1994). Modifications have been described in McGorry et al. (1996); however, considerable development has occurred subsequently. In this chapter the service model circa 1997 is described, diagrammatically represented in Figure 10.1. More detail on the rationale and the content of these therapeutic interventions is provided in the *Early Psychosis Training Pack* (McGorry & Edwards, 1997).

Early Psychosis Assessment Team (EPACT)

The Early Psychosis Assessment and Community Treatment Team (EPACT; formerly EPAT) is a mobile assessment and community treatment team which is the first point of contact with EPPIC (Drew & Howe, 1997; Yung, Phillips & Drew, in press). Functioning in its current form since August 1995, EPACT is a 24-hour 7-day-per-week service which provides immediate assessment for first presentations and, when required, intensive home-based treatment (Fitzgerald & Kulkarni, in press). Through networking and carefully targeted community education activities, EPACT seeks to raise community awareness of psychosis in young people and promote recognition and early referral. Possible cases are always assessed in person, and referrers are encouraged to re-refer if signs indicative of an early psychosis develop at a later point. EPACT strives to minimize the stress involved in what is likely to be the patient's and family's first

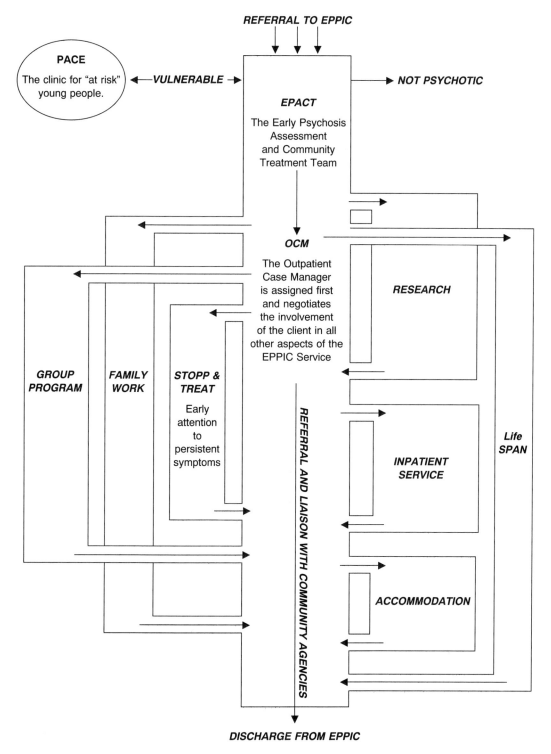

Figure 10.1   The EPPIC model

contact with psychiatric services, by: providing information and support at each stage of the assessment phase; being available to conduct assessments in the least threatening environment, for example, in the home, school or local doctor's surgery; and responding flexibly to each situation. A major focus for EPACT is promoting the patient's engagement with the treatment. For example, in cases where a young person is likely to take several weeks to be able to recognize the need for treatment and to develop sufficient motivation to attend regular appointments, home-based treatment and support is provided where possible, with transport to the clinic provided and a case manager introduced early on.

In the first 2 years EPACT received 956 referrals, of which 587 were clinically assessed and 398 were accepted into EPPIC (with additional direct inpatient intake the total number of new cases amounted to 500 in that 2-year period). This number of new cases is in the mid-range of that predicted by WHO figures. Forty per cent of the assessments took place at the young person's own home, and 21% at a agency that was not part of the psychiatric services. In the first 6 months 49.8% of referrals came outside the psychiatric sources, with 9.8% coming from family and friends; in the second 6 months, these figures had increased to 69.2% and 24.5%, respectively, indicating that the community education program was having an impact. Five per cent of referrals came from general practitioners initially, increasing to nearly 10% with more intensive education of general practitioners. In the first 12 months of the service, the mean time between receiving a call for an urgent assessment and arriving for the assessment was 68 minutes; the mean response for non-urgent referrals was 3.1 days. Only 8.5% of all involuntary admissions required police transport.

EPACT's assessment and home treatment function will soon to be incorporated within a broader Youth Access Team (YAT). YAT will also undertake a crisis assessment function for non-psychotic youth and ultimately provide a single low-stigma point of entry to psychiatric services for individuals aged 12–25 years (Women's and Children's Healthcare Network & Western Healthcare Network, 1997).

PACE

The Personal Assessment and Crisis Evaluation Clinic (PACE) has been established to identify, gain a clearer understanding of and treat individuals who are at high risk of developing a psychotic disorder in the near future (Yung et al., 1996a, b). PACE is located at a generalist adolescent health centre orientated towards health promotion in order to avoid premature labelling and stigmatization. Intake criteria were guided by a pilot phase of research and clinical experience. Young people who are thought to be at imminent risk of developing a psychotic illness on the basis of: family history of psychotic illness or a DSM-IV schizotypal personality disorder and a recent change in mental state; or sub-threshold psychotic symptoms (e.g. unusual perceptual experiences) occurring several times a week over a period of at least 1 week; or brief, limited or intermittent psychotic symptoms (BLIPS), are referred to the clinic by EPACT or other referral agencies. Assessment, monitoring, support and referral are provided. Psychological and medical treatment is offered with the aim of ameliorating symptoms, enhancing coping strategies and ultimately, it is hoped, delaying or preventing the onset of psychosis.

Research components include examining characteristics of the PACE group (e.g. pre-psychotic symptomatology, brain structure, neuropsychological processes, and drug and alcohol use) for predictive purposes (Yung et al., in 1998) and evaluating the effectiveness of a combined psychological therapy/medication intervention in reducing pre-psychotic symptomatology and delaying or preventing the onset of psychosis. PACE received 162 referrals in 1996–1997. Of the 99 assessments conducted, 44% met inclusion criteria. Patients accepted by PACE seem to have higher mean level of general psychopathology and negative symptoms and to be experiencing greater disability than patients recovering from a first episode of psychosis (Yung et al., 1996a).

Outpatient Case Management

Two teams provide case management and medical treatment based on geographical boundaries of the EPPIC catchment area. Adopting a therapist model, the outpatient case manager (OCM) is the primary treating clinician, using his/her clinical skills to assess the needs of the patient and the family, whilst using the developing relationship as part of the treatment itself. The clinician–patient relationship is the central axis around which all treatment revolves and the OCM is central to all decisions across inpatient and outpatient settings (Edwards, Cocks & Bott, in press), as can be seen in Figure 10.1.

Case management goals include: minimizing duration of active psychosis; preventing the toxic effects of medication using low-dose drug strategies, atypical neuroleptics and prophylactic anti-parkinsonian medication; avoiding inpatient admission if possible, and humanizing admission if it becomes necessary; and actively seeking and treating secondary problems. Elements of Cognitively Orientated Psychotherapy for Early Psychosis (COPE; McGorry et al., this volume) are incorporated within the OCM service. Case management in first-episode psychosis provides an opportunity to "get it right", in terms of both assessment and provision of optimal needs-based treatment *early*, thereby preventing iatrogenic effects and promoting quality of life. For example, failing to complete secondary school will impact on an individual long after the psychotic episode has resolved (Kessler et al., 1995). Early treatment while continuing to attend school may avoid "post-morbid occupational decline" (Beiser et al., 1994).

EPPIC has a steady state case-load of approximately 320 active patients, with 20 new cases accepted each month. Full-time case managers carry individual case-loads of approximately 40 patients and each patient is also assigned a psychiatrist or senior psychiatric registrar. Case allocation and case loads are carefully and systematically monitored. Caseloads of this magnitude are somewhat excessive for optimal treatment and preclude a truly assertive model. They do attest to the "real world" nature of EPPIC, and mean that assistance is frequently requested from the EPACT team. Table 10.1 summarizes case load information calculated on a weekly basis, which is further broken down for each case manager. Similar information is maintained for medical caseloads. Frequency of contact varies with phase of illness and involvement with other sub-programs. At discharge, approximately 33% of patients are referred to adult community mental health services, 17% to general practitioners, and 10% to private psychiatrists.

In-patient Unit

The inpatient service provides acute treatment for those individuals who cannot be managed in the community due to risk of self-harm or violence, refusal or inability to comply with assessment or treatment, and/or lack of adequate support in the community. The focus of the 16-bed facility is on symptom reduction and containment, emphasizing brief admission in order to prepare the person for community treatment by either EPACT or the OCM service. This is facilitated by staff members working across the different program components and the immediate assignment of the case manager at entry to the program. Currently, the average length of stay in the unit for an individual experiencing a first episode of psychosis is 18 days.

Measures instituted to help prevent or reduce secondary morbidity resulting from the experience of hospitalization include: separation of first-episode patients from older and chronically ill patients and use of a low-stigma setting (e.g. avoiding state psychiatric hospitals); provision of clear explanations about admission and other procedures, education about the roles of various professionals, and psychoeducation; and involvement of families and peers (Kulkarni & Power, in press; Merlo & Hofer, in press). Low doses of neuroleptics are standard practice during the acute phase and disturbed behaviour is managed by targeted intensive nursing interventions, use of benzodiazepines and lithium as "neuroleptic-sparing" agents, and minimal use of seclusion (Power et al., 1998).

Group Program

The EPPIC group program offers an opportunity for the client to participate in a range of group activities selected according to the individual's personal goals and stage of recovery; acute, recovery and focus groups are provided (Albiston, Francey & Harrigan, 1998; EPPIC, in press; Francey, in press). Four "streams" are represented to ensure access to a balanced and comprehensive range of group modules: vocational programs; creative expression; social recreational; and health promotion and personal development. Opportunities for the mastery of tasks according to each individual's stage of development are provided, taking into consideration the impact of the psychosis and the receptivity of the individual at a given point in time. In developing group content, attention has been given to the age of the participants. For example, the Outdoor Adventure Group (which includes abseiling, white-water rafting and rock climbing) is especially appealing to young people, significantly impacting on self-esteem and interpersonal skills (Albiston, Francey & Harrigan, in press).

A tailored program is derived from the choices expressed by the participants, who are expected to help draft and regularly review their own individual programs. The program is a loosely linked set of open groups, a structure which enables a larger population (steady state approximately 50) to be included, with a balance between cohesion and flexibility. The EPPIC group program operates on four terms per year, with approximately 10-week cycles, paralleling the term structure of schools and higher education institutions. Our data suggests that the group program is targeting a subgroup of EPPIC patients with poorer premorbid adjustment and that participation in the group program may contribute to the prevention of deterioration (Albiston, Francey & Harrigan, in press).

The EPPIC group program is nested within a set of broader Centre for Young People's Mental Health (CYPMH) group interventions (McGorry, 1996).

Family Work

Working with first-episode families is unique in the sense that families are usually naive to the experience of psychosis and its treatment. While further research is needed regarding the specific nature and extent of distress and burden experienced by first-episode families (Gleeson et al., & Burnett, in press), it can be assumed that this is often a bewildering and distressing experience for relatives (Cozolini & Nuechterlein, 1986; Wynne, 1986).

The emphasis of the family work program is to highlight the special needs of families where one of their members experiences a psychotic episode (EPPIC, 1997b). The importance of families and carers in supporting a young person through their first episode is emphasized and every effort is made to include families as collaborators in treatment. The specific needs of a family are acknowledged, not only for the impact the family environment may have on the person's experience and path to recovery, but with regard to the family's own need for support. The three key foci for family intervention in early psychosis are: the impact of the psychosis on the family system; the impact of the psychosis on individual family members; and the interaction between the family and the course of the psychosis (Gleeson et al., in press). Consideration of cultural attitudes and religious beliefs are key components of assessment (Ferrari, 1996).

These needs of families for crisis support and practical education about psychosis are addressed through multi-family group interventions and individual sessions with families, supported by specialist family workers. The model consists of an integrated approach including psychoeducation, crisis management, practical problem solving, supportive psychotherapy, and, if indicated, family therapy. Psychoeducation includes a series of evening sessions entitled "Family and Friends", scheduled over 4 consecutive weeks, covering all aspects of psychosis, treatment approaches, and the future. A second group intervention provides further support and psychoeducation for families with a relative with a more persistent illness as a component of the prolonged recovery clinic.

Accommodation

Leaving home is a normal life-stage event, the time and complexity of which is affected by the onset of psychotic illness, for example, tensions resulting from bizarre behaviours may make remaining in the family home impossible. Ideally, young people should have access to mainstream housing and ultimately have the opportunity to live in a housing environment of their choice. Recovery from psychosis is aided by decreasing the disruption to a young person's lifestyle that can result from inadequate or unstable housing (Pennell, Tanti & Howe, 1995).

A significant minority of clients have been observed to be homeless around the time of commencing treatment at EPPIC. There is a shortage of community housing in the Centre's catchment area and a young person's vulnerable psychological state and compromised income can make competing for housing, whether it be youth-specific or private, difficult. Several projects have been established to provide housing and support to young people who have experienced homelessness or who are at significant risk of homelessness. The EPPIC accommodation program provides a transitional supported accommodation service which is run in collaboration with key community agencies. The "Linkages House" Salvation Army project provides 3-month transitional accommodation for two residents, frequently aiding entry into other supported housing programs. "Evans St", a joint project with the Schizophrenia Fellowship of Victoria, comprises four self-contained one bedroom units and provides housing and support for up to a 12-month period. Both programs aim to enhance living and social skills, operating on the premise that most young people will recover from psychosis and move into independent mainstream housing.

The Accommodation Steering Group ensures that a wide range of accommodation options are available to individuals within the program. This group also provides consultation to OCMs, assisting with emergency accommodation and providing resource materials regarding medium- to long-term options, and advocates for additional housing options.

TREAT

Treatment resistance is a major contributor to prolonged and persistent disability in psychosis (McGorry & Singh, 1995). Deciding at what phase of the recovery process to define "persistent" psychotic symptoms involves consideration of appropriate passages of recovery time, given the personal and psychiatric histories of patients and, frequently, attempts to disentangle relapse from ongoing symptoms. Approximately 7% of individuals with first-episode psychosis experience persistent psychotic symptoms at 12 months; restricting diagnostic considerations to schizophrenia or schizo-affective disorder, the proportion rises to

8.9% (Edwards et al., 1998), a figure still somewhat lower than that reported by Lieberman et al. (1993).

The Treatment Resistance Early Assessment Team (TREAT) identifies individuals experiencing prolonged recovery at 3 months after entry into EPPIC, providing a consultancy service to case managers and psychiatrists which aims to accelerate recovery and prevent established treatment resistance (Edwards et al., in press). Management principles include: active pursuit of effective treatment using relatively low-dose strategies for adequate periods of time (Cocks, 1997; Remington, Kapur & Zipursky, 1998); willingness to increase dose or switch to another drug if response is delayed beyond 6 weeks; an expectation of at least two adequate drug trials (i.e. equivalent to haloperidol 10 mg/day for 4–6 weeks) within a 3 month period; augmentation with lithium over a 4-week period (Kane & Marder, 1993); use of novel antipsychotics; use of strategies to promote treatment compliance (Kemp et al., 1996); attention to substance abuse; early use of structured psychological and family approaches; and conveying hope to the patient and the family.

The Systematic Treatment of Persistent Positive Symptoms (STOPP) is a therapy developed to help treat enduring positive psychotic symptoms (see McGorry et al., this volume). The "Recovery Plus" project is the research arm of TREAT, involving examination of the relative and combined effectiveness of clozapine and STOPP (Maude et al., 1997).

LifeSPAN

Certain subgroups of patients with established psychiatric illness are at particularly high risk of suicide. For example, one in five young men with adolescent-onset schizophrenia commits suicide (Krausz, Muller-Thomsen & Maasen, 1995). Patients are at highest risk of completed suicide during the post-psychotic period (Drake et al., 1984). It seems probable that clinical care in early psychosis can significantly reduce suicide rates (McGorry, Henry & Power, in press). Beyond that, specific suicide prevention strategies may be needed for young people with mental illness at high risk, such as those recovering from a first psychotic episode (Power, in press). Accurate and effective detection of suicide risk is dependent on well-trained and skilled staff and a network of services to intercept those at high risk.

LifeSPAN is a clinical research project funded to introduce interventions and reforms in existing mental health services in order to prevent suicide among young people who suffer from mental illness. The project aims to detect and treat those individuals who attend EPPIC who are at ultra-high risk of suicide. A cognitive-behavioral therapy intervention directed towards feelings of hopelessness, suicidal ideation and depression (Beck et al., 1979; Linehan et al., 1991; Linehan et al., 1994; Salkovkis, Atha & Storer, 1990) has being specifically tailored for early psychosis patients in consultation with national and international suicide experts. The intervention is currently being piloted, with formal evaluation to commence shortly.

Statewide Services

EPPIC Statewide Services assists agencies within Victoria to incorporate an early psychosis focus in their clinical programs. This service co-ordinates all public speaking engagements undertaken by EPPIC within Victoria and also provides information about both EPPIC and early psychosis to interested persons. The service provides community education, professional education and training (through workshops, site visits and training seminars), statewide secondary and tertiary consultation, provides policy input, and develops and promotes relevant resources (e.g. early psychosis manuals, fact sheets, booklets and multimedia psychoeducational products). A postgraduate course is offered via distance education in collaboration with the Department of Psychiatry at the University of Melbourne (Graduate Diploma in Young People's Mental Health). Statewide Services facilitates and develops early psychosis projects, which involves working intensively with mental health professionals in a discrete sector for a period of 6 months to help address the needs of young people with psychotic disorders, after which the level of direct support is reduced with structures in place to continue and further develop the focus. The team work in collaboration with local services to develop models of practice and protocols of care that are responsive to local needs and integrate well with the region's service organization and direction. The effectiveness of the model is currently being evaluated in a metropolitan area mental health service using process and clinical outcome data (Haines et al., 1997). EPPIC Statewide Services hosts quarterly 2-day site visit programs, produces regular newsletters titled "*Early Psychosis News*", manages the National Early Psychosis Resource Centre, and maintains the EPPIC Website (http://yarra.vicnet.au/~eppic).

A CASE VIGNETTE: "DALE"

The case of Dale illustrates the problems of delay in the provision of adequate treatment.

Dale, a 21 year-old single unemployed man living with his elderly parents, was admitted with his first episode of psychosis after injuring his parents with the claw of a hammer in response to command hallucinations. He had been bought to hospital handcuffed by police in the back of a police van without involvement of mental health workers. On admission he had blunted affect, poverty of speech with ideas of reference, auditory hallucinations, thought insertion, delusions of persecution, and delusions of control by an unspecified outside force. He was described as having been sociable and likeable until he began multiple drug abuse (cannabis, alcohol, petrol, solvents) at age 18. He reported experiencing auditory hallucinations and feeling suspicious of others for at least 6 months prior to presentation. He is said to have been a happy child who completed school at the age of 16 and worked for 6 months as a storeman. He had no past psychiatric or medical history and no family history of psychiatric illness. Physical examination and investigations were normal.

Due to administrative circumstances, not unusual in the state psychiatric system at the time of Dale's initial presentation, he spent time in three different psychiatric hospital during his "first admission"; he was admitted to hospital A for 41 days before being transferred to hospital B for 32 days and finally to the EPPIC inpatient unit, where he remained for 105 days. In hospital A he was diagnosed as "psychotic" without elaboration and prescribed chlorpromazine in doses which rapidly increased to 1000 mg over the first 3 days of admission. Hospital B changed the medication to haldol 50 mg and later modecate 25 mg, presumably assuming non-compliance would be an issue. Not until nearly 3 months after admission is there an attempt at a personal history documented in the clinical file. At this stage it is noted that his parents do not want him home.

On admission to the EPPIC inpatient unit, a comprehensive management plan addressing drug and alcohol abuse, education regarding illness, and specifically focusing on suicidal thoughts, was designed. Psychotic symptoms had persisted throughout the admission and therefore medication was ceased and reassessed. A case manager was assigned within 2 days of admission to EPPIC, and she referred him to the group program, explored accommodation options, and linked him to an employment program within the first week. From this time he started to "come alive", judging from entries in the casenotes, with reference to his fears, interests, and goals. The OCM and family worker then had sessions with Dale's parents, who were understandably concerned about their son's potential for violence. The father attended the family and friends education sessions. Dale was soon referred to TREAT, and was commenced on clozapine. STOPP was introduced and he attended regularly for 35 sessions. STOPP initially focused on a detailed assessment of symptoms and exploration of his explanatory model. Coping strategies for the voices and psycho-education functioned to gently challenge his delusional beliefs and perceived lack of control. Later sessions explored his poor sense of self and the trauma of, as Dale painfully described it, "being mental". Improvements in symptoms, as well as an increasing sense of his having some control over his life, were further enhanced when he moved out of his family home into supported accommodation specifically established for first-episode patients.

Dale's management was far from ideal. Treatment needs to begin early and community education must focus on easing the patient's pathway into care. The incident of violence which occurred prior to the admission was clearly very traumatic for patient and family and, one could assume, may have been avoided if intervention had been early. When treatment is entered it should be effective wherever possible. Nearly all patients can expect remission or significant recovery (Lieberman et al., 1993). High doses of medication and the subsequent side effects did not give Dale confidence in those who were supposedly helping him. A process of automatically reviewing "prolonged recovery" patients by a panel of senior staff helps to avoid this situation. Treatment needs to take account of the complex interactions of drug abuse, personality, family reaction and personal understanding of illness. Even a very unwell person is responding to his/her experiences and our treatments: it must be acknowledged that "there is a person in there". A recognition of the impact of being psychotic, with the after-effects of the behaviour at the time, is essential in the recovery process.

HOW DOES EPPIC WORK?

Structure

EPPIC is currently quite substantial in terms of resources, with clinical staff numbering the equivalent of 60 full-time positions and an annual budget, including administration and provisions of AUD $3.8 million (1997). The size and

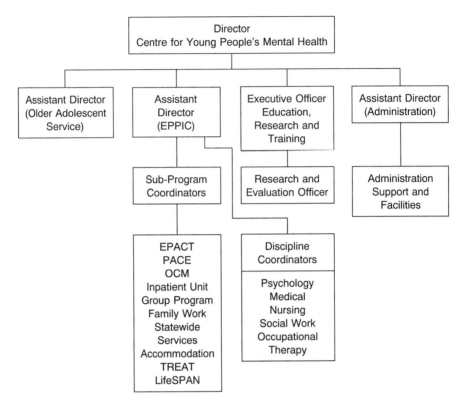

Figure 10.2   EPPIC organizational context

complexity of the service provides communication challenges for both staff and clients, particularly within a rapidly evolving youth mental health context (McGorry, 1996)

EPPIC operates on a matrix structure of sub-programs and disciplines, as illustrated in Figure 10.2, with clearly designated co-ordinators taking responsibilities for key areas and represented in the management and planning (MAP) executive. Line management responsibility lies with sub-programs co-ordinators, with discipline co-ordinators providing discipline-specific advice. Efforts are made to ensure a multi-disciplinary mix within sub-programs; however, an ethos of "best person for the job" prevails and many core roles are advertised as generic positions. The staffing composition of the various sub-programs is outlined in Table 10.1. Many clinicians work across programs, which aims to avoid marginalization of program elements. For operational purposes, Table 10.2 is broken down by individual employees and sessional allocations to sub-programs are negotiated by the sub-program co-ordinators (not illustrated here). Program co-ordinators are encouraged to adopt an empowering management style, mir-

Table 10.1 Number of clients allocated to EPPIC case management teams for the week beginning 26 August 1997

| | Number of sessions | Maximum case load | Number of clients | Discharges due over next 3 months | | | | | |
				Overdue	1 Month	2 Months	3 Months	Total	New clients past 3 months
Team A	31.5	189	162	4	8	3	6	21	38
Team B	36.07	216	174	6	10	5	11	32	35
Total	67.57	405.42	336	10	18	8	17	53	73

Session = 3 hours 48 minutes, or 0.5 day. Maximum case load calculated at six clients per session and does not reflect staff on leave or lowered caseloads due to staff entering or exiting employment at EPPIC.

Table 10.2 Clinical staff composition of EPPIC sub-programs by disciplines based on recurrent funding

	Psychology	Medical	Nursing	Social work	Occupational therapy	Total
EPACT	1	1.4	7	2.0	1	10.4
PACE		1.05				1.05
OCM	3.65	4.0	2.1	1.4	2.3	13.45
Inpatient Unit		2.9	21.5	1.0		25.4
Group Program	0.6			1.0	2.33	3.93
Family Work		0.2		1.0		1.2
Statewide Services	1.0		0.9		1.0	2.9
Accomodation			0.2	0.5		0.7
TREAT	0.20	0.1				0.30
LifeSPAN	0.15	0.1				0.25
						59.58

PACE, TREAT and LifeSPAN have additional grant-funded clinical positions not reflected here. Administrative and research staff are not included.

roring the approach considered appropriate in interactions between case managers and young people, who are frequently struggling with issues concerning autonomy and control. Twice a year the *EPPIC Information Package*, which details the internal workings of the program, is updated and distributed to all staff.

MAP is currently supported by 10 sub-committees, outlined in Figure 10.3, and each sub-committee has a nominated convenor who formally reports

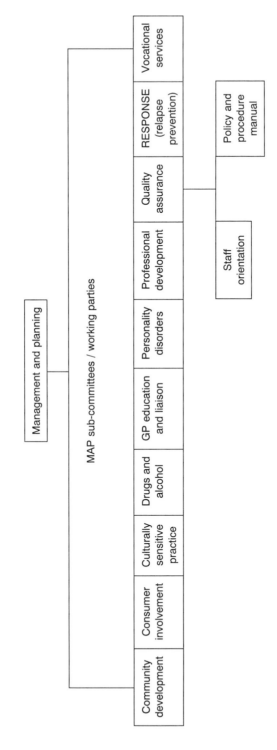

Figure 10.3   EPPIC committee structure

bi-annually to the executive. These groups have been described as the "engine room" of EPPIC—seeding ideas and driving initiatives to improve outcomes for clients. A number of areas within the program require substantial development. In particular, consumer satisfaction and consumer or "prosumer" (Davidson et al., in press) participation are high priorities. The model of consumer involvement developed in EPPIC needs to take into consideration the kind of roles appropriate for early psychosis patients who may have a relatively short experience of the service, and a consumer has been employed to assist in this process. A vocational need analysis is underway which should inform the development of a staged model for return to work or school. The possibility of implementing a supported employment model, drawing on the ideas of Becker, Drake and colleagues (Becker & Drake, 1994; Drake et al., 1994) is being actively pursued. Cannabis use is an ongoing concern, with rates being higher in this group than their local peer group (Hambrecht & Häfner, 1996). In recognition of the association of cannabis abuse with poorer outcome (Linszen, Dingemans & Lenoir, 1994), funding has been secured to develop and evaluate a brief intervention for individuals experiencing a first-episode psychosis and "problematic" substance use.

The *Stitch in Time* community video provides an 8-minute service overview (Ioannides & Hexter, 1994b) which is particularly useful in explaining the service to clients, and a more extensive 26-minute film about early psychosis featuring the stories of the consumers of the service (Ioannides & Hexter, 1994b). The *Users Guide: Everything You'll Need to Know About EPPIC*, a written service orientation document, is supplied to patients and families during the engagement process. There are also pamphlets available describing each of the individual program components, as we find some young people appreciate more select information. Increasingly, patients and families are accessing information from the EPPIC website, the website number being advertised using colourful postcards.

Staff Training

"Expectations and practice cannot necessarily be assumed to coincide" (Wooff, 1992, p. 289). Staff training is crucial for skill development, personal growth, maintaining standards and, in a busy clinical service, gives permission to reflect on practice. Group sessions promote a collective philosophy and are important in integrating program elements. Staff at EPPIC have access to weekly professional development sessions, in which internal and invited specialist speakers share their knowledge. These sessions allow collective discussion to occur on topics of particular interest, for example, substance abuse, debriefing, suicide prevention, sexual abuse. The timetable is are organized in four cycles: research and evaluation; clinical audit; theory; and practice. In addition, weekly clinical case conferences take place which provide a forum for discussion of illustrative and/or difficult cases to occur with all staff present. The two OCM teams alternatively present cases rotating through four designated phases of treatment: pre-psychotic, acute, recovery and prolonged recovery. Rosters for professional development and clinical consultation are established on a 6-monthly basis.

Most staff receive clinical supervision and the frequency and format clinical varies. Supervision arrangements have a duration for a 6- or 12-month periods only and each period of supervision episode has a stated theme. Staff have access to workshops convened by Statewide Services and visiting speakers are also engaged to undertake workshops on specific topics.

EPPIC continuously strives to improve both service delivery as well as modify factors which may hinder the high level of recovery that it aims to achieve. Annual full-scale service review days are held off-site in which the clinical model and service structures are re-evaluated, chaired by an external facilitator. Sub-programs also conduct bi-annual half-day reviews, where both professional opinions and consumer views are canvassed.

Evaluation and Quality Assurance

Evaluation and quality assurance in mental health services is becoming an increasingly important issue, as those who fund services, those who provide services and those who use services want to know whether the services provided are effective and delivered in the best possible manner. Because preventative intervention in early psychosis is a relatively new area, evaluation of outcome and quality control in service provision are particularly important, not only for their intrinsic value but as a powerful tool to influence policy makers and other clinicians.

Evaluation is an integral aspect of EPPIC's functioning and a framework has been established which involves process, impact and outcome evaluation. Each sub-program carries out process and impact evaluation, while the overall outcome for patients is assessed through formal follow-up of patients. The evaluation process is planned by the Quality Assurance Committee co-ordinated by a full-time evaluation officer.

The EPPIC Standards of Quality have been designed to achieve a streamlined and structured approach to the implementation of clinical practice, helping to smooth out inappropriate variation in clinical practice (Grimshaw & Hutchinson, 1995). The standards are based upon the centre's philosophy and were developed via consensual meetings of EPPIC staff. They are not intended to detail clinical practice, but rather to provide a shared understanding of the practice framework. Table 10.3 gives examples of clinical guidelines and measurement indicators developed to evaluate service provision for clients in the acute phase of illness.

Table 10.3 Examples of clinical guidelines and measurement indicators used by EPPIC as part of the *EPPIC Standards of Quality in Clinical Practice* (contained in the EPPIC Information Package, August 1997)

Guideline	Indicator
All patients should be assigned an OCM and medical officer within 2 working days of initial assessment	Percentage of registered clients assigned an OCM and medical officer within 24 hours of assessment
The OCM will formally liaise with the EPACT or inpatient unit within 2 working days of assignment	Mean number of days between OCM allocation and attendance of hand-over
The OCM will see a new client within 1 week of allocation	1. Mean number of days between allocations and contact with client 2. Percentage of clients seen within 1 week of allocation
The client will be seen at least weekly during the acute phase	Average numbers of days seen during acute phase
Liaison should occur between the OCM and acute treatment team which includes a joint meeting with the patient as a component of the discharge from the inpatient unit or EPACT (this should be recorded in the file)	Percentage of first presentation acute treatment discharges (inpatient unit and EPACT) in which this joint meeting occurs
Once the patient has been seen by an EPPIC clinician the family should be contacted within 48 hours to offer support and information	1. Percentage of families seen in first 48 hours at least once 2. Mean number of days between date of entry to OCM service and family contact 3. Percentage of families contacted in the first 24 hours
The families of the client should be seen at least weekly during the acute phase of illness	Mean number of times family seen
All patients and families should be given the EPPIC information kit within 1 week of initial assessment	1. Number of *Users Guide's* distributed vs. number of new registrations
Appropriate psychoeducation will be supplied by the OCM during the acute phase	Mean numbers of cases in which *Stitch in Time* community video and booklet is given to new clients
All patients should be informed of the EPPIC group program activities	1. Numbers of patients asked who know about the group program 2. Average number of new clients (<3 months in service) attending introduction group

OCM = outpatient case manager; EPACT = Early Psychosis Assessment and Treatment Team.

Global outcome evaluation is an important variable in mental health service delivery, as cost–benefit analysis supersedes simple costing methods and process indicators. Ruggeri & Tansella (1995) distinguish between efficacy (the potential of a treatment under experimental or "controlled" conditions) and effectiveness (the result obtained in "real world" clinical practice). Quite often treatments may be assumed to be effective, because their efficacy has been demonstrated, yet in naturalistic settings may be far from effective. A naturalistic effectiveness study with multidimensional outcome measures was undertaken to evaluate the effectiveness of the EPPIC program on 12-month outcome, in contrast to a previous model of care (McGorry et al., 1996). Results suggested that EPPIC clients were experiencing a significantly better outcome than their counterparts in non-EPPIC services in relation to overall quality of life, including social and role functioning. The level of post-traumatic stress disorder previously documented as associated with hospitalization was reduced and the experience of psychosis itself was reported as being less stressful. The average length of hospital stay and the mean dose of neuroleptics used had both decreased, although recovery had not been compromised as evidenced by monitoring of the patients mental state. The increased community costs of the EPPIC model were more than covered by the reduction in inpatient costs, suggesting that the intervention was an economically viable method of improving outcomes (Mihalopoulos, Carter & McGorry, submitted).

Research

Research has played a fundamental role in guiding EPPIC's development. The current program of research includes projects in suicide prevention, prolonged recovery, low-dose antipsychotic medication, treatment delay, pre-psychotic samples, cannabis use, and examination of comparison cohorts. Five randomized controlled trials of medications and/or psychosocial treatments are under way. Funding sources include the Victoria Health Promotion Foundation, the National Health and Medical Research Council, the Stanley Foundation, pharmaceutical companies (Janssen-Cilag, Novartis) and project funding from the Victoria State and Federal governments.

Over a dozen individuals are undertaking higher degrees within the service. Topic areas being studied include: relapse prevention; emotion recognition; personality and self-constructs; coping styles; vocational self-concept; enduring negative symptoms; engagement issues; and long-term outcome. A number of clinicians are pursing one-off projects for the purpose of informing clinical and/or research work, such as: psychotherapeutic interventions in first-episode psychotic mania; the prevalence of co-morbid syndromes; the outcome of a group psychoeducation intervention; and examination of individuals who refuse to participate in research! Collaboration around biological psychiatry research occurs with the Mental Health Research Institute, located only a few minutes walk from the EPPIC site.

   Additional information about research in progress is provided in the *Annual Report* (Centre for Young People's Mental Health, 1998).

SUMMARY AND CONCLUSION

EPPIC has developed an innovative comprehensive specialized treatment service for individuals experiencing their first psychotic episode residing in the Western Metropolitan Region of Melbourne. The focus placed on early detection and intensive early treatment of emergent psychosis is designed to limit the damage to personal identity, social networks and role-functioning caused by the underlying illness, while the array of services offered to promote recovery and adaptation are aimed at reducing or delaying relapse and avoiding the development of secondary consequences of having experienced a psychotic episode. An initial evaluation of the EPPIC model demonstrated a significant improvement in symptomatic and functional outcome when compared to the previous inpatient-only model and funding submissions have been prepared to enable long-term follow-up. The statewide training arm of EPPIC has undertaken pilot projects in other parts of Melbourne and rural Victoria, attempting to assist mental health services to incorporate an early psychosis focus within their settings. Interest in the development and application of best practice treatments for early psychosis is rapidly developing, with early psychosis projects under way in other parts of Australia and New Zealand, the UK, The Netherlands, Scandinavia, the USA and Canada (Edwards, McGorry & Pennell, in press). Amongst early psychosis clinicians and researchers, a number of key service delivery debates are emerging, focusing on: (a) the relative importance of early detection vs. the provision of best treatments following identification of the illness; (b) what constitutes best practice treatment for early psychosis; and (c) the appropriate length of time to provide such treatments, with opinions ranging from the "first episode" to 5 years. In EPPIC's next developmental phase the aim will be to tackle a number of these issues through collaborative projects with other mental health services. At the very least, this "real world" research generates considerable enthusiasm amongst clinicians and the evaluation process itself acts as a rigorous quality assurance exercise in the pursuit of excellence—factors important in fuelling the energy and optimism which are essential in working with this population.
   To conclude:

> As science only issues interim reports, the scientific basis of treatment may change from decade to decade but, as the predicament of someone suffering from depression or schizophrenia does not change from one decade to another, the art of treatment is likely to be more enduring, harder to teach, and probably more valuable to the practice of psychiatry than simple information about the specifics of treatment (Andrews, 1997, p. 11).

We endeavour to ensure that EPPIC contributes to both the art and the science of treatment for young people experiencing a first-episode psychosis.

ACKNOWLEDGEMENTS

We wish to thank Dominic Miller for drafting Figure 10.1; Mark Henry and Daniella Haitas for Figures 10.2 and 10.3; and Richard Bell and Mark Henry for supplying the information contained in Tables 10.1 and 10.2, respectively. Many clinicians have contributed to the development of the EPPIC model and we wish to acknowledge particularly those individuals who have allowed us to draw on unpublished writings and/or work in progress.

REFERENCES

Albiston, D.J., Francey, S.M. & Harrigan, S.M. (1998). A group program for recovery form early psychosis. *British Journal of Psychiatry* (suppl. 33), **172**, 117–121.

Andrews, G. (1997). Evidence-based medicine and the future of the practice of psychiatry. In *Mental Health in the 21st Century*, Proceedings of the Geigy Symposium, University of Newcastle, November 1996.

American Psychiatric Association (1997). Practice guideline for the treatment of patients with schizophrenia. *American Journal of Psychiatry*, **154**(suppl), 1–63.

Australian Bureau of Statistics (1991). *Census of Population and Housing Expanded Community Profile*. Canberra: Australian Bureau of Statistics.

Becker, D.R. & Drake, R.E. (1994). Individual placement and support: a community mental health centre approach to vocational rehabilitation. *Community Mental Health Journal*, **30**, 193–206.

Beck, A.T., Rush, A.J., Shaw, B.F. & Emery, G. (1979). *Cognitive Therapy of Depression*. New York: Guilford.

Beiser, M., Bean, G., Erickson, D., Zhang, J., Iacono, W.G. & Rector, N.A. (1994). Biological and psychosocial predictors of job performance following a first episode of psychosis. *American Journal of Psychiatry*, **151**, 857–863.

Beiser, M., Erickson, D., Fleming, J.A.E. & Iacono, W.G. (1993). Establishing the onset of psychotic illness. *American Journal of Psychiatry*, **150**, 1349–1354.

Birchwood, M. & MacMillan, F. (1993). Early intervention in schizophrenia. *Australian and New Zealand Journal of Psychiatry*, **27**, 374–378.

Birchwood, M., McGorry, P. & Jackson, H.J. (1997). Early intervention in schizophrenia. *British Journal of Psychiatry*, **170**, 2–5.

Carpenter, W.T. & Strauss, J.S. (1991). The prediction of outcome in schizophrenia IV: eleven-year follow-up of the Washington IPSS cohort. *Journal of Nervous and Mental Disease*, **179**, 517–525.

Centre for Young People's Mental Health (1998). *Annual Report.* Parkville, Australia.

Cocks, J.T. (1997). Use of very low dose antipsychotic in the treatment of first episode psychosis. Paper presented at conference, Schizophrenia: Toward the 21st Century, Surabaya, Indonesia.

Copolov, D.L., McGorry, P.D., Keks, N., Minas, I.H., Herman, H.E. & Singh, B.S. (1989). Origins and establishment of the schizophrenia research programme at Royal Park Psychiatric Hospital. *Australian and New Zealand Journal of Psychiatry*, **23**, 443–451.

Cozolini, L.J. & Neuchterlein, K. (1986). Pilot study of the impact of a family education program on relative of recent-onset schizophrenic patients. In M.J. Goldstein, I. Hand & K. Hahlweg (eds), *Treatment of Schizophrenia: Family Assessment and Intervention*, pp. 129–140.

Crow, T., Macmillan, J.F., Johnson, A.L. & Johnstone, E.C. (1986). A randomised controlled trial of prophylactic neuroleptic treatment. *British Journal of Psychiatry*, **148**, 120–127.

Davidson, L., Weingarten, R., Steiner, J., Stayner, D. & Hoge, M.A. (in press). Integrating prosumers into clinical settings. In C.T. Mowbray (ed.), *Consumers as Providers in Psychiatric Rehabilitation: Models, Applications and First Person Accounts*. International Association of Psychosocial Rehabilitation Services.

Drake, R.E., Becker, D.R., Biesanz, J.C., Torrey, W.C., McHugo, G.J. & Wyzik, P.F. (1994). Rehabilitative day treatment versus supported employment. I. Vocational outcomes. *Community Mental Health Journal*, **30**, 519–532.

Drake, R.E., Gates, C., Cotton, P.G. & Whitaker, A. (1984). Suicide among schizophrenics: who is at risk? *Journal of Nervous and Mental Disease*, **172**, 613–617.

Drew, L.T. & Howe, E. (1997). Description and evaluation of the early psychosis assessment and community treatment team. Poster presented at the First UK International Conference on Early Intervention in Psychosis, Stratford-upon-Avon, June.

Eaton, W.W., Mortensen, P.B., Herrman, H., Freeman, H., Bilker, W., Burgess, P. & Wooff, K. (1992). Long-term course of hospitalization for schizophrenia: I. Risk for rehospitalization. *Schizophrenia Bulletin*, **18**, 217–228.

Edwards, J., Cocks, J. & Bott, J. (in press). Preventive case management in first episode psychosis. In P.D. McGorry & H.J. Jackson (eds), *Recognition and Management of Early Psychosis: a Preventive Approach*. New York: Cambridge University Press.

Edwards, J., Francey, S., McGorry, P.D. & Jackson, H. (1994). Early psychosis prevention and intervention: evolution of a comprehensive community-based specialized service. *Behaviour Change*, **11**, 223–232.

Edwards, J., Maude, D., McGorry, P.D., Harrigan, S. & Cocks, J. (1998). Prolonged recovery in first episode psychosis. *British Journal of Psychiatry* (suppl. 33), **172**, 107–116.

Edwards, J., McGorry, P.D., Pennell, K. (in press). Models of early intervention in psychosis: An analysis of service approaches. In M. Birchwood, D. Fowler & C. Jackson (eds), *Early Intervention in Psychosis: A guide to concepts, evidence and intervention*. Chichester: Wiley.

EPPIC (1997a). *Psychoeducation in Early Psychosis: Manual 1 in a Series of Early Psychosis Manuals*. Melbourne: EPPIC Statewide Services.

EPPIC (1997b). *Working with Families in Early Psychosis: Manual 2 in a Series of Early Psychosis Manuals*. Melbourne: EPPIC Statewide Services.

EPPIC (in press). *Group Work in Early Psychosis: Manual 4 in a Series of Early Psychosis Manuals*. Melbourne: EPPIC Statewide Services.

Fava, G.A. & Kellner, R. (1993). Staging: a neglected dimension in psychiatric classification. *Acta Psychiatrica Scandinavica*, **87**, 225–230.

Fenton, W.S. (1997). Course and outcome in schizophrenia. *Current Opinion in Psychiatry*, **10**, 40–44.

Ferrari, G. (1996). Multicultural issues in first psychosis. *Conn Mental Health Matters*, **1**, 7.

Fitzgerald, P. & Kulkarni, J. (in press). Home-based treatment of first-episode psychosis. In P.D. McGorry & H.J. Jackson (eds), *Recognition and Management of Early Psychosis: a Preventive Approach*. New York: Cambridge University Press.

Francey, S. (in press). The role of day programs in recovery from early psychosis. In P.D. McGorry & H.J. Jackson (eds), *Recognition and Management of Early Psychosis: a Preventive Approach*. New York: Cambridge University Press.

Gleeson, J., Jackson, H.J., Stavely, H. & Burnett, P. (in press). Family intervention in early psychosis. In P.D. McGorry & H.J. Jackson (eds), *The Recognition and Management of Early Psychosis*. New York: Cambridge University Press.

Grimshaw, J.M. & Hutchinson, A. (1995). Clinical practice guidelines—do they enhance value for money in health care? *British Medical Bulletin*, **51**, 927–940.

Haines, S.A., Gleeson, J.F., Pennell, K.M. & McGorry, P.D. (1997). Incorporating an early psychosis focus in a mainstream psychiatric setting: Early psychosis projects in

Victoria. Poster presented at the First UK International Conference on Early Intervention in Psychosis, Stratford-upon-Avon, June.

Häfner, H., Maurer, K., Löffler, W., Bustamante, S., an der Heiden, W., Riecher-Rössler, A. & Nowotny, B. (1995). Onset and early course of schizophrenia. In H. Häfner & W.F. Gattaz (eds), *Search for the Causes of Schizophrenia*, Vol. III. Berlin: Springer-Verlag, pp. 43–66.

Hambrecht, M. & Häfner, H. (1996). Substance abuse and the onset of schizophrenia. *Biological Psychiatry*, **40**, 1155–1163.

Helgason, L. (1990). Twenty years' follow-up of first psychiatric presentation for schizophrenia: what could have been prevented? *Acta Psychiatrica Scandinavica*, **81**, 231–235.

Ioannides, T. (Producer) & Hexter, I. (Director) (1994a). *A Stitch in Time: Psychosis ... Get Help Early* (a community video). Melbourne: Early Psychosis Prevention and Intervention Centre.

Ioannides, T. (Producer) & Hexter, I. (Director) (1994b). *A Stitch in Time: Psychosis ... Get Help Early* (a video about EPPIC). Melbourne: Early Psychosis Prevention and Intervention Centre.

Jablensky, A., Sartorius, N., Ernberg, G., Anker, M., Korten, A., Cooper, J.E., Day, R. & Bertelsen, A. (1992). Schizophrenia: manifestations, incidence and course in different cultures. A World Health Organization ten-country study. *Psychological Medicine* (monograph, suppl 20). Cambridge: Cambridge University Press.

Jackson, H.J. & Judd, F. (1997). Evidence-based clinical psychiatry: the need for a balanced view. Submitted for publication.

James, N. (1996). *A Symposium on Treatment-resistant Schizophrenia: Early Identification and Appropriate Treatment* (video). XXth CINP Congress, Melbourne, June. Adelaide: Foundations Studios.

Jones, P.B., Bebbington, P., Foerste, A., Lewis, S.W., Murray, R.M., Russell, A., Sham, P.C., Toone, B.K. & Wilkins, S. (1993). Premorbid social underachievement in schizophrenia: results from the Camberwell collaborative psychosis study. *British Journal of Psychiatry*, **162**, 65–71.

Kane, J.M. (1997). The facilitation of early detection and treatment of schizophrenia: editorial review. *Current Opinion in Psychiatry*, **10**, 3–4.

Kane, J.M. & Marder, S.P. (1993). Psychopharmacologic treatment of schizophrenia. *Schizophrenia Bulletin*, **19**, 287–302.

Kemp, R., Hayward, P., Applewhaite, G., Everitt, B. & David, A. (1996). Compliance therapy in psychotic patients: randomised controlled trial. *British Medical Journal*, **312**, 345–349.

Kessler, R.C., Foster, C.L., Saunders, W.B. & Stang, P.E. (1995). Social consequences of psychiatric disorders. I: Educational attainment. *American Journal of Psychiatry*, **152**, 1026–1031.

Kosky, R. & Hardy, J. (1992). Mental health: is early intervention the key? *Medical Journal of Australia*, **256**, 147–148.

Krausz, M., Muller-Thomsen, T. & Maasen, C. (1995). Suicide among schizophrenia adolescents in the long-term course of illness. *Psychopathology*, **28**, 95–103.

Kulkarni, J. & Power, P. (in press). Initial management of first-episode psychosis. In P.D. McGorry & H.J. Jackson (eds), *Recognition and Management of Early Psychosis: a Preventive Approach*. New York: Cambridge University Press.

Larsen, T.K., McGlashan, T.H. & Moe, L.C. (1996). First-episode schizophrenia. I. Early course parameters. *Schizophrenia Bulletin*, **22**, 241–256.

Lieberman, J., Jody, D., Geisler, S., Alvir, J., Loebel, A., Szymanski, S., Woerner, M. & Borenstein, M. (1993). Time course and biological correlates of treatment response to first-episode schizophrenia. *Archives of General Psychiatry*, **50**, 369–376.

Lieberman, J.A., Koreen, A.R., Chakos, M., Sheitman, B., Woerner, M., Alvir, J. et al. (1996). Factors influencing treatment response and outcome of first-episode schizophrenia: implications for understanding the pathophysiology of schizophrenia. *Journal of Clinical Psychiatry*, **57**(suppl), 5–9.

Linehan, M., Armstrong, H., Suarez, A. & Allmon, D. (1991). Cognitive behavioral treatment of chronically parasuicidal borderline patients. *Archives of General Psychiatry*, **48**, 1060–1064.

Linehan, M., Tutek, D., Heard, H. & Armstrong, H. (1994). Interpersonal outcome of cognitive behavioural treatment for chronically suicidal borderline patients. *American Journal of Psychiatry*, **151**, 1771–1776.

Linszen, D.H., Dingemans, P.M. & Lenoir, M.E. (1994). Cannabis abuse and the course of recent-onset schizophrenic disorders. *Archives of General Psychiatry*, **51**, 273–279.

Loebel, A., Lieberman, J.A., Alvir, J.M., Mayerhoff, D.I., Geisler, S.H. & Szymanski, S.R. (1992). Duration of psychosis and outcome in first-episode schizophrenia. *American Journal of Psychiatry*, **149**, 1183–1188.

Maude, D., Edwards, J., McGorry, P.D., Cocks, J., Bennett, C., Burnett, P., Pica, S., Bell, R., Harrigan, S. & Davern, M. (1997). A randomised controlled trial using cognitive-behavioral therapy and clozapine in the early treatment of persisting positive symptoms in first-episode psychosis: preliminary results. Paper presented at the Second International Conference on Psychological Treatments for Schizophrenia, Oxford, England.

McElroy, S.L., Strakowski, S.M., West, S.A., Keck, P.E. & McConville, B.J. (1997). Phenomenology of adolescent and adult mania in hospitalized patients with bipolar disorder. *American Journal of Psychiatry*, **154**, 44–49.

McGlashan, T.H. (ed.) (1996a). Early detection and intervention in schizophrenia [Special issue]. *Schizophrenia Bulletin*, **22**, 197–352.

McGlashan, T.H. (ed.) (1996b). Early detection and intervention in schizophrenia. *Schizophrenia Bulletin*, **22**, 327–346.

McGlashan, T.H. & Johannessen, J.O. (1996). Early detection and intervention with schizophrenia: rationale. *Schizophrenia Bulletin*, **22**, 210–222.

McGorry, P.D. (1991). Paradigm failure in functional psychosis: review and implications. *Australian and New Zealand Journal of Psychiatry*, **25**, 43–55.

McGorry, P.D. (1992). The concept of recovery and secondary prevention in psychotic disorders. *Australian and New Zealand Journal of Psychiatry*, **26**, 3–17.

McGorry, P.D. (1993). Early Psychosis Prevention and Intervention Centre. *Australasian Psychiatry*, **1**, 32–34.

McGorry, P.D. (1995). Psychoeducation in early psychosis: a therapeutic process. *Psychiatry*, **58**, 329–344.

McGorry, P.D. (1996). The Centre for Young People's Mental Health: blending epidemiology and developmental psychiatry. *Australasian Psychiatry*, **4**, 243–246.

McGorry, P.D. (in press). "A stitch in time" ... the scope for preventative strategies in early psychosis. *European Archives of Psychiatry and Clinical Neuroscience*.

McGorry, P.D., Chanen, A., McCarthy, E., Van Riel, R., McKenzie, D. & Singh, B.S. (1991). Post-traumatic stress disorder following recent-onset psychosis: an unrecognized postpsychotic syndrome. *Journal of Nervous and Mental Disease*, **179**, 253–258.

McGorry, P.D., Copolov, D.L. & Singh, B.S. (1990). Current concepts in functional psychosis. *Schizophrenia Bulletin*, **3**, 221–234.

McGorry, P.D. & Edwards, J. (1997). *Early Psychosis Training Pack*. Macclesfield, Cheshire: Gardiner-Caldwell Communications.

McGorry, P.D., Edwards, J., Mihalopoulos, C., Harrigan, S. & Jackson, H.J. (1996). Early Psychosis Prevention and Intervention Centre: an evolving system for early detection and intervention. *Schizophrenia Bulletin*, **22**, 305–326.

McGorry, P.D., Henry, L. & Power, P. (in press). Suicide in early psychosis: could early intervention work? In R. Kosky, R. Goldney & R. Hassan (eds), *Proceedings of Suicide Prevention. The Global Contact*. New York: Hassan, Plenum.

McGorry, P.D. & Jackson, H. (eds) (in press). *The Recognition and Management of Early Psychosis: a Preventive Approach*. New York: Cambridge University Press.

McGorry, P.D. & Singh, B.S. (1995). Schizophrenia: risk and possibility. In B. Raphael & G.D. Burrows (eds), *Handbook of Studies on Preventive Psychiatry*. Melbourne: Elsevier Science, pp. 491–514.

Merlo, C.G. & Hoffer, H. (in press). Systematic considerations for the inpatient treatment of first-episode, acute schizophrenic patients. In M.C.G. Merlo, C. Perris & H.D. Brenner (eds), *Cognitive Therapy with Schizophrenic Patients: the Evolution of a New Treatment Approach*.

Mihalopoulos, C., Carter, R.C. & McGorry, P.D. (submitted). Is early intervention in first episode psychosis an economically viable method of improving outcome? Submitted for publication.

Moscarelli, M., Capri, S. & Neri, L. (1991). Cost evaluation of chronic schizophrenic patients during the first three years after the first contact. *Schizophrenia Bulletin*, **17**, 421–426.

Pennell, K.M., McGorry, P.D., Haines, S.A., Urbanc, A., Pound, B., Dagg, B., Handley, P., Wigg, C. & Berry, H. (1997). Australian National Early Psychosis Project: the development and promotion of a national best practice model in early intervention in psychosis—a project overview. Paper presented at the Mental Health Services Conference, Sydney, Australia.

Pennell, K., Tanti, C. & Howe, L. (1995). Housing and support for young people recovering from an episode of early psychosis: a service description. Poster presented at the Mental Health Services Conference, Auckland, New Zealand.

Power, P. (in press). Suicide and early psychosis. In P.D. McGorry & H.J. Jackson (eds), *Recognition and Management of Early Psychosis: a Preventive Approach*. New York: Cambridge University Press.

Power, P., Elkins, K., Adlard, S., Curry, C., McGorry, P. & Harrigan, S. (1998). An analysis of the initial treatment phase in first episode psychosis. *British Journal of Psychiatry* (suppl. 33), **172**, 71–76.

Rabiner, C.J., Wegner, J.T. & Kane, J.M. (1986). Outcome study of first-episode psychosis. I. Relapse rates after 1 year. *American Journal of Psychiatry*, **143**, 1155–1158.

Remington, G., Kapur, S. & Zipursky, R.B. (1998). Pharmacotherapy of first episode psychosis. *British Journal of Psychiatry* (suppl. 33), **172**, 66–70.

Rice, K., Herman, M.A. & Petersen, A.C. (1993). Coping with challenge in adolescence: a conceptual model and psycho-educational intervention. *Journal of Adolescent Health*, **16**, 235–251.

Rolfe, T. (1997). Cannabis use in first episode psychosis: incidence and short-term outcome. *Australian and New Zealand Journal of Psychiatry*, **31**(suppl 1), A74.

Ruggeri, M. & Tansella, M. (1995). Evaluating outcome in mental health care. *Current Opinion in Psychiatry*, **8**, 116–121.

Salkovkis, P., Atha, C. & Storer, D. (1990). Cognitive behavioral problem solving in the treatment of patients who repeatedly attempt suicide: a controlled trial. *British Journal of Psychiatry*, **157**, 871–876.

Takanishi, R. (1993). The opportunities of adolescence—research, interventions, and policy: introduction to the special issue. *American Psychologist*, **48**, 85–87.

Winnicott, D.W. (1965). *The Family and Individual Development*. London: Tavistock.

Women's and Children's Heathcare Network & Western Healthcare Network (1997). Strategic plan for an integrated mental health service for children and young people in the western region of the department of human services. Unpublished service document, Parkville, Australia.

Wooff, K. (1992). Service organisation and planning. In M. Birchwood & N. Tarrier (eds), *Innovations in the Psychological Management of Schizophrenia*. New York: Wiley, pp. 277–304.

Wyatt, R.J. (1991). Neuroleptics and the natural course of schizophrenia. *Schizophrenia Bulletin*, **17**, 325–351.

Wyatt, R.J., Piña, L.M. & Henter, I.D. (in press). First-episode schizophrenia: early intervention and medication discontinuation in the context of course and treatment. *British Journal of Psychiatry* (suppl).

Wynne, L.C. (1986). Working with families of acute psychotics: problems for research and reconsideration. In M.J. Goldstein, I. Hand & K. Hahlweg (eds), *Treatment of Schizophrenia: Family Assessment and Intervention*. pp. 109–115.

Yung, A.R. & McGorry, P.D. (1996). The prodromal phase of first-episode psychosis: past and current conceptualisations. *Schizophrenia Bulletin*, **22**, 353–370.

Yung, A.R., McGorry, P.D., McFarlane, C.A., Francey, S., Patton, G.C. & Jackson, H.J (1998). The prediction of psychosis: a step towards indicated prevention. *British Journal of Psychiatry* (suppl. 33), **172**, 14–20.

Yung, A.R., Phillips, L.J., McGorry, P.D., McFarlane, C.A., Francey, S., Jackson, H.J., Patton, G.C. & Rakkar, A. (1996a). Monitoring and care of young people at incipient risk of psychosis. *Schizophrenia Bulletin*, **22**, 283–351.

Yung, A.R., Phillips, L.J. & Drew, L.T. (in press). Promoting access to care in early psychosis. In P.D. McGorry & H.J. Jackson (eds), *Recognition and Management of Early Psychosis: a Preventive Approach*. New York: Cambridge University Press.

Yung, A.R., McGorry, P.D., McFarlane, C.A. & Patton, G.C. (1996b). The PACE clinic: development of a clinical service for young people at high risk of psychosis. *Australasian Psychiatry*, **3**, 345–351.

Chapter 11

An Integrated, Multilevels, Metacognitive Approach to the Treatment of Patients with a Schizophrenic Disorder or a Severe Personality Disorder

Carlo Perris*
Swedish Institute of Cognitive Psychotherapy, Stockholm, Sweden
and
Lars Skagerlind
Department of Psychiatry, Norrlands University Hospital,
Umeå, Sweden

INTRODUCTION

Previous chapters in this volume have described various approaches to the treatment of patients with a personality disorder or a schizophrenic disorder. The previous contributions have mainly dealt with the individual treatment in an outpatient setting, or with the use of strategies and techniques for dealing with specific psychopathological manifestations. The scope of this chapter, instead, is to highlight the use of a more global, integrated, multilevels psychotherapy approach to severely disturbed patients, that is cognitively based and schema-

---

*Author for correspondence.

Cognitive Psychotherapy of Psychotic and Personality Disorders: Handbook of Theory and Practice.
Edited by C. Perris and P.D. McGorry.
© 1998 John Wiley & Sons Ltd.

focused. Although there are some commonalities between the approach to be described in this chapter and that followed by Fowler and his co-workers (Fowler, Garety & Kuipers, 1996; Fowler, Garety & Kuipers, this volume) or by Kingdon & Turkington (1994) and Chambon, Perris & Marie-Cardine (1997), one major difference is that our programme is carried out at special-purpose small units, which were originally developed in Umeå in Northern Sweden in the 1980s (Perris, 1986, 1988a) and have been implemented subsequently in several other places, both in Sweden and in other European countries (e.g. Svensson, Hansson & Thorson, 1993).

Before describing the treatment program, however, it is necessary to avoid misunderstandings by spending a few words on the concept of integration as it applies to the program to be described. An integrative approach to psychotherapy can be conceived at different levels. One such level concerns the purposeful combination of different therapeutic modalities (e.g. individual, group, milieu, and family therapy) within the context of the treatment program. Another, instead, refers to the utilization, within one given therapeutic modality, of concepts and strategies which could rightly be regarded as belonging to therapies with a different theoretical orientation (e.g. the use of gestalt or behavioural techniques in the practice of individual cognitive psychotherapy). Both levels of integration occur in the treatment program that will be described in the following. It must be stressed, however, that the integration of therapeutic modalities, and therapeutic strategies in the context of the program to be described, should not be understood as a kind of unsystematic eclecticism. In fact, all therapeutic activities comprised in the program (including medication, the use of non-verbal therapeutic interventions and the use of less common strategies of the kind described by H. Perris (this volume) are linked together by a unitary, consistent theoretical principle. The adoption of a consistent theoretical framework is a necessary condition not only for the purposeful integration of various strategies at the practical level, but also, and even more important, to avoid the impending risk of epistemological confusion if integrative attempts stretch beyond the use of various strategies and techniques belonging to different therapeutic domains and also try to encompass less compatible metapsychological conceptions, especially those related to the process of change. An additional aspect of the integrated approach to treatment pursued in our units is that it involves the active participation of professionals with a different basic education (doctors, psychologists, nurses, etc.), who have received a common basic training in cognitive psychotherapy. Such a common training, should the need arise, allows for timely therapeutic interventions to be made by each member of the staff without any fragmentation in the type of response that is given to the patient.

All the components of the program, including the use of non-verbal therapeutic strategies (e.g. creative painting, or the training of body awareness), are based on a consistent use of cognitive-behavioural psychotherapy principles, basically derived from the procedures developed by Beck (1976) for the outpatient treatment of emotional disorders, and subsequently adapted by Perris (1986, 1988a, 1993, 1996a) for the treatment of severely disturbed patients.

The approach is a metacognitive one. That implies that the program is not primarily focused on the correction of basic cognitive deficits, or in the remediation of specific psychotic symptoms. Its ultimate aim, instead, is to achieve a restructuring of dysfunctional internal working models of self and others, as conceived by Bowlby (1969) and Main (1991), that the patients are assumed to have developed early in life and which represent a substantial part of their vulnerability. From this perspective, particular attention is consistently paid, in the context of each therapeutic modality, to the possible occurrence of dysfunctional interpersonal cycles, as described by Safran and Segal (1990; see also Peyton & Safran, this volume). The occurrence of such interpersonal cycles is expected, in fact, to reflect the kind of *tacit* knowledge (Polanyi, 1966) embedded in the core affective/cognitive schemata (or meaning structures, Lundh, 1988) of each patient. The role of "participant observers" assumed by all members of the staff greatly facilitates the detection of dysfunctional interpersonal cycles, independent of whether they occur in the individual-, group- or milieu-setting, and represent an important base for appropriate therapeutic interventions.

THEORETICAL RATIONALE

There seems to be a fair consensus among therapists of different ideological orientations that psychotherapy with schizophrenic patients, aiming at a restructuring of internal working models of self and others, preferably should begin in a protected setting where the possibility of letting the patient undergo a restitutive emotional experience, as emphasized by Sullivan (1931), is available. The experience we have gained during the last decade strongly suggests that a similar consideration applies to most patients with a severe personality disorder as well. Access to a setting which is therapeutic *per se* greatly facilitates the development of a purposeful therapeutic relationship at the same time as it allows for the full utilization of all the powerful therapeutic processes that may develop in such a setting (Gunderson, 1978; Perris, 1985, 1988b) and greatly reduces the risk of early dropout from treatment.

The theoretical rationale behind the treatment program that will be highlighted in the following has been reported at some length elsewhere (Perris, 1989, 1993, 1994, 1996b; Perris & Skagerlind, 1996). Briefly, the program is based on a few major premises, in the first place, awareness of the heterogeneity of the disorders subsumed under the label "schizophrenia" and hence of the need of case-specific strategies within a more general framework common to all patients participating in the treatment. The need for case-specific planning applies to patients with severe personality disorders as well. In fact, as discussed at some length elsewhere (Perris & Perris, 1997), a categorical Axis II diagnosis seldom represents a sufficient and purposeful basis for treatment. Second, knowledge derived from several investigations suggests that "chronicity" is not an unavoidable outcome intrinsic to a hypothetic disease "schizophrenia". Rather, it is largely influenced by cultural and psychosocial determinants. In our approach, we reject simplistic, unilinear causal explanations of both schizophrenic and personality disorders in favour of more complex etiopathogenetic models based on the concept of *individual vulnerability*, as described by Perris (this volume). It is important to emphasize once again, however, that individual vulnerability, as we define it, is not to be understood in exclusively biological terms. Instead, it has to be conceived as the result of the continuous interactions between biological and psychological determinants on the one side, and the continuous transactions between the individual and the environment on the other. Within this framework, vulnerability is defined both by the relatively invariant biological characteristics of the individual (including any more or less specific genetic predisposition) and by the development of dysfunctional internal working models of self and environment, which are assumed to interact in-between. Additional premisses refer to the necessity of taking into account the multifactorial nature of the global disability of the severely disturbed patients, which also encompasses deficits in interpersonal skills to a variable degree, and finally to awareness of both the facilitating and detrimental effects of concomitant medication to achieve a purposeful balance in its use.

THE GENERAL OUTLINES OF THE INTEGRATED TREATMENT PROGRAM

The general layout of the treatment program has been reported at some length in previous writings, where a more detailed description can be found (Perris, 1988a, 1989, 1993; Perris & Skagerlind, 1996). Briefly, the program is generally located in ordinary houses or flats in the community, where six to eight patients per home live in a family-style atmosphere, providing for themselves in daily chores and the preparation of meals under the supervision of the staff.

The staff at those small centres are mental nurses working on a day-time schedule. They have received formal training in cognitive psychotherapy and are responsible for all therapeutic work, including individual therapy and the conduct of therapeutic groups. In addition, one full-time occupational therapist and one part-time psychiatrically-schooled physiotherapist also trained in cognitive psychotherapy are part of the treatment team. Psychotherapy supervision in groups and continued in-service education are provided on a weekly basis. When the supervisor is not a doctor, access to medical advice is provided on a consultation basis a few hours weekly. Even though there is a general framework for treatment, valid for all partecipants, a particular emphasis on flexibility allows (as will be exemplified below) for the adaptation of the program to the particular needs of each patient participating in it.

Patients accepted to the centres are primarily in the age range 18–40 years, of either sex, who meet a DSM-III-R (or, more recently, DSM-IV) diagnosis of schizophrenic disorder, or an Axis II diagnosis of personality disorder (the last-mentioned belonging almost exclusively to clusters A or B). Although we would very much prefer to receive patients in an acute phase of illness, a majority of those referred to the centres have been preliminarly treated in some acute ward or as out-patients, mostly because of space constraints. However, they still present a psychotic symptomatology or severe disturbances of interpersonal behaviour when admitted to the units. Most patients have had several previous hospitalizations or repeated acute interventions at emergency units. Most frequently, in fact, patients with a schizophrenic disorder accepted to the units have a history of illness of 7–10 years from the first episode of manifest psychopathology. Excluded are patients with alcohol abuse or substance abuse as the main reason for care, and patients with a documented history of recurring acts of violence against others. To cope with the unavoidable problem of a waiting list, a special "socialization group" has been created. Members of the staff meet at irregular intervals with patients who expect to be admitted in order to socialize them in the therapeutic work at the centre, and in the basic principles of cognitive psychotherapy (CPT). In this way, the patients' motivation for treatment is kept alive during the waiting period.

Already the general layout of the program, in line with the conception maintained by Kingdon & Turkington (1994), is assumed to have a "normalizing" impact on the patients, as shown in Table 11.1. Also, it facilitates the training of everyday basic social skills in a natural setting, mainly through vicarious modelling and a strong emphasis on various activities to be carried out in the community.

Since space constraints do not allow for a detailed description of all the components of the program, and since most of those elements have been described at some length elsewhere (Perris, 1988a, 1989, 1993), we will summarize them in Table 11.2, in which a short characterization of each intervention is also given. In this way, it will be possible to leave more space to a closer description of the main phases of the individual psychotherapy. This description might be useful since it applies, also, to the practice of individual psychotherapy in an outpatient setting. Also, as an occasional part of the program, collective trips to other cities of a duration of 2–3 days take place once or twice each term.

As shown in Table 11.2, medication is a part of the treatment program. We agree with Coursey (1989) that psychotherapy and medication are not replacements for each other and can be purposefully combined. This stance is in line with the prevalent opinion that the strictly individualized use of medication is in many

Table 11.1 Overall "normalizing" aspects of the layout

Focus on individual vulnerability	Promoting distancing
Location in ordinary houses	Counteracting alienation from the community
Presence of pet animals	Enhancing the family atmosphere
Access to an own key of the house	Enhancing feelings of autonomy and belonging
Facultative interaction with visitors	Promoting the training of interpersonal skills and minimizing feelings of strangeness

Table 11.2 Integrating elements of the treatment program

Milieu therapy	Emphasis on a family-style atmosphere based on the concept of "secure base" (Bowlby, 1988; Perris, 1992)
Expressive painting	Aimed at facilitating communication in verbally inhibited patients, and at the monitoring of treatment progress
Physiotherapy	Aimed at the training of body knowledge, posture, setting of limits, etc. It also includes sports activities outside the units
Group therapy (includes various types of group meetings once weekly)	1. Exercises aimed at the correction of basic cognitive deficits. This kind of intervention is used only with patients who are particularly disorganized 2. Cognitively-based training of interpersonal skills 3. Training in the identification, differentiation, expression and control of emotive reactions 4. Training in the planning of leisure activities outside the units during weekends, holidays, etc.
Individual therapy	Schema-Focused, 2–3 sessions weekly
Medication	Training in the self-management of medication, which is kept at the lowest effective level, according to each patient's needs
Homework assignments	To be carried out at the unit or in real life in the community. They also include the completion of evaluation forms
Interventions with families	To reduce conflicts and to promote collaboration
Ongoing evaluation	To record progress and to document the results of treatment

cases unavoidable for effective psychotherapy with schizophrenic patients to be implemented, or for occasionally containing deleterious acting-out in personality-disordered patients. However, since participation in psychotherapy obviously requires a certain degree of alertness from the patients, along with the capacity to experience and express emotions, the dosage of drugs is kept at the lowest effective level in order to avoid negative influences on attentional processes and emotional expressivity. On the other hand, the use of cognitive psychotherapy strategies is both feasible and particularly effective when there is a need to deal with some patient's lack of compliance with medication. One subgoal of the treatment program is that each patient has to learn about the pros and cons of his/her medication and shall be able to take care of it at discharge, if continued medication is required.

One particular advantage of the approach described in this chapter is that all the members of the staff at the units, because of their common psychotherapy training, are actively involved in all therapeutic work and participate in group supervision. In this way, a thorough integration of all therapeutic elements can occur. For example, observations concerning some patient's dysfunctional behaviour made during the day, or in some group session, can easily be made a topic for discussion in the individual sessions. Conversely, difficulties evidenced at individual sessions can constitute the base of homework assignments to be carried out during the day at the unit, or in some of the group sessions.

INDIVIDUAL PSYCHOTHERAPY

Particular Adaptations of the Conduct of Therapy for Working with Severely Disturbed Patients

According to our experience of more than 10 years, the whole treatment requires a time-span ranging from about 1.5–2.5 years, roughly divided in the four phases to be described below. Before describing those phases, however, it might be appropriate to highlight some adaptations of "standard cognitive psychotherapy" (Clark, 1995) which have proved to be necessary to implement a metacognitive schema-focused approach with the type of patients dealt with in this chapter (Rothstein & Vallis, 1991, Perris, 1996a). Since most of those modifications are dealt with by Vallis (this volume), only a short mention will suffice at this juncture.

The main emphasis of a metacognitive approach is on the restructuring of *nuclear internal working models of self and others (core-schemata)*, rather than on the modification of more peripheral emotive/cognitive schemata. A distinction between peripheral basic assumptions and more central ones, which are hierarchically organized and out of awareness, underscores the crucial role that the organization of self-knowledge plays in both health and disease (e.g. Guidano, 1987). There is evidence in the literature that a rationalistic approach (of a noncritical type) may be sufficient in dealing with more peripheral psychopathological manifestations, but that it leaves almost unchanged the *core* vulnerability of the individual. To achieve a re-structuring of prevalently tacit *core schemata*, it is necessary to aim at achieving a second-order change rather than limit oneself to a first-order one (Lyddon, 1990).

One prerequisite for a correct identification of dysfunctional nuclear schemata, and for a conceptualization of dysfunctional interpersonal schemata to be modified, is that particular attention is paid to problematic aspects of development. In this context, it has to be kept in mind that in the unfolding process of development, differentiation and maturation of self, the organization of the earliest emotional-cognitive experiences is laid down in memory at the preverbal level, probably as *anoetic* procedural memory (Tulving, 1985) during the sensorimotor stage of development postulated by Piaget (1926), and as internal, generalized representations (RIGs), as described by Stern (1985). Only later during development are those experiences organized as episodic (*noetic*) memory, and even later are reorganized in the domain of semantic (*autonoetic*) memory. Thus, in practice it becomes necessary for the therapist to learn how to work with the memory of the patient (Bara, 1984) if one aim is a more adaptive integration of the various memory systems and hence a modification of core schemata.

At the structural level, the most frequent adaptations refer to the flexibility that is necessary in carrying out therapy in practice (e.g. frequency, duration and length of the sessions), and to the timing in the application of some of the techniques and strategies pertinent to cognitive psychotherapy. Also, as discussed in the chapter by H. Perris (this volume), it can be necessary to use less common strategies or to create *ex novo* new ones to suit the needs and the resources of a particular patient (Guidano, 1987). Such structural modifications are essential at the beginning of therapy, when a re-emergence of egocentrism is most marked, together with a pronounced deficit in metathinking (Perris, 1989, 1993). It would be almost impossible, in fact, to expect that patients with pronounced disturbance of the type just mentioned, should be able, early in therapy, to pinpoint automatic thoughts or to take anyone else's perspective but their own.

Patients with a schizophrenic disorder, as well as those with a severe personality disorder, frequently show a pronounced difficulty concerning the regulation of emotions, as well as impulse control. One practical consequence is that, especially at the beginning of treatment, particular attention has to be paid to validating the emotional experiences of the patient, before attempting to pinpoint the cognitive aspects related to those experiences. In the absence of such a validation, the risk of an early dropout greatly increases.

At the processual level, there is a general consensus that the development and maintenance of a valid therapeutic relationship is a crucial prerequisite for working with severely disturbed patients. One way of conceptualizing the relationship that is expected to develop between the patient and the therapist is in terms of *secure base* (Bowlby, 1988; Liotti, 1988; Isola, 1992; Perris, 1992, 1993; Perris & Perris, 1997; Liotti & Intreccialagli, this volume). Implicit in the concept of secure base is that the patient is given the opportunity to develop the certainty that his demands, when in need, will be empathically meet by the therapist, and that the therapist, in turn, is able to stimulate the patient in the exploration of even painful experiences and in promoting his/her autonomy. Meanwhile, a characteristic of the therapist acting as a secure base is that she/he must be able to set appropriate limits to the patient's dysfunctional behaviour.

The Phases of Therapy

It is current practice to schematize according to successive phases the psychotherapy of severely disturbed patients, even though there exists no clear-cut boundary between the various moments of the psychotherapeutic pathway. Most often, rather, the various phases of treatment fade into each other, and overlap can frequently occur. In particular, the boundary between the second and the third phases is to be regarded as very fluid indeed. However, a subdivision into phases might be useful as a guideline for psychotherapists in training who will work with this particular kind of patient.

In principle, four main phases can be distinguished:

1. An *attachment phase*, during which the therapeutic relationship is expected to develop and consolidate. During this phase an assessment of the patient's needs and resources is also carried out. Preliminary targets are defined, and a preliminary treatment plan is agreed upon.
2. A phase of *analysis and restructuring* of dysfunctional working models of self and others, during which the strategies and techniques of cognitive psycho-therapy are applied.
3. A phase during which the patient is coached in the *revision and re-edition of his/her life history*.
4. The phase of *preparation to termination and to a life after therapy*, during which attention is also paid to the working-through of the grief of mental illness.

Let us examine these phases more closely.

Attachment Phase and the Building-up of the Therapeutic Relationship

One major advantage of working in a therapeutic setting of the type described above is that the building-up of the therapeutic relationship can unfold in a less conventional way. There is, in fact, the possibility of meeting the patients at a level of their choice without forcing upon them an individual ther-apeutic activity for which they are still not prepared, and toward which they feel diffident.

> *Albert*, aged 20, was a very passive young man who kept mostly to himself and had difficulties in familiarizing with the other patients at the centre. Attempts at carrying out individual therapy sessions were mostly unsuccessful. Albert showed a suspi-cious attitude and gave only monosyllabic answers. His therapist discovered that one of Albert's interests was cross-country skiing. Thus, he proposed some outings together. Initially, Albert seemed to barely tolerate the company of the therapist, but later showed that he enjoyed it. After a few weeks of purely social interaction, it was possible to resume the formal individual sessions in which Albert became more co-operative.

> *Elsy*, aged 29, divorced and the mother of two daughters, accepted admittance to one of our therapeutic units after a sequence of short hospitalizations in her home town because of explosive actings-out and self-harm behaviour which had precipi-tated her divorce. During the early sessions she maintained a hostile attitude, often refusing to answer even the most neutral questions, claiming that the therapist should already know the answers without bothering her. On two occasions, without any evident provocation, she manifested explosive behaviour, throwing around whatever she had nearby, and left the therapy room. She went to her own room and committed actions of self-harm. In one of these occasions, the therapist put an arm around her shoulders and, speaking to her gently but firmly, succeeded in calming

her down before allowing her to retreat. No self-harm occurred. When they met outside the therapy room, the therapist behaved towards Elsy in as friendly a manner as before, as if the outbursts had not occurred. After a few such episodes, Elsy was able to report that because of the therapist's behaviour she had started experiencing that she could trust someone. She reached an agreement that she would try to mentally fly a "red flag" whenever she felt the impulse to explode. This strategy helped her to become more able to participate in the sessions. There were minor relapses, but Elsy proved able to put increasingly longer latency between the impulse to react and the actual reaction until her outbursts eventually came to an end. Retrospectively, she said that these experiences had helped her to successfully invalidate and then modify her self-image of being dangerous, and the image of the therapist as a fearful and a menacing attachment figure.

Adam, aged 25 and unemployed, was referred for a paranoid syndrome with manifest ideas of reference and a diffuse feeling of being persecuted by malevolent relatives and acquaintances. On a few occasions, he failed for 1 or 2 days to come back to the unit as agreed after a weekend when he was permitted to go home. He remained at home and refused to go out. On each of those occasions a member of an outpatient team had to pick him up at home and bring him back to the centre. After a couple of such incidents, the therapist decided to visit Adam at his flat on successive days and to hold the therapeutic sessions there. This action of the therapist apparently represented the critical incident which promoted Adam's definitive return to the therapeutic unit and the continuation of the therapy.

In the context of the therapeutic relationship, especially when working with patients with a schizophrenic disorder, the concept of *therapeutic distance* is of a paramount importance. This concept is well known to therapists with a psycho-analytical orientation. It has been underscored in cognitive psychotherapy by Liotti & Onofri (1987) and Perris (1996b). Within the framework of attachment theory (Bowlby, 1969; Perris, 1996b; Perris & Perris, 1997), the concept of "distance" mainly refers to the therapist's obligation of letting the patient establish the optimal degree of closeness in his/her attempt to establish contact, in order not to intrude too early on the model of attachment that the patient has developed. In practice, the regulation of an optimal distance does not exclusively refer to physical distance, even though the behaviour of severely disturbed patients in this respect is well known.

Mary, aged 28, with several years' history of persecutory delusions during which she acted against strangers, had been hospitalized several times and treated with high dosages of neuroleptic drugs. She participated without being manifestly obstructive in the therapeutic interviews, but succeeded in keeping the interviews at a superficial level. Whenever the therapist attempted to investigate more deeply into personal matters, she leaned back on the chair, turned her head at one side and started to express bizarre delusions which, in practice, made any further interaction meaningless. After several months, during which this behaviour was analysed, she admitted that her delusional incoherent behaviour was her solution to keep the therapist at distance from what was painful for her, without the risk of alienating his interest.

The Analysis of Dysfunctional Working Models and the Revision of the Patient's Autobiography

As mentioned before, the second and the third phases of treatment often overlap. Hence, we describe them together. During these phases, most of the strategies and techniques of cognitive psychotherapy can be employed, and graded home-work is assigned to facilitate the transfer to real life of hindsights gained in therapy. Also, as decentring progresses, and the ability of metathinking improves, it is possible to help the patient in becoming aware of automatic dysfunctional thoughts, and in counteracting them.

There are several strategies which can be used to facilitate the identification of dysfunctional working models of self and others. One is to analyse accurately the behaviour of the patient in the context of the therapeutic relationship. It can be assumed, in fact, that such behaviour will reflect the original pattern of attachment. In this context, "automatic behavioural reactions" could be assumed to correspond to automatic thoughts. A second approach consists of a thorough analysis of the way in which the patient tells his/her life history (e.g. in a fragmented way with many lacunae, or in an idealizing way in which the facts clearly contradict such idealizations). Particularly relevant in this context is an analysis of how the patient's memory systems appear to be intregrated with each other. A third way consists of the use of assessment instruments as the DWM Scale described by Perris et al. (this volume), or the Schema Questionnaire proposed by Young (1990).

The process pf identification of core schemata can also be facilitated by the use of less common strategies, such as creative painting (thematic or spontaneous) and the use of photographs:

> In the first of a series of self-portraits produced by *Hellen* during her 2-year stay at one of the centres, it was hardly possible even to discern the contours of a human figure. There was a hint of blond hair, and some marks indicating the legs. Successive self-portraits in the course of treatment became more and more ordinary, until there was no doubt that they referred to a girl of her age (26 years). When an analysis of the paintings was carried out, it emerged that as a child she had sported very long pigtails of which her relatives were allegedly very proud. At age 12, giving way one evening to the pressure of a classmate, she had her plaits cut off. Afterwards she was afraid to go home and to meet her parents, but had no other choice. In fact, nobody seemed to notice what she had done until the third day after the event, when her younger brother at breakfast pointed out that Hellen had had her pigtails cut off. Apparently, the only reaction by Hellen's mother was, "Oh! Has she? I hadn't noticed". Since that time one of Hellen's basic self-schemata had been one of being "invisible, unnoticed by anyone".

The use of photographs is valuable in the reconstruction of a patient's life history, especially in the early phases of treatment. They might help fill the gaps for people who may have blocked details of their past. The pictures also help patients to reconnect with family members who have died or are out of touch for other reasons. The use of family albums is particularly relevant when working with patients who have been sexually abused in childhood. Those patients, in fact, most frequently feel guilty for having been seductive, or for not having been able to set limits and stop the abuse. Looking together at pictures taken at the time when the abuse was going on, as well as by appropriate use of the Socratic method, it becomes easier to help patients to become aware of the arbitrariness of their conclusions and to realise how unjustified their guilt feelings are. Correcting their memory distortions, it is easy to make them aware that they were, in fact, helpless and powerlcss against the abuser.

At the end of the process which characterizes phases two and three, it is expected that the patient has become able to re-edit his/her life history in a more coherent and complete way, integrating in this narrative also the traumatic events which might have contributed in making him/her deviate from a pathway of normality.

The Final Phase and the Grieving of Losses

Lafond has treated at some extent the grieving of mental illness in a separate chapter (this volume), to which we refer for detail.

While one may have been able to experience the luck of being able to help a patient in leaving behind a whole life of psychopathological misery, it remains for the therapist one of the most difficult and frustrating tasks, namely, to help the patient in coming to terms with a sense of emptiness that he/she does not know how to fill. This difficulty is even more pronounced when the patient has lived for several years in the role of a psychotic without any ability to establish meaningful relationships with healthy people. Many patients do not know how to orientate themselves in an ordinary world that for them is unknown.

Therapists of a psychoanalytical orientation (e.g. Westen, 1991) agree, however, that in this context cognitive psychotherapy has a clear advantage compared with psychotherapies of a different ideological orientation. In fact, cognitive psychotherapy, as mentioned above, greatly facilitates the continuous testing in real-life situations of the hindsights developed in the course of therapy, hence facilitating the patient's re-adaptation to an ordinary life. There remains, however, the grief of opportunities which have been lost for ever and which are impossible to make up for. On such occasions the therapist must be prepared to deal with the grief of the patient as if it were a crisis following a loss, with all its well-known phases.

Separation at the end of treatment is seldom a major problem. As a rule it is spaced over a few months and does not occur abruptly. Also, if the therapeutic relationship has developed against the background of a secure attachment, the end of treatment does not simultaneously imply the definitive cutting of the emotional bond that has developed between patient and therapist. It is rather that, in a hierarchy of attachments, the figure of the therapist maintains an important role at least until new and more important attachments have developed. On the other hand, as we have pointed out elsewhere (Perris & Perris,

1997), it should be kept in mind that the more securely an attachment is experienced, the more possible it is to distance oneself from the attachment person, and the easier is the exploration of new, meaningful relationships.

A PRELIMINARY EVALUATION OF RESULTS

On previous occasions we have reported on a preliminary naturalistic 3-year follow-up study of a small series of patients, who have been treated for 1.5 years on average (Perris, 1994, 1996b; Perris & Skagerlind, 1994, 1996; Perris, Skagerlind & Johansson, 1995) and also on a small controlled trial of changes in attentional processes (Perris et al., 1990). The results of this preliminary evaluation suggest that the treatment program that we use is easily accepted by the patients, and is able to produce marked changes in social functioning which are not only maintained, but also increase during follow-up. Of particular interest is that no patient has interrupted treatment and that none of the patients treated at our units has committed suicide, either during treatment or after discharge. Recently, we have been able to add to the original series 10 additional patients who have completed a 3-year follow-up, and also some 20 patients with a personality disorder (mostly clusters A and B). A detailed report of these additional cases will be published elsewhere. It can be said, however, that in these cases the results obtained also strongly support the effectiveness of our approach. An additional study of a small series of patients treated with the same approach in a similar setting for 2 years, and with a 2-year follow-up, has been reported by Svensson, Hansson & Thorsson (1993). In this study also, the results have shown a good effect on symptoms, social functioning and quality of life.

ISSUES OF GENERALIZATION

When the approach that we pursue has been reported at international meetings, one frequent objection has been that the program could perhaps work in the hands of its proponents, and suit local conditions, but that it could hardly be generalized to other settings. In fact, the opposite has proved to be true. Since the development of our original units in Umeå, several similar units have been implemented in most Swedish regions. At present 10 of them have been implemented. Also, units where a similar approach is used have been made operative in Italy and in Finland, and others are being planned in other countries. Even though we recommend an inpatient model located in ordinary houses or flats, other alternative locations are acceptable as well, e.g. at day center facilities or in an unused ward of a hospital.

Another controversial issue in the present economic climate refers to the costs of the program. The average cost per patient/day is about US$200 at the units which have been implemented in Sweden. However, we have been able to show a tenfold decrease of inpatient stay during the 3-year follow-up for the patient series that has been evaluated. In addition, 51% of the patients at the end of the follow-up proved to be engaged in remunerated ordinary work, and an additional 19% were involved in governmental programs for unemployed.

REFERENCES

Bara, B.G. (1984). Modification of knowledge by memory processes. In M.A. Reda & M.J. Mahoney (eds), *Cognitive Psychotherapies*. Cambridge: Ballinger, Harper & Row.
Beck, A.T. (1976). *Cognitive Therapy and the Emotional Disorders*. New York: International Universities Press.
Bowlby, J. (1969). *Attachment and Loss*, Vol. 1: *Attachment*. London: Hogarth Press.
Bowlby, J. (1988). *A Secure Base*. London: Routledge.
Chambon, O., Perris, C. & Marie-Cardine, M. (1997). *Techniques de la psychothérapie cognitive des psychoses chroniques*. Paris: Masson.
Clark, D.A. (1995). Perceived limitations of standard cognitive therapy: a consideration of efforts to revise Beck's theory and therapy. *Journal of Cognitive Psychotherapy*, **9**, 153–172.
Coursey, R.D. (1989). Psychotherapy with persons suffering from schizophrenia: the need of a new agenda. *Schizophrenia Bulletin*, **15**, 349–353.
Fowler, D., Garety, P. & Kuipers, E. (1996). *Cognitive-behaviour Therapy for Psychosis*. Chichester: Wiley.
Guidano, V.F. (1987). *Complexity of the Self*. New York: Guilford.
Gunderson, J.G.(1978). Defining the therapeutic processes in psychiatric milieus. *Psychiatry*, **41**, 327–335.
Isola, L. (1992). Il setting e la sua influenza nella relazione terapeutica. In G. Sacco & L. Isola (eds), *La relazione terapeutica nelle terapie cognitive*. Roma: Melusina Editrice, pp. 119–129.
Kingdon, D.G. & Turkington, D. (1994). *Cognitive-behavioral Therapy of Schizophrenia*. New York: Guilford.
Liotti, G. (1988). Attachment and cognition: a guideline for the reconstruction of early pathogenic experiences in cognitive psychotherapy. In C. Perris, I.M. Blackburn & H. Perris (eds), *Cognitive Psychotherapy. Theory and Practice*. Heidelberg: Springer Verlag, pp. 62–79.
Liotti, G. & Onofri, A. (1987). La relazione terapeutica con il paziente schizofrenico alla luce della teoria dell'attaccamento. *Schizofrenia*, **1**, 31–35.
Lundh, L.-G. (1988). Cognitive therapy and the analysis of meaning structures. In C. Perris, I.M. Blackburn & H. Perris (eds), *Cognitive Psychotherapy. Theory and Practice*. Heildeberg: Springer Verlag, pp. 44–61.
Lyddon, W.J. (1990). First- and second-order change: implications for rationalist and constructivist cognitive therapies. *Journal of Counseling and Development*, **69**, 122–127.
Main, M. (1991). Metacognitive knowledge, metacognitive monitoring, and singular (coherent) vs. multiple (incoherent) models of attachment: findings and direction for future research. In C. Parkes, C.M. Stevenson-Hinde & P. Marris (eds), *Attachment Across the Life Cycle*. London: Tavistock & Routledge, pp. 127–159.
Perris, C. (1985). Milieu therapeutic processes and cognitive therapy. Read at the XIII International Congress of Psychotherapy, Opatija, Yugoslavia, October 6–12.
Perris, C. (1986). Intensive cognitive-behavioural in-patient treatment of young severely ill patients: presentation of a community-based treatment centre. In C. Perris & M. Eisemann (eds), *Cognitive Psychotherapy. An update*. Umeå: DOPUU Press, pp. 127–130.

Perris, C. (1988a). *Kognitiv psykoterapi vid schizofrena störningar.* Stockholm: Pilgrim.
Perris, C. (1988b). Cognitive psychotherapy and milieutherapeutic processes in psychiatric inpatient units. *Journal of Cognitive Psychotherapy*, **2**, 35–50.
Perris, C. (1989). *Cognitive Therapy with Schizophrenic Patients.* New York: Guilford.
Perris, C. (1992). Integrating psychotherapeutic strategies in the treatment of young severely disturbed patients. *Journal of Cognitive Psychotherapy*, **6**, 205–219.
Perris, C. (1993). *Psicoterapia del paziente difficile.* Lanciano, Italy: Métis.
Perris, C. (1994). Cognitive psychotherapy with schizophrenic patients: a schema-focused approach. In E. Robertson, M. Tesson, K. Kellehear, V. Miller & J. Farhall (eds), *Proceedings of the 4th Annual Mental Health Conference of Australia & New Zealand*, Melbourne, September 20–30, 15–28.
Perris, C. (1996a). Sindromi dissociative. In B. Bara (ed.), *Manuale di psicoterapia cognitiva.* Torino: Bollati-Boringhieri, pp. 685–710.
Perris, C. (1996b). Psicoterapia con pacientes esquizofrénicos. Una aproximación cognitiva, integrada, dirigida a esquemas. In *Adaptacion y homeostasis en psyquiatria: Un puente entre la biología y la psicosociología.* Córdoba: Fundacion "Castilla del Pino", pp. 87–102.
Perris, C. & Skagerlind, L. (1994). Cognitive therapy with schizophrenic patients. *Acta Psychiatrica Scandinavica*, **89**(suppl 382), 65–70.
Perris, C. & Skagerlind, L. (1996). La psychotherapie integrative & cognitive des jeunes schizophrenes. *Synapse*, **124**, 18–26.
Perris, C. & Perris, H. (1997). *Personlighetsstörningar. Uppkomst och behandling ur ett utvecklingspsykopatologiskt perspektiv.* Stockholm: Natur och Kultur.
Perris, C., Skagerlind, L. & Johansson, T. (1995). An integrative schema-focused cognitive program for the treatment of patients with a schizophrenic disorder. Read at the World Congress of Behavioural & Cognitive Therapies. Copenhagen, July 10–15.
Perris, C., Thoresson, P., Skagerlind, L., Warburton, E., Gustavsson, H. & Johansson, T. (1990). Integrating components in a comprehensive cognitive treatment program for patients with a schizophrenic disorder. In C.N. Stefanis et al. (eds), *Psychiatry: A world perspective*, Vol. 3. Amsterdam: Elsevier, pp. 724–729.
Piaget, J. (1926). *La représentation du monde chez l'enfant* [Italian translation: *La rappresentazione del mondo nel fanciullo*, 1966]. Torino: Bollati-Boringhieri.
Polanyi, M. (1966). *The Tacit Dimension.* Garden City, NJ: Doubleday.
Rothstein, M.M. & Vallis, M.T. (1991). The application of cognitive therapy to patients with personality disorders. In T.M. Vallis, J.L. Howes & P.C. Miller (eds), *The Challenge of Cognitive Therapy.* New York: Plenum, pp. 59–84.
Safran, J. & Segal, Z.V. (1990). *Interpersonal Processes in Cognitive Therapy.* New York: Basic Books.
Stern, D.N. (1985). *The Interpersonal World of the Infant.* New York: Basic Books.
Sullivan, H.S. (1931). The modified psychoanalytic treatment of schizophrenia. *American Journal of Psychiatry*, **11**, 519–536.
Svensson, B., Hansson, L. & Thorsson, C. (1993). Cognitive therapy of schizophrenia. Read at the International Symposium on Schizophrenia, Oslo, November.
Tulving, E. (1985). How many memory systems are there? *American Psychologist*, **40**, 385–398.
Westen, D. (1991). Cognitive-behavioral interventions in the psychodynamic psychotherapy of borderline personality disorders. *Clinical Psychology Review*, **11**, 211–230.
Young, J. (1990). *Cognitive Therapy for Personality Disorders: a Schema-focused Approach.* Sarasota, FL: Professional Resource Exchange, Inc.

Chapter 12

Preventively-orientated Psychological Interventions in Early Psychosis

Patrick D. McGorry, Lisa Henry, Dana Maude and **Lisa Phillips**
*Department of Psychiatry, The University of Melbourne,
Victoria, Australia*

INTRODUCTION

Following a prolonged crisis of confidence in the value of psychological interventions in psychotic disorders, we are now entering a new era in which they may find a more appropriate and enduring place. Davidson, Lambert & McGlashan have reviewed this process in another chapter in this volume and only a brief reference to it will be made here. The great weakness of earlier approaches, specifically the modified psychoanalytic model, was that they were developed at a time when there was controversy regarding the nature of psychotic disorders, and unidimensional paradigms and grand theories competed for total explanatory power. Models of disorder were unsophisticated and psychological treatment was based on the flawed foundation of psychological determinism. As effective biological treatments were developed, this foundation was progressively eroded, culminating in studies which pitted biological against psychological treatments (May, Tuma & Dixon, 1976). Principally but not totally for this reason, psychotherapeutic treatments became discredited and there was little enthusiasm for some time for more appropriate designs where combinations of biological and psychosocial treatments were evaluated. Even with the new wave of cognitive therapies, this is regrettably rare. As Coursey (1989) recognized, biological determinism has served patients equally poorly, yet a revival of interest in psychotherapeutic interventions must be soundly based on a biopsychosocial model of disorder.

Cognitive Psychotherapy of Psychotic and Personality Disorders: Handbook of Theory and Practice.
Edited by C. Perris and P.D. McGorry.
© 1998 John Wiley & Sons Ltd.

Now that the biological revolution is in ascendancy, we need to step back and reflect on what a biologically based distortion of the human spirit means for the person who suffers it, and for the intervention required. In our rush to discover the basic biology of schizophrenia, we have ignored the human experience of schizophrenia . . . I would suggest that we now need to rebuild a biologically sound, problem-specific approach to psychotherapy with schizophrenia that is grounded in the human experience of the disorder (Coursey, 1989, p. 350).

The model which informs the present chapter regards psychotic disorders as a collection of illnesses in which there is a biological disturbance of CNS function resulting in a variable mix of symptomatology and cognitive/emotional disorder. This biological disturbance derives from an interaction of biological vulnerability, which may arise on genetic or environmental grounds, such as perinatal birth complications, with environmental and psychological factors. Biological vulnerability alone, however, is usually not sufficient for the expression of the disorder (Miller, 1997). One or a series of additional contributory causes are required for onset, and a similar model influences the course of illness. It is also likely, but not yet demonstrated, that psychological and social influences can contribute to the level of vulnerability, good candidates being childhood trauma and other consequences of adverse social conditions. In summary, a psychosomatic approach to this group of CNS disorders, based on the general biopsychosocial model for disorders of all kinds (Engel, 1980), seems appropriate, and such a model was originally pioneered by Arieti (1974). This allows for a revival and realignment of psychological interventions as powerful components in the treatment of psychotic patients; particularly so, given that the biological disturbance affects the CNS and subjective experience in a fundamental and usually pervasive way. The effect on the *person* and his/her environment is often profound. As Davidson, Lambert & McGlashan (this volume) point out, psychotherapeutic interventions did not die out in real-world clinical settings in recent decades, yet they lacked empirical as well as moral support. Until the rise of the cognitive paradigm and the belated attempt to apply it to the more severe end of the spectrum of disorder, clinicians lacked a blueprint and associated specific skills for working psychotherapeutically with psychotic patients. While not everyone stopped talking to their patients, many were able to justify limiting or avoiding this cornerstone of care. This led to much neglect and alienation for patients, particularly in the English-speaking world. In other parts of the world, the persistence of psychological determinism also harmed patients and deprived many of appropriate access to effective biological treatments.

The present chapter stands on the shoulders of this welcome revival, and seeks to identify the opportunities for psychological interventions within a preventively-orientated framework of care. The focus will be primarily upon the early phases of disorder and the major advances in psychological treatment of more established illness will not be covered in detail. The chapter will consist of three sections which will focus upon cognitive interventions utilized in three distinct phases of early psychosis: first, in the pre-psychotic phase; second, early in the recovery after a first episode of psychosis; and finally, psychological treatment in people who experience prolonged or incomplete recovery, including acute relapses.

THE PRE-PSYCHOTIC PHASE

A Framework for Preventive Intervention in Psychosis

Since preventive intervention has been regarded as difficult and, until recently, beyond our present capacities, it is important to be clear about the conceptual basis for approaching it. This involves a general consideration of the spectrum of intervention in mental disorders (Mrazek & Haggerty, 1994). Broadly, interventions can be classified into prevention, treatment and maintenance.

Within prevention, drawing on the ideas of Gordon (1983), Mrazek and Haggerty subclassify interventions as universal, selective and indicated. Universal preventive interventions are targeted to the general public or a whole population group that has not been identified on the basis of individual risk, e.g. use of seat belts, immunization, prevention of smoking. Selective preventive measures are appropriate for subgroups of the population whose risk of becoming ill is above average. Examples include special immunizations, such as for people travelling to areas where yellow fever is endemic, and annual mammograms for women with a positive family history of breast cancer. The subjects are clearly asymptomatic. Indicated preventive measures apply to those individuals who on examination are found to manifest a risk factor that identifies them, individually, as being at high risk for the future development of a disease, and as such could be the focus of screening. Gordon's view was that such individuals should be asymptomatic and "not motivated by current suffering", yet have a clinically demonstrable abnormality. An example would be asymptomatic individuals with hypertension. Mrazek & Haggerty (1994), adapted Gordon's concept as follows:

> Indicated preventive interventions for mental disorders are targeted to high-risk individuals who are identified as having minimal but detectable signs or symptoms foreshadowing mental disorder, or biological markers indicating predisposition for mental disorder, but who do not meet DSM-III-R diagnostic levels at the current time.

This major definitional shift allows individuals with early and/or subthreshold features (and hence a degree of suffering and disability) to be included within the focus of indicated prevention. Some clinicians would regard this as early intervention or an early form of treatment; however, the situation with these individuals is not so clearcut. While some of these cases will clearly have an early form of the disorder in question, others will not. They might, however, have other less serious disorders, and many individuals subthreshold for a potentially serious disorder like schizophrenia may have nevertheless crossed a clinical threshold where they either require or request treatment. If we can successfully argue for interventions at this phase or level of symptoms and disability, then by current convention it should be regarded as indicated prevention and not (early) treatment *per se*.

> The best hope now for the prevention of schizophrenia lies with indicated preventive interventions targeted at individuals manifesting precursor signs and symptoms who have not yet met full criteria for diagnosis. The identification of individuals at this early stage, coupled with the introduction of pharmacological and psychosocial interventions, may prevent the development of the full-blown disorder (Mrazek & Haggerty, 1994, p. 154).

Mrazek & Haggerty clearly believe that the frontier for preventive efforts lies at this cusp just prior to the onset of frank psychosis. This is both a radical position and a conservative one. It is radical in contrast to early intervention in first episode psychosis, yet conservative in relation to the ultimate dream of primary prevention. Other preventive foci relate to early detection of fully-fledged cases, the intensive and phase-specific treatment of this group, and preventively orientated treatment of more established disorder.

The Basis for Psychological Interventions in the Pre-psychotic Phase

> I feel certain that many incipient cases might be arrested before the efficient contact with reality is completely suspended, and a long stay in institutions made necessary (H.S. Sullivan, 1927, pp. 106–107).

One of the dreams of many psychiatrists from the time of Sullivan through to the present day was to be able to identify and reverse the decline and disability associated with the prepsychotic phase of illness in people who went on to develop schizophrenia. Apart from widespread therapeutic nihilism, the greatest obstacle to the exploration of such treatment possibilities has been the difficulty in gaining access to people before the first psychotic episode. Most people do not seek help or gain access to a mental health professional until positive psychotic symptoms have developed, and even then long delays are common. In recent years, we have developed a service system which has been able to identify and treat at least a subset of young people at substantially increased risk for subsequent psychosis, usually schizophrenia. The development of this service and the criteria defining risk are described elsewhere (Yung et al., 1996), but approximately 40% of the patients treated progress to a psychotic diagnosis within 12 months of entry to the clinic. This is despite the provision of supportive needs-based psychosocial care, which may well have reduced the transition rate to psychosis from an even higher level. Indeed, our clinical impression was that in a number of patients, it was possible for them to pull back from the brink of a frank psychotic break through the provision of support, and the reduction of stress. This clinic has enabled us to learn more about the clinical characteristics of people at this phase of illness, to understand their needs more clearly, and to begin to develop phase-specific interventions to assist them and to try to influence the risk of full-blown disorder, in line with the indicated prevention model.

While our experience to date indicates that, as with the treatment of established psychoses, psychological interventions alone will not be sufficient in most cases to achieve maximum or optimal protective impact, there is a logical and clinically sound case for their development. The stress-vulnerability model is a useful framework for the development of such interventions, since stress is particularly salient at this phase of life from ambient and developmental sources. Adolescents and young adults have a range of major challenges to face as they grow, separate from their family of origin and attempt to make their way in the world. Many experience a series of "cascades of stress" and find themselves poorly equipped to cope and with inadequate support. If there is an underlying vulnerability to psychosis, these cascades may produce a downward spiral in functioning, confidence and social relatedness.

An obvious strategy is to address several elements of this dynamic situation. First, the level of stress can often be rapidly reduced by decisive environmental manipulation, e.g. taking some time off from school or work and spending time relaxing or in enjoyable leisure activities, or renegotiating a loan to ease financial pressure. Second, active teaching of more effective coping in the face of stress can be tackled over a short- to medium-term time-frame and often helps young people who have had limited experience of life and have much maturing to do. Third, there are always specific psychological issues and social conditions for each individual, and here a sophisticated formulation of the person is essential before embarking on a more individual psychotherapy. This is where more depth is required in a psychological sense, and the value of the psychodynamic paradigm and the newer schema-based cognitive models can be appreciated. Finally, a potential role for medication can be identified in treating specific syndromes such as major depression, panic disorder and obsessive-compulsive disorder, and in reducing the impact of stress on the vulnerable young person, as a holding operation while the psychological interventions are taking effect. One would hope that there may also be a role for more specific psychopharmacological treatment at this phase of illness. This could involve the use of novel antipsychotics in low dose; however, we have little understanding of the neurochemistry and neurophysiology of this phase, and it may well be, particularly in those with predominantly negative, neurocognitive and non-specific symptoms, that other agents, e.g. cognitive enhancers, may prove to be more relevant and effective. We are currently trialling a combination of specific cognitively-orientated psychological therapy and low-dose risperidone in a randomized clinical trial which may help to clarify some of these issues.

Specific Psychological Intervention for People at High Risk of Early Transition to Psychosis

The specific cognitive-behavioural intervention developed for this randomized controlled study consists of five possible modules which target separate problem areas. The modules are stress management, depression/negative symptoms, positive symptoms, co-morbidity and group work. The stress management and depression modules have been adapted from standard cognitive-behavioural therapy approaches. Other comorbidity, notably social phobia and obsessive-compulsive phenomena, are approached from the same perspective. Low-grade positive symptoms are tackled by drawing upon the various cognitive strategies developed by several British groups in relation to persistent positive psychotic symptoms in schizophrenia. Finally, group-based approaches can be offered to young people with problems with social relatedness. All patients receive the stress management module, while additional and subsequent modules are decided by the therapist and the patient, based on an assessment of the presenting problem(s) and the patients' perception of their own functioning. Full details of the approach are available on request from the authors in the form of a therapeutic manual. The intervention is brief (10–12 sessions) and consists of three phases of therapy. The initial phase involves engagement and assessment and is followed by the main therapy phase, in which the range of specific modules are drawn upon and followed. The final phase includes "lapse" prevention and termination from therapy.

Case Vignette

Ben was a 21 year-old man living with his fiancée and parents at the time of referral, and was referred to the clinic by his general practitioner. Prior to the referral, Ben had experienced a number of difficulties. First, he had been working in a meat factory, where he had had a forklift accident some 16 months prior to presenting at the clinic. This had resulted in a shattered knee and some loss of movement in that joint. At the time of referral he was seeking compensation from his employer. Second, Ben was dismissed from his job because his employer believed he had deserted his workplace without explanation. However, Ben claimed he had obtained sickness leave due to his knee injury and had given his employer medical certificates. Consequently he had subsequently sought legal advice regarding unfair dismissal. The loss of his job resulted in financial distress, causing Ben and his fiancée to move into his parents' house. Third, his car had been stolen from outside his workplace and was later found incinerated. Ben had invested time and money on the car and was distraught when it was stolen and destroyed.

At assessment, Ben's affect was very flat and he managed little eye contact, also tending to mumble his words. He sat slumped in his chair. He attended with his father, who showed a willingness to respond to questions for Ben and expressed some annoyance at his son's presentation. Ben described feeling quite depressed as a result of the above events. Normally he was a very active and happy person; he had a lot of friends and a good relationship with his fiancée. Over the past 5 months or so he said he had been feeling negative about the world and this was affecting his relationships with friends and family, which resulted in him not wanting to socialize. At present there was very little that interested him. He described a lowered libido and said that his sleep and appetite and decreased markedly. He also described difficulty in concentrating and daily experiences of "blanking out" or losing his train of thought. He described infrequent low-grade positive symptoms, which were regarded as subthreshold for frank psychosis. These consisted of fleeting auditory and visual hallucinations within the last 2 months: they were in the form of shadowy figures or a voice saying his name. No frank psychotic symptoms were elicited. It was noted that Ben's older brother had a 5 year history of experiencing schizophrenia, with continuing relapses and ongoing moderate disability.

The treatment provided was as follows. Ben was accepted by the clinic on the basis that he had a first-degree relative with a psychotic illness and was experiencing a significant decrease in functioning, as well as subthreshold positive psychotic symptoms. Ben was treated with antidepressant medication, 50 mg sertaline/day for 6 months, and psychological treatment. It was hypothesized that the stressors Ben had experienced had contributed to a major depression and fleeting psychotic symptoms. Ben's reduction in functioning, in conjunction with his family history of schizophrenia, had increased his vulnerability to developing a psychotic illness. Consideration was given to the use of low-dose neuroleptics; however, in the absence of frank psychosis, high suicide risk or aggression, it was decided that neuroleptics could be withheld pending the response to antidepressant medication and psychosocial treatments.

The focus of the psychological component of his treatment was on reducing his level of depression, improving his capacity to respond to and cope with stressful events, and restoring his normal level of functioning. Beck et al.'s (1979) cognitive-behavioural model for depression, along with other strategies, was utilized. Interactions within the family were also brought into focus, and Ben's father and fiancée were involved in his treatment.

After 6 months Ben reported feeling happier with his life, his symptoms had substantially resolved, and he was searching for work again. His depression had resolved, the subthreshold psychotic symptoms had ceased and his thinking was clearer. He was no longer taking medication and the psychological treatment had also been completed. However, there was significant continuing stress through ongoing legal battles, and Ben's father continued to put pressure on Ben to follow them through. Ben and his fiancée remained living in his parents house. He was offered continuing follow-up on a monthly basis.

THE RECOVERY PHASE FOLLOWING A FIRST EPISODE OF PSYCHOSIS

A Framework for Cognitively-orientated Psychotherapy in Early Psychosis

To design a psychological approach to assist the person attempting to recover from an initial episode of psychosis, it is worth going back to first principles and trying to put oneself in the shoes of the patient. First, the person has typically gone through powerful, disturbing and potentially traumatic experiences, has developed at least transient impairments in cognitive functioning, and may find it very difficult to trust people or relate in a stable manner. Secondly, there is the crisis element, compounded by the external stigma and the self-stigma associated with becoming a psychiatric patient, and the consequent threat to identity and self-esteem. The latter are particularly significant in young people at a critical period of psychological development, and the recovery environment, as in all crises, is highly influential. This comprises the family, the peer group and the wider society. Third, the impact on developmental and vocational tasks is often critical in this age group, during which the peak incidence of psychosis occurs. Finally, there is frequently a range of complicating premorbid and co-morbid issues which add to the distress and disability. These need to considered in any personal or individual psychotherapeutic approach.

Based upon this experiential scenario, we can draw on a range of theoretical perspectives and therapeutic strategies which flow from them. An assumption similar to that enunciated by Coursey (1989) has been made, namely that the person's more florid and cognitively disorganizing symptoms must be attenuated or resolved to enable an effective psychotherapeutic process to commence. This generally requires the use of low-dose neuroleptic medication which, through its impact on the core psychotic symptoms, can be seen as producing a holding environment and foundation for recovery. We then aim to work with the adaptive and healthy elements of the person's psychological make-up to promote integration, adaptation and recovery. A major conceptual distinction exists here between recovery-orientated psychological work as contrasted with the rehabilitation paradigm, which is more psychosocial, less psychotherapeutic, and fails to emphasize the preventive element. This is consistent with the broad strategy developed by the interpersonal school of psychotherapy for the treatment of schizophrenia (Fromm-Reichmann, 1960). Some of the newer relevant theoretical perspectives have been reviewed in McGorry (1992) and Jackson et al. (1996), but will be briefly considered here.

Key Theoretical Building Blocks for a Cognitive Approach to Recovery

Constructivism

Perris (1989) has pointed out that underlying most psychotherapeutic theories is one of two views of human nature. The first is that a person is seen as a "pilot", responsible for the direction of his/her life. The second is the view of a person as a "robot" and not responsible for the course followed. Most cognitive theories adhere to the first view, and constructivism has developed this in a particular way, such that the person is regarded as a "scientist" who is continuously forming and revising hypotheses about all aspects of his/her life, self and environment (Kelly, 1955). This is best expressed in *Personal Construct Psychology*, a theory developed by George Kelly (1955), which has given rise to a set of clear theoretical postulates and an approach to psychotherapy centred on the systems of meaning of the patient. Constructivism has been described as follows:

> The constructivist perspective is founded on the idea that humans actively create and construe their personal realities. The basic assertion of constructivism is that each individual creates his or her representational model of the world. This experiential scaffolding of structural relations in turn becomes a framework from which the individual orders and assigns meaning to new experience (Mahoney & Lyddon, 1988, p. 200).

In relation to psychosis, as the young person enters treatment for acute symptomatology he/she has to relate the experience of becoming a "patient" to his/her existing scaffolding of meaning. An additional issue is that during the acute phases of illness the scaffolding may be partially or seriously rearranged and thus be functioning in a different and inefficient way. This is less of an issue during and following recovery, when psychotherapy becomes a possibility, especially if recovery is substantial, and the "normal psychic life" referred to by Manfred Bleuler (1978) is then involved in a process of reconstruing the experience of psychosis and treatment in relation to its established construct systems. The constructivist paradigm is highly congruent with the evocative notion of "possible selves" developed by Markus & Nurius (1986). Here, cherished, while ill-defined, hoped-for future selves (e.g. becoming a teacher and eventually having children, etc.) are threatened by the reality of the onset of serious mental illness. Furthermore, a highly unacceptable possible self is dramatically presented to the young patient in the form of a life ravaged by chronic mental illness. This threat is presented through exposure to large numbers of middle-aged patients with chronic illnesses.

Crisis, Disaster and Trauma

These three related areas provide a rich theoretical and practical basis for preventively-orientated therapeutic work with "survivors" in the early stages of a psychotic disorder. Preventive psychiatry has been built on the foundations of crisis theory and there is little doubt that the onset of a psychotic illness, particularly if acute, represents a major crisis for the individual and family, resulting in transient or sustained overload of coping resources (Jeffries, 1977; Jones, Wynne & Watson, 1986).

The term "disaster" is used to denote usually overwhelming events and circumstances that test the adaptational responses of community or individual beyond their capability and lead, at least temporarily, to massive disruption of function for community or individual (Raphael, 1986). In relation to psychosis, the appropriate concept is that of "personal disaster" (Raphael, 1986 p. 97). Disastrous events give rise to a range of sequelae including loss and trauma, which in turn may produce a related spectrum of psychological morbidity. Psychological trauma is a related concept with somewhat greater specificity.

An experience is traumatic if it:

1. Is sudden, unexpected or non-normative.
2. Exceeds the individual's perceived ability to meet its demands.
3. Disrupts the individual's frame of reference and other central psychological needs and related schemas.

(McCann and Pearlman, 1990, p. 10).

Figley (1985) defined trauma as a response which represents "an emotional state of discomfort and stress resulting from memories of extraordinary, catastrophic experience which shattered the survivor's sense of invulnerability to harm". The overlapping concepts of crisis, disaster and trauma are associated with a natural process of homeostasis, regeneration and recovery, which provides a framework for preventive work aimed at promoting this process. There have been a number of attempts to evaluate the effectiveness of preventive interventions provided in the aftermath of crises and disasters and these are reviewed in Raphael (1986). An important principle is to identify groups who may be at particularly high risk of subsequent psychological sequelae. For example, those with multiple losses are at risk of pathological grief reactions, while those with the highest exposure to trauma are at particular risk of post-traumatic stress disorder (PTSD). These considerations should guide the assessment process and thus shape preventively-orientated therapy in patients recovering from their first psychotic episode. There is tremendous scope for preventively-orientated strategies at this point, prior to the development of enduring secondary morbidity. The management of the acute and recovery phases of the first episode, by both the patient and significant supports, dictates the subsequent course and nature of the illness for the rest of the person's life (Ciompi, 1988). This means that we should treat the initial episode of psychosis as a traumatic event and apply intensive, focused treatment interventions to the patient and his/her family to minimize the trauma.

The emergence of a psychotic disorder, the process of entry into treatment and being labelled as mentally ill are generally (but not always) traumatic experiences. These experiences may have a major disruptive effect upon the cognitive schemas of the individual. Schemas may be defined as beliefs, expectations and assumptions about the self, others and the world. Horowitz (1986) talks about "person schemas" which are concerned with "enduring but slowly changing views of self and of other, and with scripts for transactions between self and other". Each individual may have a repertoire of multiple self-schemas. When a traumatic event occurs, there may not be appropriate schemas available to guide adaptation to the event. Schematic change occurs by evolution, not by an erasure of existing schemas. This is important in understanding how the person is to deal with being regarded as mentally ill for the first time and with the core experiences that have accompanied this change. Many enduring schemas will have been fundamentally challenged, even shattered, leading to extreme, often maladaptive, coping measures, such as denial of the impact of having been psychotic. This resonates strongly with the concept of possible selves referred to above.

The trauma model is of potentially great heuristic value in making sense of some of the phenomena seen in early psychosis. The commonly observed tendencies toward "integration" of the psychotic experience on the one hand, or "sealing-over" (Levy et al., 1975) of the experience on the other, can also be explained using Horowitz's (1986) information-processing model of PTSD, with intrusive/re-experiencing phenomena in a generally unstable equilibrium with a denial/avoidance response. Preliminary support for the heuristic value of the PTSD model is provided by a study of the prevalence of PTSD symptoms in a recovering group of recent-onset psychosis patients (McGorry et al., 1991).

Raphael (1986) suggests that those identified as likely to be at risk from PTSD be provided with an intervention as soon as possible after the "disaster", which aims to:

1. Promote a sense of mastery of the experience.
2. Promote support from significant members of the social group.
3. Facilitate working through the traumatic experience and of the emotions of fear, helplessness, anxiety and depression that have developed as a consequence.

McCann & Pearlman (1990) suggest a range of strategies which may be adapted to the post-psychotic period. Their model of therapy blends developmental psychology, self theory/constructivism, and cognitive theory in a way which lends itself naturally to the recovery process in early psychosis.

Taylor (1983) presented a theory of cognitive adaptation to threatening events which focused on the self-curing abilities of individuals. This theory was consonant with the idea of natural recovery or homeostasis following disaster and identified three themes, around which the readjustment process is focused:

1. A search for meaning in the experience.
2. An attempt to regain mastery over the event in particular and over one's life more generally.
3. An effort to enhance one's self-esteem—to feel good about oneself again despite the personal setback.

Cognitive Therapy and Secondary Morbidity

A potentially fruitful focus for cognitive therapy with patients with psychosis is the treatment of depression, anxiety, social phobia, obsessional features, panic, substance abuse and other syndromes, utilizing similar cognitive techniques developed for these same syndromes in the absence of psychotic disorder. Essentially this involves utilizing cognitive therapies in the more comprehensive treatment of co-morbidity in psychosis. It is possible to consider these associated syndromes either as co-morbidity or as secondary morbidity; in the latter case, perhaps as a consequence of failure to adapt to the impact and disruption of the psychotic experience. This range of morbidity is a major contributor to distress and disability in people with psychotic disorders.

The time to consider this approach, as with the cognitive therapy of persistent positive symptoms (see below), is when the acute positive symptomatology is receding in response to neuroleptic treatment. This view is based on the fact that much of the co-morbidity, mainly anxiety and depression, will resolve in parallel with the psychotic symptoms (Knights & Hirsch, 1981). For the proportion of co-morbidity that fails to follow this pattern or emerges in the post-psychotic or recovery phase, a range of approaches including psychological therapies should be considered. Co-morbidity appears most commonly to take the form of depression, social anxiety, panic disorder and post-traumatic stress symptomatology.

All of these syndromes lend themselves to cognitive-behavioural interventions and yet these approaches have rarely been offered within the psychotic population.

Cognitive Therapy and General Psychological Vulnerability

The vulnerability-stress model (Zubin & Spring, 1977) can provide a useful and practical summary of the factors that may be involved in the development of psychotic illness. The premise behind the model is that the likelihood of developing a psychotic illness will depend upon the degree of vulnerability a person brings to a situation (e.g. biological, personality or neurological impairment), and exposure to a range of additional stresses, such as life events (marriage, leaving home, starting work, grieving) and environmental influences (relationship problems, conflicts at work). This notion of Zubin & Spring's concept of vulnerability in relation to psychosis, extends also to include vulnerability to a wider range of psychological problems. It also involves the notion that persons with premorbid vulnerability will be more likely to develop post-psychotic/secondary morbidity of various kinds, in addition to being more at risk of frank psychotic relapse. This pre-morbid vulnerability can be thought of in a number of ways. First, there may be compromised information-processing performance, a feature evident in many of the high-risk studies in psychosis. Second, there may be generally identifiable psychological problems, such as low self-esteem and, in cognitive terms, a vulnerability to "pathological" cognitive styles (e.g. depressive cognitions in absence of frank depression). Third, there may be specific developmental trauma or other factors which confer a particular vulnerability, consistent with a psychological "Achilles heel", which might be understood better from a psychodynamic perspective. We know that many patients have suffered such pre-morbid and concurrent traumas (Mueser et al., in press). The latter two contributors to vulnerability could be the focus of preventively-orientated psychotherapy in the recovery phase of a psychotic episode, prior to the emergence of any frank post-psychotic secondary morbidity such as depression.

Other Theoretical Perspectives

Very few authors have really centred upon the concept of self in the understanding and treatment of psychotic disorders (Coursey, 1989; Perris, 1989; Davidson & Strauss, 1992; Coursey, Keller & Farrell, 1995; Hogarty et al., 1995). Furthermore, the individuals described by these authors experienced chronic illness courses.

Most psychotic disorders emerge during adolescence and young adulthood. There are a number of key developmental tasks facing the individual at this time which are profoundly affected by the onset of illness. Adolescence is the transitional period between childhood and adulthood. It commences with the biological events of puberty and continues via a complex series of psychological and sociocultural processes and influences, which contribute towards the development of an independently functioning person. When an adolescent or young adult becomes psychotic, their psychological development, according to Erikson's (1968) psychosocial model, is inevitably disrupted. At a time when their peers are testing and achieving their independence, the young person recovering from psychosis is being monitored and treated by a range of health professionals. The family, although itself in crisis, is seen at least temporarily as a dependable and more secure environment for the adolescent to recover within. Significant regression is very common and difficult to distinguish from cognitive and emotional impairment. Additionally, the vocational or study opportunities for the adolescent are either lost or delayed. As a result of his/her illness the young person may have difficulties relating to and re-integrating with his/her peer group.

The illness experience often leads to lowered self-esteem, anxiety and depression. According to Erikson's (1968) psychosocial model, this may result in a dysfunctional self-image with core features of dependency and the incorporation of the sick role of "psychiatric patient". This process can be compounded by one of "engulfment" (Lally, 1989), through which a person with psychosis could incorporate, over time, the identity, behaviours and demeanour of the chronic psychiatric patient.

It is therefore desirable to preserve a person's sense of self and self-efficacy immediately after an illness has occurred. This is best achieved by targeting adaptation to illness as a key recovery goal at the earliest possible time, namely, as early in the first presentation of psychosis as is possible. In this way, it may be possible to prevent the disruption of the individual's identity formation and prevent further deterioration by reducing the risk of suicide, severe impairments and disabilities from emerging and solidifying (Jackson et al., 1996; McGorry, 1992, 1994, 1995).

The COPE Model

COPE is an acronym for cognitively-orientated psychotherapy for early psychosis. It was developed by a clinical research working group (Jackson, McGorry, Edwards, Hulbert, Henry, Francey, Maude, Cocks and Power) from 1992 and continues to evolve. COPE is based upon the theories outlined above as well as other influences, with an emphasis on lifespan development, identity formation and self-efficacy. COPE aims at assisting people to adjust in the wake of the first episode of psychosis, usually when their positive symptoms have abated. Psychoeducation and cognitive techniques are used to challenge self-stigmatization and self-stereotypes, thereby helping the person come to terms with understanding his/her illness experience and recommencing the pursuit of life goals. Prevention of secondary morbidity, such as depression and anxiety, is also a focus of COPE. The therapeutic approach is described in detail elsewhere (Jackson et al., 1996) and in a therapy manual available from the authors, but description of the major phases of the therapy will be provided here.

COPE is a brief (mean = 18 sessions) or focal psychotherapeutic approach to the management of older adolescents and young adults experiencing their first episode of psychosis and has four goals:

1. To *assess* and therefore understand the person's explanation of his/her disorder and gain an appreciation of his/her attitude towards psychosis in general.
2. To *engage* and develop a therapeutic relationship with the person in order to form a collaborative therapeutic framework.
3. To promote an *adaptive* recovery style from psychosis. This is promoted by focusing upon how the person is adjusting to the reality of having experienced a psychotic episode and/or the possibility of an ongoing vulnerability or continuing symptoms, and their effects upon how the person perceives him/herself now.
4. To prevent or manage *secondary morbidity*, such as depression, anxiety and stigma, which all influence self-esteem and have developed secondary to the psychotic disorder.

Consistent with the cognitive therapy approach, COPE is carefully tailored to each individual, based upon the therapeutic formulation of the problem. COPE is offered toward the end of the acute phase of the psychotic disorder as the mental state of the person has stabilized and he/she is more likely to be responsive to, and engage in, therapy. The number of sessions and length of time required for COPE will depend upon a number of factors. These include the strength of the therapeutic alliance and therefore the commitment of the person to enter and participate in therapy, and the severity and complexity of the problems presented.

COPE consists of four therapy phases. Similar to other therapies, the first phase focuses upon engaging the person. It is also at this stage that the therapist commences the assessment. This involves careful assessment, interviewing and facilitating disclosure of the person's perspective on their problem(s).

The second phase of therapy has been called the "early phase". The primary focus of this phase is to continue working upon developing a positive therapeutic alliance. People at this early stage of therapy may still be experiencing positive psychotic symptoms, so concentrating upon coping strategies may be useful (Kingdon & Turkington, 1994; Fowler, Garety & Kuipers, 1995). Adaptation and secondary morbidity issues can also be introduced during this phase.

The third phase or "mid-phase" of COPE forms the bulk of the therapy and is concerned with targeting adaptation and secondary morbidity issues. The therapist may offer a new model of the person's experiences and judgments about psychosis. Ventilation and debriefing may be relevant, perhaps simply as just "telling the story". The vulnerability-stress model is utilized here with cognitive clarification, depending upon the person's willingness to consider another perspective. This is essentially a form of psycho-education provided within a psycho-therapeutic relationship (McGorry, 1995). The aim is to decrease distress and promote an adaptive response. Secondary morbidity is identified and approached using modified cognitive-behavioural techniques.

In the fourth phase or "termination phase", the focus of therapy is upon consolidating the "new" adaptive style of understanding the person's psychosis and his/her coping strategies, which have evolved through therapy. This aim here is to ensure that a sense of mastery over the episode has been achieved, an acceptable level of meaning attached to it, and that self-esteem is more secure. Anticipating and responding to emotional responses about termination issues is important. A relapse prevention plan is also developed or reinforced.

Preliminary findings of an open trial of COPE therapy for first-episode psychosis patients provide encouraging results to clinicians and researchers focusing upon psychotherapy in early psychosis. The details of the preliminary findings are described elsewhere (Jackson et al., 1998) but a brief description is provided here. The findings suggest that the therapeutic intervention provides positive changes in the individual's attitudes towards treatment and awareness of his/her psychiatric disorder. Also, the therapy appears to lead to improvements in negative symptom scores and better psychosocial functioning at outcome. Since patients with these better outcomes may have self-selected for the therapy, these results at the moment must be regarded as indicative and not definitive. A randomized controlled trial has since been conducted in our centre and a similar study, the SOCRATES project, is well under way in the UK. Stronger conclusions regarding efficacy are therefore likely to be possible in the near future.

COPE therapy has also included a focus on the subgroup of first-episode patients with psychotic mania, with promising results. At 1-year outcome, preliminary results from an open trial suggest that those who received the therapeutic intervention had a better quality of life, showed a tendency to psychologically integrate their illness experience and had a reduced number of relapses compared to those who did not receive the treatment (Henry et al., 1997).

Case Vignette

Bill was a 17 year-old male, living with his parents, when he was admitted to a psychiatric hospital with a several-months history of positive psychotic symptoms. This was his first episode of psychosis, and it was later discovered that his psychotic symptoms had been preceded by a longer period of failing school performance and gradual reduction in energy and vitality. Two months prior to Bill's hospital admission, his parents noticed that he would not have meals with them, as he believed his food was poisoned. Around this time, Bill refused to leave the house, as he said that other people were watching him. He stopped attending school and seeing his friends. There had been a sustained attempt to engage him as an outpatient over 2–3 weeks; however, Bill had become increasingly angry, had refused further contact from the home-based treatment team, and was becoming threatening to his increasingly distressed parents.

He was commenced on 1 mg risperidone daily, which was increased after several days to 2 mg. His psychotic symptoms abated quickly and Bill was discharged from hospital into the care of his parents after 3 weeks with significant reduction in the level of psychotic symptoms. Over the next 4–6 weeks there was further improvement and the positive symptoms remitted completely, although he remained somewhat anxious, withdrawn and lacking in confidence at this stage.

Prior to becoming ill and ultimately psychotic, Bill had had a clear and positive view of himself and his future. He intended to complete school and then work in his family's courier business full-time. However, after the psychotic episode, it became increasingly clear that he had developed a quite different and highly pessimistic view of his immediate and long-term future. He now saw himself as being dependent and a burden to his family. Bill believed he was now incapable of achieving his previous plan for his future because of his psychotic illness. Bill's previous sense of self-esteem, identity and "possible self" was now lost to him and had been replaced with a markedly devalued sense of self.

The Repertory Grid, developed by Kelly (1955), was one technique used to draw out this information about his views of himself. The grid technique enables the impact of this change in life's circumstances to be assessed, monitored and kept in focus during therapy. The Repertory Grid consists of a number of headings, such as "Myself 12 months ago", "A person having a breakdown", "Myself now", "Myself in 6 months", "A person with schizophrenia". These are called grid elements and are used as a framework to build up a picture of how the recovering person construes him/herself at the moment, how this contrasts with previous modes of construing the self, and how he/she sees other kinds of predicament and possible selves. This is done by associating the elements with a series of adjectives or constructs. These are ideally drawn out individually for each new patient, but can be supplied in a more standard-ized way. In this way it is possible to associate with each element 14 adjectives and their opposites, e.g. "good–bad", "dependable–not dependable", "stable–unstable", "free–trapped", "rational–irrational". The person merely rates each element on a scale for each construct pair, so that a pattern is built up for each one which can be compared for that element over time and cross-sectionally with other elements.

This was done by Bill over different time points throughout the length of therapy. This was a way of making explicit Bill's view about his illness and its impact on his view of himself. Irrational assumptions were assessed and challenged using a cogni-tive approach. It was clear that his core beliefs about mentally ill people were a major negative influence upon his recovery. His degree of readiness rapidly to adopt the identity of a mentally ill person, rather than to deny the reality of the illness episode, was somewhat unusual and was carefully explored. This seemed to be related to witnessing the severity of disability in a number of co-patients in the hospital setting, and his memories of his grandfather, who had suffered from schizophrenia and had died in a mental hospital after many years of illness. The constructivist approach was useful for accessing Bill's core beliefs about himself and as a reference between phases of illness, so that he could see the recovery process in action by observing changes and improvements over time. His self-esteem and optimism for the future improved steadily in the wake of the resolution of his psychotic symptoms and he continued to make a steady recovery over a period of several months. Continuing problems related to difficulties re-engaging with his peer group, who had gained a year on him at school, and some minor difficulties in concentrating in class.

THE PROLONGED RECOVERY PHASE FOLLOWING FIRST-EPISODE PSYCHOSIS

A Framework for Preventative Intervention in Prolonged Recovery

There are a significant minority of first-episode patients for whom recovery is a protracted process. This group includes those patients who have initially shown some response to treatment although they continue to exhibit residual symptoms, those that show gradual improvement over an extended period, and those who seem to have experienced little change in severity of symptoms since their initial onset. The characteristics of the prolonged recovery group are not well-known at this time. The proportion of first-episode patients with an initial diagnosis of schizophreniform disorder, schizophrenia or schizo-affective disorder not achieving complete remission of symptoms after 12 months is likely to be between 9% and 17% (Edwards et al., in press; Lieberman et al., 1993). An inadequate response to treatment in the first episode appears to be related to the duration of untreated psychosis (Loebel et al., 1992), a diagnosis of schizophrenia (Lieberman et al., 1993) and poorer pre-morbid psychosocial functioning in childhood and adolescence (Jones et al., 1993).

The evidence from outcome studies implicating duration of untreated psychosis (Loebel et al., 1992) and the total period of unchecked positive psychotic symptoms over the course of illness (McGlashan, 1986) in the extent of recovery achieved, have prompted suggestions of a toxic physiological process accompanying positive symptoms. This line of argument points to the possible biological importance of shortening the duration of the first psychotic episode. The psychosocial consequences for the young person remaining actively psychotic over an extended period include the continued disruption to social, interpersonal and occupational role functioning, which is likely to seriously compound the issues related to the impact of the psychotic episode. The psychological impact of the protracted experience of powerlessness, fear, isolation and distrust of his/her mental functioning is likely to continue to undermine his/her sense of being able to cope and find a place in the world.

Given these considerations, psychological intervention for persisting symptoms during the first psychotic episode needs to occur within a broader context of a systematic early intervention approach to prolonged recovery. Where a comprehensive treatment program is in place, we would suggest that a patient who has not achieved remission of positive symptoms following 3 months of treatment be considered a prolonged recovery patient, and require an extensive review (Edwards et al., 1998). At this point in the illness course, a highly integrated biological and psychological assessment and formulation is required. Implementation of the psychological intervention then necessarily occurs in conjunction with targeted pharmacological strategies, such as changing medication and/or dose, and the early introduction of atypical agents (Edwards et al., 1998). The therapy forms one arm of an early intervention package which aims to accelerate a stalled recovery process and, for some of these patients, also aims to prevent treatment resistance from being established later in the illness course.

Psychological Interventions for the Prolonged Recovery Phase

The recent promising developments in specific cognitive-behavioural therapies for treatment of refractory symptoms in patients with longstanding illnesses, along with the perspectives offered by theorists concerned with the psychodynamics and core cognitive components of positive symptoms, and our experience in working in the recovery phase with first-episode patients, have provided the guiding frameworks for approaching persisting symptoms in the very early stages of psychotic illness.

Psychological therapies developed for patients with chronic symptoms have highlighted methods for enhancing coping strategies (Yusupoff & Tarrier, 1996), techniques for belief modification around hallucinations and delusions (Bentall, Haddock & Slade, 1994; Chadwick, Birchwood & Trower, 1996), and ways of presenting an understanding of psychotic symptoms in a way that is meaningful and acceptable to the patient (Kingdon & Turkington, 1994). The need to allow for cognitive deficits and information-processing biases, and ways of dealing with this in the therapeutic process, has been usefully emphasized (Fowler, Garety & Kuipers, 1995).

It has been speculated that these techniques and approaches may be more effective if used at earlier stages of the illness course (Haddock, Bentall & Slade, 1996); however, there have been only a few studies to date which have included or focused on patients in the early phase of illness (Drury et al., 1996; Haddock et al., in press), and none to our knowledge who have considered these types of interventions with an at-risk subgroup. We are currently conducting a randomized controlled trial where the effectiveness of introducing cognitively-orientated therapy in a first-episode group who have been inadequately responsive to treatment after 3 months, is being assessed with standard neuroleptic therapy and in combination with clozapine (the Recovery Plus Project).

In utilizing these types of approach with the first-episode group, it becomes apparent that accommodation of the needs of a younger group and issues related to recent onset and diagnosis is required. An added focus of the work becomes the prevention of further elaboration and entrenchment of symptoms. The recovery issues addressed in COPE remain relevant here. The young person experiencing a protracted recovery is viewed as being at a vulnerable stage of identity formation and development, in the process of negotiating psychosocial demands related to the late adolescent/young adult phase of life, while attempting to deal with inter- and intra-personal disruption caused by the experience of psychotic symptoms. The content of the persisting symptoms at this phase, and the nature of the therapeutic relationship, tends to reflect the developmental phase and includes issues related to independence, identity, sexuality, comparisons with peers, and intimacy. The approach is required to incorporate fluctuations in mental state, changing and evolving symptom profiles, medication compliance issues, along with prominent affective components such as intense anxiety, confusion, loss, and despair.

With the onset of symptoms occurring in the recent past with this group, there is greater access to premorbid functioning and style, allowing for closer consideration of how individual characteristics interact with treatment setting, the experience of being unwell, and the particular symptoms with which they present. Psychological formulations of onset and persistence of symptoms can have greater impact.

In line with recent cognitive models (e.g. Bentall, 1994; Perris, 1989; Trower & Chadwick, 1995) and psychodynamically influenced ideas (e.g. Arieti, 1974; Roberts, 1991), ongoing symptoms can usefully be viewed as an attempt to regain a sense of coherence and integration in the self-concept, and preservation of self-worth in the face of multiple challenges, which include those present at the onset, but also the experience of psychosis itself. In comparison with the majority of first-espisode patients, for whom symptom remission occurs within the first weeks and months of treatment, one may speculate that patients with persisting symptoms have a more vulnerable and less differentiated self-concept to begin with, poorer or less varied coping resources, more highly stigmatized views of mental illness, and/or inadequate social supports. Working with persisting symptoms following the first psychotic episode therefore requires a bridging framework incorporating both the recovery issues central to a young person in the early phase of illness, and the principles applicable to established treatment of refractory symptoms.

STOPP

The approach labelled "systematic treatment of persistent psychosis" (STOPP) was developed in parallel with COPE to address the special needs of the prolonged recovery group. The particular components of STOPP therapy include a detailed assessment of phenomenology and the person's explanatory model, personal history and self-concept, leading to a formulation of possible reasons for the persistence of the symptoms and the development of a rationale for working together. There is an active introduction of normalized models of psychotic experiences, education about coping strategies for specific symptoms, as well as dealing with heightened emotional states and ongoing stressors. The belief systems underpinning positive symptoms are then explored and indirectly challenged, while alternative explanations for experiences continue to be built upon. There is a strong focus on consolidating a sense of self by attempting to make sense of the person's story, increasing awareness of his/her individual characteristics, introducing new experiences, and/or encouraging contact with old and forgotten sources of pleasure and interest.

STOPP is usually offered on a weekly or twice-weekly basis with the content addressed at a gentle and sensitive pace. Flexibility in style and structure of sessions takes on an even greater emphasis, given a need to allow for deficits in cognitive functioning in these patients, along with the high levels of anxiety and distress which accompany this early phase in illness course and the experience of not recovering. This sense of failure to recover is heightened in our local context, which is prevention- and recovery-orientated. We have worked to emphasize that people can recover at different rates and in different ways, but our environment may create additional pressures for young people with prolonged recovery.

Case History

Paul is 23 years old. He is on sick leave from his part-time job as an administration clerk, has deferred his study from a part-time commerce course, and lives with his mother. At the time of presentation to the service he described 6 months of increasing depression, producing an increase in his drug and alcohol intake, culminating in a 3-month period of hearing multiple voices in his head, saying that he was no good, telling him not to swear, commenting on his thoughts, and giving him mundane commands. At times the voices became threatening, saying they were going to kill him. He had a vague feeling that people in the streets were looking at him strangely because they knew things about him and had some connection with the voices. He took an impulsive overdose in an attempt to stop the voices by killing himself, and was taken to hospital by his brother. Paul was commenced on risperidone, which was increased to 6 mg over a 10-week period, before side effects developed. The voices had become less frequent and more muffled at times. Paul was reluctant to discuss his experiences in much depth and wanted to get back to his work and studies as quickly as possible. He found the voices intensified at work and he needed to come home early some days. Olanzapine was then introduced to replace the risperidone, but over the next 6 weeks the voices continued to intensify and became more elaborate. They began to tell him they were being transmitted by the Mafia and a bikie gang, and that he had been singled out for an initiation test. The voices told him they were going to get him, cut him and break his legs, that they were always watching him and knew everything about him. They continued to comment on his thoughts and put other thoughts into his head, and communicated to him via the television. He felt helpless and totally powerless.

Paul is the youngest of seven children and grew up in a tense and oppressive household. His father was an alcoholic and described as a controlling, abusive and unpredictable man. He died suddenly 5 years ago. Paul's mother is a very warm, caring and resourceful women. She had suffered marked and sustained depression during her marriage, and the parenting of the younger children had often fallen to the older two children. Paul has always been a great support to his mother and continues to be very attuned to the pressures she is under and her sources of concern or stress. Paul described himself as having shut off from his own emotions a long time ago, and stated that he had always tried to manage his feelings by thinking things through rationally. He stated that he has always felt at a distance from other people, even those he loved, like his family.

At around 4 months following entry to the service, Paul was commenced on clozapine and twice-weekly STOPP therapy was initiated. The initial focus of the therapy was on offering a sense of hope and a framework for recovery. It was conveyed that his situation could be thought about and that some sense could be made of his predicament. The meaning and impact of receiving assistance in this way was explored early in the process. Much initial time was spent on developing a rationale for not engaging with, and tuning into, the voices, before coping strategies could be trialled and implemented. Information about psychotic symptoms was offered within general models of mental functioning, and ways and circumstances in which ideas become stuck and elaborated were illustrated. Myths and stigmatized views of mental illness were elicited and challenged on an ongoing basis. Inconsistencies and queries about his own model of what was occurring were discussed in depth and augmented by fact-finding expeditions, e.g. reading about how the Mafia and bikie gangs are structured and operate, etc. His own thoughts and ideas about reclaiming his life were encouraged. Suicide prevention was an ongoing issue. Gentle connections were made between uncomfortable feelings and thoughts and the experience of voices or persecution, along with connections to his personal style, e.g. strong and rigid expectations, fear of his emotional states, difficulty dealing with uncertainty, and a strong need to feel in control. Over a 3-month period, Paul's voices had diminished from occurring constantly to occurring for only brief intervals during the day, and were muffled. His conviction in, and preoccupation with, his delusional ideas had reduced significantly, and he had recommenced studying two subjects of his course. His engagement with the service and interest in discussing his personal experiences and concerns had dramatically increased.

CONCLUSION

The preventively-orientated psychological approaches described above remain relatively new and continue to evolve and undergo evaluation. While they are phase-linked to an extent, both COPE and STOPP can remain "on offer" for a longer period, since many patients become more open to a psychological approach, either when more time has elapsed between their initial episode and the present day, or in the wake of a second or third episode. This notion of "second-bite therapy" is important to keep in mind with young people with high initial levels of denial, invulnerability and sealing-over. A psychological approach to the prevention of relapse is another psychosocial treatment strategy which can be considered as part of the spectrum of psychological preventive strategies in psychotic illness. It is important that the renaissance in psychological treatment becomes as evidence-based as possible, and correspondingly efficient as well, given the large numbers of people who need to be helped in this way. For this reason, the timing and duration of therapies and the skill and activity of therapists are important parameters to consider, although the human and personal elements are almost certainly the critical ingredients. Finally, faith in the value of a personal and individual psychotherapeutic approach as an essential element in the treatment of all people with psychotic illness, a value which was lost for too long from psychiatric practice, needs to be safeguarded and actively disseminated. Provided that we can achieve a logical integration of practical psychological treatments linked by phase of illness to biological and social interventions, we may be at the dawn of a new era of sophistication in the care of people with psychotic illness.

REFERENCES

Arieti, S. (1974). An overview of schizophrenia from a predominantly psychological approach. *American Journal of Psychiatry*, **131**(3), 241–249.

Beck, A.T., Rush, A.J., Shaw, B.F. & Emery, G. (1979). *Cognitive Therapy of Depression*. New York: Guilford.

Bentall, R.P. (1994). Cognitive biases and abnormal beliefs: toward a model of persecutory delusions. In A.S. David & J. Cutting (eds), *The Neuropsychology of Schizophrenia*. London: Erlbaum.

Bentall, R., Haddock, G. and Slade, P. (1994). Cognitive behaviour therapy for persistent auditory hallucinations: from theory to therapy. *Behaviour Therapy*, **25**, 51–66.

Bleuler, M. (1978). *The Schizophrenic Disorders: Long Term Patient and Family Studies*, (Clemens SM, trans.). New York: International Universities Press.

Chadwick, P., Birchwood, M. & Trower, P. (1996). *Cognitive Therapy for Delusions, Voices, and Paranoia.* Chichester: Wiley.

Ciompi, L. (1988). Learning from outcome studies: toward a comprehensive biological-psychosocial understanding of schizophrenia. Annual meeting of the American College of Psychiatrists (1987, Maui, Hawaii). *Schizophrenia Research*, **1**(6), 373–384.

Coursey, R.D. (1989). Psychotherapy with persons suffering from schizophrenia. *Schizophrenia Bulletin*, **15**, 349–353.

Coursey, R.D., Keller, A. & Farrell, E. (1995). Individual psychotherapy and persons with serious mental illness: the clients' perspective. *Schizophrenia Bulletin*, **21**, 283–301.

Davidson, L. & Strauss, J. (1992). Sense of self in recovery from severe mental illness. *British Journal of Medical Psychology*, **65**, 131–145.

Drury, V., Birchwood, M., Cochrane, R. & Macmillan, F. (1996). Cognitive therapy and recovery from acute psychosis: a controlled trial: Impact on psychotic symptoms. *British Journal of Psychiatry*, **169**, 593–607.

Edwards, J., Maude, D., McGorry, P.D., Harrigan, S. & Cocks, J.T. (1998). Prolonged recovery in first-episode psychosis. *British Journal of Psychiatry*, (suppl. 33), **172**, 107–116.

Engel, G.L. (1980). Application of the biopsychosocial model. *American Journal of Psychiatry*, **137**(5), 535–544.

Erikson, E.H. (1968). *Identity: Youth and crisis.* New York: Norton.

Figley, C.R. (1985). *Trauma and Its Wake. The Study and Treatment of Post-traumatic Stress Disorder.* New York: Brunner/Mazel.

Fowler, D., Garety, P. & Kuipers, E. (1995). *Cognitive Behaviour Therapy for Psychosis: Theory and Practice.* Chichester: Wiley.

Fromm-Reichmann, F. (1960). *Principles of Intensive Psychotherapy.* Chicago, IL: University of Chicago Press.

Gordon, R. (1983). An operational classification of disease prevention. *Public Health Reports*, **98**, 107–109.

Haddock, G., Morison, A.P., Hopkins, R., Lewis, S. & Tarrier, N. (in press). Individual cognitive-behavioural interventions in early psychosis. *British Journal of Psychiatry* (suppl.).

Haddock, G., Bentall, R.P. & Slade, P.D. (1996). Psychological treatment of auditory hallucinations: focusing or distraction? In G. Haddock & P.D. Slade (eds), *Cognitive-Behavioural Interventions with Psychotic Disorders.* Routledge: London.

Henry, L., Edwards, J., Cocks, J., McGorry, P. & Jackson, H. (1997). Cognitively oriented psychotherapy and the recovery process in first episode mania with psychotic features. Paper presented at the International Society for the Psychological Treatments of the Schizophrenias and other Psychoses (ISPS) Conference, London, 12–16 October.

Hogarty, G.E., Kornblith, S., Greenwald, D. et al. (1995). Personal therapy: a disorder relevant psychopathology for schizophrenia. *Schizophrenia Bulletin*, **21**, 379–393.

Horowitz, M.J. (1986). Stress-response syndromes: a review of posttraumatic and adjustment disorders. *Hospital and Community Psychiatry*, **37**(3), 241–249.

Jackson, H., McGorry, P., Edwards, J. & Hulbert, C. (1996). Cognitively oriented psychotherapy for early psychosis (COPE). In P. Cotton and H. Jackson (eds), *Early Intervention and Prevention in Mental Health*, Melbourne: Melbourne Australian Psychological Society, pp. 131–154.

Jackson, H., McGorry, P., Edwards, J., Hulbert, C., Henry, L., Francey, S., Maude, D., Cocks, J., Power, P., Harrigan, S. & Dudgeon, P. (1998). Cognitively-oriented psychotherapy for early psychosis (COPE) preliminary results. *British Journal of Psychiatry*, **172**(suppl 33), 92–99.

Jeffries, J.J. (1977). The trauma of being psychotic: a neglected element in the management of chronic schizophrenia. *Canadian Psychiatric Association Journal*, **22**, 199–206.

Jones, E.E., Wynne, M.F. & Watson, D.D. (1986). Client perception of treatment in crisis intervention and longer-term psychotherapies. *Psychotherapy*, **23**(1), 120–132.

Jones P.B., Bebbington P., Foerster A., Lewis S.W., Murray R.M., Russell A., Sham P.C., Toone B.K. & Wilkins S. (1993). Premorbid social underachievement in schizophrenia results from the Camberwell collaborative psychosis study. *British Journal of Psychiatry*, **162**, 65–71.

Kelly, G. (1955). *The Psychology of Personal Constructs*. New York: Norton.

Kingdon, D. & Turkington, D. (1994). *Cognitive-Behavioural Therapy of Schizophrenia*. New York: Guilford.

Knights, A. & Hirsch, S.R. (1981). "Revealed" depression and drug treatment for schizophrenia. *Archives of General Psychiatry*, **38**(7), 806–811.

Lally, S.J. (1989). "Does being in here mean there is something wrong with me?" *Schizophrenia Bulletin*, **15**(2), 253–265.

Levy, S.T., McGlashan, T.H. & Carpenter, W.T. (1975). Integration and sealing-over as recovery styles from acute psychosis. *Journal of Nervous and Mental Disease*, **161**, 307–312.

Loebel, A.D., Lieberman, J.A., Alvir, J.M.J., Mayerhoff, D.I., Geisler, S.H. and Szymanski, S.R. (1992). Duration of psychosis and outcome in first-episode schizophrenia. *American Journal of Psychiatry*, **149**, 1183–1188.

Lieberman, J.A., Jody, D., Geisler, S.H., Alvir, J.M., Loebel, A.D., Szymanski, S.R., Woerner, M. & Borenstein, M. (1993). Time course and biological correlates of treatment response in first-episode schizophrenia. *Archives of General Psychiatry*, **50**, 369–376.

Mahoney, M.J. & Lyddon, W.J. (1988). Recent developments in cognitive approaches to counseling and psychotherapy. *The Counseling Psychologist*, **16**, 190–234.

Markus, H. & Nurius, P. (1986). Possible selves. *American Psychologist*, **41**, 954–969.

May, P.R., Tuma, A.H. & Dixon, W.J. (1976). Schizophrenia—a follow-up study of results of treatment methods. *Archives of General Psychiatry*, **33**, 474–478.

McCann, L. & Pearlman, L.A. (1990). *Psychological Trauma and the Adult Survivor: Theory, therapy, and transformation*. New York: Brunner/Mazel.

McGlashan, T. (1986). A selective review of recent North American long-term follow-up studies of schizophrenia. *Schizophrenia Bulletin*, **14**, 515–542.

McGorry, P.D., Chanen, A., McCarthy, E., van Riel, R., McKenzie, D. & Singh, B.S. (1991). Post-traumatic stress disorder following recent-onset psychosis: an unrecognised post-psychotic syndrome. *Journal of Nervous and Mental Disease*, **179**, 253–258.

McGorry, P.D. (1992). The concept of recovery and secondary prevention in psychotic disorders. *Australian and New Zealand Journal of Psychiatry*, **26**, 3–17.

McGorry, P.D. (1994). The influence of illness duration on syndrome clarity and stability in functional psychosis: does the diagnosis emerge and stabilise with time? *Australian and New Zealand Journal of Psychiatry*, **28**, 607–619.

McGorry, P.D. (1995). Psychoeducation in first-episode psychosis: a therapeutic process. *Psychiatry*, **58**, 329–344.

Miller, R. (1997). Schizophrenia: a tameable tiger? *The New Zealand Medical Journal*, **110**, 283–285.

Mrazek, P.J. & Haggerty, R.J. (eds) (1994). *Reducing Risk for Mental Disorders: Frontiers for Preventive Intervention Research*. Washington, DC: National Academic Press.

Mueser, K.T., Goodman, L.B., Trumbetta, S.L., Rosenberg, S.D., Osher, F.C., Vidaver, R., Auciello, P. & Foy D.W. (in press). Trauma and posttraumatic stress disorder in severe mental illness. *Journal of Consulting and Clinical Psychology*.

Perris, C. (1989). *Cognitive Therapy with Schizophrenic Patient*. New York: Guilford.

Raphael, B. (1986). *When Disaster Strikes: How Individuals and Communities Cope with Catastrophe*. New York: Basic Books.

Roberts, G. (1991). Delusional belief systems and meaning in life: a preferred reality? *British Journal of Psychiatry*, **159**(suppl 14), 19–28.

Sullivan, H.S. (1927).   The onset of schizophrenia. *American Journal of Psychiatry*, **6**, 105–134.

Taylor, S. (1983).   Adjustment to threatening events: a theory of cognitive adaptation. *American Psychologist*, **38**, 1161–1173.

Trower, P. & Chadwick, P.D. (1995).   Pathways to defense of self: a theory of two types of paranoia. *Clinical Psychology: Science and Practice*, **2**, 263–278.

Yung, A.R., McGorry, P.D., McFarlane, C.A., Jackson, H.J., Patton, G.C. & Rakkar, A. (1996).   Monitoring and care of young people at incipient risk of psychosis. *Schizophrenia Bulletin*, **22**(2), 283–303.

Yusupoff, L. & Tarrier, N. (1996).   Coping strategy enhancement for persistent hallucinations and delusions. In G. Haddock & P.D. Slade (eds), *Cognitive-Behavioural Interventions with Psychotic Disorders*. London: Routledge.

Zubin, J. & Spring, B. (1977).   Vulnerability—a new view on schizophrenia. *Journal of Abnormal Psychology*, **86**, 103–126.

Chapter 13

The Grief of Mental Illness: Context for the Cognitive Therapy of Schizophrenia

Virginia Lafond
MSW, CSW Schizophrenia Service, Royal Ottawa Hospital,
Ottawa, Ontario, Canada

> Because of illness, my major life events have been infused with loss. Though I was the only one in my family to graduate from university, I have not been able to continue my studies. Finally, I even lost the job I prized. The illness itself has brought many changes, including improvements, but with those, losses. With therapy and the new medication, I now have even lost that special role I thought I had—my God-sent special vocation. I now see it was a delusion. For sure, I am grieving my mental illness (statement of patient told to the author).

In psychiatric clinical practice, it is rare that we hear grief expressed as clearly as this patient has. But most of those we encounter do present us with evidence that they are living the material, emotional and psychological consequences of their mental illness experience. And whenever we pause to consider the losses experienced by people affected by mental illness, and the inevitable grieving process that accompanies this loss, we are where we as mental health professionals should want to be—in touch with the person (Strauss, 1992; 1994). However, if the literature can be trusted as an accurate reflection of practice, it seems safe to conclude, barring rare exceptions, that practitioners have confined the practice of grief work to those losses commonly recognized as such by society; e.g. death, divorce, notice of job termination (Kübler-Ross, 1969; Worden, 1982; Schwartz-Borden, 1986; Blinde & Stratta, 1992). Thus the occurrence of schizophrenia, mood disorder and other mental illnesses have, in general, not been considered apt fodder for grief work. We can conclude then that: (a) mental illness and its attendant losses meet the criteria of disenfranchised loss, in that this loss remains

Cognitive Psychotherapy of Psychotic and Personality Disorders: Handbook of Theory and Practice.
Edited by C. Perris and P.D. McGorry.
© 1998 John Wiley & Sons Ltd.

unrecognized by society, with neither rituals nor language for mourning, grieved in isolation, often in shame and stigma (Doka, 1989, 1993; Pine et al., 1990); (b) the grieving process so clearly described as healthy, normal and healing by leading grief scholars (Lindemann, 1944; Kübler-Ross, 1969; Parkes, 1972, 1986; Parkes & Weiss, 1983; Raphael, 1983) has been left untapped in terms of its potential part in psychiatry's therapeutic synergy.

The agenda of this chapter is first to put a spotlight on the profile of grief in the person's experience of mental illness and then to illustrate how the grieving process can be exploited for therapeutic work. Application of cognitive therapy methods as suggested by Perris (1989) for use in schizophrenia will be described. The underpinning of this chapter is the conviction that the grief of mental illness provides, both to the person affected and to the therapist, a healthy, natural, inexpensive and constantly available resource for therapy.

This chapter is written somewhat in the genre of a handbook. Part I offers a theoretical framework for grief work with the person who has a mental illness. (Note: Although the scope of this chapter is limited to the person directly burdened with psychosis, the grieving mental illness framework is also adaptable for practice with others affected by the experience of mental illness, e.g. the person's family members.) Part II discusses some ingredients for effective practice. Part III contains a fairly detailed description of how I have integrated into my practice the grieving-mental-illness framework and also includes vindications of its success. The chapter concludes with some further observations about the benefit of incorporating utilization of the grief of mental illness in our efforts to assist the person towards recovery.

PART I: "GRIEVING MENTAL ILLNESS": THEORETICAL FRAMEWORK

Conclusions from the Literature

When the literature is searched for that which addresses *the person* suffering mental illness—that is, where there is focus on other than strict alleviation of symptoms—one finds a body (albeit small) of critical, edifying and heartening material. Authors such as Jeffries (1977), Kanter (1985), Mohelsky (1987), Deegan (1988), Coursey (1989), Selzer et al. (1989), Dincin (1990), Corin & Lauzon (1992) and Strauss (1992, 1994) speak to certain "oversights" in the state of the art of psychiatry. All suggest some measures of correction and, in their respective ways, exhort the psychiatric community to take the person into account, not only for humanitarian reasons but also for maximization of therapeutic effect.

As mentioned previously, grief and its process has long been established in the literature as our normal, healthy and healing reaction to loss (Lindemann, 1944; Kübler-Ross, 1969; Parkes, 1972, 1986; Worden, 1982; Parkes & Weiss, 1983;

Raphael, 1983). However, in practice, as also noted above, when it comes to the loss aspects of mental illness, these and their accompanying grief experiences have been largely ignored. Exceptions are generally of three sorts: (a) that focusing on the grieving experiences of family members when mental illness occurs in a family member (e.g. Miller et al., 1990; Atkinson, 1994); (b) that which gives brief acknowledgment of the occurrence of grieving in patients (Gunderson, 1978; Selzer et al., 1989); and (c) that which proffers some hints to the therapist for adequate grief therapy (e.g. Lefley, 1987; Selzer et al., 1989; Alexander, 1991). In general, subjective reactions of patients to their own mental illness are characterized as disease process or as grief—but grief that is not allowed expression, e.g. subjective reaction as disease process is coined by Jeffries as follows:

> After an acute psychosis, a traumatic neurosis often ensues similar to that which follows back injury, or the type of cardiac neurosis that follows a real or imagined coronary infarct. In fact there may be a number of different neurotic responses to the trauma of an acute schizophrenic episode . . . (1977, p. 199).

Selzer et al. (1989) do speak about subjective reaction to mental illness, identify it as grief, and point out how it is not allowed expression:

> Grief is most often the affect patients would experience if they faced the reality of their current situation. Indeed, rage defends against that grief. "Support" from family, friends, or clinicians may be their efforts to deny schizophrenic individuals' grief. Frequently, the patients are left to bear it alone. "I'm sure you'll get better" may, on the conscious level, be meant as a friendly, helpful comment, but it can make patients less able to express their anger. Assurances from others about the future may be heard by them as an unwillingness to listen to their anger and despair (Selzer et al., 1989, p. 227).

The description by Mayer-Gross (1920) portrayed a grieving process reaction to the mental illness as experienced by patients. Jeffries (1977) notes as follows the thinking of Mayer-Gross:

> [A] phenomenological classification of the various ways in which a person may react to an acute psychotic experience [was proposed by Mayer-Gross]. He distinguished four modes: denial of the future (despair); denial of the experience itself (exclusion); creation of a "new life" after the illness; "melting" of the illness into a continuous set of "life values" (Jeffries, 1977, pp. 200–201).

More recently, a significant contribution has been made by Appelo et al. (1993). Their article entitled "Grief: its significance for rehabilitation in schizophrenia" highlights the clinical importance of the patient's grieving reaction to schizophrenia and points out how this reaction can be utilized. They make the point powerfully:

> . . . that many behaviours related to schizophrenia have been falsely interpreted as psychopathological or as a lack of motivation, while grief theory places them in a

meaningful context of reactions to loss. Consequently, awareness of this alternative alters one's attitude towards these symptoms, and signifies the use of cognitive-behavioural interventions for complicated grief in the clinical practice of rehabilitation (p. 58).

In writing *Grieving Mental Illness: A Guide for Patients and Their Caregivers* (Lafond, 1994), mine was a multipurpose task. Obviously, like Appelo et al., my aim was to promote focus on the grieving process specifically related to mental illness and to join this with suggestions for grief's constructive use for patients, their family members and other caregivers. Drawn from my personal experience in recovering from mental illness, as well as from my professional practice, my hypothesis is that those affected by major mental illness who engage consciously in their grieving process will have a better outcome than those who do not.

Loss Aspects of Mental Illness: Some Considerations

We who work day in and day out with those who suffer mental illness and with their families know that losses accompanying mental illness are both harsh and myriad in kind and number. They begin with the illness itself and can touch many, if not all, other aspects of a person's life. Depicted below are five dimensions of major loss endured through the experience of mental illness. This is offered with obeisance to practitioners' awareness of these and also to our need, once in a while, to stand still, as it were, in contemplation about them.

The Illness Itself

In speaking of his own subjective experience with depression, the renowned novelist, William Styron, puts it this way:

> To most of those who have experienced it, the horror of depression is so overwhelming as to be quite beyond expression . . . But in science and art the search will doubtless go on for a clear representation of its meaning, which sometimes, for those who have known it, is a simulacrum of all the evil of our world: of our everyday discord and chaos, our irrationality, warfare and crime, torture and violence, our pulse toward death and our flight from it held in the intolerable equipoise of history (Styron, 1990).

Patricia Deegan, clinical psychologist, speaks of what the mental illness brings to the person, also from a first-hand point of view:

> All of us who have experienced catastrophic illness and disability know this experience of anguish and despair. It is living in darkness without hope, without a past or a future. It is self-pity. It is hatred of everything that is good and life giving. It is rage turned inward. It is a wound with no mouth, a wound that is so deep that no cry can emanate from it . . . (Deegan, 1988).

Patients' reports of their illness experience serve perhaps as our best teachers when it comes to appreciating the severity of the loss that mental illness itself represents. These descriptions usually include a plethora of "absolutes" and "superlatives"—communicating both the utter meanness and unwelcome intrusiveness of mental illness. Over and over again, we learn that the feelings directly related to illness are experienced at endpoints on the emotional spectrum. Whatever the symptoms or the particular diagnostic category, the many lessons taught by those who are directly affected by mental illness include those that demonstrate how mental illness works to set in motion major life alterations, how time and use of time are markedly affected, and what it is like to become the subject of treatment and to have to learn about dealing with diagnostic facts and labels.

Losses Related to Treatment/Rehabilitation Efforts

We who are the givers of various modes of help see the help we give as good, benign, or at the very least (e.g. in cases where we recognize that the treatment contains inherent difficulties), the best of what is available. Self-reports of patients often provide a contrasting picture. Alongside mention of gains, these frequently give indication of the experience (and *feeling*) of loss *vis-à-vis* the course of treatment. Seen in the context of the grief of mental illness, messages such as "Medication will help" and "the weekly group sessions will help you" are recognized as containing messages of loss usually delivered without any acknowledgment of that loss.

Material Losses: Residence, Income, Career and Job Changes

With the advent of mental illness, material aspects of the patient's life change, sometimes slowly, sometimes quickly, but in some cases drastically. Many people find themselves residing away from their usual abode for reasons connected to the illness. The words of Unzicker (1989) echo the fears of many who suffer mental illness: "To be a mental patient is to be a resident of a ghetto, surrounded by other mental patients who are as scared and hungry and bored and broke as you are". Even if the person does not have to move, it is very common that house rules and/or expectations change. These changes range from having someone around and always monitoring the taking of medication, to having family members with new solicitous attitudes—attitudes which are palpably different from those demonstrated to others in the family.

One patient, an artist and formerly an executive secretary, frequently reminds me of the loss aspects of mental illness. Repeatedly she complains, "What I detest most about all this is being poor, having to live in this neighbourhood, and having no access to funding for anything I want to do artistically or otherwise". Also, Unzicker's comment on her financial situation speaks for itself about the material losses experienced along with mental illness: "To be a mental patient is to live on

$82 a month in food stamps, which won't let you buy the Kleenex to dry your tears, and to watch your shrink come back from lunch, driving his Mercedes Benz".

Mental illness often affects the capacity to be financially independent. Indeed, a range of changes to one's "marketability" or to career hopes occurs in most cases. Career prospects, if not altogether extinguished, are often radically altered, marking for the person a significant departure from his/her dreams and expectations. In a world where independence is extolled in expectation and prized when in hand, loss of any measure of it means for the person a loss of exceptional magnitude.

Relationship Losses

As to the quality and quantity of relationships, including those with family and close friends, mental illness is a harbinger of unwanted and unanticipated changes. Paranoid processes, bizarre behaviours, lack of initiative, and diminished ability to make oneself understood, even if occasionally present, play havoc with both existing relationships and often the capacity to make new ones. Also, all too frequently, a very unfortunate consequence of mental illness is that the person is prevented from establishing long-term partnership, and thus role loss (as a spouse, parent or grandparent) is the undesired result.

Loss Related to Sense of Self

Mental illness seriously assaults the patient's sense of self. Compounding this assault is the fact that most people have little vocabulary to express themselves coherently when loss affects their very own selves. Even for us in the mental health professions, phrases like "sense of self", "self-esteem" and "self-image" in relation to *our* selves, probably remain closer to the pages of psychology textbooks than to being of real help in our everyday language about ourselves. It follows, then, that another component to loss related to the sense of self can often be reluctance (perhaps because of lack of vocabulary or of awareness) on the part of therapists to open up for discussion the subject of just how a person is feeling, that is, about matters related to having illness to deal with.

When the subject of loss related to sense of self is opened, issues coming to the fore include: the unconscious absorption of societal stigma regarding mental illness into self-image; absence of capacity to make reasonable predictions about one's self; profound difficulties in making oneself understood in various spheres; and finding oneself in a subordinate role, which often is accompanied by a perception of oneself as an undervalued participant in one's own recovery.

The foregoing list of five particular loss aspects of mental illness endured by patients is surely not exhaustive. Omitted, for example, are losses suffered via the system of delivery of psychiatric services recounted by the anti-psychiatry movement (e.g. Unzicker, 1989; Burstow & Weitz, 1988) but also by others outside of that movement.

Reaction to Loss: the Grieving Process

The literature related to grief and its process can for the most part be classified into four categories: (a) that identifying and describing stages or phases of grief (e.g. Kübler-Ross, 1969; Parkes, 1972, 1986; Parkes & Weiss, 1983); (b) that criticizing the "stage approach" and presenting alternative conceptualization (e.g. Hodgkinson & Stewart, 1991; Rando, 1984, 1986); (c) that focusing on unresolved, pathological grief (e.g. Zisook, 1987); (d) that reporting research findings about other than human death loss—often making reference to stages of grief outlined by Kübler-Ross in *On Death and Dying* (e.g. Crosby, Gage & Raymond, 1983; Winegardner, Simonetti & Nykodym, 1984; Blinde & Stratta, 1992).

In my work with patients and their family members, I have found it helpful to elaborate upon a stage or phase model of grieving. Five categories of reaction, viz. denial, sadness, anger, fear and acceptance, are identified and defined. These are not conceptualized as strict sequential phases, but as components usually experienced in the process of grieving mental illness. However, I do suggest some semblance of sequence for two reasons; first, to convey a sense of realistic hope that one "can come to some greater feelings of peace" than one is feeling at present; second, to give at least a sketch of a roadmap for the psychological and emotional twists and turns sure to be encountered along the grieving journey. A sequential dynamic is usually quite noticeable when, for example, during the course of denial, the person becomes more aware of the realities that mental illness has brought to his/her life, and then reacts to this deepening awareness with feelings of sadness or anger. Nevertheless, it is important to make it clear: (a) that the grieving process does not progress in exact, predictable stages; (b) that moving back and forth between phases or "see-sawing" is normal; (c) that one can experience more than one phase of grieving at once; and finally (d) that, depending on circumstances, people often find themselves feeling as if they have to start all over again at the beginning of the grieving journey.

Phases of Grieving Mental Illness

Denial

Denial, usually the first stage of grieving the mental illness experience, has acquired a generally faulty reputation. Stripped of its grieving process context, it is thought of as a *state of being* or, worse, as willful negative expression—that is, a deliberate refusal to face up to the fact of the presence of mental illness in one's life. Thanks to the work of leading grief scholars, mentioned above, mental health practitioners are provided a valuable alternative, indeed, a constructive view of the role of denial. This view sees denial in a context of normal, healthy grieving acting as a kind of safety-valve or shock-absorber. As such, it allows the person successful survival of the "bad news" about having psychiatric illness. Acting as a shock-absorbing mechanism, it serves two purposes in the case of mental illness: (a) it helps the person preserve both a sense of self and sense of the world; (b) it assists with the process of integration of the shocking news as the person can manage this integration.

There can be little doubt that the course of denial is influenced by the illness. Thus the development of insight regarding the mental illness is usually less vigorous and quick in its appearance than it is in cases of other losses. Indeed, it is typical to see the initial phase of illness and that of denial working in tandem against chances of an early yielding to the grieving process or willing engagement in therapy.

Once the florid force of illness abates, denial's dynamic can still take on various levels of intensity. Whatever its intensity, absorption of bits and pieces of information specific to the experience of mental illness remains ongoing. Statements such as, "You need to take this medication indefinitely", "Your doctor recommends you live in a group home", and "I cannot live with you any more" are resisted but heard none-the-less. With the hearing comes the absorption of painful news related to illness, and with this absorption, the person experiences deepening feelings of sadness, anger and fear.

Sadness, Anger and Fear

Unlike denial, and whether in the context of grieving or not, experiences of sadness, anger and fear are usually given at least some validation by society as normal and healthy. Nevertheless, powerful misunderstandings about these emotions persist, including: (a) the fact that certain emotions are considered more appropriate, depending on one's gender; (b) frank expressions of one's anger or sadness indicate "loss of control"; (c) fear that emotions, if expressed, will be subjected to diagnosis and treatment (e.g. as Unzicker, 1989, states: "To be a mental patient is ... not cry, and not hurt, and not be scared, and not be angry, and not be vulnerable, and not to laugh too loud—because, if you do, you only prove that you're a mental patient ..."); and (d) the automatic equation of expressed emotion with unconstructive or destructive expression.

Conscious engagement with the feelings of sadness, anger and fear provides much material for therapy, including the establishment of therapeutic alliance (Appelo et al., 1993; Lafond, 1994). Indeed, as will be outlined in further detail later, cognitive therapy finds fertile ground when patients in a group context are given just a little information about these feelings, e.g. that these feelings are normal. Also, the simple act of acknowledging wherever the person is at emotionally, including if necessary at those points when the person is inclined to "act out" the feelings of grief, provides a lifeline for constructive grief expression. And, at the very least, information about the grieving process related to mental illness furnishes a needed vocabulary for what has been, and is, happening emotionally and psychologically as a result of the occurrence of illness.

Acceptance

In *On Death and Dying*, Kübler-Ross (1969) describes the acceptance stage as one in which the dying person, having proceeded successfully through stages of mourning his/her own impending death, reaches a point "almost void of feelings . . . [where] the pain is gone, the struggle is over . . ." (p. 113). Acceptance in the context of grieving mental illness radically departs in its definition from that of Kübler-Ross, as well of those of Parkes, Lindemann and others. This is in large part due to the fact that losses associated with mental illness do not have the characteristic of finality that other losses have. In other words, in the case of serious mental illness, it is often chronic loss that is being grieved. Thus, in *Grieving Mental Illness: A Guide for Patients and Their Caregivers*, I defined acceptance as ". . . facing the realities brought about by the presence of mental illness, and then building and practicing coping skills so that recovery can be achieved and maintained" (p. 77).

Early in discussions about accepting the reality of mental illness, it is necessary to clarify the meaning of acceptance; e.g. that it does not mean approval of one's mental illness. Statements such as, "I can never accept my illness" are frequent. Working from a grieving mental illness framework, such statements set the stage for explaining that acceptance: (a) begins with trying to face whatever realities have been brought into one's life by mental illness; (b) is strengthened by efforts to gain increased insight; and (c) plays a powerful role in maintaining mental health. (I often use as example here the acceptance "coping skill" of watching for and dealing with early signs of a next acute episode.) In my opinion, knowledge about acceptance is crucial for those suffering first episodes of psychosis, particularly how it can be "put to work" to assist the person to avoid further episodes. Conceptualizing acceptance as a tool for maintaining recovery makes its achievement both a real and an attractive possibility. Indeed, for some it becomes a beacon of meaningful hope on the grieving journey.

Careful observation of patients and family members who appear to have achieved some obvious peace despite the illness indicate that there are three essential elements in acceptance: insight, activity and affirmation. These continue to be present past the acute phases of illness. A person gains insight by: (a) seeking information about his/her mental illness, particularly noticing how the illness expresses itself in one's own unique circumstances, as well as keeping an eye open for information prepared for the general public's consumption; (b) discovering what can be done to manage symptoms; (c) asking questions of one's therapists. Activity, a close cousin of insight, is evident in those who choose to actualize the role they know they have to play in order to recover and sustain recovery. The practice of affirmation, taking one's own situation seriously enough to tell oneself that coping with illness is tough but "I'm doing the best I can . . .", interweaves with insight and activity to achieve a satisfactory level of acceptance. Therapists can be of help in the achievement of acceptance by encouraging patients to make serious conscious commitment to working in an acceptance mode.

PART II: CONSIDERATIONS FOR PRACTICE

Characteristics of the Therapist

The work of assisting people to engage in the grieving process associated with their mental illness is facilitated if the therapist assumes a stance which combines affirmation, teaching, encouragement and collaboration.

Stance of Affirmation

By assuming a stance of affirmation the therapist openly acknowledges the work that the individual has done and is doing to recover and maintain recovery. Expressing presumption that the patient is working toward recovery, even early on in a first inpatient admission, is important—not only for purposes of affirmation of effort but also to convey to the patient that he/she is expected to play an active part in his/her own recovery. Integral also to this stance is patent recognition of the individual's healthy side, strengths and talents. A stance of affirmation also means that the therapist's various interventions are delivered in a way that purposefully acknowledges and affirms the person's emotional and psychological struggle with mental illness. Attempts to be affirming should not wait until an individual's florid state of psychosis subsides. Observable grieving reactions are usually present alongside psychotic symptoms. As mentioned before, effort to connect with the person through his/her grieving feeling, whether expressed openly or not, can be the key to establishing therapeutic rapport. As well, therapeutic alliance is often enhanced by the therapist's affirmation of, or open agreement with, complaints about defects in the system of psychiatric service delivery. Beyond this, what also merits identification and affirmation is the person's already present constructive coping skills. These include, for example, making efforts to recognize early signs of illness, calling for help before problems reach crisis proportion, and making attempts to grapple with persistent psychotic symptoms. These come to light as patients tell their stories in response to purposely asked questions; e.g. "How have you managed so far?", "What skills have you employed to get to this point?" and "What do you do to be good to yourself?" In addition to the patient's already present constructive coping skills, further subject matter for affirmation (and other work) includes the uniqueness of the person, e.g. as exemplified through the choice of coping skill and the particular way this skill is utilized by the person, as well as the sheer effort put into choosing and exercising a coping skill. Also, in my opinion, it is necessary for therapists to give some positive acknowledgment to previously made, unconstructive coping choices. These can be framed as "lessons in life" or courses of action one takes prior to learning about a range of preferable coping options.

Teaching Stance

Because the grief of mental illness is a form of grief which is not accorded societal recognition, the therapist must always take care to convey basic points about grieving mental illness and must be prepared to do so repeatedly. Basic points to be taught include the following:

1. Mental illness is a loss to be grieved.
2. Denial, sadness, anger, fear and acceptance are normal components of grief.
3. Most people feel, at one time or another, more than one feeling.
4. Grief is a healthy process.
5. Conscious engagement in the process provides both a bridge to successful therapy and fuel for the further work involved in maintaining recovery.

Beyond these basics, it becomes essential to teach particular coping skills, and to coach the person as he/she attempts to use them. These skills include use of "key coping questions" (Lafond, 1994) and other cognitive therapy techniques such as metathinking and decentering (Perris, 1989). It is always important to remember, as Perris points out (p. 184), that these techniques are not to be taught as goals in themselves, but as methods or ways of assistance with alleviation of symptoms.

Stance of Encouragement

Encouragement springs from authentic knowledge of how the person is working and has worked with his/her strengths. It avoids what McMullin (1986) calls "irrational reinforcements", that is, assignment to the person of meaningless attribution for success. (The therapist would avoid saying, for example, "Good for you! You've done it!". Instead, the therapist says, "Good for you! Obviously, you have been and are working to keep yourself well".) Therapists operationalize encouragement in at least two interrelated ways: (a) by assisting the person to discover realistic goals (e.g. "the overall rehabilitation goal"; Farkas & Anthony, 1989); and (b) by providing hands-on assistance with the achievement of those goals. Often, for example, the therapist will need to connect the person to others for appropriate timely resources. A stance of encouragement, however, always goes beyond the functional aspects of goal achievement to touch meaningfully the person's psychological and emotional dimension.

Stance of Collaboration

Willingness to be both companion and co-worker are essential for working effectively with the person's grief of mental illness. This willingness is demonstrated to the person through the therapist's affirming, teaching and encouraging efforts. Willingness on the part of the therapist to work collaboratively is reinforced whenever we make purposeful mention of the person's grieving process associated with his/her mental illness experiences. Mentioning the presence of sadness, anger or fear, about having to deal with certain aspects of psychiatric illness, buttresses the therapeutic alliance.

Thus far in this chapter, the intent has been to convey a theoretical and philosophical framework for working with the grief of mental illness. A description of how I have applied this in my practice follows.

PART III: WORKING WITH THE GRIEF OF MENTAL ILLNESS IN A GROUP

Context of Choice for Practice: Group Work

From time to time discussions about group work for people with schizophrenia leads to the conclusion that a group is not an appropriate context. In light of experience, I disagree. We have found that these patients, like anyone else if given the chance, will make choices about attending a group or not and, once in the group, will participate as they see fit. About any given individual's attendance, I have found two guidelines helpful: (a) attendance and participation must always be voluntary—especially important in recognition of the vulnerability to stress experienced by people with schizophrenia; and (b) the person's illness can not be presenting with such force that the group would probably be extraordinarily disrupted.

Many patients with schizophrenia appear to be well served by a combination of group work and individual therapy. Such a combination, in my view, is ideal for the purpose of promoting knowledge about the grief of mental illness and its exploitation for hastening and enhancing recovery. Indeed, patients presenting on the surface as uninterested, "too down" or unable in other ways to participate in group sessions have often surprised us by their thoughtful, articulate participation. Additionally, comments expressing how a particular group session "helped me with things I wasn't ready to talk about . . ." remind us of the importance of considering each and every one for group work, no matter how uninterested he/she appears to be. However, for those who for one reason or another cannot manage a group context, individual grief work sessions remain an option.

When patients refuse to attend group sessions, respect for this response is in order, along with a statement that perhaps later they will find themselves feeling more ready for the group. Whenever time and other circumstances permit, efforts can be made to promote participation in group work, including the option of sitting silently in the group.

The Coping with Illness Group

For the past several years, the Coping with Illness Group has taken place on a weekly basis in the Schizophrenia Service, Royal Ottawa Hospital. Lasting no more that 50 minutes, it is attended by both in- and outpatients. Being an open, on-going group, participants change from week to week. There is, however, usually a steady nucleus of membership. There are normally two facilitators: one of my colleagues in social work and myself.

The group has three specific purposes: (a) to provide a regular place and space for education about the grief of mental illness; (b) to serve as a source of "moral support"; (c) to supply practical coping-with-illness suggestions, including cognitive coping skills.

There are five phases which constitute the Coping with Illness Group sessions: introductory; exploratory; educational; discussion; and wrap-up.

Phase 1: Introductory

At the beginning of each group, after a brief word of welcome, the patients are reminded that the group is a voluntary one so that they need not feel any pressure to participate by talking (e.g. "We don't want you to feel as if you're on a hot seat . . .") and that, if need be, they may leave the group room before the allotted time is up. During the introductory phase, it is also made clear that the group is "not a therapy group to resolve deep-seated personal problems but one where feelings can be talked about, feelings related to mental illness, having to come to hospital, being dependent on medication, et cetera—and what we can do with and about these feelings". As well at this point participants are reminded that everyone is welcome to come back to the group after discharge from the inpatient service. The introductory stage of the group ends as group members are invited to introduce themselves by first name.

Phase 2: Exploratory Stage

A starting point in terms of topic is solicited from the group and usually suggestions are forthcoming, the veterans leading the way. Coping, coping skills, grieving, metathinking, decentering, and working through anxiety are among the subjects most commonly identified. (In the rare case when a suggestion is not forthcoming from group members, one of the group leaders suggests beginning with reviewing what is understood of the group's purpose.) It is not exceptional that someone will express a desire to sort out a personal problem. Depending on the problem and its description, the group leaders take one of two courses of action: (a) they affirm the significance of the problem and acknowledge that it merits attention but counsel the person to address it with certain members of the team outside the group; or (b) they use it as the launching pad for making educational points related to the group's purpose.

Phase 3: Educational

The teaching methodology in the Coping with Illness Group combines lecture with a Socratic style. Typically, complementary commentary is readily supplied by one or two of the seasoned outpatient members, but also sometimes by an inpatient. Often, for example, an explanation of a particular dynamic of the grieving process (that it's normal to feel fear throughout this process) is followed by patients explaining that it is also normal to feel elements of anger and sadness throughout the process, too. Throughout the group session, use is made of a board to note the main points of core lessons and to note the contributions of the patient members.

Examples of core lessons

Core lessons used in the Coping with Illness Group are presented here in the vernacular and in their entirety for purposes of instruction and readability. In practice, because we believe the dynamics of the group to be of equal value to the teaching of core lessons, the core lessons are not always rendered as they appear below.

1. *Grieving process associated with mental illness.* Whenever we have losses, we undergo a process called grieving. Many people know that they experience grief when someone close to them dies or a divorce occurs in their family. Mental illness is a loss also, and it can bring along with it many other losses, and so there is a grieving process that comes with mental illness. What we often talk about in this group is how grieving has stages or phases—denial, sadness, anger, fear and acceptance.

   Denial happens usually when people first get sick or first come to hospital. People say things like: "I don't need to be here in hospital. I'm not sick", "Somebody's made a big mistake", "I don't need medication". When the person begins to realize that illness is present, he/she usually feels sad or angry, or both sad and angry, about what has happened. The last stage is acceptance. Acceptance means that a person has come to terms with the illness and has developed, and continues to develop, coping skills. Most people still have some of the early grieving feelings even when they've arrived at an acceptance stage. The big difference for those who have arrived at acceptance is that these feelings are not so much a driving force once they've been through the grieving process. They know better how to make a peaceful, happier life for themselves through the use of their coping skills.

   Another important feeling that is probably present for most of us throughout our grieving process is fear—fear of a lot of things, like never getting well again, or of getting sick again. It helps us if we know that fear can be tamed and that we can learn to use it as a guide.

   One of the most important things to remember about the grieving process is that it is completely healthy and normal. It's absolutely okay to feel sorry for yourself—sorry that you have had difficult struggles because of illness, as indeed you may be having right now. It's okay to be very sad or even enraged about it. The trick is to be looking continuously for ways to help yourself cope constructively—so that you can make a better life for yourself and you don't hurt yourself or somebody else.

   Sometimes in grieving our losses we return to an earlier stage, even after we feel we've arrived at acceptance. In other words, we can feel as if we're going to have to go through the whole grieving process again. This too is quite normal. In any case, if this happens to you, it's good to remember that although you may feel like it, you're not at "square one". All along the way of this grieving process, whether we actually realize it or not, we are all building some coping skills.

2. *Problematic grieving.*   There can be one major problem with grieving—getting stuck, for example in anger and sadness, or seesawing back and forth between anger and sadness. This can and does happen—especially if we don't know much about denial or acceptance. This is why it's very important to know as much as possible about how our grieving process works.

3. *Building coping skills/mechanisms.*   When we are convinced that it's perfectly okay to have feelings about having mental illness, having to come for treatment, etc., we are then in a position to ask the key coping questions:

   (a)   How can I help myself cope with _____?
   (b)   Are there ways I can use my experience of _____ constructively?

   The blanks can be filled in with any feelings, aspects of feelings, or other situations you encounter. It's good to make what you put into the blanks as specific as possible. Often, answers to these questions surface as we think about how we've managed successfully before. Sometimes we might need the advice of a friend or a professional helper to arrive at ways of coping that are satisfying and constructive.

   Since 1993, when I became acquainted with the practice of cognitive therapy related to schizophrenia (Perris, 1989), teaching about the cognitive skills of metathinking and decentering has been incorporated into the work of the group. In fact, at the request of group members, discussion of these coping mechanisms often takes center-stage. Requests for review of what they mean, how and in what circumstances they work, are often quickly accompanied, with little or no prompting, by examples of how these skills have helped.

4. *Metathinking.*   Metathinking simply means thinking about your thoughts. In other words, we stand back from ourselves so that: (a) we get different views of our thoughts, our perceptions, our thinking—that is, the way we interpret the world around us; (b) we give ourselves a chance to test out whether there might be other possible ways of thinking about certain events. Metathinking is useful whenever people feel pressured. In fact it can be very helpful if we're bothered with depression, schizophrenia, manic-depressive illness, paranoid thinking or some kinds of delusional thinking.

5. *Decentering.*   Some people who are bothered by problems of mental illness can have a tendency to think that they, their problems and/or other qualities, make them more important than they are. [At this point, a number of same-sized circles are drawn on the board to illustrate others "on the bus or around us in a shopping centre" along with one large circle to depict the perceived

disproportionately larger self.] The skill of decentering has two steps: (a) we first recognize that from time to time we will see ourselves as more important than we are, e.g. when we believe we are getting special messages, or that "everybody is talking about *me*"; (b) we try to bring our ideas about ourselves and our problems down to size. By picturing yourself as the same size as the other people on the bus, problems like delusional thinking and paranoid thinking can sometimes be reduced. We help ourselves decenter by noticing that some on the bus are reading or looking out the windows, and by imagining what others might be thinking about other than about ourselves. It stands to reason that some might be planning supper for that night or thinking about the argument they had with a co-worker yesterday.

Phase 4: Discussion

Discussion in the group reflects both success and struggle. Group participants are encouraged to describe their success stories as they have tried to use the various coping skills. Subject matter also often includes dealing with voices and other symptoms, the chronicity of mental illness, living with labels, symptom self-management, dealing with feelings related to suffering mental illness, stigma, being misunderstood, family relationship problems, medication problems, and feelings of hopelessness and powerlessness. Also, acknowledged are the hassles inherent in day-to-day coping, leading into discussion usually involving affirmation of ways and means practiced to successfully cope with these hassles. Among the range of coping skills are the following: (a) "Phoning a friend and talking things over" is noted as the exercise of a coping skill (and thus disabused of dependency behaviour connotation); (b) finding keys to manage symptoms of schizophrenia like finding and practicing ways of keeping stress level in check; (c) using the key coping questions as guides, thinking about how and what someone can do to cope constructively through a difficult experience; (d) discovering how to follow through as best one can, and also how to routinely give oneself "pats on the back" for doing so. What is also pointed out on a regular basis during the discussion phase of the group is that all the while we are reaching for identification of how we feel, how we are going to constructively process this feeling, and, importantly, how we are being compassionate to ourselves as we cope, that we are engaged in the business of building self-esteem.

Phase 5: The Wrap-up

When the group session is brought to a close, points covered are mentioned in summary fashion. Sometimes a point for next week's group is suggested. Then, besides acknowledging with thanks everyone's presence and contribution, participants are routinely given two further items of information: (a) if anyone feels upset because of something that was said in the group, he/she is welcome to talk to one of the leaders on an individual basis; (b) everyone is welcome to come back next week.

Evaluation of the Coping with Illness Group

Formal evaluations of the Coping with Illness Group are conducted periodically by asking participants whether the group makes a difference in their lives, and if so, what the differences are. These are planned sessions, so that group participants are given advance notice of time and place and also that a tape recorder will be used. These evaluation sessions serve two purposes: (a) for the patient participants, provision of structured opportunity for articulation of what in particular about the group works for them; (b) for the facilitators, provision of feedback which not only serves to guide the facilitation of future sessions, but also serves to contribute, as it has in the past, to the continuing development of the grieving mental illness model. Recent examples of the patients' feedback will illustrate:

> Each of us has had a psychotic episode. I heard voices. Medication from the doctors has helped. Now by coming to the group and talking, I learn how *I* can cope with my illness. It's becoming easier for me to live with my illness. I'm able to solve some of the problems by opening up and talking about what I can do to treat my illness, e.g. by metathinking and decentering. I've also learned it's normal to have feelings about having an illness.

> I find metathinking and decentering help a lot, especially the metathinking. This means thinking about your thoughts. Now I am a very thoughtful person. When I am alone I think a lot, and I am able to think out my thoughts and reason with myself. I find that by thinking my thoughts through, and taking what is bothering me, without worrying about the pros and cons, helps a lot. The decentering I am not fully up to date on, but I do realize that you are not the only person in the world and that other people are involved. That helped a lot too. But I think the metathinking has helped me more than anything else.

> I get the message from this group that we can take some responsibility in helping ourselves to be healthy again. When it comes to a breakdown in mental health, you don't really think much about it, except that you put all your eggs in one basket letting the doctor take care of you. You don't think of asking, "What can I do to help myself get better?" When I first came to the group I realized that some of the things that you were teaching us, like metathinking and decentering, involve a lot of skills that can be used when you are at home by yourself. These help you stay well. For the first time in 15 years, I felt I had the skills to manage my illness.

> I was already practicing some coping mechanisms like reaching out to somebody. But before coming to the group, I always felt that I was being over-dependent when I called somebody.

> Learning in this group that my feelings were normal, actually how the grieving process works, gave me a sense of safety. When I learned about the grieving process I wrote it down and tacked it up on my bulletin board to remind myself that no matter what, my feelings about being in hospital, about being struck with this blasted illness, are normal.

> In the group, we've talked a lot about self-coaching. I have been out of hospital for years. I am, though, still struggling with a few things. Anyway, yesterday at my new

volunteer job I was very nervous. But I remembered that we were talking about how to self-coach. So I did the self-coaching thing: I told myself that I should try my best, ask a few questions—and not be ashamed to ask—and just work as well as I could. I also told myself that if I made a mistake I would talk it over later. Talking lots of things over helps, like we do in this group. When we are still recovering, we run into a lot of obstacles. If you have coping skills to help you through, especially if you are feeling sad or angry, frustrated or scared, then it is very helpful to find out ways of putting things in perspective.

Both the dynamic of the Coping with Illness Group and its continuing evolution have proven most valuable "partners" for me as I have worked to develop this grieving mental illness model. Indeed, the group has served both as catalyst and laboratory for a number of therapeutic forays. What was once an unsuccessful group meeting (unsuccessful because the group's former focus, discharge planning, held no inherent substantive quality for participant cohesion) has been transformed into a group where participants feel comfortable sharing their emotional and psychological experience with mental illness, as well as showing a clear willingness to learn a variety of cognitive coping skills. What accounts for this success? I believe the answer lies not only in the collaboration between and among the participants and the two group leaders, but also and probably in greater part, in the participants' hunger for coping skill knowledge and coaching. As is evidenced in the feedback above, sound coping skills are often already part of the person's repertoire. Participation in the group promotes "self-respecting" characterization of these practices—i.e. strategies (like reaching out to talk to someone) are acknowledged as *bona fide* coping skills, and not as "dependent behaviour". Other skills such as those that involve purposeful use of the grieving feelings have prompted both men and women to become open about bouts of tearfulness and anger. And, as the feedback also indicates, "metathinking" and "decentering" are now not only "household" names for some afflicted with serious mental illness but also play central parts in coping.

PART IV: CONCLUSION

Hopefully, this chapter has persuasively articulated a constructive use of the grieving process related to suffering mental illness with methods for cognitive therapy skill teaching and coaching. As I was writing it I found myself fueled by hope that this articulation would be of assistance to other mental health practitioners who are interested in working with *the person* suffering serious mental illness.

Thus far, for a number of reasons, I have been inclined to study the efficacy of this therapeutic model using qualitative methodology. If the experience of success as expressed by the Coping with Illness Group participants in formal group evaluation sessions is allowed to stand as indication, work with the grief of mental illness would appear to bode well for further application of cognitive therapy in schizophrenia and other serious psychoses.

ACKNOWLEDGMENTS

The author extends heartfelt thanks to Jo Weston MSW CSW and to Raymond Lafond MSW for their constructive suggestions, as well as to William Masson MSW particularly for his collaboration in working with patients in group context.

REFERENCES

Alexander, K. (1991). *Understanding and Coping with Schizophrenia: 14 Principles for the Relatives.* Melbourne: Schwartz & Wilkinson.
Appelo, M.T., Sloof, C.J., Woonings, F.M.J., Carson, J. & Louwerens, J.W. (1993). Grief: its significance for rehabilitation in schizophrenia. *Clinical Psychology & Psychotherapy*, **1**(1), 53–59.
Atkinson, S.D. (1994). Grieving and loss in parents with a schizophrenic child. *American Journal of Psychiatry*, **151**(8), 1137–1139.
Blinde, E.M. & Stratta, T.M. (1992). The "sport career death" of college athletes: involuntary and unanticipated sport exits. *Journal of Sport Behavior*, **15**(1), 3–20.
Burstow, B. & Weitz, D. (eds) (1988). *Shrink Resistant: the Struggle Against Psychiatry in Canada*, Vancouver, BC: New Star Books.
Corin, E. & Lauzon, G. (1992). Positive withdrawal and the quest for meaning: the reconstruction of experience among schizophrenics. *Psychiatry*, **55**(August), 266–278.
Coursey, R.D. (1989). Psychotherapy with persons suffering from schizophrenia: the need for a new agenda. *Schizophrenia Bulletin*, **15**(3), 349–353.
Crosby, J.F., Gage, BA. & Raymond, M.C. (1983). The grief resolution process in divorce. *Journal of Divorce*, **7**(1), 3–18.
Deegan, P.E. (1988). Recovery: the lived experience of rehabilitation. *Psychosocial Rehabilitation Journal*, **11**(4), 11–19.
Deegan, P.E. (1996). Recovery as a Journey of the heart. *Psychiatric Rehabilitation Journal*, **19**(3), 91–97.
Dincin, J. (1990). Speaking out. *Psychosocial Rehabilitation Journal*, **14**(2), 83–85.
Doka, K.J. (1989). *Disenfranchised Grief: Recognizing Hidden Sorrow.* Lexington, MA: Lexington Books.
Doka, K.J. (1993). *Living with Life-threatening Illness: a Guide For Patients, Their Families and Caregivers.* New York: Free Press.
Farkas, M.D. & Anthony, W.A. (eds) (1989). *Psychiatric Rehabilitation Programs: Putting Theory into Practice.* Baltimore, MD: Johns Hopkins University Press.
Gunderson, J.G. (1978). Defining the therapeutic process in psychiatric milieus. *Psychiatry*, **41**(4), 327–337.
Hodgkinson, P.E. & Stewart, M. (1991). *Coping with Catastrophe: a Handbook for Disaster Management.* London and New York: Routledge.
Jeffries, J.J. (1977). The trauma of being psychotic: a neglected element in the management of chronic schizophrenia. *Canadian Psychiatric Association Journal*, **22**(5), 199–206.
Kanter, J.S. (ed.) (1985). Clinical issues in treating the chronically mentally ill. In *New Directions for Mental Health Services*, No. 27. San Francisco: Jossey-Bass.
Kübler-Ross, E. (1969). *On Death and Dying.* London: Tavistock.
Lafond, V. (1994). *Grieving Mental Illness: a Guide for Patients and Their Caregivers.* Toronto: University of Toronto Press.
Lefley, H.P. (1987). Behavioral manifestations of mental illness. In A.B. Hatfield & H.P. Lefley (eds), *Families of the Mentally Ill: Coping and Adaptation.* New York: Guilford.

Lindemann, E. (1944). Symptomatology and management of acute grief. *American Journal of Psychiatry*, **101**, 141–148.

Mayer-Gross, W. (1920). Uber die Sellungnahme zur Abgelanfenen akuten Psychose. *A Ges Neurol Psychiat*, **60**, 160–212 (cited by Jeffries, 1977).

McMullin, R.E. (1986). *Handbook of Cognitive Therapy Techniques*. New York and London: W.W. Norton.

Miller, F., Dworkin, J., Ward, M. & Barone, D. (1990). A preliminary study of unresolved grief in families of seriously mentally ill patients. *Hospital and Community Psychiatry*, **41**(12), 1321–1325.

Mohelsky, H. (1987). The functionalist approach to psychiatric rehabilitation. *Psychosocial Rehabilitation Journal*, **X**(4), 17–29.

Parkes, C.M. (1972). *Bereavement: Studies of Grief in Adult Life*. New York: International Universities Press.

Parkes, C.M. (1986). *Bereavement: Studies of Grief in Adult Life* (revised edn). London: Penguin Books.

Parkes, C.M. and Weiss, R.S. (1983). *Recovery from Bereavement*. New York: Basic Books.

Perris, C. (1989). *Cognitive Therapy with Schizophrenic Patients*. New York: Guilford.

Pine, V.R., Margolis, O.S., Doka, K., Kutscher, A.H., Schaefer, D.J., Siegel, M.E. & Cherico, D.J. (1990). *Unrecognized and Unsanctioned Grief: the Nature and Counseling of Unacknowledged Loss*. Springfield, IL: Charles C. Thomas.

Rando, T.A. (1984). *Grief, Dying, and Death: Clinical Interventions for Caregivers*. Champaign, IL: Research Press Company.

Rando, T.A. (1986). *Loss and Anticipatory Grief*. Lexington, MA: Lexington Books.

Raphael, B. (1983). *The Anatomy of Bereavement*. New York: Basic Books.

Schwartz-Borden, G. (1986). Grief work: prevention and intervention. *Social Casework: the Journal of Contemporary Social Work*, **67**(8), 499–505.

Selzer, M.A., Sullivan, T.B., Carsky, M & Terkelsen, K.G. (1989). *Working with the Person with Schizophrenia: the Treatment Alliance*. New York: New York University Press.

Strauss, J.S. (1992). The person—key to understanding mental illness: towards a new dynamic psychiatry, III. *British Journal of Psychiatry*, **161**(18), 19–26.

Strauss, J.S. (1994). The person with schizophrenia as a person. II: Approaches to the subjective and complex. *British Journal of Psychiatry*, Suppl 23, 103–107.

Styron, William (1990). *Darkness Visible: A Memoir of Madness*. New York: Random House.

Unzicker, R. (1989). On my own: a personal journey through madness and re-emergence. *Psychosocial Rehabilitation Journal*, **1**(13), 71–77.

Winegardner, D., Simonetti, J.L. & Nykodym, N. (1984). Unemployment: the living death. *Journal of Employment Counseling*, **21**(4).

Worden, J.W. (1982). *Grief Counseling and Grief Therapy: a Handbook for the Mental Health Practitioner*. New York: Springer.

Zisook, S. (ed.) (1987). *Biopsychosocial Aspects of Bereavement*. Washington, DC: American Psychiatric Press.

Chapter 14

A Systematic Cognitive Therapy Approach to Schizo-affective Psychosis

Douglas Turkington
St Nicholas Hospital, Newcastle upon Tyne, UK
and
David Kingdon
Mental Health Group, University of Southampton, UK

Schizoaffective psychoses are defined in ICD-10 (WHO, 1992) as being episodic disorders in which both affective and schizophrenic symptoms are prominent within the same episode of illness. The symptoms need to be present simultaneously, or at least within a few days of each other, and because of the mixture of symptoms, criteria cannot be met for schizophrenia or an affective disorder. All clinicians recognize clinical presentations of schizo-mania, schizo-depression and schizo-affective psychosis (mixed), as being extremely common. Whereas there has been good progress in the clinical practice of cognitive therapy with affective disorders (e.g. Blackburn & Twaddle, 1996), building on the classical work of Beck et al. (1979), there was a long gap in cognitive therapy of psychosis work after Beck's original single case study (Beck, 1952). Interest in this area was triggered again by Milton's description of the effect of confrontation vs. belief modification in the treatment of delusions (Milton, Patwa & Hafner, 1978). Ground-breaking work then followed with the treatment of a cohort of schizophrenic patients in Bassetlaw with cognitive-behavioural therapy (CBT) (Kingdon & Turkington, 1991). At about the same time, Carlo Perris was describing a cognitive therapy approach to schizophrenia and personality disorder within therapeutic communities in Umeå (Perris, 1988). Psychologists in Liverpool, Manchester and Birmingham then advanced the theory and practice of CBT with psychotic patients using a series of well-designed experimental studies,

Cognitive Psychotherapy of Psychotic and Personality Disorders: Handbook of Theory and Practice.
Edited by C. Perris and P.D. McGorry.
© 1998 John Wiley & Sons Ltd.

e.g. Bentall, Kinderman & Kaney (1994), Tarrier et al. (1993) and Drury et al. (1996). Our own clearly defined process of therapy and techniques for CBT in schizophrenia and delusional disorder (Turkington et al., 1996a) are most closely paralleled by the work of Fowler and colleagues in London and Norwich in relation to an emphasis on collaboration, formulation and schema-focused approaches to psychotic symptoms (Fowler, Garety & Kuipers, 1995). Despite these advances, CBT of psychotic disorders remains very much in its infancy in comparison to CBT of affective disorders, in terms of both models and technique application. Recent advances in describing CBT of bipolar disorder (Scott, 1995) have not yet filtered through into the literature in terms of description of techniques, case work or well-designed research methodology. In general terms, schizo-affective psychosis is greatly neglected in the research literature and there has only been one single case study of the use of CBT with this patient group, described by Fowler, Garety & Kuipers (1995). In this chapter I will attempt to describe the process of therapy and potential pitfalls of CBT in schizo-affective psychosis and illustrate the theory with a case example. It seems helpful to have an overview of the stages of CBT in schizo-affective psychosis (see Fig. 14.1).

Although the flow diagram given need not be applied in the sequence shown, most of these stages will need to be negotiated in order for maximum symptom resolution to occur. In a patient who is extremely suicidal, however, this would become the immediate focus of therapy. On the other hand, an extremely paranoid patient would perhaps be so preoccupied and distressed by the delusion that he/she would be immediately working on the delusion itself, intermingling assessment, engaging and delusion-focused techniques. The therapist, therefore, must pick and choose the order of technique application, but two factors seem paramount. First, the case must be thoroughly assessed and deemed suitable, and second, a shared formulation requires to be generated, which includes a clear and believable explanation of symptomatology. At all times, even good therapists find themselves wavering into mild collusive or mild confrontational stances in their approach, and keeping an eye on the collusion/confrontation parameter is important. Beck's collaborative empiricism in relation to psychotic patients seems an extremely therapeutic posture for the development of explanations and reality testing.

ASSESSMENT

The patient will come to the assessment interview with a combination of schizophrenic (e.g. thought insertion, delusional perception, running commentary auditory hallucinations) and affective (e.g. depressive, manic or mixed affective) symptomatology. The first 4–6 sessions usually involve a mixture of assessment and engaging techniques. This is because a single one-off (impersonal) assessment session can seriously damage the engaging process. This can happen because often in the delicate early stages of engagement the patient might feel that his/her own current concerns are not being given adequate time or consideration

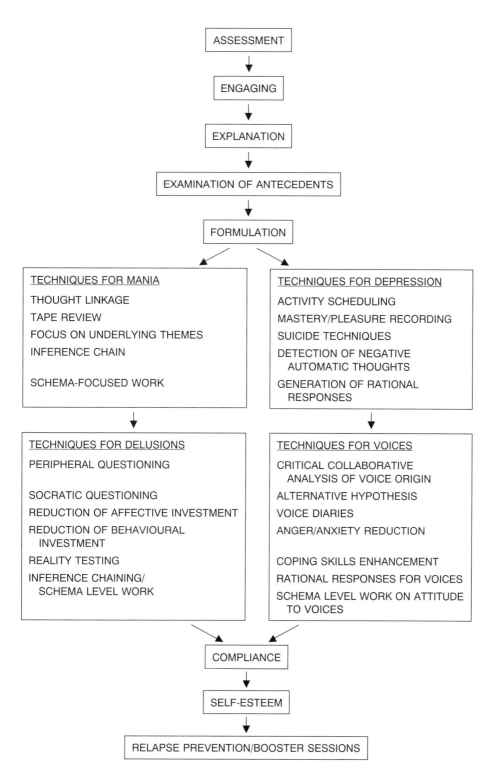

Figure 14.1 The stages of CBT in schizo-affective psychosis

within assessment. It is, of course, useful for a standard psychiatric assessment to have been completed by a House Officer in order that the full range and impact of symptomatology can be catalogued and understood. Issues such as life events, family and personal history and premorbid personality can all be documented before the patient has the first cognitive therapy session. The cognitive therapist can then set about the generation of a problem list, with all this background knowledge in place. An assessment of depression and in particular of suicidal thoughts, intent and plans seems paramount. The Beck Depression Inventory (Beck et al., 1961) and the Hopelessness Scale (Beck et al., 1974) are particularly pertinent. Early sessions will focus immediately on suicidality if this seems necessary. We find the most useful techniques in this group to be:

1. Pros and cons of suicide.
2. The corpse (Who will find it? How will they react? Will it be messy?).
3. Effect of the death on key friends/relatives (the concept of not getting rid of the pain, only passing it on to a loved one).
4. Increased risk of depression/suicidality in relatives. Usually the depressed patient will say that the children will get over it because he/she is so worthless and useless as a parent anyway. The high levels of depression and suicide in the relatives of successful suicides needs to be pointed out and de-centring can be used to see what the patient would feel like if his/her own father had committed suicide when young (the concept needs to be got across that the suicide may plague him/her forever, i.e. he/she won't get over it easily).
5. Religious and philisophical aspects (Is suicide a sin? What will happen after death? Do we know enough to answer this question?).
6. Most suicide bids do not succeed and the person can end up worse off than he/she currently is, sometimes with permanent physical and mental damage (things could get worse).
7. The usefulness of the concept of suicide. We can consider suicide as a helpful concept but as a destructive actuality, in that the concept of "there is always a way out" can help the patient through periods of deep despair, without him/her ever coming to the point of actually carrying it out.

It is interesting that our recent study of CBT vs. befriending in neuroleptic-resistant schizophrenia (Turkington et al., 1996b) showed clearly that those people with psychosis who drop out of cognitive therapy tend to do so at this early assessment/engaging stage. That group tend to have very high depression and hopelessness scores but they are not more psychotic on CPRS ratings (Asberg et al., 1978). Failure of assessment/engagement with psychotic patients seems to be related to hopelessness and depression and this subgroup constitutes a very high risk group for completed suicide. A number of therapist attitudes facilitates engagement and allows a thorough assessment:

1. Warmth, genuineness, unconditional positive regard.
2. Open-mindedness and respect for the symptoms and for what they might mean to the patient.

3. Experience of psychotic interaction and an attitude of relaxed hopefulness about session work.
4. Gentle, slow pacing of sessions.
5. Provision of material in written form.
6. Informing the community key worker that CBT is commencing and providing appropriate background reading. Often the Community Psychiatric Nurse/social worker will be very important in helping the patient to complete key homework assignments.

Assessment dovetails into engaging where we start to set agendas for sessions, e.g. in mania:

- "The mind seems very active just now. Should we look at the kind of things you're thinking about?" (techniques for mania, see Fig. 14.1); or:
- "The sadness seems very deep. Shall we try something to attempt to lift the mood?" (activity scheduling, mastery and pleasure recording/rational responses, etc.); or:
- "What do you understand by your symptoms? Shall we try to come to a common understanding of them?" (de-catastrophize madness label, generate explanations).

Very often patients will, however, not want to pursue what they regard as peripheral issues and they will want to tackle the main symptoms on the agenda straight away. It is of course a basic principle of cognitive therapy that there is no point in working on a target problem when the patient wants to work on something else. Therefore, it can be appropriate to work on hallucinations or delusions very early in treatment, if these symptoms are dominating the clinical picture.

If the usual process of therapy is followed, then assessment and engaging will be followed by specific focused sessions on the patient's understanding of his illness. Written material is useful, e.g. "What's happening to me?" (Kingdon, pers. comm.) can be supplemented by material on sleep deprivation causing paranoid ideation and hallucinations in normal volunteers (Oswald, 1974). Specific handouts on stress and psychotic symptoms can be helpful for the patient to understand that his/her symptoms are not categorically different from those experienced by anyone else under situations of extreme stress, e.g. hostage situations (Siegel, 1984), sensory deprivation (Leff, 1968) or solitary confinement (Grassian, 1983). The purpose of this work on generating explanations is to help the patient to feel human again and not to label him/herself as "a loony" or "a nut case". These labels are often being used by patients in a critical automatic way linked to cognitions of hopelessness, untreatability and steady deterioration into neglect, violence and homelessness. Recent surveys (e.g. Furnham & Bower, 1992) of attitudes of clinicians and of the general population to schizophrenia show that the old dementia praecox diagnosis is still very much alive in many clinicians' minds, fostering clinical approaches involving distancing, humouring and over-reliance on biological approaches and a generally pessimistic/guarded demeanour. Attitudes hopefully will be improved by the initiative on schizophrenia (Sartorius, 1997) but currently the community views schizophrenia as "Jekyll and Hyde", i.e. two people inside one mind or "demonic possession". Illness views do not dominate cultural thinking on the subject. The patient therefore needs help to understand what schizophrenia is exactly, how there can be a genetic predisposition and what the prognosis is for recovery or good outcome. Depending on the study, it would appear that 20–30% of definite schizophrenic cases completely recover. Another similar proportion have good outcome, with relapses but no ongoing disability between episodes. Romme & Escher (1996) have shown that good coping strategies with auditory hallucinations are directly related to having an explanation, which the patient believes, as to what the cause of the voices might be. Freudian, Jungian, mystical and para-psychological explanations were often found acceptable by patients; however, a number of possible explanations should be generated, with percentage belief allocation attributed to each one, as collaborative discussion proceeds in a guided discovery modality as to which belief fits each patient's pattern of symptoms most closely.

The presence of sleep deprivation correlates closely with the severity of psychotic symptomatology at the time of admission (Meltzer et al., 1970) and this is often the best starting point. Then, of course, it makes more sense to the patient as to why they should take tranquillizing medication at night time as an aid to symptomatic improvement through improved sleep pattern. Sulpiride, risperidone and olanzapine seem to the author to be the medications most often accepted by patients due to their good profile of side effects, and this can be the beginning of the compliance component of treatment, presented as part of an integrated treatment strategy, grounded in critical collaborative analysis of the psychotic and affective subject material.

It seems important to disentangle psychotic and culturally syntonic explanations, e.g. explanations concerning alien abduction can no longer be necessarily considered delusional. Witchcraft and religious explanations have always been culture-syntonic and should be accepted into cognitive therapy work as one of the alternative hypotheses. Discussing these issues very much aids the engaging process and hopefully shows the patient an example of systematic hypothesis testing and deductive reasoning which should generalize out into future homework tasks. A normalizing explanation can be helped by personal disclosure of hypnagogic or hypnopompic hallucinations, which can be seen to be similar phenomena occurring in the therapist.

At the end of the phase of generation of hypotheses and a decision on a personal explanation, one of the cornerstones of future progress will have been laid. Trust, self-esteem and hope will all have improved to some degree and it is then time to move towards a case formulation through a thorough examination of the antecedents of the schizo-affective breakdown. Normally a patient will report no particular stresses leading up to the emergence of symptomatology on normal history taking, but on a more thorough examination of the pre-psychotic period, key schema invalidating/traumatizing life events are often detectable. These events can trigger the emergence of psychotic symptoms and influence the psychotic content. The techniques for the examination of the pre-psychotic period include inductive questioning, imagery and role play. Inductive questioning involves guiding the patient through the pre-psychotic period from an identified starting date, e.g. a birthday, and trying to clarify what events took place thereafter, e.g. a period of over-work, a successful relationship, relationship breakdown, sexual orientation conflict, arguments with a family member, death of a close friend, failure at a job interview, etc. This technique gently allows the patient to explore the particular stressors which seem to be linked to the emergence of psychosis, and the understanding of this link can be an important integrative experience (Fig. 14.2).

If an invalidated schema is activated by this process of questioning, then it is possible for some of the symptoms to become worse for a period and necessitate the need for therapist withdrawal into a supportive/behavioural stance, using relaxation, distraction, general support, etc., until gently reaffirming the link and moving on to a full case formulation. Role play can be useful if, for example, failure at a job interview is reported, but there is no emotional content expressed. Role play and imagery in such a circumstance can allow the patient to detect particular negative automatic thoughts and related schemas. From the examination of the prodrome and the earlier normalizing explanation, a full and shared formulation is collaboratively generated. An example of such a formulation is given in Fig. 14.3.

This formulation relates to the schizomanic presentation of *David*, a young man aged 20 who was admitted as an emergency from a local Buddhist monastery, where the monks were becoming increasingly concerned about his bizarre meditation rituals and grandiose pronouncements. The chief monk informed me that David "was not following the middle way". On informal admission, which he accepted with ambivalence and under parental pressure, he was in a state of poor self-care with formal thought disorder, including accelerated tempo of thought, intermingling of themes, derailment and "Knight's move thinking" (an incomprehensible link between two thoughts). He had the grandiose delusion of being spiritually enlightened, "a Buddha". There was episodic depressive swings and reduced drive. Pseudomystical thinking was prominent and linked to a very severe social anxiety. There was also a hypochondriacal delusion of spinal damage, which could be used to opt out of any attempts at normal social interaction. This man spent hours pacing the ward and engaging in bizarre meditative postures. Six brief engaging sessions were mostly spent on discussion of meditative practice and Buddhist theory, and trust was gradually built up. Thought disorder techniques (Turkington & Kingdon, 1991) were useful to help David to link themes and attempt to maintain a focus in CBT. In the hope of achieving a case formulation, he agreed to review his life history

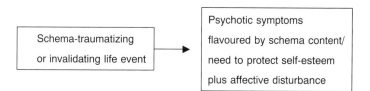

Figure 14.2   The link between stressors and the emergence of psychosis

INDUCTIVE FORMULATION

0–3 years	Moved house. Slept on landing
3–5 years	Felt superior to other kids. Felt "left out" by peers. Couldn't do handstands. Not included in games. Episodic feelings of *inadequacy*/uselessness
7–11 years	"Started battling with it". Strong fear that he would be rejected. Mother/father raging all the time. "Felt that they were living their lives through me". Felt he had to support mother/father: felt inadequate to do so. Constant feeling of depression/tiredness. "No space to feel, so I *cut off all feelings*"
11–13 years	Boarding—okay
13–18 years	At harrow. Constant *humiliation* by six bullies: "bastards". No friends at all. Feeling like crying, not being able to. Exhaustion. Homosexual encounter with very charismatic/evil individual. Felt he took over. Felt that he was trying to make me socially good. Felt "programmed"/experimented with, Manipulated. Emotions so suppressed. Screaming inside
18–18$^1/_4$ years	In pain. "Bodily distortion"/*back pain* starts. Breakdown Began. Unable to think, very detached
18$^1/_4$–18$^1/_2$ years	At home. "Put on a front"
18$^1/_2$–19 years	Holiday in Greek Islands. Back pain/severe *anxiety*. "Floating mentally"
19–20 years	At university. Involved in *Buddhist* monastery. Increasing *withdrawal*. Increasingly bizarre meditation rituals. Increasingly incomprehensible

Figure 14.3   Inductive formulation of a case

inductively (see Fig. 14.3). With the generation of this case formulation, which was by far our longest session yet, engagement was greatly improved and there seemed to be more common ground for discussion. David started to become more verbal and less socially anxious and more motivated to interact in CBT. He also agreed, for the first time, to anxiolytic medication (lorazepam), but not to a neuroleptic.

Figure 14.4 shows a schematic case formulation, which was generated collaboratively. On the basis of the formulation, David suggested that the Buddhist practice was his way of coping with these very powerful anxiety symptoms and the back pain was accepted as being due to severe tension in the large muscles at the base of the spine. A mixture of anxiety-reducing rational responses, graded exposure to social interaction and activity scheduling, linked to mastery and pleasure recording, were commenced. An MRI scan of the lumbar spine revealed a congenital bony deficit, which allowed David a validating explanation for his excessive focus on his back and his use of the symptom to avoid interaction. Having made some progress in anxiety reduction with lorazepam, and having had many hours of CBT, he became amenable to receive sulpiride for the treatment of ongoing symptomatology. Imagery techniques were used to allow the experience of affect, linked to the memories of family difficulties and systematic bullying. He started to experience increased recall, dreams and nightmares, which allowed the formulation to be gradually elaborated. By now, more effective coping strategies had been put in place and the back pain and Buddhism were rarely mentioned. Symptoms steadily improved and much hostility expressed against a perceived cold mother and systematic bullying.

Schema-level work seemed vital in an attempt to work with the powerful drives for success and approval, which eventually led to a psychotic (schizo-affective) breakdown. The compensatory schemas were tackled initially before the core schema of inadequacy was attempted. David was in agreement that an absolute demand for career success was a dysfunctional belief, in that it led to lack of pleasure from normal activities and was inefficient, through its tendency to stifle spontaneity and creativity in the workplace. Having agreed to this, the continuum of beliefs

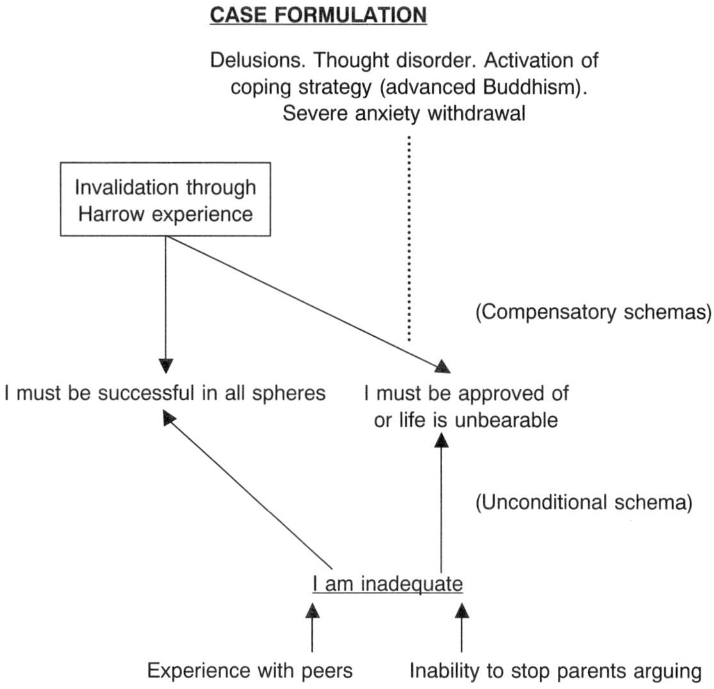

CASE FORMULATION

Delusions. Thought disorder. Activation of
coping strategy (advanced Buddhism).
Severe anxiety withdrawal

Invalidation through
Harrow experience

(Compensatory schemas)

I must be successful in all spheres   I must be approved of
or life is unbearable

(Unconditional schema)

I am inadequate

Experience with peers   Inability to stop parents arguing

Figure 14.4 A schematic case formulation, generated collaboratively

concerning success were explored. The chapter "Dare to be Average" (from Burns, 1980) was read as homework. Activity scheduling was pursued with mastery and pleasure recording to look for feelings of success with day-to-day projects. In relation to the absolute demand for approval, this was underpinning much of his poor social performance due to anxiety related to hypervigilance over signs of perceived disapproval from others. Again, he could agree that the person who demanded approval at all times from all others was bound to be disappointed, as there are natural variations in the kind of personality each individual is attracted to or gets on with. Also at times, everyone has to be assertive and stand their ground if they do not agree with another person's comments or actions, and such confrontation usually does not leave the assertive individual being liked. It was accepted that the person who does not have clear and honest communications with others would end up being "walked all over" in an emotional sense. Role play and imagery linked to rational responses allowed a reduction in the intensity of this demand for approval, and again these were tested out in real-life situations, using diary recording of emotional severity, negative automatic thoughts, rational responses and behavioural efficacy.

The underlying core dysfunctional assumption concerning personal inadequacy was tackled next and, having made progress with compensatory schemas, there was reasonable motivation to tackle this. However, enormous amounts of anger towards the mother and a deep pervasive sadness had to be worked with. Evidence against the belief was articulated and positive logging revealed a number of day-to-day personal skills and achievements which had never been considered in relation to this pervasive assumption of inadequacy. Adequacy was tested in a wide variety of mastery situations and the negative construct of complete inadequacy was operationalized and compared to his day-to-day activity mastery schedule. Gradually, some shift in this underlying pervasive schema was achieved, with a reduction in the related anger and sadness.

This young man, at the time of discharge from hospital, had been through 26 CBT sessions of varying length over an 11-week admission. Total CPRS score fell from 110 to 17, compliance with medication and booster sessions remained good, but unfortunately further relapse did occur in relation to personal, familial and occupational stressors. The process of therapy and case study described show how classical Beckian cognitive therapy can be adapted to the treatment of schizoaffective presentations. Much further research is needed in this area.

REFERENCES

Asberg, M., Montgomery, S.A., Perris, C., Schalling, D. & Sedvall, G. (1978). A comprehensive psychopathological rating scale. *Acta Psychiatrica Scandinavia*, **271**(suppl), 5–69.
Beck, A.T. (1952). Successful out patient psychotherapy of a chronic schizophrenic with a delusion based on borrowed guilt. *Psychiatry*, **15**, 305–312.
Beck, A.T., Wiseman, A.N., Lester, D. & Trexler, L. (1974). The measurement of pessimism: the hopelessness scale. *Journal of Consulting and Clinical Psychology*, **42**, 861–865.
Beck, A.T., Ward, C.H., Mendleson, M., Mock, J.E. & Erboff, J.K. (1961). An inventory for measuring depression. *Archives of General Psychiatry*, **4**, 561–571.
Beck, A.T., Rush, A.J., Shaw, B.F. & Emery, G. (1979). *Cognitive Therapy of Depression: A Treatment Manual*. New York: Guilford.
Bentall, R.P., Kinderman, P. & Kaney, S. (1994). The self. Attributional processes and abnormal beliefs: towards a model of persecutory delusions. *Behaviour Research and Therapy*, **32**(3), 331–341.
Blackburn, I.M. & Twaddle, V. (1996). *Cognitive Therapy in Action. A Practitioner's Case Book*. London: Souvenir.
Burns, D. (1980). *Feeling Good: the New Mood Therapy*. New York: William Morrow.
Drury, V., Birchwood, M., Cochrane, R. & McMillan, M. (1996). Cognitive therapy and recovery from acute psychosis: a controlled trial. 1. Impact on psychotic symptoms. *British Journal of Psychiatry*, **169**, 593–601.
Fowler, D., Garety, P. & Kuipers, E. (1995). *Cognitive Behaviour Therapy for Psychosis*. Chichester: Wiley.
Furnham, A. & Bower, P. (1992). A comparison of academic and lay theories of schizophrenia. *British Journal of Psychiatry*, **161**, 201–210.
Grassian, G. (1983). Psychopathology of solitary confinement. *American Journal of Psychiatry*, **140**, 1450–1454.
Kingdon, D.G. & Turkington, D. (1991). The use of cognitive behavioural therapy and a normalising rational in schizophrenia: a preliminary report. *Journal of Nervous and Mental Disease*, **179**, 207–211.
Leff, J.P. (1968). Perceptual phenomena and personality in sensory deprivation. *British Journal of Psychiatry*, **114**, 1499–1508.
Meltzer, H.Y., Kuipher, D.J., Wyatt, R. et al. (1970). Sleep disturbance and serum CPK activity in acute psychosis. *Archives of General Psychiatry*, **22**, 398–405.
Milton, F., Patwa, V.K. & Hafner, R.J. (1978). Confrontation versus belief modification in persistently deluded patients. *British Journal of Medical Psychology*, **51**, 127–130.
Oswald, I. (1974). *Sleep*, 3rd edn. Harmondsworth: Penguin.
Perris, C. (1988). *Cognitive Therapy with Schizophrenic Patients*. New York: Cassell.

Romme, M. & Escher, S. (1996).   Empowering people who hear voices. *Cognitive Behavioural Interventions with Psychotic Disorders.* G. Haddock & B.D. Slade (eds), London. Routledge.

Sartorius, N. (1997).   Fighting schizophrenia and its stigma: a new World Psychiatric Association educational programme. *British Journal of Psychiatry*, **170**, 297–298.

Scott, J. (1995).   Psychotherapy for bipolar disorder. *British Journal of Psychiatry*, **167**, 581–588.

Siegel, R.K. (1984).   Hostage hallucinations. *Journal of Nervous and Mental Disease*, **172**, 264–271.

Tarrier, N., Beckett, R., Harwood, S., Baker, A., Yusopoff, L. & Ugateburu, I. (1993).   A trial of two cognitive-behavioural methods of treating drug resistant residual psychotic symptoms in schizophrenic patients. 1. Outcome. *British Journal of Psychiatry*, **162**, 524–532.

Turkington, D. & Kingdon, D.G. (1991).   Ordering thoughts in thought disorder. *British Journal of Psychiatry*, **159**, 160–161.

Turkington, D., Sensky, T., Siddle, R., O'Carroll, M., John, C., Dudley, R., McPhilips, M., Barnes, T., Scott, J. & Kingdon, D.G. (1996a).   A randomised controlled trail of cognitive behaviour therapy in the management of treatment resistant schizophrenia. Presented to the European Psychiatry Annual Meeting of the Royal College of Psychiatrists, London, 7–12 July 1997.

Turkington, D., John, C.H., Siddle, R., Ward, D. & Birmingham, L. (1996b).   Cognitive therapy in the treatment of drug resistant delusional disorder. *Clinical Psychology and Psychotherapy*, **3**(2), 118–128.

WHO (1992).   *The ICD-10 Classification of Mental and Behavioural Disorders.* Geneva: World Health Organization.

Chapter 15

Cognitive-behavioral Approaches to the Treatment of Personality Disorders

James Pretzer
*Department of Psychiatry, Case Western Reserve University
School of Medicine, and Cleveland Center for Cognitive
Therapy, Cleveland, OH, USA*

At one time, the term "personality disorder" rarely appeared in cognitive-behavioral discussions. Marshall & Barbaree (1984) wrote:

> No more than 15 years ago, a behavioral perspective of the personality disorders would have seemed far-fetched both to the proponents and opponents of behavioral analysis ... [T]he behavioral approach at that time saw learning as situationally specific so that it was anathema to suggest that personality disorders controlled behavior in various settings (pp. 406–407).

However, behaviorists could not ignore personality disorders for long, since individuals diagnosed as having "personality disorders" are commonly encountered in clinical practice, constituting up to 50% of all cases seen in some clinical centers (Turkat & Maisto, 1985).

The treatment of personality disorders presents a challenge whatever one's theoretical orientation. Therapy with clients diagnosed as having personality disorders is often described as being complex, time-consuming and frustrating (Fleming & Pretzer, 1990). Early reports suggested that personality disorders are a major source of a negative outcome in psychotherapy (Mays & Franks, 1985), that at least some personality disorders are not responsive to cognitive-behavioral interventions (Rush & Shaw, 1983) and that the presence of a personality disorder has important effects on the outcome of treatment for Axis-I disorders (e.g. Giles, Young & Young, 1985). Over the past 15 years, a variety of

Cognitive Psychotherapy of Psychotic and Personality Disorders: Handbook of Theory and Practice.
Edited by C. Perris and P.D. McGorry.
© 1998 John Wiley & Sons Ltd.

behavioral and cognitive-behavioral approaches to the treatment of personality disorders have been developed and even radical behaviorists are beginning to address this topic (e.g. Koerner, Kohlenberg & Parker, 1996).

Recent advances in theory, research, and practice show considerable promise for the development of effective, empirically validated approaches to the treatment of individuals with personality disorders. This chapter will provide an overview of the current status of cognitive-behavioral theory, research and practice regarding personality disorders.

THE EVOLUTION OF COGNITIVE-BEHAVIORAL PERSPECTIVES ON PERSONALITY DISORDERS

At first, the term "personality disorder" itself presented problems for cognitive-behaviorists, since it seemed to imply that the individual who is so diagnosed "has" a "personality" which is "disordered" and that his/her problems result from this disordered personality. However, this presented less of a problem when personality disorders were defined in DSM-III-R as "enduring patterns of perceiving, relating to, and thinking about the environment and oneself" which "are exhibited in a wide range of important social and personal contexts" and which "are inflexible and maladaptive and cause either significant functional impairment or subjective distress" (American Psychiatric Association, 1987, p. 335). With this definition of personality disorder, one need not presume that a "disordered personality" is central to the disorder. Cognitive-behavioral conceptualizations of personality disorders have evolved through a series of iterations in recent years. At this point, there have been important advances, but significant controversy remains regarding how to best conceptualize personality disorders.

Personality Disorders as a Collection of Symptoms

One early approach to understanding and treating clients with personality disorders was simply to apply established behavioral conceptualizations and interventions to one symptom after another. After all, the problematic behaviors and symptoms characteristic of clients diagnosed as having personality disorders, such as impulsive behavior, poor social skills and inappropriate expression of anger, are not unique to these individuals. Furthermore, behavioral treatments for such problems have received considerable empirical support. One example of this type of approach is that advocated by Stephens & Parks (1981). They discuss treating clients with personality disorders symptom by symptom, without presenting any broader conceptualization of personality disorders. This view suggests that an individual who presents with problems including depression, anxiety and lack of assertion, and who meets DSM-IV diagnostic criteria for dependent personality disorder, simply needs treatment for depression, treatment for anxiety, and assertion training. Since cognitive-behavioral interventions are effective with each of these problems, this perspective implies that treating this client should be fairly straightforward.

Stephens & Parks cite empirical evidence of the efficacy of behavioral interventions for the treatment of 10 categories of maladaptive behavior characteristic of individuals with personality disorders. However, they note that the vast majority of the studies cited were conducted either with subjects not diagnosed as having personality disorders or with mixed samples of subjects. Obviously, the finding that a particular symptom or problematic behavior can be treated effectively in a heterogeneous sample of subjects does not necessarily imply that the intervention in question will be equally effective when applied with clients diagnosed as having personality disorders.

In fact, outcome studies which have examined the effectiveness of "standard" cognitive-behavioral treatment protocols with subjects diagnosed as having personality disorders have produced results which challenge the view that one can simply approach personality disorders symptom by symptom. For example, in a study of the cognitive-behavioral treatment of social phobia, Turner (1987) found that patients without personality disorders improved markedly after a 15-week group treatment and maintained their gains at a 1-year follow-up. However, patients with personality disorder diagnoses in addition to their social phobia showed little or no improvement both post-treatment and at the 1-year follow-up. Turner concludes:

> In summary, the present pilot data suggest that what is an effective treatment for a social phobia is not necessarily an effective treatment for a social phobia mixed with a personality disorder . . . If the results of this study can be cross-validated under more exacting conditions, then behavior therapists' long-standing opposition to the concept of personality disturbance will require rethinking. This would be a major change in behavioral psychotherapy theory and practice (p. 142).

Personality Disorders as Resulting from "Ordinary" Conditioning and Social Learning

An important limitation of symptomatic approaches to the treatment of personality disorders is that individuals with personality disorders typically manifest a broad range of symptoms and problems. A client may seek treatment in the midst of a personal crisis and describe problems with depression, anxiety and significant interpersonal problems. Without a coherent conceptualization, it is difficult for the clinician to decide which symptoms to address first or to develop a comprehensive treatment plan.

A number of authors (Koerner, Kohlenberg & Parker, 1996; Marshall & Barbaree, 1984; Turner & Hersen, 1981) note that many of the problems experienced by individuals with personality disorders are interpersonal in nature. They conceptualize personality disorders as disorders of social behavior acquired in accord with operant conditioning and social learning principles and hold that complex, combined schedules of both direct and vicarious reinforcement and punishment establish behavior patterns which generalize across situations and which can be quite persistent. This perspective asserts that personality disorders are acquired and maintained in the same ways as other interpersonal behavior and that persons with personality disorders differ from other persons primarily in terms of their learning history. It suggests that in order to effectively treat personality disorders, it is necessary to modify naturally occurring contingencies so that adaptive social behavior will be established and maintained and that it may also be necessary to help the client to master the skills needed for adaptive social behavior.

In discussing personality disorders in terms of traditional principles of operant conditioning and social learning, Turner & Hersen (1981) cite a number of studies as providing empirical support for their views. These studies show that contingency management can produce persistent behavioral improvement with institutionalized offenders and juvenile delinquents, that social skills training can be used effectively with individuals labeled passive-aggressive, aggressive or explosive, and that a behavioral treatment can be effective with individuals diagnosed as having histrionic personality disorder. However, as was the case with the studies cited by Stephens & Parks (1981), these studies did not use subjects who were shown to meet DSM-III criteria for personality disorder diagnoses and therefore it is not possible to determine whether the interventions used in these studies provide effective treatment for individuals with personality disorders.

Studies using subjects who clearly satisfy criteria for personality disorder diagnoses have produced conflicting results. The idea that "standard" behavioral or cognitive-behavioral interventions can provide adequate treatment for clients with personality disorders is challenged by studies showing that even when cognitive-behavioral interventions focus specifically on client's interpersonal problems, the presence of personality disorders can have an impact on the effectiveness of treatment (e.g. Edelman & Chambless, 1995). Other studies which have found that the presence of personality disorders does not influence treatment outcome (e.g. Mersch, Jansen & Arntz, 1995) are more consistent with the idea that personality disorders can simply be conceptualized as disorders of interpersonal behavior.

Personality Disorders as Resulting from Dysfunctional Cognitions and Social Learning

Purely behavioral understandings of personality disorders have been difficult to develop, since so many behavioral concepts are situation-specific and personality disorders involve cross-situational consistencies in behavior. One can attempt to explain cross-situational consistencies in behavior in terms of generalization, the persistence of behavior acquired through intermittent reinforcement, or the effects of environmental reinforcement. However, it is difficult to explain the long-term persistence of maladaptive behavior across a range of disparate situations. Most behavioral perspectives would predict that behavior which is truly maladaptive would eventually be replaced by more adaptive behavior, or would be manifested primarily in situations where the maladaptive behavior is actually reinforced. Cognitive-behavioral approaches have an advantage in attempting to account for cross-situational consistencies in behavior since important concepts (variously termed schemas, dysfunctional beliefs or irrational beliefs) are hypothesized to be persistent across a range of situations.

Turkat and his colleagues (e.g. Turkat & Maisto, 1985) have presented an empirically based, cognitive-behavioral approach to the understanding and treatment of the various personality disorders. They develop detailed formulations of individual clients' problems on the basis of a thorough initial assessment, generate specific hypotheses and test these hypotheses individually using the most appropriate available measures. Then a treatment plan is developed on the basis of the case formulation and, as this treatment plan is implemented, successful intervention is seen as validating the therapist's formulation of the case, while unsuccessful interventions spur re-evaluation of the formulation. The result is a series of single-case experimental designs intended both to test hypotheses regarding personality disorders and to provide effective treatment for individual clients.

Turkat & Maisto provide empirical evidence that cognitive-behavioral interventions based on an individualized conceptualization can be effective in treating clients with personality disorders, with both behavioral observation and established measures used to document changes at both post-test and follow-up in some of the cases. A careful reading of several of the cases shows that interventions based on an individualized conceptualization were effective when previous symptomatic treatment had not been effective. In addition, the results reported suggest that Turkat & Maisto's approach can provide a comprehensive treatment for some clients with personality disorders, rather than simply treating specific symptoms. However, the results also make it clear that treatment was ineffective with many personality disorder clients. The most common difficulties mentioned by the investigators were: inability to develop a formulation-based treatment approach; the subjects being unwilling to engage in treatment; and the subjects terminating therapy prematurely.

Turkat and his colleagues present individualized conceptualizations and treatment strategies which were used with particular clients but they are cautious about generalizing these ideas to other individuals with the same diagnoses. This is an important limitation of Turkat's approach. Since all interventions are based on unique individualized conceptualizations rather than a conceptualization of personality disorders in general or a conceptualization of a specific personality disorder, the clinician must "start from scratch" with each client in developing a conceptualization and treatment plan. If it were possible to develop valid conceptualizations, either of personality disorders in general or of specific personality disorders, this might facilitate the development of treatment protocols which would be less time-consuming to apply than a completely individualized approach to treatment.

A number of authors have expanded established cognitive perspectives to apply directly to the personality disorders, such as Padesky's (1986, 1988) adaptation of Beck's cognitive theory (Beck, 1976; Beck et al. 1979). A comprehensive approach to conceptualizing personality disorders in a cognitive framework has been presented recently (Pretzer & Beck, 1996), and detailed cognitive-behavioral conceptualizations and treatment strategies for specific personality disorders have been based on Beck's cognitive therapy (Beck et al., 1990; Fleming, 1983, 1985, 1988; Freeman et al., 1990; Layden et al., 1993; Pretzer, 1983, 1985, 1988; Simon, 1983, 1985). These authors expand established cognitive-behavioral perspectives by emphasizing the interplay between cognition and interpersonal behavior. Personality disorders are seen as the result of "self-perpetuating cognitive/interpersonal cycles" and it is argued that a strategic approach to intervention based on a clear conceptualization of the client's problems is necessary for effective intervention.

Other cognitively-orientated authors have argued that in order to adequately account for the characteristics of individuals with personality disorders, cognitive therapy needs significant revision and have proposed their own modifications of cognitive therapy (Liotti, 1992; Lockwood, 1992; Lockwood & Young, 1992; Rothstein & Vallis, 1991; Safran & McMain, 1992; Young, 1990; Young & Lindemann, 1992). These approaches, variously termed "structural", "constructivist" or "post-rationalist" by their advocates, propose adding new concepts or concepts borrowed from other theoretical systems to existing cognitive-behavioral approaches. For example, Young (1990; Young & Lindermann, 1992) has advocated adding a "fourth level of cognition" which he terms "early maladaptive schemas" (EMS); Lockwood (1992) advocates integrating concepts from object-relations theory into cognitive therapy; and Liotti (1992) emphasizes the role of egocentrism in the personality disorders.

These various modifications of cognitive therapy's theory and therapeutic approach have not been greeted with universal enthusiasm. For example, Padesky (1986, 1988) has argued that there is no need to hypothesize that EMS are qualitatively different from other schemas in order to account for the persistence of dysfunctional cognitive and interpersonal patterns observed in clients with personality disorders. She points out that the tendency of schemas, beliefs and behavior patterns to persist even after they have become seriously dysfunctional can easily be understood in terms of the effect they have on the perception and processing of new experiences.

Cognitive conceptualizations of personality disorders are of relatively recent vintage, and research into the role of cognition in personality disorders in its initial stages. Early studies (Gasperini et al., 1989; O'Leary et al., 1991) have examined the role of cognitions in personality disorders in an exploratory way and have provided support for the general proposition that dysfunctional cognitions play a role in personality disorders. However, these studies did not test hypotheses derived from any of the current cognitive-behavioral conceptualizations of personality disorders. More recent research has examined the relationship between specific personality disorders and the beliefs and thoughts hypothesized by Beck et al. (1990) to play a role in personality disorders. These studies have produced encouraging results but only preliminary results are available so far (Beck et al., 1996; Huprich & Nelson-Gray, 1996). Most importantly, none of these studies have examined the interplay between cognition and interpersonal behavior, which plays a central role in cognitive conceptualizations of personality disorders (Pretzer & Beck, 1996).

It is interesting that many of the authors cited above who argue that cognitive therapy needs substantial revision in order to deal adequately with personality disorders make no reference to the extensive work which has been done on conceptualizing and treating personality disorders within the existing cognitive framework. Many of the points which the constructivists emphasize, such as the strongly self-perpetuating nature of personality disorders, the role of family relationships in the etiology of personality disorders, and the importance of the therapist–client relationship in treating these disorders, have been emphasized for some time by the authors who are working within the existing cognitive model. Since those who advocate revising cognitive therapy have yet to present detailed conceptualizations of specific personality disorders or to propose treatment strategies which are tailored to the characteristics of specific personality disorders, it is too early to determine whether or not their proposals contain important new contributions. However, early studies provide preliminary evidence that the EMS hypothesized by Young (1990) are related to borderline personality disorder in a clinical sample (Bauserman et al., 1996) as well as to anxiety, depression and personality disorder in a university sample (Schmidt et al., 1995).

Other theorists are developing cognitive perspectives on the personality disorders which either are based on other cognitive-behavioral approaches, which entail major revisions of established approaches, or which are independent of established approaches. For example, Murray (1988) asserts that personality disorders can be understood in terms of a "core rubric" incorporating self-perception, world-view and instructions for action; Proeve (1995) advocates a Multimodal treatment approach; Wessler (1993) presents an approach he terms "cognitive appraisal therapy"; and Safran & McMain (1992) propose a cognitive-interpersonal approach to treatment.[1]

---

[1] One theory that might appear to be cognitive-behavioral at first glance is Millon's influential "biosocial-learning theory". Millon's groundbreaking work has influenced much of the contemporary work on personality disorders, including the categorizations of DSM-III and DSM-IV. In his comprehensive work on personality disorders, Millon (1981) emphasizes the role of "vicious circles" in which the cognitive, affective and behavioral aspects of personality disorders perpetuate each other and result in the disorders being persistent and inflexible. His work is vividly descriptive and many of his concepts can be translated into cognitive-behavioral terminology. However, Millon considers himself to be psychoanalytically-orientated (Millon, 1987) and, while he frequently discusses the effects of social learning, his views of some of the personality disorders include psychodynamic concepts which are not easily reconciled with a behavioral approach.

A particularly promising approach is Linehan's "dialectical behavior therapy", which she and her colleagues have developed specifically as a treatment for borderline personality disorder (Linehan, 1987a, 1987b, 1993). This approach combines a cognitive-behavioral perspective with concepts derived from Dialectical Materialism and from Buddhism. The result is a somewhat complex theoretical framework and a contemporary cognitive-behavioral, problem-solving approach to treatment. It includes an emphasis on collaboration, skill training and contingency clarification and management, with a number of features designed to address issues which are believed to be important in treating individuals with borderline personality disorder. These include frequent, sympathetic acknowledgment of the individual's sense of desperation, a matter-of-fact attitude towards parasuicidal and other dysfunctional behavior, and an attempt to reframe suicide attempts and other dysfunctional behaviors as part of the individual's learned problem-solving repertoire. Therapists actively teach emotion-regulation skills, work to increase the individual's interpersonal effectiveness, encourage increased affect-tolerance, and attempt to maintain contingencies which support more adaptive behavior and extinguish dysfunctional behavior (for a detailed presentation of this treatment approach, see Linehan, 1993).

In a series of papers (Linehan et al., 1991; Linehan, Heard & Armstrong, 1993; Linehan, Tutek & Heard, 1992), Linehan and her colleagues have reported a controlled comparison of the effects of dialectical behavior therapy with the effects of "treatment-as-usual" in the community mental health system in a sample of chronically parasuicidal borderline subjects. Following 1 year of treatment, the patients in the dialectical behavior therapy condition were found to have a significantly lower drop-out rate and significantly less self-injurious behavior than subjects receiving "treatment as usual" (Linehan et al., 1991). The dialectical behavior therapy subjects also were found to have significantly better scores on measures of interpersonal and social adjustment, anger, work performance and anxious rumination (Linehan, Tutek & Heard, 1992). However, the two groups showed only modest overall improvement in depression or other symptomatology and did not differ significantly in these areas (Linehan et al., 1991). Throughout a 1-year follow-up, the dialectical behavior therapy subjects were found to have significantly higher global functioning. During the initial 6 months of the follow-up study they showed less parasuicidal behavior, less anger, and higher self-rated social adjustment. During the second 6 months, they had fewer days of hospitalization, and better interviewer-rated social adjustment.

These findings are quite encouraging given that the subjects not only met diagnostic criteria for borderline personality disorder but also were chronically parasuicidal, had histories of multiple psychiatric hospitalizations, and were unable to maintain employment due to their psychiatric symptoms. These subjects clearly were more disturbed than many individuals who meet diagnostic criteria for borderline personality disorder but are not parasuicidal, are rarely hospitalized, and are able to maintain productive employment.

THE EFFICACY OF COGNITIVE-BEHAVIOR THERAPY AS A TREATMENT FOR PERSONALITY DISORDERS

Cognitive-behavior therapy has been found to provide effective treatment for a wide range of Axis I disorders. However, most research into the effectiveness of cognitive therapy and related approaches as treatments for individuals with personality disorders is of recent vintage, and empirical evidence regarding the effectiveness of cognitive-behavioral approaches to treating individuals with personality disorders is fairly limited. Table 15.1 provides an overview of the available evidence regarding the effectiveness of cognitive-behavioral interventions in the treatment of individuals diagnosed as having personality disorders. It is immediately apparent from this table that there have been many uncontrolled clinical reports which assert that cognitive-behavioral therapy can provide effective treatment for personality disorders, many of which propose specific treatment approaches. However, there are a few controlled outcome studies to provide support for these assertions. This has led some to be concerned about the risks associated with a rapid expansion of theory and practice which has outstripped the empirical research (Dobson & Pusch, 1993).

Effects of Co-morbid Personality Disorders on the Treatment of Axis I Disorders

A number of studies have examined the effectiveness of cognitive-behavioral treatment for Axis I disorders with subjects who are also diagnosed as having

Table 15.1 The effectiveness of cognitive–behavioral treatment with personality disorders

	Uncontrolled clinical reports	Single-case design studies	Effects of personality disorders on treatment of Axis I disorders	Controlled outcome studies
Antisocial	+	−	+	a
Avoidant	+	±	±	+
Borderline	±	±	+	+
Dependent	+	+	+	
Histrionic	+		−	
Narcissistic	+	+		
Obsessive–compulsive	+	±	−	
Paranoid	+	+		
Passive–aggressive	+		+	
Schizoid	+			

+ = Cognitive-behavioral interventions found to be effective; − = cognitive-behavioral interventions found not to be effective; ± = mixed findings; a = cognitive-behavioral interventions were effective with antisocial personality disorder subjects only when the individual was depressed at pretest.

personality disorders and have found that the presence of an Axis II diagnosis greatly decreases the likelihood of treatment being effective. For example, Turner's (1987) study cited previously found that socially phobic patients without personality disorders improved markedly after a 15-week group treatment for social phobia and maintained their gains at a 1-year follow-up. However, patients with personality disorder diagnoses in addition to social phobia showed little or no improvement, both post-treatment and at the 1-year follow-up. Similarly, Mavissakalian & Hamman (1987) found that 75% of agoraphobic subjects rated as being low in personality disorder characteristics responded well to a time-limited behavioral and pharmacological treatment for agoraphobia, while only 25% of the subjects rated as being high in personality disorder characteristics responded to this treatment.

A number of other studies have also found that well-established cognitive-behavioral treatments are less effective with individuals who have personality disorders in addition to their Axis I diagnoses (e.g. Black et al., 1994; Giles, Young & Young, 1985; Tyrer et al., 1993). However, the evidence regarding the impact of co-morbid personality disorders on the treatment of Axis I disorders is more complex than this. Some studies have found that the presence of personality disorder diagnoses did not influence outcome (Dreesen et al., 1994; Mersch, Jansen & Arntz, 1995). Other studies have found that personality disorder diagnoses influenced outcome only under certain conditions (Fahy, Eisler & Russell, 1993; Felske et al., 1996; Hardy et al., 1995), that clients with personality disorders are likely to terminate treatment prematurely, but that those who persist in treatment can be treated effectively (Persons, Burns & Perloff, 1988; Sanderson, Beck & McGinn, 1994), and that some personality disorders predicted poor outcome while others did not (Neziroglu et al., 1996).

Some studies provide evidence that focused treatment for Axis I disorders can have beneficial effects on co-morbid Axis II disorders as well. For example, Mavissakalian & Hamman (1987) found that four of seven subjects who initially met diagnostic criteria for a single personality disorder diagnosis no longer met criteria for a personality disorder diagnosis following treatment. In contrast, subjects diagnosed as having more than one personality disorder did not show similar improvement. A major limitation of the studies which have examined the effectiveness of cognitive-behavioral treatment for Axis I disorders with individuals who also have personality disorders is that the treatment approaches used in these studies typically did not take the presence of personality disorders into account. This leaves unanswered the question of whether treatment protocols designed to account for the presence of personality disorders would prove to be more effective.

Studies of Cognitive-behavioral Treatment of Axis II Disorders

A number of studies have focused specifically on cognitive-behavioral treatment of individuals with personality disorders. Turkat & Maisto (1985) used a series of single-case design studies to investigate the effectiveness of individualized cognitive-behavioral treatment for personality disorders. Their study provides evidence that some clients with personality disorders could be treated effectively, but the investigators were unsuccessful in treating many of the subjects in their study. A recent study has attempted to test the efficacy of the intervention approach advocated by Beck et al. (1990) using a series of single case studies with repeated measures (Nelson-Gray et al., 1996). The nine subjects for this study were diagnosed with major depressive disorder and one or more co-occurring personality disorders. Each subject was assessed pre-therapy, post-therapy, and at a 3-month follow-up for level of depression and for the number of diagnostic criteria present for their primary personality disorder. After receiving 12 weeks of treatment, six of the eight subjects who completed the 3-month follow-up manifested a significant decrease in level of depression, two subjects manifested a significant decrease on both measures of personality disorder symptomatology, two failed to show improvement on either measure, and four showed mixed results. As the authors note, 12 weeks of treatment is a much shorter course of treatment than Beck et al. (1990) would expect to be required for most clients with personality disorders.

Much of the theory and research on the treatment of personality disorders has focused on outpatient treatment. However, inpatient treatment has received some attention as well. Springer et al. (1995) report that a short-term cognitive-behavioral therapy group produced significant improvement in a sample of hospitalized subjects with various personality disorders and that a secondary analysis of a subset of subjects with borderline personality disorder revealed similar findings. They also report that clients evaluated the group as being useful in their life outside the hospital.

At least three personality disorders have been the subject of controlled outcome studies. In a study of the treatment of opiate addicts in a methadone maintenance program, Woody et al. (1985) found that subjects who met DSM-III diagnostic criteria for both major depression and antisocial personality disorder responded well to both cognitive therapy and a supportive-expressive psychotherapy systematized by Luborsky et al. (1985). The subjects showed statistically significant improvement on 11 of 22 outcome variables used, including psychiatric symptoms, drug use, employment and illegal activity. Subjects who met criteria for antisocial personality disorder but not major depression showed little response to treatment, improving on only three of 22 variables. This pattern of results was maintained at a 7-month follow-up. While subjects not diagnosed as having antisocial personality disorder responded to treatment better than the sociopaths did, sociopaths who were initially depressed did only slightly worse than the non-sociopaths, while the non-depressed sociopaths did much worse.

Studies of the treatment of avoidant personality disorder have shown that short-term social skills training, and social skills training combined with cognitive interventions, have been effective in increasing the frequency of social interaction and decreasing social anxiety (Stravynski, Marks & Yule, 1982). These authors interpreted this finding as demonstrating the "lack of value" of cognitive interventions. However, it should be noted that the two treatments were equally effective, that all treatments were provided by a single therapist (who was also principal investigator), and that only one of many possible cognitive interventions (disputation of irrational beliefs) was used. In a subsequent study, Greenberg & Stravynski (1985) report that the avoidant client's fear of ridicule appears to contribute to premature termination in many cases, and they suggest that interventions which modify relevant aspects of the clients' cognitions might add substantially to the effectiveness of intervention.

The studies, cited previously, by Linchan and her colleagues (Linehan et al., 1991, 1993; Linehan, Tutek & Heard, 1992) on the treatment of borderline personality disorder have been widely recognized as providing evidence that cognitive-behavioral interventions can be effective with clients who have severe personality disorders. The finding that 1 year of cognitive-behavioral treatment could produce significant improvement in subjects who not only met diagnostic criteria for borderline personality disorder but who also were chronically parasuicidal, had histories of multiple psychiatric hospitalizations and were unable to maintain employment due to their psychiatric symptoms, is quite encouraging.

The Effect of Personality Disorders on "Real Life" Clinical Practice

In clinical practice, most therapists do not apply a standardized treatment protocol with a homogeneous sample of individuals who share a common diagnosis. Instead, clinicians face a variety of clients and take an individualized approach to treatment. A recent study of the effectiveness of cognitive therapy under such "real world" conditions provides important support for the clinical use of cognitive therapy with clients who are diagnosed as having personality disorders. Persons, Burns & Perloff (1988) conducted an interesting empirical study of clients receiving cognitive therapy for depression in private practice settings. The subjects were 70 consecutive individuals seeking treatment for Dr Burns or Dr Persons in their own practices. Both therapists are established cognitive therapists who have taught and published extensively, and in this study both therapists conducted cognitive therapy as they normally do. This meant that treatment was open-ended, was individualized rather than standardized, and medication and inpatient treatment were used as needed.

The primary focus of the study was on identifying predictors of dropout and treatment outcome in cognitive therapy for depression. However, it is interesting for our purposes to note that 54.3% of the subjects met DSM-III criteria for a personality disorder diagnosis and that the investigators considered the presence of a personality disorder diagnosis as a potential predictor of both premature termination of therapy and therapy outcome. The investigators found that while patients with personality disorders were significantly more likely to drop out of therapy prematurely than patients without personality disorders, those patients with personality disorder diagnoses who persisted in therapy through the completion of treatment showed substantial improvement and did not differ significantly in degree of improvement from patients without personality disorders. Similar findings were reported by Sanderson, Beck & McGinn (1994) in a study of cognitive therapy for generalized anxiety disorder. Subjects diagnosed with a co-morbid personality disorder were more likely to drop out of treatment, but treatment was effective in reducing both anxiety and depression for those who completed a minimum course of treatment.

It has recently been argued that Beck's cognitive therapy (Beck et al., 1979) does not provide an adequately effective treatment for individuals with personality disorders (McGinn, Young & Sanderson, 1995). It is interesting to note that, in criticizing cognitive therapy, McGinn, Young & Sanderson choose to criticize a treatment approach (Beck et al., 1979), which was developed as a treatment for depression. The critics do not even mention the treatment protocols for cognitive therapy with personality disorders which have been developed (e.g., Beck et al., 1990; Freeman et al., 1990; Layden et al., 1993).

Beck's cognitive therapy for depression was not developed as a treatment for individuals with personality disorders, and Beck and his colleagues have not claimed that it provides adequate treatment for personality disorders (or for anxiety disorders, or for substance abuse, etc.). Instead, Beck and his colleagues have developed specific treatment protocols for a number of different disorders, including cognitive protocols for the treatment of personality disorders (Beck et al., 1990; Freeman et al., 1990; Layden et al., 1993). The empirical research cited above which tests these recently-developed treatment protocols is limited, but the results thus far are encouraging.

COGNITIVE-BEHAVIORAL APPROACHES TO SPECIFIC PERSONALITY DISORDERS

Many authors suggest that it is important to develop conceptualizations and treatment approaches tailored to specific personality disorders, rather than trying to develop a "generic" approach which does not distinguish between the various personality disorders. A discussion of each of the personality disorders is beyond the scope of this chapter. The following references should provide a good starting point for readers who are interested in exploring current conceptualizations of specific personality disorders:

- *Antisocial personality disorder.*   Beck et al. (1990, Chapter 8); Brantley & Sutker (1984); Freeman et al. (1990, Chapter 10); Gorenstein (1991); Marshall & Barbaree (1984); Sutker, Archer & Kilpatrick (1981).
- *Avoidant personality disorder.*   Alden (1992); Beck et al. (1990; Chapter 12); Freeman et al. (1990, Chapter 12); Turkat & Maisto (1985).
- *Borderline personality disorder.*   Beck et al. (1990, Chapter 9); Davis & Schrodt (1992); Farrell & Shaw (1994); Freeman et al. (1990, Chapter 8); Linehan (1987a, 1987b, 1993); Turner (1987, 1992).

- *Dependent personality disorder.* Beck et al. (1990, Chapter 13); Freeman et al. (1990, Chapter 12); Overholser (1987); Turkat & Carlson (1984); Turkat & Maisto (1985).
- *Histrionic personality disorder.* Andrews & Moore (1991); Beck et al. (1990, Chapter 10); Freeman et al. (1990, Chapter 9); Turkat & Maisto (1985).
- *Narcissistic personality disorder.* Beck et al. (1990, Chapter 11); Bux (1992); Carey, Flasher, Maisto & Turkat (1984); Freeman et al. (1990, Chapter 10); Turkat & Maisto (1985).
- *Obsessive-compulsive personality disorder.* Beck et al. (1990, Chapter 14); Digiuseppe et al. (1995); Freeman et al. (1990, Chapter 11); Turkat (1986); Turkat & Maisto (1985).
- *Paranoid personality disorder.* Beck et al. (1990, Chapter 6); Freeman et al. (1990, Chapter 7); Turkat (1985, 1986, 1987, 1990); Turkat & Banks (1987); Turkat & Maisto (1985).
- *Passive-aggressive personality disorder.* Beck et al. (1990, chapter 15); Burns & Epstein (1983); Freeman et al. (1990, Chapter 13); Perry & Flannery (1982).
- *Schizoid personality disorder.* Beck et al. (1990, Chapter 7); Freeman et al. (1990, Chapter 7).
- *Schizotypal personality disorder.* Beck et al. (1990, Chapter 7); Freeman et al. (1990, Chapter 7); Greenberg (1992).

IMPLICATIONS FOR CLINICAL PRACTICE

As was noted previously, the past 15 years have seen advances in theory and practice outstrip the empirical research (Dobson & Pusch, 1993). While this provides grounds for legitimate concern, it would hardly be feasible to suspend theoretical and clinical work until more empirical research is available. The practicing clinician faces a difficult situation in that one can hardly refuse to provide treatment for a class of disorders which may be present in as many as 50% of clients seen in many outpatient settings. However, the available treatment approaches are less fully developed and less well-validated than is the case with many of the Axis I disorders. Fortunately, there is an increasing body of evidence that cognitive-behavioral treatment can be quite effective for clients with personality disorders.

A series of general guidelines for cognitive therapy with clients who have personality disorders have been presented, most recently in Pretzer & Beck (1996). These guidelines appear to apply equally well to other cognitive-behavioral approaches to intervention:

1. *Interventions are most effective when based on an individualized conceptualization of the client's problems.* In working with clients who have personality disorders, the therapist is often faced with choosing among many possible targets for intervention and a variety of possible intervention

techniques. A clear treatment plan which is based on a thorough evaluation, on clinical observation, and on the results of clinical interventions, minimizes the risk of the therapist being confused by the complexity of the client's problems.

2. *It is important for therapist and client to work collaboratively towards clearly identified, shared goals.* Clear, consistent goals for therapy are necessary to avoid skipping from problem to problem without making any lasting progress. However, it is important for these goals to be mutually agreed upon in order to minimize the non-compliance and power struggles which often impede treatment of clients with personality disorders. The time and effort spent developing mutually acceptable goals can be a good investment.

3. *It is important to focus more than the usual amount of attention on the therapist–client relationship.* A good therapeutic relationship is as necessary for effective intervention in cognitive therapy as in any other approach to therapy. Behavioral and cognitive-behavioral therapists are generally accustomed to being able to establish a fairly straightforward therapeutic relationship at the outset of therapy and then to proceed without paying much attention to the interpersonal aspects of therapy. However, this is not usually the case when working with clients who have personality disorders. The client's perception of the therapist may be biased at times, and the dysfunctional interpersonal behaviors which clients manifest in relationships outside of therapy are likely to manifested in the therapist–client relationship as well. While the interpersonal difficulties which are manifested in the therapist–client relationship can disrupt therapy if they are not addressed effectively, they also provide the therapist with the opportunity to do *in vivo* observation and intervention (Freeman et al., 1990; Linehan, 1987c; Mays, 1985; Padesky, 1986).

4. *Consider beginning with interventions which do not require extensive self-disclosure.* Clients with personality disorders often are quite uncomfortable with self-disclosure due to a lack of trust in the therapist, discomfort with intimacy, fear of rejection, etc. While it is sometimes necessary to begin treatment with interventions which require discussion of deeply personal thoughts and feelings, it can be useful to begin treatment by working on a problem which does not require extensive self-disclosure. This allows time for the client to gradually become more comfortable with therapy and for the therapist to gradually address the client's discomfort with self-disclosure (Freeman et al., 1990; Chapter 8).

5. *Interventions which increase the client's sense of self-efficacy[2] often reduce the intensity of the client's symptomatology and facilitate other interventions.* The intensity of the emotional and behavioral responses manifested by

---

[2]The term "self-efficacy" refers to expectations regarding one's ability to deal effectively with a specific situation (Bandura, 1977). An individual's level of self-efficacy regarding a particular situation is believed to have an important effect both on the individual's anxiety level and his/her coping behavior in that situation.

individuals with personality disorders is often exacerbated by the individual's doubting his/her ability to cope effectively with particular problem
situations. If it is possible to increase the individual's confidence that he/she
will be able to handle problem situations if they arise, this often lowers the
client's level of anxiety, moderates his/her symptomatology, enables him/
her to react more deliberately, and makes it easier to implement other
interventions. The individual's sense of self-efficacy can be increased
through interventions which correct any exaggerations of the demands of
the situation or minimization of the individual's capabilities, through helping the individual to improve his/her coping skills, or through a combination
of the two (Freeman et al., 1990, Chapter 7; Pretzer, Beck & Newman,
1990).

6. *Do not rely primarily on verbal interventions.* The more severe a client's
problems are, the more important it is to use behavioral interventions to
accomplish cognitive as well as behavioral change (Freeman et al., 1990,
Chapter 3). A gradual hierarchy of "behavioral experiments" not only
provides an opportunity for desensitization to occur and for the client to
master new skills but also can be quite effective in challenging unrealistic
beliefs and expectations.

7. *Try to identify and address the client's fears before implementing
changes.* Clients with personality disorders often have strong,
unexpressed fears about the changes they seek or are asked to make in the
course of therapy. Attempts to induce the client to implement changes
without first addressing these fears are often unsuccessful (Mays, 1985). If
the therapist makes a practice of discussing the client's expectations and
concerns before each change is attempted, this is likely to reduce the client's
level of anxiety regarding therapy and to improve compliance.

8. *Help the client deal adaptively with aversive emotions.* Clients with personality disorders often experience very intense aversive emotional reactions in
specific situations. These intense reactions can be a significant problem in
their own right but, in addition, the individual's attempts to avoid experiencing these emotions, his/her attempts to escape the emotions, and his/her
cognitive and behavioral response to the emotions often play an important
role in the client's problems in living. Often, the individual's unwillingness
to tolerate aversive affect blocks him/her from handling the emotions
adaptively and perpetuates fears about the consequences of experiencing
the emotions. Individuals with personality disorders may need to acquire
some of the cognitive and/or behavioral skills needed to handle the emotions effectively (Farrell & Shaw, 1994; Linehan, 1993).

9. *Anticipate problems with compliance.* Many factors contribute to a high
rate of non-compliance among clients with personality disorders. In addition to the complexities in the therapist–client relationship and the fears
regarding change which were discussed above, the dysfunctional behaviors
of individuals with personality disorders are strongly ingrained and often
are reinforced by aspects of the client's environment. However, rather than

simply being an impediment to progress, episodes of non-compliance can provide an opportunity for effective intervention. When non-compliance is anticipated, one can improve compliance by identifying and addressing the issues beforehand. When non-compliance arises unexpectedly, it provides an opportunity to identify issues which are impeding progress in therapy so that they can be addressed.

10. *Do not presume that the client exists in a reasonable environment.* Some behaviors, such as assertion, are so generally adaptive that it is easy to assume that they are always a good idea. However, clients with personality disorders are often the product of seriously atypical families and live in atypical environments. When implementing changes, it is important to assess the likely responses of significant others in the client's environment, rather than presuming that they will respond in a reasonable way.

11. *Attend to your own emotional reactions during the course of therapy.* Interactions with clients with personality disorders can elicit emotional reactions from the therapist, ranging from empathic feelings of depression to strong anger, discouragement, fear or sexual attraction. It is important for the therapist to be aware of these responses so that he/she does not unduly influence or disrupt the therapist's work with the client and so that the therapist can be used as a source of potentially useful data. Therapists may benefit from using cognitive techniques themselves (see Layden et al., 1993, Chapter 6) and/or seeking consultation with an objective colleague.

12. *Be realistic regarding the length of therapy, goals for therapy, and standards for therapist self-evaluation.* Many therapists using behavioral and cognitive-behavioral approaches to therapy are accustomed to accomplishing substantial results relatively quickly. One can easily become frustrated and angry with the "resistant" client when therapy proceeds slowly or become self-critical and discouraged when therapy goes badly. Behavioral and cognitive-behavioral interventions can accomplish substantial, apparently lasting, changes in some clients with personality disorders, but more modest results are achieved in other cases and little is accomplished in others. When therapy proceeds slowly, it is important neither to give up prematurely nor to persevere with an unsuccessful treatment approach. When treatment is unsuccessful, it is important to remember that therapist competence is not the only factor influencing the outcome of therapy.

CONCLUSIONS

While the number of published studies is quite limited and some studies suffer from methodological problems, several general conclusions are suggested by the available research. First, many reports indicate that standard cognitive-behavioral treatments for Axis I disorders may not prove effective for individuals with co-morbid Axis II disorders, even if the treatments are quite effective with subjects who do not have Axis II disorders. Second, the available findings suggest that for some individuals with an Axis I disorder and a concurrent Axis II disorder, behavioral or cognitive-behavioral treatment for the Axis I disorder not only can be effective as a treatment for the Axis I disorder but can result in overall improvement in the Axis II disorder as well. Third, clinical reports assert that cognitive-behavioral therapy can provide an effective treatment approach for most of the personality disorders. We do not yet have adequate empirical data to support this enthusiasm but a growing body of evidence shows that cognitive-behavioral treatment can be effective for some individuals with personality disorders. Finally, we have little evidence to provide grounds for comparing cognitive-behavioral therapy with alternative approaches to treating personality disorders.

A decade ago, Turkat & Levin (1984) concluded that "in most of the personality disorder literature, there are so few data that conclusions cannot even be attempted" (p. 519). In a similar vein, Kellner (1986) concluded that there were too few adequately controlled studies of behavioral treatment approaches with subjects clearly diagnosed as having personality disorders to provide an empirical basis for recommending specific interventions for such clients. In the few years since these two reviews were conducted, the situation has improved slowly but steadily. In particular, the findings reported by Persons, Burns & Perloff (1988) are quite encouraging. They suggest that while the presence of a personality disorder increases the likelihood of cognitive-behavioral therapy proving ineffective (if the client discontinues therapy prematurely), when it is possible to induce the client to persist in treatment, cognitive-behavioral therapy can prove quite useful.

It should be noted that the subjects in Persons et al.'s study received treatment in the period of time before the recent advances in the treatment of personality disorders were widely published. As treatment approaches specifically designed to address the needs of individuals with personality disorders (Beck et al., 1990; Linehan, 1993) are tested, we can hope to learn much more about the strengths and weaknesses of our current approaches to understanding and treating clients with personality disorders.

REFERENCES

Alden, L.E. (1992). Cognitive-interpersonal treatment of avoidant personality disorder. In L. VandeCreek, S. Knapp & T.L. Jackson (eds), *Innovations in Clinical Practice: a Sourcebook*, Vol. II. Sarasota, FL: Professional Resource Press.

American Psychiatric Association (1987). *Diagnostic and Statistical Manual of Mental Disorders*, 3rd edn, revised. Washington, DC: American Psychiatric Association.

Andrews, J.D.W. & Moore, S. (1991). Social cognition in the histrionic/overconventional personality. In P.A. Magaro (ed.), *Cognitive Bases of Mental Disorders*. Newbury Park, CA: Sage.

Bandura, A. (1977). *Social Learning Theory*. Englewood Cliffs, NJ: Prentice-Hall.

Bauserman, S.A.K., Hayes, A., Harris, M. & Schaeffer, A. (1996). Early maladaptive schemas and borderline personality disorder. Paper presented at the 30th Annual

Conference of the Association for the Advancement of Behavior Therapy, New York, November.

Beck, A.T. (1976). *Cognitive Therapy and the Emotional Disorders*. New York: International Universities Press.

Beck, A.T., Butler, A.C., Brown, G.K. & Dahlsgaard, K.K. (1996). The Personality Belief Questionnaire: Evidence of validity for five axis II disorders. Paper presented at the 30th Annual Conference of the Association for the Advancement of Behavior Therapy, New York, November.

Beck, A.T., Freeman, A., Pretzer, J., Davis, D.D., Fleming, B., Ottaviani, R., Beck, J., Simon, K.M., Padesky, C., Meyer, J. & Trexler, L. (1990). *Cognitive Therapy of the Personality Disorders*. New York: Guilford.

Beck, A.T., Rush, A.J., Shaw, B.F. & Emery, G. (1979). *Cognitive Therapy of Depression*. New York: Guilford.

Black, D.W., Wesner, R.B., Gabel, J., Bowers, W. & Monahan, P. (1994). Predictors of short-term treatment response in 66 patients with panic disorder. *Journal of Affective Disorders*, **30**, 233–241.

Brantley, P.J. & Sutker, P.B. (1984). Antisocial personality disorder. In H.E. Adams & P.B. Sutker (eds), *Comprehensive Handbook of Psychopathology*. New York: Plenum.

Burns, D.D. & Epstein, N. (1983). Passive-aggressiveness: a cognitive-behavioral approach. In R.D. Parsons & R.J. Wicks (eds), *Passive-aggressiveness: Theory and Practice*. New York: Bruner/Mazel.

Bux, D.A. (1992). Narcissistic personality disorder. In A. Freeman & F. Dattilio (eds), *Comprehensive Casebook of Cognitive Therapy*. New York: Plenum.

Carey, M.P., Flasher, L.V., Maisto, S.A. & Turkat, I.D. (1984). The *a priori* approach to psychological assessment. *Professional Psychology: Research and practice*, **15**, 515–527.

Davis, M.H. & Schrodt, G.R. Jr (1992). Inpatient treatment. In A. Freeman & F. Dattilio (eds), *Comprehensive Casebook of Cognitive Therapy*. New York: Plenum.

Digiuseppe, R., Robin, M., Szeszko, P.R. & Primavera, L.H. (1995). Cluster analysis of narcissistic personality disorders on the MCMI-II. *Journal of Personality Disorders*, **9**, 304–317.

Dobson, K.S. & Pusch, D. (1993). Towards a definition of the conceptual and empirical boundaries of cognitive therapy. *Australian Psychologist*, **28**, 137–144.

Dreesen, L., Arntz, A., Luttels, C. & Sallaerts, S. (1994). Personality disorders do not influence the results of cognitive behavior therapies for anxiety disorders. *Comprehensive Psychiatry*, **35**, 265–274.

Edelman, R.E. & Chambless, D.L. (1995). Adherence during sessions and homework in cognitive-behavioral group treatment of social phobia. *Behavior Research and Therapy*, **33**, 573–577.

Fahy, T.A., Eisler, I. & Russell, G.F. (1993). Personality disorder and treatment response in bulimia nervosa. *British Journal of Psychiatry*, **162**, 765–770.

Farrell, J.M. & Shaw, I.A. (1994). Emotion awareness training: a prerequisite to effective cognitive-behavioral treatment of borderline personality disorder. *Cognitive and Behavioral Practice*, **1**, 71–91.

Felske, U., Perry, K.J., Chambless, D.L., Renneberg, B. & Goldstein, A.J. (1996). Avoidant personality disorder as a predictor for treatment outcome among generalized social phobics. *Journal of Personality Disorders*, **10**, 174–184.

Fleming, B. (1983). Cognitive therapy with histrionic patients: resolving a conflict in styles. Paper presented at the meeting of the American Psychological Association, Anaheim, CA, August.

Fleming, B. (1985). Dependent personality disorder: managing the transition from dependence to autonomy. Paper presented at the meeting of the Association for the Advancement of Behavior Therapy, Houston, TX, November.

Fleming, B. (1988). CT with histrionic personality disorder: resolving a conflict of styles. *International Cognitive Therapy Newsletter*, **4**(4), 8–9, 12.

Fleming, B. & Pretzer, J. (1990). Cognitive-behavioral approaches to personality disorders. In M. Hersen, R.M. Eisler & P.M. Miller (eds), *Progress in Behavior Modification*, Vol. 25, 119–151. Newbury Park, CA: Sage.

Freeman, A., Pretzer, J.L., Fleming, B. & Simon, K.M. (1990). *Clinical Applications of Cognitive Therapy*. New York: Plenum.

Gasperini, M., Provenza, M., Ronchi, P., Scherillo, P., Bellodi, L. & Smeraldi, E. (1989). Cognitive processes and personality disorders in affective patients. *Journal of Personality Disorders*, **3**, 63–71.

Giles, T.R., Young, R.R. & Young, D.E. (1985). Behavioral treatment of severe bulimia. *Behavior Therapy*, **16**, 393–405.

Gorenstein, E.E. (1991). A cognitive perspective on antisocial personality. In P.A. Magaro (ed.), *Cognitive Bases of Mental Disorders*. Newbury Park, CA: Sage.

Greenberg, D. & Stravynski, A. (1985). Patients who complain of social dysfunction. I. Clinical and demographic features. *Canadian Journal of Psychiatry*, **30**, 206–211.

Greenberg, R. (1992). Schizotypal personality disorder. In A. Freeman & F. Dattilio (eds), *Comprehensive Casebook of Cognitive Therapy*. New York: Plenum.

Hardy, G.E., Barkham, M., Shapiro, D.A., Stiles, W.B., Rees, A. & Reynolds, S. (1995). Impact of Cluster C personality disorders on outcomes of contrasting brief therapies for depression. *Journal of Consulting and Clinical Psychology*, **63**, 997–1004.

Huprich, S.K. & Nelson-Gray, R.O. (1996). Distinctive dysfunctional thoughts associated with different personality disorders. Paper presented at the 30th Annual Conference of the Association for the Advancement of Behavior Therapy, New York, November.

Kellner, R. (1986). Personality disorders. *Psychotherapy and Psychosomatics*, **46**, 58–66.

Koerner, K., Kohlenberg, R.J. & Parker, C.R. (1996). Diagnosis of personality disorder: a radical behavioral alternative. *Journal of Clinical and Consulting Psychology*, **64**, 1169–1176.

Layden, M.A., Newman, C.F., Freeman, A. & Morse, S.B. (1993). *Cognitive Therapy of Borderline Personality Disorder*. Boston, MA: Allyn and Bacon.

Linehan, M.M. (1987a). Dialectical behavior therapy in groups: treating borderline personality disorders and suicidal behavior. In C.M. Brody (ed.), *Women in Groups*. New York: Springer.

Linehan, M.M. (1987b). Dialectical behavioral therapy: a cognitive behavioral approach to parasuicide. *Journal of Personality Disorders*, **1**, 328–333.

Linehan, M.M. (1987c). Commentaries on "the inner experience of the borderline self-mutilator": a cognitive-behavioral approach. *Journal of Personality Disorders*, **1**, 328–333.

Linehan, M.M. (1993). *Cognitive-behavioral Treatment of Borderline Personality Disorder*. New York: Guilford.

Linehan, M.M., Armstrong, H.E., Suarez, A., Allmon, D.J. & Heard, H.L. (1991). Cognitive-behavioral treatment of chronically suicidal borderline patients. *Archives of General Psychiatry*, **48**, 1060–1064.

Linehan, M.M., Heard, H.L. & Armstrong, H.E. (1993). Naturalistic follow-up of a behavioral treatment for chronically parasuicidal borderline patients. *Archives of General Psychiatry*, **50**, 971–974.

Linehan, M.M., Tutek, D.A. & Heard, H.L. (1992). Interpersonal and social treatment outcomes in borderline personality disorder. Paper presented at the 26th Annual Conference of the Association for the Advancement of Behavior Therapy, Boston, MA, November.

Liotti, G. (1992). Egocentrism and the cognitive psychotherapy of personality disorders. *Journal of Cognitive Psychotherapy*, **6**, 43–58.

Lockwood, G. (1992). Psychoanalysis and the cognitive therapy of personality disorders. *Journal of Cognitive Psychotherapy*, **6**, 25–42.

Lockwood, G. & Young, J. (1992).   Introduction: cognitive therapy for personality disorders. *Journal of Cognitive Psychotherapy*, **6**, 5–10.

Luborsky, L., McLellan, A.T., Woody, G.E., O'Brien, C.P. & Auerbach, A. (1985). Therapist success and its determinants. *Archives of General Psychiatry*, **42**, 602–611.

Marshall, W.L. & Barbaree, H.E. (1984).   Disorders of personality, impulse, and adjustment. In S.M. Turner & M. Hersen (eds), *Adult Psychopathology and Diagnosis*. New York: Wiley.

Mavissakalian, M. & Hamman, M.S. (1987).   DSM-III personality disorder in agoraphobia. II. Changes with treatment. *Comprehensive Psychiatry*, **28**, 356–361.

Mays, D.T. (1985).   Behavior therapy with borderline personality disorders: one clinician's perspective. In D.T. Mays & C.M. Franks (eds), *Negative Outcome in Psychotherapy and What to Do About It*. New York: Springer.

Mays, D.T. & Franks, C.M. (1985).   Negative outcome: what to do about it. In D.T. Mays & C.M. Franks (eds), *Negative Outcome in Psychotherapy and What to Do About It*. New York: Springer.

McGinn, L.K., Young, J.Y. & Sanderson, W.C. (1995).   When and how to do long-term therapy . . . without feeling guilty. *Cognitive and Behavioral Practice*, **2**, 187–212.

Mersch, P.P.A., Jansen, M.A. & Arntz, A. (1995).   Social phobia and personality disorder: severity of complaint and treatment effectiveness. *Journal of Personality Disorders*, **9**, 143–159.

Millon, T. (1981).   *Disorders of Personality: DSM-III: Axis II*. New York: Wiley.

Millon, T. (1987).   On the genesis and prevalence of the borderline personality disorder: a social learning thesis. *Journal of Personality Disorders*, **1**, 354–372.

Murray, E.J. (1988).   Personality disorders: a cognitive view. *Journal of Personality Disorders*, **2**, 37–43.

Nelson-Gray, R.O., Johnson, D. Foyle, L.W., Daniel, S.S. & Harmon, R. (1996).   The effectiveness of cognitive therapy tailored to depressives with personality disorders. *Journal of Personality Disorders*, **10**, 132–152.

Neziroglu, F., McKay, D., Todaro, J. & Yaryura-Tobias, J.A. (1996).   Effect of cognitive behavior therapy on persons with body dysmorphic disorder and comorbid Axis II diagnosis. *Behavior Therapy*, **27**, 67–77.

O'Leary, K.M., Cowdry, R.W., Gardner, D.L., Leibenluft, E., Lucas, P.B. & deJong-Meyer, R. (1991).   Dysfunctional attitudes in borderline personality disorder. *Journal of Personality Disorders*, **5**, 233–242.

Overholser, J.C. (1987).   Facilitating autonomy in passive-dependent persons: an integrative model. *Journal of Contemporary Psychotherapy*, **17**, 250–269.

Padesky, C.A. (1986).   Personality disorders: cognitive therapy into the 90s. Paper presented at the Second International Conference on Cognitive Psychotherapy, Umeå, Sweden, September 18–20.

Padesky, C.A. (1988).   Schema-focused CT: comments and questions. *International Cognitive Therapy Newsletter*, **4**, 5,7.

Perry, J.C. & Flannery, R.B. (1982).   Passive-aggressive personality disorder: treatment implications of a clinical typology. *Journal of Nervous and Mental Disease*, **170**, 164–173.

Persons, J.B., Burns, B.D. & Perloff, J.M. (1988).   Predictors of drop-out and outcome in cognitive therapy for depression in a private practice setting. *Cognitive Therapy and Research*, **12**, 557–575.

Pretzer, J.L. (1983).   Borderline personality disorder: too complex for cognitive-behavioral approaches? Paper presented at the meeting of the American Psychological Association, Anaheim, CA, August. (ERIC Document Reproduction Service No. ED 243 007.)

Pretzer, J.L. (1985).   Paranoid personality disorder: a cognitive view. Paper presented at the meeting of the Association for the Advancement of Behavior Therapy, Houston, TX, November.

Pretzer, J.L. (1988). Paranoid personality disorder: a cognitive view. *International Cognitive Therapy Newsletter*, **4**, 4, 10–12.

Pretzer, J.L. & Beck, A.T. (1996). A cognitive theory of personality disorders. In J.F. Clarkin & M.F. Lenzenweger (eds), *Major Theories of Personality Disorder*. New York: Guilford.

Pretzer, J.L., Beck, A.T. & Newman, C.F. (1990). Stress and stress management: a cognitive view. *Journal of Cognitive Psychotherapy: An International Quarterly*, **3**, 163–179.

Proeve, M. (1995). A multimodal therapy approach to treatment of borderline personality disorder: a case study. *Psychological Reports*, **76**, 587–592.

Rothstein, M.M. & Vallis, T.M. (1991). The application of cognitive therapy to patients with personality disorders. In T.M. Vallis, J.L. Howes & P.C. Miller (eds), *The Challenge of Cognitive Therapy: Applications to Non-traditional Populations*. New York: Plenum.

Rush, A.J. & Shaw, B.F. (1983). Failures in treating depression by cognitive therapy. In E.B. Foa & P.G.M. Emmelkamp (eds), *Failures in Behavior Therapy*. New York: Wiley.

Safran, J.D. & McMain, S. (1992). A cognitive-interpersonal approach to the treatment of personality disorders. *Journal of Cognitive Psychotherapy: An International Quarterly*, **6**, 59–68.

Sanderson, W.C., Beck, A.T. & McGinn, L.K. (1994). Cognitive therapy for generalized anxiety disorder: significance of co-morbid personality disorders. *Journal of Cognitive Psychotherapy*, **8**, 13–18.

Schmidt, N.B., Joiner, T.E. Jr, Young, J.E. & Telch, M.J. (1995). The Schema Questionnaire: investigation of psychometric properties of a measure of maladaptive schemas. *Cognitive Research and Therapy*, **19**, 295–322.

Simon, K.M. (1983). Cognitive therapy with compulsive patients: Replacing rigidity with structure. Paper presented at the meeting of the American Psychological Association, Anaheim, CA, August.

Simon, K.M. (1985). Cognitive therapy of the passive-aggressive personality. Paper presented at the meeting of the Association for the Advancement of Behavior therapy, Houston, TX, November.

Springer, T., Lohr, N.E., Buchtel, H.A. & Silk, K.R. (1995). A preliminary report of short-term cognitive-behavioral group therapy for inpatients with personality disorders. *Journal of Psychotherapy Practice and Research*, **5**, 57–71.

Stephens, J.H. & Parks, S.L. (1981). Behavior therapy of personality disorders. In J.R. Lion (ed.), *Personality Disorders: Diagnosis and Management*, 2nd edn. Baltimore, MD: Williams & Wilkins.

Stravynski, A., Marks, I., & Yule, W. (1982). Social skills problems in neurotic outpatients: social skills training with and without cognitive modification. *Archives of General Psychiatry*, **39**, 1378–1385.

Sutker, P.B., Archer, R.A. & Kilpatrick, D.G. (1981). Sociopathy and antisocial behavior: theory and treatment. In S.M. Turner, K.S. Calhoun & H.E. Adams (eds), *Handbook of Clinical Behavior Therapy*. New York: Wiley.

Turkat, I.D. (1985). The case of Mr P. In I.D. Turkat (ed.), *Behavioral Case Formulation*. New York: Plenum.

Turkat, I.D. (1986). The behavioral interview. In A.R. Ciminero, K.S. Calhoun & H.E. Adams (eds). *Handbook of Behavioral Assessment*, 2nd edn New York: Wiley.

Turkat, I.D. (1987). Invited case transcript: the initial clinical hypothesis. *Journal of Behavioral Therapy & Experimental Psychiatry*, **18**, 349–356.

Turkat, I.D. (1990). *The Personality Disorders: a Psychological Approach to Clinical Management*. New York: Pergamon.

Turkat, I.D. & Banks, D.S. (1987). Paranoid personality and its disorder. *Journal of Psychopathology and Behavioral Assessment*, **9**, 295–304.

Turkat, I.D. & Carlson, C.R. (1984).   Data-based versus symptomatic formulation of treatment: the case of a dependent personality. *Journal of Behavior Therapy and Experimental Psychiatry*, **15**, 153–160.

Turkat, I.D. & Levin, R.A. (1984).   Formulation of personality disorders. In H.E. Adams & P.B. Sutker (eds), *Comprehensive Handbook of Psychopathology*. New York: Plenum.

Turkat, I.D. & Maisto, S.A. (1985).   Personality disorders: application of the experimental method to the formulation and modification of personality disorders. In D.H. Barlow (ed.), *Clinical Handbook of Psychological Disorders: a Step-by-step Treatment Manual*. New York: Guilford.

Turner, R.M. (1987).   The effects of personality disorder diagnosis on the outcome of social anxiety symptom reduction. *Journal of Personality Disorders*, **1**, 136–143.

Turner, R.M. (1992).   Borderline personality disorder. In A. Freeman & F. Dattilio (eds), *Comprehensive Casebook of Cognitive Therapy*. New York: Plenum.

Turner, S.M. & Hersen, M. (1981).   Disorders of social behavior: a behavioral approach to personality disorders. In S.M. Turner, K.S. Calhoun, & H.E. Adams (eds), *Handbook of Clinical Behavior Therapy*. New York: Wiley.

Tyrer, P., Seivewright, N., Ferguson, B., Murphy, S. et al. (1993).   The Nottingham Study of Neurotic Disorder: effect of personality status on response to drug treatment, cognitive therapy and self-help over two years. *British Journal of Psychiatry*, **162**, 219–226.

Wessler, R.L. (1993).   Cognitive appraisal therapy and disorders of personality. In K.T. Kuehlwein & H. Rosen (eds), *Cognitive Therapies in Action: Evolving Innovative Practice*. San Francisco, CA: Jossey-Bass.

Woody, G.E., McLellan, A.T., Luborsky, L & O'Brien, C.P. (1985).   Sociopathy and psychotherapy outcome. *Archives of General Psychiatry*, **42**, 1081–1086.

Young, J. (1990).   *Cognitive Therapy for Personality Disorders: a Schema-focused Approach*. Sarasota, FL: Professional Resource Exchange.

Young, J.E. & Lindemann, M.D. (1992).   An integrative schema-focused model for personality disorders. *Journal of Cognitive Psychotherapy*, **6**, 11–24.

Chapter 16

The Assessment of Personality Disorder: Selected Issues and Directions

Henry Jackson
Department of Psychology, University of Melbourne and Early Psychosis Research Centre, Parkville, Victoria, Australia

A personality disorder is defined as: " . . . an enduring pattern of inner experience and behavior that deviates markedly from the expectations of the individual's culture, is pervasive and inflexible, has an onset in adolescence or early adulthood, is stable over time, and leads to distress or impairment" (American Psychiatric Association, 1994, p. 629).

INTRODUCTION

During the 1960s and 1970s the study of *personality* was disparaged in academic circles as being largely unscientific (Millon, 1984). Anti-personological sentiment was consonant with the prevailing *Zeitgeist*, in which it was asserted that virtually all behaviour was under the control of environmental contingencies (Millon, 1984), with the publication of Walter Mischel's (1968) damning volume on *Personality & Assessment* being particularly influential in strangling interest in personality for quite a time. Examination of Mischel's (1968) work points to two major themes: that behaviour was *neither consistent across situations nor across time*, leading in turn to the conclusion that there was no coherency or cogency to the notion of personality. Over time it became clear that Mischel's argument was specious. Personality theorists did not disagree that the underpinning behavioural manifestations of personality could vary over time and situation, but argued that if a sufficiently large number of "behaviours" were measured, then a coherency and temporal consistency would emerge, thereby pointing to the

Cognitive Psychotherapy of Psychotic and Personality Disorders: Handbook of Theory and Practice.
Edited by C. Perris and P.D. McGorry.
© 1998 John Wiley & Sons Ltd.

existence of a latent "trait" that, taken in concert with other co-existent latent traits, constituted the "entity" we label *personality* (see Millon, 1984). In short, one behavioural indicator by itself is insufficient to make a judgement about someone's personality with any conviction, but one's confidence in concluding that an individual has a certain personality *trait* increases with the amassment of similar data in a variety of situations and across time.

However, the situation as regards *personality disorders* was little better. Throughout the same period, and although psychiatrists and nurses paid lip-service to the concept of personality disorder, their clinical *modus operandi* was to reserve the term for those patients who either did not have a florid Axis I disorder or who elicited extreme countertransference reactions, e.g. those patients with borderline and antisocial personality disorders. In other words, personality disorder was a diagnosis of exclusion. This state of affairs improved somewhat with the publication and eventual dissemination of DSM-III (APA, 1980) and its progeny (APA, 1987, 1994), which explicitly defined personality disorders and highlighted the need for a clinician to consider personality disorders when conducting a diagnostic evaluation of a patient.

DSM-III (American Psychiatric Association, 1980) described the characteristics of personality disorders as being inflexible, long-standing, pervasive and most importantly maladaptive, causing the person functional impairment or subjective distress. Secondly, the multi-axial system of DSM-III was a major breakthrough because it explicitly permitted the *simultaneous* diagnosis of Axis I conditions, such as depression and personality disorders. These features have remained in the two subsequent DSM editions (American Psychiatric Association, 1987, 1994).

This emphasis on the importance of personality disorders presupposed that we were able to *assess* the presence of a "personality disorder" as defined at the masthead of this chapter. Clearly, the accurate measurement of personality disorder is important. Thus, the focus of this chapter is on documenting major research themes as regards the assessment of personality disorder and describing selected issues and directions. Although there are available numerous instruments that measure a particular personality trait/disorder, such as perfectionism (Blatt, 1995; Hewitt et al., 1991) or schizotypy (Chapman & Chapman, 1985), these will not be the focus of this chapter. Instead, the emphasis is on broad-span measures which attempt to index the entire spectrum of personality disorders.

The chapter begins by briefly covering *some* of the background leading to the development of semi-structured instruments for personality disorder assessment, describes two such instruments, and then covers some of the themes of the research pertaining to the *measurement* of personality disorders generated by DSM-III, DSM-III-R, and DSM-IV (American Psychiatric Association, 1980, 1987, 1994) and ICD-10 (World Health Organization, 1992). Problems with that research will be briefly discussed. A dimensional alternative to the categorical DSM-III/R/IV and ICD-10 approach is proposed. Two dimensional instruments are then described (Costa & McCrae, 1992a, b; Cloninger, Svrakic & Przybeck, 1993). Then, a further alternative theoretical approach is described—that of

Theodore Millon (Millon, 1990; Millon with Davis, 1996; Millon & Davis, 1997), together with the proposal that a cognitive approach to assessing personality disorders (Beck, Freeman & Associates, 1990; Young, 1994) could dovetail with one layer of Millon's model. Hints for the busy clinician in assessing clients for a possible personality disorder are provided and conclusions drawn as to the state of the field and possible future directions.

THE ROLE OF DSM-III IN STIMULATING THE DEVELOPMENT OF INSTRUMENTATION FOR THE MEASUREMENT OF PERSONALITY DISORDERS

As previously noted, personality disorder was neglected in the mental health domain as a diagnostic "entity" until the publication of DSM-III (American Psychiatric Association, 1980). This gave a great fillip to the study and measurement of personality disorder—putting it back on the mental health agenda and raising awareness of the importance of both the concept and the measurement thereof, to epidemiologist, researcher and clinician alike. Yet, it is worth remembering that the empirical literature existent up until 1980 was rather limited. This meant that for DSM-III, the personality disorders and their constituent criteria sets were not decided empirically, or from a unified theoretical position. Instead, they were based on the decisions of a Committee of the American Psychiatric Association. This Committee consisted of notable scholars in the field such as Allan Frances, Donald Klein, John Lion, Theodore Millon and Robert Spitzer (American Psychiatric Association, 1980). The end result was that DSM-III (American Psychiatric Association, 1980) described 11 personality disorders, namely: paranoid, schizoid, schizotypal, antisocial, borderline, histrionic, narcissistic, avoidant, dependent, compulsive and passive-aggressive personality disorders. These are arranged in three clustering arrangements (labelled Clusters A, B and C). With relatively minor modifications, both the personality disorders and clusters have remained with us through the two subsequent DSM revisions (American Psychiatric Association, 1987, 1994) with the exception of passive-aggressive personality disorder. The latter has been removed from the text of DSM-IV and placed in "Appendix B: Criteria Sets and Axes for Future Study" of DSM-IV (American Psychiatric Association, 1994) for reasons touched on by Millon (Millon with Davis, 1996). It should be emphasized that, as with the Axis I disorders and criteria sets, changes to the personality disorder section of the DSM-IV were much better informed by the more substantial empirical literature existent at the time of revision (American Psychiatric Association, 1994, pp. xviii–xxi). ICD-10 (World Health Organization, 1992) includes eight personality disorder categories, specifically: paranoid, schizoid, dissocial, emotionally unstable (with two subtypes—impulsive and borderline), histrionic, anxious (avoidant), dependent and anankastic. Unlike DSM-IV, ICD-10 recognizes no *a priori* clustering arrangement.

DSM-III and its subsequent revisions provided a set of criteria for each personality disorder, but strictly speaking these criteria were not operationalized, and doubtless this allowed raters' idiosyncratic biases to creep into the assessment procedure. Without standardized instrumentation, moderate kappas of 0.56–0.65 were reported for personality disorders as a *class* (i.e. the presence/absence of personality disorder of any kind) in the DSM-III Field Trials (American Psychiatric Association, 1980, pp. 470–471). Also, in a seminal study, reliability using DSM-III (American Psychiatric Association, 1980) criteria was generally low and variable, with the reported kappas for *specific* DSM-III personality disorders ranging from 0.05 to 0.49 (Mellsop et al., 1982). Concern over poor inter-rater reliability gave impetus to the development of semi-structured instrumentation aimed at improving the assessment of personality disorders.

Development of Measures to Assess Personality Disorders

In the last two decades, the instrumentation available for interested clinicians and researchers has burgeoned but is widely variable in conceptual bases and rating format. The tools range on one end from those instruments which require clinician judgement (i.e. are externally rated by an assessor) and are based completely on DSM-III/R-IV (American Psychiatric Association, 1980, 1987, 1994) criteria, e.g. Personality Disorder Examination (PDE: Loranger et al., 1987), the Structured Interview for DSM-III Personality (SIDP: Pfohl, Stangl & Zimmerman, 1983; see updates by Pfohl et al., 1989; Pfohl, Blum & Zimmerman, 1997), and the Structured Clinical Interview for DSM-III-R (SCID: Spitzer et al., 1992; and SCID-II: First et al., 1995a,b). Then there are those instruments which are based on the same nosologies but adopt a self-report format such as the Personality Diagnostic Questionnaire (Revised) (PDQ-R: Hyler et al., 1983, 1988, 1992), and also those instruments which are grounded in alternative conceptual models, such as Millon's Multiaxial Clinical Inventory, of which there have been three successive editions (Millon, 1977, 1987; Millon, Millon & Davis, 1994). Instruments developed in the UK are the Standardized Assessment of Personality (SAP: Mann et al., 1981) and the Personality Assessment Schedule (PAS: Tyrer et al., 1979). New important alternative instruments based on broader concepts are the Dimensional Assessment of Personality Pathology—Basic Questionnaire, of Livesley & Jackson (in press) and Clark's Schedule for Non-adaptive and Adaptive Personality (SNAP: Clark, 1993).

The development of semi-structured instruments such as the PDE and SIDP to assess DSM-III, DSM-III-R or DSM-IV personality disorders (American Psychiatric Association, 1980, 1987, 1994) has led to improved inter-rater reliability for personality disorder *categories* and *dimensions* (Zimmerman, 1994). To date, apart from inter-rater reliability data obtained from the International version of the PDE for ICD-10 criteria (see Loranger et al., 1994), inter-rater reliability data for ICD-10 personality disorders are lacking.

Research Work Undertaken with Personality Disorder Instruments

The last 17 years or so has witnessed a rapidly accumulating data base using DSM-III/-R/IV-based instrumentation (American Psychiatric Association, 1980, 1987, 1990) or instrumentation developed from other theoretical orientations which attempt to measure DSM-III/R/IV disorders (MCMI and MCMI-II: Millon, 1977, 1987) but next to nothing has been reported for ICD-10-based instruments (for an exception, see Loranger et al., 1994). Apart from examining inter-rater reliability data, there have been a number of other major themes throughout the personality disorder literature. One seam of work has been concerned with determining the proportions of patients in various settings with various Axis I problems or co-morbidities who have certain types and numbers of personality disorders, e.g. between schizophrenia and schizotypal personality disorder, and between affective disorders and borderline personality disorder (Black et al., 1993; Jackson et al., 1991b; Morgenstern et al., 1997).

A second theme in this literature has centred on discussion around whether sex differences represent genuine gender differences in personality disorder prevalences or whether these are due, in part, to diagnostic stereotyping or bias (Bornstein, 1996, 1997; Widiger & Spitzer, 1991). With some qualifications, DSM-IV (American Psychiatric Association, 1994) stipulates that females are more likely to be diagnosed with borderline, histrionic and dependent personality disorders, whereas males are more likely to be diagnosed with paranoid, schizoid, antisocial, narcissistic and obsessive-compulsive personality disorders (see also American Psychiatric Association, 1980, 1987). Corbitt & Widiger (1995) provide an excellent overview of the issues concerning gender differences and also review extant empirical studies. Two examples of relevant empirical work are Alnaes & Torgersen (1988) and Jackson et al. (1991b).

A third major theme has focused on the concordance between self-report of personality disorders and semi-structured instrument assessments of the same. Concerns have been raised about the ability of self-report questionnaires, including the MCMI-I and its successors, to accurately and completely cover the personality disorders as measured by assessor-rated structured instruments such as the PDE and the SIDP (Jackson et al., 1991a; Zimmerman, 1994).

State effects have been the focus of a fourth line of investigation. Zimmerman (1994) concluded that in contrast to semi-structured instruments, self-report inventories, e.g. MCMI and PDQ, are far too susceptible to state effects. Loranger et al. (1991) found that a semi-structured instrument, namely the PDE, was not influenced by state factors such as depression and anxiety. However, this finding is not consistent (e.g. Peselow et al., 1994).

A fifth line of research endeavour has been concerned with internal validity (i.e. regarding the extent to which the criteria for a disorder cohere) and the diagnostic efficiency of criteria, i.e. the degree to which individual personality disorder criteria (i.e. features) carry comparatively stronger or weaker weightings for indicating the presence or absence of a given personality disorder, when compared to other features in the same criteria set for that personality disorder. Studies conducted within this area of research commonly examine the inter-rater reliability data for specific personality disorder features; the internal consistency of those features; and the base rates of both those features and categorically-defined personality disorders in a given population. Those same studies have then examined the *sensitivity, specificity, positive predictive power* (PPP) and *negative predictive power* (NPP) of a personality feature (for examples of this work see Jackson & Pica, 1993; Pfohl et al., 1986).

A sixth line of investigatory activity has focused on predictive validity, i.e. treatment response (Donat, 1997; Perry, 1993). In general, the presence of a personality disorder indicates poorer end-state functioning and poorer response to treatment than in patients without personality disorders (Baer et al., 1992; Zimmerman et al., 1986).

A seventh line of research endeavour has revolved round various attempts to reduce DSM-III personality disorders to their quintessential components through multidimensional scaling, cluster analysis, factor analysis or principal components analysis (Bell & Jackson, 1992; Ekselius et al., 1994; Widiger et al., 1987).

Some Conclusions Concerning DSM-III/-R/IV Research into Measuring Personality Disorders

A number of conclusions can be reached about assessment issues within this particular area. A primary concern is that the base-rates of personality disorders appear to vary according to the instrument used, it being generally true that self-report instruments tend to yield a higher number of personality disorders than semi-structured or structured instruments (Zimmerman, 1994). Even when two semi-structured instruments are used there is low concordance, as can be seen in the study of Pilkonis et al. (1995), where both the PDE and SIDP were used. In essence, there is no gold standard for the measurement of personality disorders as formalized by the DSM-III/-R/IV system, although the SIDP and PDE measures *appear* to afford the strongest approximation to DSM-III/-R/IV (American Psychiatric Association, 1980, 1987, 1994) when one considers inter-rater reliability data and content validity. In reviewing the literature, interested clinicians would be advised to keep in mind which measure was used to assess personality disorders in specific studies. The lack of an "industry" gold standard represents a real Achilles heel for personality disorder research. Two other related factors could affect the base-rates of diagnosed personality disorders. The first pertains to the nature of the treatment facility (i.e. state hospital, fee-for-service clinic, general hospital, free community clinic, private practice), whilst the second is the use of convenience samples compared to consecutive patient referrals.

Another problem is the general lack of concern for the phase of illness. This, in combination with the lack of formal assessment of state effects (e.g. depression, anxiety, psychosis, or residua of the same) in a number of studies, might mean that patients are overdiagnosed with certain types of personality disorders, or are assigned higher personality disorder dimensional scores than is truly the case. This problem is amplified if the person is young and developed an Axis I illness early in his/her life, rendering difficult attempts to distinguish between state and trait (Hulbert, Jackson & McGorry, 1996).

SOME ALTERNATIVE METHODS OF MEASUREMENT

Although semi-structured interviews such as the SIDP and PDE can yield dimensional scores for each of the personality disorders, at root they are based on a particular categorical conceptualization of personality disorders. Nevertheless, there is increasing recognition that the Neo-Kraepelinian conceptualization of mental disorders that undergirds the DSM-III/-R/IV nosology may not be the optimal guide to diagnosing, measuring or understanding personality disorders (e.g. Widiger, 1993; Widiger & Costa, 1994; Widiger & Frances, 1994; Widiger et al., 1994).

Ultimately, of course:

> "Whether or not the entities, properties, and processes of a particular domain (such as psychopathology, or vocational interest patterns) are purely dimensional, or are instead a mix of dimensional and taxonic relations, *is an empirical question*, not to be settled by a methodological dogma about "how science works" (Meehl, 1992, p. 119).

Yet in the early stages of development Meehl argues, we can't define the *core* concepts, which remain *open* concepts (Meehl, 1990, 1992). Therefore, I believe it behoves us to contemplate the worth of concepts and measures other than those based on the DSM-III/-R/IV.

One initial step would be to turn to the so-called "normal" personality domain because, for the best part of this century, the study of personality has constituted a major strand within academic psychology. Yet it is both surprising and alarming that there has been little interchange between researchers in the respective fields of personality and personality disorder until the last few years. With exceptions it would be true to state that the *personality* field has been dominated by a dimensional or trait approach, with an emphasis on factor-analytic techniques, typically of an exploratory kind. Conversely, in the *personality disorder* field there has been an explicit acceptance of a categorical model which, until the last two decades, has not been subjected to psychometric analysis.

Five-factor Model (FFM)

Over a period of time, and notwithstanding dissidents (Block, 1995; Cloninger, Svrakic & Przybeck, 1993), it has been asserted that five robust basic factors of personality are consistently extracted from factor-analytic procedures, namely: neuroticism; extraversion; openness to experience; agreeableness; and conscientiousness (Costa & McCrae, 1990, 1992a, b; Widiger & Trull, 1997).

Widiger, Costa and their colleagues (e.g. Widiger, 1993; Widiger & Costa, 1994; Widiger & Frances, 1994; Widiger et al., 1994) have asserted that dimensional models like the FFM, but also including other dimensional models (e.g. Clark, 1993; Cloninger, Svrakic & Przybeck, 1993; Jackson et al., 1996) permit retention and flexibility of information. This in turn, enables one to determine the patient's position on a stipulated dimension or trait relative to their own scores on the other dimensions, and relative to other people's scores on the various dimensions, the latter being gauged through norms supplied in manuals. The NEO-PI-R (Costa & McCrae, 1992b) is one measure of the FFM.

The Neuroticism, Extraversion, Openness Personality Inventory—Revised (NEO-PI-R) Measure

The NEO in its revised form (NEO-PI-R: Costa & McCrae, 1992b) contains 240 items, each of which is scored on five-point scales. There are five factors and six constituent subscales or facets for each of the five factors. These are outlined in Table 16.1. High alpha correlations have been reported. Equally impressive stability across a 6-year time period has been reported, the correlational values for the latter ranging from 0.55 to 0.87 (see McCrae & Costa, 1990, Table 10, p. 88). Results have been replicated across self, peer, spouse and observer ratings, across age groups and across certain languages and cultures (McCrae & Costa, 1990, 1997).

Widiger et al. (1994) and Widiger & Costa (1994) have shown that DSM-III-R personality disorders map onto these five personality dimensions and their constituent subscales or facets, overcoming the problems of personality disorder overlap and co-morbidity, and providing clinicians with fuller descriptions of a patient than would otherwise be available. Individuals with diagnosable personality disorders are found to differ in predictable ways on the five factors (Widiger & Costa, 1994; Widiger et al., 1994) and this has formed a major line of research endeavour (see e.g. Costa & McCrae, 1990; Duijsens & Diekstra, 1996). To some extent, implicit in this line of research is the notion that personality disorders comprise more *extreme* "personality" traits occurring in consistent combinations and configurations with one another (Widiger & Frances, 1994).

Clinically, tools like the NEO-PI-R may be more useful for the practising therapist or clinician because although they allow us to see how extreme that person is on so-called "negative" traits, they are not tied to the deficit model of pathology implicit in psychiatric nosologies. Rather, they allow us to grasp a broader picture of the person by obtaining scores continuous with those of others in the community (although naturally, that person may score higher or lower on those same scales and in differing trait or facet combinations than others in the community).

Table 16.1   The five factors and constituent facets of the NEO-PI-R (Costa & McCrae, 1992b)

The NEO-PI-R contains six facets for each of the five factors. They are as follows:

1. *Neuroticism facets* include: (i) Anxiety—this comprises nervousness and free-floating anxiety; (ii) Angry–hostile—anger, frustration and bitterness; (iii) Depression—guilt, sadness, hopelessness; (iv) Self-consciousness, shame, embarrassment; (v) Impulsiveness—low frustration to tolerance; (vi) Vulnerability— unable to cope with stress, becoming dependent, hopeless or panicked under stress.
2. *Extraversion facets* include: (i) Affectionate—friendly, likes people; (ii) Gregariousness—prefers other people's company; (iii) Assertiveness—dominant, forceful and socially ascendant activity; (iv) Energy—rapid tempo; (v) Excitement seeking—craves excitement and stimulation, bright colours and noise; (vi) Positive emotions—joy, happiness, love and cheerfulness.
3. *Openness to experience facets* include: (i) Fantasy—has a vivid imagination and an active fantasy life; (ii) Aesthetics—a deep appreciation for art and beauty; (iii) Feelings—experiences deeper and more differentiated emotional states; (iv) Actions—willingness to try different activities, go to new places, or eat unusual foods; (v) Ideas—Intellectual curiosity, a willingness to consider new, perhaps unconventional, ideas; (vi) Values—an openness to values means the readiness to re-examine social, political and religious values.
4. *Agreeableness facets* include: (i) Trust—believes that others are honest and well-intentioned; (ii) Straightforwardness—frank, sincere and ingenuous; (iii) Altruism—an active concern for others' welfare, generous, considerate; (iv) Compliance—defers to others, inhibits aggression, forgives and forgets; (v) Modesty and self-effacing; (vi) Tendermindedness—sympathy and concern for others.
5. *Conscientiousness facets* include: (i) Competence—capable, sensible, prudent and effective; (ii) Order—neat, tidy and well-organized; (iii) Dutifulness—"governed by conscience" duty; (iv) Achievement striving—high aspiration levels and works hard to achieve their goals; (v) Self-discipline—an ability to motivate themselves, no matter what; (vi) Deliberation—a tendency to think carefully before acting.

To take an example, a clinician is about to embark on therapy with a client. This client presents with an obsessive-compulsive disorder but also has an obsessive-compulsive personality disorder, according to the PDE. The therapist gives the client the NEO-PI-R to complete. That NEO-PI-R may inform us that the client is indeed high in conscientiousness, but it may tell us in more detail the extent and extremeness of his conscientiousness by allowing us to compare his scores on conscientiousness against the published norms, and provide us with more information at the constituent facet level. For example, is the client extreme across all six facets of conscientiousness or only on one or two of those facets? Yet the chief advantage of the NEO-PI-R is that it may inform us additionally about potentially redeeming or mitigating personality features, such as a high degree of openness to ideas or values or warmth and trust, with which the therapist can work. Openness to ideas might suggest that the client is able and willing to consider other ways of thinking about his problems. Higher degrees of warmth and trust might indicate that the client is able to form a therapeutic relationship with the therapist—a critical component for effective therapeutic outcome (Binder & Strupp, 1997; Luborsky et al., 1997). Although empirical data supporting the predictive validity of the NEO-PI-R when used in a configurational manner has yet to be undertaken, it does have a certain degree of face validity, resonating with the approach clinicians might take in treatment planning and in rendering prognostic judgements in clinical practice. Examples of this approach at the case level are provided by Bruehl (1994) and Corbitt (1994).

The Temperament and Character Inventory (TCI)

The TCI (Cloninger, Svrakic & Przybeck, 1993; Cloninger et al., 1994) can be seen as an alternative dimensional measure to the NEO-PI-R and is a development of the theoretical and empirical work of Cloninger (1987; Cloninger, Svrakic & Przybeck, 1993). The TCI (Cloninger et al., 1994) comes in a number of versions, but the major and most current one contains 240 items which are scored true or false. The items constitute a total of 25 facet scales, which in turn load on one of seven dimensional measures, four of them being temperament dimensions (novelty seeking, harm avoidance, reward dependence and persistence) and three labelled character dimensions (self-directedness, cooperativeness and self-transcendence). The seven dimensions and the 25 constituent facets are shown in Table 16.2.

Temperament dimensions characterize heritable features manifested early in life and involve biases in perceptual memory and habit formation. The character

Table 16.2 The seven scales and constituent facets of the Temperament and Character Inventory (TCI: Cloninger et al., 1994)

1. *Novelty-seeking facets* include: (i) Exploratory seeking vs. stoic rigidity; (ii) Impulsiveness vs. reflection; (iii) Extravagance vs. reserve; (iv) Disorderliness vs. regimentation.
2. *Harm avoidance facets* include: (i) Anticipatory worry vs. uninhibited optimism; (ii) Fear of uncertainty vs. confidence; (iii) Shyness with strangers vs. confidence; (iv) Fatiguability and asthenia vs. vigour.
3. *Reward dependence facets* include: (i) Sentimentality vs. insensitivity; (ii) Attachment vs. detachment; (iii) Dependence vs. independence.
4. *Persistence* (This is a one-facet scale).
5. *Self-directedness facets* include: (i) Responsibility vs. blaming; (ii) Purposefulness vs. lack of goal direction; (iii) Resourcefulness; (iv) Self-acceptance vs. self-striving; (v) Congruent second nature.
6. *Co-operativeness facets* include: (i) Social acceptance vs. social intolerance; (ii) Empathy vs. social disinterest; (iii) Helpfulness vs. unhelpfulness; (iv) Compassion vs. revengefulness; (v) Integrated conscience.
7. *Self-transcendence facets* include: (i) Self-forgetfulness vs. self-conscious experience; (ii) Transpersonal identification vs. self-isolation; (iii) Spiritual acceptance vs. rational materialism.

dimensions represent those features of personality that mature in adulthood and influence social and personal effectiveness, such as insight and self-concept. The instrument is theoretically driven, the items being rationally generated and subsequently subjected to empirical testing (Cloninger, Svrakic & Przybeck, 1993; Cloninger et al., 1994). The manual (Cloninger et al., 1994) provides a theoretical exposition, background development to the instrument, norms, the TCI's factor structure, reliability and validity data, discussions of the use of the instrument for clinical subjects and normal subjects, together with a bibliography of research using the TCI or variants thereof. Like the NEO-PI-R, the TCI can be mapped onto traditional personality disorder categories, e.g. anxiety disorder patients consistently obtain high harm avoidance scores, bulimic patients score high on novelty seeking and harm avoidance. Again, like the NEO-PI-R, configural analyses can be derived from the TCI and used by clinicians in treatment planning. Case examples illustrating this approach can be found in a manual (Cloninger et al., 1994). Considered together, they show that the higher order "facets" of the "Big Seven" dimensions may prove very useful to the working clinician, in similar ways as described previously with the NEO-PI-R.

Both the NEO-PI-R and the TCI bridge the realms of normal and abnormal personality with their dimensional approaches but we should not neglect other more complex theoretical approaches which may add "conceptual depth and breadth" to the understanding and measurement of personality disorders. One such approach is that proposed by Millon (1990; Millon & Davis, 1997).

THINKING AHEAD—THEODORE MILLON

Theodore Millon (1986, 1990; Millon with Davis, 1996, Millon & Davis, 1997) is the most eminent personality disorder theorist of our times. His integrative and developmentally-grounded theory (Millon, 1986, 1990; Millon with Davis, 1996) represents the most comprehensive and theoretically compelling alternative to the atheoretical DSM and ICD systems of conceptualizing and organizing personality disorders. One of the most powerful aspects of his work is his emphasis on the multi-layered nature of personality disorders. He makes the incisive point that not one personality disorder instrument measures *all* domains of personality (and this holds true for *normal* personality as well). In his view, such instruments should not be limited to behaviours, cognitions or interpersonal conduct, but instead encompass the complete range of all relevant or potentially relevant personological characteristics.

Millon, whilst not providing such a highly desirable measurement tool, has detailed in his most recent work a conceptual template that might well give impetus to the realization of this goal (Millon with Davis, 1996; Millon & Davis, 1997). Personality features are portrayed within eight "prototypal diagnostic domains" (Millon with Davis, 1996; Millon & Davis, 1997) embedded within a four-by-two matrix. Four levels, as set out in Figure 16.1, correspond to the "four historic approaches that characterize the study of psychopathology" (Millon with

Davis, 1996, p. 138), these being behavioural, phenomenological, intrapsychic, and biophysical. Two "systems" are labelled the "structural" (akin to "anatomical" systems) and "functional" (akin to "physiological" systems). This produces the eight "prototypal diagnostic domains" and, as shown in Figure 16.1, these fall within different sectors of the matrix arrangement. So, to take an example, schizoid personality disorder is represented as follows: *expressive acts* = impassive; *interpersonal conduct* = unengaged; *cognitive style* = impoverished; *self–image* = complacent; *object representations* = meagre; *regulatory mechanisms* = intellectualization; *morphologic organization* = undifferentiation; *mood/temperament* = apathetic (Millon with Davis, 1996, p. 139).

To reiterate, such a comprehensive measure is not yet available, but for the cognitively-orientated practitioner, there are signs that such measures and approaches are being developed in the regulatory (defence) mechanisms domain (Berman & McCann, 1995; Soldz et al., 1995) and the cognitive domain that might, with further development and psychometric testing, be invaluable in the assessment of patients' cognitive schemas and in the judicious selection of foci for therapy. Two such cognitive approaches are represented by the work of Beck, Freeman & Associates (1990) and of Jeffrey Young (1994).

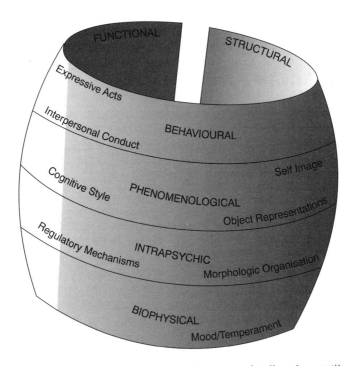

Figure 16.1   The eight "prototypal diagnostic domains' of Millon (from Millon with Davis, 1996; copyright © 1996 John Wiley & Sons Inc.; reproduced and adapted with permission)

A Cognitive Approach

Beck, Freeman & Associates (1990) have described cognitive styles and attributions which, they aver, are associated with particular personality disorders. So, for avoidant personality disorder, Beck, Freeman & Associates (1990) assert that key schemata are considered to be: "I am socially inept and undesirable", "Other people are superior to me and will reject or think critically of me if they get to know me", "I can't handle strong feelings", "You'll think I'm weak", "Most people don't have feelings like this" (Beck, Freeman & Associates, 1990, p. 257) and "I'm inadequate", "I'm unlikeable" (p. 261). Beck developed his Belief Questionnaire (BQ: Beck, 1990) on the basis that there were relatively unique schemata for each personality disorder, but this remained empirically untested until Trull et al. (1993) examined the psychometric properties of the BQ, finding high internal consistency (0.77–0.93) and test–retest reliability (0.63–0.82), but little evidence of discriminant validity.

A similar approach has been developed and enunciated by Young (1994), who has developed a cognitive therapy for persons with personality disorders. He has pointed out the need to identify early maladaptive schemata which he construes as unconditional beliefs about oneself in relation to the environment and the world. They are implicit, part of self, and go unchallenged by the person. Because of those three factors, over time these recurrent, dysfunctional schemata become more resistant to change. There are four (admittedly crude) criteria that define an early maladaptive schema: they usually trigger high levels of emotion (e.g. anxiety, depression, guilt); almost always they are closely linked to the most distressing, pervasive and enduring life problems experienced by the patient; and they are usually tied to the patient's most serious developmental problems with parents, siblings and peers during the early years of life. Typically, these schemata are triggered by events in the environment relevant to the particular schema. There are said to be 18 schemata and these are displayed in Table 16.3.

Although it is hinted that these schemata are linked with certain types or clusters of personality disorder, this is not explicitly described in Young's (1994) work. In fact, in view of the problems with categorical approaches referred to earlier, it may be a better option to link identified cognitive schemas with "supertraits", e.g. an avoidant interpersonal style that might underpin several so-called personality disorders, rather than belong to a specific type of personality disorder, e.g. avoidant personality disorder. An apparently earlier version of Young's (1994) schema questionnaire was examined and found to have adequate psychometric properties (Schmidt et al., 1995) but the relationship of each schema with each specific personality disorder or, alternatively, "supertrait", was not examined.

Despite the paucity of empirical data, there is much to recommend the approach advocated by Beck, Freeman & Associates and Young. It seems to afford a potential link between the idiographic and the nomothetic and potentially provides clinicians with a useful clinical tool for the assessment of personality

Table 16.3 Young's (1994) 18 Early Maladaptive Cognitive Schemata (grouped under five general areas)

Impaired autonomy and performance
    Dependence/incompetence; vulnerability to danger; enmeshment/undeveloped self; failure

Disconnection and rejection
    Emotional deprivation; abandonment/instability; mistrust/abuse; social isolation/alienation; defectiveness/shame

Impaired limits
    Insufficient self-control/self-discipline; entitlement/domination

Other-directedness
    Subjugation; self-sacrifice; approval-seeking

Overvigilance and inhibition
    Vulnerability to error/negativity; overcontrol; unrelenting standards

disorders at a cognitive level—one which also affords immediate intervention targets for cognitively-orientated practitioners. One can see how this approach might usefully complement the assessment and treatment of patients with borderline personality disorders (e.g. Linehan, 1993; Perris, 1994) by helping to identify core early maladaptive schemas.

"HINTS" FOR THE BUSY CLINICIAN IN ASSESSING CLIENTS FOR A POSSIBLE PERSONALITY DISORDER

The utility of the various assessment tools discussed so far is in their standardization, the provision of norms, and so forth. Yet, this writer appreciates that the busy clinician may not have access to the various standardized instrumentation or the time or money to expend on detailed assessments as discussed to date in this chapter. Hence there is a need for some "handy hints for busy clinicians" which are based more on the standard psychiatric interview approach that is the mandatory cornerstone of the working clinician's "toolbox".

1. Take a detailed full history, rather than a cursory and superficial recording of chronology (Jackson, Robinson & Pica, 1996). Information must be registered under the usual rubrics/headings: presenting problem and referral source; history of the presenting problem; past psychiatric/psychological history; medical history; alcohol and drug abuse; forensic history; family—including a genogram of the structural arrangements within the family, history of psychiatric conditions, relationships, atmosphere, quality of care, etc.; personal—including developmental, educational, occupational, social, sexual, intimate, etc.; personality, which can be assessed less formally via judgements according to the patient/client, the interviewing clinician and, if possible, by interviewing an informant; mental state examination (MSE); and

formulation. The entire history is of key importance in clarifying the presence of personality dysfunction, but social and intimate relationships, work record, emotional expression and control and coherency of self might be key foci in assessing the presence of personality dysfunction. The MSE (incorporating a cognitive screen) is particularly important in the determining of "trumping conditions", e.g. organic disorder. A very brief history of someone with avoidant personality disorder is provided at this point:

> *Kathy*, a 33 year-old medical practitioner, presented complaining of fears of oral examinations—one of which was imminent and the passing of which was a necessary prerequisite hurdle for continuing in her specialist training in neurology. Obtaining an extensive history and mental status examination revealed that what appeared to be, on the face of it, a simple and circumscribed condition (perhaps social phobia) was, in fact, a complex and extensive avoidant personality disorder. Her family, who lived interstate, were overprotective and she was the only one of her family to attend university. She had always felt that she had been "lucky" to gain entry into a school of medicine in a prestigious university. Although she had successfully passed each year of her medical course, she continued to feel that she "had fluked it". This "feeling" continued throughout her internship years and now into the specialist training in neurology she had chosen to pursue.
>
> She had some friends, but closer questioning revealed that they were relationships in which she did not, and would not, reveal her feelings or discuss important and intimate issues in her life, fearing that she would be ridiculed or rejected. As regards this point, it was important to establish whether this fear was a paranoid one; in fact, it was not.
>
> Kathy had experienced three sexual relationships and these had failed. In retrospect, although very tentative and apprehensive about entering all of them, it transpired that they were non-intimate relationships in which the men had maintained "prime" relationships with other women. Kathy now felt she had been exploited in these relationships but was not expecially angry, maintaining that she had felt lucky that someone had found her desirable. She did not host parties, was reluctant to attend them, was fearful of appearing in formal situations, e.g. weddings, or in situations where she might be the centre of attention. Her social life was in the main quite barren and, to be brief, most of Kathy's life had been spent forestalling potentially difficult interpersonal or social situations.

2. Try to ensure that Axis I conditions, most notably depressive and anxiety conditions, are not causing a "pseudo-personality disorder" picture to arise. The use of a brief inventory, e.g. the Beck Depression Inventory (Beck & Steer, 1987), may be helpful in clarifying the situation or at least in alerting the clinician to the possibility that the information about the self may be somewhat suspect. In the case of Kathy, it was important to exclude Axis I disorders, particularly depression and anxiety disorders (although she did in fact meet the additional diagnosis of Social Phobia), and rule out that she did not have paranoid ideation indicative of a psychotic disorder or schizotypal or paranoid personality disorder.

3. Wherever possible, arrange for a single interview with a "significant other". The selection of this "significant other" is critical; it should be someone who is reliable and knows the client well, say a parent or older sibling, spouse or

partner—someone who is both able and willing to supply "accurate" bio-graphical material about the client. In the case of Kathy, her family lived interstate and an interview was not easy to arrange. Neither was it thought to be particularly necessary.

4. Much of what we do in psychiatry focuses on the negative. We need to "accentuate the positive" by determining the strengths (interpersonal and otherwise) of the client, on the basis of what the client tells the interviewer, what the clinician devines during the conduct of the interview(s) and over subsequent sessions (i.e. during actual therapy sessions), and what we deter-mine from a suitable informant if one is available. In the case of Kathy, it was her tenacity in pursuing her medical studies and maintaining some forms of extra-curricular interests, e.g. her interest in theatre, in being part of a bush-walking club, and in maintaining some forms of social contact, albeit, in real terms, somewhat "distant" ones.

5. One needs to use the therapeutic situation not only for therapy but for ongoing assessment (Beck, Freeman & Associates, 1990). The progression of therapy should presumably enhance the therapist's understanding of the client's issues, themes and so on. Tracing the developmental antecedents of the disorder and deepening comprehension of the client's themes can be accomplished via a variety of techniques, all individually tailored to the client's needs. Techniques might include logbooks, diaries, guided imagery and guided retrospective life-history reporting (which involves systematically working through each year of the client's life—tagging each year to any significant life events). One can elicit automatic thoughts during the session by asking the client to reveal what he/she is thinking about the therapist at a particular point in time or during discussion of a particular topic. What are the affects tied up with a particular topic? How confident is the person that the "feared" beliefs are true? These techniques were used with Kathy. As her relationship with the therapist deepened, more and more detail emerged about her family life, her academic life and her relationships. Her fears of being rejected or disapproved by the therapist also emerged and these be-came a focus for therapy.

SUMMARY AND CONCLUSIONS

The first wave of research into personality disorders and assessment of the same was stimulated by DSM-III and its successors. It has provided us with some instrumentation and, as a consequence of that, some information about the prevalence of personality disorders to be found in various settings, about gender differences in personality disorders, and about the predictive validity of person-ality disorders in determining treatment outcomes, and so forth. Yet, we should be aware that, at best, the DSM-III/-R/IV Personality Disorder criteria sets offer a simulacrum of reality. Therefore, we should not be content to sit back and accept current DSM conceptualizations (and tools like the PDE which index the DSM and are, *ipso facto*, similarly innately limited) as the *sine qua non* of PD conceptualization. The DSM provides useful working models for us but there exist increasingly competitive and potentially useful alternatives to the DSM-based tools. For instance, Parker et al. (1996) have presented an ongoing attempt to develop further the definition and classification of the personality disorders by including all DSM-IV and ICD-10 descriptors, but by adding other items drawn from Millon's (1986) work and items derived from various anxiety, depression and dysfunctional attributional measures (Parker et al., 1996, p. 828). The outcomes are awaited with interest.

Although interest is increasing in the work of Cloninger, Svrakic & Przybeck (1993) and Widiger & Costa (1994), further encouragement needs to be given to forming an anastomosis between the research base pertaining to personality disorders and that research and theorizing that pertains to the so-called study of "normal personality". A tool such as the NEO-PI-R is an example of a measure that has been derived from the so-called "normal" personality area that may prove useful to the clinician. The strengths of the NEO-PI-R, and also the TCI for that matter, are in being able to identify a client's positive attributes—not only their negative ones—as both instruments provide configurational profiles. Treatment planning can be implemented in a way which is inherently more appealing to the clinician.

Much work needs to be done at the conceptual level in elucidating the multi-layered structure of personality disorders. Ultimately, measurement tools need to be developed along the lines promised by the theorizing of Millon (Millon with Davis, 1996; Millon & Davis, 1997). For epidemiologists, and arguably researchers, spotlighting superfactors or traits may suffice; but for the clinician, what is inarguably of considerably more benefit is the development of fine-grained tools that provide configurational analyses *but* that yield scores in the eight domains stipulated by Millon (Millon with Davis, 1996; Millon & Davis, 1997). Scores in these domains could suggest appropriate targets for intervention. The challenge will be how to take such a complexity of constructs and develop a practical and "user-friendly" tool for practitioners. Future research needs to address which domains may be more amenable to treatment than others.

Finally, we need to broaden our horizons, not only in terms of the numbers and types of dimensions, classes, or "depths" of personality/disorder traits, but in terms of the methods we will use to measure them. Block (1995) has argued that we should be inclusive of data derived from a variety of epistemiological methods, including those garnered from autobiography, observations, neuro-physiology, from psychiatric insights, from personal introspection, as well as from theoretical considerations. I concur. In my opinion, it would be far too premature to foreclose on both the *conceptualization* and *measurement* of personality disorders.

REFERENCES

Alnaes, R. & Torgersen, S. (1988).   DSM-III symptom disorders (Axis I) and personality disorders (Axis II) in an outpatient population. *Acta Psychiatrica Scandinavica*, **78**, 348–355.

American Psychiatric Association (1980). *Diagnostic and Statistical Manual of Mental Disorders (DSM-III)*, 3rd edn. Washington, DC: American Psychiatric Association.

American Psychiatric Association (1987). *Diagnostic and Statistical Manual of Mental Disorders (DSM-III-R)*, 3rd edn, revised. Washington, DC: American Psychiatric Association.

American Psychiatric Association (1994). *Diagnostic and Statistical Manual of Mental Disorders (DSM-IV)*, 4th edn. Washington, DC: American Psychiatric Association.

Baer, L., Jenike, M.A., Black, D.W., Treece, C., Rosenfeld, R. & Greist, J. (1992). Effect of Axis II on treatment outcome with clomipramine in 55 patients with obsessive-compulsive disorder. *Archives of General Psychiatry*, **49**, 862–866.

Beck, A.T. (1990). *Belief Questionnaire*. Unpublished manuscript.

Beck, A.T. & Steer, R.A. (1987). *BDI: Beck Depression Inventory Manual*. San Antonio, TX: The Psychological Corporation.

Beck, A.T., Freeman, A. & Associates. (1990). *Cognitive Therapy of Personality Disorders*. New York: Guilford.

Bell, R.C. & Jackson, H.J. (1992). The structure of personality disorders in DSM-III. *Acta Psychiatrica Scandinavica*, **85**, 279–287.

Berman, S.M.W. & McCann, J.T. (1995). Defense mechanisms and personality disorders: an empirical test of Millon's theory. *Journal of Personality Assessment*, **64**, 132–144.

Binder, J.L. & Strupp, H.H. (1997). "Negative process": a recurrently discovered and underestimated facet of therapeutic process and outcome in the individual psychotherapy of adults. *Clinical Psychology: Science and Practice*, **4**, 121–139.

Black, D.W., Noyes, R. Jr, Pfohl, B., Goldstein, R.B. & Blum, N. (1993). Personality disorder in obsessive-compulsive volunteers, well comparison subjects, and their first degree relatives. *American Journal of Psychiatry*, **150**, 1226–1232.

Blatt, S.J. (1995). The destructiveness of perfectionism: implications for the treatment of depression. *American Psychologist*, **50**, 1003–1020.

Block, J. (1995). A contrarian view of the five-factor model approach to personality description. *Psychological Bulletin*, **117**, 187–215.

Bornstein, R.F. (1996). Sex differences in dependent personality disorder prevalence rates. *Clinical Psychology: Science and Practice*, **3**, 1–12.

Bornstein, R.F. (1997). Dependent personality disorder in DSM-IV and beyond. *Clinical Psychology: Science and Practice*, **4**, 175–187.

Bruehl, S. (1994). A case of borderline personality disorder. In P.T. Costa Jr & T.A. Widiger (eds), *Personality Disorders and the Five-factor Model of Personality*. Washington, DC: American Psychological Association, pp. 189–197.

Chapman, L.J. & Chapman, J.P. (1985). Psychosis proneness. In M. Alpert (ed.), *Controversies in Schizophrenia: Changes and Constancies*. New York: Guilford, pp. 157–174.

Clark, L. (1993). *Manual for the Schedule for Nonadaptive and Adaptive Personality (SNAP)*. Minneapolis, MN: University of Minnesota Press.

Cloninger, C.R. (1987). A systematic method for clinical description and classification of personality variants. *Archives of General Psychiatry*, **44**, 573–588.

Cloninger, C.R., Svrakic, D.M. & Przybeck, T.R. (1993). A psychobiological model of temperament and character. *Archives of General Psychiatry*, **50**, 975–990.

Cloninger, C.R., Przybeck, T.R., Svrakic, D.M. & Wetzel, R.D. (1994). *The Temperament and Character Inventory (TCI): a Guide to its Development and Use*. St Louis, MO: Center for Psychobiology of Personality, Washington University.

Corbitt, E.M. (1994). Narcissism from the perspective of the five-factor model. In P.T. Costa Jr & T.A. Widiger (eds), *Personality Disorders and the Five-factor Model of Personality*. Washington, DC: American Psychological Association, pp. 199–203.

Corbitt, E.M. & Widiger, T.A. (1995). Sex differences among the personality disorders: an exploration of the data. *Clinical Psychology: Science and Practice*, **2**, 225–238.

Costa, P.T. Jr & McCrae, R.R. (1990). Personality disorders and the five-factor model of personality. *Journal of Personality Disorders*, **4**, 362–371.

Costa, P.T. Jr & McCrae, R.R. (1992a). Four ways five factors are basic. *Journal of Personality and Individual Differences*, **13**, 635–665.

Costa, P.T. Jr & McCrae, R.R. (1992b). *NEO PI-R*®: *Professional Manual. Revised NEO Personality Inventory (NEO-PI-R) and NEO Five Factor Inventory (NEO-FFI)*. Odessa, FL: Psychological Assessment Resources, Inc.

Donat, D.C. (1997). Personality traits and psychiatric rehospitalisation. A two-year follow-up. *Journal of Personality Assessment*, **68**, 703–711.

Duijsens, I.J. & Diekstra, R.F.W. (1996). DSM-III-R and ICD-10 personality disorders and their relationship with the big five dimensions of personality. *Personality and Individual Differences*, **21**, 119–133.

Ekselius, L., Lindstrom, E., von Knorring, L., Bodlund, O. & Kullgren, G. (1994). A principal component analysis of the DSM-III-R personality disorders. *Journal of Personality Disorders*, **8**, 140–148.

First, M.B., Spitzer, R.L., Gibbon, M. & Williams, J.B.W. (1995a). The Structured Clinical Interview for DSM-III-R Personality Disorders (SCID-II). Part I: Description. *Journal of Personality Disorders*, **9**, 83–91.

First, M.B., Spitzer, R.L., Gibbon, M., Williams, J.B.W., Davies, M., Borus, J., Howes, M.J., Kane, J., Pope, H.G. Jr & Rounsaville, B. (1995b). The Structured Clinical Interview for DSM-III-R Personality Disorders (SCID-II). Part II: Multi-site test–retest reliability study. *Journal of Personality Disorders*, **9**, 92–104.

Hewitt, P.L., Flett, G.L., Turnbull-Donovan, W. & Mikail, S.F. (1991). The Multidimensional Perfectionism Scale: reliability, validity, and psychometric properties in psychiatric samples. *Psychological Assessment: A Journal of Consulting and Clinical Psychology*, **3**, 464–468.

Hulbert, C.A., Jackson, H.J. & McGorry, P.D. (1996). Relationship between personality and course and outcome in early psychosis: a review of the literature. *Clinical Psychology Review*, **16**, 707–727.

Hyler, S., Reider, R., Spitzer, R.L. & Williams, J.B.W. (1983). *The Personality Diagnostic Questionnaire*. New York State Psychiatric Institute.

Hyler, S.E., Reider, S.D., Williams, J.B.W., Spitzer, R.L., Hendler, J. & Lyons, M. (1988). The Personality Diagnostic Questionnaire: development and preliminary results. *Journal of Personality Disorders*, **2**, 229–237.

Hyler, S.E., Skodol, A.E., Oldham, J.M., Kellman, H.D. & Doidge, N. (1992). Validity of the Personality Diagnostic Questionnaire—Revised: a replication in an outpatient sample. *Comprehensive Psychiatry*, **33**, 73–77.

Jackson, D.N., Paunonen, S.V., Fraboni, M. & Goffin, R.D. (1996). A five-factor versus six-factor model of personality structure. *Personality and Individual Differences*, **20**, 33–45.

Jackson, H.J., Gazis, J., Rudd, R.P. & Edwards, J. (1991a). Concordance between two personality disorder instruments with psychiatric inpatients. *Comprehensive Psychiatry*, **32**, 252–260.

Jackson, H.J., Whiteside, H.L., Bates, G.W., Bell, R., Rudd, R.P. & Edwards, J. (1991b). Diagnosis of personality disorders in psychiatric inpatients. *Acta Psychiatrica Scandinavica*, **83**, 206–213.

Jackson, H.J. & Pica, S. (1993). An investigation into the internal structure of DSM-III antisocial personality disorder. *Psychological Reports*, **72**, 355–367.

Jackson, H., Robinson, T. & Pica, S. (1996). State psychiatric hospitals and psychiatric wards in general hospitals. In P.R. Martin & J.S. Birnbrauer (eds), *The Practice of Clinical Psychology: Profession and Practice in Australia*. Melbourne: Macmillan Education Australia, pp. 103–128.

Linehan, M.M. (1993). *Cognitive-behavioral Treatment of Borderline Personality Disorder*. New York: Guilford.

Livesley, W.J. & Jackson, D. (in press). *Manual for the Dimensional Assessment of Personality Pathology—Basic Questionnaire.* Port Huron, MI: Sigma.

Loranger, A.W., Susman, V.L., Oldham, J.M. & Russakoff, L.M. (1987). The Personality Disorder Examination: a preliminary report. *Journal of Personality Disorders*, **1**, 1–13.

Loranger, A.W., Lenzenweger, M.F., Gartner, A.F., Susman, V.L., Herzig, J., Zammit, G.K., Gartner, J.D., Abrams, R.C. & Young, R.C. (1991). Trait-state artifacts and the diagnosis of personality disorder. *Archives of General Psychiatry*, **48**, 720–728.

Loranger, A.W., Sartorius, N., Andreoli, A., Berger, P., Buchheim, P., Channabasavanna, S.M., Coid, B., Dahl, A., Diekstra, R.F.W., Ferguson, B., Jacobsberg, L.B., Mombour, W., Pull, C., Ono, C. & Regier, D.A. (1994). The International Personality Disorder Examination. The World Health Organization/Alcohol, Drug Abuse, and Mental Health Administration Pilot Study of Personality Disorders. *Archives of General Psychiatry*, **51**, 215–224.

Luborsky, L., McLellan, A.T., Diguer, L., Woody, G. & Seligman, D.A. (1997). The psychotherapist matters: comparison of outcomes across twenty-two therapists and seven patient samples. *Clinical Psychology: Science and Practice*, **4**, 53–65.

McCrae, R.R. & Costa, P.T. Jr (1990). *Personality in Adulthood.* New York: Guilford.

McCrae, R.R. & Costa, P.T. Jr (1997). Personality trait structure as a human universal. *American Psychologist*, **52**, 509–516.

Mann, A.H., Jenkins, R., Cutting, J.C. & Cowen, P.J. (1981). The development and use of standardised assessment of abnormal personality. *Psychological Medicine*, **11**, 839–847.

Meehl, P.E. (1990). Schizotaxia as an open concept. In A.I. Rabin, R.A. Zucker, R.A. Emmons & S. Frank (eds), *Studying Persons and Lives.* New York: Springer, pp. 248–303.

Meehl, P.E. (1992). Factors and taxa, traits and types, differences of degree and differences of kind. *Journal of Personality*, **60**, 117–174.

Mellsop, G., Varghese, F., Joshua, S. & Hicks, A. (1982). The reliability of Axis II of DSM-III. *American Journal of Psychiatry*, **139**, 1360–1361.

Millon, T. (1977). *Millon Multiaxial Inventory Manual.* Minneapolis, MN: National Computer Systems.

Millon, T. (1984). On the renaissance of personality assessment and personality theory. *Journal of Personality Assessment*, **48**, 450–466.

Millon, T. (1986). Personality prototypes and their diagnostic criteria. In T. Millon & G.L. Klerman (eds), *Contemporary Directions in Psychopathology.* New York: Guilford, pp. 671–712.

Millon, T. (1987). *Millon Clinical Multiaxial Inventory Manual II.* Minneapolis, MN: National Computer Systems.

Millon, T. (1990). *Toward a New Personology: an Evolutionary Model.* New York: Wiley.

Millon, T., Millon, C. & Davis, R.D. (1994). *Millon Clinical Multiaxial Inventory—III.* Minneapolis, MN: National Computer Systems.

Millon, T. with Davis, R.D. (1996). *Disorders of Personality: DSM-IV™ and Beyond*, 2nd edn. New York: Wiley.

Millon, T. & Davis, R.D. (1997). The MCMI-III: present and future directions. *Journal of Personality Assessment*, **68**, 69–85.

Mischel, W. (1968). *Personality & Assessment.* New York: Wiley.

Morganstern, J., Langenbucher, J., Labouvie, E. & Miller, K.J. (1997). The comorbidity of alcoholism and personality disorders in a clinical population: prevalence rates and relation to alcohol typology variables. *Journal of Abnormal Psychology*, **106**, 74–84.

Parker, G., Hadzi-Pavlovic, K., Wilhelm, K., Austin, M-P., Mason, C., Samuels, A., Mitchell, P. & Eyers, K. (1996). Defining the personality disorders: description of an Australian database. *Australian and New Zealand Journal of Psychiatry*, **30**, 824–833.

Perris, C. (1994).   Cognitive therapy in the treatment of patients with borderline person-
    ality disorders. *Acta Psychiatrica Scandinavica*, **379**(suppl), 69–72.
Perry, J.C. (1993).   Longitudinal studies of personality disorders. *Journal of Personality
    Disorders*, **7**(suppl), 63–85.
Peselow, E.D., Sanfilipo, M.P., Fieve, R.R. & Gulbenkian, G. (1994).   Personality traits
    during depression and after clinical recovery. *British Journal of Psychiatry*, **164**, 349–
    354.
Pfohl, B., Stangl, D. & Zimmerman, M. (1983*).   Structured Interview for DSM-III Per-
    sonality (SIDP)*. Ames, IA: University of Iowa.
Pfohl, B., Coryell, W., Zimmerman, M. & Stangl, D. (1986).   DSM-III personality dis-
    orders: diagnostic overlap and internal consistency of individual DSM-III criteria.
    Comprehensive Psychiatry, **27**, 21–34.
Pfohl, B., Blum, N., Zimmerman, M. & Stangl, D. (1989).   *Structured Interview for DSM-
    III-R Personality (SIDP-R)*. Iowa City, IA: University of Iowa.
Pfohl, B., Blum, N. & Zimmerman, M. (1997).   *Structured Interview for DSM-IV Person-
    ality (SIDP-IV)*. Washington, DC: American Psychiatric Press.
Pilkonis, P.A., Heape, C.L., Proietti, J.M., Clarke, S.W., McDavid, J.D. & Pitts, T.E.
    (1995).   The reliability and validity of two structured diagnostic interviews for person-
    ality disorders. *Archives of General Psychiatry*, **52**, 1025–1033.
Schmidt, N.B., Joiner, T.E. Jr, Young, J.E. & Telch, M.J. (1995).   The Schema Question-
    naire: investigation of psychometric properties and the hierarchical structure of a
    measure of maladaptive schema. *Cognitive Therapy and Research*, **19**, 295–321.
Soldz, S., Budman, S., Demby, A. & Merry, J. (1995).   The relation of defensive style to
    personality pathology and the Big Five personality factors. *Journal of Personality
    Disorders*, **9**, 356–370.
Spitzer, R.L., Williams, J.B.W., Gibbon, M. & First, M.B. (1992).   The Structured Clinical
    Interview for *DSM-III-R* (SCID). I: History, rationale and description. *Archives of
    General Psychiatry*, **49**, 624–629.
Trull, T.J., Goodwin, A.H., Schopp, L.H., Hillenbrand, T.L. & Schuster, T. (1993).   Psy-
    chometric properties of a cognitive measure of personality disorders. *Journal of
    Personality Disorders*, **61**, 536–546.
Tyrer, P., Alexander, M.S., Cicchetti, D., Cohen, M.S. & Remington, M. (1979).   Reli-
    ability of a schedule for rating personality disorders. *British Journal of Psychiatry*, **135**,
    168–174.
Widiger, T.A. (1993).   The DSM-III-R categorical personality disorder diagnoses: a cri-
    tique and an alternative. *Psychological Inquiry*, **4**, 75–90.
Widiger, T.A. & Costa, P.T. Jr (1994).   Personality and personality disorders. *Journal of
    Abnormal Psychology*, **103**, 78–91.
Widiger, T.A. & Frances, A.J. (1994).   Toward a dimensional model for the personality
    disorders. In P.T. Costa Jr & T.A. Widiger (eds), *Personality Disorders and the Five-
    factor Model of Personality*. Washington, DC: American Psychological Association, pp.
    19–39.
Widiger, T.A., Trull, T.J., Hurt, S.W., Clarkin, J. & Frances, A. (1987).   A multidimen-
    sional scaling of the DSM-III personality disorders. *Archives of General Psychiatry*, **44**,
    557–563.
Widiger, T.A. & Spitzer, R.L. (1991).   Sex bias in the diagnosis of personality disorders:
    conceptual and methodological issues. *Clinical Psychology Review*, **11**, 1–22.
Widiger, T.A., Trull, T.J., Clarkin, J.F., Sanderson, C. & Costa, P.T. Jr (1994).   In P.T.
    Costa Jr & T.A. Widiger (eds), *Personality Disorders and the Five-factor Model of
    Personality*. Washington, DC: American Psychological Association, pp. 41–56.
Widiger, T.A. & Trull, T.J. (1997).   Assessment of the five-factor model of personality.
    Journal of Personality Assessment, **68**, 228–250.
World Health Organization (1992).   *The ICD-10 Classification of Mental and Behav-
    ioural Disorders: Clinical Descriptions and Diagnostic Guidelines*. Geneva: WHO.

Young, J.E. (1994). *Cognitive Therapy for Personality Disorders: a Schema-focused Approach.* Sarasota, FL: Professional Resource Press.

Zimmerman, M. (1994). Diagnosing personality disorders: a review of issues and research methods. *Archives of General Psychiatry*, **51**, 225–245.

Zimmerman, M., Coryell, W., Pfohl, B., Corenthal, C. & Stangl, D. (1986). ECT response in depressed patients with and without a DSM-III personality disorder. *American Journal of Psychiatry*, **143**, 1030–1032.

Chapter 17

Less Common Therapeutic Strategies and Techniques in the Cognitive Psychotherapy of Severely Disturbed Patients

Hjördis Perris
Swedish Institute of Cognitive Psychotherapy, Stockholm, Sweden

INTRODUCTION

One strength of cognitive psychotherapy (CPT), emphasized very early by Beck (1976) and others (Arnkoff, 1981; Glass & Arnkoff, 1982; Perris H, 1985; Perris C, 1986/96), is its flexibility. Another is its integrative power (Alford & Beck, 1997). Both these characteristics allow for the choice by the therapist of appropriate strategies and techniques which are particularly tailored to suit the needs of an individual patient, independently of whether those techniques were originally conceived within the CPT framework or more properly belong to other psychotherapeutic domains. One prerequisite underscored by Beck, however, is that those techniques or strategies have always to be used having the goals of CPT in mind. Arnkoff (1981) emphasizes that "flexibility in marrying procedures (from different sources) need not imply the practice of atheoretical, trial-and-error therapy (p. 203)".

As pointed out in previous papers (Perris H, 1985; Perris & Perris, 1998) as well as has been underscored by other authors (e.g. Vallis; Pretzer; Perris & Skagerlind, this volume), it can be necessary when working with severely disturbed patients to make adaptations of the standard conduct of therapy. These

Cognitive Psychotherapy of Psychotic and Personality Disorders: Handbook of Theory and Practice.
Edited by C. Perris and P.D. McGorry.
© 1998 John Wiley & Sons Ltd.

adaptations also imply the use, in different phases of the therapy (e.g. in the initial phase when working with uncommunicative patients), of less conventional techniques or, as Guidano (1987) points out, the creation of new ones whenever the necessity arises.

In this chapter some exemplifications will be given of how such techniques as the keeping of a daybook, or writing letters, or the use of photographs, tables from the Thematic Apperception Test (TAT, Morgan & Murray, 1935), drawings and creative paintings, metaphors, dreams and fables can be easily integrated into the practice of cognitive psychotherapy with severely disturbed patients. The particular purpose of each technique will also be emphasized.

A more general observation, which probably applies to the whole group of patients with a personality disorder, is that most of them have pronounced emotional difficulties. Some of them have difficulties in expressing their emotions, whereas others are overwhelmed in an uncontrolled way by their emotions. Looking at these patients from the perspective of attachment theory (Bowlby, 1969–1980; Crittenden, 1994; Perris & Perris, 1998), it could be said that the former are prominently *cognition-directed*, whereas the latter are prominently *emotion-directed*.

In the conduct of CPT there is a strong emphasis in making the patient an active partecipant in the therapeutic work, epitomized in the concept of *collaborative empiricism* (Beck et al., 1979). A prerequisite for his/her active collaboration is that the patient has been socialized for therapy. The process of socialization implies that the therapist has to make treatment as comprehensible as possible, providing clear explanations for each step in the treatment in order for the patient to become able to participate actively in identifying his/her problems.

Strategies for Conveying Theoretical Information to the Patient

In this section a few examples will be given of techniques which can be used to convey theoretical information to the patient in order to promote his/her active participation in the identification of his/her problems and in the search of appropriate ways of approaching them.

When patients who, at the beginning of therapy, appear to be mostly cognition-directed (e.g. patients with an anxious-avoidant attachment pattern and a Axis II personality disorder belonging to cluster A) reach a point when they experience the therapeutic relationship as a *secure base* (Bowlby, 1988), they may also begin to experience emotions of which they had previously been unaware. The strength of such experiences can be frightening, even when the experienced emotions are positive ones. When this occurs (e.g. when the patient experiences security and trust in the unit where the treatment takes place), then the therapist attempts to explain for the patient what is happening in order to reduce his/her anxiety about losing control.

A sketch of the type presented in Figure 17.1 can be a suitable base for explanation. The explanation usually given to the patient is as follows:

All of us are born with a cognition- and an emotion-instrument (*pointing at the same time to the head—cognitions—of person A and to the keyboard down on the belly—emotions*). These instruments were, however, untuned when we were born. The tuning of these instruments occurs with help from our parents or from other persons taking care of us as children. When the tune is perfect, there is harmony between the cognition- and the emotion-instrument, as in subject A. He appears to be happy and confident because he can trust that his instruments will guide him safely through life. He can trust either cognitions or emotions because he "knows" that they are in harmony with each other. But for person "B", harmony between the instruments does not occur. For some reason, he did not get appropriate help. Thus, because the instruments were dysharmonic, he decided to turn off one of them—in your case the emotion-instrument. Person B tries now to follow only one instrument, relying "on his head", e.g. he does whatever others do without paying any attention to his feelings. Those around him might think that it is strange, and he himself in the long run has an experience of emptiness and dullness. In the end it might happen that he applies for help without knowing what is actually wrong. He just feels this emptiness.

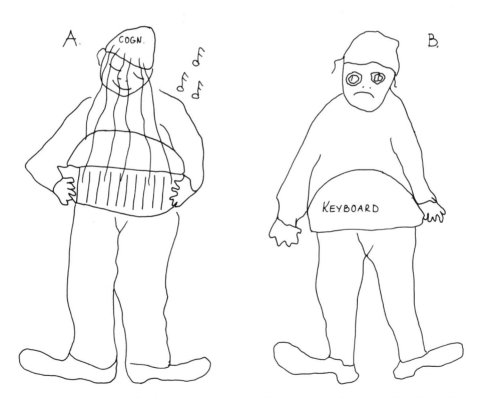

Figure 17.1 A sketch that has proved to be useful to explain to the patient the relationship between cognitions and emotions

What I think is happening to you is that you are in the same situation as person B. One difference is that because of the emotional warmth here at the unit, your frozen-over emotion-instrument has begun to thaw. As a consequence it emits sounds which frighten you because they are untuned and because you had probably forgotten that you actually had an emotion-instrument. We will help each other so that your emotion-instrument will be tuned and your quality of life will become more similar to that of person A.

One instance when I was able to use this technique occurred when a patient who apparently had completely excluded his emotions from awareness came back from a walk to the unit where he was admitted and expressed with some surprise: "How strange! I have been down-town and people looked so happy. Now I am back at the unit and everyone looks happy here as well" (no change in the level of emotions had occurred at the unit during the patient's short absence, and very likely, not down-town either).

Another patient of the same type as the previous one came back one day to the unit almost ecstatic. He had watched some small children playing in a sandpit and "it was the most beautiful thing he had ever seen".

Sometimes, however, it happens that frightening aggressive feelings occur. In such instances, the occasional addition of a low dosage of a neuroleptic drug might be appropriate to contain "the pressure of the emotion-instrument threatening to explode".

What has been said so far illustrates how, with the aid of elementary sketches and metaphors, it is possible to help the patient to cope with sudden emotional changes which are experienced as frightening. The examples reported above refer to patients with a disturbed attachment pattern of the A type (cognition-directed). A similar strategy can be used, however, even with patients with an anxious-ambivalent attachment pattern—type C—who are assumed to be emotion-directed. The difference is that the emphasis in the latter case is put upon helping the patient in using his/her cognitions to moderate his/her emotions.

When it is necessary to convey to the patient theoretical CPT notions that he/she has to learn in order to actively participate in the therapeutic work, there are obviously several strategies which can be applied. To an intellectually well-developed patient it is possible, for example, to give, as homework, some appropriate booklet to read. It sometimes happens, however, that despite the patient being able to carry out the assigned homework, it is evident that the knowledge so acquired remains at an intellectual level and the patient is unable to assimilate it. In other words, it could be said that no harmony between the two instruments (person B) in Figure 17.1 has occurred.

A patient with an obsessive-compulsive personality disorder maintained that he had fully understood how the therapeutic work should proceed in order to get the help he wanted. Despite this affirmation, he manifested a pronounced difficulty in following the therapist's explanations, which he continuosly met with counterarguments that he had previously tried without any success. Speaking metaphorically, it could be said that he went around with "a frozen head without a body", that is, without being in touch with his emotions.

A change occurred, however, when the therapist told him about a dream that another patient had reported. This last-mentioned patient had applied for help for a depressive reaction following his divorce. From the very beginning of treatment, he mentioned that he had the feeling of wandering through life as "a loser". In the course of therapy, it was possible to evidentiate how this attitude of being a loser had informed all the patient's life to become a self-fulling prophecy. He reported, for example, that when he get married he already "knew" that his marriage would not last, since his wife was "superior to him". In a similar way, he had started three different research projects to achieve a doctorate without succeeding in carrying out any of them. Also in this respect, he "already knew from the beginning that he would be unable to carry them out".

In a later session he reported the following dream: He was on the icy surface of a lake, carrying a small child in his arms. The ice cracked and rumbled and there was the risk that it would crack altogether at any moment. He hauled himself towards the shore with the child in his arms, under the constant menace that the ice would crack. At some point during his effort he happened to turn his head and see at some distance three men wearing black top-hats dancing and leaping, delighted at the cracking ice. At that point a thought occurred to him: "It could have been like that for me if had I not had this child to carry".

With the help of the image given by this dream, dreamed by another person, the patient was able to realize that his own difficulties were related to the child he himself was carrying inside, without being able to see it. He was also able to realize that the child in the other patient's dream symbolized the self-image of a loser, that is, his own dysfunctional attitude of self-unworthiness. The ice, i.e. his life, could have been different if he had not had that child to carry, that negative self-image. Also, the three men with their black top hats (in Sweden the sign of a doctoral degree) could have been himself.

After this episode the further course of therapy markedly changed. The patient became aware that he had to actively train, with the help of appropriate homework, to learn how to leave behind him the responsibility for the child that he had been carrying.

A concept that often recurs in the context of psychotherapies of a different ideological orientation is that of "the child within oneself". In CPT that "child", as in the example of the dream reported above, corresponds to a dysfunctional self-schema, or a dysfunctional internal working model of self and others, according to Bowlby's terminology (Bowlby, 1969–1980), which negatively informs one attitudes towards oneself and one's relationships to others and to life in general. Such a dysfunctional basic attitude is mostly outside the individual's awareness. Hence, it (automatically) influences all one's actions. Such an attitude is easy to identify from the patient's automatic thoughts, which often are of the type: "I am unable to do anything"; "Everything I do is wrong"; "Others are able to do things, not I"; that is, "I am uncapable", "I am a loser". In other people's styles of self-expression the therapist can recognize a "Messiah" or a "Batman". On the surface, one sees a person who pursues impossible goals or who is uncapable of refusing to do something because of being afraid of appearing a weak person. One patient said, "There is a colonel within myself criticizing whatever I do".

The ultimate goal of CPT is to identify dysfunctional basic assumptions of which the patient has been unaware and to help him/her in developing more functional ones which would allow the questioning of dysfunctional patterns of thoughts. Basic dysfunctional assumptions (or working models) are assumed to have developed in the past as a result of early interactions when the patient was a child. It is on the strength of such dysfunctional working models that the *child inside* still survives.

One way to make such concepts understandable for the patient could be the use of a sketch of the type shown in Figure 17.2.

Two cartoon human figures are drawn hand-in-hand, the one bigger and the other smaller, separated by a partition wall. In the upper left of the paper the therapist draws a symbol of himself, and in the upper right he draws symbols of the patient's parents. Afterwards, the therapist asks the patient whether he/she understands what the picture symbolizes. If the patient is unable to catch the meaning, the therapist explains that the figures symbolize both the "adult" patient and the child with his self-image. The line between the figures symbolizes a partition wall that has been responsible of the fact that the child has remained invisible until now.

But now (*the therapist adds*) we shall together pull down the wall (*this is marked with a few crosses*) because we shall together investigate how the child that has remained with you from the past influences your present life. We shall together look at various situations in your everyday life to discover whether, when you stumble on road-

Figure 17.2 A sketch to help the patient to discover. The hitherto invisible "child inside"

blocks, it is the "child inside" who is responsible. We shall also, from time to time, look backwards at how your life was when you were a child and try to understand how it comes about that your present life has become what it is.

Your parents (*put a mark on their symbol*), who should have helped you when they had their opportunity, tried to do their best according to their abilities. Here am I (*the therapist points to the symbol of himself*). What do you believe my task will be? Who do you think will take care of that small child now? *A frequent answer from the patient after a short hesitation is*: I will have to do that myself. Right (*adds the therapist*) with my guidance you will do that.

In the course of therapy there are several occasions to go back to that metaphor to make therapy more alive. The formal cognitive therapy language can be translated into that metaphor in many ways, e.g. "The dysfunctional basic assumptions are by the child, the functional ones by the adult". When the patient feels distressed, or has difficulties in coping with everyday problems, it can be said that, "Now it is the cry from the small child that we hear".

One could suspect that the patient would feel ashamed or offended by the use of such a simple drawing, and by the image of an adult with a small child. In my experience of a few decades, this is not so. Rather, many patients experience having been "seen" for the first time. Therapists in training, who have been instructed to use this approach under supervision, have most often been positively surprised by the new course that therapy has taken after the use of this strategy.

Strategies for Collecting Relevant Information and for Helping the Patient in Dealing with Emotional Experiences and Gain Control

In the previous section, a few less common strategies for helping the patient's understanding of the main tenets of CPT have been presented. In the following, some strategies will be highlighted which can be useful in the further conduct of therapy.

The main guiding principle of CPT is the *conceptualization* of the individual case, which begins with the early interviews. Most often, a skilled interview strategy is sufficient for collecting the information that will allow a conceptualization of the patient's problem within a cognitive theoretical framework. Working with severely disturbed patients, who most often are not communicative, other strategies have to be employed to gather the information on the patient's assumptions, in various respects, that is necessary for the planning of appropriate therapeutic strategies. For this purpose the use of creative painting, or that of a table from the TAT, may be very useful means.

The Use of Creative Painting

By asking the patient to paint simple pictures in watercolours it is possible to get access to useful information that can help in the conceptualization of the individual case and hence the planning of treatment. For example, a tree without leaves or well-marked roots can easily reveal that the appearent image of sclf-assurance that the patient shows, in reality conceals another side of him/her. Later, a repetition of the same painting as treatment proceeds allows the monitoring of changes which go hand-in-hand with successive changes in the patient's self-image. Hence, the painting becomes an indirect measure of the progress of therapy.

What has been just pointed out suggests that creative painting can be used to gather such information concerning the patient that he/she is unable to convey in words, however he/she would like to. Creative painting, however, can also be used as a therapeutic technique, especially with patients with a personality disorder who have difficulties in verbalizing their emotions. One way of using this technique is to ask the patient to paint as homework something concerning a topic currently on the focus in therapy, e.g. "to be stuck". The painting that the patient shows in the next session can then be used as a basis for further developments in successive homework assignments and in relation to questions put by the therapist, for example, "How can you illustrate how to get through loss?". In this way, especially in an early phase of treatment, it is possible through a series of pictures/homework assignments to help the patient to work with his/her problems on a symbolic plan, until he/she becomes able to do that verbally.

The Use of TAT Tables

Selected tables from the TAT, judged by the therapist to be appropiate for the patient's problems, are shown to the patient, who is asked to write a short history answering the following questions: "What has happened before the situation you are seing in the table?"; "What is going on right now?"; "What will happen afterwards?"; "What could be the thoughts and the feelings of the person/s in the picture?" The idiosyncratic history told by the patient suggests a picture of his/her specific way of thinking, and most often mirrors his/her current "dilemma".

Thus, the TAT-induced production of comments by the patient can serve to give him/her a preliminary hint about his/her core problems. The therapist, in his/her turn, can choose between openly confronting the patient with those problems as hypotheses to be tested or, for a while, continuing to work through those problems on the symbolic level that the patient him/herself has chosen in his/her interpretation of the table. In this last-mentioned instance, the therapist proceeds in a similar way as described above concerning the use of creative painting. That is, he/she lets the patient verbalize and elaborate his/her thoughts or fantasies around the theme that he/she had previously narrated. In that way, an indirect working-through of the patient's problems can take place at a greater distance, especially when a more direct confrontation with the core dilemmas could be experienced by the patient as forbidden or frightening. Even though the patient, at the beginning, may be unaware of the meaning of the histories he/she writes or tells, a point is eventually reached when he/she realizes that, in reality, the history concerns him/herself. Such a discovery might be surprising, but is never dramatic.

Writing a Daybook

To let the patient write instead of, or in parellel with, talking can sometime be a purposeful technique in many respects. On a previous occasion (Perris H, 1985), I have reported on the use of a daybook as a basis for therapeutic work with two uncommunicative cluster A patients. For several months the therapy was conducted mostly in writing, putting comments on the margins and asking questions to which the patients, still in writing, had to answer at home.

Another very chaotic patient, who was unable to communicate but in a torrent of words asked for help, when it appeared almost impossible to keep her on track, and to agree on some topic for the session's agenda, presented with a borderline personality disorder and a severe eating disorder. The strategy adopted in her case was to ask her as a homework, between sessions, to write down, in as few words as possible, just one topic from the coming agenda. Also, she was given the task of limiting, during a given time-frame, her bothering of other patients and the staff at the unit with her incessant talk. The patient reacted with humour to these suggestions and accepted them as a challenge. It worked, and the patient very soon learned to be more logical and to the point.

In this case the problem was to promote some structure in the patient's way of presenting her problems. A different problem arises when the patient is tongue-tied. With patients of this kind it takes a very long time indeed before getting access to their thoughts and feelings. As mentioned above, with this type of patient the strategy of letting them write down what they would have liked to tell the therapist about may be very useful. The patient is asked to write down, in general terms, what he/she does and what happens around him/her during the periods between the therapy sessions, together with his/her reactions, thoughts and deliberations concerning those events. Not only concrete situations, but also thoughts and ruminations may be included. At the next session, the patient submits his/her notes to the therapist, who read them through, making comments and asking questions in the margins in much the same way as he/she would have done if the patient had reported on the same events and thoughts in a conventional interview. Afterwards, the notes are returned to the patient by mail. He/she, in turn, makes amendments and further comments according to the questions and suggestions that the therapist has proposed. In the following session, therapist and patient together go through those points that the patient has found to be unclear. In this way, the therapist is able to judge whether the patient has been able to correctly elaborate on his/her comments and hence decide to what extent further discussion is required.

With this approach it is also possible to further the progress of therapy with uncommunicative patients, thus enhancing its long-term effects in a way that is beneficial to them. Its disadvantage lies in the extra work entailed for the therapist. This disadvantage, however, can be reduced in different ways and during different stages of the treatment as therapy proceeds and the patient's complete trust is acquired. One particular advantage of this approach, however, is that it can also be exploited to extend oneself as a therapist. For example, during vacations or other circumstances when occasional disruptions in therapy are unavoidable, the therapist encourages the patient to continue to keep notes so that he/she can follow various aspects of his development and reactions during the break of therapy.

Writing Letters

With the previous examples an attempt has been made to show how the strategy of *writing* can be used to contain push forward thought processes. Another context in which the strategy of writing is applicable is when it is appropriate to help the patient in sorting out his/her thoughts and feelings towards someone (dead or alive).

> One patient had an image of self as a nasty woman and accordingly behaved very thornily towards people in her environment. During the course of therapy, it emerged that she had developed that self-image when her parents suddenly divorced when she was 8 years old. She was convinced that the parents' divorce was her fault. Her father had walked out on the family and had never since been heard of. During the sessions, she recalled that she had pondered a lot on why the father had left, until she had reached the conclusion that it must have been her fault. One contributing factor to such a conclusion was that as a child she used to go to the parents' bedroom when she woke up at night asking to be allowed to stay with them. On those occasions her father apparently reacted with anger.

With the progress of therapy it became clear that she had missed her father very much at the same time as she had been torn between feelings of guilt and anger. The therapist suggested that she should write a letter to him, speaking her mind. It was not planned, however, that the letter should be mailed because she did not know her father's current adress. The patient wrote several letters of various tenor. Later, the thought occurred to the patient that she could try to learn about the father's present whereabouts and send him a real letter. This letter also was rewritten several times before it was eventually mailed.

In this case the patient was able to get in touch with her father. He explained thoroughly to her the circumstances surrounding the divorce and was able to reassure her that it had never been her fault that the family had split. In this way, the negative self-image that the patient had developed could be restructured. Accordingly, also, her behaviour towards others changed in a marked way.

To write a letter to someone who no longer is alive is sometimes the only way to be able to get in touch and express something that had never been said. Many personality-disordered patients have a history of abuse or neglect from their parents or some close relative. They find it difficult to speak about those events "because it would be of no use since they are dead". Secluded feelings (cf. Bowlby's concept *defensive exclusion*) make it difficult for those patients to feel alive and participating in life. They go through life as a "robot" directed by powerful feelings which they try to keep out of their awareness, but which from time to time threaten to come thronging in. The following vignette may serve as an illustration.

> A man aged 40 applied for the first time for psychiatric help, complaining of "a strange sensation in the head". He was diagnosed as suffering from depression and referred for cognitive psychotherapy. The patient's condition, however, deteriorated almost immediately. He became psychotic and manifested the delusion that his skin at the wrists could be turned around. As a consequence of that he was admitted into a psychiatric ward and treated with a series of electroconvulsive therapies. When the psychotic condition remitted, the patient was referred back to the cognitive treatment unit where I was working, for further treatment with cognitive psychotherapy.

From the history at the intake interview, it emerged that the patient's mother had died of cancer when the patient and his brother were aged 10 and 12, respectively, and that their father had committed suicide about 1 year after the death of his wife. The children were then put into the care of relatives that they did not know very well. They had grown up in that milieu. The patient had lived in a childless marriage for several years.

During therapy, very strong feelings of anger mixed with guilt, directed toward the father, soon became manifest. For this patient, who had not been accostioned to expressing any emotion, the task of writing letters to the dead father became an opportunity for working through strong feelings which had been there all the time, threatening to come thronging in. When he had sought help for his "strange sensations in the head" he had apparently reached a breaking point.

After about 3 months of cognitive psychotherapy, people around him experienced the patient as completely transformed. He became frank and spontaneous in a way he had never been before. On own initiative he participated, together with his middle-aged wife, in a fertility analysis, which in due time resulted in the birth of a daughter. It can easily be assumed that without the *delivery* of the feelings towards the father that had occurred in therapy, that little girl would probably never have been born.

Even though the patient just mentioned cannot be regarded as a clear-cut case of personality disorder, his experiences very closely resemble those which can occur in personality-disordered patients, leading to an acute breakdown. Hence, the case may serve as an illustration of how the writing of letters can be used to bring strong feelings to awareness and help the patient in revising them.

The Use of Photo-albums and Photographs

Photographs may be used as a method enabling the patient and therapist to more readily explore feelings, work through conflicts, and mobilize affect. Access to a patient's family album, or photographs from the patient's childhood, can give a lot of unexpected information.

A severely depressed patient, although not a personality-disordered one, was referred for CPT. She was completely locked in her depressive thoughts and did not deny that she had thought of suicide at the same time as she refused any medication. There were in her history several stressful events that had occurred to her during the past years. In particular, she and her husband had become the adoptive parents of two small children within a very short time-frame and their life had completely changed. Also, there was the prospect of having to attend an important celebration that she could not avoid. The patient's negative thoughts revolved almost exclusively around having been badly treated by her mother as a child. She repeatedly maintained that she had been unjustly treated in comparison with her siblings. She had a grudge against her mother and siblings and it was almost impossible to get anything else out of her. An interview with her mother revealed an ordinary woman in upper middle-age, who was very concerned about the daughter's present condition and about her accusations. She sincerely tried to ransack her memory but could not recall anything that could support the daughter's allegations.

First when the patient was asked to bring photographs from her childhood and her youth, it became possible to make a more appropriate reconstruction of the patient's past and of her real problems. In the first place, there was nothing in the several photographs that could support the patient's distorted memories. In every picture in the album, there was the image of a happy little girl engaged in all sorts of thrilling situations which had been caught by the parents' camera. However, when a photograph from the patient's confirmation day appeared in the album, the image of a despondent and seemingly depressed girl in a group of happy young people could be seen looking into the camera. It was the patient. With the help of this picture, it was possible to reconstruct that the patient's depression had already begun when she was in her teens and that she had suffered from recurrent depressive episodes while at high school. It was also revealed that the patient had not started her periods spontaneously, but only when treated with hormones. She had stopped her medication because she was afraid of becoming pregnant, with the result that she had a few pregnancies which all ended with miscarriages. After this reconstruction, the therapy went smoothly. The patient became aware of her distortions and of her maladaptive dysfunctional view of self and others. She resumed her hormone medication and was able to be discharged after a few weeks, completely free from her depression.

In this example, access to photographs had the function of checking on the accuracy of recollections of past family events (Meloche, 1973). In a similar way, access to photographs might allow for the reconstruction of events or situations which otherwise would pass undetected. This is particularly the case when the patient omits to report facts or past experiences which to him/her seem irrelevant. The following case vignette might serve as an illustration of this process:

A personality-disordered patient of the paranoid type had been repeatedly subjected to insults and rejection by members of his family. This was something he could not speak about, partly because he felt ashamed, but mostly because he was sufficiently used to such treatment to regard it as an ordinary occurrence. His paranoid ideas, which were focused on his workmates, concealed a very strong restrained wrath following all the adverse events he had had to suffer previously in life and from which he had been unable to defend himself. With the help of photographs from his childhood it was possible to trigger memories from that period that could be worked through in therapy. In one of these pictures the patient, aged 5, was sitting between an older pair on a sofa in the family's parlour. At one corner of the sofa there is a young woman looking with tenderness at a small blond child on her knees. The patient seems to glance enviously at the woman and the child. The picture reproduces a visit from some neighbours (the older pair). The young woman with the child is the patient's mother with his younger brother.

The patient admitted that there had been a strong rivalry between him and his brother when they were growing up and that the parents had had to watch him to avoid him damaging his little brother. During their youth the brothers had feuded with each other. These negative feelings were evident in another photograph, in which the patient was watching a dog that he regarded as belonging to him, while the brother attempted to attract it to himself. The hostility towards the brother was still lasting. It became a main topic during the therapy. The opening given by the photographs allowed a focus on the patient's real problems, whereas the patient's paranoid ideas concerning his workmates were relegated to the background and, eventually, faded out completely.

Space constraints do not allow for a more thorough discussion of the different ways in which photographs can be used to further the progress of therapy, e.g. their use with patients who have been abused in childhood (Berman, 1993; Perris C, 1996; Perris & Perris, 1998); to establish rapport with elderly patients (Gerace, 1989); or to promote change through feedback and self-confrontation (Hunsberger, 1984). I expect, however, that the few examples reported above may suffice to give an idea about the powerful dynamics concealed in this technique.

Dreams and Fables

Even though it was just the analysis of the content of dreams of depressed patients that prompted Beck (1967, 1971; Beck & Ward, 1961) to develop cognitive therapy, the use of dreams is with a few exceptions (e.g. Freeman, 1981; Perris, 1986/96; Perris & Perris, 1998) seldom mentioned in CPT textbooks among the useful CPT strategies.

Metaphors, dreams and fables can be said to belong to a similar kind of strategy. The patient undoubtedly tells something about him/herself in reporting his/her dreams when the therapist is able to listen. The therapist in turn, as shown earlier in this chapter, can convey important information to the patient with the help of metaphors or by relating some dream reported from some other person. Another strategy is to tell some *ad hoc* fable that bears some relation to the patient's current problems.

It happens quite often that by using such strategies, a process is set in move that can lead to radical changes in a patient's condition.

The Use of Dreams

Many patients maintain that they never dream. When one such patient eventually reports that he has started dreaming, it is often because he has begun to experience feelings which were unknown to him.

Recurrent dreams most often reveal a current dilemma that the patient is unable to solve. Such a dilemma can have as its object some real worry for something that might happen, or it can also reflect more diffuse anxiety coupled to feelings of unworthiness, or of being caught in some relationship, or to fear of rejection. Becoming a parent, for example, might induce such a diffuse anxiety in someone who feels in need of being cared for and who must instead act as a *secure base* for someone else who is in a higher need of care to survive. If the person who feels anxious is unable to deal with this experience, there is a risk that such deeply rooted anxiety will become bound to some secondary external problem that the person unsuccessfully attempts to solve. As a therapist, there is also the risk of "going astray", focusing exclusively on the presented symptomatology without becoming aware of what might lie behind the symptoms. It is in instances of this kind that the use of dreams can be a signpost of where the patient's dilemma has to be sought. In agreement with other authors (e.g. Freeman, 1981), dreams do not need to be interpreted. They can be understood in thematic rather than symbolic terms. Moreover, the patient, most often, well knows what the dream is about.

The content of a dream can be used in therapy as a metaphor in a similar way as when using TAT tables. The patient, for example, can be asked to "continue his/her dream" when awake during the session. A question of the type, "How would you have liked that dream to continued if you had dreamed further?" can prompt the patient's inner thoughts.

The report of dreams can, also, give some information on the progress of therapy. The following case vignette is an illustration:

A patient with diffuse psychopathological manifestations, mostly characterized by generalized anxiety, and who had been in therapy for a long time without any improvement, was referred for cognitive psychotherapy. The patient was a freelance professional artist. He took each day has it came, devoting himself to philosophic speculation at a higher level of abstraction. When he started CPT he suddenly found himself in a situation in which he was expected to collaborate actively in a setting characterized by structure, problem-formulation, goal direction and a lot of pedagogic elements. Also, he was expected to deal with down-to-hearth problems in his very chaotic present life. Despite some doubts, he was prepared to give it a trial. After five trial sessions he was asked whether he felt any advantage with the treatment and whether he wanted to continue. His answer was that he willingly wanted to continue. To the precise question about what he felt he was getting from the treatment, he could only give a vague answer. He maintained that his previous experience had been that everything conspired against him and that he could not help it. Now, instead, he felt that he himself could decide what he wanted. At the next session the patient wanted to report on a remarkable dream that he had had.

It was summertime and he was in the middle of a meadow. He happened to open his mouth, when suddenly a swarm of bees appeared in his mouth, taking possession of his head. He became terribly afraid, then he happened to see an "instructor" nearby, holding an anatomical chart which showed what was going on in the patient's head. The "instructor" related what would happen, what the bees were doing, etc. The patient felt shaken, but when he realized that the "instructor" is calm and seems to have control over the situation he felt reassured. He discovered, also, that there was, also, a double present: the "other" as a shadow of himself, obliquely to one side.

The therapist received the message conveyed by the dream without interpreting it. Instead, she used its metaphorical language both on that occasion, and later on during the course of therapy whenever the patient was "assaulted by a swarm" in his real life. The patient in a double image can be seen as a metaphor of the therapeutic relationship, within which the therapist helps the adult in taking care of the child (the "instructor" instructs the one, while the "other" watches and learns).

The Use of Fables

Stories, fairy tales, myths and fables are tools of folk therapy, with which people helped themselves long before the development of psychotherapy. Within the psychoanalytic tradition (e.g., Bettelheim, 1975), telling fables and other tales is one powerful tool in the practice of strategic therapy as developed by Milton Erickson (Gordon, 1978; Rosen, 1982). Fairy tales or fables can be therapeutic because they help the patient in finding his/her own solutions through contemplating what the story seems to imply about him/her and his/her innermost problems at this moment in his life. Also, appropriate fables may metaphorically convey solutions to problems that the patient thinks are unsolvable. Comprehension of those problems and of their possible solution can be fostered by the verbal image. Peseschkian (1986) suggests that, since fables are free from the direct world of the patient's experience, they do not trigger his/her resistance to the uncovering of his/her weakness, and can help him/her in developing a new attitude to his/her problems.

Flexibility in therapy involves tailoring interventions to the therapist's current understanding of the patient. Elsewhere (Perris & Perris, 1997), I have emphasized that most patients with a personality disorder have the experience of not having been seen, of having been unwanted or rejected. It has been difficult for them to follow some direction in life, and this has made them afraid. Feelings such as frustration, anger, rejection and shame related to those experiences have been screened off. Remaining is only a self-image of being unwanted, unlovable, of being someone to despise.

Amongst other things, therapeutic work with such patients obviously has to aim at helping them to become aware of painful feelings they have screened off. The patient, now an adult, has to be helped to understand that the inner working models he has developed as a child are largely depending upon a child's egocentric perspective. First, then, a purposeful grieving can begin. Fables constructed *ad hoc* for this purpose have to include themes which touch on the exposed position one has had as a child if they are expected to be a source of relief and a stimulus to development.

In the following section, and as a conclusion for this chapter, I would like to relate an *ad hoc* fable that was written for a severely anorectic girl in treatment with CPT. She presented, also, a marked aggressive and acting-out behaviour which made it impossible for her to establish any meaningful interpersonal relationship.

A Fable for Carin: "The Little Baby Dragon"

Once upon a time, there was a little baby dragon who lived all alone and abandoned in a desolate cave, high up on a mountain on a desert island far out at sea. In the country on the other side of the sea, people had heard of the lonely, abandoned baby dragon in the desolate cave on the desert island out at sea. There were many rumours about it—about how it got there—but no-one know for sure. According to one rumour, its mother had given birth to it on the beach, but it was so weak and puny that the mother was convinced that it was not going to survive, hence she had left it there to die. Despite its smallness, however, the baby dragon had a very strong will to live. So, when it had gathered some strength and the mother dragon had disappeared back into the sea again, it had started the difficult climb up the steep and slippery rocks, not knowing where it was heading, but instinctively aware that the sea, to which it really wanted to go, could crush it.

After many days and nights filled with all kinds of dangers and without any food but a little grass that grew here and there amongst the rocks, the little baby dragon had finally managed to reach the top. There it had found an uninhabited cave, so small that it would soon outgrow it. For despite the lack of food, the little baby dragon gradually grew bigger. People said that other baby dragons which had been abandoned had lived in that very cave earlier, but no-one knew how they got there or how they got away.

It was said that many attempts had been made to rescue the little baby dragon but none had been successful. Some of those who tried had died in storms and tempests on the great sea that surrounded the island. The few expeditions that had managed to land on the island, and had even climbed half-way up the cliffs, had been forced to turn back because they could not stand the pain of the venom which the little baby dragon, entrenched in its cave, sprayed over them. Neither had anyone succeeded in speaking to the little baby dragon, since the only language it understood was the one it had thought out for itself in its loneliness. Thus, people had tried various strategies to get the little baby dragon to understand that they only wanted to help. Some of these had even involved forcing the little dragon to leave its cave so that they could capture it. They had, for example, thrown a rope round its neck when it had put its head out of the cave, but no rope was strong enough to hold it. The more people tried to force it to come out, the deeper the baby dragon withdrew into its cave.

Someone had the idea that instead of forcing it out of the cave, they should lure it out. To this end, they sought advice from all kinds of experts who knew what dragons liked to eat, and prepared a meal that they were sure the baby dragon would be unable to resist. And it worked, at least partly. When the aroma of the delicious meal reached the little baby dragon through the opening of the cave, where it lay feeling scared and lonely, unaware that it could be anywhere else, it felt an almost irresistible urge to approach the food that had been laid out to satisfy its enormous hunger. But something—it didn't know what it was—stopped it.

Not until much later, when it had been rescued from its cave, did the little baby dragon realise that what it had been afraid of was that, if it ate the good food, it would risk getting so big that there would no longer be room for it in its little cave, which was its sole protection from the dangers that lurked outside. The little baby dragon did not yet understand that once it grew big, all the dangers that it knew about and feared would become less threatening than they were when it was little and cowed.

The little dragon had never experienced the feeling which a baby dragon gets from cuddling up to a big mummy dragon, with its tummy full of rich and nourishing mother's milk. Then it would have been able to go to sleep without any trouble even in the open, with the sound of the sea in its ears, and all the threatening dangers around it, knowing beyond doubt that its mother was all-powerful.

Thus, time after time, people had tried to rescue the little dragon from its imprisonment in the narrow cave high up on the mountain on the desert island far out to sea.

People probably did not give up because they could not accept that life could let an innocent creature like a little baby dragon meet such a tragic fate. If someone did not find a way to save the baby dragon, it would be forced to live a very monotonous and isolated life in the cave, with the constant threat hanging over it of not knowing where it could go if the cave got too small. Yes, people wept and wailed over the fate that awaited the little baby dragon if they failed to find a way to gain its confidence. It would never live among the others on the far side of the sea where there were riches and life was full of possibilities. They knew that once the little baby dragon had arrived there and learned the language that they spoke, thousands of wonderful changes would present themselves.

But everything seemed hopeless!

But then something happened. Early one morning, no-one really knew how, but someone had seen it. . . . An incredible beast rose slowly out of the sea and climbed up onto the beach of the desert island. They did not really know what kind of beast it was. No-one had ever seen anything like it before. It looked like a terrifying monster—huge and mighty—but at the same time it was attractive in its appearance.

As it left the sea it had turned round and people had noticed its big, soft eyes. Its fur was long and soft as silk and glistened red in the early dawn. Its great paws left deep imprints in the windswept sand when, with heavy, determined steps, it began its journey up to the top of the mountain. For the whole day the unknown creature made its way over sharp rocks and sudden water-filled ravines, but as early as dusk of the first day it had reached its goal. Without hesitating it got the little baby dragon out of its cave, held it to its bosom and lay down to wait for morning.

Never in its life had the little baby dragon felt anything like this. Paralysed by fear mixed with an undefined hope it had not tried to defend itself as it usually had done before. Now, all of a sudden, it found itself completely enveloped in the softness of the great creature's fur. Large, mild eyes that watched it steadily spoke a language that the little baby dragon understood without any difficulty.

Its whole body vibrated when the long fear and terror slowly released their grip. In their place came sensations that reminded it of burbling streams that surged through every fibre of its tense and dried-up body. In the enormous lap of the great creature, the baby dragon drank its first drop of the life-giving nourishment that it had not thus far been allowed.

Worn out with exultation, the little baby dragon finally fell asleep, tucked into the great creature's fur, to the beat of its big, warm heart . . . and when the new day came, the little baby dragon saw that the cave it had lived in was nothing more than a fragile clam's shell, already beginning to disintegrate . . . "Thank you for coming in the end", said the little baby dragon to the creature, in whose shining eyes it could see mirrored something it liked very much.

REFERENCES

Alford, B. & Beck, A.T. (1997). *The Integrative Power of Cognitive Therapy*. New York: Guilford.

Arnkoff, D.B. (1981). Flexibility in practicing cognitive therapy. In G. Gamery, S.D. Hollon & R.C. Bedrosian (eds), *New Directions in Cognitive Therapy*. New York: Guilford, pp. 203–223.

Beck, A.T. (1967). *Depression: Clinical, Experimental and Theoretical Aspects.* New York: Hoeber.

Beck, A.T. (1971). Cognitive patterns in dreams and daydreams. In J.H. Masserman (ed.), *Science and Psychoanalysis*, Vol. XIX. New York: Grune & Stratton, pp. 2–7.

Beck, A.T. (1976). *Cognitive Therapy and the Emotional Disorders.* New York: International Universities Press.

Beck, A.T. & Ward, C.H. (1961). Dreams of depressed patients. *Archives of General Psychiatry*, **5**, 462–467.

Beck, A.T., Rush, A.J., Shaw, B.F. & Emery, G. (1979). *Cognitive Therapy of Depression.* New York: Guilford.

Berman, L. (1993). *Beyond the Smile: the Therapeutic Use of Photograph.* London: Routledge.

Bettelheim, B. (1975). *The Uses of Enchantment. The Meaning and Importance of Fairy Tales.* New York: Vintage Books.

Bowlby, J. (1969–1980). *Attachment and Loss*, Vols 1–3. London: Hogarth.

Bowlby, J. (1988). *A Secure Base.* London: Routledge.

Crittenden, P.M. (1994). Peering into the black box: an exploratory treatise on the development of self in young children. *Rochester Symposium on Developmental Psychology*, **5**, 79–148.

Freeman, A. (1981). Dreams and images in cognitive therapy. In G. Emery, S.D. Hollon & R.C. Bedrosian (eds), *New Directions in Cognitive Therapy*. New York: Guilford, pp. 224–238.

Gerace, L.M. (1989). Using family photographs to explore life cycle changes. *Nursing and Health Care*, **10**, 245–249.

Glass, R. & Arnkoff, D.B. (1982). Think cognitively: selected issues in cognitive assessment and therapy. In P.C. Kendall (ed.), Advances in *Cognitive-behavioral Research and Therapy*, Vol. 1. New York: Academic Press, pp. 36–75.

Gordon, D. (1978). *Therapeutic Metaphors.* Cupertino, CA: Meta Publications.

Guidano, V.F. (1987). *Complexity of the Self.* New York: Guilford.

Hunsberger, P. (1984). Uses of instant print photography in psychotherapy. *Professional Psychology: Research and Practice*, **15**, 884–890.

Meloche, M. (1973). Utilisation de l'album de photos dans l'évaluation clinique. *La Vie Medicale au Canada Francaise*, **2**, 865–870.

Morgan, C.D. & Murray, H.A. (1935). A method for investigating phantasies. *Archives of Neurology & Psychiatry*, **34**, 289–306.

Perris, H. (1985). The use of experiential diaries in the cognitive therapy of uncommunicative patients. Paper presented at the 13th International Congress of Psychotherapy, Opatija, Yougoslavia, October 6–13.

Perris, C. (1986/96). *Kognitiv terapi i teori och praktik*, 3rd edn. Stockholm: Natur och Kultur.

Perris, C. (1996). Sindromi dissociative. In B.G. Bara (ed.), *Manuale di psicoterapia cognitiva.* Torino: Bollati-Boringhieri, pp. 685–739.

Perris, C. & Perris, H. (1998). *Personlighetsstörningar. Uppkomst och behandling ur ett utvecklingspsykopatologiskt perspektiv.* Stockholm: Natur och Kultur.

Peseschkian, N. (1986). *Oriental Stories as Tools in Psychotherapy.* Heidelberg: Springer-Verlag.

Rosen, S. (ed.) (1982). *My Voice Will Go with You. The Teaching Tales of Milton H. Erickson.* New York: Norton.

Chapter 18

Metacognition and Motivational Systems in Psychotherapy: A Cognitive–Evolutionary Approach to the Treatment of Difficult Patients

Giovanni Liotti and Bruno Intreccialagli
SITCC, Rome, Italy

Some patients are difficult to treat in individual psychotherapy because of their defective metacognitive capacity. Metacognition may be broadly defined as the ability to monitor one's thoughts and emotional experiences, and to reflect about them (i.e. as thinking about thinking; for a more formal definition of metacognition, see Eysenck, 1990).

Serious deficits in metacognitive capacity—coupled with high mutability of mood and attitudes as well as with dramatically instable interpersonal styles—are typical of the dissociative identity disorder (also known as multiple personality disorder, MPD) and of the borderline personality disorder (BPD), as Fonagy (1991, 1995) and Liotti (1994) have discussed. According to many clinicians and theorists (e.g. Ross, 1989), these conditions constitute a psychopathological continuum, sometimes referred to as the "borderline continuum". They constitute a continuum because they share some fundamental clinical features and the underlying psychological processes of dissociation (Buck, 1983; Fink & Galinkoff, 1990; Horevitz & Braun, 1984; Ross, 1989). They share also aetiological roots. BPD and MPD have been both interpreted as chronic post-traumatic stress disorders

Cognitive Psychotherapy of Psychotic and Personality Disorders: Handbook of Theory and Practice.
Edited by C. Perris and P.D. McGorry.
© 1998 John Wiley & Sons Ltd.

(Gunderson & Sabo, 1993; Ross, 1989). Both may be rooted in an early disorganization of attachment behaviour (Cotugno & Benedetto, 1995; Fonagy, 1995; Liotti, 1992).

A defective metacognitive capacity, i.e. a deficit in the capacity to monitor and reflect on one's own thoughts, is particularly troublesome for the process of cognitive therapy. The ability to monitor one's thoughts and feelings is the necessary prerequisite of the classic cognitive techniques. When treating patients in the borderline continuum, therefore, cognitive therapists are often confronted with the need to correct the impairment in the metacognitive processes, before they can try to help patients correct irrational beliefs, dysfunctional cognitions or pathogenic basic assumptions.

This chapter describes a way of using the therapeutic relationship in order to foster metacognitive capacities. The theoretical rationale for aiming at cognitive and metacognitive changes through interpersonal experiences is expressed by many developmental studies of cognitive and metacognitive processes in interpersonal contexts. Attachment theory and research have been particularly concerned with the interrelationships of cognitive, emotional and interpersonal processes in personality development (Bowlby, 1985, 1988; Fonagy, 1995; Fonagy et al., 1995; Liotti, 1994). Guidano & Liotti (1983), Gilbert (1989, 1992) and Safran & Segal (1990) have studied, in clinical and theoretical contexts, the possibility of weaving together evolutionary epistemology, cognitive-developmental perspectives, interpersonal approaches, and therapeutic strategies. All these studies contribute to the theoretical underpinnings of our approach to the analysis of the therapeutic relationship.

THEORETICAL UNDERPINNINGS

The concept of "interpersonal motivational system" is the hardcore of our theoretical underpinnings.

Evolutionary and ethological considerations strongly support the hypothesis that humans have multiple inborn algorithms for the processing of socio-emotional information (Cosmides, 1989). Human beings, in other words, are endowed with the innate disposition to engage in a few basic forms of interpersonal interaction (Gilbert, 1989, 1992). Innate dispositions give way, as a function of learning in interpersonal contexts, to complex control systems, each of which regulates a particular domain of interpersonal behaviour. The development of simple innate relational dispositions into complex, goal-corrected behavioral control systems has been masterfully illustrated, in the case of the attachment system, by Bowlby (1982, 1988). The innately-based control systems are goal-corrected, in the sense that each of them orientates behaviour toward a particular interpersonal goal (protective proximity of a potential caregiver, sexual mating, high social rank, cooperation in the prospect of shared advantages) through cybernetic principles of feed-back and feed-forward. Since the interpersonal behavioural systems are defined by their goal, it is useful to conceive them as interpersonal *motivational* systems.

Ethological observation, evolutionary considerations and across-species comparison concur in identifying at least five distinct interpersonal motivational systems (Gilbert, 1989):

1. *The attachment system* (activated by global feelings of vulnerability, and aiming at the achievement and maintenance of proximity to a caregiver).
2. *The caregiving system* (activated by emotional signals of distress emitted by a well-known member of one's social group or family, and aiming at reducing such distress).
3. *The agonistic or competitive system* (aimed at defining social ranks of reciprocal dominance and submission, it implies various sub-routines: ritualized aggression, yielding, withdrawal, dominance).
4. *The sexual mating system.*
5. *The cooperative system* (this implies the ability to cooperate, on equal grounds, toward the achievement of a shared goal; social play may be the precursor of cooperative behaviour in both philogenesis and ontogenesis).

For a cognitive psychotherapist, it is particularly interesting to consider that the cooperative system implies a way of constructing the self and other people on equal grounds, whilst the attachment, caregiving and agonistic systems imply asymmetrical interpersonal schemas. The self, when the caregiving system is operative, is constructed as stronger or wiser than the other person, and willing to provide help, while the other is perceived as vulnerable. The attachment system conveys a view of the self as weak or endangered. The agonistic system, in its yielding sub-routine, facilitates a cognitive construction of the self as subjugated, defective or even menial, whilst in its dominance sub-routine induces a view of the self as basically powerful and proud.

Interpersonal life may be conceived as governed by the sequential operation of the five motivational systems. Each system, when the appropriate interpersonal context activates it, substitutes for another in controlling thoughts, feelings and behaviour. The shift from a given motivational system to another one is regulated by:

1. *Inner needs* (e.g. rising levels of sexual hormones facilitate the shift from any other motivational system to the sexual system).
2. *Environmental contingencies* (e.g. the evaluation that a given environmental resource is available in limited amounts facilitates the activation of the agonistic system; the perception of environmental dangers activates the attachment system).
3. *Emotions expressed by other people* (e.g. a child's tears activate the parent's caregiving system).

Each interpersonal motivational system comprises an inborn component (a set of innate rules attributing meaning to socio-emotional signals, and value to particular interpersonal goals) and a learned one (cognitive schemas summarizing past experiences in the exercise of that system, and shaping expectations as to the likelihood of success in the strivings for the system's goal). Bowlby (1982, 1988) called the learned component of an interpersonal motivational system an "internal working model". Safran & Segal (1990), in order to emphasize its being a cognitive structure concerned with the representation of self and other people, call it an "interpersonal schema". Interpersonal schemas variously articulate and develop the basic way of constructing the self and other people that are coordinated by the different interpersonal motivational systems. For instance, the schemas developed on the basis of a secure attachment convey a view of the self as both vulnerable and trusting when the careseeking system is active. The vulnerability of the self, in other words, is regarded as transient and above all not undermining basic trust in self and other people when self-knowledge has been constructed on the basis of positive attachment relationships. The schemas of an insecure attachment, on the contrary, may induce a representation of the self as unworthy of help and of the potential caregiver as intrusive, threatening or rejecting (Bowlby, 1988; Guidano & Liotti, 1983).

The innate algorithms constituting the foundation of the interpersonal motivational systems process, at the beginning of human life, only *procedural* (implicit, non-verbal) knowledge (see Eysenck, 1990, for the definition of procedural and declarative knowledge). The processing of procedural knowledge takes place mainly at the unconscious or preconscious level of mental operations. Emotions—as Bowlby (1982) has convincingly argued—are often the first phase of the processing of procedural information, governed by an inborn algorithm, which becomes conscious.

The development of internal working models, usually starting from the second year of life, allows for the processing also of *declarative* (explicit or propositional) knowledge within the operations of an interpersonal motivational system (declarative knowledge is to be further studied in the two categories of semantic and episodic, or autobiographical knowledge: see Eysenck, 1990).

The smooth development of declarative knowledge ("knowing that") on the basis and in relation to the corresponding procedural knowledge ("knowing how", which comprises the innate capacity of attributing value and meaning to basic interpersonal emotions) is likely to be the condition for the growth of metacognitive capacities.

There is a possibility that the types and contents of declarative knowledge implied in the operations of a mature interpersonal system are at strong variance with the original structure and meaning of the system's procedural knowledge (see Bowlby, 1985; Gilbert, 1989, 1992; Liotti, 1991). If interpersonal experiences produce such a dissociation between the procedural and the declarative aspects of a motivational system's cognitive processing, then it is likely that the system will become dysfunctional. Interpersonal difficulties, then, can be analysed in terms of the cognitive abnormalities characterizing the operations of the various interpersonal motivational systems.

One of the chief, negative developmental outcomes of an interpersonal system's dysfunction can be the impairment of metacognitive monitoring in the meaning domain of that system. One's own interpersonal attitudes, emotional experiences and motives, as well as those of people one is interacting with, then become topics on which it is difficult or impossible to reflect.

Empirical findings (Fonagy, 1995), clinical observations and theoretical reflections (Liotti, 1994) converge in indicating that secure attachment in childhood, and cooperative relationships later on, are the ideal interpersonal background for developing high metacognitive capacities. Since metacognitive development is related to the functioning of the interpersonal motivational systems, it is in principle possible to foster a patient's metacognitive capacities through the shaping of a proper therapeutic relationship. The following clinical case illustrates such a process.

CASE DESCRIPTION

Silvia Q, a 30 year-old single woman, was referred to one of us (B.I.) by her former psychiatrist. The referring psychiatrist reported the following:

Silvia is the younger of three sisters. Their father died 15 years ago. Silvia had scarcely met him since she was 4 years old. At that time, Silvia's parents went through a conflictual conjugal separation, motivated by the father's emotional difficulties (a psychotic breakdown could be inferred). Silvia's mother, having to earn a living, was forced to leave her daughters in the care of the maternal grandparents. To grow up in such a home environment seemed to foster the three girls' wishes for autonomy. When about 20, each of the three sisters got a job and was able to live on her own.

Silvia was offered employment by an international business firm on the basis that her excellent knowledge of a foreign language allowed her to work abroad for a while. This she did successfully. At the age of 27, Silvia reached such a level of expertise in her work that she was called back to Italy by the main branch of her firm. Her mother retired at about the same time. Silvia and her mother decided to live together. Shortly thereafter, Silvia fell in love with Giulio, a 35 year-old bachelor still living with his widowed mother.

In this interpersonal context—living with her mother, which was quite new, and beginning a relationship with Giulio—Silvia fell emotionally ill. She became dysphoric, was verbally aggressive toward her mother, and grew morbidly jealous of Giulio. Then at times she became incoherent in her speech and thought, and occasionally uttered the ungrounded suspicion that people at work might be covertly hostile to her. She also felt that the numbers and numerals she met with in her daily life (phone numbers, street numbers, number-plates, totals in bills, numerals printed in clothes and shoes) could have concealed meanings. She yielded to the compulsion of ruminating for hours on the fancied cabbalistic connections of these numbers. At times, Silvia looked deeply absorbed in her thoughts, as if she was in a trance: she was then unable, even for as long as 1 hour, to respond to her mother's, her sisters' or Giulio's invitations to pay attention to outside reality. Abrupt changes of mood and attitudes were also noticed by Silvia's relatives.

Not surprisingly, her work performance, which had been so good for over 7 years, began to deteriorate, and Silvia received negative evaluations from her boss. As a consequence, she voiced the idea of quitting her job. This prospect alarmed her mother, who insisted that Silvia consulted a psychiatrist. Silvia reacted with fear and expressed distrust in the possibility that psychiatry could help her. She eventually agreed, however, to meet a psychiatrist for a joint interview together with her mother. In this way an attempt at helping Silvia through conjoint family therapy could begin. Two years of conjoint sessions, however, did not yield significant benefits. The only positive result of the family sessions was Silvia's new acceptance of individual psychotherapy.

In the two years of treatment, various psychotropic drugs were prescribed. Although Silvia's compliance with the drugs had been far from satisfactory, it had been possible to assess that neither antidepressant nor neuroleptic drugs, either alone or in combination, could significantly reduce Silvia's ailments.

As far as the diagnosis is concerned, the referring psychiatrist hypothesized first a schizophrenic disorder, then a borderline syndrome with severe dissociative symptoms. However, since Silvia sometimes expressed the vague feeling that a concealed will or personality, somehow related to her inner world but separated from her self, was competing with her own will in determining her choices and the direction of her own thoughts, the diagnosis of a dissociative identity disorder (formerly called multiple personality disorder: see American Psychiatric Association, 1994) could not be ruled out.

The First Phase of the Treatment

When Silvia Q sat for the first time in front of her new psychotherapist, it soon became evident that her cooperative motivational system was difficult to access. Silvia moved her chair to about 1 metre from the therapist's desk, and started to talk hesitantly, with her gaze at times fixed in the middle distance, at times instead inexpressively fixed on the therapist's face. She soon stated her sceptical attitude toward psychotherapy. However, when the therapist suggested that he and Silvia could try jointly to identify an area of her experience that both of them could regard as worthy of exploration, Silvia did not refuse the suggestion. After a brief pause of reflection, she replied: "I would like to know why I am so jealous of my boy-friend".

At the end of the first session, the therapist had reason to believe that Silvia could, at least for a moment, conceive herself and the therapist as people sharing a common goal and engaged in a common enterprise (exploring the meaning of her jealousy). This observation, whilst it suggested that the prospect of establishing a therapeutic alliance was not a desperate one, did not imply that the cooperative system could stably motivate their interpersonal behaviour and guide Silvia's interpersonal cognition. Rather, Silvia's psychopathological problems, and her behaviour during most of the first session, clearly suggested that a motivational system implying asymmetrical interpersonal schemas (i.e. either the attachment or the agonistic system) would govern Silvia's future attitude toward the therapist.

In the following sessions, Silvia continued to move her chair away from the desk. The therapist had the impression that she was frankly afraid of meeting him and talking to him. Her gaze expressed fear, her voice was trembling, her words few, fragmented, incoherent. She seemed unable to concentrate her attention on the topic of her attitudes toward Giulio, or on any other topic, for more than a few minutes. Her ability to report on emotions and thoughts, not to mention her capacity to reflect on them (metacognition), was almost nil. Confusedly, she turned time and again to the idea that a sort of hidden, malevolent will—she was not clear on whether she regarded it as extraneous or as somehow connected to her inner world—was threatening her work and her love relationship. Maybe— sometimes she whispered with a trance-like expression on her face—the concealed meaning of numbers and numerals could reveal the intentions of this malignant will.

Paying close attention both to his own emotions, evoked by Silvia's behaviour in the session, and to Silvia's interpersonal attitudes in the therapeutic relationship (in a way much alike to the one suggested by Safran & Segal, 1990), the therapist was able to hypothesize that the attachment motivational system was guiding his patient's behaviour in the therapeutic relationship. Silvia's interpersonal (non-verbal) behaviour was such as to make her therapist feel protective (rather than cooperative, annoyed, dominant, or seductive) toward her. Since emotions expressed as a function of a person's attachment system tend to activate the caregiving motivational system in his/her partner, the therapist's protective feelings were a hint that the attachment system was regulating Silvia's behaviour in the therapeutic relationship. Moreover, the expressive quality of Silvia's fear in the therapeutic relationship was more suggestive of the type of fear characterizing disorganized–disorientated attachment (Main & Hesse, 1990; Liotti, 1992, 1995) than of the type of fear that might be expressed in competitive interactions (i.e. interactions motivated by the agonistic system, and aimed at defining ranks of dominance or power in the relationship: Gilbert, 1989, 1992).

A metaphor summarizes the therapist's impressions and hypotheses concerning the motivational systems governing Silvia's behaviour in the therapetic relationship: Silvia acted like a frightened child who hopes to find comfort in a parent's arms, but is also afraid of some obscure threat if she yields to this hope and approaches the attachment figure. This form of fearful attachment in a child has been found by developmentalists to be related to a parent's frightened and/ or frightening attitudes, which in turn are often due to an unresolved mourning process, or to a post-traumatic stress reaction plaguing the parent's emotional life while he/she is taking care of the child (Main & Hesse, 1990; Liotti, 1992). As a consequence of being frightened by the same person who is providing comfort and protection from fear, the child's attachment behaviour becomes disorganized and disoriented. Very likely, the internal working models related to disorganized attachments are multiple, fragmented and dissociated. A predisposition to dissociative reactions may be set in motion by early disorganized–disorientated attachment (Liotti, 1992, 1993, 1995).

Silvia's therapist was aware that an unexamined internal working model of fearful, disorganized attachment may become the basis for a patient unconsciously construing either the self or the attachment figure as threatening, frightening, or evil (Liotti, 1995). If the therapist takes an attitude in the therapeutic relationship such as to foster the activation of the patient's attachment system (e.g. trying explicitly to offer comfort and reassurance), the result could then be, paradoxically, an increase of the patient's fear. On the other hand, if the therapist takes a straightforwardly directive role in the relationship with a frightened patient, he/she could induce the activation of the yielding sub-routine (Gilbert, 1992) of the agonistic system in the patient. This, too, could be counterproductive if the therapist's aim is to reduce the likelihood of the patient's experiencing fear and discomfort in the therapeutic relationship.

On the basis of these assumptions, Silvia's therapist decided to limit himself to listening to his patient's confused discourse with an inner empathic attitude. He did not try to dispute Silvia's beliefs in the concealed operations of a malevolent "will", neither did he explicitly try to reassure and convince her that she had nothing to fear in the therapeutic relationship. He also abstained from explanations, critical comments, or interpretations of any sort. He hoped that Silvia could gradually and spontaneously acknowledge that he was available to *listen* and, whenever possible, to *understand* and *help* her. If the possibility emerged, for Silvia, of construing the therapeutic relationship either as one of secure (instead of fearful and disorganized) attachment, or as a cooperative one, then it could be hoped that the therapeutic relationship would foster the exercise and development of Silvia's metacognitive capacities.

The Second Phase of the Treatment

After 2 months, and nine sessions, Silvia Q gave up the habit of moving her seat from the therapist's desk before starting to speak. During the tenth session, looking more relaxed, for the first time she asked if she could smoke a cigarette. Her therapist did not smoke, and there was no ashtray in the therapy room.

The therapist thought that Silvia's request could mean that she was (consciously or not) testing his way of experiencing the therapeutic relationship. The therapist imagined that something like the following question could be tacitly taking shape in Silvia's thoughts: "Are you so rigidly dominant as to forbid any request of mine that could even slightly annoy you? Are you going to judge me negatively if I show a bit of slightly improper behaviour?" Perhaps, at the deeper (mainly unconscious) level of the inborn algorithms governing the construing of interpersonal events, the attachment system (in Silvia until then functioning according to an internal working model of fearful, disorganized attachment) was giving way to the agonistic system. It was important not to allow Silvia the possibility of construing the therapeutic relationship according to the mentality governed by the agonistic system (i.e. of construing the therapist as overwhelming and the self as either rebellious or subjugated).

The therapist took out an ashtray from his desk drawer and answered: "Yes, you can. I do not smoke, however. If the smoke begins to annoy me, I'll let you know". Silvia lit her cigarette, and started to speak—and then answer to the therapist's comments and questions—in a way that was decidedly more syntonic and coherent than had ever been the case before. Since that tenth session, she has seemed more able to concentrate on the theme that had been selected in the first session as the goal of joint exploration, namely, her jealousy. The therapist thought (and, monitoring his own emotions, also felt) that he was witnessing a major change in the motivational attunement within the therapeutic relationship. From the original alternation of attitudes related to a fearful, disorganized attachment and agonistic attitudes related to issues of dominance and submission, an interpersonal atmosphere created by moments of cooperation and moments of a more secure attachment seemed to emerge. Correspondingly—and in keeping with hypotheses relating the optimal development of metacognitive capacity to secure attachments and to cooperative interactions (Fonagy, 1995; Liotti, 1994)—Silvia's thought processes became more orientated and wider in scope.

Noticing this progress, the therapist thought that his patient could now be ready for an investigation of her own memories. Silvia was still unable to observe her present automatic thoughts, or to relate emotional experiences to her way of construing interpersonal events. Perhaps, however, in the more relaxed atmosphere of the therapeutic relationship, she could apply her limited metacognitive capacity to a reflection on memories of her childhood experiences. The therapist, then, invited Silvia to dwell on her past family interactions: "I would understand your present experiences better if you could tell me something of your past family history". She seemed willing to comply with this invitation. However, whenever Silvia tried to offer information concerning family events, her thought processes again became confused, incoherent, full of logical lapses and time lapses. For instance, Silvia would narrate a given interaction with her mother in such a way as to give the impression that she was reporting a quite recent episode. Then, cues emerged in her narrative which suggested that the episode could actually have happened when Silvia was a child. She seemed either unconcerned with the need to make the time-scale of her reported memories clear to the listener, or unable to orientate herself in such a time scale. As a consequence, the therapist sometimes experienced a trance-like state while trying to make sense of Silvia's narratives. He had to make an intense attentional effort in order to avoid disorientation. He had to ask for dates, periods of the year, names of the persons involved, in order to make sense of Silvia's flow of confused memories. His patient did not seem troubled or annoyed by these questions. Rather, she looked grateful for his requests for clarification. Thanks to the fact that another person was striving to orientate himself in the reconstruction of her past, Silvia seemed to begin to make sense, for the first time, of her own personal memories.

It is important to emphasize that Silvia's therapist, although aware of alternative theoretical approaches that could explain what was happening in the therapeutic process, was committed to the cognitive, developmental and interpersonal model outlined above. He knew that Kohut's self psychology (see e.g. Wolf, 1988) could explain both Silvia's difficulties and her uncertain progress in psychotherapy in terms of empathy, empathic failures, and consequent cohesion or loss of cohesion of the self. He, however, was committed to interpreting the same observations in terms of interpersonal motivational systems active at a given moment, interpersonal cognitive schemas connected to the operations of those motivational systems, and hindrances or facilitations to the exercise and development of metacognitive capacities. His goal, as a consequence of this theoretical orientation, was to maintain the motivational set-up on the register of secure attachment and/or cooperation, and thereupon to facilitate the exercise of his patient's metacognitive capacity. Once Silvia could learn to monitor her own thoughts and feelings metacognitively, the classic techniques of cognitive therapy could eventually be applied.

The Third Phase of the Treatment

In order to maintain the motivational set-up of the therapeutic relationship on the register of secure attachment and cooperation, considerable therapeutic skills had to be exerted. Silvia often betrayed, in the therapeutic relationship, the tendency to motivational shifts from cooperation to dominance-submission and to sexual seductiveness, or from secure attachment to insecure, disorganized attachment. For instance, on one occasion (during the twenty-second session) she asked her therapist not to address her any more as to "Miss Q", but to call her "Silvia". To this, the therapist replied, rather warmly but firmly, that this could be accepted provided that she: (a) was prepared to remember that their relationship was a cooperative and professional one, aimed at the joint goal of clarifying the roots of her jealousy; and (b) was prepared to reciprocate by calling him "Bruno" rather than "Doctor I". To this, Silvia replied that she felt unable to call him "Bruno". Then, the therapist said, it seemed more sensible to refute her request, and to go on with "Miss Q" and "Doctor I": in such a way of addressing each other resided the possibility of constantly remembering that the positive feelings and the mutual appreciation that they both could legitimately experience in their relationship should not make them forget what the main aim of their joint enterprise was.

Also in instances such as the one described above, the therapist was aware of alternative theoretical models that could have guided his responses to Silvia's interpersonal moves. Weiss's theory of psychotherapy (Weiss, 1993) would have suggested that Silvia was unconsciously testing the therapist's capacity to disconfirm one of her irrational, tacitly held, pathogenic beliefs. For instance, Silvia could tacitly (unconsciously) harbour a pathogenic belief of the type: "If I get close to another person and expect his/her acceptance, help and comfort, then he/she will either reject or deservedly downgrade me, and I should accept being downgraded in order not to be rejected". If Silvia's request to be addressed by her first name, and to continue addressing her therapist as "Doctor I", had been accepted, such an irrational belief would have been confirmed, and the unconscious test would not have been passed. To pass the test would, according to Weiss, both reduce Silvia's level of anxiety in the therapeutic relationship and facilitate her conscious access to the previously unconscious irrational belief that had guided her request.

The therapist was sympathetic to Weiss's theory. However, he based his decision not to accept Silvia's proposal on the simpler idea that to resist the motivational shift toward dominance-submission (a patronizing "Doctor I" and an inept "Silvia"), and to foster the operations of the cooperative motivational system, could facilitate his patient's resort to metacognition. The central aim of the therapeutic strategy was to assist the development of Silvia's metacognitive capacities.

Metacognition entails, among other capacities, the ability to monitor the relationships one's thinking processes may establish between a given piece of autobiographic memory (episodic knowledge) and the inner world of generalized meaning structures (semantic structures). In order to foster Silvia's metacognitive capacities, and taking into account her difficulty in reporting childhood memories in a meaningful way, the therapist suggested basing the reconstruction of Silvia's memories on a series of old family photographs. (Silvia—perhaps in accordance with Weiss' hypothesis that a search for previously unconscious episodes and meanings may follow the therapist's passing a test—had spontaneously brought and shown the therapist, during the twenty-fourth session, one of these old photographs, portraying Silvia, when 5 years old, with her mother). Episodes of Silvia's childhood could be evoked by each photograph. They could be defined—as to time, place and persons involved—more clearly than Silvia had previously been able to do. Meaning could be attributed or re-attributed to these episodes. Such a simultaneous exercise of episodic memory and semantic knowledge, taking place in an interpersonal atmosphere of cooperation or of secure attachment, could foster the development of Silvia's metacognitive capacities. A similar cognitive approach to the psychotherapeutic problem of how to help a patient to develop the higher integrative functions of memory and consciousness, may stem from Bucci's (1985, 1993) work on the relationships between non-verbal and verbal coding.

Silvia and the therapist spent part of each of the following 50 sessions observing and commenting on two or three of her family photographs, both old and recent. The rest of each session was usually devoted to commenting on Silvia's present relationships with her mother and her boy-friend, Giulio. In the process of examining the photos, Silvia became progressively more clear, concise and coherent in her speech, and better orientated as to time, place and attribution of meaning. Interestingly, during this process she suggested a change in the joint goal of therapy: rather than be concerned mainly with the meaning and causes of her abnormal jealousy, she now wished to know why other people find it so difficult to understand her, why she felt "mixed up" so often, and why such a confusion had come to plague her subjective experience of herself and other people just in that period of her life. This request for a change of the set goal for the therapeutic dialogues was a clear sign of a major growth of Silvia's metacognitive capacities. To be aware of one's own confusion, and to wish to regain a more lucid state of mind, is possible, of course, only when the disorder of the higher integrative functions of consciousness and memory is remitting. Not surprisingly, Silvia's complaints related to feelings of depersonalization diminished drastically.

Silvia's Family History

Ordering the family photographs (there were hundreds of them, portaying uncles, aunts, grandparents, cousins, family friends, besides of course Silvia's parents and sisters) in a clear time sequence, and reflecting on each of the persons portrayed in them on the basis of her therapist's questions and comments, restored the continuity and coherence of Silvia's memory of herself and of meaningful people of her past.

Particular care and time was spent by the therapist in trying to explore Silvia's memories of her father. As will be remembered, the father had left home after a dramatic conjugal quarrel, of which Silvia had only a vague but still frightening memory, when she was aged 4. Thereafter she met him only rarely—allegedly because he was often emotionally or physically very ill—until he died when Silvia was 14. Notwithstanding the care and time the therapist employed in trying to reconstruct Silvia's memories of her father, her comments on the pictures in which he was present remained laconic and emotionally cold, in striking contrast with the flow of emotion-ridden memories often evoked by the pictures of other people. "Here he was still at home"; "Here he was already ill"; "Here we were visiting him . . . I was probably 6 or 7 years old . . . I remember having spent almost all day on his shoulders . . . He used to carry me around like that, since I was the little one"; "Here Giulio, my mother's younger brother, had accompanied the three of us (namely, Silvia and her two sisters) to visit him".

There was, then, another Giulio in Silvia's life, besides her boy-friend. Giulio, the brother of Silvia's mother, was about the same age as Silvia's older sister. He was, for most of the sessions spent examining the photos, the only other person besides Silvia's father who did not evoke emotion-ridden memories, but only rather laconic comments. When about 1 year had elapsed since the beginning of therapy, Silvia casually examined a photo portraying her father when still at home immediately after having dwelled on a recent picture of "Uncle Giulio" (now a young man). Only then did she notice the striking resemblance between the two men. The therapist had already observed the likeness, which was quite surprising for two supposedly unrelated persons as a man and his brother-in-law, but abstained from making a remark about it until Silvia, too, explicitly came to notice it.

For Silvia, to acknowledge the striking resemblance between her father and "uncle Giulio" came as a shock. Not only did "Uncle Giulio" resemble her father: he also resembled Silvia and her sisters, while he did not show any likeness of features with people in the lineage of Silvia's mother. Reflecting on this resemblance, Silvia expressed a sequence of strong emotions—surprise, shame, fear, anger and sadness—while a hypothesis on the reasons for such a likeness of features emerged: Giulio had been born from the secret sexual relationship between Silvia's father and her maternal grandmother.

This hypothesis, which later found confirmation from the dialogues between Silvia and her mother, became the new organizing principle for the reconstruction of the patient's early developmental history. The sexual affair between

Silvia's father and his mother-in-law had been kept secret. The secret was unveiled shortly after Silvia was born, when the resemblance between Giulio (then about 5 years old) and Silvia's father became all too evident. Silvia's mother was obviously deeply distressed by the discovery of the twofold betrayal by her mother and her husband. The emotional turmoil that followed affected all Silvia's caregivers, who were all frightened (and therefore frightening to an infant) by the consequences of the misdeed. Being frightened of all her caregivers, Silvia's early patterns of attachment—to her mother, her father and her grandparents—all became disorganized and disoriented (Main & Hesse, 1990). Disorganized attachment is related to the construction of a multiple internal working model of self and other people (Main, 1991), and is the antecedent of dissociative processes deeply affecting the integrative functions of consciousness and memory (Lichtenberg, Lachman & Fosshage, 1992, pp. 164–168; Liotti, 1992, 1993, 1994, 1995).

Other negative factors then added to the predisposition to dissociate that had been set in motion by the early experience of a disorganized attachment. The prolonged, conflictive process of separation between Silvia's parents offered plenty of occasion for traumatic experiences, to which the young child reacted with the dissociative processes already facilitated by her multiple, incoherent internal working models. The family secret (Giulio being the son of Silvia's father and maternal grandmother) was maintained in the communication between the older family members and the four children (Giulio, Silvia and her sisters). The deeply distorted family communication very probably further hindered Silvia's already threatened integrative functions of consciousness and memory. Silvia's metacognitive capacity, as a consequence, could not develop properly. It is likely that Giulio and the two older sisters, not having experienced disorganization of early attachment (the frightening secret was discovered by Silvia's mother and her maternal grandfather when the other children were already aged 3 or older, while Silvia was just an infant), were relatively less affected with regard to the coherence of internal working models and the development of metacognitive capacities.

The Meaning of Silvia's Symptoms

During the reconstruction of the "family secret", Silvia and her therapist shared the feeling of a cooperative striving toward a common goal: to understand the meaning of the strange and distressing experiences that had started to plague the patient's life shortly after going to live with her mother.

As a result of these reflections, Silvia came to believe that, as soon as she had the opportunity of living with her mother after having spent so many years far apart from her, she *felt* that there was a secret that her mother was keeping concealed from her. However, Silvia was then unable to reflect consciously on this feeling, or intuition. She had, very likely, the semi-conscious intuition that the secret had to do with being unfaithful in a love relationship. The fact that in that very period of her life she was for the first time involved in a sentimental relationship—moreover, with a man who bore the same name, Giulio, as the man she believed to be her uncle and whose birth was part of the secret—created the basis for her abnormal, irrational, ego-dystonic jealousy. Her cabbalistic obsession for the meaning of numbers could have been the result of the semi-conscious intuition that the secret had to do with *dates*: the strange closeness of the dates of birth of her older sister and of "Uncle Giulio", for instance. How come that, after more than 20 years after her mother's birth, her grandparents had decided to have another child? Was it not strange that her maternal grandmother and her mother were pregnant almost at the same time? And what about the unacknowledged resemblance between "Uncle Giulio" and Silvia's father?

All this emotion-ridden and doubt-inducing information, we can now hypothesize, was processed outside Silvia's consciousness (see Dennett, 1991, for a brilliant and up-to-date treatise of the relationships between conscious and unconscious cognitive processes). This information was also shut off from the communication with her mother and other relatives (see Bowlby, 1985, for a discussion of the cognitive-emotional consequences of such distortions in family communication). Therefore, they tended to emerge in Silvia's consciousness and communication only as chaotic, irrational fragments of ideation and affect. Silvia's reduced metacognitive capacities did not allow for a sufficiently critical evaluation of her now very unusual and distressing subjective experience of herself and of significant others. Both her relational and her subjective life began to deteriorate. So, the stage was set for the development of her serious psychiatric disorder.

This process of self-reflection, which took place within the context of a therapeutic relationship that was now both supportive and cooperative, clearly fostered the development of Silvia's metacognitive capacity. The newly developed metacognitive resource allowed for the solution of her relational problems.

The Final Phase of the Treatment

Silvia became able to monitor her thoughts and feelings carefully during and after the often disappointing interactions with her boyfriend Giulio. Thanks to such a metacognitive monitoring, the state of mind that was once globally experienced as "jealousy" revealed itself to be quite a complex one.

Silvia had many quite justified negative thoughts and feelings related to her boyfriend's attitudes. Giulio, who was 35 years old, had never been able to complete his University studies, to find a job or to live on his own (he was still living with his widowed mother, totally depending on her for his financial support). He was egocentric, prone to daydreaming, socially rather withdrawn. When Silvia reflected on these aspects of Giulio's style of life, she often came close to concluding that she would have to finish such an unpromising relationship. She came close to, but did not clearly formulate, such a conclusion in her mind, because as soon as the mental representation of herself leaving Giulio forever began to take form, she felt intense emotions of fear and sadness. After this painful emotional experience, Silvia had fantasies of Giulio being unfaithful to her, deserting her for another woman, or otherwise betraying their love. These fantasies, which actually were just the last ring of a complex chain of thoughts and feelings, were the only mental contents that she had been able to recover from her memory when required to provide reasons for her aggressive behaviour toward Giulio. However, when Silvia became capable of proper metacognitive monitoring, the whole chain of thoughts and feelings became easily retrievable. It then became possible to reflect on why such intense feelings of anguish accompanied the prospect of leaving Giulio.

The final phase of Silvia's treatment mainly consisted in the application of classic cognitive therapy techniques to her catastrophizing way of construing the prospect of separation from a lover or a husband. She was now able to detect automatic thoughts and to reflect critically on the related pathogenic beliefs (e.g. "If I abandon a man who loves me, I'll prove my unworthiness, and nobody will love me in the future").

As a result of this process of revision of irrational beliefs related to the themes of loneliness, Silvia decided to put an end to her unhappy relationship with Giulio. Shortly thereafter, she also decided to live on her own. She had forgiven her mother for having kept the events that led to the divorce, and the real identity of "Uncle Giulio", a secret for so long. However, Silvia now felt that it was impossible to create a trusting relationship with her mother, and that she would appreciate the freedom of living apart from her mother more than she feared the consequent loneliness. She also felt that she had regained her capacity to go on in life without depending on other people's support, and that it was therefore possible to end the therapy. The whole therapeutic process had lasted about $2^{1}/_{2}$ years.

At a follow-up interview, about 1 year after the end of the treatment, Silvia reported her satisfactory adaptation to work, and about a new and much happier sentimental relationship. None of her former symptoms had recurred.

REFERENCES

American Psychiatric Association (1994). *Diagnostic and Statistical Manual of Mental Disorders, 4th edn (DSM-IV)*. Washington, DC: American Psychiatric Association.
Bowlby, J. (1982). *Attachment and Loss, Vol. 1*, 2nd edn. London: Hogarth.
Bowlby, J. (1985). The role of childhood experience in cognitive disturbance. In M.J. Mahoney & A. Freeman (eds), *Cognition and Psychotherapy*. New York: Plenum, pp. 181–200.
Bowlby, J. (1988). *A Secure Base*. London: Routledge.
Bucci, W. (1985). Dual coding: a cognitive model for psychoanalytic research. *Journal of the American Psychoanalytic Association*, **33**, 571–607.
Bucci, W. (1993). The development of emotional meaning in free association: a multiple code theory. In A. Wilson & J.E. Gedo (eds), *Hierarchical Concepts in Psychoanalysis* New York: Guilford, pp. 3–47.

Buck, O.D. (1983).   Multiple personality as a borderline state. *Journal of Nervous and Mental Disease*, **171**, 62–65.

Cosmides, L. (1989).   The logic of social exchange: has natural selection shaped how humans reason? *Cognition*, **31**, 187–276.

Cotugno, A. & Benedetto, A.M. (1995).   *Il paziente borderline* [*The Borderline Patient*]. Milan: Angeli.

Dennett, D.C. (1991).   *Consciousness Explained*. Boston, MA: Little, Brown.

Eysenck, M.W. (1990).   *The Blackwell Dictionary of Cognitive Psychology*. Oxford: Basil Blackwell.

Fink, D. & Galinkoff, M. (1990).   Multiple personality disorder, borderline personality disorder and schizophrenia: a comparative study of clinical features. *Dissociation*, **3**, 127–134.

Fonagy, P. (1991).   Thinking about thinking: some clinical and theoretical considerations concerning the treatment of borderline patients. *International Journal of Psychoanalysis*, **72**, 639–656.

Fonagy, P. (1995).   The influence of attachment on the representational world in the pre-school years. Paper presented at the Conference "Attaccamento: Teoria, ricerca e implicazioni cliniche" [Attachment: Theory, Research and Clinical Applications]. Rome, June 23.

Fonagy, P., Steele, M., Steele, H., Leigh, T. et al. (1995).   The predictive specificity Of the Adult Attachment Interview: implications for psychodynamic theories of normal and pathological development. In S. Goldberg & J. Kerr (eds), *John Bowlby's Attachment Theory: History, Research and Clinical Applications*. Hillsdale, NJ: Analytic Press.

Gilbert, P. (1989).   *Human Nature and Suffering*. London: Erlbaum.

Gilbert, P. (1992).   *Depression: The Evolution of Powerlessness*. New York: Guilford.

Guidano, V.F. & Liotti, G. (1983).   *Cognitive Processes and Emotional Disorders*. New York: Guilford.

Gunderson, J.C. & Sabo, A. (1993).   The phenomenological and conceptual interface between borderline personality disorder and post-traumatic stress disorder. *American Journal of Psychiatry*, **150**, 19–27.

Horevitz, R.P. & Braun, B.G. (1984).   Are multiple personalities borderline? *Psychiatric Clinics of North America*, **7**, 69–87.

Lichtenberg, J., Lachman, F. & Fosshage, J. (1992).   *Self and Motivational Systems: Toward a Theory of Technique*. Hillsdale, NJ: Analytic Press.

Liotti, G. (1991).   Insecure attachment and agoraphobia. In C.M. Parkes, J. Stevenson-Hinde & P. Marris (eds), *Attachment Across the Life Cycle*. London: Routledge.

Liotti, G. (1992).   Disorganized/disoriented attachment in the etiology of the dissociative disoders. *Dissociation*, **5**, 196–204.

Liotti, G. (1993).   Disorganized attachment and dissociative experiences: an illustration of the ethological-developmental approach to cognitive therapy. In K.T. Kuehlvein & H. Rosen (eds), *Cognitive Therapies in Action*. San Francisco, CA: Jossey-Bass, pp. 213–239.

Liotti, G. (1994).   *La dimensione interpersonale della coscienza* [*The Interpersonal Dimension of Consciousness*]. Rome: NIS.

Liotti, G. (1995).   Disorganized attachment in the psychotherapy of the dissociative disorders. In S. Goldberg & J. Kerr (eds), *John Bowlby's Attachment Theory: History, Research and Clinical Applications*. Hillsdale, NJ: Analytic Press.

Main, M. (1991).   Metacognitive knowledge, metacognitive monitoring and singular (coherent) vs. multiple (incoherent) model of attachment. In C.M. Parkes, J. Stevenson-Hinde, P. Marris (eds), *Attachment across the Life Cycle*. London: Routledge.

Main, M. & Hesse, E. (1990).   Parents' unresolved traumatic experiences are related to infant disorganized attachment status: is frightened and/or frightening parental behavior the linking mechanism? In M.T. Greenberg, D. Cicchetti & E.M. Cummings (eds), *Attachment in the Preschool Years*. Chicago: University of Chicago Press, pp. 161–182.

Ross, C. (1989). *Multiple Personality Disorder: Diagnosis, Clinical Features and Treatment*. New York: Wiley.

Safran, J. & Segal, Z. (1990). *Interpersonal Process in Cognitive Therapy*. New York: Basic Books.

Weiss, J. (1993). *How Psychotherapy Works*. New York: Guilford.

Wolf, E.S. (1988). *Treating the Self*. New York: Guilford.

Chapter 19

A Cognitive-behavioural Approach to the Understanding and Management of Obsessive-compulsive Personality Disorder

Michael Kyrios
*Departments of Psychology and Psychiatry,
University of Melbourne, Royal Melbourne Hospital, Parkville,
Victoria, Australia*

INTRODUCTION

Description of Clinical Presentations

Obsessive-compulsive personality disorder (OCPD) is one of the common personality disorders that present in clinical practice, and frequently constitutes a major hurdle to successful treatment of clinical syndromes, although outcome data for its treatment from controlled studies is virtually non-existent. Much debate exists as to the nature of the obsessive-compulsive personality, with a range of definitions, each focusing on particular aspects of the syndrome (Pfohl & Blum, 1991). Furthermore, there is even debate as to the categorical vs. dimensional nature of the syndrome (Nestadt et al., 1991; Pitman & Jenike, 1989; Pollack, 1987), although a nosological approach has been used most commonly in the psychiatric literature. Nonetheless, Nestadt et al. (1994) found that OCPD

Cognitive Psychotherapy of Psychotic and Personality Disorders: Handbook of Theory and Practice.
Edited by C. Perris and P.D. McGorry.
© 1998 John Wiley & Sons Ltd.

was the only DSM-III personality disorder that withstood a confirmatory factor analysis as a single factor. From epidemiological research, a prevalence of 1.7% was found for the DSM-III Compulsive Personality Disorder in a non-patient community sample (Nestadt et al., 1991). DSM-IV (American Psychiatric Association, 1994) cites a prevalence of 1% for OCPD in community samples, and 3–10% in mental health clinic presentations. OCPD has been found more commonly in males, married and working individuals (Nestadt et al., 1991).

Numerous expressions have been used since the mid-1800s to describe the clinical phenomena now termed OCPD and, even to this day, ICD-10 and DSM-IV classification systems use different nomenclature to describe similar patterns of personality dysfunction. One will often encounter the terms "obsessional", "compulsive", "anakast", "anal", "conforming", or "passive-ambivalent" to describe variants of the dysfunctional personality syndrome characterized by rigidity, a preoccupation with perfectionism, excessive personal and moral standards, an inflated concern about matters of control and order, extremes in emotional control and constriction, interpersonal reticence, and indecisiveness "at the expense of flexibility, openness and efficiency" (Pfohl & Blum, 1991). Obsessive-compulsive patterns can be seen to lie on a continuum ranging from normal and adaptive through to pathological and maladaptive, although sociocultural factors may determine what constitutes dysfunction (Pollack, 1987).

Individuals with OCPD often present with Axis I disorders, particularly anxiety disorders, mood syndromes and disorders (most notably, dysthymia, agitated depression and anger), adjustment disorders (particularly during stressful periods requiring a degree of flexibility), somatoform disorders (especially hypochondriasis), dissociative syndromes and, on occasion, brief reactive psychoses and schizophreniform disorders. Clinical and community studies consistently report a distinct relationship between OCPD and both unipolar major depression and anxiety disorders (Alnaes & Torgersen, 1988; Corruble, Ginestet & Guelfi, 1996; Gasperini et al., 1990; Nestadt et al., 1992; Sanderson et al., 1994; Tyrer et al., 1983). With regard to substance abuse, the results are somewhat less consistent. While Nestadt et al. (1992) report a decreased risk for alcohol abuse in a community study of OCPD, Romach et al. (1995) report that 45% of chronic users of alprazolam and lorazepam entering an outpatient discontinuation program were diagnosed with OCPD.

OCPD is not to be confused with obsessive-compulsive disorder (OCD), which was once considered to be a more severe form of the personality syndrome. While estimates of comorbidity between OCPD and OCD vary considerably (Black et al., 1993), comorbidity rates between OCPD and other anxiety or depressive disorders are consistently higher (Corruble, Ginestet & Guelfi, 1996; Nestadt et al., 1992; Sanderson et al., 1994). In fact, Black et al. (1993) concluded that the data do not support a specific relationship between OCD and OCPD. Nonetheless, there are similarities in the characteristics of OCPD and OCD. OCD subjects may exhibit OCPD traits as distinct from the full OCPD criteria, while OCPD subjects may exhibit behavioural and cognitive patterns commonly seen in OCD. Hence, the cognitive-behavioural treatment of OCD may have much to offer in terms of techniques and strategies for the management of OCPD, and *vice versa* (Guidano & Liotti, 1983).

OCPD also commonly presents with other personality disorders and characteristics, most notably avoidant, dependent, paranoid and Type A personality, but also borderline, schizotypal, histrionic, narcissistic disorders and traits. Pfohl (1996) notes that the overlap between OCPD and other personality disorders may occur because other disorders are relatively homogeneous and may contain elements of OCPD. While the actual relationship between OCD, OCPD and other personality disorders remains a contentious research issue, this may not be particularly important from a treatment perspective. Of greater significance, particularly from a cognitive-behavioural perspective, is the identification of cognitive, behavioural, affective and lifestyle issues that require intervention in any particular individual. While a diagnostic label will give some indication of some such relevant therapy issues, there are obvious limitations to taxonomic approaches and the assumption of homogeneity within nosological categories.

In fact, there appears to be a great deal of heterogeneity within the OCPD spectrum. Millon (1996) differentiates eight clinical domains in which the OCPD patient can manifest dysfunction, and which require clinical attention, although various OCPD subtypes may present with specific salient features. Characteristic patterns include: (a) a highly regulated expressiveness and appearance (e.g. a tense, constrained and serious demeanour) which hides an inner ambivalence and insecurity, a fear of disapproval, and intense feelings of anger; (b) an overly respectful interpersonal manner (i.e. a highly developed sense of morality, formality and social correctness, with a high degree of outer respect for those in authority); (c) a regulated and narrow cognitive style (e.g. a rigid adherence to conventional rules, schedules and hierarchies); (d) a conscientious self-image (i.e. a highly responsible and disciplined self, with a high degree of devotion to perfection and productivity, and an aversion for recreational activities); (e) a high degree of defence against the conscious awareness of inner impulses or internalized representations seen as socially unacceptable; (f) the activation of a wide range of defences, including reaction formation with regard to feelings of defiance, rebelliousness, resentment and anger; identification with socially acceptable models; sublimation, especially with regard to the ventilation of hostile impulses; and the use of isolation and undoing to control negative emotional responses; (g) a compartmentalized morphological organization allowing little interaction between the various constellations of drive, memory and cognition (i.e. rigid compartmentalization of one's inner world to avoid the spilling over into consciousness of ambivalent images, feelings and attitudes); and (h) a solemn, overly sensitive or anhedonic mood or temperament, which may be constitutionally based.

Numerous OCPD subtypes have been identified which may present the therapist with different challenges and may require differential management strategies. Millon (1996) discusses prototypal variants ranging from normal through to childhood syndromes and adult subtypes. Five adult subtypes have been identified: (a) *the conscientious subtype*, characterized by a willingness to conform to others' rules and authority for fear of rejection or failure; (b) *the puritanical subtype*, who is typically austere and punitive, highly controlled and self-righteous, with severe judgemental attitudes; (c) *the bureaucratic subtype*, who welcomes tradition, formal establishments and bureaucracy, which provide not only a powerful identification but also established sets of rules and regulations and firm boundaries to contain feared inner impulses; (d) *the parsimonious subtype*, who is distinguished by a meanness and self-protectiveness that shields from the possibility of loss, and defends against the possibility of others recognizing their self-perceived inner emptiness; and (e) *the bedevilled subtype*, who constantly experience a deep internal struggle between the need to comply with the wishes of others and the desire to assert their own interests, leading to chronic feelings of hostility and conflict. While the identification of these subtypes may be clinically useful, research has yet to establish their validity, the need for idiosyncratic interventions, or even their distinctive aetiologies.

Theories of Aetiology

Neurobiological, ethological or evolutionary, genetic, developmental, cognitive, psychoanalytic and interpersonal theories have been proposed for the development of personality disorders in general and OCPD specifically (Clarkin & Lenzenweger, 1996). While most theories are not incompatible with each other, each specific theory contains elements of other theoretical positions, and their associated management approaches are generally easily integrated in clinical practice. The reality of clinical practice and the difficulties presented by OCPD is that clinicians need to incorporate different types of formulations for different individuals at various stages throughout treatment.

Neurobiological theories suggest that heritable or inborn defects in information processing, regulation of affect, and/or interpersonal behaviour are important in the aetiology of OCPD. Although a higher prevalence has been reported in first-degree relatives (for review, see Black et al., 1993), estimates of genetic influence have varied (Nigg & Goldsmith, 1994; Pfohl, 1996). Nonetheless, neurobiological theories offer heuristic value in ways other than providing arguments and evidence for the genetic basis of OCPD.

For instance, Cloninger (1987) defines obsessional personality in terms of low novelty seeking, high harm avoidance and low reward dependence, which are associated with rigidity, alienation and self-effacement. The second-order cluster of rigidity, characterized by low novelty seeking and high harm avoidance, is associated with lack of assertiveness and preoccupation with order and safety through the overuse of rules and detail. Cloninger regards novelty seeking, harm avoidance and reward dependence to be related to the dopamine, serotonin and noradrenaline systems, respectively. Similarly, Depue (1996) proposes that three major personality superfactors (specifically, positive emotionality, negative emotionality and constraint) interact in the development of personality and, possibly, personality disorders. Positive emotionality (related to incentive-reward motivation and active goal facilitation) is thought to be mediated by the dopamine system. Animal studies have suggested a relationship between norepinephrine activity in the locus coeruleus and negative emotionality (conceptualized as a warning-alarm system which aims to facilitate the direction of attention under conditions of environmental uncertainty or threat). Furthermore, animal studies of serotonin suggest its role in increasing the threshold for facilitation of behavioural and emotional responding. Hence, the serotonergic system is thought to play an important role in constraint. Each of these systems is seen to have a modulatory, as distinct from a mediating, role in influencing the flow of information in neural networks.

Such approaches may be viewed as "important building blocks for more complex future modelling of personality traits" (Depue, 1996, p. 373); however, "at the same time, it is completely unclear if the same neurobiological processes thought to underlie normal personality are functionally and structurally similar to those involved in personality pathology" (Depue, 1996, p. 379). Furthermore, the degree of dysfunction associated with particular personality patterns will depend to a great extent on sociocultural criteria for adjustment and/or maladjustment. Any purported neurobiological disruption underlying a particular behavioural complex must be seen within the environmental and developmental contexts which mould not only the manifestation of behaviour, but also its interpretation. Hence, while many consider that a neurobiological approach will provide future directions for the pharmacological treatment of personality disorders, as is the case with Axis I disorders, it will always be necessary to have an arsenal of psychosocial strategies to deal effectively with the individual within his/her context. Hence, psychological conceptualizations of personality disorder are necessary to guide individual clinical interventions.

Psychologically-orientated theorists differ in the emphasis that they put on various internal personality structures, the subjective experience of the self, and the effect of social expectations and other external influences on inter- and intrapersonal functioning.

Focusing on internal personality structures, Freud considered compulsive symptoms to result from a breakdown in the individual's efforts to repress prohibited impulses and thoughts, whereas anal character reflected successful repressions with supplementary reaction formations and sublimations. Obsessive-compulsives exhibit excesses in the use of particular defensive styles (sublimation, reaction formations), behavioural patterns (scrupulousness, procrastination, avoidance of affect) and deficits in their ability to deal effectively at cognitive and behavioural levels with impulses and feelings, especially those that are related to moral issues (e.g. anger, sexuality).

Kernberg (1996), a contemporary psychoanalytic theorist who also focuses on internal personality structures, regards the neurotic personality organization, which includes the obsessive-compulsive personality, as characterized by:

> ... normal ego identity and the related capacity for object relations in depth, ego strength reflected in anxiety tolerance, impulse control, sublimatory functioning,

effectiveness and creativity in work, and a capacity for sexual love and emotional intimacy which is disrupted by unconscious guilt feelings reflected in specific pathological patterns of interaction in relation to sexual intimacy (Kernberg, 1996, p. 121).

With regard to aggression, in OCPD specifically, a well-integrated but exceedingly punitive superego attempts to neutralize excessive aggression, leading to self-doubts and a preoccupation with perfectionism and control. When the neutralization is incomplete, the resulting severity of the aggression leads to regression and an unstable personality organization (i.e. the mixed obsessive, paranoid and schizoid features which often maintain a borderline personality organization). Interestingly, Kernberg also integrates neurobiological conceptualizations of distortions in affect activation, and posits that such inborn dispositions are complemented by early traumatic experiences which lead to the development of severe manifestations of aggression.

In contrast to psychoanalytic theorists who emphasize internal structures and experiences of self, Millon has focused on the external aspects of aetiology and presentation in the obsessive-compulsive, taking an evolutionary and developmental perspective on the emergence of personality. Millon & Davis (1996) distinguish various polarities relating to basic human instincts: (a) existential aims (e.g. enhancement and preservation of life); (b) modes of adaptation (ranging from active to passive); and (c) replication strategies (ranging from propagation to nurturance of self and/or others). The obsessive-compulsive is seen to be concerned with a passive accommodation and other-orientation where existential issues are dealt with adequately. Obsessive-compulsives are considered to experience conflict between hostility towards others and a fear of social disapproval. Hostility towards others develops from an assumed coercion to accept the standards imposed by others, an assumption deriving from their early experiences of constraint and discipline but only when they contravened parental rules. Fear of social disapproval evolves from their other-directedness, and their assumption of rejection following any possible infringement of strict and restrictive moral codes. Hence, obsessive-compulsives become preoccupied with perfectionism, control of self and environment, order, rules and regulations in order to resolve their ambivalence towards others.

Attachment theory (Bowlby, 1969, 1973, 1980), based on the principle that anxiety about attachment and dependence on significant others is an important developmental and evolutionary influence, has been used by numerous theorists to integrate various biological and psychosocial approaches to the aetiology of personality disorders. The interaction between temperamental dispositions and child-rearing practices influences the quality of attachments with significant implications for cognitive, behavioural and social development (Ainsworth, 1979, 1989). According to Guidano & Liotti (1983), obsessive-compulsive personality is characterized by ambivalent attachments which derive from parents who exhibited rejecting attitudes camouflaged by an outward mask of absolute devotion. Typically, the parents of obsessive-compulsives are highly verbal, motorically underactive, rarely spontaneous, and emotionally undemonstrative. Despite early over-indulgence, parents set high ethical standards, make unrealistic demands for maturity and responsibility, and forbid not only the expression but also the feeling of emotions. Unconditional positive regard is foreign to the obsessive-compulsive, and rewards are difficult to obtain in such a family environment. The resulting internalized sense of self of obsessive-compulsives is characterized by a split pattern of self-recognition. At one polarity they believe that they are loved, accepted and worthy of love. Simultaneously, they believe that they are unloved, rejected and not worthy of love. Furthermore, active attempts are made to exclude feelings and emotional expressions from their experience. Because of their nature, feelings are obviously inescapable; hence, any emotional modulation is likely to be experienced as uncontrollable, further encouraging the obsessive-compulsive to use verbal/analytical information processing and decision making. The verbal/analytical modality leads necessarily to the exclusion of free fantasy, imagery, emotions and impulses, counteracting the obsessive-compulsive's ambivalence and chronic need for certainty. Furthermore, a range of diversionary strategies (e.g. ruminations, doubts, rituals) selectively divert attention away from the affective modality, creating an internal experience devoid of warmth, creativity and flexibility.

While noting the influence of attachment in the developmental history of the typical obsessive-compulsive, constructivist theorists (Guidano, 1991; Guidano & Liotti, 1983; Mahoney, 1991) emphasize the importance in treatment of targeting constructions about the self. Other cognitive theorists, on the other hand, have emphasized the need to target a range of constructions that are related to information processing patterns. Such constructions, termed "schemas", refer to cognitive and affective complexes which assign meanings to events by selecting and integrating incoming data, and which direct actions and organize patterns of response. As they develop, "schemas" tend to become "closed" to "other" unrelated or disconfirmatory information or meanings, hence maintaining themselves and their influence on individual functioning. Personality, a broader construct, may be viewed, at least partly, as a function of conglomerates of basic schemas (Beck & Freeman, 1990).

Cognitive theorists consider cognition or, more broadly, information processing, to be a basic component of schemas and, hence, at the basis for shaping individuals' constructions of the world and themselves, as well as their emotional and behavioural responses to environmental situations (Beck, 1976). Faulty beliefs or assumptions, and systematic errors, biases and distortions in perceiving and interpreting events, will result in dysfunction and psychopathology. It is usually posited that these are learnt through experience or vicarious means, although some theorists hold to the notion of beliefs as dispositions towards evolutionarily-based and ethologically advantageous biases in information processing. Whatever their origins, faulty beliefs and distorted information-processing styles will result in negative automatic thoughts, often outside of the individual's awareness, which will direct dysfunctional emotional and behavioural responses. It is also held that mood influences cognitive processes such as recall, perception and interpretation (Eysenck, 1992; Teasdale &

Barnard, 1993), and that behaviours will modify events by eliciting environmental responses.

Cognitive therapists have identified a number of beliefs, cognitive distortions and strategies that characterize obsessive-compulsives. For instance, obsessive-compulsives exhibit rigidity in thinking, typically using dichotomous thinking, overattention to detail and applying inflexible rules. They exhibit a strong belief in correct solutions, demanding that they avoid mistakes and failures at all costs. "Mistakes" or "failures" are misperceived, regarded as intolerable, and dealt with through the use of self-punishment. Obsessive-compulsives are inherently concerned about criticism, engaging in extremes of personal criticism, setting up unrealistic expectations for themselves and others in all domains, and thinking in terms of "shoulds" and "musts". They believe in overcompensating for low self-esteem and possible criticism through overachievement. They are perfectionistic, and often exhibit an inflated sense of personal responsibility resulting in extremes of worry, morality and scruples. If the perfect course of action is not clear, they regard it best to do nothing, resulting in procrastination. They will overestimate the amount of risk, particularly in relation to the experience of emotion, hence overemphasizing the need for self-control. Their need for control also generalizes to the external world, where they insist on certainty, rules and regulations or well-practised rituals, and are often regarded as dogmatic, opinionated and inflexible.

The cognitive model, which is eclectic in its therapeutic strategies, can also be a useful model for the integration of different aetiological formulations. Our own approach, which is aimed at identifying and modifying faulty beliefs or assumptions, cognitive distortions, disadvantageous information-processing styles, and the associated behavioural patterns which maintain such maladaptive cognitive processes (e.g. procrastination, avoidance), incorporates a number of theoretical frameworks but is still "cognitive" in its orientation.

In our own approach, we consider that early attachments, influenced by the interaction between temperament and biological dispositions, lead to the development of core beliefs about one's self, the world and others. These core beliefs, which need to be targeted in treatment, relate to at least five significant and interrelated cognitive domains which contain various belief polarities and hold strong affective associations (see Figure 19.1). These are presented below.

Worth and Defectiveness

The characterization of this domain borrows from the theoretical work of Guidano & Liotti (1983). At the core of obsessive-compulsives is the uncertainty about their own inherent regard and self-worth, and the constant checks to establish for themselves whether they are worthy. The obsessive-compulsive believes that, at best, worth has to be earned by effort. At worst, the obsessive-compulsive believes that he/she is inherently defective and unworthy of regard or rewards. With reference to others and the world, obsessive-compulsives doubt whether they themselves are capable of providing affection and nurturance; however, obsessive-compulsives often try to put others and the world to the test. These attempts to establish whether the world or others are defective or not can

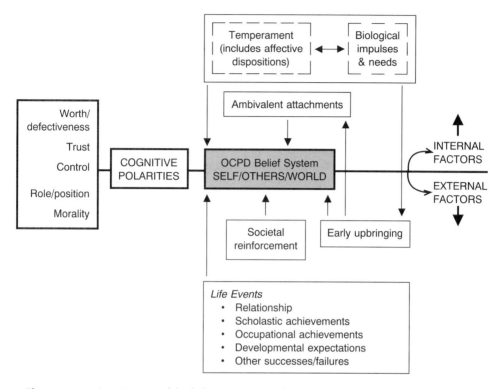

Figure 19.1 Cognitive model of obsessive-compulsive personality disorder

also be seen as checks on the trustworthiness surrounding the individual. Such checking provides the compulsive background which, despite its advantages of serving as a distraction from one's sense of ambivalence or possible emptiness, also maintains the sense of ambivalence. This sense of ambivalence, in turn, is used as evidence for the inherent defectiveness of the individual and the external world. Obsessive-compulsives who are also depressive have developed an additional sense of helplessness in themselves and the external world. To some extent, depressive and obsessive-compulsive phenomena may be seen as different reactions to similar belief structures. Whereas depression is perhaps the result of a depreciated self-concept, obsessive-compulsive phenomena may be the result of trying to rectify the discrepancy between the ideal and actual self or the ideal and actual world. Hence, obsessive-compulsive phenomena may be conceptualized as a maladaptive means of preserving a sense of self-worth, in the face of a perceived hostile social world which induces a sense of worthlessness (Bhar & Kyrios, 1996).

Trust

If one truly feels that they are worthy of love and that others or the world are capable of providing such love, then the ability to trust begins to develop between the individual and the external world and, hence, within the individual. With reference to the external world, the consistent and appropriate gratification of the individual's needs helps to build a sense of safety and nurturance, in contrast to a sense of danger and rejection. The individual can begin to feel a sense of reliance on the external world for the provision of biological and, ultimately, emotional needs. With reference to oneself, not only is trust in the external world internalized in time, but trust in one's ability to elicit caring from the external world is also important in developing a sense of self-efficacy. Obsessive-compulsives typically attempt to compensate totally for the lack of trust in themselves and the external world through the use of various strategies: becoming overly independent or dependent, establishing unattainable ideals or unrealistic goals (i.e. becoming perfectionistic), constantly checking or testing themselves or others, establishing and adhering inflexibly to rules and regulations. The net result is often procrastination and a lack of creative freedom rather than reliable problem-solving options which develop out of a body of experiences.

Control

Having developed a sense of trust in oneself and in the external world, the individual can begin to explore his/her possibilities and, hence, develop a sense of control over him/herself and the external environment. For instance, children with secure attachments are more likely to explore their environment and help develop their cognitive and social skills. They can begin to put order to the chaos around them from a firm base of security. They learn that lack of familiarity is not necessarily fraught with danger and, even when there is uncertainty, they can always return to their secure base. In time, with some experimentation, individuals learn to deal effectively with increasing degrees of difficulty, complexity and uncertainty. Rarely having experienced a sense of security internally or externally, the obsessive-compulsive, on the other hand, fears disorganization or even uncertainty, and overcompensates by establishing unrealistic, unattainable and/ or unsustainable control strategies for themselves and the external world. Obsessive-compulsives need to learn that perfect control is not possible, and that lack of perfect control is not catastrophic. They need to feel less threatened and deal more flexibly with increasingly chaotic or unpredictable situations, as well as trust in their ability to deal with situations where control is not in their hands. In any given situation, they need to learn to focus less on issues of control and attend more to situation-relevant and situation-specific factors, with less emphasis on self-referent control issues.

Role/Position

One outcome of exploring one's possibilities is the eventual acquisition of a variety of satisfying and stimulating roles within one's environment which provide the individual with structure, rewards, support and ongoing possibilities. The acquisition of various roles also provides some balance between autonomy and dependence which can allow for a sense of social security and confidence in one's ability to deal with situations where one might feel insecure. Nonetheless, one needs some flexibility in the roles that one acquires in order to deal with changing environmental, developmental and personal circumstances. Hence, borrowing from the work of Erikson (1950, 1959), extremes of role cohesion and role diffusion are not adaptive. Through their procrastination, obsessive-compulsives may secure role diffusion. Alternatively, through their obsession with control, they might develop extremes of role cohesion by taking on inflexible roles.

Morality

Individuals who have not been able to achieve satisfying roles or positions might acquire an albeit vulnerable and unstable sense of self through their adherence to rules and regulations, particularly those relating to morality and responsibility, which generalize to others and the world. Such adherence simplifies life for the obsessive-compulsive by averting the need to take account of complex and confusing reality. Obsessive-compulsives, with their ambivalent sense of self, are prone to inflexible and perfectionistic adherences which consistently produce self-doubts and, hence, maintain an ambivalent sense of self. The inflexible adherence to ethical, religious or moral codes is often established in early childhood through interactions with parents who, on the one hand, outwardly espouse devotion on the grounds of moral obligation but, on the other hand, fail to show emotion in any immediate sense, preferring verbal modes of communication (Guidano & Liotti, 1983; Guidano, 1991). The moral high ground may also compensate for an ambivalent self-image, as it allows for identification with external authority which is seen to be devoid of the need for the defences to which the obsessive-compulsive holds.

In summary, ethologically-important instincts, biological dispositions and temperament, and life experiences (particularly significant or recurrent events), perhaps at strategic developmental stages, play an important role in the development of dysfunctional schemas about self, others and the world. In planning interventions, clinicians need to consider the obsessive-compulsive's constructions of self and the external world, his/her maladaptive defences, and the cognitive, behavioural and interpersonal strategies used to guarantee his/her safety and combat the experience of emotion.

COGNITIVE-BEHAVIOURAL STRATEGIES IN THE MANAGEMENT OF OCPD

Philosophy and Rationale

Behaviour therapy aims to increase the individual's adaptive behavioural repertoire, while decreasing maladaptive behaviour patterns. In addition, more adaptive contingencies are developed which will encourage the adaptive behavioural repertoire while discouraging maladaptive behaviour patterns. Cognitive therapy, on the other hand, directly addresses the irrational beliefs or assumptions (the "what" of thinking) and the cognitive distortions (the "how" of thinking) that are exhibited by the obsessive-compulsive, as well as the attentional and other cognitive processes that maintain the cognitive dysfunctions. The restricted affective features of the obsessive-compulsive can be modified by targeting these behavioural and cognitive features. In this sense, cognitive-behavioural therapy for OCPD is not essentially different to that for any other condition where discrepancies between perceptions, expectations and reality can serve as the content of sessions. However, one also needs to account for the special characteristics of personality disorders (e.g. vicious cycles, inflexibility, etc.) that have been discussed by various authors (Clarkin & Lenzenweger, 1996; Millon, 1996; Young, 1990). Hence, the treatment of the obsessive-compulsive needs to go beyond traditional cognitive and behavioural techniques. It needs to address issues relating to identity, attachment and self-knowledge, in addition to traditional symptom reduction approaches (Guidano, 1991; Guidano & Liotti, 1983).

Nonetheless, cognitive-behavioural therapy is not a restrictive melange of techniques; rather, it is a philosophical or theoretical framework which can guide the creative use of interpersonal processes and existing therapeutic techniques (e.g. behavioural, gestalt, psychodynamic) or the creative development and integration of new techniques. However, the actual techniques utilized within therapy sessions can differ from client to client and from therapist to therapist. Given that OCPD is a heterogeneous disorder and obsessive-compulsive patterns are seen in a range of other disorders, an individualized approach to treatment is obviously necessary to account for variations in presentation. However, there are characteristic OCPD patterns which the therapist needs to consider targeting specifically, irrespective of the actual therapeutic techniques utilized. Furthermore, there are numerous cognitive-behavioural strategies that can be employed at some stage in the treatment of OCPD within the context of a therapeutic relationship.

All dealings with obsessive-compulsives need to be characterized by a consistency in one's approach that cuts through the core cognitive domains described above. Obsessive-compulsives need to be helped to feel understood and safe, worthy of unconditional positive regard and trust, and to develop a sense of confidence in dealing with possible loss of control. The importance of their various roles and positions needs to be acknowledged but not to the extent that their unconditional worth is undermined. They need to feel worthy by due fact of their existence and not merely because of their compliance with perceived social and moral codes. Their emotions and impulses, which they might find abhorrent or intolerable, need to be acknowledged, normalized and accepted. They need to be given the time and attention which they often report having missed out on in their early years. They need to feel that, when rules are transgressed, they can learn to cope with the perceived chaos, potential danger or possible rejection. They need to acknowledge that self-rejection and the obligation to please the external world in order to avoid rejection will, ultimately, lead to ongoing difficulties for themselves. Above all, they need to acknowledge, in the context of self-acceptance, the limitations of their current coping strategies, and the need to adopt strategies characterized by self-efficacy, empowerment and realistic responsibility.

Diagnosis, Assessment and Initial Management

With regard to diagnosis, attempts to develop assessment measures for OCPD have not been particularly successful. The MMPI has not been successful in differentiating OCPD from non-obsessive-compulsive inpatients (Schotte et al., 1991), neither have structured clinical interviews been reliable in the diagnosis of OCPD (First et al., 1995). While both the MMPI and the revised Millon Clinical Multiaxial Inventory (MCMI-II; Millon, 1987) contain obsessive-compulsive scales, there is little evidence for their convergent validity (McCann, 1992), with the two scales appearing to assess different aspects of OCPD.

Nonetheless, it is often useful to administer a number of self-report inventories, particularly those relating to symptoms which often precipitate the referral for treatment (e.g. Beck Depression Inventory; State-Trait Anxiety Inventory; Derogatis Symptom Checklist—Revised). It also useful to administer measures of general or specific beliefs and assumptions such as the commonly used Beliefs Inventory and Dysfunctional Attitudes Scale, the more inclusive Schema Questionnaire (Schmidt et al., 1995; Young, 1990), or the newly developed Obsessional Beliefs Questionnaire (Obsessive-Compulsive Cognitions Working Group [OCCWG], 1997). The Daily Record of Dysfunctional Thoughts can be useful during later stages of the assessment phase to examine the appraisals patients make of daily events and situations, although many therapists prefer to design monitoring sheets to suit the individual's situation or presenting problems. Use of diaries to increase awareness of feelings and associated thoughts is often useful, and can act as a springboard for reinforcing the importance of free thoughts and emotion in one's life. However, some obsessive-compulsives may do poorly with monitoring sheets because of performance fears ("not doing it right"), their lack of awareness or insight, the tendency towards overdetailed monitoring, etc. Lack of awareness or insight can often be dealt with through an educative process, discussing the differences between common intrusions, feelings, beliefs and thoughts.

Any effective intervention begins with a complete history and analysis of current difficulties. It is necessary for the history-taking to take a developmental perspective which will allow for the identification of early maladaptive schemas, particularly those relating to attachments and self. Quality of attachments and child-rearing, early traumatic events, early socialization, progress through school, work and relationship histories are particularly useful foci. A useful strategy is to ask the patient to write a "life" history, pointing out significant positive and traumatic events from birth to his/her present situation. Another useful strategy is the identification and detailed description of significant others in the individual obsessive-compulsive's life, including the individual's past and present reactions to these significant others.

It is important to note that, even with a thorough history, the obsessive-compulsive will often first present as a motivated, diligent and compliant patient; only in time will the dysfunctional idiosyncrasies of the obsessive-compulsive (e.g. inflexibility, rigidity) be revealed to the therapist. However, during all phases of assessment and treatment, it is important to distinguish between adaptive and maladaptive manifestations of the obsessive-compulsive syndrome. For instance, many of the positive prognostic features associated with cognitive-behavioural therapy success are the very features which, obviously in a more extreme form, are often indicative of OCPD (see Safran & Segal, 1990). OCPD has also been found to be a positive prognostic factor in depressed outpatients completing a sequential pharmacotherapy intervention (Hoencamp et al., 1994). Furthermore, in many psychotic patients, obsessive-compulsive patterns are associated with containment of the clinical syndrome, and their amelioration is followed by a deterioration in the patient's psychological state.

With regard to intervention, as most obsessive-compulsives will present for treatment with specific difficulties or symptoms (e.g. anxiety states, substance abuse, adjustment disorder, depression), immediate symptom reduction through prescriptive behavioural techniques are often the immediate focus (relaxation and controlled breathing techniques; activity scheduling, including activities of pleasure and mastery, exercise and other physical activities; and contingency management). While this is a necessary step, it is important to note that, as symptoms resolve or as the therapist becomes more aware of maladaptive obsessive-compulsive manifestations, the need for a broadening of the scope of therapy will become evident. A useful strategy for introducing the need to deal with the broader OCPD-related issues, as distinct from the clinical symptoms, is to gauge the discussion in terms of relapse prevention, a concept which might appeal to the control-conscious obsessive-compulsive. However, even the clinical symptom-reduction stage comprises a good opportunity to discuss chronic OCPD-related patterns or problems. For example, activity scheduling in response to a depressive episode would by necessity deal with the OCPD-related aversion for recreational activities and overemphasis on productive pursuits.

Hence, traditional behavioural strategies can be used in conjunction with simple cognitive strategies to deal with initial presenting problems, often with beneficial implications for the more chronic personality problems. In the longer term, such techniques can also form the basis for dealing with dispositions associated more closely with OCPD.

Conducting Cognitive-behavioural Therapy (CBT)

Treatment Aims

From a broader perspective, effective treatment for any psychological disorder needs to account for associated neurobiological dispositions, maladaptive behavioural patterns, and dysfunctional cognitive styles. In the case of OCPD, neurobiological and affective dispositions such as low novelty seeking, high harm avoidance, low reward dependence, restricted emotional expression and negative mood states can be modified by the use of various behavioural techniques which can be further facilitated with cognitive strategies. The aim of such interventions are:

1. To increase the use of rewards and tolerance for novelty by gradually widening the individual's range of activities, particularly those which the obsessive-compulsive views as "non-productive" (e.g. recreational activities, exercise, relaxation). This can be regarded as both a short-term and a long-term goal.
2. To decrease avoidance tendencies by a graded exposure program which can be applied equally to specific situations and psychophysiological triggers (e.g. emotion). Relaxation strategies are useful for dealing with the physical component of anxiety, while cognitive strategies can deal with the cognitive component.
3. To increase emotional awareness and expressive skills via a skills-based shaping framework, and through monitoring strategies (e.g. via the use of diaries). Process issues during the progress of therapy can also act as an important context for the targeting of interpersonal and affective issues.
4. To decrease negative mood states such as irritability and dysthymia through the use of cognitive and relaxation or visualization strategies, as well as activity scheduling and mood monitoring through the use of dairies. Teasdale, Segal & Williams (1995) describe an attentional focusing technique for the management and prevention of depression which can form the basis for encouraging patients to expose themselves to moderately negative feelings, as a way of increasing tolerance of negative affective states and of decreasing more intense negative affective states.

The obsessive-compulsive's reward base needs to be broadened through a gradual build-up of their repertoire of enjoyable, spontaneous, rewarding activities. Activities need to be scheduled and regulated, and built up slowly. To avoid procrastination relating to ambivalence about making a decision, activities may initially need to be structured and gently prescribed by the therapist. This is particularly true for relaxation strategies which the obsessive-compulsive often views as "non-productive" and unnecessary. Relaxation time can be built up slowly, especially given the diligence of the obsessive-compulsive, although the therapist needs to beware of various relaxation pitfalls. For instance, the obsessive-compulsive may become more tense as a result of instigating relaxation exercises. This is possibly due to their trying too hard, and feeding into their somatization tendencies. It is generally best to provide a psycho-educational package comprising accurate explanations of sympathetic and parasympathetic nervous system activity, the "fight–flight" response, and the need for a balanced lifestyle. Such a package forms the rationale for many of the prescriptive interventions which the obsessive-compulsive is initially keen to pursue. The net result of these changes is to counter the narrow fixed attention of the obsessive-compulsive by providing experiences outside his/her usual routines.

As patients build up their repertoire of activities and rewards, they will begin to encounter previously avoided or fear-provoking situations. It is best to deal with these in a structured and graded manner through the use of *in vivo* or imaginal exposure. The patient identifies "high-risk" situations which are associated with a range of predicted negative outcomes. The patient predicts which outcomes are most likely and, with the help of the therapist, plans and rehearses coping strategies should negative outcomes result. After placing the risk situations on a hierarchy, the individual exposes him/herself to those situations associated with lowest risk and tests out his/her predictions about outcomes and coping levels. Progress to higher risk situations is contingent on dealing effectively with lower placed situations. It is recommended that patients are exposed only to situations in the 40–60 range of subjective units of discomfort or distress (out of a possible range of 0–100), although it needs to be remembered that obsessive-compulsives will usually underestimate their expected distress. Relaxation techniques can be used in conjunction as part of a wider anxiety-management strategy, although they are neither sufficient nor necessary components of an exposure regime. Ultimately, patients need to develop skills in dealing with anxiety/discomfort or with specific situations, in addition to building up a sense of confidence in their ability to deal with threat and ambivalence. The behavioural concepts of graded exposure and shaping are particularly important in dealing with neurotic conditions (Barlow & Lehman, 1996; Zimbarg et al., 1992).

As part of facilitating an exposure regime, it is useful to instigate simple cognitive strategies to counter the obsessive-compulsive's rationale for continuing with avoidance strategies and, hence, facilitate his/her motivation to sustain an active "exposure" or "approach" framework as distinct from his/her "avoidance" or "withdrawal" tendencies. More advanced cognitive strategies may also be required to deal with the obsessive-compulsive's low threshold for perception of harm or threat. Specifically, the patient identifies a range of situations which are considered to be "risky". The associated risks are then examined in detail, and estimates of the likelihood and severity of negative outcomes are made for each risk. Patients are made aware of their tendency to focus only on possible negative outcomes, and are gradually helped to develop an awareness of potential positive outcomes. The possibility for positive outcomes increases the obsessive-compulsive's tolerance for "threat" situations. It is also useful to examine inconsistencies in the patient's avoidance patterns. For instance, most patients will have driven to his/her appointment (high likelihood and severity of a negative outcome such as a motor car accident) but will avoid "imperfection" or spending some "free time" during the weekend when they feel that they should be doing something productive (low likelihood and severity of negative outcome). The knowledge that they are prepared to cope with negative outcomes of a higher likelihood and severity can increase the obsessive-compulsive's sense of self-efficacy and increase his/her motivation to face feared situations. This type of approach can also be used to increase emotional awareness and expressive skills. Faulty beliefs surrounding the expression of emotion (e.g. "Emotions must be kept tightly controlled") can be targeted through the use of graduated behavioural experiments. Various gestalt techniques (e.g. the "empty chair" technique) are also often useful for bringing the client's emotions into the "here-and-now", and can be utilized easily within a shaping or graded approach.

Because of the rigid compartmentalization of various elements of their personality, obsessive-compulsives lack awareness of inconsistencies in their cognitive functioning. Cognitive distortions and irrational assumptions can be addressed initially in a didactic and structured manner, with initial directives by the therapist to complete reading and monitoring exercises. The authority which the obsessive-compulsive projects onto the therapist is usually sufficient initially to ensure adherence to treatment directives, as long as the rationale for the therapist's directions are coherent. The therapist guides the patient to identify maladaptive thinking patterns and, through a Socratic dialogue described by numerous cognitive therapists (Beck, 1976; Safran & Segal, 1990), develop alternative adaptive and rational thinking which is practised during sessions. Together with the therapist, relevant homework assignments of an appropriate level of difficulty are set, which will allow the patient to apply the newly developed rational thinking in planned situations using a shaping framework. Gradually, a more spontaneous and flexible examination of the individual patient's cognitive patterns can be instigated, with a more flexible view of homework assignments.

The progress towards more spontaneous therapy sessions by implication sets the scene for an examination of interpersonal dynamics. It is important to note the difficult situation with which the therapist is faced. Taking too little or too much control of the sessions threatens the possible engagement of the patient with therapy. While the therapist–patient relationship has traditionally been considered the realm of the interpersonal therapist, a cognitive approach can be utilized to target more directly the obsessive-compulsive's cognitive set regarding interpersonal aspects of self and other. Such process issues will be examined after detailing the content of cognitive-behavioural therapy sessions.

Content of CBT Sessions

As stated previously, specific strategies may be required for specific cognitive and behavioural patterns. For instance, inflated responsibility, extremes of morality and scruples can be targeted by use of the "pie-chart of responsibility", more often used in the treatment of OCD (van Oppen & Arnzt, 1994). Patients identify a negative outcome which they believe they are personally responsible for causing. A discussion or survey is then conducted to identify all potential causes for the negative outcome, starting off with the patient as the causal agent. A pie-chart is then constructed whereby each identified cause is attributed a proportion of the total contribution to the negative outcome. It is advisable to rate the patient's causal contribution last. Many patients will find it difficult going beyond themselves as contributing 100% to the negative outcome. One way around this difficulty is to pretend that the patient is taking on the role of a defence lawyer who is trying to minimize perceptions about his/her client's contribution to the negative outcome (i.e. arguing the "beyond a reasonable doubt" defence).

Typically, arguments can be built up around minimizing the individual's contribution by attributing some responsibility to others, one's family, various social agencies and governments, medical services in the case of negative health outcomes, etc. An alternative process involves the use of the "empty chair" technique, whereby the client argues for and against his/her "total guilt", depending on which chair he/she is sitting. The therapist can then take over the opposing arguments while the client takes on the role of arbiter with the aim of developing more reasonable contentions. At the end of such processes, the individual patient's contribution to a negative outcome has generally been downgraded significantly from 100%.

The pie-chart of responsibility technique can also be combined with other strategies targeting three further questions: (a) the likelihood that the perceived negative outcome will occur; (b) the identification of other outcomes that might be more realistic; and (c) the likelihood that the patient will fail to cope with the predicted negative outcomes. Any negative event will consist of a series of steps, each of which is associated with a probability. The likelihood of the negative event occurring is the product of each individual probability which, in most cases, will be trivial and smaller than the likelihood of winning a large lottery. Furthermore, as neurotic individuals tend to predict events on the basis of cognitive distortions (i.e. using catastrophizing, dichotomous thinking, and emotional reasoning) rather than realistic evidence, alternative outcomes (i.e. other than those identified) are often more likely to occur. A survey of friends or others may help the patient identify alternative outcomes, some of which may even be positive.

The futility of predicting the future and of emotional reasoning can be targeted through a discussion of likelihoods and the concomitant use of behavioural experiments. For instance, the patient is asked to buy a lottery ticket and fantasize about winning, after which a discussion is held as to how it "feels", and predicted and actual outcomes are contrasted. Should the patient be lucky enough to win the lottery, this can only further facilitate the process, as the next purchase of a lottery ticket is unlikely to lead to a win even though the patient might feel at some level that they are more likely to win. This technique can also be used to allow the obsessive-compulsive to develop and express an internal fantasy life.

With regard to coping with negative outcomes, patients are asked how they have dealt with other stressful events in their life. The reality is that most people find ways of dealing with adversity (e.g. death of loved one, wars, unemployment, relationship break-up, other losses, etc.), and that the patient has dealt with difficult issues in the past. Furthermore, the patient has in all probability continued to expose him/herself to situations where there is a high likelihood of danger but where he/she assumes that all will turn out well. It is useful to point out such inconsistencies in such a way as to give the obsessive-compulsive a sense of self-efficacy, control and self-trust. A list of already existing adaptive coping mechanisms can be made up which helps to improve the patient's self-efficacy and confidence. However, this needs to be placed in the context that we all face adversity and experience times of stress, emotional upheaval or ambivalence. Hence, the normalization of "imperfect control" needs to be stressed to the obsessive-compulsive. It is also useful for the therapist to use the obsessive-compulsive's dependency on him/her to facilitate the build-up of tolerance for uncertainty and confusion. For instance, when patients ask therapists for instructions as to how to deal with specific problems or suggested answers to dilemmas, therapists can gently repel such requests, guiding patients into a more independent problem-solving approach and then attending to the working-through of their uncertainty, self-doubts, ambivalence, confusion, etc. Such strategies also have implications for perfectionism and procrastination.

Perfectionism can be further targeted by graduated purposeful mistakes or trying harder to be "more perfect". The aim of such interventions is to point out to the patient that purposeful mistakes do not lead to catastrophe, and that trying too hard will not guarantee improved performance or moral superiority. Thought suppression exercises will illustrate that total mental control is not possible, and that increased attempts at mind control actually lead to decreased control (Wegner, 1992; Wegner & Pennebaker, 1993). Alternatively, less concentrated thought suppression can be shown to lead to decreased frequency and intensity of negative thoughts. It is useful to note, perhaps through the use of graphs, the general relationship between performance and pressure or control and anxiety. Cost–benefit analyses, where the limitations and adaptive features of specific obsessive-compulsive strategies are contrasted, are particularly useful for intervening with avoidance patterns and procrastination. This cognitive strategy is facilitated through the concomitant use of behavioural interventions such as graded exposure to previously avoided situations or to situations regarded as threatening. In addition, normalizing or providing a rationale for the initial development of obsessive-compulsive strategies (i.e. a discussion of the initial benefits or adaptive value of these now often maladaptive strategies), may help the obsessive-compulsive develop a less punitive attitude to him/herself.

The general tendency to ruminate or worry can be dealt with via thought-stopping, distraction and refocusing techniques or via the "putting-off" technique used in conjunction with "timed worrying/ruminating". A dieting analogy can be used effectively with patients by explaining, for instance, that worrying (like eating) can be put off for a time, although at some point we all need to worry (or eat). However, we can limit the amount of worrying (or eating) that we do. Patients are instructed to "put off" their worrying for a gradually increasing amount of time, leading to a set "worry time" during, say, the early evening which is gradually decreased from 1 or 2 hours down to 5 or 10 minutes. The issues which patients worry about during the day are noted in their diaries for reference during the set worry time. The quality of "worry" can also be improved, with instructions in problem-solving approaches to the issues noted in the diary. It is often useful to experiment with ruminating over a non-personal issue, initially without a problem-solving approach. Once a problem-solving approach is instigated, the patient's experiences are discussed. Did they find a better solution to the problem any faster by worrying? Hence, at this point, a cost–benefit analysis can be instigated. More emotionally-laded and more personal issues can be dealt with in the usual hierarchical manner.

As discussed earlier, obsessive-compulsives will often report the experience of intrusive thoughts, urges or images which are appraised in a manner which leads to distress and/or attempts to use neutralizing responses (e.g. suppression). Such intrusions are commonly related to themes of aggression, sexuality, personal responsibility, safety and morality. In the case of OCPD, there is likely to be little consciously-experienced distress, although the aversion to such intrusions will be evident, as will the aversion or defences against the expression of distress. Before working on the intrusions themselves, it may be necessary to deal first with the extreme aversion to distress, specifically, and emotion in general. Freeston, Rheaume & Ladouceur (1996) have identified a number of strategies that can be used successfully to reappraise such intrusions in a more rational manner. Freeston et al. (1997) have further illustrated the usefulness of these techniques in decreasing obsessive-compulsive symptoms in an OCD cohort. The adaptive reappraisal of intrusions can be used in conjunction with loop tapes, whereby the obsessive-compulsive is exposed to repetitions of the identified intrusion by listening to the loop tape for 30–60 minutes. It is useful for the patient to keep a log of their level of anxiety and ability to concentrate on the distressing intrusion every 5 minutes. It is imperative that the obsessive-compulsive is encouraged not to work with intrusions causing distress above the 60–70 out of 100 range. This type of exposure can be augmented by the use of relevant objects to intensify and make the experience more realistic. For example, in the case of an aggressive intrusion, it might be useful for the patient to be handling an object such as a knife or a reminder of an angry incident. Gradually more distressing objects can be used in the familiar graded exposure regime. A second phase can also be introduced as an option, particularly for those with poorly regulated emotional responses to the distressing intrusions. Firstly, negative appraisals of the intrusion are identified through monitoring or via the use of the Interpretation of Intrusions Inventory (OCCWG, 1997). Positive or adaptive reappraisals are developed and perhaps placed on a cue card. A second phase of exposure to the loop tape is accompanied by repetition of the positive reappraisals (first, overtly via use of the cue card and eventually, covertly). The patient monitors, every 5 minutes for each exposure session, his/her level of anxiety, ability to concentrate on the distressing intrusion, and level of belief in the positive reappraisals. As before, augmentation of the exposure can be achieved through the use of relevant objects.

This technique is also useful for dealing with suppressed or avoided emotions. The patient is exposed to a description of an emotionally-laden issue via the loop tape (e.g. description of parent's funeral). Objects relevant to the situation (e.g. deceased parent's favourite ring) can magnify the experience. The general lack of threat associated with extremes of emotionality can be illustrated by such scheduled blocks of increasingly high emotionality. It is often useful to combine this technique with an exploration of increasingly emotionally-laden early childhood traumas or the patient's relationship with an authoritarian parent. The "empty chair" technique is particularly useful towards this end. The limitations of extremes of emotional avoidance can also be illustrated by comparing such scheduled "blocked" periods of exposure time to "timetabled" avoidance episodes. An exploration of differences in problem-solving potential of these two approaches then ensues (i.e. a cost–benefit analysis).

Experiential techniques can also be used to facilitate cognitive change. One technique already mentioned, the "empty chair" technique, can be used to deal with both dichotomous thinking patterns and the individual's sense of ambivalence (Hyer, Brandsma & Shealy, 1995), although this technique needs to be used carefully with patients who exhibit poor emotional regulation (e.g. borderline or psychotic patients). One of the aims of this technique is to identify and express the affect associated with the dichotomy. Such affect is usually associated with the belief domains identified previously (e.g. feelings of defectiveness and worthlessness, fears of rejection, loneliness and loss of control, etc.).

As with any problem or perceived "failure" that arises in the context of psychotherapy with the obsessive-compulsive, a combined approach of providing accurate information, problem-solving, unconditional positive regard and debriefing of affective responses will help to build up more adaptive responses. However, therapists need to accept that obsessive-compulsives will experience difficulty in building up adaptive thinking because of "yes . . . but" responses and their characteristic inflexibility. Obsessive-compulsives often go from maladaptive "black" to equally maladaptive "white", rather than developing a flexible "grey" framework. While patience on the part of the therapist will be necessary, creative therapy will also need to be instigated from time-to-time. At other times, it will be necessary to use obsessive-compulsive characteristics or strategies to change aspects of the obsessive-compulsive. For instance, it is sometimes useful to ask the patient to write an essay or report (e.g. "Write an essay on positive aspects of yourself"). One might also choose to use cue cards during behavioural rehearsals or exposure exercises.

Hence, behavioural strategies in conjunction with cognitive strategies can be utilized to achieve short-term goals, as well as deal with the underlying psychological issues thought to be at the basis for the development and maintenance of obsessive-compulsive phenomena. Together with a patient engaged in therapy, an effective therapist will be able to design and implement an individualized program. However, successful treatment is as much about effective techniques (i.e. the "what" of therapy), as it is about timing, process and the development of a beneficial therapeutic alliance (i.e. the "how" of therapy).

Progress, Process and the Therapeutic Alliance

As obsessive-compulsives suffer a basic insecurity in their perception of the external world, their appraisal of self and their relative ability to deal with emotions, it is important to provide, particularly in the early stages of treatment, an interpersonal environment characterized by safety and structure. This will: (a) help the obsessive-compulsive stay with feelings and impulses until a new aware-ness and acceptance is reached; and (b) help develop the expression, experience and working-through of uncomfortable feelings. Hyer, Brandsma & Shealy (1995, p. 231) state the importance of "making the ineffable real and felt". Ultimately, such awareness and expression will encourage adaptive regression, allowing for the development of more beneficial defences.

Initially, obsessive-compulsives will often reveal only socially acceptable atti-tudes, impulses and behaviour to the extent that therapists may wonder about the reasons for referral. Fears about aggressive and sexual impulses lead to a tight control over all emotion and impulses. Such fears and their associated defences require that the therapist starts off with relatively "safe" material (e.g. the patient's account of the reason for referral and presenting problems), gradually leading into an exploration of increasingly emotional material. This latter process can be facilitated through structured means (e.g. patient lists of the important events or individuals in his/her life from birth to the present time). Eventually, once the therapist has a good understanding of the patient's early learning history and the underlying personality issues, a structured program of exposure to increasingly confusing or threatening situations and potential mistakes (e.g. behavioural experiments targeting personal responsibility) can be developed and implemented. Initial use of therapist authority can be utilized to explain the treatment rationale and to prescribe homework tasks, with a gradual retreat to shared and ultimately patient-initiated responsibility for progress. Homework tasks during the initial sessions, which are obviously characterized by assessment and an exploration of issues, can take the form of reading psycho-educational material, completing monitoring sheets, and undertaking relaxation training. Psycho-education (including ethological explanations of emotion) can provide information and an opportunity for normalizing emotions and repressed impulses (i.e. "giving permission"), while relaxation strategies constitute useful anxiety management and body awareness strategies. Monitoring sheets are also useful for the purpose of gaining baseline information and facilitating awareness.

In the initial stages, patients may continuously ask the therapist for reassur-ances about prognosis, somatic complaints and any other issue. While the temp-tation on the therapist's part may be to ignore or give in to such requests, it is important for the therapist to acknowledge that whatever they decide will have some impact on rapport and progress. There is no correct solution to the issue of whether therapists should or should not respond to the client's demands for reassurance in the first instance. From a therapeutic perspective, what is important is that the patient's intrapsychic concerns are brought to conscious awareness within a hierarchical framework and are dealt with within a shaping framework. Often it is useful to work out the meaning underlying such obsessional demands. Through their demonstrations of the need for reassurance, patients are often expressing their anxiety about being in therapy, their concerns about negative social evaluation, their fears about losing control, and/or their relative inability to deal with the pace set in the sessions. Empathic statements and education about normal processes in psychotherapy will often alleviate anxiety, leading to a decrease in reassurance seeking. Alternatively, therapists can take a baseline of reassurance-seeking, and gently bring their observations into the focus of discussion once rapport has confidently been established. A non-critical examination of the issues underlying reassurance-seeking within the session will usually be of great value in planning subsequent interventions, as well as making the sessions more time-effective.

In addition to the initial need to exhibit a sense of organization and control over the process of therapy, therapists need to convey unconditional positive regard as an important step in facilitating self-acceptance and self-trust in the obsessive-compulsive. Furthermore, an attitude of adaptation of current defences rather than the need for drastic change is less frightening and, ultimately, more useful to the obsessive-compulsive. Hence, it is important to use current strategies and adapt them to be more flexible (i.e. the tendency to use lists, rules, agendas, etc. can be used more adaptively in cognitive-behavioural therapy).

Once rapport has been established, it is important for the therapist slowly to introduce more humanizing elements (e.g. encouragement of fantasy life, use of dreams to decode underlying true object relations, use of humour) before the use of confrontation can be used effectively. Non-critical confrontation, using the Socratic dialogue strategy, can be used primarily to link inconsistencies in affect and thinking. However, therapists need to avoid responding in kind to intellectualized defences. Ultimately, it is the adaptive utility of the obsessive-compulsive defence that ought to be questioned, not the rationalization *per se*.

After the initial period of assessment and initial focus on immediate symptom reduction, when therapist and patient have much to discuss which is conducive to a structured approach, a period of long silences often follows when an agreed focus for therapy is being sought. At this stage, patient and therapist may be searching for a different focus; the therapist is often searching to broaden the therapy focus, while the obsessive-compulsive is searching for short-term certainty and guarantees. The long silences are often anxiety-provoking for obsessive-compulsives as they may fear being swamped with abhorrent thoughts, feelings or urges. Alternatively, the obsessive-compulsive might fear that the therapist will see his/her inner emptiness through his/her defensive veneer. The therapist needs to reassure the patient that this is a common phenomenon during the course of therapy. Furthermore, the therapist needs to provide a rationale for the patient to continue working through this difficult period (e.g. explaining the difficulties within a hierarchical exposure framework). It is this phase that constitutes a high risk for premature termination as the patient–therapist relationship reaches an important impasse in its development.

The patient–therapist relationship and, in particular, transference analysis have been the central concern of psychoanalytic approaches. This involves analysing the reactivations (in the "here-and-now") of past internalized object relations, be they real or fantasized or distorted internalizations. From a cognitive-behavioural perspective, it makes sense to help patients understand and integrate components of their dispositions, existing skills, defences and beliefs/

attitudes deriving from early developmental events, and their intra- and inter-personal conflicts. Furthermore, transference can be seen as an assumed generalizability of the patient's pre-existing beliefs and attitudes, particularly those relating to the interpersonal domain, from his/her past significant relation-ships to the therapist. Moreover, in any long-term therapy, the patient's frame of reference will naturally turn towards the therapist–patient relationship. Given the obsessive-compulsive's sensitivity to issues relating to the interpersonal domain, it is imperative for the cognitive-behavioural therapist to deal effectively with any transference issues resulting in intense negative emotions. It is impera-tive not to trivialize patients' emotional reactions, or to criticize them for their "misconceptions". Nonetheless, one can normalize such misconceptions, try to understand the patient's perspective and the process leading to their conclusions. However, it is equally valid, through a Socratic dialogue, to help the patient reach alternative understandings of the interpersonal issue or situation to which he/she has reacted.

Therapists need also be aware of countertransference traps where they become angry and irritated by patient's defences, identify with their patients' reaction formations and intellectualization, or become captivated by pressure to be the "perfect" therapist. Therapists also need to be aware of their own "blind spots" (i.e. cognitive distortions especially relating to obsessive-compulsive beliefs or patterns). It is important for therapists to remember that clients are not coping with the extremity of their beliefs which ultimately cause them psycho-logical pain. While therapists might often find themselves arguing points of detail, becoming confused, or feeling frustration or anger towards their clients, an acknowledgement of countertransference processes can be extremely useful. A useful image for therapists experiencing hostility is to visualize the patient as a lonely vulnerable child hiding in fear behind well-defended walls pining for nurturance and acceptance. The patient's intransigence and inflexibility often derives from his/her defences, which are constructed by the patient as necessary for the survival of his/her sense of self.

Of particular importance is the need for therapists to deal with their own frustration at the slow pace of progress and the need for repetition. This is only possible if therapists keep salient, in their own cognitive sets, that progress needs to be gradual, particularly in the early stages of treatment, as the obsessive-compulsive will easily manifest anxiety, avoidance or hostility in response to rapid changes or perceived rejection. Rejection is easily interpreted by the obses-sive-compulsive when the therapist is seen to take too much control by setting unrealistic demands. Whilst this may set up an important transference with great potential for significant change, it is not advisable to move too fast in the early stages as the therapist risks missing the opportunity to establish adequate engage-ment with the patient.

It is important to restate that a CBT approach to psychological treatment is not merely comprised of theory-specific techniques, tactics or methods; rather, CBT encompasses techniques from a range of theoretical approaches. In a cogni-tive approach, the commonality between these various techniques is that they are guided by cognitive theory, which asserts that the patient's construction of a particular technique and the cognitive processes being targeted by that technique are the important issue, rather than the initial theoretical basis for that technique. Hence, in any "constructivist" approach to therapy, the therapist needs to be constantly aware of the constructions that clients put on the therapy process, the techniques being utilized and the impact of those techniques on cognitive distortions and faulty appraisals. As the interpersonal domain is an important context of cognitive distortions and faulty appraisals in the obsessive-compulsive, it is imperative that therapists also place a deal of import on patients' constructions about interpersonal and other process issues, regardless of the theoretical approach to the management of obsessive-compulsive disorder.

CONCLUSION

OCPD is associated with a range of dysfunctional patterns in affective, cognitive and behavioural domains, with an emphasis on the development of rigid defences to harbour the individual from the experience of inter- and intrapersonal conflict or distress. OCPD commonly presents with anxiety and mood disorders, although it is seen with a range of Axis I and II conditions. Although formal psychological assessments of OCPD require further development, its early diagnosis is important, particularly given its potentially detrimental effect on treatment outcomes. It is more likely that the obsessive-compulsive's patterns will emerge in treatment over time, especially once acute clinical problems are beginning to resolve, or through the taking of a thorough developmental history.

The aetiology of OCPD is not yet fully understood, although various models have been proposed. An integrated approach offers the greatest heuristic value, particularly with regard to ongoing management. Treatment options include the targeting of dysfunctional cognitions, restricted behavioural repertoires, lack of appropriate contingencies, negative affective dispositions, and issues relating to attachment and identity. While a cognitive-behavioural approach is especially useful towards these ends, treatment needs to be implemented within the context of a safe interpersonal environment characterized by acceptance, trust, consistency and encouragement of both self-efficacy and self-worth. Hence, therapists need to be highly skilled in interpersonal aspects of psychological treatment, and to be aware of transference and countertransference traps.

REFERENCES

Ainsworth, M.D.S. (1979).   Infant–mother attachment. *American Psychologist*, **34**, 932–937.
Ainsworth, M.D.S. (1989).   Attachments beyond infancy. *American Psychologist*, **44**, 709–716.

Alnaes, R. & Torgersen, S. (1988).   The relationship between DSM-III symptom disorders (Axis I) and personality disorders (Axis II) in an outpatient population. *Acta Psychiatrica Scandinavica*, **78**, 485–492.

American Psychiatric Association (1994).   *Diagnostic and Statistical Manual of Mental Disorders (4th edn)*. Washington, DC: American Psychiatric Association.

Barlow, D.H. & Lehman, C. (1996).   Advances in the psychosocial treatment of anxiety disorders. *Archives of General Psychiatry*, **53**, 727–735.

Beck, A.T. (1976).   *Cognitive Therapy and the Emotional Disorders*. Madison: International Universities Press.

Beck, A.T. & Freeman, A. (1990).   *Cognitive Therapy of Personality Disorders*. New York: Guilford.

Bhar, S. & Kyrios, M. (1996).   Cognitive schemata and depressed mood in the development of obsessive-compulsive phenomena: a cross-sectional study in a non-clinical population. Paper presented at the 19th National Conference of the Australian Association for Cognitive & Behavioural Therapy. Sydney, Australia, July.

Black, D.W., Noyes, R. Jr, Pfohl, B., Goldstein, R.B. & Blum, N. (1993).   Personality disorder in obsessive-compulsive volunteers, well comparison subjects, and their first-degree relatives. *American Journal of Psychiatry*, **150**, 1226–1232.

Bowlby, J. (1969).   *Attachment and Loss, Vol. 1. Attachment*. New York: Basic Books.

Bowlby, J. (1973).   *Attachment and Loss, Vol. 2. Separation: Anxiety and Anger*. New York: Basic Books.

Bowlby, J. (1980).   *Attachment and Loss, Vol. 3. Loss: Sadness and Depression*. London: Hogarth.

Clarkin, J.F. & Lenzenweger, M.F. (eds) (1996).   *Major Theories of Personality Disorder*. New York: Guilford.

Cloninger, C.R. (1987).   A systematic method for clinical description and classification of personality variants: a proposal. *Archives of General Psychiatry*, **44**, 573–588.

Corruble, E., Ginestet, D. & Guelfi, J.D. (1996).   Comorbidity of personality disorders and unipolar major depression: a review. *Journal of Affective Disorders*, **37**, 157–170.

Depue, R.A. (1996).   A neurobiological framework for the structure of personality and emotion: implications for Personality Disorders. In J.F. Clarkin & M.F. Lenzenweger (eds), *Major Theories of Personality Disorder*. New York: Guilford, pp. 347–390.

Erikson, E. (1950).   *Childhood and Society*. New York: Norton.

Erikson, E. (1959).   Growth and crises of the healthy personality. In G.S. Klein (ed.), *Psychological Issues*. New York: International University Press.

Eysenck, M. (1992).   *Anxiety: The Cognitive Perspective*. Hove: Erlbaum.

First, M.B., Spitzer, R.L., Gibbon, M., Williams, J.B.W. et al. (1995).   The Structured Clinical Interview for DSM-III-R Personality Disorders (SCID-II): II. Multi-site test–retest reliability study. *Journal of Personality Disorders*, **9**, 92–104.

Freeman, A., Pretzer, J., Fleming, B. & Simon, K.M. (1990).   *Clinical Applications of Cognitive Therapy*. New York: Plenum.

Freeston, M., Rheaume, J. & Ladouceur, R. (1996).   Correcting faulty appraisals of obsessional thoughts. *Behaviour Research & Therapy*, **34**, 433–446.

Freeston, M., Ladouceur, R., Gagnon, F., Thibodeau, N., Rheaume, J., Letarte, H., Bujold, A. (1997).   Cognitive-behavioural treatment of obsessive thoughts: a controlled study. *Journal of Consulting & Clinical Psychology*, **65**, in press.

Gasperini, M., Battaglia, M., Diaferia, G. & Bellodi, L. (1990).   Personality features related to generalised anxiety disorder. *Comprehensive Psychiatry*, **31**, 363–368.

Guidano, V.F. (1991).   *The Self In Process*. New York: Guilford.

Guidano, V.F. & Liotti, G. (1983).   *Cognitive Processes and Emotional Disorders*. New York: Guildford.

Hoencamp, E., Haffmans, P.M., Duivenvoorden, H., Knegtering, H. & Dijken, W.A. (1994).   Predictors of (non-)response in depressed outpatients treated with a three-phase sequential medication strategy. *Journal of Affective Disorders*, **31**, 235–246.

Hyer, L., Brandsma, J. & Shealy, S. (1995). Experiential Mood Therapy with the MCMI-III. In R.D. Retzlaff (ed.), *Tactical Psychotherapy of the Personality Disorders*. Boston, MA: Alyn & Bacon, pp. 210–233.

Kernberg, O.F. (1996). A psychoanalytic theory of Personality Disorders. In J.F. Clarkin & M.F. Lenzenweger (eds), *Major Theories of Personality Disorder*. New York: Guilford, pp. 106–140.

Mahoney, M.J. (1991). *Human Change Processes*. New York: Basic Books.

McCann, J.T. (1992). A comparison of two measures for obsessive-compulsive personality disorder. *Journal of Personality Disorders*, **6**, 18–23.

Millon, T. (1996). *Disorders of Personality: DSM-IV and Beyond*. New York: Wiley.

Millon, T. & Davis, R.D. (1996). An evolutionary theory of Personality Disorders. In J.F. Clarkin & M.F. Lenzenweger (eds), *Major Theories of Personality Disorder*. New York: Guilford, pp. 221–346.

Millon, T. (1987). *Millon Clinical Multiaxial Inventory Manal II*. Minneapolis, MN: National Computer Systems.

Nestadt, G., Romanoski, A.J., Brown, C.H., Chahal, R., Merchant, A., Folstein, M.F., Gruenberg, E.M. & McHugh, P.R. (1991). DSM-III compulsive personality disorder: an epidemiological survey. *Psychological Medicine*, **21**, 461–471.

Nestadt, G., Romanoski, A.J., Samuels, J.F., Folstein, M.F. & McHugh, P.R. (1992). The relationship between personality and DSM-III Axis I disorders in the population: results from an epidemiological survey. *American Journal of Psychiatry*, **149**, 1228–1233.

Nestadt, G., Eaton, W.W., Romanoski, A.J., Garrison, R. et al. (1994). Assessment of DSM-III personality structure in a general population survey. *Comprehensive Psychiatry*, **35**, 54–63.

Nigg, J.T. & Goldsmith, H.H. (1994). Genetics of personality disorders: perspectives from personality and psychopathology research. *Psychological Bulletin*, **115**, 346–380.

Obsessive-Compulsive Cognitions Working Group (1997). Cognitive assessment of obsessive-compulsive disorder. *Behaviour Research and Therapy*, **35**, 667–681.

Pfohl, B. (1996). Obsessiveness. In C.G. Costello (ed.), *Personality Characteristics of the Personality Disordered*. New York: Wiley, pp. 276–288.

Pfohl, B. & Blum, N. (1991). Obsessive-compulsive personality disorder: a review of available data and recommendations for DSM-IV. *Journal of Personality Disorder*, **5**, 363–375.

Pitman, R.K. & Jenike, M.A. (1989). Normal and disordered compulsivity: evidence against a continuum. *Journal of Clinical Psychiatry*, **50**, 450–452.

Pollack, J. (1987). Obsessive-compulsive personality: theoretical and clinical perspectives and recent research findings. *Journal of Personality Disorders*, **1**, 248–262.

Romach, M., Busto, U., Somer, G., Kaplan, H.L. & Sellers, E. (1995). Clinical aspects of chronic use of alprazolam and lorazepam. *American Journal of Psychiatry*, **152**, 1161–1167.

Safran, J.D. & Segal, Z.V. (1990). *Interpersonal Process in Cognitive Therapy*. New York: Basic Books.

Sanderson, W.C., Wetzler, S., Beck, A.T. & Betz, F. (1994). Prevalence of personality disorders among patients with anxiety disorders. *Psychiatry Research*, **51**, 167–174.

Schmidt, N.B., Joiner, T.E., Young, J.E. & Telch, M.J. (1995). The Schema Questionnaire: investigation of psychometric properties and the hierarchical structure of a measure of maladaptive schemas. *Cognitive Therapy & Research*, **19**, 295–321.

Schotte, C., DeDoncker, D., Maes, M., Cluydts, R. & Cosyns, R. et al. (1991). Low MMPI diagnostic performance for the DSM-III-R obsessive-compulsive personality disorder. *Psychological Reports*, **69**, 795–800.

Teasdale, J. & Barnard, P. (1993). *Affect, Cognition, and Change*. Hove: Erlbaum.

Teasdale, J., Segal, Z.V. & Williams, J.M.G. (1995).   How does cognitive therapy prevent depressive relapse and why should attentional control (mindfulness) training help? *Behaviour Research & Therapy*, **33**, 25–39.

Tyrer, P., Casey, P. & Gall, J. (1983).   Relationship between neurosis and personality disorder. *British Journal of Psychiatry*, **142**, 404–408.

van Oppen, P. & Arnzt, A. (1994).   Cognitive therapy for obsessive-compulsive disorder. *Behaviour Research & Therapy*, **32**, 79–87.

Wegner, D.M. (1992).   You can't always think what you want: problems in the suppression of unwanted thoughts. In M. Zanna (ed.), *Advances in Experimental Social Psychology*, Vol. 25. New York: Academic Press, pp. 193–225.

Wegner, D.M. & Pennebaker, J.W. (eds)(1993).   *Handbook of Mental Control*. Englewood Cliffs, NJ: Prentice-Hall.

Young, J.E. (1990).   *Cognitive Therapy for Personality Disorders: A Schema-focused Approach*. Saratosa, FL: Professional Resource Exchange.

Zimbarg, R.E., Barlow, D.H., Brown, T.A. & Hertz, R.M. (1992).   Cognitive-behavioural approaches to the nature and treatment of anxiety disorders. *Annual Review of Psychology*, **43**, 235–267.

Chapter 20

Interpersonal Process in the Treatment of Narcissistic Personality Disorders

Elizabeth Peyton
New School for Social Research, New York, USA
and
Jeremy D. Safran
New School for Social Research and Beth Israel Medical Center, New York, USA

> The individual would have an easy time changing his early "inauthentic" style if he could somehow disengage his own commitment to it. But rules, objects, and self-feeling are fused—taken together they constitute one's "world". How is one to relinquish his world unless he first gains a new one? This is the basic problem of personality change (Becker, 1964, p. 179).

The treatment of personality disorders poses a paradox. To the extent that an individual's sense of self is constituted by his or her personality, any attempts to change the personality will be experienced as a threat to the self. Creation occurs in the context of destruction. What is destroyed is nothing less than the very structures, schemas and self-experience one has relied on, no matter how maladaptively, for a lifetime. Thus, when treating someone with a personality disorder, a therapist must respect the individual's subjective sense of risk and the need to negotiate a balance between continuity and change.

Personality refers to the structures of a person's experiencing. Conceptualized as systems of organizing principles or cognitive-affective schemas, these structures serve to generate the forms and meanings of one's experience of self and other (Atwood & Stolorow, 1984). Developmentally, these structures are formed in an interpersonal context through patterns of interaction between infant and

Cognitive Psychotherapy of Psychotic and Personality Disorders: Handbook of Theory and Practice.
Edited by C. Perris and P.D. McGorry.
© 1998 John Wiley & Sons Ltd.

attachment figures. Interpersonal schemas (Safran, 1990a) comprise the nucleus of what will become the varied and complex dimensions of personality functioning. Drawing upon Bowlby (1969, 1973, 1980) and Stern (1985), Safran has conceptualized interpersonal schemas as generalized representations of self–other interactions that have been abstracted from repeated exchanges with attachment figures and that organize an individual's expectations regarding possible forms of relatedness. Formed by one's early experiences, these schemas continue to shape one's experience of self in relation to others, both internal and external, as well as patterns of interpersonal engagement. In healthier individuals, schemas are equally subject to continual expansion, differentiation and revision in response to new and varied experiences with others. The processes of accommodation and assimilation are relatively balanced. The schemas of people with personality disorders, however, are extremely rigid, such that much of what they experience is assimilated to pre-existing, often maladaptive, structures.

Infants enter the world with two sets of basic needs, self-needs and relational needs, which function as the twin motivational poles of personality development.[1] These needs in fact reflect basic human capacities which, when adequately fostered, evolve through different maturational stages. Developmental research (Stern, 1985; Trevarthen, 1993) has documented the neonate's innate capacity for social interaction. Attachment needs are the most fundamental of relational needs, forming the foundation upon which other relational needs (i.e. attunement, mutuality, intimacy) develop and unfold. Self-needs include needs for self-cohesiveness, individuation, and autonomy.[2] While these two sets of needs are interdependent, tensions may arise between them—and often do to varying degrees. The infant and growing child is totally dependent on parent figures to respond to his[3] evolving needs. Where these needs are not met, the child experiences not only pain and frustration, but also the fear of losing his vital connection to the parents. In such instances, self-needs may be sacrificed (i.e. concealed, distorted, dissociated) in the interest of maintaining a connection. For example, the child who is unable to get positive attunement from parent figures for his spontaneous self-expression, may adapt himself to the image these figures require for their own needs and comfort. The child sacrifices his own natural feelings and impulses, in order to obtain some semblance of the attunement he is seeking. In gratifying his parents, he guarantees connection. It may work the other way around as well. When parents are overly stimulating or otherwise

---

[1] Many personality theorists have postulated two principal motivational processes informing personality development (Angyal, 1941; Bowlby, 1969, 1973; Blatt & Blass, 1992). While they have been variously labeled, they all share the basic distinction between needs for interpersonal relatedness and those for self-definition.

[2] This distinction between self-needs and relational needs maps fairly well onto Sullivan's (1953) distinction between satisfaction and security needs. It seems to us, however, that while relational needs may largely reflect security issues, and self-needs satisfaction issues, one may also find satisfaction in relational experiences and security in certain self-experiences.

[3] For the sake of simplicity, we will selectively use masculine or feminine pronouns throughout this chapter, rather than employ both in each instance.

impinging on the child's ability to self-regulate, a child may resort to some form of withdrawal, thereby impairing the quality of relatedness.

It is through the interactive patterning of a child's self and relational needs, her attachment figures' responses, and the child's counter-responses and experiences, that interpersonal schemas are formed. Many different self–other configurations will be represented over time, in relation to various stage-appropriate needs. These are not merely passive registrations of interactional events, but rather reflect both real features of these interactions and the individual's interpretations of them. Within this view, it is conceivable that a child could form competing representations of the same experience. For example, if a child's expression of a need for help is met with rejection, ridicule or withdrawal, the child may encode two different versions of the interaction. In one, the child may represent the parent as tough but good, responding as she did because of the child's wrong or bad behavior. Expressions of need will be interpreted as bad. In the other, the child may represent the parent as cruel and uncaring, and herself as hurt, angry and even hateful. Because a child's sense of security is so dependent on her attachment to parental figures, viewing them negatively can feel very threatening. Therefore, the more negatively toned representations may be less elaborately encoded—and effectively banished from awareness. Another possibility is that the rejecting parental behavior will be encoded, but the painful feelings originally connected with it will be dissociated. A truncated, affect-less representation remains.

The ways in which various interpersonal interactions are encoded can be seen as a function of anxiety. Intense levels of anxiety can interfere with the individual's capacity to fully encode an interpersonal event in all its various dimensions. Anxiety that pervades the dyadic system (between parent and child) is particularly noxious and disabling. Infants and children are extremely sensitive to anxious reactions in parental figures, becoming anxious themselves in turn (Sullivan, 1953). The extent to which attachment figures are able to tolerate difficult interactions and accept the child's range of experiences will significantly influence the degree to which these different representations are encoded, as well as linked or dissociated. The child whose expressions of disappointment or rage in response to parental rejection or misattunement successfully brings about a restoration of concern or attunement, is able to more elaborately and consciously represent the other as rejecting and self as angry (in addition to other as responsive and self as effective). The affective repair detoxifies the pain and anxiety, allowing the individual to establish a representational matrix that generates multiple, shifting, non-exclusive experiences of self and other. In other words, the greater the non-anxious reception and reflection of a child's various affects and self-other experiences a parent can provide, the less reliant the child will be on defensive exclusion or dissociation.

Henry Stack Sullivan (1953, 1956) emphasized the role of dissociation in relation to interpersonal anxiety and the development of the personality. According to his theories, self-experience which creates anxiety in one's attachment figures is felt to threaten relatedness and the security of the self. Dissociation of such experience functions to restore the vital connection and sense of self-coherence. While Sullivan saw dissociation as the process through which the psyche was organized into "me" and "not me", we conceptualize it as a spectrum phenomenon generating various degrees and qualities of "me" and "not me".[4] If the mind is inherently complex, consisting of multiple representations of self and other, dissociation affects the extent to which each of these is symbolically elaborated and interrelated. An inherent tension exists between associative and dissociative processes. A child may have multiple interactional experiences with attachment figures, some of which are organized into relatively stable, available self–other schemas, while others may be defensively dissociated.

In our view, an individual's interpersonal schemas consist of those representations that can be associated, averaged and affectively modulated. More elaborately encoded and linked, they constitute the medium through which the individual experiences a sense of psychological continuity and integrity. Dissociated self–other representations, while not contributing so directly to one's typical ways of construing, experiencing and engaging with the interpersonal world, nevertheless exert considerable influence. Paradoxically, it is their very silence that creates "noise" in the system.

The phenomenon of *dissociation*, understood as a process intrinsic to the schematization of self–other representations, adds greater dimensionality to our understanding of personality functioning. It allows for a view of personality that encompasses both presence and absence. Just as negative space is crucial to the compositional quality of a painting, dissociated experience is intrinsic to the structures and processes of the personality (Stern, 1983). Far from being mere absences, these gaps in the encoding or linking of experience become essential parts of one's self-functioning. The means by which certain desires, needs and feelings remains to various degrees unsymbolized and disconnected from other areas of self-experience, dissociation functions along a continuum of intensity and pervasiveness. At the extreme end of the continuum, dissociation functions like a negative organizing principle which inhibits certain configurations of experience from emerging into awareness at all. It thereby denies access to cognitive and affective states that would be experienced as disruptive and destructive of one's continuous sense of self. To the extent that dissociation inhibits symbolization and awareness, experience will be constricted and one's emotional life impoverished. Maintaining this dissociative structure, however, is crucial to the *experienced* integrity of the self. As will be elaborated later, the need to perpetuate dissociative structures accounts in part for the difficulties attending the work of personality change.

What distinguishes a personality disorder from normal personality functioning is the degree to which one's psychological structures generate rigid and redundant, rather than situationally-sensitive, forms of experience and behavior. As

---

[4] Recently, Irwin Hirsch (1994) has argued that for Sullivan, too, dissociation existed in degrees along a continuum. While extreme anxiety led to "not me" experience, lesser degrees of anxiety led to "bad me" integrations (p. 779).

defined in DSM-IV, a personality disorder is a "pattern of inner experience and behavior that . . . is inflexible and pervasive across a broad range of social situations" (American Psychiatric Association, 1994). We attribute this redundancy and inflexibility to two interrelated dimensions of personality functioning: the presence of dysfunctional interpersonal schemas and a extreme reliance on dissociative processes. These two dimensions clearly work in concert. Interpersonal schemas structure one's experience of and interaction with others along established lines, lines that were at one time an important means of maintaining relatedness and a stable sense of self. In other words, they were originally highly adaptive. Subsequently, if too fixed and inflexible, they become extremely maladaptive. By definition, dissociated experience will not be generated by these schemas, and because such experience remains unformulated, it forever fails to revise them in adaptive ways. Dissociation thus works to reinforce existing schemas by preventing access to perceptual and emotional experiences that might lead to their modification.

The concept of the cognitive-interpersonal cycle (Safran, 1984; Safran & Segal, 1990) refers to the phenomenon in which an individual's typical construal processes lead to characteristic behaviors and communications which elicit predictable responses. While dissociated thoughts and feelings remain outside the individual's awareness, they are nonetheless expressed in non-verbal ways. Such incongruent communication tends to elicit characteristic responses from others which confirm the person's underlying expectations of self–other interactions. In other words, interpersonal schemas activate and in turn are maintained by cognitive-interpersonal cycles in which the individual evokes schema-consistent responses from others. The more rigid the individual's expectations and associated behaviors, the more likely he will pull complementary and schema-confirming responses from a range of people. This cyclical phenomenon explains in large measure the self-perpetuating quality of personality disorders.

For example, if according to the individual's schemas she believes that keeping her own desires out of the interactional field and accommodating to the other's wishes is necessary for maintaining a sense of relatedness, her dissociated frustration and anger in response to not having her own needs met will likely be conveyed in non-linguistic ways. Her surface presentation of eager people-pleasing and compliance may be silently countered by a subtle, begrudging attitude conveyed through a cold, piercing stare or rigid and resentful body postures. Confused and uncomfortable in the midst of these mixed messages, the other person may retreat from and in some way reject her, unwittingly confirming an implicit assumption of being inadequate or unlikeable. Such an experience paradoxically leads to the reinforcement of existing schemas rather than their revision. Instead of learning to be more relaxed and assertive, the person will likely redouble her efforts at being vigilantly and rigidly accommodating.

The original motivations of connection and self-regulation that informed the creation of interpersonal schemas continue to play a major role in their maintenance. Resistance to change reflects the fear of relinquishing those modes of being which, while maladaptive in many respects, one has long associated with feelings of security and integrity. For example, the individual who as a child split off feelings of warmth and intimacy because they evoked anxiety in attachment figures, continues to dissociate such experience despite the paradoxical fact that in the present, this very way of functioning tends to keep others at a distance. It is precisely because this distance was originally necessary to maintaining an acceptable form of interpersonal connectedness that it continues to feel optimal. Experiences that threaten one's sense of interpersonal relatedness equally threaten to disturb and fragment one's sense of self. The paradox of dissociation is that by dividing self-experience into relatively unlinked parts, a sense of self-continuity and coherence is maintained (Bromberg, 1993).

TREATMENT: AN INTERPERSONAL PROCESS APPROACH

Our approach to the treatment of personality disorders emphasizes the relational qualities of the therapeutic situation. Not merely a precondition for the change process, the therapeutic relationship is integral to it. While conceptually distinct, techniques and relational factors cannot be distinguished in clinical practice (Butler & Strupp, 1986). The interpersonal impact of an intervention is always as significant, if not more so, than its manifest content. The principal goal of treatment is to create a relational context in which new experiences of self and other can emerge. Through a collaborative process, patient and therapist work to elaborate these experiences symbolically and to allow them to enter into a productive dialogue with other parts of the patient's personality. In so doing the patient's core cognitive-affective structures, namely his dysfunctional interpersonal schemas, are gradually modified.

At the heart of this treatment approach is the therapist's role as participant-observer. Never fully objective, the therapist's observations arise from a position embedded within an interpersonal process. It is crucial that he acknowledge his contributions to the interpersonal field and recognize the value of his own feelings and impulses in generating hypotheses about interpersonal cycles that are typical for the patient. Because people with personality disorders are particularly rigid in their interpersonal styles, therapists commonly find themselves pulled into these characteristic relational configurations. In order to illuminate and understand this process, the therapist must first be able to observe his participation in it. This entails an honest exploration of one's feelings, attitudes, and actions, many of which may be unpleasant or distasteful.

Identifying feelings and responses repeatedly evoked by the patient is the essential first step in the therapist's efforts to understand the often subtle interpersonal processes characterizing the therapeutic interaction. Being aware of, rather than just caught up in, one's experience with the patient allows the therapist to reflect on the nature of the processes informing it. An attitude of genuine curiosity guides the therapist in his consideration of the patient's behaviors and communications and the way in which they engender certain responses. These communications, which are often subtle, non-verbal behaviors, can be thought of as *interpersonal markers* (Safran, 1990b). An interpersonal marker represents a point in the interpersonal process where mutual exploration of one's experience in the moment may lead to enhanced understanding of the beliefs and feelings underlying the patient's typical behaviors and interpersonal style. They are ideal junctures for in-depth exploration because the patient's relevant cognitive-affective processes are likely to be most available to reflective awareness.

For example, a patient who implicitly believes that fully experiencing and expressing sadness or anger will cause others to reject him, may deaden these feelings and speak in a flat, monotonous tone of voice. Efforts by the therapist to engage the patient in a deeper exploration of his feelings may meet with dull, unelaborated responses. By noting and inquiring about the patient's vocal quality, the therapist initiates a discovery-oriented process through which the masked feelings, as well as the patient's anxieties about expressing them, may gradually emerge. This requires that the therapist be able to recognize the patient's non-verbal behavior as significant—although its meaning may not be immediately clear. Often, such recognition only occurs after the therapist has been "caught" in the interaction and begins to reflect on what is going on. In the example just described, the therapist may begin to feel distanced by the patient's communication style, frustrated, and inclined to give up trying to make contact. If the therapist is able to identify her experience as a response to this non-verbal behavior, and communicates this awareness rather than acting on it, she opens up the possibility for greater understanding as well as increased vitality in the therapeutic process. Mutual exploration here may lead not only to important insights but to a greater sense of relatedness between patient and therapist. This relational experience is crucial to the change process.

In communicating one's experience, the therapist must be genuinely open to hearing any number of possible responses from the patient. Sorting through the complexities of the interpersonal process will invariably involve traveling down many unanticipated paths of inquiry. For this reason, we stress the importance of an open attitude and a willingness to invite surprise. In a situation very similar to the one described above, one of the authors communicated to the patient her experience of feeling stuck: she felt reluctant to continue asking questions in the face of his apparent apathy and disinterest, but worried that if she remained silent he would feel neglected or abandoned. The patient's initial response was to say, despondently, that he felt the therapist had given up on him. Immediately, an affective engagement, previously lacking, was established. When asked in what way it seemed that the therapist had given up on him, the patient communicated that perhaps he had stumped the therapist, that his problems were too complex for her to figure out. While the content of his words suggested a certain degree of despair, the smile that swept across his face while speaking conveyed something else. This smile represented a new interpersonal marker and a new twist in the interpersonal process.

In our approach we stress the importance of remaining attuned to whatever is emerging in the moment. Signs of emerging experience may be subtle and easily overlooked. In the example above, the smile was intense but fleeting. If one were to focus purely on the words rather than his expression, one might naturally continue to discuss his despair and fears of being beyond repair. Attending to the smile, however, allowed a previously unseen part of the patient to emerge and be known. When the therapist inquired about the smile and his experience, the patient seemed a bit flustered and suggested that it was embarrassment. The therapist shared that she had experienced it as a little teasing and sensed that there was a hint of pleasure in the patient's expression. At this point the patient's smile returned and he began to laugh. He said this was true and began to recall many instances in his life where he derived pleasure from frustrating people. Often, he explained, this assumed the form of his withholding information from another person, which gave him a sense of power and control. The therapist and he began to understand that he was withholding aspects of himself from her, and in so doing protecting himself from feelings of vulnerability and disempowerment. In addition to learning about how this experience and behavior serve him, the patient and therapist found themselves relating to one another in a much more alive and immediate fashion.

We emphasize two principal means of facilitating change. The first is interpersonal in nature and involves the disconfirmation of dysfunctional schemas. To the extent that the therapist becomes aware of the interpersonal pull to act in schema-confirming ways and effectively "unhooks" herself from the cycle by choosing to metacommunicate about her experience, rather than acting on it, she creates the opportunity for the patient to experience a different kind of response than was expected. For example, if in response to a patient's pedantic, intellectualized and abstract style of speaking the therapist is able to communicate her experience of distance and disconnection, while at the same time expressing genuine interest in the patient's experience, the therapist will initiate a process of disconfirmation. The therapist may learn that prior to the patient's shift into this more intellectualized mode of speaking, she had been experiencing warm feelings towards the therapist. She had felt anxious that any display of these feelings would be unreciprocated or outright rejected, leading in turn to feelings of hurt and humiliation. The therapist is then able to help the patient see the way in which her anticipation of rejection has led to distancing behavior. Equally important is the therapist's ability to convey interest in and acceptance of the patient's warm feelings.

The second means of facilitating change, while related to the first, is more intrapersonal in nature. This involves helping the patient to access, symbolize and integrate affects and self-states that have typically remained outside awareness. Failure to integrate emotional experience deprives the individual of information that may potentially motivate adaptive behavior (Safran & Sagal, 1990). Moreover, it restricts and diminishes one's sense of self and self-agency. By enlarging his range of emotional experiencing, the patient expands his sense of self. This expansion of self is a crucial aspect of the change process, for it ultimately leads to greater freedom and flexibility in one's behavior and more direct forms of interpersonal communication (Levenson, 1983; Muran, 1997).

This process, however, is frequently experienced as threatening. The emergence of normally dissociated affects may feel like an invasion of alien and disruptive forces. Relinquishing one's dissociative structures risks a sense of psychic fragmentation and disorientation.

Helping the patient access dissociated emotional experience, therefore, requires an exquisite sensitivity on the part of the therapist. He must be attuned not only to the subtle signs of unexpressed feelings, but also to the anxiety and avoidance attending his attempts to explore them. Often, the indicators are non-verbal: facial expressions, body posture, tone of voice or sudden shifts of attention. In order to notice these, the therapist must focus as much on "the action of telling" (Schafer, 1983, p. 228) as on what is being told. The example given earlier of a patient's triumphant smile while talking about being too difficult to be helped illustrates the often discrepant relationship between what is being communicated through verbal and non-verbal channels. Although initially unable or reluctant to articulate the smile's significance, the patient was later able to access his pleasure in the context of the therapist's interested and accepting attitude. The relative ease with which he was able to access this aspect of himself suggests it may have been dissociated only moderately, forming part of what Sullivan called the "bad me" (as opposed to the "not me"). Although ashamed of this part of himself, the patient also recognized its spirit and vitality, qualities lacking in his more typical self-experience.

In other instances, the individual may be unable to so readily acknowledge disowned feelings or attitudes. The same patient had great difficulty allowing angry feeling to emerge in therapy. The dissociated anger was often palpable to the therapist in the form of the patient's tone of voice and his cold, confrontational stare. Commenting on these non-linguistic features, however, frequently led to denial, minimization, or a claim that he was angry at himself. Following these inquiries about possible anger, the patient often reported that he was drifting, spacing out, and unable to focus. In our treatment approach, such avoidant measures are respected as necessary—albeit maladaptive—means by which the patient maintains his security and sense of self. The therapist points out the shift, asking if the patient has any sense of how the shift occurred. Exploring the difficulties and anxieties attending the exploration of dissociated feelings becomes the relevant focus, rather than the disowned feelings themselves. Increasingly, as the anxieties are felt and articulated within an accepting relational context, a greater tolerance for the dissociated aspects of experience develops.

Clearly the interpersonal and intrapersonal dimensions of facilitating change work together. In exploring an interpersonal interaction, the therapist and patient may discover intrapersonal processes that inhibit more adaptive forms of relating. For example, a patient who repeatedly responds dismissively to a therapist's observations, effectively communicating "Yeah, I already know that", may be disowning an experience of pleasure or gratitude in response to being empathically understood. An examination of the interpersonal dynamics through which the therapist feels devalued and distanced, may lead to an exploration of the patient's self-experience. It may emerge that feelings of appreciation lead to a sense of dependency or vulnerablity which undermines the patient's self-image as strong and self-reliant.

An individual's need to experience himself in rigidly prescribed ways clearly shapes his interpersonal relationships. To the extent that someone can begin to experience himself more fully and with greater flexibility, his other relationships will be also transformed. As the patient expands his awareness of himself, he simultaneously achieves a richer, more real awareness of others. This change in intrapersonal functioning, however, requires a new interpersonal context for its facilitation. Both the therapist's willingness to respond in new ways to the patient, and her interest in and acceptance of previously disowned affects and self-states, create the relational field in which the patient can increasingly feel safe to experience himself in more authentic ways.

The change process is always just that—a process. It requires time, patience and very likely the repetition of similar sequences of interactions. Existing schemas are not restructured in response to a single disconfirming experience. Neither are newly accessed affects or other experiences likely to be integrated as the result of a single "cathartic" session. By remaining focused on and interested in where the patient is at any given time, i.e. the ongoing stream of his experience, rather than on where one would like him to be, the therapist not only conveys an implicit acceptance of who and how the patient is at the present time, but also helps further the change process itself. Paradoxically, the more aware, accepting and understanding the patient becomes of his own current ways of being, the more free he will be to change.

TREATING THE NARCISSISTIC PERSONALITY

In the following section, we discuss how our therapeutic approach might play out in the treatment of individuals diagnosed with Narcissistic Personality Disorder. Rather than advocating specific strategies or techniques for working with narcissistic personalities, we maintain that our approach inherently addresses the most salient and problematic features of an individual's personality functioning, regardless of how they constellate with respect to specific diagnostic categories. The therapist's attention and responsiveness to interpersonal and intrapersonal dynamics in and of itself facilitates the emergence of a therapeutic process uniquely suited to the specific needs of the patient. In certain respects, preconceptions regarding a given diagnostic category can interfere with one's ability to attend to what is actually unfolding in the here and now of the therapy. Nonetheless, we believe that an understanding of narcissistic pathology and its relational origins is useful insofar as it sensitizes the therapist to crucial, often complex features of the therapeutic process.

Narcissistic Personality Disorder, as defined in the DSM-IV, represents one variant of what many consider to be a spectrum of narcissistic disturbances (Bach, 1985; Fiscalini, 1994; Gabbard, 1990). Broadly conceived, pathological narcissism may consist, in various patterns, of the following core dynamics:

"grandiosity, cyclic idealization and contempt for oneself and others; self-centeredness and lack of empathy for others; abnormal self-esteem vulnerability; psychological inaccessibility and imperviousness, attitudes of entitlement—assumed special rights or privileges; controllingness and coerciveness; and other-directedness—the ceaseless search for the attention, approval, and admiration of others" (Fiscalini, 1994, pp. 748–49). What these qualities generally reflect is a fundamental disturbance in an individual's sense of self and his continuous efforts to regulate and consolidate it.

While the spectrum has been divided and labeled in different ways, two principal prototypes have emerged. Variously referred to as "overt" and "covert" (Gabbard, 1990) or "inflated" and "deflated" (Bach, 1985) narcissists, the two are distinguished by the extent to which an individual's grandiosity and egocentricity are consciously experienced and explicitly expressed. The overt type corresponds closely to the clinical picture described by DSM-IV criteria. Arrogant, insensitive and demanding of admiration, the overt narcissist clings to his inflated sense of entitlement and omnipotence, keeping his dissociated sense of vulnerability and inadequacy at bay. In contrast, the covert narcissist's grandiose strivings are more disguised. Inhibited and self-effacing, sensitive and prone to feelings of shame and humiliation, the covert narcissist's longing for mirroring and admiration are largely dissociated, often lived out through attachments to idealized others with whom he can identify. Each prototype reflects a profound disturbance in early relationships through which the individual was required to forfeit whole dimensions of his actual needs and feelings. Despite their manifest differences, both types of narcissistic personality suffer a profound alienation from their real experience and an impaired sense of their intrinsic self-worth.

The development of a healthy resilient sense of self requires an empathic environment of optimal "illusioning" and "disillusioning" responses to the child's naive grandiosity. Heinz Kohut (1971) identified two fundamental developmental needs—"mirroring" and "idealizing"—which, if inadequately met, lead to impairments of the self. Unconditional adoration and approval of the infant or young child, along with the parents' enjoyment and acceptance of the child's reciprocal idealization, create the non-verbal core of the interpersonal self. As long as this early mirroring approval is a response to the actual child—as opposed to what the parent wants him to be—the child internalizes these reflected appraisals as a solid sense of self-worth. Appropriate and empathic disillusionment is also necessary as the child matures. The parent who can help the child confront his real limitations, while empathically responding to the child's inevitable frustrations and disappointments, facilitates in the child an emerging acceptance of his vulnerabilities as well as his strengths.

Fiscalini (1993) has described several patterns of parent–child interaction that inform the development of narcissistic personalities, among them the shamed and special child. The etiological pattern of the special child characterizes many of those individuals most typically diagnosed as narcissistic personalities. The special child is one who is selectively prized and admired for his real or illusory special attributes or abilities, while neglected or devalued for his more ordinary qualities and needs. Such a child feels that connection is contingent upon his being superior and omnipotent. In other words, the inflated "false" self is rewarded, while the child's "real" self—his more multi-dimensional actuality—remains largely unloved and admired. Such a person ends up feeling special, yet fundamentally insufficient and unworthwhile. Behind his cherished sense of uniqueness and brilliance lies the shadow of an intolerably inadequate and depleted self. Anxious and ashamed about his "ordinary" human qualities, the special narcissist relies on such defenses as rage, aloofness, control and contempt to protect and reinforce the distorted superior self.

In contrast, the shamed child experiences chronic disapproval and premature disillusionment of many developmentally appropriate needs. Attaching, depending, asserting and individuating needs may all be rejected and ridiculed because of parental anxiety, envy or hate. Even the child's fundamental needs for mirroring and idealizing may become shamefully unacceptable. These shameful needs and feelings are dissociated and become "not-me" experience. Often, a precocious form of pseudo-independence and self-sufficiency develops to defend against intolerable feelings of need. This experience describes the etiology of the covert narcissist, the individual who tends to comply with the expectations of others, while harboring unconscious resentment for not being sufficiently recognized, loved and admired.

In summary, narcissistic disorders result from severe or prolonged injury to a child's emerging sense of self, which requires for its normal development respect for and responsiveness to a range of experiential states. Both the special and shamed child suffer the relational effects of parents more invested in their own needs and interests than those of their child. Optimal responsiveness to the child's phase-appropriate needs and experiences is impeded by the parents' preoccupation with more self-orientated motivations (Rothstein, 1986). For the toddler going though the separation–individuation process, this lack of empathy creates an experience of more intense separation anxiety; he is deprived of the basic reflective functions necessary for the formation of a stable, core identity. Illusions of perfection and self-sufficiency are conjured (consciously or unconsciously) to protect a fragile, poorly differentiated self. The acute sensitivity of the narcissist reflects his intense need to regulate his self experience in very rigid and controlling ways.

It is this characteristic sensitivity (signaled variously by detachment, shame or rage) that many clinicians consider the primary obstacle to working with narcissistic personalities. From our perspective, however, it constitutes the leading edge of the therapeutic engagement and exploration. The patient's sensitivity and the therapist's reactions to it define fundamental features of an interpersonal relationship which, before it can be explored, understood and perhaps transformed, must be lived out between them. Whatever pull the therapist feels to respond in a circumscribed, cautious and empathic manner constitutes a crucial dimension of the interpersonal process. Whether she responds to that pull, resists it or metacommunicates about it, the therapist's participation will further reflect and shape the ongoing process in which they are mutually engaged.

As is the case in the treatment of all personality disorders, the therapist working with the narcissistic individual needs always to remain mindful of the patient's need to balance continuity and change. In the case of the narcissist, however, what needs to be maintained is often the entirety of his subjective experience. It is not simply that certain kinds of self-experience must remain dissociated (which is also true), but moreover that any expression of a point of view other than the patient's own subjective experience—because it threatens the experienced omniscience and integrity of the self—cannot be tolerated. In other words, it is the form as much as the content of the therapeutic interventions that feels threatening. Presenting a narcissistic patient with an observation that differs from his own experience may engender intense feelings of shame, rage and/or envy.

The controversies about the proper role of empathy in the treatment of narcissistic personalities seem almost moot when one views therapy as an organically unfolding interpersonal process in which interventions are formed in a context-specific, relational fashion. We view empathy not so much as a particular technique, but rather as a mode of relating. It is often a natural or spontaneous form of relating, but in the treatment of narcissists the therapist may begin to feel controlled. Attending to the discrepancy between what feels genuine and what feels forced or coerced with respect to one's empathic communications may help the therapist develop initial hypothoses about important aspects of the interpersonal process. A sense of being locked into a very circumscribed role may reflect an experiential counterpart to the patient's own restricted range of feeling and behaving. While the patient's need for empathic reflection may feel excessive and even infuriating, premature attempts by the therapist to question or confront the patient about this need will prove counter-therapeutic. How the therapist uses her feelings about the interaction to therapeutic ends is a matter of considerable artistry and tact.

Therapy with narcissistic personalities often requires prolonged periods of empathic responsiveness to issues of self-esteem. By empathic responsiveness we do not mean a total mirroring of the patient. Rather, we mean the therapist's attunement to subtle shifts within both herself and the patient, particularly those that seem to reflect mounting anxiety and threatened self-esteem. Direct inquiry into such shifts may or may not lead to mutual exploration. When a patient's capacity for reflective awareness is limited (many narcissists have considerable difficulty separating from their own subjectivity), the therapist may need to rely on empathic conjectures. Comments that acknowledge the patient's difficulty or discomfort in being, for example, in the vulnerable position of needing help, contribute both to the patient feeling understood and also to his beginning to view himself from an external, interpersonal perspective. Overall, the early phase of treatment involves engaging the patient in a process where a just tolerable degree of anxiety and frustration is maintained through "maximal verbal and non-verbal responsiveness to his need to be accepted and understood on his own terms" (Bromberg, 1983, p. 380), all the while inviting the patient's curiosity about this controlling need.

By responding to the patient's "need to be accepted and understood in his own terms", the therapist has already begun the interpersonal process of disconfirming dysfunctional schemas. The narcissistic patient often has the expectation that his own genuine (i.e. non-defensive) experience will be rejected or invalidated by others. Of course, the painful irony is that his compensatory attitudes of aloofness, grandiosity and self-sufficiency are what in fact tend to irritate and distance others. The therapist who responds to these attitudes critically, however, will unwittingly confirm and reinforce the underlying schema. Thus, the tendency of the therapist to be pulled into a critical or confrontational stance *vis-à-vis* the patient's defensive attitudes represents a common and serious pitfall of the therapeutic process. If the therapist can notice but refrain from acting on her urge to puncture the patient's inflated self-image, instead acknowledging his needs for acceptance, she establishes the conditions for a new relational experience.

The therapist's awareness of her own feelings and inclinations is crucial. Typical responses vary from feeling irritated and desiring to puncture the patient's grandiose "bubble" to feeling distanced and wanting to break through his barriers to make contact, to feeling devalued and longing to blame the patient for his lack of appreciation. Sufficient groundwork must be done in terms of establishing an alliance before the therapist should consider metacommunicating about her experience. Even so, the therapeutic alliance is likely to be tested and strained by the attempt to introduce the therapist's subjective reactions into the discussion. The capacity to work through the resulting tension or rupture in the alliance, however, will itself be of enormous therapeutic value (Safran & Muran, 1995). In fact, attending to disfluencies in the therapeutic relationship is one of the therapist's most critical functions.

While metacommunication may appear to *create* tension between therapist and patient, it might also be seen as the means by which existing but previously unacknowledged tension is made manifest. To the extent that the therapist's reactions are always embedded within an interpersonal field, her feelings of discomfort and unease typically reflect a fundamental tension in the dyadic interaction, a tension that the two participants have tacitly and collusively "agreed" to ignore. In this context, metacommunication initiates a process of demystification. By sharing her responses to her patient in a spirit of genuine curiosity about what they may signify, she is implicitly stating her interest in answering the question, "What's going on around here?" (Levenson, 1983). For the patient whose childhood relationships required a defensive inattention to what was really transpiring (for example, the chronic neglect of the narcissist's real feelings and needs), the therapist's commitment to exploration and clarification, while threatening on one level, offers comfort and relief on another.

Metacommunication is most effective when it is done in reference to a specific interpersonal marker. For instance, if in response to the therapist's comment, "It sounds as though you were feeling lonely and confused", the patient replies, "Those are good words" in a flat and disengaged voice, the therapist may feel paradoxically complimented and devalued, recognized and distanced. In calling the patient's attention to his response and her own reaction to it, while at the same time expressing interest in the patient's experience, the therapist may deepen the process of schema disconfirmation. The patient may report that he had begun to feel sad and tearful, but had cut these feelings off for fear of being considered weak or pathetic. He also may have begun to feel angry at the therapist for eliciting these more vulnerable feelings, but worried that his anger would drive her away. The patient's response reflects both an effort to mask these feelings and their unwitting expression.

Of course, especially early on, it is just as likely that the patient will respond to the therapist's inquiry with either a very concrete (i.e. unreflective) understanding of the interaction, irritation or contempt. The capacity to stand back from an interpersonal interaction, reflecting on both one's own mind and the other person's mind, is not one that comes naturally to many narcissistic individuals (Bach, 1985). Facilitating the growth of this capacity is in fact one of the major goals of the treatment with such patients. At the point in therapy when the narcissist is able to engage in a mutual exploration of an interaction with interest and emotional presence, much of the therapeutic work will have already been accomplished.

Acknowledging and reclaiming disowned aspects of self-experience plays a central role in the narcissist's developing this capacity to relate more fully to others. Experiences and affects relating to loss, deprivation, dependency and vulnerablity are often those the narcissist has most trouble accepting as part of who he is. The therapist's role is not only to reintroduce the individual to his more vulnerable feelings, but to help him understand how and why he avoids them. In exploring a moment where a patient cuts himself off from an emerging sense of loss and loneliness, the therapist may learn that the patient has begun to feel like a "loser", i.e. small and self-pitying. In addition to helping the person see how he distances himself from his own experience, the therapist implicitly communicates an acceptance of feelings the patient cannot himself tolerate.

The task of helping someone become more open to his feelings of loss and longing is in many ways fraught with as much peril as potential. Narcissistic patients have disowned such feelings, based on their early experiences of rejection and unmet needs. Therapists, despite their best intentions, are likely to fall short of their patient's hopes and desires. Encouraging a patient to be more aware of his deep-seated longing for unconditional love, the therapist is inevitably inviting the patient to experience disappointment—albeit in a new context. "Optimal disillusionment" was the term used by Winnicott (1965) to describe the mother's gradual frustration of the infant's needs for absolute attunement. Working through the inevitable disillusionments of the therapeutic relationship in a constructive, non-traumatic fashion becomes one of the most important means of change.

The kinds of change the narcissistic patient and his therapist have in mind are likely to be quite different at the outset of treatment. Narcissistic people generally enter treatment when their narcissistic strategies have failed them. Depression, somatic complaints and relationship difficulties are among the many manifest reasons the narcissist seeks help. Demoralized and desperate, he regards the therapist as someone who can help restore and perfect his narcissistic stance, rather than someone who can help him live and relate more fully and genuinely. While to the therapist an increased awareness of internal experience means greater vitality and potential for intimacy, to the patient it threatens to create a sense of shame and weakness. The very act of seeking help feels like an admission of defeat; to offset this inherent humiliation, the narcissist often makes large and unrealistic demands that the therapist make him perfect, powerful and successful—anything but who he actually is.

Negotiating the inevitable tension between these disparate aims is a matter of considerable delicacy. The therapist must respect the manifest wishes of the patient, while gradually facilitating new kinds of experience that open the narcissist's eyes to previously unimagined possibilities of being and relating. But the tension is not something simply to be cleverly managed; rather, it must be lived out, experienced and explored between patient and therapist. The patient's expectations of the therapist, that she magically transform him, and the therapist's inability to do so will inevitably lead to feelings of frustration, anger and disappointment. Exploring and identifying these feelings with the patient in a spirit of genuine and empathic interest, the therapist creates the means by which the individual can live through his narcissistic patterns in a new and therapeutically reconstructive way (Fiscalini, 1994).

The relationship between patient and therapist constitutes the heart of the change process. The patient's narcissistic schemas need to be played out within the therapeutic relationship itself in order for them to be articulated, understood and reworked. The therapist's willingness to collaboratively live out and inquire into the meaning of the patient's narcissistic patterns creates the context for the emergence of new relational experiences. The therapist's attitude of openness, curiosity and humility—of never presuming to know what can only be mutually discovered—guides the process and models new and non-narcissistic ways of being. Together, the therapist and patient create a rich relational "world", one which over time comes to hold sufficient value and promise that the patient is willing to surrender his old "world"—the only world he has ever known—and to live fully in the new.

REFERENCES

American Psychiatric Association (1994). *Diagnostic and Statistical Manual of Mental Disorders*, 4th edn. Washington, DC: American Psychiatric Association.

Angyal, A. (1941). *Foundations for a Science of Personality*. New York: Commonwealth Foundation.

Atwood, G.E. & Stolorow, R.D. (1984). *Structures of Subjectivity: Explorations in Psychoanalytic Phenomenology*. Hillsdale, NJ: Analytic Press.

Bach, S. (1985). *Narcissistic States and the Therapeutic Process*. New York: Jason Aronson.

Becker, E. (1964). The human personality: a contemporary critique. In *Revolution in Psychiatry*. New York: Free Press, pp. 163–198.

Blatt, S.J. & Blass, R.B. (1992).   Relatedness and self-definition: two primary dimensions in personality development, psychopathology, and psychotherapy. In J.W. Barron, M.N. Eagle & D.L. Wolitzky (eds), *Interface of Psychoanalysis and Psychology*. Washington, DC: American Psychological Association.
Bowlby, J. (1969).   *Attachment and Loss, Vol. 1. Attachment*. New York: Basic Books.
Bowlby, J. (1973).   *Attachment and Loss, Vol. 2. Separation, Anxiety and Anger*. New York: Basic Books
Bowlby, J. (1980).   *Attachment and Loss, Vol. 3. Loss, Separation and Depression*. New York: Basic Books.
Bromberg, P.M. (1983).   The mirror and the mask: on narcissism and psychoanalytic growth. *Contemporary Psychoanalysis*, **19**, 359–387.
Bromberg, P.M. (1993).   Psychoanalysis, dissociation, and personality organization. *Psychoanalytic Dialogues*, **5**, 511–528.
Butler, S.F. & Strupp, H.H. (1986).   Specific and non-specific factors in psychotherapy: a problematic paradigm for psychotherapy research. *Psychotherapy*, **23**, 30–40.
Fischalini, J. (1993).   Interpersonal relations and the problem of narcissism. In J. Fiscalini & A.L. Grey (eds), *Narcissism and the Interpersonal Self*. New York: Columbia University Press.
Fiscalini, J. (1994).   Narcissism and coparticipant inquiry: explorations in contemporary interpersonal psychoanalysis. *Contemporary Psychoanalysis*, **30**, 747–776.
Gabbard, G.O. (1990).   Psychodynamic Psychiatry in Clinical Practice, Washington, DC: American Psychiatric Press.
Hirsch, I. (1994).   Dissociation and the interpersonal self. *Contemporary Psychoanalysis*, **30**, 777–799.
Kohut, H. (1971).   *The Analysis of the Self*. New York: International Universities Press.
Levenson, E. (1983).   *The Ambiguity of Change*. New York: Basic Books.
Muran, J.C. (1997).   Multiple selves and depression. *In-Session: Psychotherapy in Practice*, **3**, 53–64.
Rothstein, A. (1986).   The theory of narcissism: an object-relations perspective. In A.P. Morrison (ed.), *Essential Papers on Narcissism*. New York: New York University Press.
Safran, J.D. (1984).   Assessing the cognitive-interpersonal cycle. *Cognitive Therapy and Research*, **8**, 333–348.
Safran, J.D. (1990a).   Towards a refinement of cognitive therapy in light of interpersonal theory: I. Theory. *Clinical Psychology Review*, **10**, 87–105.
Safran, J.D. (1990b).   Towards a refinement of cognitive therapy in light of interpersonal theory: II. Practice. *Clinical Psychology Review*, **10**, 107–122.
Safran, J.D. & Muran, J.C. (1995).   Resolving ruptures in the therapeutic alliance: Diversity and integration. *In-Session: Psychotherapy in Practice*, **1**, 81–92.
Safran, J.D. & Segal, Z.V. (1990).   Interpersonal Process in Cognitive Therapy. New York: Basic Books.
Schafer, R. (1983).   *The Analytic Attitude*. New York: Basic Books.
Stern, D.B. (1983).   Unformulated experience. *Contemporary Psychoanalysis*, **19**, 71–99.
Stern, D.M. (1985).   *The Interpersonal World of the Infant: a View from Psychoanalysis and Developmental Psychology*. New York: Basic Books.
Sullivan, H.S. (1953).   *The Interpersonal Theory of Psychiatry*. New York: W.W. Norton.
Sullivan, H.S. (1956).   *Clinical Studies in Psychiatry*. New York: W.W. Norton.
Trevarthen, C. (1993).   The self born in subjectivity: the psychology of an infant communicating. In U. Neisser (ed.), *The Perceived Self: Ecological and Interpersonal Sources of Self-Knowledge*. Cambridge: Cambridge University Press.
Winnicott, D.W. (1965).   The Maturational Process and the Facilitating Environment. London: Hogarth.

Chapter 21

Cognitive Psychotherapy in the Treatment of Personality Disorders in the Elderly

Lucio Bizzini
Department of Psychiatry, University Hospitals of Geneva,
Geneva, Switzerland

PERSONALITY, LIFE-SPAN AND MENTAL DISORDERS

Aging and Personality

Allport (1937) defines personality as "the internal dynamic organization of the individual's psychological systems which determine his actual adjustment to the environment". As Vézina, Cappeliez & Landreville (1994) rightly stated, this view of personality immediately comes down on the side of stability as far as the development of adult personality is concerned. An individual's personality would therefore remain steady with age when considered from the point of view of its features or, as it is commonly described, of its character. Nevertheless, Costa et al. (1986) demonstrate a slight but significant drop in the personality traits of neuroticism, extraversion and openness towards experience. These results, acquired from a cross-sectional study wherein the effects of age, of the time period and of the cohort could tend to confusion, have apparently been confirmed by a recent longitudinal study carried out by Spiro et al. (reported by Sadavoy et al., 1996), especially as far as extraversion is concerned.

It would be more interactionist to regard personality as a dynamic process which evolves in terms of adaptation and which is successful when external demands meet internal resources or, as Piaget (1967) reminds us, when assimilation and accommodation are in a state of cooperation and equilibrium.

Cognitive Psychotherapy of Psychotic and Personality Disorders: Handbook of Theory and Practice.
Edited by C. Perris and P.D. McGorry.
© 1998 John Wiley & Sons Ltd.

Along the same lines, Jung (see Spagnoli, 1995) adopts a more developmental outlook on personality, considering that it evolves throughout one's life, suggesting that the older we get, the more the two poles (internal and external) balance each other out. On the one hand, we slide progressively towards the outside world, while at the same time modes of thought and behavior proper to each sex (due to less stringent social demands) are reduced. With maturity, the individual becomes less impulsive, his whole system of emotions becomes more complex and more subtle than in his youth, feelings become more interiorized, along the lines of what Erikson, Erikson & Kivnick (1986) call *involved disinvolvement*, a form of wisdom that prepares us for the end of life ("Wisdom is detached concern with life itself, in the face of death itself" (p. 37)).

Research into life course and personality for their part has emphasized the importance of the cohort and sex factors. Some authors have concluded that people born towards the beginning of the century tend to be more measured and restrained but also less assertive. Other authors have made the point that men maintain higher personality stability throughout life, whereas women reorganize their lives more. Other studies into the elderly show that women become more affirmative and independent and men more affectionate and caring (see Vézina, Cappeliez & Landreville, 1994).

An important contribution to the study of personality in the aging process has been made by Hans Thomae (1980), who, within a cognitive perspective, puts forward the idea that the motor responsible for personality change resides in the perception the individual has of the need for, and the possibility of, change. As a result of longitudinal research (Bonn Longitudinal Study), Thomae puts forward three basic postulates for personality development and adaptation to one's own aging. He points out the importance of personal beliefs, as well as of preoccupations which dominate each period of life, and points to the need for equilibrium between the cognitive and motivational components of personality as being the deciding factor in adaptation. This study therefore brings out the deciding influence which one's perception of the need for change has over the modification of certain personality traits. It further emphasizes the importance of the representation that the individual has of his/her own aging process. It is through this subject–environment articulation process, determined by an ongoing desire for change, that Thomae offers possible explanations for successful aging.

In conclusion, personality development can be regarded as a dialectical process between stability and change. Stability prevails if adaptation to life's circumstances is not too costly, whereas personality change takes place under the pressure of difficult life events. The aging process increases the individualization of one's lifecourse, not only from a professional but also from a family and relational point of view. Already part of the social environment, interpersonal differences become more and more profound. The likelihood of somatic problems increases, representing the most dominant factor in the danger to well-being. Even more than with the young adult, everything depends upon how the outside and the inside worlds are articulated and upon maintaining a coherent life course where beliefs, desires and conflicts are balanced. The task of adapting can turn out to be a very difficult one for the elderly person.

Aging and Personality Disorder

Little research has been carried out concerning the prevalence of personality disorders in aging. Fogel & Sadavoy (1996) consider that "nosological problems associated with personality disorder diagnoses are worse when older people are studied, because recall may be worse, informants less available, and diagnostic behavioral criteria less typical of the manifestations of personality disorder seen in later life" (p. 646). Moreover, the authors insist that the diagnosis of organic disorders considerably reduces the chances that any personality diagnosis be made along Axis II.

Epidemiological data that we have available seems to indicate that the elderly person has less tendency towards personality disorder than the young adult would appear to have. Moreover, it has been found that there are more psychiatric consultations for elderly people with personality disorder than for those without (Ames & Molinari, 1994). Furthermore, Vine & Steingart (1994) have shown that the diagnosis of personality disorder is often associated with chronic depression within the elderly person and they conclude that personality is a decisive factor in the onset of chronic depression with age. Finally, Abrams et al. (1994), in their study of groups of geriatric patients with late- (first incidence over the age of 60) or early-onset depression, show that the latter patients have undergone more episodes of personality dysfunctioning. It must also be noted that with age there is a certain "cooling down" of classical psychiatric symptoms (schizophrenia, manic-depressive psychosis), either in terms of better everyday coping (greater skill in adapting to the outside world) or in terms of an exacerbation of one of the affective poles and the adoption of a monopolar mode. This tendency is also seen for personality disorders, which often diminish with the elderly subject. Moreover, some personality diagnosis criteria appear to be worsened by behavioral features common to the elderly (Léger & Clément, 1990). From our clinical experience, personality disorders within the elderly are very common and we often see certain Axis II characteristics. This impression would seem to be confirmed both by the data given by Molinari & Marmion (1993), who found that 58% of all personality disorders within their sample were found in elderly psychiatric outpatients, as well as those given by Fogel & Westlake (1990), who found obsessive-compulsive disorders within 46% of their elderly depressed patients.

A high percentage of the elderly patients we come to see show personality disorders or at least certain pathological aspects within their personalities. These may well be chronic psychiatric patients, the victims of regular—and especially depressive—relapses. As far as treatment is concerned, Thompson, Gallagher &

Czirr (1988) emphasize the fact that elderly patients with personality disorders are less likely to have reduced depressive symptoms after short-term psychotherapy, which Kunik et al. (1993) did not find this in their study of depressive patients.

It seems wrong to us to consider modifying the psychological functioning of such patients, especially within the cognitive context. On the contrary, it would appear more realistic and apt to help the elderly patient re-employ the resources he/she has previously used successfully, at least in periods when symptoms receded. In other words, we advise the therapist to maximize the adaptive potential of the schema (which is, by definition, dysfunctional) that the individual has built up throughout his/her existence, rather than to set about establishing a whole new schema to deal with the outside world.

There is, however, another group of patients that we regularly come across in our clinical practice. They have no long psychiatric history behind them but some personality disorder has been attributed to them. This phenomenon may be explained by the fact that adapting to the changes in lifestyle brought about by age requires more and more resources. In trying to adapt, certain mechanisms of psychological dysfunctioning may develop and cause pseudo-personality disorders. It therefore seems to us that the main problem is not the influence of personality disorders on the process of adaptation. The elderly person has more chance of a balanced personality if his/her repertoire for coping (allowing him/her to integrate the self, the others and the outside world) is sufficiently large. While addressing the importance of mid-life crisis, during which the individual has to cope with the subjective and/or objective processes of change pertaining to that age, Guidano (1992) insists that the experience of living is a constant process of personal growth in which the many aspects of the self must be at all times integrated. Sadavoy et al. (1996), in their study of the psychotherapeutical treatment of personality disorders within the elderly, remind us that, even before attributing certain symptoms to Axis II, the therapist must carefully assess Axis I disorders for which prognosis is more favorable, as treatable depressions and psychoses can easily be masked by apparent signs of personality disorder. This vision of things corroborates our idea that the principal elements to be taken into account while working with the elderly are the life course and the adaptation style that the individual has developed throughout his/her existence in the context of his/her personal vulnerability (Perris, this volume).

The aim of this chapter is, first, to present our conceptual and clinical framework and then to show the different characteristics of the psychological treatment we are offering elderly patients with emotional disorders arising out of a critical moment in their life courses (namely, the loss of a close relative, a conflict within the couple, retirement, or the onset of severe health problems), and whose strategies of adaptation are at a loss. We have chosen to present the clinical case of a 70 year-old man, whose personality comprised obsessional-compulsive and perfectionist traits and who within 18 months underwent three severe episodes of depression in the context of a conflictual family environment.

OUR CONCEPTUAL AND CLINICAL FRAMEWORK FOR THE TREATMENT OF GEROPSYCHIATRIC PATIENTS

Life-span and Development

In order to have a better understanding of the principles of psychotherapy for the elderly, we must be aware of the psychological and the sociological conditions of the aging process. How has the elderly person developed throughout his/her life, which models describe his/her course? What are the most pertinent aspects to be taken into consideration when working with older patients? These are some of the questions we have sought to answer from within the scientific literature.

Psychological Aspects

It must be said that the study of the psychological development of adults has been long overlooked. This can be put down to a certain number of ideas that have dominated twentieth century psychology: those of Freud, for example, for whom everything is determined by the age of 6 and for whom the rigidification of structures with age makes cure and change impossible; those of Binet, who claimed with good reason that "the child is no miniature adult", thus stimulating a current of research focusing on the child's world. Finally, there are those of Piaget, who, in the context of his epistemological project, studied how children acquire knowledge by constructing it. Moreover, preconceived ideas about the development of the human being stopping at 18, the understanding of how important educating the young can be, as well as methodological difficulties in research, have all held back work on the psychology of the adult and the elderly. It has only been in the last 25 years that several approaches have been put forward in the study of the cognitive development of the adult (see Sternberg & Berg, 1992, for a literature review):

- The so-called *psychometric approach*, which focuses on the IQ notion, indicating that certain abilities decline with age while others do not. This approach favors a quantitative method which, despite modifications concerning the age categories, cannot account for the changes that take place with aging.
- The so-called *information-processing approach*. Centered around the computer metaphor, it is based on problem-solving capacity and memory. This approach lacks ecological validity, as Baddeley (1981) stated, human functioning being more complex. Moreover, any developmental perspective is missing altogether, as is the metacognitive dimension (namely, the way people think). The comparison between elderly and young students is, to say the least, inadequate, since it draws on material aimed at the latter.

- The *approach based on the notion of learning*, focusing on the accumulation of knowledge, is purely descriptive. This approach maintains—and rightly so—that learning is a long process, but its interest is exclusively geared towards content rather than to the process itself. No theoretical framework within this approach is able to account for the mechanisms of post-adolescent development.
- The *Piagetian approach* (Piaget, 1972), according to which no new developmental stages emerge in adulthood. The adult applies the mental operations constructed to adolescence to different settings. Importance is therefore laid on the gaining of experience through the notion of expertise. Mistakes in reasoning and logic made by children and adolescents may also be found in adults. This approach overestimates the importance of the logical aspect of reasoning. Moreover, the somewhat vague concept of *horizontal décalage* that Piaget uses in order to explain the differenciated applications of operations does not seem convincing, given the complexity of the problem.
- The *neo-Piagetian approach*, according to which there is a fifth stage in intellectual development that authors call "post-formal" (Labouvie-Vief, 1992). It is defined, depending on the context, as a "metasystematic, dialectical or epistemic" stage integrating emotions and cognitions. The accent is put on the task-solving priorities with which the adult is confronted. It is indeed the overcontextual nature of the aspects of growth that restricts this approach. At this stage, the lack of any global integrated vision is to be regretted. Moreover, little agreement is found for the definition of this stage.
- The so-called *life-span approach*, which studies the whole range of psychosocial development in late life, provides us with useful information, be it from a *sensorial* point of view (the study of the effect of diminished sensorial capacity on learning, the search for compensating strategies, the implementation of new strategies); from a *cognitive* point of view (the analysis of information processing with age; Salthouse, 1985), the study of the development of notions such as wisdom (Baltes & Smith, 1990; Baltes et al., 1995) creativity (Ruth & Birren, 1985) or curiosity (Zinetti, 1989); from a *conative* point of view (studies on the consequences of life changes and undesired life events; Holmes & Rahe, 1967; Norris & Murrel, 1987); from an *interactionist* point of view (description of the characteristics of a stressor—the adaptation tasks are more frequent with age—and of the characteristics of a person—cognitive assessment, repertoire of available strategies, adaptive style).

Sociological Aspects

Literature concerning a sociological perspective on aging and old age focuses first and foremost on the actual generational context. Indeed, when studying the aging and old age phenomena, one ought not to forget that some of the differences that are observed between classes of age can be explained by life habits, the educational system subjects were brought up in and the level of education achieved, or even by the degree of familiarity with a test situation, rather than by the mere age factor (see studies by Schaie, 1974, 1980, or by Baltes, 1987). We are living in a period of over-aging (which will go on, according to the demographic forecasts that indicate that in 2020 a quarter of the population will be over 65 years of age). We are also living at a time when women are over-represented and when life expectancy will constantly increase (presently, in Western countries, it corresponds to 80 for women and 73 for men; Vieillir en Suisse, 1995).

Psychosocial theories (see Mishara & Riedel, 1984), in a context of well-being, endeavor to explain optimal aging through different theories: the theory of *disengagement*, in which it is inevitable, healthy and universal for the older person to adhere to the retiring- and preparation-for-death models and to commit him/herself to new relationships with more distance; the theory of *activity*, in which old age is successful as long as one maintains or replaces activities and roles; the theory of *continuity*, in which there is a the search for a balance which is characterized by changes that match the older person's adaptive capacities. Other sociological studies have underlined the role of the socioprofessional, economic and cultural context (for a review, see Baltes & Brim, 1983).

To sum up, research into the development of the adult and the elderly and the description of a life course account for the great cognitive (relativistic and dialectical thought) and emotional (progressive internalization of feelings) complexity and call for the integration of both dimensions. This development and complexity can be observed particularly when the person has to adapt to the different tasks of adult life, such as choice of career, management of one or more intimate relationships, assuming complex social roles, acceptance of possible disillusions at work, in the couple, in the children's upbringing, reorientation of priorities that takes into account sensorial and cognitive changes, and the ability to cope with health problems. These tasks are even more numerous in old age.

Among these studies, we retain in particular that the notion of wisdom is destined to represent a key concept in accounting for development in aging. Wisdom refers to human affairs (philosophical and existential aspects), but also to managing human relations and society. It entails a cognitive component (an increase in relativistic or reflective thought has been seen in aging) and an affective component (the distinction between the needs of the other and those of oneself is more evident, the defense mechanisms more elaborate). It allows the integration of the rational and the emotional components, the solving of conflicts between "despair" and "integrity", according to Erikson's (1959) terms, and it is meant to account for the adaptative mechanisms in the final stage of the life cycle.

Cognitive Psychotherapy with the Elderly

Psychotherapy with the elderly is becoming more and more common practice, be it institutional or private, and many authors have defended the soundness of such treatment. As suggested by Vézina, Cappeliez & Landreville (1994) on the subject of depression, "Current knowledge would seem to indicate that psycho-therapy can be beneficial to the depressive elderly, either as full treatment or in combination with pharmacotherapy" (p. 340, our translation). More especially, the psychotherapeutical approach with the elderly has benefited in recent years from the emergence of short-term therapy centered around real problems and considered more effective for coping with everyday problems. Of these, cognitive therapy has without doubt contributed most to the acceptance of psychological care for the elderly.

Beck et al., (1979) define cognitive therapy as:

> ... an active, directive time-limited, structured approach, used to treat a variety of psychiatric disorders ... The therapeutical techniques are designed to identify, reality-test, and correct distorted conceptualisation and dysfunctional beliefs (schemas) underlying these cognitions ... The cognitive therapist helps the patient to think and act more realistically and adaptively about his psychological problems and thus reduces symptoms (pp. 3–4).

This type of treatment has shown itself to be particularly effective with depressive, anxious, phobic or obsessional patients. The cognitive therapist calls, on the one hand, upon behavioral techniques (i.e. assigning graduated tasks, problem solving programs, activity plans, muscular relaxation, etc.) and, on the other hand, upon cognitive techniques (i.e. identifying automatic thoughts, written self-observation, widening of interpretations, explanation of cognitive models, etc.). A "scientific" type of collaboration between patient and therapist develops throughout therapy, a sort of partnership in which both play active roles, centered around cognitive restructuring and adaptive changes. At the present time, we are seeing new theoretico-practical elements (widening of the epistemological framework, the therapeutical relationship, the patient's emotions and background as therapeutic fulcra). Thus, in cognitive psychotherapy, more cognition, emotion and action are integrated, and going back into the past is advised in order to seek out particular moments of exploration as well as to find an answer to the cognitivo-emotional blockage (Guidano & Liotti, 1983; Safran & Segal, 1990; Mahoney, 1991; Sookman, Pinard & Beauchemin, 1994; Favre & Bizzini, 1995; Bizzini & Myers-Arrázola, 1996; Pezzati, 1996). Beck, Freeman et al. (1990) also recommend delving into the past and taking into account historical data in work with patients exhibiting personality disorders in the sense of DSM-III psychiatric diagnosis. In this case, cognitive psychotherapy is carried out over a longer period of time, the average number of sessions per treatment going from 20–30 over 6 months or a year to 40–60 over 2 or 3 years. The efficacy of cognitive therapy is scientifically proven. For example, as far as the treatment of depression within the general public is concerned, Murphy et al. (1984) show that its effect is greater than that of medicine and come to the conclusion that a modification of the central cognitive process is a necessary prerequisite for any chemical or psychological treatment to be effective.

With the elderly, a number of studies, centered essentially upon depression, have shown the efficacy of cognitive psychotherapy over other psychotherapeutic and biological treatments (Beutler et al., 1987; Gallagher-Thompson, Hanley-Peterson & Thompson, 1990; Perris, 1990; Thompson, Gallagher & Steinmetz Breckenridge, 1987; Thompson et al., 1991; for discussion, see Cappeliez, 1993). Moreover, it must be noted that cognitive-behavioral treatment of the depressed elderly has obtained as much success with the young (60–80% success rate) and the schemas and basic postulates on which all cognitive work is based are the same as for younger patients (Vézina & Bourque, 1984). The phases of cognitive psychotherapy, as well as the techniques and therapeutic styles, are thus similar to those found in the treatment of younger patients. Nevertheless, the therapist who is working with the elderly has to consider the sensorial and information-processing changes that occur in old age, the specific content of dysfunctional thought patterns, the older patient's expectations toward therapy and the therapist, as well as his/her own representations of old age. In other words, the therapist who works in psychotherapy with the elderly has to be familiar with the specific data of the neuropsychological assessment and rehabilitation, as well as with psychogerontological models used to describe the aging process and old age.

Neuropsychological Point of View

The therapist must pay particular attention to the slowing down of information processing (in the sense of Salthouse, 1985), to the increased likelihood of organic intellectual deterioration, as well as to the higher frequency of strokes within the elderly. Furthermore, he must be able to distinguish between senescence and senility, and between mnesic modifications and mnesic loss, as well as understand the specific characteristics of the third and fourth age (Bizzini, 1990). He must therefore avail himself of the necessary assessment tools and choose the more adequate treatment between psychotherapy and neuropsychological rehabilitation. The clinician is very often confronted with patients who complain of cognitive incapacity. Difficulties in the processing of information (perception, memory, attention span, concentration, representation, etc.) are found in everyday situations and are closely linked to emotions and behavior. Cognitive incapacities are thus responsible for inhibiting strategies of adaptation and problem-solving as well as the understanding of new situations. As soon as the first signs appear, the clinician must explore what is behind the complaint:

- Is it a cognitive-emotional blockage associated with a depressive episode?
- Is it the incapacity to face up to changes due to age?
- Are we faced with other somatic and/or behavioral problems?
- Is it the onset of intellectual deterioration in the context of organic etiology?

Within these different contexts, treatment strategies will obviously not be the same. The problem must be set within a nosographic framework and we must be sure not to overlook the most relevant therapy adapted to the case. For example, we are often faced with an elderly patient suffering from depression in the context of a neuropsychological disorder (cerebral stroke, onset of dementia) for which it is all the more important to adapt any proposal of psychotherapy (Hibbard et al., 1990; Teri & Gallagher-Thompson, 1991; Myers-Arrázola & Bizzini, 1995).

Psychogerontological Point of View

The therapist must be familiar with different models: Wechsler's decline model (1958) and the criticisms made of it by Horn & Cattell, and Schaie & Baltes (see Vézina, Cappeliez & Landreville, 1994), as well as Baltes's successful aging model (1987, Baltes & Baltes, 1990), which stresses the importance of the processes of selection, optimization and compensation which are favorable to the elderly person's adaptation to his/her environment. The therapist must also be aware of his/her own negative stereotypes concerning age and revise his/her therapeutical approach when faced with old-old or young-old.

A number of authors (Emery, 1981, Steuer & Hammen, 1983; Thompson, et al., 1986; Perris, 1990) have proposed modifications of cognitive psychotherapy applied to the elderly. They advise psychotherapists to take into account the particular way the elderly patient has of processing information, the transitions (i.e. bereavements, retirement, moving house, physical illness) that the elderly must face in later life, as well as the poor level of psychotherapeutic culture the current cohort may have, and consider the expectations the elderly patient has towards therapy. It is often the patient's first taste of psychotherapy and for this reason it is in our interest to explain the "rules of the game" from the very start in order to avoid, for example, passiveness or feelings of inferiority (Latour & Cappeliez, 1994). The little that the current elderly know about psychotherapy has led therapists to conduct psychotherapy sessions (Cappeliez, 1991) and to suggest group treatment. So it is that this type of approach has gradually spread within hospital and outpatient institutions. In particular, the group context represents an alternative to loneliness, as well as helping to install feelings of solidarity and exchange among participants (Bizzini, Droz & Richard, 1990). However, it must be remembered the first post-war generation has just reached the age of 60 and that outlooks on psychotherapy which we have just been discussing have to be modified somewhat, although it must be said that each person develops, whatever his/her age, within the culture of the society he/she lives in. Whatever the case may be, the pessimism which therapists long held *vis-à-vis* the psychological treatment of the elderly today seems very much a thing of the past.

The UTCA Concept

After working for over 15 years with the elderly we are convinced that, without integrating neuropsychological and psychogerontological approaches, the therapist tends to over- or under-estimate intellectual impairment or to forget that the patient's perception and values concerning the world are probably not the same as his/her own. We suggest that therapists be familiar with psychogerontological and neuropsychological models in order to be aware of certain special characteristics of older adults.

Created in 1993, the UTCA (Unité de Therapie Cognitive de l'Agé or Cognitive Therapy Unit for the Aged), composed of five psychologists and one psychiatrist, was designed to offer an age-appropriate psychological treatment for inpatients and outpatients suffering from depression, anxiety, personality disorders or the onset of encephalopathy, for all of which cognitive psychotherapy is prescribed. Our main aim was to integrate and articulate knowledge from the psychogeront-ology, neuropsychology, psychopathology and psychiatry fields into the cognitive model (Table 21.1.)

From the epistemological point of view, the Piagetian approach allows us—among other things—to avoid a certain reductionism where human behavior is concerned, to which cognitive therapy has often been prone, as well as avoiding the simplistic metaphor of man as a computer. Piaget considers that any theory of the mind is above all constructive, which is to say that the individual, through his active influence over his environment, develops by confronting internal and external resistances, by balancing out his assimilating and accommodating tendencies, and by overcoming conflicts during his development by the emergence of a higher level of knowledge. Thus we have a developmental and interactionist conceptual framework particularly well adapted to the integration of lifecourse and adaptation tasks, which are central notions both in work with the elderly and in fully understanding psychological mechanisms and the processes of change. Theoretical, neuropsychological and psychogerontological aspects, which we have gone into in detail above, had been developed elswhere in the literature from a clinical point of view (Richard, Droz & Bizzini, 1984; Bizzini, 1990).

We provide individual or group psychotherapies and offer all our patients the same intervention protocol (Table 21.2). This protocol is essential to all our

Table 21.1 Theoretical model of UTCA intervention

- Epistemological basis (Piaget): constructivism and interactionism
- Neuropsychological: evaluation and rehabilitation
- Psychogerontological: life-span and cohorts
- Psychotherapeutical: case conceptualization and settings

Table 21.2 UTCA protocol

1. Psychiatric diagnosis (DSM-III-R/ICD 10)
2. Assessment of patient's cognitive competence (neuropsychological examination
3. Assessment of suitability (Safran & Segal's SSCT Scale, 1990)
4. Quantitative assessment (self-assessment questionnaires)
5. Synthesis of data (case conceptualization)
6. Individual or group cognitive psychotherapy (cognitive therapy with decentering strategies, CTDS)

psychotherapeutical work. It enables us from the very start to be sure of the nosographic framework (psychiatric diagnosis) and of the patient's cognitive competence (neuropsychological examination). Then, after examination of the semi-structured interview based on Safran & Segal's (1990) Suitability for Short-term Therapy Scale and the quantitative assessment (self-assessment questionnaires), the members of the UTCA draw up a synthesis of the data (case conceptualization) and propose an intervention strategy (individual or group therapy). The case conceptualization enables us to determine the main therapeutic objectives for each patient, as well as to decide on the most relevant strategies for the case in hand. Thereafter, we will need to find, in one-to-one collaboration with the patient, the most appropriate content and form of therapy.

Adapting cognitive therapy to age entails, along with the usual cognitive therapy characteristics, a wider use of psycho-educational models and problem-solving, frequent recourse to redundancy and multimodality, to the use of the blackboard as well as setting up a therapy note book. This therapeutical approach is especially suited to combined treatments.

CLINICAL VIGNETTE

The following clinical vignette is intended to demonstrate how cognitive psycho-therapy can be carried out with elderly patients suffering from psychiatric disorders. More especially we will discuss the diagnosis and assessment, the case conceptualization and the aims of therapy as well as the intervention and its results. We will show in concrete terms how we integrate psychogerontological models into our psychological work and will illustrate through this example the functioning of the UTCA.

> *Mr A* is married, a musician, born in 1925, who has been hospitalized in our clinic for a third episode of depression. Over the last year, he has already been hospitalized twice and has been diagnosed as suffering from major depression with obsessive-compulsive personality disorder (DSM-III-R).
>
> During his first hospitalization, the patient remains for 2 months and receives psychotropic treatment (neuroleptics and antidepressants), psychomotricity and occupational therapy. Upon discharge, he is referred to a psychiatrist, but relapses after 1 month. During the second hospitalization lasting 1 month, the patient undergoes the same therapeutic treatment, to which a number of couple interviews are added. After his second discharge, in March, he resumes psychiatric treatment that entails, apart from medication, psychoanalytically-inspired support psychotherapy. Three months later he breaks off all treatment. In September he relapses and is hospitalized again. During the first 2 months, treatment consists of anti-depressive medication and a series of interviews with a psychiatrist, focusing on the problems within the couple. He and his wife finally take the decision to stay together. Mr A nevertheless continues to feel depressed and is therefore referred to the UTCA. Thus, we see the patient for the first time 1 month after the beginning of his third hospitalization.
>
> Safran & Segal's (1990, see also Segal et al., 1995) semi-structured SSTC interview brings out Mr A's ideas of uselessness, loss of interest, social withdrawal and absence of projects. The patient can mention automatic thoughts but shows few

emotions linked with his thoughts. According to him, change is difficult to envisage, as he sees himself as imprisoned in a vicious circle, although he still hopes to resume playing his musical instrument. He agrees to begin psychotherapy and, despite his reticence, has no negative attitudes toward the therapists.

His score on the BDI (Beck's Depression Inventory, 21-item version) is 40, which corresponds to severe depressive mood.

We envisage integrating him into a group therapy that starts a month later. In the meantime, one of the UTCA psychologists offers him some individual cognitive psychotherapy sessions,. During these, Mr A expresses a lot of feelings of guilt, sadness, and suicidal tendencies. He insists on his past incompetence (he says that he has always suffered from performance anxiety: "I won't be able to play, I will play like a pig and drop my bow") and on the difficulties within the couple. As far as the latter are concerned, he disagrees with his doctor, who advises separation. After four individual sessions, he joins in group treatment. At that moment, the BDI score is down to 30 (moderate depressive mood). Neuropsychological assessment reveals that the patient has full mastery of his cognitive capacities, his MMSE being 29 (out of 30).

CTDS Group Treatment (17 Sessions over 5 Months)

CTDS stands for "cognitive therapy with decentering strategies", a kind of treatment that we apply within the framework of the National Research Programme of The Swiss National Science Foundation. The treatment objectives consist of helping the patient develop specific decentering strategies that increase the probability of re-constructing more adaptive visions of self, of the world and of the future. As far as the therapeutic aspect is concerned, this corresponds to enriching traditional group cognitive therapy by integrating sessions specifically devoted to decentering strategies. These sessions focus on elaborating both a definition and a model of decentration, and on establishing and training decentering strategies. CTDS is a group treatment that involves three to six depressed patients aged 60–80, whom we meet as outpatients or who are referred to us by the Day Hospital. Treatment comprises 17 sessions of $1\frac{1}{2}$ hour each, twice a week for the first eight sessions, and then once a week for the following nine.

Our patient immediately addresses his inability to resume playing his instrument ("I shut the violin case, I can't play it any more"). He does not mention his problems within his couple in front of the group. He says that, in his struggle against depression, he sleeps a lot, avoids company, does not listen to music but still thinks about certain melodies. He acknowledges that depression is not a state that is meant to last, but at the same time he states that he "can't take it any more". During the second session, he defines with our help his own therapy goal: "To look for the sequence of stages that it will take me to resume playing the violin". We note that he tends to minimize the few successful moments he has achieved (he was able to go back home for the weekend and he enjoyed doing so). We point it out to him. At the fourth session, the patient suggests in a triple-column exercise (Beck et al., 1979) that he has begun going out for walks and observing nature. He makes the difference between "before" ("I didn't want to go out, I walked slowly, I was always engrossed in my thoughts") and "now" ("I try to observe nature a little bit, and the people around me"). Together we point out the importance of activity as a means of changing emotional complexion. We call this the "acting-before-understanding" strategy. During the fifth session of group therapy, we notice that he withdraws a lot of his emotions, but he admits to feeling better and tells of moments of pleasure during his walks. In the seventh session, we propose talking about old age and growing old. The patient says, "On retiring, I told myself—I hope things will work out up until then, afterwards I might just as well disappear". He adds that he committed himself so much to his profession, that self-confidence had always been lacking, that he always had those one-track thoughts ("I am a no good musician") and that the compliments he usually got were not credible (" Ah, it worked out fine today, another concert over!"). Shortly before the eighth session, the doctor announces to him that he is not ready to discharge the hospital yet. We analyze this through a triple column exercise and notice that the patient can successfully make use of alternative thought ("After all, it's for my own good, and anyway I am going back home for the weekend"). During the ninth session, as we ask him to tell us which strategies he has been most receptive to, he says the alternative thought strategy and the activity strategy. He then quotes something that he claims he wants to enforce: "1800 times he found a way of failing and did not find the light bulb, but the 1801st time he found it". As far as his personal objective goes (to look for the sequence of stages that will take him to resume playing the violin), the patient concedes that he thinks about it "all the time, I have to get down to it but am afraid, and that blocks me". At this time, BDI score is 26 (moderate depressive mood). During the tenth group session, we teach an initial decentering strategy, which we call "the strawberry effect". We define it as self-distancing by focusing and concentrating upon the activity at hand. Thus, we propose to the patient that he eat a strawberry while focusing on the different sensations he feels. By doing so, namely by focusing on the activity, he can experience the interruption of the flow of negative thoughts and depressive ruminations. At this stage of treatment, the patient is allowed to be discharged from the hospital and continues the CTDS group therapy as an outpatient. He will also be seen by a new psychiatrist. During the eleventh session, Mr A declares that, "Thought is an evil thing when you don't feel well. The strawberry effect means playing music, because with music you forget everything, you are totally caught up and you never feel like sneezing". Thus, he acknowledges the soundness of activity as a way of facing up to depression. In the twelfth session, a role-play shows how much the patient has realized the importance of a second decentering strategy, namely "putting one-self in someone else's place". He mentions the Matterhorn metaphor (thirteenth session) to illustrate his progress towards his personal objectives: "I got as far as the cabin: I actually opened the violin case and then I shut it". He adds that "One must absolutely do something, it is simply not possible to have played all one's life and to stop like that. Every night I dream that I am going to play but there is always an obstacle". During the fourteenth session, the patient reckons that up to now he had been able to decenter 20% but that now he has reached 80%. In fact, he goes for a walk every day, but still avoids meeting people, because he fears having to talk about what has happened. He is not spontaneously willing to accept the possibility that others will not ask him all sorts of questions. In the fifteenth session, he admits that "if I acted on my feelings, I would just stay in bed; nothing gives me pleasure any more, everything demands an effort on my part; nevertheless I put things in perspective by telling myself I have no right to feel bad, because I don't have a hard life".

At the end of the CTDS treatment, the patient has resumed playing music with a colleague of his, but he says he still feels depressed. His BDI score is 35 (severe depressive mood). We therefore decide to offer him individual cognitive therapy to continue the previous therapeutic work, which he accepts.

Individual Treatment (17 Sessions over 8 Months)

During the first individual session, Mr A mentions many ways of overcoming negative ideas, which he learnt in the group (activity, putting oneself in someone else's place, dedramatizing). He also says that it is easier for him to express personal things in an individual therapy setting. To the question, "How does Mr A see himself, what are his basic rules?", he admits that $1\frac{1}{2}$ years ago he would have said to himself things like "I feel useless, a nuisance, out of place every-where, worthless since I am not able to play any more". He feels that this state of mind has ruined him, that his life has shifted from *dream* (violin and music) to *reality* (family and social relations). Following this discussion, he is confronted with three possible solutions: to accept reality as it is (no longer a dream); to refuse reality (despair); or to accept a new relationship between dream and reality through the notion of fun (by playing with others without necessarily thinking that it is a concert, by "lowering standards"). Progressively, the patients feels less imprisoned, endeavors to go beyond the blockage by adopting the principle of pleasure (second session). We use the triple column technique to explore the story he tells about a friend who has played lots of concerts and who recently asked him to accompany him. At this stage, the patient acknowledges that he has made some progress as he has been able to switch from a performance model ("I can't play the way I used to") that involved him in absolute, egocentric and negative thoughts, to the current, more adaptive and decentered situation, which is closer to a model of pleasure ("I am looking forward to it"). By now, he estimates that the latter model is present at 60% in the way he functions. In the third session, we work on the basic beliefs on which all his professional approach has been based. At first he proposes the schema, "I am not allowed to make any mistakes". He gives the example of a gala concert for an oboe soloist, during which he missed his entry by four beats. Outraged and disappointed with himself, he thought "I've ruined his concert!". It must be said that the soloist did not make any remark, which nonetheless did not lower Mr A's disappointment. Throughout his career, the patient has always considered performance anxiety as an enemy and has taken psychotropes to cope with his fear of "choking".

Perfectionism has been in the front line all his musical life. An event which he considers crucial is brought to therapy 2 months into individual treatment. The patient recalls that one of his first violin teachers, 2 weeks before the final examination, told him that he had not acquired the necessary technical skills to pass. This event had such an enormous effect upon him that it was from that moment that he lacked self-confidence. Moreover, the patient goes on to say that the mere fact that he holds the bow in his left hand (a very rare phenomenon) has always been difficult for him to assume. We notice that as far as his activities are concerned, he pays regular visits to a friend, he has started playing again with another friend ("just for fun") and is keeping up his healthy walks. On the other hand, he still avoids social events.

The patient has taken up the violin again on his own and manages to perform a few exercises. He has realized that it is not as hard as he previously thought but he admits that playing alone is a thankless task and that he is no longer obliged to do it. In the fourth session, Mr A says that he has less rumination and fewer negative thoughts. We work on the schema "I am not allowed to make any mistakes" using the descending-arrow technique. This leads to "If you make a mistake, then it's serious, then you are no good. If you are no good, then you lose your job and you won't be able to make a living out of it, and that's vital". The patient distances himself from this way of thinking and is able to elaborate and express alternative thoughts. He then sets out another basic belief that structures his world: "I need to be alone." He recognizes this as being part of his own nature. When he was a child, caught between school and his music, he preferred to be alone. He thinks he has somewhat compensated for this withdrawal with another very strong schema: "I must help others". Thus, he notices that, when he had his breakdown 2 years before, there was no stable environment. He had reached the end of his helping approach and considered himself of little or no use. Today he says that he is trying to see the world in a different light and is convinced that this is worthwhile. Nevertheless, he insists that it is still very difficult for him to take up his violin: he says to himself: "I don't want to do it, I daren't do it, What will become of me?" I suggest he use the "acting-before-understanding" strategy, which he successfully applied during CTDS. He says he cannot enforce it now because what really motivates him is accompanying others. Moreover, he says that he has had a lot of fun recently and felt especially comfortable chatting to colleagues he had met at a dinner party. During the sixth session, I introduce the idea of life course, which we divide into three principal stages.

1935–1991   Great intrinsic motivation (from the very beginning).
                   Singularization (bow held in left hand since age 10).
                   High self-expectations (progressively, and mainly since his nomination to the orchestra, 1947).
                   Strong sense of responsibility (an obligation, since 1947).
                   Role of mentor (he has been giving lessons since 1955).
1991–1996   Sense of tiredness (progressively since retirement, substitute role in the orchestra).

Depression (no more desire to play, loss of motivation for the violin, isolation).

Hospitalization (difficult to accept).

New way of perceiving things (CTDS).

Accepts help and commits himself to the relationship.

1996–future   Reorientation of motives (from a performance to a pleasure model).

Personal ways to be found (new role of music, leisure).

During the seventh session, the passage from the performance model (judgment, pressure, success, fear of failure) to the pleasure model is achieved. The patient uses the "Matterhorn metaphor" and distinguishes three ways of climbing the mountain. The first one, the easiest, consists of taking up the violin again and that has already been achieved. The second one, playing with others, is taking place with more difficulty but is working out well with the support of friends and colleagues. The third way, the most difficult of all, involves resuming work on his own with the instrument, and that has yet to begin. During the eighth session, the patient realizes that retirement has modified the relationship between pleasure and obligation. At first, when he was in the orchestra, the ratio was 20% pleasure, 80% obligation. Now, it is 50%/50%. The patient does not consider the schema "I am not allowed to make any mistakes" to be as absolute as before and he no longer assesses himself as severely, saying "Everyone makes mistakes." In the same time period, concerning the schema "I am very much isolated", Mr A informs us that he took the train (for the first time in 3 years) to go to a party and that he enjoyed it very much. He admits that when he was "in the depths of depression", as he says in the ninth session, he felt indifferent, egocentric and self-orientated. Now, after seeing a film like *Il Postino*, he feels moved but does not necessarily identify with the characters as he used to. He even admires the actors' performances. He describes his change using the boat metaphor. "If I imagine myself on a boat, before I used to be tossed about by the wind and the waves. Now, I allow myself to take over the helm." After 4 months of individual sessions, Mr A indicates that he has "forced himself" to go to a concert using the "acting-before-understanding" model. He enjoyed it and was able to see and talk to a few colleagues. At this time, his BDI score is 15 (moderate depressive mood), the self-deprecation items especially having diminished. At the thirteenth session, only one thing casts a shadow over him. He says, "I have no more feeling for the violin". He recognizes that there has been progress in other areas so we go back to the "taking up the violin again" objective. Mr A has been able to play with other people again (with pleasure and competence) but has not been able to do it alone. He says, "It doesn't work. I don't have any goals. Even so, I should be able to maintain the current level". He suggests finding another therapy objective which, for the moment, he defines as "finding something to replace the activity which has occupied my whole life". During the fourteenth session, concerning this new goal, he indicates that his days are very full and that reading, going out for walks and watching television allow him to get rid of his negative thoughts and to accept his life course where "being productive or effective reduces the effect of what is meant to be". We stress the importance of the progress that has been brought about by strategies such as "acting-before-undestanding" or the strawberry effect, among others. His friends tell him that he is more energetic and more open at social events. And the patient says that he has begun telling jokes again.

Over the summer, he has spent 3 weeks in the mountains and is very happy about it. He has been walking a lot, been close to nature and has met a few old acquaintances. He feels much better, describes himself as more serene, doing things without brooding over them. This positive state has gone on after he got back from holiday. He says he has become more patient, doing things more slowly and making the most of his spare time. His idea now is to begin playing his instrument at his own pace; he is planning a concert with some friends for next year. The patient no longer feels useless, saying he has changed and no longer thinks about it in these terms. We talk about his life course and the fact that he has had to go through a deep crisis. In this respect, we mention some psychosocial models of retirement (decommitment, activity, continuity) and Mr A admits that he had never prepared for his retirement simply because he never envisaged life continuing after his career.

We decide to tackle the final phase of treatment, which aims at reinforcing what has been learnt and following up with booster sessions. The patient is clearly feeling better and does not face aging as negatively as he used to. We therefore lengthen the time between sessions to 1 month. During the sixteenth session, the patient's well-being is confirmed to us as he tells of many events that show that he has completely recovered his psychological equilibrium. He plays the violin every day as if it were a sort of physical exercise, and generally enjoys life. Eight months after the beginning of the individual therapy and 13 months after the beginning of CTDS (seventeenth session), we look back over the group and individual sessions. From the CTDS interviews, he says he has drawn the idea of working on thoughts and has integrated the possibility of changing his state of mind. The strategies that seem most effective for him are activity and alternative thinking. He adds that in the group, he was able to compare himself with others and see that they too were changing. The individual sessions have allowed him to restructure the basic schema "I am not allowed to make any mistakes". The patient says that he is relieved to have come out of depression, he is happy at having time to devote to himself and happy at being able to envisage things patiently. Now, he can devote time to things that he has always put to one side in the past. The shift from the performance to the pleasure model is taking place, especially by reinvesting his motivation in life. He no longer has thoughts of uselessness and considers that not being a professional musician does not deprive life of meaning. As for the "Matterhorn metaphor", he says he has managed to climb it and is satisfied with it, but right now, he says, "I am watching the mountain from Zermatt". At this time, his BDI score is 5, which indicates absence of any depressive mood. We will see the patient again in 6 months' time for a final post-evaluation. The psychiatrist who has continued to follow him (and who has also progressively increased the time between sessions) has now stopped all medical treatment. It must be added that it was only at the final assessment that the DAS (Dysfunctional Attitudes Scale)—which has been applied four times (before CTDS, after CTDS, 3 months later and 6 months later)—finally indicated no significant presence of dysfunctional beliefs.

To sum up, we have seen the patient 17 times within CTDS, which consists of group cognitive psychotherapy, during which we use, apart from the usual strategies in this form of therapy (activity, becoming aware of the link between emotion and thought, understanding the cognitive model of depression, implementing alternative thinking, searching for basic schemas), the defining and use of explicit decentering strategies. At the end of the group intervention, we offered the patient a series of individual sessions (17) in order to provide stability for the changes that were observed during group therapy and in order to explore the basic beliefs in greater depth. The patient was able progressively to reinvest his motivations and modify his relationship with his musical instrument. We observed that Mr A replaced the performance and excellence schema, on which his whole career as a violinist had been based, with the schema of pleasure and maintenance of skill level. He thus came to be aware of the fact that setting himself free from the first model released him from psychological pressure and allowed him to develop his interest for activities that had remained at the stage of pure intentions. In addition, he has reintegrated a social network and lost the feelings of shame and fear of being judged by others. The patient judges himself less severely and, above all, states that he functions normally without forcing himself to do so. Finally, he says, he can enjoy life and no longer mentions his marital problems. The adaptive breakdown that occurred 2 years ago would appear to have been solved.

CONCLUSIONS

In our psychotherapeutical work at the UTCA, our specific treatment of the elderly may be considered similar to those carried out with young adults. Nevertheless, certain adaptations are deemed necessary in order to maximize the potential for change within the elderly. In the clinical case presented here, we have shown how important the conceptualization phase is and just how much the period of construction of therapeutical alliance is to be respected. We have also stressed that the incidence of personality disorders is to be put in perspective with the elderly where the undesirable events of life represent the main source of stress and misadaptation. We therefore deem it necessary to guide the patient in reinvesting his/her motivations and vital impulses. We have increased the ecological validity of our treatment with an assessment adapted to the patient, with the awareness of pacing within session, and with an appropriate level of language. We have been able to confirm the findings of a previous study (Bizzini, Droz & Richard, 1990), namely that the patient lightened his depressive mood, raised his rate of activity, found new personal resources, reintegrated social circles and set out new projects. During psychotherapy, we first noted an increase in the hold that certain basic schemas had over him (phase of awareness) then towards the end of therapy, a drop in and modification of these schemas (restructuring phase).

Cognitive psychotherapy usually takes 15–25 sessions, although this is by no means a hard and fast rule (Freeman & Dattilio, 1992). However, when dealing with an elderly person suffering from mood disorders, with or without personality disorders, we must expect therapy to last even longer. The cognitive therapist's task is an ongoing one of patient cognitive restructuring as well as support to activity. Therapy with this type of patient is necessarily longer, on the one hand because of the possible chronic aspect of the problem, and on the other hand due to certain personal schemas which may be particularly resistant to change. Moreover, with depression, the fact that the patient has already had to confront earlier periods of depression increases personal vulnerability to depression, which then necessitates even longer work upon self-schemas (Teasdale, 1988).

In our opinion, the above experiment proves that psychotherapeutical work is not only possible with the elderly but also beneficial to the patient as well as being challenging for the therapist. The amount of adaptation with which the elderly person is confronted late in his/her life makes his cognitive-emotional balance even more fragile and calls for the setting-up of appropriate psychological aid. Cognitive psychotherapy is one such aid. After a number of years involved in this form of psychotherapy and clinical work with the elderly, we have come to the conclusion that it is fully relevant to the reality of the aged. Its application in geriatric psychiatry demands some adaptations specific to the culture and nature of old age. Its effectiveness has been proved by scientific methodology and what is now needed is research into the mechanisms responsible for particular therapeutic changes at this stage in life.

All in all, the clinical therapist working with the elderly is first of all confronted with his/her own personal aging as well as with the matter of respect due to different generations. He/she must be familiar with specific psychogerontological knowledge, which is indispensable for overcoming misconceptions in the aging process. He/she must also be prepared to adapt his/her therapeutic and assessment methods to the elderly person's psychological reality. To finish, I would like to quote Bob Knight (1996) who maintains that "working with older clients in therapy is challenging and rewarding for the therapist, who may well find learning about later life in the intimate context of psychotherapy a maturing experience." (p. 177).

REFERENCES

Abrams, R.C., Rosendhal, E., Card, C. & Alexopoulos, G.S. (1994). Personality disorders correlates of late and early onset depression. *Journal of American Geriatrics Society*, **42**(7), 727–731.

Allport, G.W. (1937). *Personality: a Psychological Interpretation*. New York: Holt, Rinehart and Winston.

Ames, A. & Molinari, V. (1994). Prevalence of personality disorders in community-living elderly. *Journal of Geriatry, Psychiatry and Neurology*, **7**(3), 189–194.

Baddeley, A.D. (1981). The cognitive psychology of everyday life. *British Journal of Psychology*, **72**, 257–269.

Baltes, P.B. (1987). Theoretical propositions of life-span developmental psychology: on the dynamics between growth and decline. *Developmental Psychology*, **23**(5), 611–626.

Baltes, P.B. & Baltes M.M. (1990). *Successful Aging: Perspectives from the Behavioral Sciences*. New York: Cambridge University Press.

Baltes, P.B. & Brim, O.G. (1983). *Life-span Development and Behavior*. New York: Academic Press.

Baltes, P.B. & Smith, J. (1990). Toward a psychology of wisdom and its ontogenesis. In R.J. Sternberg (ed.), *Wisdom: Its Nature, Origins, and Development*. New York: Cambridge University Press. pp. 87–120.

Baltes, P.B., Staudinger, U.M., Maerker, A. & Smith, J. (1995). People nominated as wise: a comparative study of wisdom-related knowledge. *Psychology and Aging*, **10**(2), 155–166.

Beck, A.T., Rush, A.J., Shaw, B.F. & Emery, G. (1979). *Cognitive Therapy of Depression*. New York: Guilford.

Beck, A.T., Freeman, A. et al. (1990). *Cognitive Therapy of Personality Disorders*. New York: Guilford.

Beutler, L.E., Scogin, F., Kirkish, P., Schretlen, D., Corbishley, A., Hamblin, D., Meredith, K., Potter, R., Banford, C.R. & Levenson, A.I. (1987). Group cognitive therapy and alprazolam in the treatment of depression in older adults. *Journal of Consulting and Clinical Psychology*, **55**, 550–556.

Bizzini L. (1990). Les pertes mnésiques dans l'âge. *Geriatrica*, **3**(6), 11–16.

Bizzini L., Droz, P. & Richard, J. (1990). Thérapie cognitive et dépression de l'âge avancé. *Cahiers Psychiatriques Genevois*, **8**, 71–82.

Bizzini, L. & Myers-Arrázola, L. (1996). Psychothérapie cognitive et dépression dans l'âge: un modèle d'intervention en psychiatrie gériatrique. *La Revue Canadienne du Vieillissement*, **15**(2), 183–197.

Cappeliez, P. (1991). Interventions psychothérapeutiques auprès de personnes âgées déprimées. *Journal of Psychiatry and Neuroscience*, **16**(3), 170–175.

Cappeliez, P. (1993). Depression in elderly persons: prevalence, predictors and psychological intervention. In P. Cappeliez & R.J. Flynn (eds), *Depression and the Social Environment*. Montréal: McGill-Queen's University Press, pp. 332–368.

Costa, P.T., McCrae, R.R., Zondeman, A. et al. (1986). Cross-sectional studies of personality in a national sample. II: Stability, in neuroticism, extroversion and openness. *Psychology of Aging*, **1**, 144–149.

Emery, G. (1981). Cognitive therapy with elderly. In G. Emery, S. Hollon & R. Bedrosian (eds), *New Directions in Cognitive Therapy*. New York: Guilford pp. 84–98.

Erikson, E.H. (1959). *Identity and the Life Cycles*. New York: Norton.

Erikson, E.H., Erikson, J.M. & Kivnick, H.Q. (1986). *Vital Involment in Old Age*. New York: W.W. Norton.

Favre, C. & Bizzini, L. (1995). Some contributions of Piaget's genetic epistemology and psychology to cognitive therapy. *Clinical Psychology and Psychotherapy*, **2**(1), 15–23.

Fogel, B.S. & Sadavoy, J. (1996). Somatoform and personality disorders. In J. Sadavoy, L.W. Lazarus, L-F. Jarvik & G.T. Grossberg (eds), *Comprehensive Review of Geriatric Psychiatry* Vol. II. Washington, DC: American Psychiatric Press, pp. 637–658.

Fogel, B.S. & Westlake, R. (1990). Personality disorder diagnosis and age in inpatients with major depression. *Journal of Clinical Psychiatry*, **51**, 232–235.

Freeman, A. & Dattilio, F.M. (1992). Cognitive therapy in the year 2000. In A. Freeman & F.M. Dattilio (eds), *Comprehensive Casebook of Cognitive Therapy*. New York: Plenum, pp. 375–379.

Gallagher-Thompson, D., Hanley-Peterson, P. & Thompson, L.W. (1990).   Maintenance of gains versus relapse following brief psychotherapy for depression. *Journal of Consulting and Clinical Psychology*, **58**, 371–374.

Guidano, V. (1992).   *Il sé nel suo divenire*. Turin: Bollati Boringhieri.

Guidano, V. & Liotti, G. (1983).   *Cognitive Processes and Emotional Disorders*. New York: Guilford.

Hibbard, M.R., Grober, S.E., Gordon, W.A. & Aletta, E.G. (1990).   Modification of cognitive psychotherapy for the treatment of post-stroke depression. *Behavior Therapist*, **13**(1), 15–17.

Holmes, T.H. & Rahe, R.H. (1967).   The Social Readjustment Rating Scale. *Journal of Psychosomatic Research*, **11**, 213–218.

Knight, B.G. (1996).   *Psychotherapy with Older Adults*. Thousand Oaks, CA: Sage.

Kunik, M., Mulsant, B.H., Rifai, A.H., Sweet, R.A. et al. (1993).   Personality disorders in elderly inpatients with major depression. *American Journal of Geriatric Psychiatry*, **1**(1), 38–45.

Labouvie-Vief, G. (1992).   A neo-Piagetian perspective on adult cognitive development. In R.J. Sternberg & C.A. Berg (eds), *Intellectual Development*. Cambridge: Cambridge University Press, pp. 197–228.

Latour, D. & Cappeliez, P. (1994).   Pretherapy training for group cognitive therapy with depressed older adults. *La Revue Canadienne du Vieillissement*, **13**(2), 221–235.

Léger, J.-M. & Clément, J.P. (1990).   DSM-III, DSM-III-R et pathologie mentale du sujet âgé: intérêts et limites. *Psychologie Médicale*, **22**(7), 617–624.

Mahoney, M. (1991).   *Human Change Process*. New York: Basic Books.

Molinari, V. & Marmion, J. (1993).   Personality disorders in geropsychiatric outpatients. *Psychological Reports*, **73**(1), 256–258.

Myers-Arrázola, L. & Bizzini, L. (1995).   Psychothérapie cognitive et patients atteints de démence débutante. *Psychologie Médicale*, **27**(3), 178–179.

Mishara, B.L. & Riedel, R.G. (1984).   *Le Viellissement*. Paris: P.U.F.

Murphy, G.E., Simons, A.D., Wetzel, R.F. & Lustman, P.J. (1984).   Cognitive therapy and pharmacotherapy. Singly and together in the treatment of depression. *Archives of General Psychiatry*, **41**, 33–41.

Norris, F.H. & Murrell, S.A. (1987).   Transitory impact of life-event stress on psychological symptoms in older adults. *Journal of Health and Social Behavior*, **28**, 197–211.

Perris, C. (1990).   Cognitive-behavioural psychotherapy with elderly patients. Principles, feasibility and the limits. *The European Journal of Psychiatry*, **4**(2), 95–104.

Pezzati, R. (1996).   L'anziano. In B.G. Bara (ed.), *Manuale di psicoterapia cognitiva*. Turin: Bollati Boringhieri, pp. 511–550.

Piaget, J. (1967).   *Biologie et Connaissance*. Paris: Gallimard.

Piaget, J. (1972).   Intellectual evolution from adolescence to adulthood. *Human Development*, **15**, 1–12.

Richard, J., Droz, P. & Bizzini, L. (1984).   Current approaches to treatment of the psychologically handicapped elderly. In J. Wertheimer & M. Marois (eds), *Senile Dementia: Outlook for the Future*. New-York: A.R. Liss, pp. 253–265.

Ruth, J.-E. & Birren, J.E. (1985).   Creativity in adulthood and old age: relations to intelligence, sex and mode of testing. *International Journal of Behavioral Development*, **8**, 99–109.

Sadavoy, J., Lazarus, L.W., Jarvik, L.F. & Grossberg, G.T. (1996).   *Comprehensive Review of Geriatric Psychiatry*, Vol. II. Washington, DC: American Psychiatric Press.

Safran, J. & Segal. Z.V. (1990).   *Interpersonal Process in Cognitive Therapy*. New York: Basic Books.

Salthouse, T.A. (1985).   *A Theory of Cognitive Aging*. Amsterdam: North Holland.

Schaie, K.W. (1974).   Translations in gerontology. From lab to life: intellectual functioning. *American Psychologist*, **29**, 802–807.

Schaie, K.W. (1980). Intelligence and problem solving. In J.E. Birren & R.B. Sloane (eds), *Handbook of Mental Health and Aging*. Englewood Cliffs, NJ: Prentice-Hall. pp. 263–284.

Segal. Z.V., Swallow, S.R., Bizzini, L. & Weber Rouget, B. (1995). How we assess for short-term cognitive behaviour therapy. In C. Mace (ed.) *The Artaud Science of Assessment in Psychotherapy* London: Routledge, pp. 106–120.

Sookman, D., Pinard, G. & Beauchemin, N. (1994). Multidimensional schematic restructuring treatment for obsessions: theory and practice. *Journal of Cognitive Psychotherapy*, **8**(3), 175–194.

Sternberg, R.J. & Berg, C.A. (1992). *Intellectual Development*. Cambridge: Cambridge University Press.

Spagnoli, A. (1995). *... e divento sempre più vecchio*. Turin: Bollati Boringhieri.

Steuer, J.L. & Hammen, C.L. (1983). Cognitive-behavioral group therapy for the depressed elderly: issues and adaptations. *Cognitive Therapy and Research*, **7**(4), 285–296.

Teasdale, J. (1988). Cognitive vulnerability to persistent depression. *Cognition and Emotion*, **2**, 247–274.

Teri, L. & Gallagher-Thompson, L. (1991). Cognitive behavioral interventions for the treatment of depression in Alzheimer's patients. *The Gerontologist*, **31**(3), 413–416.

Thomae, H. (1980). Personality and adjustment to aging. In J.E. Birren & R.B. Sloane (eds), *Handbook of Mental Health and Aging*. Englewood Cliffs, NJ: Prentice-Hall, pp. 285–309.

Thompson, L.W., Davies, R., Gallagher, D. & Krantz, S. (1986). Cognitive therapy with older adults. *Clinical Gerontologist*, **5**, 245–279.

Thompson, L.W., Gallagher, D. & Steinmetz Breckenridge, J.S. (1987). Comparative effectiveness of psychotherapies for depressed elders. *Journal of Consulting and Clinical Psychology*, **55**, 385–390.

Thompson, L.W., Gallagher, D. & Czirr, R. (1988). Personality disorder and outcome in the treatment of late-life depression. *Journal of Geriatric Psychiatry*, **21**, 133–146.

Thompson, L.W., Gantz, F., Florsheim, M., DelMaestro, S., Rodman, J., Gallagher-Thompson, D. & Bryan, H. (1991). Cognitive behavioral for affective disorders in the elderly. In W. Myers (ed.), *New Techniques in the Psychotherapy of Older Patients*. Washington, DC: American Psychiatric Association Press, pp. 3–19.

Vézina, J., Cappeliez, P. & Landreville, P. (1994). *Psychologie gérontologique*. Montréal: Gaëtan Morin.

Vézina, J. & Bourque, P. (1984). The relationship between cognitive structure and symptoms of depression in the elderly. *Cognitive Therapy and Research*, **8**(1), 29–36.

Vieillir en Suisse (1995). Rapport de la commission fédérale. Berne: Office central fédéral des imprimés et du matériel.

Vine, R.G. & Steingart, A.B. (1994). Personality disorders in the depressed elderly. *Canadian Journal of Psychiatry*, **39**, 392–398.

Wechsler D. (1958). *The Measurement and Appraisal of Adult Intelligence*. Baltimore, MD: Williams and Wilkins.

Zinetti, A. (1989). Curiosité et âge. University of Geneva: Unpublished thesis.

Author Index

Where a reference in the text is indicated by "et al.", e.g. Abrams "et al.", the subsequent authors are indexed. If there is more than one "et al." on the page, the first three letters of the first author's name are added to the page number. So, Baker, A. 6Tar can be found on page 6 under Tarrier "et al.".

Subject Index

acceptance, in grieving psychiatric disorders 245
accommodation, for homeless young people 177–8
ACI (Antecedent and Coping Interview) 116
activity scheduling, as treatment for hallucinations 121
adolescents *see* young people
affect *see* emotions
affective disorders *see* schizoaffective psychosis
affective-logical systems of reference 28
affirmation, in therapy 246
aggression, in obsessive-compulsive personality disorder 356
aging
  neuropsychological aspects 405–6
  and personality 397–9
  and personality disorders 399–400
  psychological aspects 401–2, 406
  sociological aspects 402–3
  theories of 403
  see also elderly people; Unité de Thérapie Cognitive de l'Agé
agonistic system, as an interpersonal motivational system 335, 342–3
agreeableness, assessment, measures 300–302
AHRS (Auditory Hallucination Rating Scale) 114, 118
American Psychiatric Association *see* *Diagnostic and Statistical Manual*
anger, in grieving psychiatric disorders 244
Antecedent and Coping Interview 116
antisocial personality disorder, cognitive-behavioural therapy for 277, 279, 281
anxiety
  cognitive-behavioural therapy for 369–70
  in personality development 381–2
  see also fear

art *see* creative painting
assessment
  and creative painting 321–2
  and diaries 323–4
  and dreams 327–9
  during therapy 118–19, 307–8
  and letters 324–5
  measures *see* rating scales
  and photographs 325–7
  services 172–4
  and TAT tables 322–3
  techniques 113–19, 136, 306–8, 321–9
asymmetrical interpersonal schemas 335, 338
attachment
  avoidant 154–5
  needs of infants 380
  and obsessive-compulsive personality disorder 356–7
  theory of 31–2, 42
attachment motivational system 335, 339–42, 345
attachment phase
  in integrated treatment 205–6
  see also therapeutic relationships
Auditory Hallucination Rating Scale 114, 118
auditory hallucinations *see* hallucinations
autobiographies *see* histories; life events
aversive emotions, in cognitive-behavioural therapy 284
avoidance
  of knowledge invalidation 152–3, 155
  in obsessive-compulsive personality disorder 366, 387
avoidant attachments 154–5
avoidant personality disorder, cognitive-behavioural therapy for 277, 279–80, 281
Axis I disorders
  cognitive-behavioural therapy for 277–8
  in elderly people 400

Indexes compiled by Sylvia Potter